T0328379

The Guidance of an Enterprise Economy

The Guidance of an Enterprise Economy

Martin Shubik and Eric Smith

The MIT Press
Cambridge, Massachusetts
London, England

This book was set in Times Roman by diacriTech, Chennai.

Library of Congress Cataloging-in-Publication Data is available.

ISBN: 978-0-262-03463-0, 978-0-262-54677-5 (paperback)

To my wife Julie and daughter Claire and her family. Julie bore the brunt of the various ego flights and depressions associated with attempts to get things right.

To Nerissa, for forbearance in a marathon she didn't ask to run.

Contents

Acknowledgments

This could not have been written without many discussions and collaborations with colleagues in different disciplines and occupations. Many of the conversations were at Princeton, Yale, the Institute for Advanced Study in the Behavioral Sciences, General Electric, IBM research, the Rand Corporation, the Cowles Foundation, and the Santa Fe Institute. We note by name only coauthors whose direct contributions helped us to meld together a considerable number of diverse elements into a whole integrated entity to give meaning to a mathematical institutional economics that must underlie any evolving society. Our specific thanks are to Lloyd Shapley, Pradeep Dubey, Siddhartha Sahi, William Sudderth, Ioannis Karatzas, Ward Whitt, Gerald Thompson, Matthew Sobel, Lode Li, Sidney Siegel, Charles Wilson, John Rogowski, Gerrit Wolf, John Miller, John Geanakoplos, Imre Baranyi, Andreu Mas-Colell, Dimitri Tsomocas, Charles Goodhart, Michael Powers, Rabah Amir, Jingang Zhao, Thomas Quint, Chen Zhong Qin, Per Bak, Maya Paczuski, Kai Nagel, Doyne Farmer, Duncan Foley, Alok Kumar, David Schizer, Martin Whitman, Shyam Sunder, Supriya Krishnamurthy, Rogier Braakman, Harold Morowitz, Benjamin Good, and Juergen Huber. Eric Smith gratefully acknowledges Jerry Murdock for support over more than a decade of our joint work, and William Melton for support during its completion. We wish to thank Glena Ames for her constant aid involving manuscript preparation.

1 The Context of Competition

1.1 Prologue: The Reality That Lies beyond General Equilibrium

This volume is devoted to the study of control, guidance, and coordination problems of government for an enterprise economy. Our basic approach requires an understanding of the roles of money and financial institutions. Our viewpoint differs from most current approaches in stressing together specifically game theory, methods of physics and experimental gaming, and more generally a broader evolutionary viewpoint from the biological and behavioral sciences.

Our intended audiences are economists, physicists, experimental gamers, accounting theorists, legal scholars, and other behavioral scientists willing to explore beyond their own specialist disciplines. In a single book it is not possible to be all things to every audience. Our biases run primarily to an exposition most congenial to mathematical economists, experimental gamers, and physicists, but we aim to make the concepts we consider understandable regardless of the technical approach. We provide a map through these diverse approaches below in this chapter.

As admirers of general equilibrium theory as expounded in the elegant book of Gerard Debreu [79], we are aware of both its great strengths and weaknesses. Initially we were tempted to consider that style, but we believe that the mathematical elegance and tight abstraction aimed only at equilibrium analysis and not at process can strangle the development of our understanding of a living, mutating economic system acting and interacting with the polity and society through many formal and informal institutions. Our goal is the understanding of economic dynamics and the institutions called forth by the many mutations it has to face in an environment replete with contingencies. This is a daunting task and will not be achieved for many years to come. Here we offer two steps beyond the abstraction of the general equilibrium system that are necessary before we can even start to consider anything more than an ad hoc approach to some low-dimensional models of economic dynamic processes.

For the most part we have purposely shied away from utilizing only the theorem-proof style of mathematical economics because most of the theorems are proved elsewhere and references are given. The details of the treatment of finitely many agents versus a continuum of agents for the noncooperative equilibrium models are more or less variants on well-developed fixed-point theorems and are unneeded for those who know this approach, or for those who do not but just want an overall picture of the economic argument. Furthermore we use the noncooperative equilibrium model primarily to make the connection with the previous theories and to point out institutional contexts where such behavioral models may or may not be reasonably adequate. This also connects with some experimental literature that is noted.

1.2   Contact with Sciences of Both the Material World and Other Domains of Behavior

It is not the purpose of economics to describe all aspects of life. It should be the purpose of economics to treat those domains it does describe with concepts and models that can be made consistent with sound scientific understanding of the other aspects of life, when these are needed to provide context.

At a minimum, economic behavior is embedded within the organic system we call the society; it affects extraction, production, utilization, exchange, consumption, and disposal of physical entities and services which exist in the material world and in time; it is supported by both informal and formal institutions, both of which rely on cognitive propensities and frequently on supporting artifacts of people, both individual and socially conditioned. Finally, the economy itself, as well as the people, things, and organizational states which are its context, has intrinsic dynamics, sometimes of a mechanical and sometimes of an evolutionary character.

Two main questions about how to contextualize economics are: what conceptual frameworks outside of economics should guide our representation of formal systems; and do these affect what we think economics itself is?

It could be argued that the economy is a mechanism to organize a subset of the decisions in a larger, highly distributed society. The social organization obeys no simple model of control flow; its dynamics is often evolutionary at many scales of time, space, and material content; and with these, it is subject to both historical contingency and great complexity.

Within this dynamic context, the economy can be an organ of memory and of control (particularly to enable coordination), but we must understand what conditions on society support the emergence of institutions for memory or stabilize control functions, and how these conditions may *limit* capacities for memory or control. (This discussion is already ongoing in biology, and there is nothing in the nature of the argument that would make it less relevant to the economy within society.) Such limitations are often reflected in historical contingency of the institutions that support economic life, and a contextualized economics should reflect the dependence on institutions when their contingencies can have consequences.

Within the economy as well as in its embedding in context, actors with different natural scales interact. Differences in scale exist between private citizens, firms, central banks, and the government. In cases of incomplete contract—which should be regarded as the norm rather than the exception— any of these may also interact informally with social norms, cognitive constraints, or other frameworks that carry *power*. Although such cases are difficult to model formally, it must be acknowledged that they reflect much of reality. Our models will typically contain only two levels, private citizens and a central government, but they are intended to represent the more general case of interaction between agents of different scale.[1] In reality there are many other legal persons beyond government that are not natural persons.

The interface of economics with both cognition and social institutions should reflect the quantitative consequences of a realization that *economic organization is not the only kind that exists*. Many economic models assume both a law of one price (i.e., well-formed prices) and exponential discounting, and it may indeed be that efficient market function involving intertemporal loans requires exponential discounting over short terms.[2] However, both the default cognitive discount structure for individuals, from pigeons to citizens of industrialized countries, and that for societies in the aggregate may well be hyperbolic, inducing a mismatch between market and agent discounting. In such cases it is possible even for ideal markets to produce systematic mispricing accompanied with far larger trading than the conventional assumptions would predict, and mechanisms other than markets might also be required to compensate. A theory of "rational" participation which assumes that individual cognition is entrained onto market discount structures is unscientific when it is systematically denied by observation, for reasons that the theory cannot incorporate. Leaving explicit roles for both government and cognition within the formal structure of economic theory can acknowledge this mismatch without necessarily having to explain it, and can provide a starting point to study scientifically the *limitations* of markets as well as their capabilities.

One of the defining features of governments is precommitment as an alternative to contract, with mechanisms of policing based on power to enforce commitments. In this respect governments are fundamentally different from either markets or the other participants in market activity, though they may play roles as participants in formal models. A scientifically valid approach to the limitations of markets can also be part of a theory of the functions of governments as, among other things, their complementary institutions. We emphasize discounting mismatch here only because it is perhaps the easiest to formalize within existing economic thought; incompleteness of contract, and cognitive deficits in dealing with extremely large, rare, or long-term events, may be even more important defining contexts for a theory of governance, along with notions of moral value and power which are not naturally represented within the economy.

It is somewhat of a side note, but the larger goal of a properly contextualized economics is a valid theory of the dynamics of the society within which it is embedded. It is well understood within evolutionary dynamics that the mechanistic constraints on economic life can feed back, through cognitive development and social niche construction, to determine the foundations of habit and relations on which the economy rests.[3] The evolutionary dynamics of policing is already an active area of study, and one in which economics and theories of power naturally meet.

While most of our models treat the "physical" function of institutions that support the economy, it is not incidental that such "physical" description also refers to the physical world in a way that constrains economic reality. Long-range constraints in physics arise because both resources and wastes are often conserved, and conversion processes must be performed jointly or they cannot take place at all. The rich webs of joint transformation which make up the state space over which agents choose actions can themselves be the source of much economic regularity.[4]

1.3   General Equilibrium and Its Natural Generalizations

The three conceptual foundations of general equilibrium (GE) are preferences, production technologies, and price systems. Koopmans [212] has perhaps most clearly abstracted the roles of these, explaining price systems as the boundary surfaces that separate production from consumption decisions. Production and consumption then provide contexts of convexity from which notions of optimality can be defined.

Simplifications which GE has made include the assumption of complete and costlessly produced and enforced contracts, and the elimination of time through contract mechanisms. Through the assumption of completeness, it has separated itself from the formal treatment of contingency, both in the sense of the complexity with which outcomes can depend on prior circumstance, and in the dependence on history that contingency permits them to record. The same assumption has made institutions epiphenomenal, in that both the concept of optimal allocation and the proof of existence of such allocations come directly from preferences and production technologies, with no role for institutions except perhaps as compact descriptions of aggregated consequences of preference. GE has only separated itself from *formal treatment* of these realities in placing them outside the domain of solutions for price systems; they are still required as inputs to problem specification.

In these senses, GE may be considered an attempt at a formally *closed* theoretical system, and yet one which is in practice excessively open because of the limitations of its formalism. The closure arises from the exclusion of boundary inputs through any formal representations except preferences or production methods. The implicit openness comes because GE takes for granted without accounting for them the mechanisms of signaling, computation, coordination, and enforcement which, in life as we know it, carry significant costs.

A major goal for a new paradigm beyond GE should be to render both its formal closure and its implicit openness less artificial, and in that sense bring the formal representation more explicitly into line with the description it purports to give of the world. This may be done by enriching the treatment of the interaction between the economy and its *boundaries*, in institutions, in cognition, and in the material world. A criterion for good institutional modeling is that institutions should be the carriers of process, and in that sense capable of representing contingent constraints on economic function which do not come from its preferences or production methods alone, but from a variety of other sources "outside" these. Another criterion is that solutions should be *constructive*, rather than emphasizing only existence as GE has done. This is not merely an aesthetic preference. In some cases the existence of a solution is sufficient for it to be found by a number of informal mechanisms, but in other cases the absence of a constructive algorithm for the members of a society to use results in paralysis. It can be argued that much of the function of institutions is to make such algorithms publicly available. In this way institutions can be used to formalize more of the structure that GE takes as given, as well as accounting for the necessity and costs of such structure.

Boundaries may exist either within the economy, between sectors such as decisions made at different times, or between the economy and fundamentally noneconomic modes of organization such as social norms or government. The formal representation of boundary conditions is not itself a representation of dynamics, but it is a precondition for representing most forms of dynamics, which are mediated by boundary conditions.

1.4   A Change in Paradigm

We believe in the importance of abstraction and invariance in economics. The invariance is manifested in function, not form. Form is manifested in the multitude of institutions mutating at different rates in order to adjust to the many vicissitudes of the societies in which the economies are embedded. General equilibrium analysis presented the right level of abstraction to start to understand efficient prices. It was a preinstitutional first step which paid a great price to obtain the right level of abstraction for the appropriate mathematization and proof. In particular it suppressed dynamics and randomness, both of which are needed to reconcile models of economic optimization with an evolving uncertain world.

The modeling constraints in general equilibrium theory were too great to take the next broader steps toward dynamics. It concentrated on the existence of efficient equilibria—and in doing so it failed to describe process, it had no explicit role for dynamics, no role for information, and government was at best only implicit in the context of the model.

The mathematization of microeconomics was given a great impetus by the work of Arrow and Debreu and McKenzie [12, 13, 79, 257] and other mathematicians and economists such as von Neumann and Morgenstern [410, 411], Nash, Shapley, Scarf, David Gale, and others. Unfortunately, to a certain extent unlike the use of mathematics in much of physics, in economics the mathematics almost took on a life of its own, and the gap between elegant mathematical models and the ongoing reality of the phenomena has widened.[5]

The approach here calls for a change of paradigm, in two phases, first from a general equilibrium formulation of exchange with n nonstrategic agent types trading in m commodities[6] to the construction of full process models. We utilize strategic market games with n types of small strategic agents trading in m commodities and utilizing various forms of money and credit to do so. We then introduce government explicitly into the model as a large controlling player, formulating the economy as a strategic market game with n types of small agents plus one large atomic agent.

The switch from a timeless equilibrium model stressing efficiency to a process model with control requires a switch in mathematical emphasis away from the perfect balance of equations. Instead, in a process economy the system often has positive shadow prices measuring the pressures calling for the change in constraints, or perhaps signaling slack conditions of oversupply. The constraints themselves may reflect financial or economic shortages, or government laws and impositions.

Through the property of closure, GE is permitted to be the mathematics of equalities, which in the narrow sense means the unconstrained clearing of all markets. Boundaries on the economy often take the form of constraints on inequality, such as budget constraints or bankruptcy conditions. In that sense, an open-system description of the economy will be based on the mathematics of inequalities. The sense in which the inequalities are not new is that they all ultimately arise from convexity of preferences or production functions. The sense in which they are new is that they are quantitatively represented in a range of shadow prices dual to institutionally imposed constraints.[7]

Shadow prices in open-economy modeling play a parallel role to equilibrium prices in the Koopmans abstraction: they represent the transfer of constraint between a focal sector of the economy and something else. This transfer may occur across time, as when a budget constraint sets an interest rate for intertemporal loans, or it may take place between the economy and a noneconomic actor such as government, when a consumption cap rather than a tax is used as a regulatory mechanism. Ensuring that a sensible—and generally, that an explicit—interpretation is available for the shadow prices is a major part of checking that the economic paradigm is compatible with those of the other aspects of reality to which it has interfaces.

1.5 The Relationship between Micro- and Macroeconomics

A critical question in economics and in physics concerns the relationship between the behavior of the individual person or particle and the aggregate or mass behavior of these entities. The desire in economics has been to reconcile the theories of microeconomic behavior with the macroeconomic models of economic control. We take some preliminary steps in this direction, stressing that the carriers of process are the institutions of a society. Thus unlike in a preinstitutional general equilibrium theory of an efficient price system, institutions cannot be avoided when considering process. As the carriers of process, institutions provide much of the context for individual economic competition and reflect the rules of the game by which the government provides guidance to the individual agents and helps to provide means to coordinate behavior.

The study and utilization of macroeconomics has been directed primarily toward the practical problems of the running and control of the everyday economy. There is a considerable distance between application and theory. Some steps that differ from conventional monetary and macroeconomic theory are needed to bridge this gap. We suggest that the contributions of theory at this time are in the understanding of function and in relating function to minimal form. The role of applied macroeconomists is to understand the actual complex institutional forms that exist in contemporary economies and to base their advice on the governance and change of these institutions on detailed empirical knowledge; but these may be modified with insights gleaned from the analysis of highly abstracted models of the minimal institutions required to perform the basic functions of a control system.

1.6   On Minimal Institutions

Both the introduction of boundary conditions and then the introduction of dynamics can introduce a bewildering array of distinct models, and also an indeterminacy of solution paths within even a single model. Part of this is not new. As a basis for definition of a competitive equilibrium, GE chooses a restrictive and rather arbitrary assumption about market clearing that is at odds with the generality of treatment given to preferences, production, and prices, and also is empirically invalid for most markets. If that assumption is removed, trading paths to equilibrium become completely indeterminate in the general case [172, 270, 378], a much more fundamental indeterminacy than the acknowledged discrete indeterminacy among many competitive equilibria. The admission of that indeterminacy, and the weakness it implies for GE without a Walrasian mechanism for price setting, is a major motivation for specifications of process. However, some of the indeterminacy may persist even when explicit mechanisms for market clearing have been introduced and validated. The latter form prevents us from naively associating formal understanding with prediction, leaving us to emphasize problems of control.[8]

The potential problem of model diversity is of a different kind and bears on how complex the world really can be, and how much of that complexity economic models can or should represent. Attempts to weaken the assumption of complete and symmetric information but otherwise retain GE methodology led to the coinage of *bounded rationality* by Simon [371]. The model diversity met even within this sphere has been correspondingly referred to as "the wilderness of bounded rationality."

We approach the problem of model diversity from the dual perspectives of *function* and *form* (again closely mirroring the way similar problems have been studied in biology). The function of a market, an institution, or a whole economy can be defined from the transformations it makes possible in a society supplied with resources and production capabilities, and driven by preferences for consumption. In general many formal models provide the same or similar functions, and among these we focus on those that are minimal by some criteria of cost or complexity. We refer to a formal model of minimal complexity, associated with some function, as a *minimal institution*.

Counterparts to the concept of minimal institution have been independently derived in many sciences. Typically they use domain-specific measures of complexity, but many of them are broadly applicable outside their domain of origin. Formal criteria of minimal complexity exist for the problem of communication, leading to the notions of *minimum description length* for messages [305] and the associated *algorithmic information content* [222] for programs.[9]

It is worth remembering that both the map from form to function and its converse can be many-to-one. It has long been appreciated in biology that opportune reuse of old forms for new functions, known as *exaptation* [170], is one of the leading determinants of evolutionary possibilities. Because we do not attempt to treat dynamics fully in this volume, we give less attention to the latter kind of degeneracy than it deserves.

In many domains it has been found—despite the fact that opportunities for bewildering complexity appear to exist—that a relatively small diversity of attested forms actually describes much of nature.[10] In some cases evolutionary dynamics can be invoked to explain such simplicity, on the grounds that only coarse-grained and modular forms can adapt before drifting to extinction. It is reasonable to look for similar forms of convergence or universality in social institutions, such as norms for property rights or symmetries in market-clearing function. In such cases, minimal institutions serve not only as convenient models but sometimes as class-level descriptions of certain aspects of function. The freedom to make quantitative predictions about a functional class from any representative instance has led to the extremely important concept of *universality classification* in statistical systems.

1.7   An Observation on Structure and Behavior

Rational behavior: greed modified by sloth surrounded by formless fear and justified ex post by rationalization.

In the first five chapters we use (with caution) the usual economic assumptions of the population being composed of a set of highly intelligent agents, without personality but able to compute and remember without bound. They are furthermore assumed to be endowed with coherent well-defined preferences that can be expressed by utility functions. These strong simplifying conditions are useful to start with: they enable us to connect closely with equilibrium theory; but our interest is far more in mechanism structure than in details about imaginary utility functions and ideal economic agents. As we approach actual dynamics they undoubtedly need modification. Although we do not deal with these modifications at this point, we suggest that a breakdown of the population into several behavioral types is called for.

Much work in mathematical economics and in game theory has been based explicitly or implicitly on an abstract *homo oeconomicus* or von Neumann man. This individual has perfect recall and an ability to compute everything. We suggest that for the development of economics it is probably worthwhile to recognize around eight different behavioral types:

- The random player with the state space unknown,
- The random player with the state space known,
- The optimal response player with global scope,
- The optimal response player with local scope,
- The nonspecialist human,
- The specialist human,
- The expert specialist human,
- The von Neumann player.

The lower and upper bounds on intelligence are usually the easiest to study and serve as useful benchmarks when studying behavior in experimental games. A market such as a one-commodity double-auction market provides an example of institutional design where the average random player with state space known appears to do approximately as well as the ideal utilitarian player (see [163, 189]).

The first player noted is the random player with the state space unknown. This is noted as a reminder that the statement that a player chooses randomly, to be made precise, requires the assumption that the player knows the domain over which she is randomizing. If the domain is not specified, an individual must provide some subjective closure to take care of the uncertainty.

In experimental gaming considerable use has been made of the random player. This is seen in the work of Gode and Sunder (1993) [163] and others.

Even the concept of a know-nothing cannot be modeled easily without taking some context into consideration. The know-nothing can be so ignorant that he or she does not even know the bounds on the choice to be made. Fortunately in many economic situations the bounds are given by mechanism and context. Thus the economically naïve is prevented by the mechanism from bidding a negative amount and cannot bid more than she has plus the amount she can borrow.

1.8   A Guide to a Multiple Technique Approach

As our intent is to connect intangibles and quantifiable features involving economic institutions and the society in which they are embedded, we are forced to utilizing different techniques. In order to cover the scope we wish to cover, we mix essay sections and purely verbal descriptions with numerical models to illustrate specific points, with formal mathematical models, and when it is feasible to do so with proof.

We argue explicitly with illustrations why certain techniques from physics, game theory, operations research, and biology are useful. Our attitude is opportunistic; different facets of the same topic may require different approaches that depend on scope and detail.

In our concern for the study of the control mechanisms over a dynamic economy we note that the apparent generality of general equilibrium analysis was bought at the cost of the omission of time, government, and process. By utilizing the strategic market game constrained to a single time period, it is possible to construct a set of minimally complex process models whose solutions, under the appropriate qualifications, include those of general equilibrium. But out of equilibrium, with money and credit as part of the models, they are loosely coupled. Furthermore the mechanisms in each of the models can be interpreted as minimal institutions.

Limited to one period these models are few in number, but as soon as one wishes to consider several periods there is a hyperastronomical proliferation of models, where the quantitative change signals a qualitative change. In the dynamics we enter the domain of a multiplicity of fluid institutions.

The techniques of mathematical economics can at best assist in the exploration of ad hoc models. The link from general equilibrium statics to dynamics exists and can be cleanly expounded mathematically, but once that is done the steps into the exploration of both structure and behavior call for the change in paradigm discussed here and for considering links to evolutionary processes.

1.8.1   Some "puzzles and questions"

A point stressed in this work is that the approach presented may help to straighten out several items that appear trivial to many an economist eager to tackle "real-world" phenomena. Problems such as normalization of a price system (dimension checking), selection of units of quantity and time (grid selection), completeness of the strategy set (conservation and compactness), and what is meant by disequilibrium dynamics (equations of motion) are not trivia. Omission of these items is why previous basic theories of money have failed.

1.9   A Sketch of Chapters

Chapter 2 discusses the properties of money together with further observations on minimal institutions. An extension is constructed of the model given by Jevons to illustrate the failure of the double coincidence of wants in binary trading. This extension enables us to use considerations of symmetry to examine the basically simple market trading structures utilizing different forms of money and credit.

A key link is described between the static general equilibrium approach and the process-oriented strategic market game approach. The latter supplies process models but not full dynamics, as the models cover only one period. This is sufficient to illustrate general equilibrium and noncooperative equilibrium solutions, but not sufficient to illustrate trajectories.

Chapter 3 provides the physics background to the approach to the economic problems considered here. This involves discussing the basics of measurement, aggregation, and the concept of dimension. The role of scaling is dealt with, and the uses of symmetries are explored. These are all useful in exploring a generalized version of the Jevons failure of the double coincidence of wants.

In many of our models we make the assumption of a linear separable term that for the exploration of many monetary control problems provides a considerable simplification of the mathematics and appears to be a reasonable simplification. It also provides an analogy with the physical concept of work.

Chapter 4 applies basic game theory in concert with the methods described in chapter 3 to the one-period models. The roles of symmetry and efficiency are considered and the asymmetric imposition of constraints is considered in their relationship with money and credit. Information and clearing rules are discussed. We consider graphical representations of the basic models, and a partial taxonomy of the one-period exchange mechanisms is presented. Comments are made on the relationship between the concepts of trading structures that have been called the trading post [339, 352] and the windows model of trade [336]. However, a full comparison of these two models is given in chapter 12.

Chapter 5 presents two fully developed models that illustrate the organizational distinctions between a commodity and fiat money. The first considers the control problem in an economy utilizing gold or any other commodity of value employed as a money where the production of the means of exchange is left in private hands. The second considers an economy where the government controls the means of exchange and contrasts this with the more laissez-faire economy with gold and no direct government ability to produce money.

Historically there has been an evolution from barter to the use of an evolving monetary medium, involving a governmentally issued coinage and eventually to a governmentally controlled symbolic money or fiat. This chapter offers the first opportunity to consider multistage processes with different interacting timescales where we can still offer a full analytical treatment.

The first five chapters and chapter 11 constitute an exposition, advocacy, and execution of a change in modeling and analysis that leads to a generally scoped set of mathematically rigorous but context-rich and institutionally open economic models. They are still explored for their equilibrium properties but are structured to be amenable to use as experimental games and simulations and to provide a platform for dynamics.

The remaining chapters are more tentative. They intermix a large set of open questions, many of which still need tighter definition, with work in progress.

Chapter 6 returns to the theme of control or prediction in the economy. Switching from the emphasis on static equilibrium, the first steps are taken in a sequence of three developments beyond general equilibrium needed to comprehend economic dynamics. They are: the production and exchange economy in a process setting; the economy with innovation, or Schumpeter revisited; and finally a change in emphasis from innovation to evolution. In this chapter a mathematical exemplar of the first item is dealt with in some detail. The other two are dealt with in chapters 9 and 10.

Even at the relatively simple level of production treated here, in the light of chapters 2 to 4 we have entered into the realms of mathematical institutional economics, in the sense that even at their simplest the multistage models with more than one timescale present require considerable parametric description. We provide a checklist of around twenty items that need specification before one can develop the equation of motion of even a reasonable ad hoc model of production. For our ad hoc production and control model we consider a rural community building a communal good, such as a farming valley constructing communal silos, with gold currency with and without elementary banking.

A reasonably complete model and dynamic noncooperative equilibrium solution shows the interplay between the technology, the demographics, and the monetary aspects of the model. Full mathematical details of the model are presented in the text, with much of the analysis and graphics consigned to the appendices.

Chapter 7 leads off with the observation that the strength and attraction of the general equilibrium analysis is that it is not a solitary model, but rather a set of principles for building models. When we consider dynamics, this is the goal to which we believe the methodology of strategic market games contributes.

With the introduction of capital stock (already in chapter 6) and a monetary system with government, a further change away from the general equilibrium paradigm becomes central. That is the relationship between ownership and control.

In a previous publication one of us [356] suggested that a useful way to connect trade with financial instruments represented by contracts and physical goods and services would be by considering a sequence of one-period transformation matrices. This is in keeping with the dynamic approaches of von Neumann [410] and Leontief [218]. A 20×21 description of the economy is sketched and linear production spaces are discussed.

We turn to the consideration of the catalytic function of capital stock in economic dynamics with finance, and in doing so we take something of a detour in attempting to devise a satisfactory linguistic structure for economic and financial activities. A transformation description for capital stock is presented, and as this is somewhat of a work in process we consider some further examples in an appendix.

The contrast between game-theoretic and general equilibrium analysis is illustrated in the need to be explicit about the state space. In dynamics this shows up in the ability to handle velocity, loose coupling, and transients. We illustrate the application of our methodology to two old classics: Adam Smith's "Real bills only" and the equation of exchange $PQ = MV$ first formulated mathematically and discussed by Simon Newcomb [274].

We close with some comments on income distribution in the economy and the problem of indexing the complexity of an economy.

Chapter 8 begins with a discussion on time, dynamics, and uncertainty, noting Marshall's comments on the melding of the long and short run. A sketch of the many types of risk is given. Possibly the key task of a financial system is to provide for the smooth functioning of a loosely coupled dynamics involving perception as well as choice in an uncertain environment.

A central problem in monetized economies has been the presence of bubbles and panics and how to control them. Diamond and Dybvig [84] provided a seminal example in terms of a simple game with two equilibrium points. Morris and Shin [267] embedded their model in a larger extensive-form game and considered correlated equilibria. We connect this analysis to an evolutionary game theory solution.

In the last part of the chapter the meaning of liquidity and the usefulness of the concept of the velocity of money are considered. In each instance the definitions of these blanket terms appear to be highly context- and question-sensitive. In particular we suggest that what may pass for a change in the velocity of money may be better described as changes in the various sources for the creation and destruction of credit. The customary lack in distinction between fiat money and various forms of bank and other credit reported in the multi-dimensional monetary statistics make any simple interpretation of velocity of dubious value.

Up until this point progress has been made from games in strategic form solved for their noncooperative equilibria to multistage models with mass agents and a government player. The solution concept has still been a modified equilibrium, in particular a perfect or Markovian equilibrium where history does not matter. In chapter 9 we take the next step toward an evolutionary economics by incorporating the concept of economic innovation into a process model. We show that this can be done for a single innovation still utilizing the concept of a noncooperative equilibrium; but an important new phenomenon appears. It is, in general, not possible to avoid having to deal with transient periods of virtually any length caused by the dynamics of the introduction of an innovation.

The viability of the innovation may well depend on the speed of adjustment. We contrast the innovation possibilities for Robinson Crusoe in a nonmonetary economy and for a small firm in a monetary economy. This brings out the relationship between the physical economy and the physical and financial economy where trade of both goods and risk may vastly enlarge the strategic possibilities. This type of model opens up the vistas toward finance as providing a control, sensing, and evaluating mechanism on top of the physical economy. In this enlargement of a loose structure, the door is opened to an array of different structures in which management and ownership are separated.

The intellectual task in attempting to explore analytically a fully mathematized version of a multistage process involving uncertainty calls for radical simplification. There is just one type of manufacturing firm and one innovation which involves replacing one process with another. This amounts to reassigning the utilization of the existing resources.

The central point of this chapter is to show that while in the Robinson Crusoe economy innovation poses a well-defined operations research optimizing problem, innovation in a monetary economy is not only far more complex but involves, as Schumpeter suggested, "the breaking of the circular flow of capital" and calls for the introduction of more money and credit into the system. There are many ways in which the gist of his verbal statement can be mathematized; we note the proliferation and then consider one model with a relatively simple computable example fully worked out.

The models and analysis presented were based on the presence of one random variable. Noted, but not solved, is the model with a repeated stream of investment opportunities, but even without formal solution it may be seen that an overlay of transient states may leave the whole system in constant turmoil with a history-dependent dynamics.

Chapter 10 continues the theme of chapter 9 but with emphasis on growth and control. This chapter is primarily verbal, sketching many of the new factors that fit in an evolving economy as further differentiated functions require further elaborated institutions. A review is given of the new aspects of an innovation economy, starting with a reconsideration of the utility function that underlies so much of economics and finance. We argue that the utility for money must dominate economic concerns after needs and most wants are satisfied.[11] It supplies a natural measure that is of considerable help locally in time and space, even though globally its worth varies. Furthermore the presence of many assets that are means of production and do not enter directly into individual preferences provides security for many assets whose "worth" is being estimated constantly to determine how wealthy individuals are. Such a question may seem to be almost metaphysical to the careful theorist; yet its one-number or scalar answer is of considerable operational interest to the tax collector.

Reinforcing the comments on money, it is noted that fiduciary decision making dominates the economy. The fiduciaries need to consider their constituencies in some form of aggregate. Given other people's money as a quasi-linear abstraction, the role of a quasi–side payment game is noted where, in essence, ownership claims to the means of production are redistributed. A sketch is given of the many subproblems in dealing with innovation in an asset-rich economy, including the possibility of two-way causality where either finance leads innovation or vice versa. The key role of bankruptcy as the delimiter of risk in a loosely coupled system is noted.

Section 10.4 touches on the role of increasing returns in its many forms. Section 10.5 notes the importance of a far more elaborate banking system than in chapter 9. Even the basic coverage of the institutional variations feasible here merit a separate volume. An elementary discussion of the problems involved in varying the money supply is given. Sections 10.8 and 10.9 provide an opening primer on the relationship between economics and biology as means to understanding complex emerging systems.

Chapter 11 provides an integration and overview of the previous chapters. It commences with a basic consideration of what is meant by a theory, in science in general and economics in particular.

It picks up in sections 11.5 and 11.6 an even more basic theme on strategic market games than was developed in chapters 2–5. By considering the nature of the transmission of messages in a trading network, utilizing several reasonably natural axioms provided by Dubey and Sahi [98], we note the special roles of the trading post and windows models as *G-mechanisms*. By adding some simple measures of the complexity of trading mechanisms and of trading messages, the emergence of markets and a single trading good is established [104]. The basic distinction between a highly decentralized and highly centralized mechanism for price formation is clarified.

Chapter 12 lays out our approach to the problems encountered in integrating the description of the structure of financial and other economic institutions and the behavior of the economic agents. We have stressed describing and understanding mechanisms (the current rules of the game); one can learn much from structure without going into details on motivation and behavior, but if economic motion is to be described they must be described. The conditions assumed about behavior are implicit in a rational-expectations approach to dynamics, but attached to it are the many simplifications acceptable in producing a proof of an efficient price system in a static utopian world but woefully inadequate and counterfactual in this world.

We argue that the transition from the unique abstract specification of the general equilibrium formulation of a one-period exchange economy into a full process model involves "one model, then few models," and then the opening of the floodgates to the multitude of institutions.

The step from general equilibrium to strategic market games (SMGs) involves the elaboration of an austere GE model devoted to the study of equilibrium conditions to a small set of SMGs that portray minimal institutions where the key is the accommodation of models with process. The emphasis is no longer on equilibrium but on compatibility with process.

The hyperastronomical proliferation of process models commences as soon as many periods and information conditions are considered. At this point further understanding calls for further detail relevant to the institution and questions about it. Our predominant stress has been on structure as providing the carriers for behavior. The use in this work of the behavioral assumption of simple noncooperative behavior illustrates how the process models fit with equilibrium analysis. What constitutes a good behavioral solution to an economic model brings with it context-laden problems in perception, learning, and teaching that are not amenable to broad generalization at this time.

The production of dynamic models conforming with our methods is, however, amenable to ad hoc dynamics, where each parameter-laden model is directed toward helping to answer some appropriate question. We note that the dynamic models selected throughout our chapters provide exemplars of this approach.

We close this chapter with comments on dynamics and complexity, stress the danger of the false dichotomy between "rational" and behavioral agents (they are all behavioral), stress again the central importance of context in describing dynamics and the key relationship between the existence of process and a basic role for money.

In chapter 13 we permit ourselves the luxury of some *obiter dicta*, including some comments on fads in theorizing and "the king has no clothes." In keeping with our concern with invariant properties of economic systems and the delicate relationship between abstract theory and practice, we make some notes on current affairs and the relevance of our theorizing to policy. Some observations on economics and its relationship to a general theory of organization are also made.

1.10   A Multidiscipline Reading Map

In this volume we deliberately have taken the risk of writing for an interdisciplinary audience, attempting to supply formally sound connections among macroeconomic, microeconomic, and game-theoretic methods and the appropriate aspects of both physics and biology, taking into account that the economy is embedded in a polity and society with laws and customs. We acknowledge but have not tried to supply in any detail the called-for formal connections with social psychology, psychology, political science, law, and history.

Ideally we would welcome all readers to read the whole volume in order to appreciate our central theme that money and financial institutions provide the guidance and coordination mechanism for an enterprise economy. However, we note that there are many approaches to viewing the themes presented here at different technical, mathematical, and disciplinary depths. Chapter 1 needs to be read by all as a general introduction. Beyond that there are several paths, a few of which are noted below.

1. An economist or game theorist concerned with appreciating the role of money and minimal financial institutions in providing the basis for strategic models of a market economy with government as well as a private sector may obtain a reasonably complete formal set of mathematical models of strategic market games in chapters 2, 4, 5, and 11.

2. A microeconomist, econophysicist, or biologist interested in how innovation fits with economic competition and how evolution fits with economic innovation could confine their reading primarily to chapters 2, 4, 9, 10, and 12.

3. An econopyhysicist or economist interested in the measurement and symmetry properties of money could read chapters 2, 3, 4, 5, 7, and 11.

4. A literary political economist could keep mathematics at a minimum but still see the full structure of the approach to evolutionary models in political economy by reading chapters 1, 2, 6.1–6.5, 12, and 13.

5. A mathematical economist or an experimental gamer concerned with fully worked out multistage models can use the models in chapters 5, 6, and 9 with little modification as experimental games to examine the predictive power of rational-expectations or other hypotheses.

Notes

1 Power in particular may be one of the most important contexts that economics should acknowledge explicitly. The assumptions of complete contract and symmetric information attempt to define economics as the sphere of decision making that remains after power has been excluded. However, correct conceptualization of many of the spheres with which the economy interacts depends inherently on the characterization of one or another form of power.

2 It is possible that the discount rate may vary, and that averages over longer times with a stochastic discount factor can yield nonexponential aggregate discounting [123].

3 The concept of human capital can be seen as an attempt to represent this relation at some level.

4 To emphasize that this is not a light observation, we consider that the input-output matrices of von Neumann-Gale growth theory are equivalent to the stoichiometric matrices of chemistry, whose structure is responsible for the vast array of chemical complexity, which is studied in its own right and involves no notions of strategic agency. In particular, the equivalence of these two representations renders capital stocks formally equivalent to reaction catalysts, which are responsible for all of physiological complexity in ways that are far from understood.

5 The preponderant development of general equilibrium theory, as well as much of game theory and finance, has been on equilibrium models, to such an extent that little is known even about the convergence of the formal systems when out of equilibrium beyond some turnpike results [256].

6 We stress exchange models because exchange and production models already introduce considerable extra complications.

7 The transformation from preferences to their dual representations in constraints and shadow prices is the *Legendre transform*, and it distinguishes closed from open representations of the economy in the same manner as it distinguishes closed from open systems in physical thermodynamics.

8 Two directions can be developed in the absence of predictability for particular trajectories of prices and exchanges. One is the development of theories of distributions, and of the behavior of samples that are in principle not predictable, a theme that has dominated evolutionary biology [169, 220]. A second direction is to recognize that, even if the individual motivations that jointly determine coordination outcomes cannot be understood or dictated, it may be possible to place bounds on the possible outcomes which leave markets within a regime of acceptable function.

9 In the statistical mechanics of many-particle systems, functionality has been learned to derive from the symmetries and dimensionality of the degrees of freedom which are active, and minimum-complexity models are those with the lowest-order algebraic representations consistent with these symmetries and dimensions. Apologies to the reader for the shortness of this description. These will be familiar to physicists as the *effective field theories* [165, 294, 415]. They are minimal in the sense of Taylor series expansions for functions such as an energy or action, being expanded to the lowest consistent powers of both fields and derivatives in time and space. We will use an organizing scheme very similar to this when considering the function of market clearing in chapter 4.

10 Examples from other disciplines include: theories with Lie-group symmetry in fundamental physics [157]; an apparently universal set of $\sim 1,000$ protein folding motifs which coarse-grain the protein space of typical amino acid chains of length ~ 100, whose nominal sequence diversity is 20^{100} [81]; or small numbers of cell states produced by regulatory networks seemingly capable of much greater diversity in cell development [407].

11 At some point the somewhat ill-defined but nevertheless omnipresent drive for power may intermix with the desire for wealth. An adequate discussion of this is beyond the scope of this work.

2 Minimal Institutions: Game Theory and Gaming

2.1 An Approach to Money and Credit

Prior to beginning the formal modeling and analysis, we present an overall sketch of our approach and how it unfolds. We argue that the general equilibrium system provides the appropriate preinstitutional modeling structure to start to study the allocative properties of the price system. The economies we live in are encompassed by their polities and societies. They involve dynamics and strategic behavior. Our task is to build process models of the economy that are consistent with the general equilibrium basis, but build out in a systematic manner toward the multitude of institutions that are the carriers of process in an ongoing society.

We argue that this can be done in such a manner that there is a natural cascade of process models consistent with general equilibrium; but these become progressively more complex as new functions are required to support the dynamics of a society.

The first step of our venture into a mathematical institutional economics involves the invention of money and markets and the endogenization of price formation. A nonzero supply of money is a critical ingredient in providing the extra degree of freedom to permit the functioning of the system out of equilibrium.

The distribution of money as well as the sufficiency of the amount of money both have roles in determining efficient trade. Questions concerning the presence of enough money raise problems involving the type of money. The possibility appears of switching from a valuable commodity such as gold to a symbolic currency such as fiat. This calls into question the roles of custom, trust, power, and government in the management of the money supply. And this in turn raises consideration of the powers of, and trust in, government involvement with the means of payment.

If the distribution of money is skewed, there will be pressures to borrow and lend. We may expect a loan market to appear. In an economy with a loan market, if we attempt to describe all points in the outcome space there will often be situations where an individual is unable to repay a loan. The "rules of the game" require that default and bankruptcy conditions be specified.

We show that the presence of default rules destroys the property that the level of the prices can be scaled up or down without affecting the distribution of real assets.[1] Furthermore the price system links the utility of fiat to the preference system of an individual. In turn the specifications of the societal rules of default have considerable influence on an individual's risk and rewards in managing any risky enterprises.

By considering the possibility of a risky outcome to an investment, even if we limit ourselves to just one random variable being manifested only once, it is possible to illustrate the essence of Schumpeter's observations on the breaking of the circular flow of capital. This in turn leads to the need to specify the sources of the extra capital required to break the circular flow, and this poses problems of ownership and power if financial investment is required to procure real resources in the process of innovation.

Once the Pandora's box of process models is opened, it is easy to demonstrate that hyperastronomical numbers of potential institutions appear as soon as one considers the alternative constructions with even two or three time periods. This is consistent with an evolving, adapting society; but it is also consistent with only a few minimal institutions appearing with the first attempts to build a minimal playable game form. Without worrying about the specific strategic behavior of the individuals, many of the basic functions of a financially guided economy appear in the one-period models. Our approach stresses the presence of basic financial functions in the political economy; the financial guidance mechanism provides the functions clothed in a myriad of institutions congenial to the specifics of the society, its laws and customs.

In this chapter the stress is on the economic and institutional aspects of trade. In the somewhat more technical chapters 3 and 4 we relate these observations and the solutions to the strategic market games to phenomena encountered in physics. In particular in section 4.4.2 we show that an important distinction in physics, between locally and globally defined symmetries, arises in the solution of market games in the same mathematical form. In all cases symmetries reflect the presence of apparent strategic degrees of freedom, which actually have no effect on allocations. When these are locally defined, it is possible for agents individually to factor them out of decision making, and arrive at the noncooperative equilibria of the game. When they are globally defined, they are under the control of no one, and the uncertainty they create for each agent can make it highly unlikely for the economy to arrive at any pure-strategy equilibrium. This is reflected in chapter 11 in the discussion of the trading post and windows models of trade.

2.2 Some Preliminaries

Here we give the usual definitions of the properties of a money, including an extra game-theoretic consideration along with system properties. Observations are made on minimal institutions, and a technical question concerning the modeling of many agents is considered.

2.2.1 Some of the properties of a money

In any elementary textbook, three usual properties of money are spelled out: that money is

1. A means of payment,
2. A store of value,
3. A numéraire.

There is a fourth item that needs to be considered when we examine its role in any strategic game required to reflect the basics of a monetary economy:

4. Money provides a way to distinguish the strategic power of agents.

You, your bank, and the central bank do not have the same strategy sets with respect to money.

Cognitive factors also enter. Money is a universal measure of economic worth. The national government is, in essence, the only institution in society that is recognized by all, along with its legitimized powers. The money it issues may be fiat or a commodity; but in either instance it exists in a positive quantity with the stamp of government on it. Total monetization of individual assets, while logically feasible, is highly improbable in societal and technological reality.

2.2.2   Further comment on minimal institutions

In chapter 1 we noted the concept of a minimal institution. Here the concept of a minimal market is considered. We are concerned with the minimal level of complexity at which a phenomenon of relevance appears. This relatively imprecise statement will be clarified below in examining the simplest mechanism for producing a market price.

2.2.3   On the treatment of finite size in economics

Many of the statistical methods that have been successful in physics have not been expected to do as well in economics, not only because agents are intentional, but because economic systems are comparatively *small* compared with mass biological and physical phenomena. Nonetheless, it is often a great simplification in problem solving first to assume a large population of agents[2] and then to treat the population as a *continuum*, so that granularity of agents or of actions is ignored. Similarly, it is often convenient to be able to pass between discrete-period and continuum models of time, or between a large finite time horizon and a formally infinite horizon. This only becomes a hazard when solution concepts rely on removable singularities[3] in the agent continuum or time horizon that are not properties of their regular, finite or discrete limits.[4] It is not a conceptual innovation but merely a matter of care not to use solutions that rely on singular limits or removable singularities.

In approaches to modeling rooted in principles of statistical inference, there is a close relation among the regular treatment of the continuum, principled treatment[5] of ignorance, and the concept of robust model selection and analysis.

Some formal methods, akin to manual sensitivity analysis but with a fuller axiomatic and technological foundation, exist to ensure that subtle limits such as continuum spaces or infinite horizons do not introduce artifacts that merely reflect ambiguities in the definitions of the limits. As with other robustness criteria derived from ad hoc sensitivity analyses, the formal methods identify results that characterize *classes of cases* or models rather than isolated cases.

Many formal methods of robust modeling consist either of replacing definite model specifications with distributions over parameters, or replacing deterministic dynamics with stochastic dynamics, usually evaluated in a suitable small-fluctuation limit. The distributions over parameters or stochastic events are often chosen to maximize some axiomatically defined measure of *entropy*[6] as a principled way to introduce least systematic bias over quantities that are left ambiguous by the coarse-grained model specification [193, 194]. Robustness of the properties derived from coarse-grained models against unknown (and generally infinite-dimensional) possibilities for model refinement may be analyzed by using a variant on the central-limit theorem to determine which higher-order model parameters are self-averaging under aggregation, an approach that is known as *universality classification* where it has been formalized [165, 294, 419].

A use of minimum-bias (or equivalently, maximum-ignorance) methods in economics comes from the zero-intelligence approach to finance from Gode and Sunder [163] and others [52].[7] We have applied minimum-bias methods to the selection of simplified stochastic models of game solutions derived from stochastic replicators, and have used self-consistent averaging of solution trajectories in the distribution of fluctuations generated by the system's own dynamics, to show which continuum limits are robustly approximated by naïve estimates of expected payoffs, and which take on systematic offsets from the naïve estimates due to fluctuations, even in the continuum limit [380].

2.3   Playable Games, Prediction, and Control

The phenomena of money and financial institutions are essentially associated with dynamics. Trade is carried out by two interlinked networks that are often considered as one. These are the system of market mechanisms that initiates the trade and provides for physical delivery, and the payments network that settles the trade. The first deals with the sale and purchase of goods and services while the second handles credit evaluation and the nature of the means of payment and the settlement and accounting for the trade.

In this work we represent both the activities of trade and settlement by means of fully defined playable games. Our concern is explicitly with games that can be played in a laboratory or classroom. The incentive to do this is twofold. It enables us to consider whether we can obtain evidence to confirm or refute conjectures about economic behavior in extremely simple situations, and it provides a valuable debugging device for formal economic models. In setting up a playable game one must include items such as the specification of what constitutes a bid or offer, when and why bankruptcy and default conditions must be specified, and what happens to price in a market when there are bids but no offers.

2.4   The Jevons Failure of the Double Coincidence of Wants

Jevons [195] provided a critical example illustrating a key difficulty in utilizing barter in an economy with more than two individuals. He considered three individuals trading in three commodities. He was able to select conditions to show that bilateral trade with utility improvement after each exchange was not sufficient to bring about optimal trade.[8] A simple example illustrates this:

Let x_{ij} = the amount of commodiy j held by individual i. The individuals' initial endowments are $(0, 1, 0)$, $(0, 0, 1)$, $(1, 0, 0)$. Consider three utility functions of the form

$$u_1(x_{11}, x_{12}, x_{13}) = 2x_{11} + x_{12}$$
$$u_2(x_{21}, x_{22}, x_{23}) = 2x_{22} + x_{23}$$
$$u_3(x_{31}, x_{32}, x_{33}) = 2x_{33} + x_{31}.$$

No pair has an incentive to trade, yet the competitive equilibrium solution is $(1, 0, 0)$, $(0, 1, 0)$, $(0, 0, 1)$.

In our analysis we contrast the generalized Jevons example with the situation in which all individuals own a general supply of all commodities. In our notation the starting allocation of commodity j to individual i will be a_i^j. We consider both the extended Jevons example $a_i^j = a\delta_i^j$,[9] which we denote by a vector a_{spec}, and a more general endowment (a_i^j) denoted by a_{gen}.[10] We generally consider m consumable goods to which m types of producers correspond in the specialist case. The total number of traders is set to rm, with $r > 1$ traders of each type. A goods type $(m + 1)$ may be introduced when money is not one of the consumables. Using the intrinsically symmetric setup of the Jevons example enables us to carry out an exploration of the basic structure behind several elementary models of trade.[11]

2.4.1   Games with aggregated strategies

Among the desirable properties of a market, anonymity and aggregation are suggested. These properties alone are sufficient to provide considerable structure to games in strategic form. They provide an important link between micro- and macroeconomic models of economic behavior. In general the payoff function for an individual i is a function of n variables, the strategies of each player. If a strategy amounts to naming a quantity of one or more goods, then each individual's payoff depends upon only two strategic variables, his own and an aggregation of the actions of the others. The simple classical Cournot oligopoly game illustrates this property. The key features of aggregation and anonymity are provided by a strategic market game. It becomes meaningful to talk about the individual playing against "the market," a faceless aggregate. Without the presence of exogenous uncertainty, the macroeconomic concept of the "representative agent" and the type-symmetric behavior of many identical individual agents may be treated mathematically in the same way. When exogenous uncertainty is present, the behavior of the representative agent and identical individual agents may differ fundamentally (see for example [199]).

2.4.2 Strategic market games and payment systems

In the past few years, one of us together with several colleagues [94, 339, 352] developed a set of games called strategic market games. They are fully formulated games that can be played, simulated, and analyzed. They serve to contrast a game theory and gaming approach to the functioning of competitive markets for the exchange of individually owned economic goods and services with the general equilibrium analysis [79]. The stress in the formulation of strategic market games is upon the explicit specification of the mechanisms for trade: in other words, upon the complete definition of the state space or the outcome set of an economy considered as a process model.

Let N stand for the set of all n agents; Ω^m represents an m-dimensional endowment space; R is the set of real numbers. A strategic market game for traders $i \in N$, with endowments $a_i \in \Omega^m$ and utility functions $u_i : \Omega^m \to R$, is defined by specifying the market structure M and the strategy sets S_i for each $i \in N$.

Under fairly weak assumptions indicated below [97], it can be shown that noncooperative equilibria exist for all of the class of games described above, where the participants in the markets use only simple messages. The conditions required are:

(A) Each u_i is concave and nondecreasing in each variable.

(B) $\sum_{i \in N} a_i > 0$.

(C) For any $(j,k) \in M$, there exist at least two traders who have positive endowments of j and desire k, as well as two traders who have positive endowments of k and desire j. (A trader i is said to desire commodity j if u_i is a strictly increasing function of the jth variable.)

There are three minimal market forms that produce price from simple strategies. They are called (1) the sell-all market, (2) the buy-sell market, and (3) the bid-offer or simultaneous double auction.

The sell-all model, where all goods except money are put up for sale, is the tax collector's dream. All assets (excluding the individuals themselves) are put up for sale, thus giving the tax collector his much-needed accurate evaluations of what anything will sell for. The size of the individual's strategy is one number per good bought, his bid. The buy-sell game as defined by Dubey and Shubik [94] requires a strategy of dimension 2 for each good. An agent names a quantity of each good he wishes to sell and names an amount of money he wishes to spend to buy each good. The simultaneous sealed bid or offer (dimension 4) or the somewhat more complex sequential double auction market have been favorites in much experimental gaming and have moves involving four numbers per good: a price bid and amount or bound on the amount to be bought, and a price offered together with an amount for sale. Details concerning why these three representations can be regarded as minimal mathematical representations of exchange, with slightly different functions satisfied, have been given elsewhere [356].

2.5   Degrees of Freedom and Symmetry in Cash and Credit Markets

In our discussion here we limit our concern to simple one-period Cournot-Nash equilibria and observe how some of the set of the noncooperative equilibria may approach the competitive equilibria when the number of small agents becomes large.[12]

In the economics of money and financial institutions there have been several problems that have for the most part eluded careful modeling and have been treated primarily by verbal methods and historical commentary. They include, with some exceptions, items such as what difference it makes to the economy if different goods or instruments are selected as the numéraire; whether a system can operate with everyone being an issuer of money, using their own IOU notes as a means of payment; whether the bankruptcy and default laws are institutional curiosities or represent logical necessities in a system designed to promote trade; and how the roles of a central bank differ from or overlap with those of a money market and what a merchant banker is. In our analysis these questions are answered in the development of models of a competitive system assisted and coordinated with a government sector and a financial system.

2.5.0.1   Price taking and a noncooperative equilibrium solution   The GE formulation assumes price taking. All individuals regard themselves as without influence on price. A way to make this precise is to consider each of the n

consumer/trader agents as being composed of a continuum of small agents and prove that the lack of influence on price is true. We may then show that with some additional modeling the GE and SMG solutions can be linked (see [97]).

2.5.0.2   A distinction with or without a difference?   When the modeling decision is made to consider that all agents are so small that they are represented as being on a continuum, there is a temptation to conclude that there is no operational distinction between the GE and SMG models of the economy. This has to be considered with extreme care. In almost all of the references given here, the underlying SMG considers a finite number n of traders and then passes to some form of limit to illustrate how direct power over price attenuates. Even then, as is illustrated in [8], the relationship between the type-symmetric noncooperative equilibria of the SMG and the competitive equilibria of the GE may not be 1 : 1.

Non-game theorist economists often view the distinction between a GE model and an associated SMG with a continuum of agents as a distinction without a difference, yet the whole procedure of modeling is essentially different as are many results. The GE tradition has purposely (and usefully for their problems) ignored the detail that the process models of the SMG cannot ignore.

2.5.1   Functions and institutional forms

Mass economies with mass (more or less anonymous) markets require many functions to be performed in facilitating the completion of trade. Among the functions are:

1. Aggregation of bids and offers;
2. Identification, verification, and auditing;
3. Credit evaluation;
4. Record keeping;
5. Insurance, storage, and transportation;
6. Credit granting;
7. Clearance and payment;
8. Final settlement and default resolution.

These functions are necessary parts of a financial system designed to facilitate trade in a dynamic economy involving both space and time.

In many economies these functions are supplied by a variety of institutions and individuals. For example there are individual traders, retailers, wholesalers, and nonfinancial firms. There are markets, credit evaluation agencies, banks, central banks and other government agencies, insurance companies, clearinghouses, accountants, lawyers, notaries, and courts. At first glance the names on the list appear to be peculiarly institutional, yet the functions they perform are an integral part of defining the dynamics of trade.

In our analysis here we do not propose to dwell in any detail on all of these institutions, but we show that even with extremely stripped-down models considered at a high level of abstraction several institutions are called for. In particular some form of credit evaluation agency, a clearinghouse, goods markets, a money market, the central bank, and the courts must appear even in relatively simple models.

2.5.2   Barter, commodity money, IOUs, and clearing

By limiting ourselves to a single-move game we are able to provide a formal structure to cover many institutional differences in monetary systems. Yet, as shown in table 2.1, there are only a small number of structures that cover most of the essentials of monetary institutions found in the history of economics and finance.

In table 2.1 the salient features of eight market structures are illustrated. They are each considered below in some detail.

2.5.2.1   Barter   Barter involves bilateral trade between pairs of agents or coalitions. It describes a state before the existence of formal markets. As exchanges are postulated to be face-to-face with value given for value received, there is no need for institutions. No numéraire is needed and all agents are implicitly in the same position.

The emergence of markets and financial institutions poses empirical problems in economic anthropology, history, and in the investigation of long-term economic dynamics. There is little hard evidence about pretribal trade, and much economic writing from Adam Smith on appears to be, at best, plausible conjecture cut from the whole cloth and not particularly germane to our understanding of trade in highly organized societies. In chapter 11 we report on an axiomatic approach to derive both markets and money that we took as primitive concepts in the SMG noted above.

2.5.2.2   Money: gold   The formal buy-sell game [94], where individuals offer quantities of goods for sale and amounts of money to buy them, provides

Table 2.1
Primitive structures covering most essential functions of monetary institutions

	Barter	One commodity	Bimetallism	(a) All goods as money	(b) All goods as money	Money market and gold	(a) All IOUs with with default	(b) All IOUs with clearing
Markets	not defined	$m-1$	$m-2$	$m(m-1)/2$	$m(m-1)$	m	m	m
Numéraire	free "ideal"	gold	gold linked to silver	free "ideal"	free "ideal"	gold	free "ideal"	free "ideal"
Means of payment	all	gold	gold and silver	all	all	gold	all IOUs	all IOUs
Store of value	all	yes	yes both	all	all	yes	no	no
Agent types	1	2	3	1	1	2	1	1
Financial markets	no	no	no	no	no	yes	no	no
Credit evaluation	no	no	no	no	no	no (variant yes)	no	yes
Clearinghouse	no	no	no	no	no	yes	yes	yes
Courts for default	no	no	no	no	no	yes	yes	no
Efficiency	not always	sometimes	generically no	generically no	yes	yes if enough money	yes	yes
DOF a_{spec}	not defined	$2(m-1)$	$3(m-2)$	$m(m-1)$	$2m(m-1)$	m^2+m-1	m^2-1	m^2-1
DOF a_{gen}	not defined	$2m(m-1)$	$2m(m-1)$	$m^2(m-1)$	$2m^2(m-1)$	$2m^2$	$(2m+1)(m-1)$	$(2m+1)(m-1)$

Note: Column (a) refers to markets that do not differentiate roles of money and goods, treated in section 2.5.2.4. Column (b) refers to markets in which these roles are differentiated, treated in section 2.5.2.5.

an abstract description of trade with gold. An initial allocation to agent i is given by the vector

$$a_i = \left(a_i^1, \ldots, a_i^m, a_i^{m+1} \right),$$

with gold as the $(m+1)$th good. The numéraire may also be set in terms of some measure of gold, such as a new sovereign. A strategy for a trader i is a vector (q_i, b_i) of dimension $2m$ such that:

$$b_i^j \geq 0, \qquad 0 \leq q_i^j \leq a_i^j \text{ for } j = 1, \ldots, m \text{ and } \sum_{j=1}^{m} b_i^j \leq a_i^{m+1}$$

where b_i^j is the bid for and q_i^j is the offer of good j by i. A money is utilized to bid in all markets, while a nonmonetary good is offered for sale only in its own market. Thus, in general, a strategy for an individual i whose good is not the means of exchange is:

$$\left(b_i^1, q_i^1; \ldots; b_i^{m-1}, q_i^{m-1} \right).$$

This has dimension of $2(m-1)$.

In the special extended Jevons example, a strategy is of the form

$$\left(b_i^1, 0; \ldots; b_i^{m-1}, 0 \right)$$

for the moneyed individual. This has dimension $m-1$, while the individuals without money each have a strategy of dimension of 1.

Even in this simple model a question concerning bidding and offering appears. It involves the possibility of wash sales. A wash sale occurs when an individual both buys and sells the same commodity, thus creating the impression that the net market activity is greater than it is. Price formation for commodity j in general is given by:

$$p^j = \sum_{i=1}^{n} b_i^j / \sum_{i=1}^{n} q_i^j.$$

A minor item which requires comment is that we have not included the spot market of gold for gold. Such a market is not ruled out by logic, but will be inactive by virtually any type of optimizing solution.[13]

2.5.2.3   Bimetallism: an economy with both gold and silver as money

The medium-of-exchange function can tolerate more than one money without too much trouble; the unit of account function cannot.
—Kindleberger [207], p. 55

A well-known old question in monetary theory has been the feasibility of using two or even three metals simultaneously as a means of payment. The usual physical argument is that individuals need to make three types of payment: large payments to buy a house, for instance; middling payments to buy a bicycle; and small payments to buy a glass of beer. Gold is too valuable for the last two; silver fits best in the middle range and copper fits at the bottom.

Unfortunately, if two or more commodities are used as a means of payment and there is any change in the endowments of any commodity of value, as there almost certainly will be, the relative prices between the various monies will change. If a country has open trade with others, silver or gold may flow in or out as a function of relative prices (see Kindleberger [207], ch. 4 for a nice summary). A central government will have to adjust the relative prices of silver and gold coinage if it wishes to keep both in circulation. In 1717, Sir Isaac Newton, Master of the Mint, observed that a lewidor (louis d'or) was worth 17s and 3f (f = farthing) in France, but 17s 6d in England, which brought a large inflow of gold to London (Kindleberger [207], p. 54). Newton set the price of an English Troy ounce of gold at £3 17s $10\frac{1}{2}$d in an attempt to adjust the ratio between gold and silver.

If we are concerned only with a one-period market with fixed endowments, then an all-seeing government could do the appropriate calculations and announce a fixed mint price between gold and silver. The number of free markets in an m-commodity world would be reduced to $m - 2$. At equilibrium, in this special case law, custom and free markets would coincide and there would be no net inflow or outflow of gold or silver if there were no arbitrage opportunities. The static equilibrium theory shows that it is logically feasible for a country to impose an extra constraint by fixing the price between gold and silver. But the hope for running a dynamic economy without constant readjustment is negligible.

In terms of the buy-sell model, the concept of a single money is well defined strategically. If good m is the money, it can be used to purchase all other goods directly. It enters the numerator of the price formation mechanism for all the goods it purchases. Thus if an individual i of type m has as his initial endowment $(0, 0, \ldots, a)$ where the mth good is deemed to be the money, his strategy is of the form $\left(0, b_{im}^1, 0, \ldots, 0, b_{im}^{m-1}\right)$ where

$$\sum_{j=1}^{m-1} b_{im}^j \le a$$

and $b_{im}^j \ge 0$. The bid has dimension $m - 1$.

Suppose, however, that there are two monies, say gold and silver, the mth and the $(m - 1)$th commodities. For simplicity our remarks are confined to our closed one-period-economy model. If a money is a means of payment but is not sold as a commodity then we can construct a well-defined playable one-period game for the extended Jevons example as follows.

An individual i of type m has as his initial endowment $(0,0,\ldots,a)$ where the mth good (gold) is deemed to be the money; his strategy is of the form $\left(0, b^1_{im}, 0, \ldots, 0, b^{m-2}_{im}\right)$ where

$$\sum_{j=1}^{m-2} b^j_{im} \le a.$$

The bid has dimension $m-2$. Similarly an individual i of type $m-1$ (who owns silver and has an endowment $(0,0,\ldots,a,0)$) has a bid of dimension $m-2$.

A strategy of a trader of type g where $g = 1,2,\ldots,m-2$ is of the form $\left(0, 0; 0, 0; \ldots; q^g_{ig}, 0; \ldots; 0, 0\right)$ which is of dimension 1.

With the two monies, how is price formed? We can specify generally for good j where $j = 1, 2, \ldots, m-2$:

$$p_j = \frac{f\left(\sum_{i=1}^k b^j_{i,m-1}, \sum_{i=1}^k b^j_{im}\right)}{\sum_{i=1}^k q^j_{ij}}.$$

If by government law a linear relationship in the valuation of gold versus silver has been set (for example, around 1700 the gold/silver ratio was in the range of 1 to 15 or 16), then the price formation is specified as:

$$p_j = \frac{\sum_{i=1}^k b^j_{i,m-1} + \alpha \sum_{i=1}^k b^j_{im}}{\sum_{i=1}^k q^j_{ij}}.$$

We now have a completely well-defined game whose solution will depend on a parameter α. It is here that law clashes with custom and free markets and context-free mathematical economic models may mislead us away from institutional understanding. If governments rule out by law market structures, black markets will spring up and ways to avoid the laws will be devised. The legal restrictions will become a cost of doing business and not a pure barrier.

In economic history, as the relative prices of gold and silver moved, coins or ornaments were melted down and recast as ornaments or coin. This suggests that gold and silver could be considered as both monies and commodities for sale. If we were to consider them as both, then a somewhat different model from the above can be considered. We may add in two extra markets: the market where the commodity silver is sold for the money gold, and the market where the commodity gold is sold for the money silver. The strategy of an individual i of type m (those who own gold) now becomes of the form $\left(0, b_{im}^1, 0, \ldots, 0, b_{im}^{m-1}, q_{im}^m, 0\right)$ where

$$\sum_{j=1}^{m-1} b_{im}^j + q_{im}^m \leq a \text{ where } b_{im}^j \geq 0 \text{ and } q_{im}^m \geq 0.$$

The bid has dimension m. Similarly an individual i of type $m-1$ (who owns silver and has an endowment $(0, 0, \ldots, a, 0)$) has a bid of dimension m.

Can the government enforce the fixed rate between the two numéraires? If the government mint had a large supply of gold and silver and were willing to buy or sell in unlimited quantities at the rate it had set, it could control the ratio with some effort. The tradeoff between the convenience of the simultaneous use of gold, silver, and copper as legal currencies and the motion of their relative prices could have been "good enough" within limits in an error-correcting (and -generating) economy.

2.5.2.4   All goods a money? Case 1: money or goods?

In some writings ([58] for instance), it has been suggested that when all goods can be used as a means of payment then every good acting as a money is the equivalent of barter. This misses the important distinction concerning the existence or nonexistence of mass markets, which produce a single price for many agents trading simultaneously through some form of aggregating/disaggregating mechanism (see [8]).

Restricting ourselves to the buy-sell game when all goods may be utilized as a means of payment, we have complete markets. There is a market between every pair of goods. But at the risk of nitpicking, we must distinguish between a unidirected and a bidirected graph. In the former A may buy B, but B cannot buy A. In our extended Jevons example, if an individual has only one commodity, say oranges, which may be used as a money to make purchases, can it also be sold as a good? If a good selected as a money can only be used for bidding, then in the extended Jevons example nothing can be offered for sale as all individuals have only a money. We have a pathological but well-defined case. The game is completely symmetric, but requires one of two breaks with our treatment of all the other markets. If bids and offers retain a unique definition, so that the notation agrees with the other cases, then any individual i of type g has a strategy of the form: $\left(0, b_{ig}^1; \ldots; 0, b_{ig}^{g-1}; 0, 0; 0, b_{ig}^{g+1}; \ldots; 0, b_{ig}^m\right)$. This has a dimension of $m-1$ and the only equilibrium is inactive. By definition only $m(m-1)/2$ markets can be considered, and none of them can go active because there are no goods for sale; there are only monies which can be bid. Although it is logically feasible, cost, custom, and common sense would rule out this structure.

2.5.2.5   All goods a money? Case 2: money and goods   If any money utilized for purchasing can also be used as a good for sale, then it is reasonable in this instance to consider the existence of all $m(m-1)$ markets, not $m(m-1)/2$. The owner of oranges buys apples in the oranges/apples market but can, if she wishes, sell oranges in the apples/oranges market. There is no need to specify a numéraire. The game is completely symmetric and each individual has a strategy of $2(m-1)$ dimensions.

2.5.2.6   A commodity money and a money market   In an economy which employs a single commodity money such as gold without other money substitutes, the equilibrium will be interior if there is enough money which is well distributed. If the distribution of money is inappropriate, even if there is a sufficiency of money a boundary solution will exist.[14] Efficiency can be improved by introducing a money market. A money market is a financial market. It requires a new instrument, the individual IOU note, and calls for both a collection agency and the courts to fully specify its functions under all contingencies. The price in the money market can be regarded as an endogenous rate of interest. It is formed by bidding IOU notes for a supply of money offered in the money market. In the extended Jevons example the rate of interest will be:

$$1 + \rho = \frac{\sum_{i=1}^{r} \sum_{g=1}^{m-1} z_{ig}^m}{\sum_{i=1}^{r} w_{im}^m},$$

where the z are the IOU notes for which the money is offered and w_{im}^m denotes the amount of commodity money an individual i offers for loan in the money market.

We must consider that the IOU notes are redeemed after trade. But it is possible that the economy could reach a state where an individual would not be in a position to redeem her IOUs. The default rules must be specified. The dimensions of the penalty will be utility/money.

The simplest game can still be defined with only one information set per individual. The extensive form has the individual borrow before bidding in the goods market. Realistically he would be informed before he bids, but this information can be finessed if we permit the individual to allocate percentages of his (unknown) buying power. In the extended Jevons example the strategy of a borrower is of the form: $\left(0, b_{ig}^1; 0, \ldots; q_{ig}^g, b_{ig}^g; 0, b_{ig}^{m-1}; z_{ig}^m, 0\right)$, where $b_{ig}^j \geq 0$ and $z_{ig}^m \geq 0$. The strategy has dimension $m + 1$. The strategy of a lender is of the form: $\left(0, b_{im}^1; 0, \ldots; 0, b_{im}^{m-1}; w_{im}^m, 0\right)$ which has dimension of m.

In this model, as all transactions are for cash, all sellers can be paid directly from the market posts in cash, but then a collection agency must solicit each borrower for repayment and the courts must take care of any defaults.

A variation of this model can have accurate credit evaluation which attaches a discount to each individual bid in a manner that avoids bankruptcy. We discuss this variation for the model in section 4.4.

2.5.2.7   Everyone their own banker (a): all issue IOUs with no credit evaluation but default rules   Suppose that each individual is permitted to issue her own IOU notes as a means of payment. We may impose some arbitrary upper bound M on the amount of notes that any individual can bid. Furthermore we select an imaginary money, "the Ideal," as the numéraire; thus an individual IOU is a promise to redeem the paper in Ideals. The utilitarian value of the Ideal in default is established by the laws or rules of default.

We consider the extended Jevons example. A strategy by an individual i of type g, $g = 1, 2, \ldots, m$, is of the form $\left(0, b_{ig}^1; 0, \ldots; q_{ig}^g, b_{ig}^g; 0, b_{ig}^{m-1}; b_{ig}^m, 0\right)$. It is of dimension $m + 1$.

We develop two models. In this model each market immediately ships all goods to all the bidders, but before it settles with the suppliers it sends all of the IOU notes to a clearinghouse together with its intended payments. The clearinghouse nets all IOUs along with the intended payments. If all net to zero, its work is done. The clearinghouse informs all individuals who are in default and all individuals who are creditors and it turns over these accounts to be settled by the courts.

The symmetry among all agents in this model is obtained by introducing the two societal agencies, the clearinghouse and the courts. In institutional fact the clearinghouse could be an agency of the government such as the Fedwire of the United States, or it could be a privately owned institution such as CHIPS (Clearing House Interbank Payments System).

The courts should reflect their society; at any moment of time the laws are part of the rules of the game, but in a longer horizon they will be subject to change. The modeling and analysis of such a system are highly dependent on the time horizon considered. If only a few months or years are under consideration, it is reasonable to accept the institutions as given. If several decades or centuries are being considered, it makes sense to investigate the tradeoff between law and custom.

2.5.2.8   Everyone their own banker (b): all issue IOUs with credit evaluation to balance the books

Suppose that, as in the preceding case, each individual is permitted to issue her own IOU notes as a means of payment. We may impose some arbitrary upper bound on bids as was done above. The strategy sets of the individuals are as before; but settlement rules are changed and we are able to introduce a credit evaluation agency to dispense with the courts and default rules by imposing a balancing of all accounts under all circumstances. This is done by utilizing the clearinghouse as both a clearing agency [311, 391] and a credit evaluator.

All markets receive rm different IOU notes in bids for the goods for sale. In order to make this game reasonably playable, we envision that each market bundles all of the IOU notes and sends them to the central clearinghouse where they are all matched and netted. As they are all denominated in the Ideal, which does not have a physical existence, the clearinghouse can impose a settlement rule by solving a simple linear system requiring the full balance of each individual by imposing a relative valuation of the notes. There are some technical problems with division by zero when individuals offer no goods whatsoever for sale but nevertheless bid. We may evaluate all bids accompanied with a zero offer as of zero value, and 0/0 is interpreted as no trade.

2.5.3   A comment on the clearinghouse versus cash in advance

The explicit introduction of a clearinghouse is consistent with the no-transactions-costs aspects of general equilibrium theory, the difference being that we present a formal process-oriented model where, in essence, the clearinghouse provides a zero-interest loan in clearinghouse credit for the small period of time during which accounts are netted [395]. The clearinghouse approach contrasts with the cash-in-advance models where a full time period lag is attributed to settlement.

A fundamental social distinction between the trading post model using gold, such as that described above, and the model with a central clearinghouse is in the amount of information and trust required. The economy with gold is far more decentralized. The gold itself is a substitute for trust and removes the need for calculation, centralization of information, and matched clearing. In a related investigation, experimental games have been run with all individuals issuing their own IOU notes as money and a central clearinghouse balancing the books [10]. The experimental results indicate that if the combination of a perfectly efficient clearinghouse is present with a system that has sufficiently harsh penalties against those who fail to deliver, the experimental subjects (university students) act in a manner that supports the basic economic theory.

2.6 Summary Comment

In this chapter we have attempted to illustrate the power of utilizing a highly stripped-down set of models of trade where the basic physical considerations of symmetry and degrees of freedom in the various systems point out the need for and nature of elementary financial instruments and institutions such as a commodity money, government or fiat money, and individual IOU notes as well as commodity markets, a money market, a central bank, bankruptcy and default laws, the commercial code, and a central clearinghouse. These appear as a manifestation of a mathematical institutional economics. The models have been examined primarily from the viewpoint of more or less conventional economic theory. In the next chapter these models are revisited with more concern for their relationship with the underlying physics relevant to the economics.

Notes

1 The GE system has the $h(0)$ property.

2 How many this means often depends on context. In the economics of competition, "many" is often between 2 and 20. In macroeconomic control the object of attention may be the whole or part of the population of the nation-state. When international agencies attempt to deal with items such as climate control, they face a world population of less than 2^{33} represented by around 200 nation-states. In biology, in investigating the internal control problems of a single human there are of the order of 2^{42} or 2^{43} cells in the organism.

3 The term is drawn from the mathematical domain known as analysis, and is defined as follows. Let $\{x_n\}$, $n \in 1, \ldots, \infty$ be a sequence with limit $\lim_{n \to \infty} x_n \equiv \bar{x}$. (For our purposes, the x will be either real scalars or vectors with real components.) Let $f(x)$ be a function defined on all x_n and on $\bar{x}$. Suppose that the limit $\lim_{n \to \infty} f(x_n) \equiv \bar{f}$ exists. If $f(\bar{x}) \neq \bar{f}$, then f is said to have a *removable singularity* at $\bar{x}$. The singularity is removable in the sense that the function f could be replaced by a function $\tilde{f}$ defined by $\tilde{f}(x_n) \equiv f(x_n) \forall n$ and $\tilde{f}(\bar{x}) \equiv \bar{f}$, with $\tilde{f}$ uniquely defined from f and nonsingular.

4 Such problems have arisen in providing a salvage value for commodity money to resolve the Hahn paradox, or in obtaining cooperation in certain infinitely repeated games such as the Prisoner's Dilemma. We illustrate a further such case for stabilizing correlated equilibria such as bank runs in chapter 8.

5 By a principled treatment we mean that the formulation of problem statements and models is itself constrained by criteria that limit the extent of ad hoc formulation permitted. Generally these criteria are chosen so that the treatment is consistent within some larger body of theory that uses the same concepts.

6 Maximization of entropy may be shown in many situations to be equivalent to minimizing the *information* implicit in the prior distribution [63, 333].

7 For the most recent review we are aware of, stressing in particular the perspectives from multiple disciplines, see [51].

8 This paradox can be overcome by the invention of a middleman in trade; see [356].

9 Here δ_i^j is the the Kronecker δ-function, equal to one if $i = j$ and zero otherwise. That is, with specialist endowments, each type of agent is endowed with a unique good characterizing his or her type.

10 If all $a_i^j = a$ and utilities are the same there will be no trade, but shadow prices can be established.

11 It is of interest to note that Mrs. Robinson [306] in her attempt to study oligopolistic competition introduced the model of a "world of monopolies" where each individual was endowed with a different commodity. This relatively unnatural model where the number of individuals equals the number of commodities has the advantage that it exposes clearly the aspects of symmetry in trying to define markets and trade.

12 Underlying all of the variations of the buy-sell market given here is the presence of an inactive equilibrium where no one trades. This is easily seen by observing that if all but one individual stay out of the market then the last individual has no motivation to enter. This is a highly implausible state, but formally fits the definition of a noncooperative equilibrium. It disappears with a small randomization.

13 If individuals are assumed to act not fully rationally—randomly or in error or under misperception—it is possible to design games such as the "Dollar auction game" where in an open auction the highest bidder obtains the object, yet the second highest bidder also pays [351]. There are variations such as where all bidders are required to pay a small "entry fee" for each bid. Actual play appears to be irrational, yet a profitable business has been based on this.

14 The specific inequalities are given in [356], ch. 9.

3 Formalizing Measurement and Modeling: The Preinstitutional Society

3.1 Concepts That Enter in Formalizing the Preinstitutional Society

In this chapter we introduce the concepts of symmetry, dimensions, and scaling, which will be fundamental to principled construction and interpretation of minimal models in the remainder of the book. Here we also introduce formal models for production and preferences, which we call the "preinstitutional society." Society defines the context within which the institutions of the polity and the economy exist. The preinstitutional society is meant to represent the shared layers of constraint within which different economic institutions must function.

3.1.1 On the role and interpretation of simple models

Economic life is potentially complex in all its dimensions: material, strategic, institutional, and behavioral. In comparison to reality, the space of tractable models is small and in most respects drastically oversimplified. If we wish to develop an empirically grounded theoretical economics capable of representing dynamics and in some cases capable of prediction, we must answer two classes of questions. First, is the purpose of simple models to suggest what *can happen* in an economy or what *does happen*, and how can we know whether simple models are even capable of representing a much more complex reality? Second, is there a systematic way to construct, classify, and select simple models to represent—in whatever approximate way—the behavior of *identifiable* classes of more complex cases? The subject of this chapter will be criteria for categorizing models, and the interpretation of minimal models as representatives of categories.

Models may be oversimplified in many ways. They may substitute homogeneity for heterogeneity, coarse few-parameter descriptions for more refined ones, or deterministic decisions and actions for stochastic ones. An example of oversimplification by homogenizing is the representative-agent assumption of general equilibrium. A famous example of parameter oversimplification is the Newcomb-Fisher equation $MV = PQ$ for money supply and velocity, which has become the basis of the quantity theory of money. Both the competitive equilibrium concept of general equilibrium theory and almost all solution concepts in game theory are based on precise choice and reliable action; solution concepts based on stochastic action are less developed and mostly elaborate the paradigm of the "trembling hand."[1]

If simple models are to provide an adequate theory of more complex reality in any of these respects, we must be able to show that their results are *universal*, in the technical sense of the term. Technical universality is the formal theory of abstraction.[2] Its underlying idea is that, while models that differ in detail will generally show some differences of behavior, sometimes a particular set of questions and a particular classification of models can be demonstrated for which all models in a class provably behave in the same way.

The greatest successes of universality classification have been achieved for problems of aggregation in stochastic processes.[3] The intuition that aggregated systems approach universal behaviors is the motivation behind the representative-agent theory and the Fisher equation, but the problem of validation in these more complicated cases has not been formalized. The problem of proving convergence of chaotic or stochastic dynamical systems to low-dimensional deterministic behaviors (the "as if rational" assumption of general equilibrium) is considerably more difficult, because convergence must be demonstrated in the context of structured dynamics.[4]

If a universality classification can be derived, then representative models may be chosen for convenience within each universality class. In general there will be a unique simplest model in each class, which we will call a *minimal model*. Specific, and sometimes predictive, theory based on minimal models becomes possible when we know the set of questions that can be asked within each class for which the answers will not depend sensitively on complexity within the class.

In much of economic theory, models are used as "proofs of principle" to illustrate that a particular response to incentives or constraints is possible in a highly simplified example. The interpretation of significance for simple models in a complex world is left to the judgment of experts, and is not itself formalized as part of economic methodology.[5] This situation has a certain resemblance (which some believe is intentional [265]) to the use of "toy" models in statistical physics, and more generally to the "phenomenological" models that have arisen in the formative decades of all natural sciences. It is possible that lessons about minimal modeling may be learned from these other fields, but for this empirical validation will be the key. Toy models have pointed the way toward universality classification in the natural sciences only in cases where their predictive accuracy or generality was far greater than their simplicity seemed to warrant. In addition to an emphasis on aggregation and averaging, the concepts of measurement, dimensionality and scaling, and symmetry have proved to lead to the most reliable criteria for model categorization and simplification in the natural sciences. We will make extensive use of these concepts in this and the following chapters.

3.2   Measurement, Aggregation, and the Concept of Dimension

The concept of measurement is closely related to the process of aggregation, in the multiplicity of ways this idea can be applied in economics. Continuously measured quantities such as endowments of goods, or bids or offers at market, may be aggregated if the goods are of the same type, but not necessarily if they are of different types.[6] Aggregation is unavoidable if the time period can be varied over which production and consumption occur. The measure of time itself can be aggregated, a topic which we will consider in depth in chapter 7. Combined aggregation of time, and of amounts of production and consumption in the same proportion, provides a principled distinction of *stocks* from *flows* in models. In particular, it may be used to test for well-defined *continuum limits*, in which the discrete periodization of time is a model artifact, not fundamental to observable economic facts. The distinction between monetary systems which have continuum limits and those which do not will reflect in a formal way the increased independence of fiat money as compared to commodity money as developed in chapter 5, which frees fiat to take on functions of control.

We will use the term *measurement* to refer to operations that quantify the count or the volume of something, and which possess three properties: (1) the measurement operation is performed in essentially the same way, no matter how much is measured; (2) measurement consists of comparing one quantity against another—called the *unit of measure*—and the unit of measure may be switched without changing the meaning of the measurement; (3) either measured quantities or the units of measure may be subdivided without changing the meaning of the measurement.

The concept of a *dimension* arises out of the process of measurement. It is the criterion by which elementary quantities either may or may not be aggregated while retaining the same measurement operation. Measurement and dimension are fundamental to the use of quantitative models in all sciences, a point which is both subtle and underappreciated. In the natural sciences, it is taken for granted that quantities with different dimensions cannot sensibly be added or subtracted. Yet at the same time, it has been possible to reduce so many natural phenomena to descriptions in terms of a few universal dimensions, enabling modes of aggregation where none had been suspected,[7] that it is often forgotten within the natural sciences how much freedom can exist to identify new dimensions. In contrast, in the social sciences where observables are often complex and heterogeneous, the difficulty is deciding when two quantities are similar enough to justify aggregating them and adding their respective measures. We believe that the only reliable notions of measurement and dimension are those based on an operational understanding of the problems of aggregation.

Dimensionality is among the most robust criteria for categorizing models. It must be respected by both deterministic and stochastic processes, and indeed by any quantitative process model. When aggregation is expressed by means of averages, many complex details may be suppressed, and the coarsest description of a system consistent with its dimensions may survive as the only robust description at the aggregate scale. Examples of drastic reduction of model complexity as a result of aggregation include both the Lévy family of solutions to the central-limit theorem and the Fisher-Tippet extreme-value distributions. The most general possible limiting distribution in either family is specified by only a few parameters. The model of the representative agent assumes that individual actions that are both complicated and unpredictable on the microscale average to aggregate behavior that is both simpler and more deterministic. Importantly, however, it assumes that the consistency of *utilitarian preferences* is a property preserved under aggregation, which is known to be true in some cases and not in others [166, 404].

The use of dynamically simple models is similar in spirit to the use of the representative agent. It is assumed that the detailed consequences of complex interactions will be more fragile under averaging than the results of simple or coarse interactions. Simple models of agent behavior are then hoped to describe aggregates better than they describe individuals. While results of this kind have been shown for important classes of dynamical systems [165], in general they are more difficult, and less is known about when they are true than is known about aggregation in utility theory.

We do not formally derive a universality classification of models in this volume, nor are we able to prove that this idea applies to general problems in game theory and gaming. We have chosen, however, to organize models on the basis of dimensions and symmetry, because these have proved to be the most robust properties under aggregation in other areas of stochastic processes. A somewhat fuller discussion of our motivation is provided in [383].

3.2.1 Aggregation and scaling symmetries

Aggregation of continuous quantities such as produced goods or monies leads to the concept of *rescaling* and the possibility of *scaling symmetries*.[8] Dimensions in the sense familiar from physics (such as mass, length, time) are usually derived from measurements of continuous quantities, including continuous changes over time in dynamical systems.

The primary use we will make of dimensions associated with continuous rescaling is the selection of minimal utility functions and price formation rules. We will consider distinct consumable goods to be incommensurable and so to have different dimensions. Prices, which reflect rates of exchange, must have dimensions that are the ratios of dimensions of two traded quantities. These dimensional consistency requirements act as primary constraints on the possible forms of price formation rules. When they constitute the *only* information about those rules, they may uniquely specify price formation to be of some minimal form, as we demonstrate below.

Similarly, the dimensions associated with utility, whether they are regarded as economically meaningful or not, are distinct from those of any goods. If the components of the marginal utility, which define offer prices, are chosen to be specified *only* by the dimensions of those prices, the resulting utilities are uniquely determined up to monotone transformation. Our construction of utilities in this manner has the character of a minimum information prescription. Their indifference surfaces are *homothetic*, meaning that they are self-similar under rescaling of the demands [404]. As a result, the general equilibrium problem defined by such utilities has a strong property known as *aggregatability*, which we will use to define natural measures of the value of trade and the efficiency of suboptimal allocations. Aggregatability thus follows directly from minimizing the description of an economy to the least complex form consistent with its scaling dimensions.

These utilities lead to Marshallian demand functions that are diagonal,[9] meaning that a change in the price of any good at fixed wealth leads to a demand change only for the corresponding good. (Equivalently: the income effect exactly compensates the substitution effect for all demand levels.) While this response to prices is highly restrictive and thus cannot be taken to reflect general economies, it is restrictive in an *appropriate way* to reflect a minimum-information assumption about preferences governed only by the dimensions of goods. More general substitution and income effects require us to specify additional information about relations among goods.

3.2.1.1   Other continuous symmetries   In this chapter we will concentrate on symmetries associated with dimensions, which affect game definitions and minimal forms.

A different, important class of symmetries arises when a game (or class of games) has a set of noncooperative equilibrium solutions in which the strategic variables may take different values but the economically relevant outcomes are indistinguishable. In this case the change in values of the strategic variables (which may only be defined as a joint change of several variables in a coordinated manner) is a symmetry with respect to the outcome. Such symmetries can make noncooperative solutions unidentifiable by agents, a topic considered in depth in chapter 4 and illustrated particularly in Market 5. Such cases can arise when private rather than centralized credit is used for exchange, but no mechanism is provided to compute the relative denomination of IOU notes written by different agents. A global symmetry from rescaling the numéraire relates any noncooperative equilibrium to any other, but precisely the symmetric nature of the change makes the determination of this scale factor impossible within noncooperative solution concepts. Only upon the introduction of further institutions can the symmetry be removed into appropriate constraints or mechanisms, so symmetry is a key link between institutions and the existence of market-clearing solutions.

3.2.2   Dimensional analysis for estimation and prediction

Consistent use of dimensions leads to one of the most universally useful systems in science, known as *dimensional analysis*. Recall that addition or subtraction of quantities is justified only if it reflects their aggregation in the material world. Similarly, setting two quantities equal must represent their comparison by some operation of measurement. If these two conditions are met, the *causal* influence that components exert over the behavior of systems comprising them can sometimes be inferred from their dimensions alone. Dimensional analysis has been presented for use in economics [75], and has been shown in applied problems (in finance [128, 377]). It can provide surprising predictive power for absolute magnitudes and relations among quantities such as prices and price volatilities, transaction costs, and rates of order flow through markets. We will provide an explicit illustration of the method for estimation of money supply and velocity in the fiat money model of chapter 5, and will make extensive use of arguments involving dimensions and continuum limits in our approach to dynamics in chapter 7.

3.3   Discrete Symmetries in Society and in the Economy

A distinct class of symmetries from those associated with aggregation and scaling is the class of *permutations*. Permutations apply to collections of discrete entities, such as agents or goods, when their particular identities or types are of interest rather than their aggregate magnitudes. Symmetry under exchange of agents or goods does not lead to a dimensional analysis and resulting minimal forms such as those we will derive for utility or price formation. Instead, it leads to criteria of simplicity and complexity based on counting. Symmetric treatment of all agents and all goods requires no parameters to distinguish subsets. Permutation symmetry may also be used to study markets for equal treatment, which in turn may be related to their allocative efficiency.

3.3.1   Uses of symmetry in analysis

Our main use of symmetry in the model of preeconomic society, and in the subsequent analysis of market models, is to *separate sectors and their effects on outcomes*. We will suppose as high a degree of permutation symmetry among agents and among the goods they produce as is compatible with distinguishing durable from nondurable goods, or goods from monies. It is important to emphasize that this does not mean we suppose that the actual societies on which markets act are symmetric in any similar degree, or that our model analyses apply only to permutation-symmetric classes of agents and goods. Rather, the use of symmetry in society is to study *sources of asymmetry* which first enter with the economic coordination and control system.

Asymmetry due to economic mechanism can be important in two respects. First, it can be a source of systematic distortion from the competitive equilibrium which reduces allocative efficiency. The economy may act directly in an asymmetric manner on agents of different types, as happens when one commodity among many is selected to serve as money. Alternatively, it may act symmetrically on all agents and all goods, but it may cause agents to treat goods they produce differently from those they must buy through markets, leading to correlations between agents and goods which impair allocative efficiency in a different way.[10] The form of this effect that we will see repeatedly is reservation of some goods from passing through the common economy. The tendency is for producers to overconsume goods they produce and to underconsume goods purchased from others, to save on transaction costs and discounted future utility associated with trade. The mechanism that produces this asymmetry is a wedge in prices.

The asymmetry that is created by a price wedge will also be a source of model simplification that we use. Trading posts in which the same commodity is used as money and as goods are a logical possibility and, like wash selling, there are cases in which they should be considered. However, in the minimal models developed here, agents never trade in such trading posts for the same reason they reserve goods that they can attain without trading. For simplicity we therefore omit such unused trading posts at the outset in defining our games.

The second way in which asymmetry can create distortions is essentially political, and we will not attempt to formalize it even though it is important, because it falls outside the scope of the strategic market games we use. Asymmetric treatment of agents or the goods they produce under economic rules can provide a reason to reject those rules, in the political or social domains.

A symmetric society provides a tabula rasa which imprints the symmetry properties of the economy on allocation outcomes. In some circumstances a normative goal in society may be to make the interfaces between society, economy, and polity as symmetric as possible, on the grounds that it will not be possible to anticipate asymmetries in the various sectors, or to correlate them across sectors in an equitable way. Asymmetric rules at any level are then regarded as a source of systematic bias which is better avoided rather than hoping it can be useful.

3.4   On Counting Degrees of Freedom

Symmetries form an abstract algebra of transformations that leave the structure of a system (a society, economy, etc.) invariant. This algebra alone is not enough to specify the consequences of symmetry for complexity. One must also know the number of *degrees of freedom* (DOF) on which the symmetry acts. The same symmetry group may have a range of *representations* when acting on different numbers of DOF. The complexity or structure of a society or economy will generally depend on how many types of goods or agents it distinguishes and, more important for our purposes, on how many strategic-choice variables are made available to the agents by the institutions of market clearing or monetary control.

Independent strategic choices count as (positive) DOF, and controls such as budget, or the absence of credit in cash-only markets, count as negative DOF. In strategic market games, the strategy choices are represented by continuous-valued variables (bids, offers, loans, etc.), while constraints are enforced by continuous-valued Kuhn-Tucker multipliers. For these the counting of DOF is straightforward. In a few cases that will be of conceptual importance to us, unconstrained variables which have no affect on economic allocations—similar to the numéraire in general equilibrium theory—will arise and will require to be identified by other means than counting of variables. We will find that negative DOF which are *not* explicitly reflected in constraints and Kuhn-Tucker multipliers often lead to serious problems of strategic indeterminacy in process models. Therefore it will often be possible to guess whether a process model is strategically well defined simply by checking whether all of its DOF, both positive and negative, are fully represented by strategy variables and explicit constraints.

3.5   The Generalized Jevons Failure in Preeconomic Society

In the next two chapters we adopt a standard model of society based on production technologies for m distinct nondurable, consumable goods. This production model, together with utilities of consumption for these goods, will define a basic set of capabilities and preferences, which it is the goal of all economic mechanisms to serve.

The m basic consumable goods are augmented in more specialized model economies by production of a single durable good, or by production of services such as formally modeled contract enforcement. The lifetime of nondurable goods—termed a "day"—is the basic timescale in the society, whose under-lying activity will consist of an indefinitely repeated daily cycle of production, trade, and consumption of these goods. Durable goods, when we need to introduce them, have a longer persistence period which is some (usually large) number of days. Their persistence will allow them to mediate many daily periods of production and consumption.

In this chapter we introduce notation for the generalized Jevons failure using the base case of m nondurables and a single-day time period as an example. Our emphasis is the kinds of symmetry that may be used to reduce models to minimal forms, and the meanings attached to such symmetries. When extra goods or rules are introduced, primarily in chapter 5, they will extend this basic pattern in a natural way, which we will define as required.

Following the general equilibrium paradigm, we suppose that goods are associated with *production functions*, which simply furnish endowments of goods in each period, in fixed quantities per agent. In cases where the number of agents is conserved but the adoption of production functions is modeled as a strategy choice, it is convenient to think of each production function as a map from a quantity of *labor*, measured in (agent numbers) × (trading periods), to consumable goods.

Situations corresponding to the Jevons failure arise because limits to time and energy place joint constraints on productivity, of whatever kind. Such constraints are effectively a form of interaction between production functions without regard to their type. We wish to define models in which low complexity is enforced by imposing high degrees of symmetry, and which will capture the two opposing cases: those in which productivity constraints are not binding on trade and the satisfaction of consumer wants, and those in which they are. We refer to these minimal idealized cases, respectively, as the alternatives of *generalist* and *specialist* production.

All goods are considered essential. In models this is expressed in marginal utilities of consumption that diverge when the demand for any good goes to zero. The generalist "production function" assigns a small and equal quantity of all goods to the agent who adopts this production strategy. Specialist production functions come in m types, and each type assigns an endowment (also equal for all types) of only one good to the agent for whom it is her production strategy. We treat the production functions for generalists and for each specialist type as mutually exclusive. Informally generalists may be considered as autarchic agents who pay for being jacks-of-all-trades with relatively low productivity in comparison with the specialists, who stand to benefit considerably from coordinating their division of labor.

The Jevons failure only arises if production generates *returns to specialization*, else all agents would simply be generalists. Therefore we choose the amounts of endowment from specialist versus generalist production functions so that specialist production, equally divided over the members of a society, yields a larger aggregate output of consumable goods than could be produced by an equal number of generalist producers. The essentiality of all goods ensures that an individual specialist, without the ability to obtain the goods she does not produce, is much worse off than a generalist, because distinct goods are not substitutable. A society of specialists who can achieve symmetric allocations through trade is then much better off than one of generalists. These three levels of welfare may be made arbitrarily divergent. We do not assume a particular origin for the returns to specialization, but because the relative magnitudes of production will be fixed beforehand, we are not attempting to represent open-ended sources of return such as innovation. Inovation requires a different treatment, as is noted in chapter 9.

3.5.1   Goods, agents, production, preferences

In the models of chapter 4, agents have preassigned production functions.[11] Agents like goods therefore come in a number m of types. We assume that for each type, a number r of *replicas* make up the population, whose total size will be $n \equiv mr$. Replication allows treatment of those aspects of competition not arising from specialization. Each agent is indexed by a subscript $i \in (1, \ldots, mr)$. In the one-period models of chapter 4, it is frequently convenient to arrange the replicas serially, so that agent indices $i \in (1, \ldots, m)$ may also be taken to represent types. The m types of goods are indexed with superscript $j \in (1, \ldots, m)$.

Market trade in all cases takes place in a single period. All the models solved in detail will use a "buy-sell" model for market price formation defined in [94]. We compare this clearing process to both simpler and more complex market mechanisms in later sections, when measures of market complexity are of interest.

3.5.1.1   Notation for endowments and demands   The initial allocation of good j to agent i will be called an *endowment* and denoted a_i^j. The final allocations resulting from interaction with the markets are denoted A_i^j. A utility for agent i is a function of the final allocations of i's consumable goods $\mathcal{U}_i(A_i^1, \ldots, A_i^m)$.

Markets aggregate and disaggregate both consumable goods offered for sale and *bids*, which may be consumable or may be essentially financial in nature. Even nonconsumable bids are treated by the mathematical models as goods in one important respect: they enter and leave the system according to specified rules, and are preserved in the act of exchange. Nonconsumable goods, however, are distinguished from consumable goods because we assume no direct utility from the holding of nonconsumables.

Either consumable or nonconsumable goods may function in the markets as monies; indeed, the comparison of the cost and flexibility afforded by the two is central to much of our analysis. For nonconsumables, their use as money is their only function. We therefore denote the amounts of these goods held with a different letter. For each agent i the initial holding will be m_i (possibly zero), and the holding after a cycle of trade will be M_i.

3.5.1.2   Agent symmetry, dimension, and minimal utilities   We will suppose that both the types of goods and the types of the agents who produce them are interchangeable—formally, we wish to consider problems in which both the statement of the problem and all properties of its solution are preserved under *permutation* of either the goods index j or the agent index i. Permutation symmetry among the production technologies is ensured by equality of the various endowments. Generalist production by agent i yields an endowment $a_i^j = \epsilon$, equal for any i and j. Similarly, specialist production will yield an amount $a_i^j \equiv a$, the same for all types of goods, if the good j is produced by agent i, and zero otherwise.

Full permutation symmetry of goods then requires that each agent have a utility which is a symmetric function of all m demand components. Permutation symmetry among agents, as long as only ordinal utilities are required, is a weaker requirement that all agents share the same set of indifference functions. For a utility $\mathcal{U}_i\left(A_i^1, \ldots, A_i^m\right)$ of agent i, the relative offer prices of goods j and j' are given by the ratios

$$\frac{\partial \mathcal{U}_i / \partial A_i^j}{\partial \mathcal{U}_i / \partial A_i^{j'}} \equiv -\left.\frac{\partial A_i^{j'}}{\partial A_i^j}\right|_{\mathcal{U}_i}. \tag{3.1}$$

The unique form of relative price that

- Is symmetric in all goods,
- Is constrained by the dimensions of relative price,
- Involves no other dimensional or dimensionless parameters

is given by

$$-\left.\frac{\partial A_i^{j'}}{\partial A_i^j}\right|_{\mathcal{U}_i} = \frac{A_i^{j'}}{A_i^j}. \tag{3.2}$$

The most general utilities producing this form are

$$\mathcal{U}_i = f_i \left(\prod_j A_i^j \right). \tag{3.3}$$

The f_i may be any monotone, concave functions. In many cases involving default, for which we model penalties as direct impacts on utility, the cardinality of f_i will be significant. In such cases, essentiality of all goods requires that f_i be unbounded below as its argument $\prod_j A_i^j \to 0$. Adopting utilities of the form (3.3) will enable us in chapter 5 to use dimensional arguments to easily estimate quantities such as money supply and velocity, for which the derivation of exact forms at noncooperative equilibria may be quite complicated. We use a dimensional argument similar to the one motivating Eq. (3.2) to choose a minimal market-clearing rule (3.4) in the next section.

3.5.2   Trading, borrowing, and default

The primitive unit which forms prices and clears goods is called a *trading post*. A single post will receive all offers of one good to be sold. Each agent i strategically chooses a set of offer quantities q_i^j for all posts j, and in the models below we will restrict $0 \le q_i^j \le a_i^j$. That is, consumable goods cannot be lent or borrowed.

Each post clears all bids and offers at a common price. The institutional guarantee of a law of one price distinguishes market trading from barter, even in cases where independent posts provide direct exchange of any good for any other.

The buy-sell trading post algorithm is our first concrete example of a unique minimal institution defined by dimensional analysis together with the number of strategic degrees of freedom assumed. The unique clearing rule consistent with the dimensions of price, synchronous strategy choice by each agent without knowledge of other agents' choices, and the absence of any other dimensional or dimensionless constants is

$$p^j \equiv \frac{\sum_i b_i^j}{\sum_i q_i^j} \equiv \frac{B^j}{Q^j}. \tag{3.4}$$

The final allocation for agent i resulting from trade at the post for good j is

$$A_i^j = a_i^j - q_i^j + \frac{b_i^j}{p^j}. \tag{3.5}$$

Post j delivers a fraction of the total goods to agent i proportional to i's fraction of the total bids at that post. In addition, i may retain any excess of his endowment that he did not offer for trade.[12] The final allocation of i's means of payment is

$$M_i = m_i - \sum_j b_i^j + \sum_j q_i^j p^j. \tag{3.6}$$

Each trading post disburses a fraction of its total bids to i in proportion to i's fraction of the goods delivered to that post.[13]

In chapter 4, we introduce promissory notes as well as bids denominated in consumable goods. Notes require processing at a clearinghouse, which represents a further level of centralization beyond the trading posts. When clearinghouses are used, the clearing rule for the means of payment becomes

$$M_i = \max \left[m_i + \sum_j \left(q_i^j p^j - b_i^j \right), 0 \right]. \tag{3.7}$$

The purpose of promissory notes is to operationalize various forms of *credit*. In many of our models incorporating personal or bank credit, it is impossible to exclude agent move profiles that result in default on promises to repay debt obligations. The default may result intentionally from the first-order conditions on utility (termed "strategic default"), or it may result from badly defined market mechanisms that leave agents unable to identify a mutually consistent scale for bids at trading posts, even if they do not intend to default. Whatever its source, default conditions must be handled by a well-defined process model. We adopt a uniform model of a *linear default penalty*, represented as a direct subtraction of utility in the form

$$U_i \to U_i + \Pi \min \left[m_i + \sum_j \left(q_i^j p^j - b_i^j \right), 0 \right]. \tag{3.8}$$

The penalty constant Π formally induces a relation between market structure and the scale for cardinal agent utilities. In market models that do not involve uncertainty, no-default solutions may often be found in which the constraint (3.8) is tight but not binding.[14] In these cases, neither the constant Π nor the cardinalization of utility enters quantitatively, and we may consider utilities to be ordinal so long as their gradients are sufficiently small compared to Π. In chapter 5 it becomes necessary to consider the magnitude of Π, but in that chapter we introduce an intertemporal context where the comparison of utilities across time periods already requires limited use of the cardinal forms.

In reality, courts and police provide penalties corresponding to Eq. (3.8), whereas clearing of goods and notes happens at markets. In the minimal models we consider, it does not matter whether the action of the clearinghouse is represented as a combination of a pure clearing activity with a court activity or the court is represented as a degenerate clearinghouse with no requirement to handle goods.

We find (Market 5 in chapter 4) that while clearinghouses and courts may lead agents to "prefer" consistent solutions without bankruptcy, these institutions alone may not make such solutions identifiable from the information available to agents within a noncooperative game. This limitation leads us to introduce a degenerate form of credit evaluation agency (degenerate in the sense that no exogenous uncertainty is assumed). Surprisingly, such an agency has nontrivial function, though it is intuitively closer to that of a foreign-exchange pricing body than a risk-assessing credit evaluator.

3.6 The Value of Trade and Quantifiers of Allocative Efficiency

The competitive equilibria (CE) furnish the most general standard of allocative efficiency possible in general equilibrium theory. For any endowment, the associated CE are the discrete set of wealth-preserving Pareto optima. These are the allocations at which no agent can propose a utility-improving trade that any other agent will voluntarily accept. At the CE, the value of the demand bundle for each agent is further required to equal the value at her endowment point, as computed *at the equilibrium prices*. Pareto optimality is a criterion by which to identify endpoints of trade, which applies to continuous recontracting as well as to one-shot clearing. However, in keeping with the general equilibrium emphasis on existence but not on attainability, the CE definition provides no algorithm by which agents can act noncooperatively to determine prices or to move toward optimal allocations. Moreover, in general cases where multiple equilibria exist, no constructive algorithm—decentralized or centralized—exists within the general equilibrium paradigm to select among them.

Process models that provide constructive solutions for noncooperative equilibria will generally produce outcomes that lie off the Pareto set. At such allocations, the offer prices of different agents will generally differ, both from each other and from the prices at any competitive equilibrium. Therefore, it is not meaningful to speak of preserving the value of the initial endowments at noncooperative equilibria. No preferred price system exists to define such a value. The very limited criteria by which "efficiency" is formalized in general equilibrium therefore become inapplicable to such noncooperative equilibrium allocations.

For noncooperative equilibria, one does not need a binary classification that separates the CE (a set of measure zero) from all other allocations, but rather a way to quantify the *inefficiency* of any allocation attainable by the society. If we wish to define quantitative measures of efficiency for general allocations, it will be necessary to have a standard reference for welfare, and it makes sense if the Pareto optima are ideally efficient under this standard. It is well known from game theory [177] and from the economic literature on aggregation [166, 172, 270, 378, 404] that no unique measure of the relative efficiency of Pareto optima exists outside the domain of aggregatable economies. Therefore we assume aggregatability in our minimal models.[15] Within the class of aggregatable economies, it is possible to define quite natural efficiency measures that do not rely on the cardinalization of utility, and which may be computed entirely from measurable quantities. By these measures, all competitive equilibria will be perfectly efficient and therefore equivalent.

The basis for welfare measures in aggregatable economies is the *money-metric* cardinalization for utilities [404]. One assigns to each indifference surface a utility level equal to the expenditure an agent would willingly make to attain the equilibrium allocation in that indifference surface. The efficiency of any allocation is then defined as a ratio between the sum of money-metric utilities for agents at that allocation and their utilities at a Pareto optimum.

In the same spirit as our other assumptions of minimality, our construction of a unique, natural efficiency measure associated with aggregatable economies enables us to understand how symmetries and the strategic freedoms offered to agents can affect allocative efficiency. The aspects of our use of money-metric utilities that may be retained under weaker assumptions than aggregatability are worked out in [378].

3.6.1   Aggregatable economies and money-metric utility

If our concern were primarily directed at consumer choice, rather than wealth and the overall functioning of a financially guided economy, we would hesitate in assuming away the income effect central to the microeconomic study of consumer demand. As details of consumer choice are played down in much that follows, we believe that the limitations on the utility function noted here are well worth considering, and they are discussed further in the appendix to this chapter.

Economists have justified the use of representative-agent models formally in economies where any collection of agents, having well-defined utilities and having arrived at some competitive equilibrium with each other, engage as a group in trade activities with the outside world that can be rationalized as the trades of a single representative agent who also has well-defined utilities. Economies in which all subsets of agents have this property are called *aggregatable*. A general property of aggregatable utilities is that all allocations in the Pareto set differ by reallocations among the agents of a *single* bundle of goods, which we will refer to as the *Gorman bundle*.[16]

The Cobb-Douglas indifference surfaces defined by utilities (3.3) are within the aggregatable class. In much of chapter 5, we will use the cardinalization $f_i(x) = \log(x)$ in Eq. (3.3) for convenience.

A different cardinalization, $f_i(x) = mx^{1/m}$, corresponds to the *direct money-metric* utility for level $\mathcal{U}_i$, as we show in the appendix. If we adopt a coordinate system for demands in which the Gorman bundle serves as a numéraire, the direct money-metric utility will equal the value of the unique Pareto optimum within any indifference surface. Because the Pareto set is a linear subspace in the $m \times n$-dimensional space of possible allocations, the sum of direct money-metric utilities in the economy is constant for all points in this set. The sum of direct money-metric utilities therefore furnishes a social welfare function that increases with all voluntary trade, and equals a constant value at all competitive equilibria. We will assign a money-metric value to any allocation for the whole society which is the sum of the direct money-metric utilities of the agents. The sum is a social welfare measure, and the contribution from any single agent is illustrated in figure 3.1.

3.6.2   Legendre transforms of utility and the economic quantity corresponding to physical "work"

The economic notion of efficiency was originally an analogy to the use of this term in engineering. In engineering, efficiency is the fraction of the possible useful work an energy store can provide that is successfully extracted by a physical process. The limits to work arise both from the finite capacity of the energy store and from the parasitic sources of waste and loss in the extraction process. Loosely, trade has been envisioned as a process to extract economic surplus, and the "efficiency" of trade has been intended to capture the degree to which surplus is not "wasted" by failures of economic coordination.

In aggregatable economies subject to individual utility maximization, these terms need not be used metaphorically. It is possible to show [378] that the

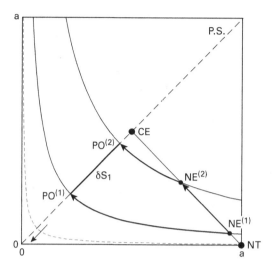

Figure 3.1

Edgeworth box construction for two specialist producers with utilities of the form (3.3). Hyperbolae are preference surfaces for agent 1, whose origin is in the lower left corner. NT identifies the initial allocation, which is also the no-trade solution for the final allocation. $NE^{(1)}$ and $NE^{(2)}$ are two final allocations that might arise from noncooperative equilibria in two different market situations (if this pair is replicated $r > 1$ times). The dashed line P.S. is the Pareto set, and $PO^{(1)}$ and $PO^{(2)}$ are points (also Pareto optima) to which a speculator external to the system could move agent 1 by voluntary trading, from the corresponding NE allocations. CE is the competitive equilibrium for this system. The limit of the thin dashed hyperbola indicated by the small arrow suggests a regularization of the speculator's actions from the initial endowments. In this limit, agent 1 is indifferent between his initial endowment and the origin, in which case the speculator can extract a. δS_1 is the profit the speculator would lose from such external manipulations, if the agents were somehow able to attain $NE^{(2)}$ by internal trading, instead of $NE^{(1)}$.

optimization problem in such economies is *mathematically equivalent*, in all essential respects, to the maximization problem that underlies the notion of work in physics and engineering. Samuelson [313] appreciated both this equivalence and the importance of the restriction that aggregatability entails, but he did not import into economic analysis the large range of useful comparative methods that have been developed for optimizing systems, based around the notion of work. In this section, we sketch the equivalence and use it both to define and to interpret a general measure of efficiency.

The details of our construction are presented in appendix 3.7. Here we summarize the result, which is easy to understand, for the specialist endowments $a_i^j = (a, 0)$ and utilities (3.3) as illustrated in figure 3.1. A given allocation, such as a no-trade solution (NT) or a noncooperative equilibrium (NE), is less than perfectly efficient if agents have potential welfare that remains unrealized at that allocation. A natural measure of the unrealized welfare for each agent is some bundle of goods that an external speculator could extract from her by a sequence of infinitesimal trades along her indifference surface from that allocation. (These are the worst kind of trading sequence she could be induced to accept voluntarily.) If the agent is left at some point on the contract curve[17] by the speculative extraction of goods, the speculator can then decouple. Even if all agents are allowed subsequently to trade internally, *by any algorithm*, no further advantageous trade will be possible. Since the price vector for goods at the final allocation will be common to all the agents, it defines (up to a normalization) the value of the bundle of goods that a speculator can extract together from all the agents.

We therefore define the welfare gain of each agent, resulting from internal trade, as *the value of the goods bundle that she has kept a speculator from extracting*, relative to what would have been extractable from the NT solution. In the case of specialist production, every agent's endowment is indifferent to an all-zero allocation bundle. Thus, from the NT solution a speculator could extract all of $\sum_j \sum_i a_i^j = rma$ from the collection of agents. The value of these extracted goods could be computed from the prices normalized to $p^j = 1$, $\forall j$ on the contract curve. In comparison, if the agents can trade internally to *any* point on the contract curve, by *any* path, the sum of their final allocations will be the entire endowment. Hence their gains from trade, expressed in money-metric terms, are rma. Note that for each agent, this gain is just the length of the segment of contract curve from the origin to the Pareto optimum, obtained by taking the inner product of the allocation vector with the normalized price vector. While this result is immediately clear for the CE by symmetry, a moment's reflection shows that it is true for any other Pareto optimum as well. Relative to the CE, these differ only by exchange among the agents of a uniform bundle $\delta A_i^j = \delta A_i^{j'}$, $\forall j, j'$, for each i. Thus we verify that the (wealth-preserving) CE has no special role in the welfare definitions relevant to allocative efficiency.

The value of a bundle extractable by an external speculator is the economic equivalent of the physical notion of *work* extracted by a load from a thermal system. The agents' utility gain in trading to the contract curve is measured by the reduction in work they could do on an external speculator (i.e., by profit they could voluntarily surrender). The reduction in the amount surrendered to any speculator who trades with a single agent will depend on the Pareto optimum at which the collection of agents finally arrives. However, the reduction in work (speculative profit) from combined exploitation of all the agents is an invariant. This invariant shared gain provides the reference standard from which efficiency may be measured. Although our measure of welfare is written as a utility gain, it is expressed in a money metric induced by voluntary trade, and it sensibly aggregates to a measure of social welfare. The welfare gain by the agent shown in figure 3.1, in going from $NE^{(1)}$ to $NE^{(2)}$, is just the length of the dark segment labeled δS_1. This quantity is also the increase in the utility version of agent 1's *entropy* S_1 from the transition $NE^{(2)} \rightarrow NE^{(1)}$.[18]

We therefore define the *efficiency* η of any allocation as the ratio of the sum of utility gains by all the agents from the NT solution to the gain *rma* that they could realize upon trading to the contract curve. This definition provides an intrinsic measure to the fraction of the contract curve for the endowments captured by any other allocation bundle. We show in appendix 3.7 (following this verbal description) that

$$\eta \equiv \frac{\sum_i m \left(\prod_j A_i^j \right)^{1/m}}{rma} = \frac{1}{rm} \sum_i \frac{m}{a} \left(\prod_j A_i^j \right)^{1/m}. \tag{3.9}$$

By construction, $\eta = 0$ at the NT solution, and $\eta = 1$ anywhere on the contract curve. The index η will be computed for each distinct allocation bundle that arises in the analyses of chapters 4 and 5.

For allocations of goods that are symmetric under exchange of agent roles, the results of our efficiency measure will be unsurprising: increasing distance from the contract curve monotonically decreases efficiency. The index (3.9) will also allow us, however, to compare such symmetric outcomes with the more complex agent-nonsymmetric solutions produced by some of the markets in chapter 4. When we come to consider intertemporal decisions, where the natural utilities of durable and nondurable consumables will differ, we will extend the one-period utilities in this chapter to what we call "effective" utilities for committed decisions. These also have Cobb-Douglas form, so it will remain appropriate to apply the efficiency measure (3.9) to the allocation sequences that result from repeated trades. The derivation of efficiency for these cases is performed in appendix 5.15 in chapter 5.

3.7   Appendix: Optimizing Systems, Wealth Extraction as Economic Work, and Natural Measures of Value and Efficiency

Walras originally [413] conceived utility as a measurable quantity, a kind of economic counterpart to the potential energy of Newtonian mechanics [265].

Economic equilibrium achieved by utility maximization was to correspond to minimization of total energy.[19] The local description of equilibrium at the level of interagent interactions was to be a kind of force balance, in which forces (the gradients of the potential) would be expressed as prices in utility theory.

The neoclassical program culminating in the formulation of Arrow, Debreu, and McKenzie, demonstrating the existence of an efficient price system, has had no need for the idea of measurable utility and the interpretation of prices as (normalized) gradients of utilities. When we consider monetary economies, however, many questions are naturally answered by labeling utility levels with the amounts of wealth that agents would voluntarily spend to reach them. This program restores many of the Walrasian concepts concerning utility. It replaces unmeasurable ordinal utilities with values derived from market prices and transfers of real goods among agents. The indeterminacy that rendered the Walrasian potential idea untenable, and that led to the abandonment of cardinal utility in much of neoclassical theory, reappears as a path dependence of money-metric cardinalizations, which may be characterized explicitly. For aggregatable economies, no path dependence arises in the welfare measure defined from money-metric utilities, so that in fact the Walrasian potential formulation can be carried as far as the construction of social welfare functions.[20]

When a potential formulation of utility exists in economics, it has many mathematical correspondences with the theory of thermodynamic potentials, as has been recognized imperfectly by many economists starting with Irving Fisher.[21] The correspondence is useful because thermodynamic potentials not only describe internal relaxation to equilibrium; they also provide ways to characterize the states separated by irreversible, internal transformations in terms of work and heat flows that, if permitted as exchanges with the environment, achieve the same state changes through reversible transformations. In the economic correspondence, an analysis with the same overall structure enables us to express welfare as a function of offer prices—the quantities actually constrained by utilities—and removes references to exchange prices which are not central for disequilibrium trades in closed economies.

The welfare measures we will obtain correspond numerically to Debreu's *coefficient of resource utilization* [78] for Cobb-Douglas economies. Our construction by means of money-metric utilities, and our emphasis on the role of offer prices, differ from Debreu's, as does the range of extensions for our approach outside the domain of aggregatable economies [378].

3.7.1   How seriously does one ever take cardinal utilities?

Our attitude toward cardinal utilities, social welfare measures, and efficiency in this chapter reflects our approach in the book as a whole. Maximization of utilities subject to constraint provides a formal exposition of certain classes of economically relevant structures of institutions and the decisions they support. It formalizes questions we may ask about processes in real economies, but we do not mistake severely simplified formal systems for the real world.

We do not assign much validity to utility functions as a prespecified, global, and invariant trait of economic decision makers. On the other hand, agents do make tradeoffs and often attempt to perform certain (usually short-term) optimizations, and indifference surfaces may capture in approximate form certain habitual tradeoffs, at the same time as aggregate expenditures and incomes may reflect aspects of agents' perceived welfare as it affects their behavior. The statement that cardinal utilities are probably not a realistic characterization of the global properties of most agents' economic decision making does not mean that all cardinalizations for a given set of preferences are equally unrealistic. Money-metric cardinalizations provide several desirable characteristics in models, and are reasonable coarse guesses at measurable variables that may be correlated with agent preferences in real economics.

Social welfare functions based on money-metric cardinal utilities address the important general problem of defining a partial order on nonequilibrium allocations, to express *how far* they are from the Pareto set (as does Debreu's coefficient of resource utilization through different measures). Our measures have the feature of uniqueness in aggregatable economies, and in economies that are not aggregatable their contour dependence provides a quantitative measure of how far welfare functions can deviate while still being derived from measures of expenditure. In real economies, ambiguity and context dependence as much as habit affect real decisions, so having ways to model them may be useful.

3.7.2   The dual system of expenditure functions and money-metric utilities

The totally symmetric Cobb-Douglas economy is simple enough that the form of direct money-metric utility could be inferred from symmetry alone. By extension of the Cobb-Douglas property that the Pareto set is a linear space to the more general class of Gorman-aggregatable economies, the form of the direct money-metric utility in the more general case could then be inferred as well. Such an approach yields a valid welfare measure, but it makes no connection to the concept of work, the relation between internal trade and wealth extraction when the economy interacts with outside agents, or with the meaning of offer prices in the context of nonequilibrium trades.

We therefore develop the potential formulation of utilities and money metrics systematically from the more fundamental property of *duality* between prices and demands in utility theory.[22] Samuelson [313] refers to systems in which convex objective functions are maximized subject to linear constraints as *minimum systems*. Their essential structure is mostly the same in utility theory and physical thermodynamics. Duality in minimum systems means that a given solution may be specified either by the demands $\left\{A_i^j\right\}$ held by agents or by the utility levels $\mathcal{U}_i$ and the offer prices $\left\{p_i^j\right\}$ which are the gradients of utility functions of those demands.[23] Not only do demands and prices furnish alternative ways to specify any allocation within an economy, but their roles as arguments and gradients are also dual. That is, it is possible to construct a function of prices so that its gradient gives the demands at those prices. In particular, it is the dual potential to utility that characterizes wealth extraction from open economies, and that corresponds to the work potential in thermodynamics.

The mathematical relation between dual potentials is known as the *Legendre transform*. Its general structure is that a potential function $f(x)$ generates a dual $\tilde{f}(p) \equiv x \partial f / \partial x - f$, where $p \equiv \partial f / \partial x$ and x is expressed as a function of p. Then $\partial \tilde{f} / \partial p = x$. Prices and demands play strictly symmetric roles under a Legendre transform, and, as emphasized by Samuelson [313], in a multivariate minimum system an entire suite of mixed Legendre transforms may be used to describe mixed quantity and price constraints. The asymmetry between prices and demands in economic theory arises from their interpretation in terms of the behavior of economies under aggregation. When economies in mutual equilibrium are aggregated, their demand variables from the original factor economies add to form the demand variables of the aggregated economy. The price variables, which are required to be equal in the factor economies as a condition for their mutual equilibrium, remain unchanged in the aggregated economy. For this reason, demands are sometimes referred to as *extensive* variables and prices as *intensive* variables, to distinguish their meanings in the dual representation.

The potential function of demands in neoclassical economics, whose gradient is proportional to prices, is of course the utility. The dual potential function of prices, whose gradient gives demands, is called the *expenditure function*. Its form is

$$e_i(p, \mathcal{U}_i) \equiv \sum_j p^j A_i^j, \tag{3.10}$$

in which $p \equiv [p^j]$ is a vector of prices and the demands are evaluated as functions $A_i^j = A_i^j(p, \mathcal{U}_i)$, which minimize e_i on the utility level $\mathcal{U}_i$ at prices p. These are known as the *Hicksian demands* at prices p and utility level $\mathcal{U}_i$. $\mathcal{U}_i$ is required as an explicit argument of e_i because the price vector has one fewer meaningful degree of freedom (the normalization, which sets the numéraire) than the demand vector.

The utility level sets the magnitude of a particular combination of the demand components. For Cobb-Douglas utilities, under the cardinalization given in Eq. (3.3), the product of the demands for all goods is set by the relation $\prod_j A_i^j = f_i^{-1}(\mathcal{U}_i)$. The remaining independent components of offer price are then determined from the remaining independent components of the Hicksian demand (and vice versa) by the relation

$$\frac{p^j}{\left(\prod_{j'} p^{j'}\right)^{1/m}} = \frac{\left(\prod_{j'} A_i^{j'}\right)^{1/m}}{A_i^j}. \tag{3.11}$$

The resulting explicit expression for e_i becomes

$$e_i(p, \mathcal{U}_i) = m \left(f_i^{-1}(\mathcal{U}_i) \prod_j p^j \right)^{1/m}. \tag{3.12}$$

If Eq. (3.12) is inverted to express $\mathcal{U}_i$ as a function of p and e_i, the resulting function is known as an *indirect utility* of prices and expenditure.

For quasi-concave utilities, the choice of price vector used in $e_i(p, \mathcal{U}_i)$ to create the indirect utility is arbitrary. For aggregatable economies, however, a natural choice will be the vector of competitive equilibrium prices. Not only are the competitive equilibria the unique points where the offer prices of all agents coincide, but it is a property of aggregatable economies that the price system is also the same at all of their competitive equilibria [378].

The expenditure function at equilibrium prices is used to create a utility function of demands $\{A_i^j\}$ known as the *direct money-metric utility*. It is perhaps easiest to understand the duality between this utility and the expenditure function by thinking of the direct money-metric utility as the integral $\int p \cdot dA_i$

of the expenditure needed to acquire a vector of goods A_i along some path in the Pareto set, which terminates at the utility surface $\mathcal{U}_i$. It is clear, then, why the gradient of the direct utility with respect to A_i should be the vector of prices. This construction is path-independent for aggregatable economies. The most general construction possible in nonaggregatable economies is a path-dependent cardinalization that we have termed the *contour money-metric utility* [378]. The contour utility preserves many desirable properties of the path-independent utility of aggregatable economies, and represents the most general extension of Negishi's prescription for constructing social welfare functions [270].

To compute an expression for the direct money-metric utility in the Cobb-Douglas economy, we restrict to the case that preferences are symmetric in all goods (as in the main text), and we suppose that labor is allocated among the production functions (whether generalist or specialist) so that the endowments of all commodities are also symmetric. This situation will represent the competitive-equilibrium labor allocation in chapter 5, and it serves as a natural reference case for the calculation of surplus. Under these assumptions, the vector of equilibrium prices p^* is likewise symmetric:

$$p^{*j} = p^{*j'}, \; \forall j,j'. \tag{3.13}$$

Using Eq. (3.11), the Hicksian demands at equilibrium prices (at any point in the Pareto set) also take equal values, which we denote

$$B_i^j = B_i^{j'}, \; \forall j,j'. \tag{3.14}$$

The vector of demands that passes through the same indifference surface as any bundle of demands $\left\{ A_i^j \right\}$ for agent i is therefore given by

$$\left(B_i^j \right)^m = \prod_j A_i^{j'}. \tag{3.15}$$

The direct money-metric utility (at equilibrium prices p^*) for the bundle $\left\{ A_i^j \right\}$ is defined as the expenditure function of the bundle $\left\{ B_i^j \right\}$ satisfying Eq. (3.15):

$$\mu_i \left(\left\{ A_i^j \right\} \right) = \sum_j B_i^j = m \left(\prod_j A_i^j \right)^{1/m}. \tag{3.16}$$

The utility μ_i defines the cardinalization f in Eq. (3.3) by $f_i\left(\prod_j A_i^j\right) = \mathcal{U}_i \equiv \mu_i\left(\left\{A_i^j\right\}\right)$. With this choice for f, and taking the money-metric values μ_i to quantify the utility levels, the expenditure function (3.12) (at any prices) becomes linear in utility,

$$e_i\left(p, \mathcal{U}_i\right) = \mu_i \left(\prod_j p^j\right)^{1/m}. \tag{3.17}$$

3.7.3 Measures of value based on expenditure

Let $w^j = \sum_i A_i^j$ denote the endowment of good j in a closed economy, for whichever case is of interest. Generally, we will be interested in symmetric, specialist production, for which $w^j = ra, \forall j$, since this case leads to the highest level of social welfare attainable in our minimal models. It is straightforward to check that the sum $\sum_i \mu_i$ of direct money-metric utilities is equal at all allocations on the Pareto set, and indeed that $\sum_i \mu_i = rma$ everywhere in this set for specialist production. Therefore we could simply declare $\eta \equiv \sum_i \mu_i / rma$ to be our efficiency measure, and it would be both unique and natural for aggregatable economies.

Although we will, ultimately, use this definition of efficiency, we develop it indirectly in this and the next section in order to make efficiency an *operational* concept, as we have made direct money-metric utility an operational concept by defining it as an integral of expenditures $\int p^* \cdot dA_i$ in the Pareto set. Our economic goal is to define efficiency in terms of wealth transfers that are constrained by the agents' *offer prices*—recalling that these are the subjects of theory and estimation in utility economics—eliminating reference to exchange prices that are unconstrained for disequilibrium trade. In the course of fulfilling this economic goal, we make contact with the thermodynamic notion of *work*, which is the mathematical counterpart to wealth transfers constrained by offer prices. This way of constructing measures of value in terms of constrained wealth transfers applies to nonaggregatable as well as to aggregatable economies, though in general these transfers will become path-dependent.

We begin by noting a property of aggregatable economies that is related to the property that they lead to constant price systems p^* at all competitive equilibria.[24] All points in the Pareto set differ only by the transfer among agents of a bundle of goods in fixed proportions—that is, the Pareto set is a linear space.

We will refer to this transferred bundle as the *Gorman bundle*. For the Cobb-Douglas economy, it is the bundle from Eq. (3.14), with all goods in equal portions. An agent's budget constraint at a Pareto optimum is the value of the Gorman bundle at equilibrium prices, here $\sum_j p^{*j} A_i^j = \left(\frac{1}{m} \sum_j p^{*j}\right)\left(\sum_j A_i^j\right)$, by symmetry of p^*.

In any competitive equilibrium, agents optimize utility against their budget constraint, conditionally independent of each other's choices given equilibrium prices p^*. In aggregatable economies, this property extends to configurations in which goods are *extracted* from the economy, as long as all agents have the allocations they could have at some competitive equilibrium. In other words, the agents cannot "see" whether their optimization problem is constrained by other agents or is constrained by an outside actor who has extracted wealth from the system. This property only holds, however, if the bundle of goods that has been removed from the system is the Gorman bundle. Therefore, we identify the value of the Gorman bundle at equilibrium prices as a natural measure of the wealth kept within an aggregatable economy, or extracted from it. We wish to establish the relation between the social welfare function and the wealth of the economy when multiples of its Gorman bundle are removed from it through voluntary trade.

We first consider the optimization problem of a single agent, since the whole-economy problem will factor into such optimization problems. We choose, for convenience, a normalization convention for prices $\sum_j p^j = m$ that will produce $p^{*j} = 1, \forall j$, in the symmetric Cobb-Douglas economy. Denote the projection of an agent i's allocations onto the Gorman bundle by $U_i \equiv \sum_j A_i^j$.[25] U_i will function as a natural numéraire for values. We now choose a "rotated" coordinate system for demands and prices such that the demand vector A_i may be written in terms of U_i and a transverse component $\vec{A}_i$ as $A_i \equiv \left[A_i^j\right] \equiv \left(U_i, \vec{A}_i\right)$. In the same coordinates, the normalized price vector becomes $p \equiv (1, \vec{p})$.

Now consider the decomposition of the expenditure function, where we take p and A_i to be offer prices and Hicksian demands related by Eq. (3.11),

$$p \cdot A_i \equiv \sum_j p^j A_i^j$$

$$\equiv \left(\frac{1}{m} \sum_j p^j\right)\left(\sum_j A_i^j\right) + \vec{p} \cdot \vec{A}_i$$

$$= U_i + \vec{p} \cdot \vec{A}_i. \tag{3.18}$$

Because offer prices are always normal to the indifference surface at the corresponding Hicksian demands, the variation of Eq. (3.18) under any change $\delta A_i \equiv \left[\delta A_i^j\right]$ may be written in terms of a change in the direct money-metric utility, as

$$p \cdot \delta A_i = \left(\prod_j p^j\right)^{1/m} \delta \mu_i. \tag{3.19}$$

Simply by decomposing $p \cdot \delta A_i$ in terms of its components (3.18), and using Eq. (3.19), we obtain an expression for the change of the Gorman bundle in terms of offer prices, Hicksian demands, and money-metric utility, in the form

$$\delta U_i \equiv \delta \left(\sum_j A_i^j\right) = -\vec{p} \cdot \delta \vec{A}_i + \left(\prod_j p^j\right)^{1/m} \delta \mu_i. \tag{3.20}$$

Eq. (3.20) is an identity, which follows from the definition of Hicksian demands as utility-maximizing arguments, and from the money metric for μ_i. Readers familiar with thermodynamics will recognize that it has the same form as the *conservation of energy* relation for a system i whose extensive quantities (corresponding to demands) are internal energy U_i and volume V_i. The thermodynamic version,

$$\delta U_i = -p\delta V_i + T\delta S_i, \tag{3.21}$$

is likewise an identity, and follows from the definitions of temperature T and pressure p as gradients obtained by maximizing entropy S_i. The correspondence between aggregatable economies and thermodynamic systems in equilibrium is only partial,[26] but it is sufficient that we may legitimately (and without making analogies) map temperature $T \leftrightarrow \left(\prod_j p^j\right)^{1/m} = \exp\left\{-\frac{1}{m}\sum_j \log\left(1/p_j\right)\right\}$ and entropy $S_i \leftrightarrow \mu_i$ to money-metric utility. Note, for later reference, that the fixed-temperature surfaces $T = $ const. correspond to $(m-1)$-spheres in the space of Hicksian demands. These spheres are "centered" on points in the Pareto set, where T attains its maximum value of unity.

The correspondence to thermodynamics is useful because it alerts us that the combination $p\,\delta V_i$ in Eq. (3.21) measures the physical quantity known as *work* which an expanding system can do on its surroundings. The quantity of work that a system can deliver is completely specified by its state transformation, because the values of both pressure p and volume V_i are uniquely defined for any (thermodynamic) equilibrium state. We have similarly constructed Eq. (3.20) so that the term $\vec{p} \cdot \delta \vec{A}_i$ is a function of offer prices which are uniquely defined at any demands A_i. Therefore we expect that the wealth change captured in $\vec{p} \cdot \delta \vec{A}_i$ will correspond to a maximal measure of extraction that an economy can provide. We need only make explicit the class of transformations for which it has this interpretation. Clearly, $\vec{p} \cdot \delta \vec{A}_i = -\delta U_i$ (the numéraire) whenever $\delta \mu_i = 0$, so these will be the class of *reversible* transformations in which agents are moved along their indifference surfaces, making infinitesimal trades at their offer prices.[27]

3.7.4 Measures of value in "open" aggregatable economies, and Walras's "potential functions" for prices

At this stage, before considering the meaning of welfare improvement from internal trading in a closed economy, we first consider the possibilities for wealth extraction by an external speculator who can dictate prices to agents, under situations when the agents cannot trade with one another. Examples of such agents might be uncoordinated individuals who deal with monopoly or monopsony firms, or agents in a country with missing markets, whose trade is conducted through the government. We will assume, however, that trades remain voluntary so that utilities remain meaningful.

The speculator's goal is to extract the maximum possible wealth from an economy, contingent on the allocations $\left\{A_i^j\right\}$ at which he finds it. Maximum extraction will be attained only if he leaves agents with equal offer prices, so that when the speculator decouples they have no further utility-improving trades to pursue. This is always possible if the agents are left at bundles (3.14) satisfying the conditions on the Pareto set. Because, in this section, we have introduced the speculator as a device to analyze the value of competitive equilibria, we will furthermore assume that he has no way to convert other demand bundles to the numéraire U, so that he seeks to extract *only* the numéraire, and maintains zero inventory of other bundles of goods.

The speculator can induce each agent i to exchange a bundle $\delta \vec{A}_i$ by paying δU_i given by

$$\delta U_i = -\vec{p}_i \cdot \delta \vec{A}_i, \tag{3.22}$$

where $\vec{p}_i$ are that agent's offer prices at her particular A_i. The increment $\delta \vec{A}_i$ obtained from one agent may be sold to others at equal or better prices, leaving the speculator with a net bundle $-\sum_i \delta U_i$ of the numéraire. The process terminates when the speculator leaves all agents with their offer prices $p_i = p^*$, or equivalently, $\vec{p}_i = 0$.

Suppose we consider the speculator's best outcome if the agents start with specialist endowments (an allocation in amount a of a single good to each agent), and no trade has occurred within the economy. Each agent is indifferent at the endowment point to having zero endowment of *all* goods, from the form (3.16) of utility. Therefore the speculator can extract, at best,

$$-\sum_i \int \delta U_i = rma, \tag{3.23}$$

leaving each agent i at the origin,[28] where

$$U_i(0) = 0. \tag{3.24}$$

We may now make use of the particular cardinalization given by money-metric utility to relate the welfare gain to the previously considered speculator's problem of extraction. In the process, we will obtain an expression that relates the change in value to the offer prices, even if these are not the prices at which agents trade.

By the identity (3.20), if we construct the quantity

$$\mathbf{A}_i \equiv U_i - TS_i$$

$$= \sum_j A_i^j - m \left(\prod_j p^j A_i^j \right)^{1/m}, \tag{3.25}$$

with (as usual) p and A_i in the relation of offer prices to demands, then its variation under any change δA_i is just $-\vec{p} \cdot \delta \vec{A}_i$. This identity arises in open-economy trades where $\delta S_i = 0$ and agents trade at their offer prices. It also arises in closed-economy trades, where $\sum_i \delta U_i = 0$ because total endowments do not leave the system, no matter what exchange prices are used. Thus the role of the offer prices, when properly normalized, is to assign a value to the gains that agents attach to any change δA_i relative to the component δU_i.

(As something of an aside regarding the normalization of prices, note that Eq. (3.25) is equivalent to a partial derivative along the contours $\delta T = 0$,

$$\left. \frac{\partial \mathbf{A}_i}{\partial A_i^j} \right|_T = -p^j. \tag{3.26}$$

That is, $\mathbf{A}_i$ is a *potential function* whose gradient along $\delta T = 0$ gives the actual-market prices of goods. This potential function is as close as one can get, in general, to Walras's conception of utilities as potentials for prices, and of utility maximization as a kind of force balance that obtained when agents' offer prices were equal and oppositely directed. Note, however, that $\mathbf{A}_i$ is not simply the utility, which corresponds to S_i, and that the gradient is subject to the restriction $\delta T = 0$.)

In thermodynamics, $\mathbf{A}_i$ is known as the *Helmholtz free energy*, and it is constructed as the Legendre transform of the entropy S_i. The sum of free energies $\sum_i A_i$ of a collection of subsystems measures the maximum work that an external load can extract from the collection. Similarly in utility economics, $\sum_i A_i$ measures the maximum wealth that an external speculator can extract. Thus we arrive at the operational definition of welfare: If agents can trade internally by any mechanism, the sum $-\sum_i \delta \mathbf{A}_i$ is the wealth (counted in numéraire U) that an external speculator can no longer extract through voluntary trade with them.

The relation between extraction and social welfare can be most immediately checked for allocations within the Pareto set, where $T = 1$. These are the allocations to which the speculator can bring an agent from any initial value $\left\{A_i^j\right\}$ by exchanging the agent's original allocation incrementally for one that consists only of the Gorman bundle,

$$U_i\left(\left\{B_i^j\right\}\right) = S_i\left(\left\{A_i^j\right\}\right). \tag{3.27}$$

Joint changes $\left\{\delta A_i^j\right\}$ that agents might make through internal trade, which increase their welfare by $\sum_i \delta \mu_i$, fix total $\sum_i U_i$, but reduce the fraction of this numéraire that the speculator can extract by trade at their raised utility levels. The amount of the reduction is $\sum_i \delta U_i = \sum_i \delta S_i$ governed by Eq. (3.27).

We have now assigned a meaning to direct money-metric social welfare, and to offer prices at nonequilibrium allocations, operationally in terms of wealth extraction. Finally, we return to the use of this measure to define efficiency. From symmetric, specialist production, the sum of agents' holdings of the numéraire at any Pareto-optimal distribution is

$$\sum_i U_i|_{\text{P.O.}} = \sum_i \sum_j a_i^j = rma. \tag{3.28}$$

If we suppose that *any* allocation $\left\{A_i^j\right\}$ results from trade beginning at the same initial conditions, it is natural to define the efficiency of trade η as the ratio between the sum of their money-metric utilities at the outcomes $\left\{A_i^j\right\}$ and the sum on the Pareto set,

$$\eta = \frac{\sum_i U_i\left(\left\{B_i^j\right\}\right)}{\sum_i U_i|_{\text{P.O.}}} = \frac{\sum_i S_i\left(\left\{A_i^j\right\}\right)}{rma}. \tag{3.29}$$

The efficiency (3.29) may be further interpreted as a weighted average of the efficiencies with which all agents satisfy their wants, in which the weight functions are the fractions of the equilibrium value each holds. Define the normalized relative allocation for any agent i by

$$\hat{A}_i^j \equiv \frac{A_i^j}{\sum_{j'} A_i^{j'}}. \tag{3.30}$$

Then we may express the economic entropy (the direct money-metric utility) as a product

$$
\begin{aligned}
S\left(\left\{A_i^j\right\}\right) &= \left(\sum_j A_i^j\right)\left(\prod_j m\hat{A}_i^j\right)^{1/m} \\
&= \left(\sum_j A_i^j\right) e^{-D\left(1/m\|\hat{A}_i\right)},
\end{aligned} \tag{3.31}
$$

in which the expression

$$D\left(\frac{1}{m}\middle\|\hat{A}_i\right) \equiv \sum_j \frac{1}{m}\log\left(\frac{1/m}{\hat{A}_i^j}\right) \tag{3.32}$$

is called the Kullback-Leibler divergence [63] of the distribution $\hat{A}_i$ from the uniform distribution over goods, whose components all equal $1/m$. $\sum_j A_i^j$ is agent i's share of the economy's value, and the exponential is the efficiency of her relative distribution. In terms of these individual efficiency measures, the efficiency of the allocation in the whole society then decomposes as

$$\eta = \sum_i \left(\frac{\sum_j A_i^j}{rma}\right) e^{-D\left(1/m\|\hat{A}_i\right)}. \tag{3.33}$$

3.7.5   Mixed boundary conditions and the use of economic "reservoirs"

Readers familiar with thermodynamic methods will recognize that our use of the Helmholtz potential and the notion of work in the previous section were slightly different from their usual use in physics. The Helmholtz potential $\mathbf{A} = U - TS$ is generally derived as a Legendre transform of the entropy $S(U, V)$ with respect to only *one* of its extensive arguments: the energy U. $\mathbf{A}$ measures the maximum possible work extracted from a system when its extensive argument V is used as a control variable, and the *gradient* value T is held fixed by contact with an external reservoir. In economics such transformations correspond to expansion paths controlled by mixed price and demand (or budgetary) boundary conditions.

An economic construction of this form could not be performed while preserving the permutation symmetries (in i and j) of the totally symmetric Cobb-Douglas economy. In that economy only one good—the Gorman bundle—has a fixed price at all competitive equilibria. In this section we extend the Cobb-Douglas economy, in a way that addresses three elements not present in the previous example. (1) Our extension incorporates the use of monetary variables and linear terms in the utility, which in the following chapters arise from budget constraints and bankruptcy penalties. (2) By introducing a separate, linear good (which we will think of as money) in the utility construction, we may naturally introduce a market for trades between money and the Gorman bundle U_i at fixed prices, permitting the usual use of the Helmholtz potential along expansion paths with mixed boundary conditions. (3) By making the utilities quasi-linear with money as the linear good, we arrive at economic models that are strictly equivalent to thermodynamic systems. The pure Cobb-Douglas example without money was equivalent in the necessary respect to define a consistent welfare function, but not in the computation of elasticities, as reviewed in [378].

We introduce a money which we call "cash" and extend the description of an agent's demands to a vector $x_i \equiv \left(M_i, \left\{ A_i^j \right\} \right)$. We suppose that agents are given no endowment of cash, but that they can trade the Gorman bundle U_i with a large market at a fixed price π. Thus, all exchanges with the large market satisfy the constraint

$$\sum_j \delta A_i^j + \pi \delta M_i = \delta U_i + \pi \delta M_i = 0. \tag{3.34}$$

The large market offers trades only between the Gorman bundle and cash.

Extending the model of the disaggregated agents and the speculator to include these cash trades we may think of a small country selling an export good on a world market large enough to stabilize prices. Internal exchanges by the agents in the small country may be subject to missing markets, so that their trade in other goods is mediated by the government (the speculator), which can now exchange wealth for cash on the world market as well.

For simplicity, we do not suppose in this appendix that cash has direct utilitarian value. We suppose, however, that (as "cash") the value of $M_i \geq 0$ for all agents i in all situations. This constraint on purchases is enforced by adding a Kuhn-Tucker multiplier to the utility

$$\mathcal{U}_i(x_i) \equiv m \left(\prod_j A_i^j \right)^{1/m} + \kappa_i M_i, \tag{3.35}$$

making the resulting function effectively quasi-linear in M_i, with a marginal utility of wealth κ_i that will be determined dynamically by budget constraints. κ_i runs over the range $[0, \infty)$ and is chosen to minimize the expression (3.35).[29] We have also assumed the direct money-metric form for utility as a convenience, though this is not essential.

The utility maximization problem subject to a budget constraint $\sum_j p^j A_i^j + \pi M_i$, which now includes the value of cash, is defined by variation of the modified Lagrangian

$$\delta \left[\mathcal{U}_i - \lambda_i \left(\sum_j p^j A_i^j + \pi M_i \right) \right] = 0, \tag{3.36}$$

in which λ_i is a second Kuhn-Tucker multiplier enforcing the total budget constraint.

Solving Eq. (3.36) gives the marginal utility of M_i in units of the numéraire $\mathcal{U}_i$,

$$\kappa_i = \frac{\pi}{\left(\prod_j p^j \right)^{1/m}} \leftrightarrow \frac{\pi}{T}. \tag{3.37}$$

The expenditure function now depends on m prices (including π) and on utility $\mathcal{U}_i$, and takes the form

$$e_i(\pi, p, \mathcal{U}_i) = \pi M_i + \sum_j p^j A_i^j$$

$$\equiv \pi M_i + U_i + \vec{p} \cdot \vec{A}_i. \tag{3.38}$$

The direct money-metric utility is simply $\mathcal{U}_i$ of Eq. (3.35), evaluated at $\kappa_i = \pi$. The Helmholtz potential is now constructed strictly as in thermodynamics, as $(\pi,p) \cdot (M_i, A_i) - \vec{p} \cdot \vec{A}_i - T\mu_i \equiv U_i - TS_i{}^{30}$ taking the form

$$\mathbf{A}_i = e_i - \left(\prod_j p^j\right)^{1/m} \mu_i - \vec{p} \cdot \vec{A}_i. \tag{3.39}$$

Terms involving M_i cancel exactly, recovering the form (3.25) above. The economic counterpart to entropy remains the function of the previous section, though it is now significant that it is a function *only* of the nonlinearly valued goods of the original Cobb-Douglas economy,

$$S_i = \mu_i - \frac{\pi}{\left(\prod_j p^j\right)^{1/m}} M_i = m \left(\prod_j A_i^j\right)^{1/m}. \tag{3.40}$$

We see that it is now possible for the (formal) utility level μ_i to change together with M_i while leaving the entropy function of the nonlinearly valued goods unchanged.

The extraction problem for a speculator interacting with an economy coupled to a world market for cash is worked out in [378]. There it is shown that money flows between the agents and the world market have the same relation to entropy change as heat flows do in thermodynamics. This correspondence is only possible in all respects for quasi-linear economies, in which the path dependence of disequilibrium trades to the Pareto set affect the linear part of the utility level, which can be entirely projected out of the first-order conditions and hence of the agents' decision processes. These more elaborate uses of the correspondence to thermodynamics and work will not be needed in the models we develop here.

Notes

1 For significant departures from this pattern, see [133] for a statistical model of price formation and [199] and [379] for inherently statistical definitions of equilibrium. The formulation of statistical equilibria has been extensively pursued in finance and the econophysics literature [91–93], as an explanation for widely observed exponential or lognormal distributions of income and wealth [392]. Several other robust distributions have also been associated with characteristic wealth generation and shuffling mechanisms. It was shown in [50] that uniform saving propensity of the agents constrains the entropy-maximizing dynamics in such a way that the distribution becomes gamma-like, while (quenched) nonuniform saving propensity of the agents leads to a steady-state distribution with a Pareto-like power-law tail [56]. A detailed discussion of such steady-state distributions for these and related kinetic exchange models is provided in [49].

2 By "abstraction" we mean the substitution, for each of a set of particular detailed cases, of a less-detailed description that refers to the set as a whole. In a formal theory of abstraction, specific and falsifiable claims should be provable from the simplified description, and they should be shown to follow as well for each particular member in the set for which the abstract description stands.

3 Examples that were the starting points of universality classification include the Lévy-Khinchin proof of convergence of summed variables under the central-limit theorem, and the Fisher-Tippet proof of convergence to the class of extreme-value distributions.

4 The required convergence is convergence of measure, both for stochastic processes and for deterministic chaos. In the theory of stochastic processes, the emergence of low-dimensional deterministic behavior is the domain of large-deviations theory. Convergence of chaotic dynamic systems onto low-dimensional attractors corresponds qualitatively to the emergence of compact summary statistics for stochastic processes.

5 We feel that the econometric practice of "calibration" should not be mistaken for the more fundamental and much more difficult process of genuine model validation. Calibration amounts to identifying the best-predictive parameters within an arbitrarily specified model class. It is a weaker process than model comparison [6, 328], which asks how much complexity is justified by prediction, or than model justification [156].

6 The question of the equivalence of goods for purposes of aggregation is the difficult economic problem of assessing *fungibility*. When are red and white billiard balls perfect substitutes, and when not?

7 The reduction of complex dimensions to simpler universal factors is the basis of *dimensional analysis*. We introduce this system in section 3.2.2, and develop its general form and apply it to economic problems in the following chapters.

8 The concept of *homogeneity* used throughout economics is defined by the behavior of equations under the rescaling of their arguments. The homogeneity of order zero of real goods and prices in general equilibrium theory with respect to the scale of the numéraire reflects a symmetry under scale change. Examples where we will use scaling symmetries to make nontrivial choices in later chapters include section 4.4.2 on the foreign exchange solution to market clearing among markets with multiple currencies; section 5.9 on the dimensional analysis predictions for relations between the money supply and the institutional scales in a society; and section 7.13.2 on the implications of time-continuously-accessible markets for the assumptions of quasi-linear utilities.

9 Let u be a utility function of demands $\{x_i\}$, denote the corresponding prices $\{p_i\}$, and denote wealth as $w \equiv \sum_i x_i p_i$. Then we say the Marshallian demand is diagonal if $\partial x_i / \partial p_j \big|_w \propto \delta_{ij}$, where δ_{ij} is the Kronecker δ, equal to one if $i = j$ and zero otherwise.

10 In the case where markets act asymmetrically on goods, the distribution of the consumption levels of goods breaks permutation symmetry among agents. In the case where markets produce correlation between self-production and consumption level, agents' internal allocations are asymmetric and therefore inefficient, but there remains a joint permutation symmetry acting on both agents and goods.

11 The models of chapter 4 are all one-period exchange models, which are not rich enough to capture the adoption of specialist production as a strategic action.

12 The ability to withhold endowments distinguishes the buy-sell model from the simpler sell-all model of [356]. The sell-all model requires only one strategic degree of freedom per trading post (the bid level), whereas buy-sell requires two degrees of freedom (amount bid and amount offered). A subset of the most symmetric exchange models considered in chapter 4 are not definable within a sell-all trading post model, because they treat bids and offers identically.

13 In Markets 1 and 2 of chapter 4, where each good serves both as commodity traded and as means of payment, this rule will require minor modification, though its overall form and its property of proportional clearing will be retained.

14 It is shown in [356] that as long as Π is sufficiently harsh to preclude strategic bankruptcy by some limiting agent, such interior solutions are assured.

15 The Cobb-Douglas preferences that we have already presented, motivated by symmetry and dimensional analysis, are also aggregatable.

16 See [378] for a proof of this property and further discussion.

17 The contract curve is the subset of the Pareto surface contained in the interior of the lens formed by the union of the indifference surfaces of all agents in the economy. No sequence of voluntary exchange, within the economy or interacting with the external world, can take agents outside this lens.

18 See [378] for motivation, and appendix 3.7 for derivation of this case.

19 Energy minimization turns out not to be a principle of Newtonian mechanics, but this was not understood in Walras's day.

20 Money-metric utility does not extend the Walrasian potential formulation as far as dynamics, even in general aggregatable economies. Only in the subclass of quasi-linear economies are both welfare and the preferences that may affect arbitrary trades rendered path-independent in money metric.

21 Fisher was a student of J. W. Gibbs, the inventor of modern statistical mechanics and, with Boltzmann, among the first to understand its connection to classical thermodynamics. Yet Fisher's attempt to map economics to thermodynamics was fraught with many elementary misunderstandings and conceptual inconsistencies, which precluded his ever recognizing the actual deep differences that make such a correspondence problematic. Fisher's writing formed part of a long sequence of analogy making that drove the topic of a correspondence between utility and thermodynamics into disrepute. Some of the correct observations and fundamental errors in this literature are reviewed in [378].

22 The dual structure of expenditure and utility economics is reviewed by Varian [404], and its parallels with the theory of stability and extremization in thermodynamics are reviewed by Samuelson [313]. The Samuelson treatment is concerned with revealed preference in the most general case, for which unique equilibria will not generally exist. Therefore he does not pursue analytic methods based on the parallels to thermodynamic work. These are therefore developed in [378].

23 Here we sketch the common features of duality that are shared between utility economics and thermodynamics. We will return below to idiosyncratic features of the economic case, including the arbitrary normalization of prices and the role of utility level in the dual relation.

24 See [378] for a derivation of these properties in terms of the usual Gorman conditions for aggregatability.

25 U_i corresponds to the internal energy state variable in physics, not to be confused with the utility $\mathcal{U}_i$. This unfortunate notation may be due in part to a belief by Walras that utility would be the economic counterpart to physical internal energy. We now know that this correspondence is not the correct one, as explained in [378].

26 This correspondence is exact only for the subset of aggregatable economies that are quasi-linear, as proved in [378].

27 We will return in a later section to the relation of μ_i to entropy, and to the economic counterparts to "heat transfers" as flows coupled to changes in entropy.

28 This is not an artificial limit. It may be obtained by considering the regular limit of extraction along the indifference surface indicated by the dashed hyperbola in figure 3.1.

29 In later chapters, where we consider finite-range Kuhn-Tucker multipliers to model bankruptcy, we discuss the interpretation of the Kuhn-Tucker variational problem as a game. Agents choose their decision variables to maximize constrained utility, while an adversary chooses the Kuhn-Tucker multiplier to minimize constrained utility. For unbounded multipliers such as κ_i, this minimax problem requires that agents always keep $M_i \geq 0$.

30 This construction is worked out and explained in detail in [378].

4 Supporting Attainable Solutions: Symmetry and Complexity in One-Period Exchange Mechanisms

4.1 From the Preinstitutional Society to the Simplest Level of Market Exchange

In chapter 3 we introduced a system of types, along with basic symmetrized models of production and preferences, which will form the social foundation for our comparative analysis of economies in this and the next chapter. In this chapter we begin to compare economies at the least-structured level of dynamics: market systems characterized by one-shot clearing and hence a single timescale for strategic choices. We choose that timescale to coincide with the social "day" that is the natural cycle of production and consumption.

The one-shot clearing mechanisms differ in the tradeoffs they make between simplicity and allocative efficiency. We compare different clearing mechanisms according to a number of structural properties that can be used as measures of complexity. We use the measure of allocative efficiency from the previous chapter to quantify distortions from the competitive equilibrium for each mechanism, arising both within agents' consumption bundles and in relative distribution among agents.

4.2 Symmetry, Equity, and Efficiency

The attainability of an allocation equilibrium can have two facets. One is the efficiency of an attainable solution relative to the solution at a competitive equilibrium. It is well understood that the competitive equilibria for an arbitrary endowment in an arbitrary economy cannot be constructively computed or selected in general. Therefore constructive solutions must deviate from some competitive equilibria in some economies. General constructions such as the noncooperative equilibria of strategic market games will deviate from Pareto optima even in cases where the competitive equilibria are unique and could in principle be identified from the information assumed.

The second facet of attainability is that apparently constructive solution concepts may have harmful or even fatal ambiguities in the selection of rational strategies. Agents may be able to work out the desired equilibria in goods, and market mechanisms may provide them strategies which determine prices and allocations. Yet these mechanisms may admit a *range* of strategic actions that are strictly equivalent with respect to allocation. If such solutions require coordination among agents, and are surrounded by suboptimal solutions at all coordination failures, the very degeneracy of solutions may make identification of strategies impossible in principle.

Both facets of attainability of solutions involve symmetry in a fundamental way. The deviations from competitive equilibrium that are the cost of constructive solutions often result from asymmetric treatment of agents by markets, or from correlations between agent production and trading strategies that lead to asymmetric treatments of goods. Symmetry in the treatment of agents can in principle be restored, but, without considerable centralization of information, doing so generally leads to ambiguities in the strategic path toward optimization, which undermine coordination.

In this chapter, we will use a comparative analysis of one-period trading mechanisms to study how arbitrary degrees of freedom are removed by market mechanisms or constructive solution concepts—whether they are taken out of the choice sets of individual agents or are somehow distributed over the economy—and how this difference affects the equity of the allocation or the need for complex market redundancies or information centralization. We will also compute the consequences of asymmetry for allocative efficiency. The tradeoff between attainability and efficiency will be considered from a different perspective (existence or nonexistence of rules) in chapter 5.

4.2.1   Counting degrees of freedom, and the problem of the undetermined numéraire

Much of the importance of process analysis can be illustrated with a single dilemma: the meaning and determination of the value of the numéraire for exchange. In an exchange economy with m goods and a corresponding m types of agents who produce them, the general equilibrium solution fixes $m - 1$ components of the price vector. The specification of these is exact at any given equilibrium, even if it is ambiguous up to the choice of equilibrium within a countable set. The $m - 1$ components are those corresponding to the ratios of marginal utility among any of the m goods. The value of the numéraire component of prices is arbitrary, and is defined in general equilibrium to be meaningless.

The duality of prices and demands in neoclassical economics[1] directly relates not only the counts but also the meanings of these two properties of any equilibrium. Each agent nominally expresses m offer price components, which are the gradient components of her utility function at its m demand arguments. The $m - 1$ components in the tangent space to the indifference surface correspond to relative prices, while the magnitude of the last component depends on the cardinalization of utility, which is irrelevant to the existence of a competitive equilibrium.

If a noncooperative and constructive procedure is required to arrive at an equilibrium, however, agents must make either bids or offers on each of m goods, and so must contribute to formation of m price components. This is true even if they hold only ordinal preferences, so that in the gradient of their utilities one component is considered economically irrelevant. One of the price components will indeed be irrelevant even to the specification of noncooperative equilibria, but agents have no way to know *ahead of time* (that is, while making their strategic choices at market) which component will be the irrelevant one. The market mechanism must therefore provide a way to make clearing independent of the irrelevant component, or else to ensure that it never arises. If the market cannot do this, agents have no way to rationally choose strategies, and coordination on a noncooperative equilibrium becomes impossible. The models below will illustrate cases of both possibility and impossibility of constructing noncooperative equilibria, which will depend on the approach taken to fix or eliminate the arbitrary numéraire.

4.2.2   Symmetric versus asymmetric imposition of constraints: equity and efficiency considerations

In general we see that three considerations are in conflict in removing or specifying the arbitrary choice variable. These are: (1) redundancy and therefore cost in the trading algorithm itself, (2) the symmetry with which the choice variable is denied to agents, and (3) the information-intensiveness of centralized institutions that promote market clearing.

In an economy where goods and agents are symmetric a priori, the ambiguous numéraire is not anyone's to specify or anyone's to be individually denied. Yet choice variables are discrete, and a single choice variable cannot be denied to each agent without removing too many choices. If it is denied as a strategy variable to one type of agents while it is permitted to the others, the denied type will have fewer choices at market and will be arbitrarily disadvantaged by the market structure. In markets where one of the goods is used as a commodity money, this asymmetry generally arises to the disadvantage to the agents who are money providers. In the one-period setting illustrated by Market 3 below, this asymmetry can be so severe that noncooperative equilibria approach the no-trade solution. Asymmetries of this kind may be removed at the cost of using all goods equivalently as monies (illustrated as Market 1), or of providing a central clearinghouse which monetizes personal credit consistently (Market 6). The former is costly in redundancies of trading post markets and monies, while the latter requires extensive information gathering and processing.

Asymmetry of the market opportunities offered to agents violates the *equal treatment* property of competitive equilibria, which assures that all a priori equivalent agents arrive at equal allocations at an equilibrium. Equal treatment may be considered a normative requirement for trading mechanisms, and its violation by a market design may constitute a reason not to adopt that design. Equal treatment also underpins the economic notion of a *representative agent*. While precisely equal treatment will usually be unrealistic, purely random violations of the equal treatment property (as by search or sampling effects) may permit some version of representative-agent modeling to be retained with equal treatment in the aggregate [379]. Systematically unequal treatment which is structurally essential would, in contrast, be expected to apply similarly to aggregates as to individuals.

4.3   Components of a One-Period Taxonomy

4.3.1   A complexity hierarchy for information and clearing rules

We will not attempt in this chapter to provide a formal definition of the complexity of a market's function.[2] The six market models presented here have been chosen to illustrate the constraints on rational action from asymmetry of the market mechanism, or from strategically ambiguous degrees of freedom. The models have sufficiently many shared features that they roughly represent successive stages in the elaboration of a few common ideas. Therefore we may choose a small number of criteria based on the degree of elaboration of a market's strategy sets or information requirements, which will provide a commonsense complexity ordering of the models. In some cases these have an obvious mapping onto measures based on description length for data or for algorithms. We will use the following rules:

- Simultaneous actions are simpler than serial actions.

- Fewer decision variables for agents in their interactions with markets are simpler than more variables. The least number of nontrivial variables is one per agent-market pairing, and it is natural to make this a choice of a bid for goods. Markets at this level, to be nontrivial, must require that agents put their entire initial allocations up for sale, removing the choice of how much to offer. Such cases, called "sell-all" markets, are treated thoroughly in [356] and will not be reconsidered here.

  The next simplest structure creates two variables per agent-market pairing, and it is natural to make these bids and amounts of supply. These markets include the sell-all case, and allow a broader and more interesting set of possible means of payment. The examples in the following taxonomy will all be of this type.

  The next simplest market structure admits four decision variables, which may be taken as bids and quantities offered, and prices for these whose limits must be specified. For these four decision variables, however, the simplest clearing mechanism requires clauses for incomplete clearing, through either queuing or cancellation of orders. These more complex games include examples in [95], and references therein, and lead into auction theory.

- Within the realm of solution concepts, noncooperative concepts are simpler than cooperative ones.

- Finally, among noncooperative solution algorithms, pure-strategy Nash equilibria with full knowledge of other-agent utilities and endowments are the simplest possible. While the mechanics of the computation may be more involved than that for more knowledge-restricted algorithms, the full-knowledge Nash equilibrium is *theoretically* simpler than a bounded-rationality concept, because it does not require the additional distinction between shared knowledge and knowledge particular to each agent.

4.3.2   Some notation for handling dimensions

Chapter 3 introduced the concept of dimension, its relation to measurement and scaling symmetry, and its use in the estimation procedure known as dimensional analysis. There we argued for a minimal form of one-period utility with homothetic indifference surfaces, and a minimal price formation rule associated with the buy-sell game. The example market mechanisms presented below require a somewhat richer treatment, because a variety of goods, promissory notes, and bank credit are considered as means of payment at trading posts. To perform an equivalent analysis of minimal price formation rules in this more diverse setting, it is helpful to have a standard notation for referring to dimensions and the operations performed by market-supporting institutions that interconvert them. This notation will also permit a compact presentation of all market forms, and easy comparison among them.

- Each consumable good is given a dimension, and the *name* given to the dimension of the jth good will be g^j (think: "apples," "oranges," "bananas").

- There is in general a numéraire, which is a specific quantity of a specific good (think "one orange"). The numéraire therefore has both quantity and dimension (in this case, the name of the dimension is "oranges"). The numéraire is denoted N.

- Personal credit takes the form of promissory notes denominated in the numéraire. Specification of the game must include defining who may produce these, when they are to be paid, how they are exchanged for the denominated goods, and when or whether they may be destroyed. Promissory notes may be written by individual agents or institutions such as central banks, and in general these are not substitutable and thus have different dimensions. The name given to the dimension of a promissory note written by agent i in numéraire N is $I_i(N)$. Promissory notes from a central bank will be given dimension $I_{CB}(N)$.

- The notation [ ] is used for the operator on a dimensional quantity that gives the name of its dimension (example: $\left[\text{"one orange"}\right] = $ "oranges").

- The notation $C(\ )$ is used for the *clearing operator* that maps a promissory note for a good to an amount of that good. The operator represents the actions of a clearinghouse, and the need for it will become apparent when we demand dimensional homogeneity of equations. An example will illustrate the relation of clearing operators, promissory notes, and dimensions: If b_i^j is a promissory note from agent i for one unit of the numéraire N, $\left[b_i^j\right] = I_i(N)$, and $C\left(b_i^j\right) = N$.

4.3.3 Graphical representations

A complete specification of a minimal market may now be done easily, by listing the dimensions of the bids, offers, and numéraire and diagrammatically representing which goods are directly exchangeable for which others. Rather than do this merely with lists, we introduce a graphical representation that makes visual comparison of the market forms easy. Only goods, penalties, and the institutional relations between them require graphical representation, since the interaction of agents with the institutions is uniformly applied according to the clearing rules given above, and since all markets will follow a uniform event sequence that we describe in the next subsection.

- A good, whether consumable or financial, is represented by a filled dot ●.

- The penalty variable applied by the courts is an open circle ○.

- A trading post that takes in two goods is represented by a solid line between the dots representing the goods ●———●. The goods may be consumables directly exchanged, or consumables offered and notes used in payment. They may have specifically assigned roles as bids and offers, or there may be freedom in this assignment, as in Market 2 below. When there is more than one market between the same two goods, as in Market 1 below, the specification of which is bid and which offer distinguishes the posts, in which case the line between them is made into a directional arrow ●———►●.

- A clearinghouse relation between goods is a dashed line between the dots representing the goods ● - - - ●. In all the models built here, one of the goods will be a promissory note and the other the underlying consumable.

- A court relation between a balance of goods and a penalty assignment is also a dashed line ● - - - ○. The court and the clearinghouse share a line style that is different from that of the trading posts, as a reminder that their relation to the agents is essentially coercive within the rules of these games, whereas the market relation is essentially voluntary.

- A credit evaluation relation between two forms of promissory notes is given the same graphical representation as a market relation. Since they are both goods, and the action of the credit evaluator is linear (involves no threshold relations), it functions in the same way as a different type of market with a different clearing rule.

4.3.4   Structure of moves within a single trading period

Markets, clearinghouses and courts, and credit evaluators all participate in trade with a definite sequence, which may be stylized by dividing a single period into a sequence similar to Hicks's "week" [184]. We will refer to this period as a "trading day." Offers and bids are delivered by agents to the trading posts "in the morning." If bids are in promissory notes and a credit evaluation agency is used to evaluate their worth, this takes place through an exchange between the trading posts and the evaluation agency "at noon" (if not, noon is an irrelevant time). Bought goods and disbursements of payment for sold goods are delivered from the markets to the agents "in the afternoon." If bids are in promissory notes and these notes must be cleared, an exchange takes place between the agents and clearinghouses "in the evening." This is the time when promissory notes are returned to their creators and, if necessary, penalties are assessed (if payment is in consumables, evening is an irrelevant time). Agents consume their final allocation bundles entirely "at night." Passage of one day defines one complete period of production, exchange, and consumption.

Agents' ignorance of each other's strategies is formalized by supposing that agents choose their q_i^j and b_i^j sets before going to market in the morning. If bids are in promissory notes, agents also write these de novo at the time of determining b_i^j.

The goal of clearinghouses is to exchange promissory notes, possibly at an exchange rate determined by a credit evaluator, so as to allow each agent to "buy back" his own promissory notes by paying with the notes of others. Agents are then free to destroy notes of their own writing at night, together with consuming their final allocations. The rules of the game prohibit agents from destroying any promissory notes besides their own.

4.4   A Partial Taxonomy of One-Period Exchange Mechanisms

We now present the taxonomy of one-period exchange mechanisms, emphasizing in each the counting of its degrees of freedom and its dimensional content. The price formation and clearing rules described in general form in chapter 3 will be refined where necessary to be consistent with the dimensional structure of each market. In all cases, however, the basic structure of the buy-sell game will be retained, and the clearing rules will continue to be the simplest ones consistent with dimensional homogeneity and having no additional arbitrary constants.

Market 1   (all-for-all, directed)

$$\left[q_i^{jk}\right] = g^j \qquad \forall j,k$$

$$[N] = \text{various}$$

$$\left[b_i^{jk}\right] = g^k \qquad \forall j,k$$

$$\left[p^{jk}\right] = \frac{g^k}{g^j} \qquad \forall j,k$$

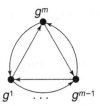

Features $m\,(m-1)$ markets. Payment in goods; no short sales, no credit. NE constructable, symmetric, and robust to allocation constraints.

This is the market structure that most closely resembles barter; it differs from barter and defines a true market only in that it aggregates all bids and offers and enforces a law of one price at each trading post. Direct-exchange trading posts exist between all commodities j and k, and are indexed superscript jk. Offers q_i^{jk} in these markets thus have dimension g^j and bids have dimension g^k. Each commodity serves as means of payment in $m-1$ markets, and is offered for sale in $m-1$ others. No credit is offered in this market system, meaning that $0 \le \sum_{k \ne j}\left(q_i^{jk} + b_i^{kj}\right) \le a_i^j$, for all agents i and all goods j.

At general endowments a_{gen}, each agent i has $2m\,(m-1)$ strategic degrees of freedom (DOF), the $\left\{q_i^{jk}, b_i^{jk}\right\}$ in all markets. Markets accepting bids and offers in the same quantity (which would appear as self-loops in the diagram) are not considered, because the only sensible clearing rule would simply return to each agent what he had delivered. The total number of strategic DOF for all m agents is therefore $2m^2\,(m-1)$.

The price for the jk market is defined by the notational generalization of Eq. (3.4),

$$p^{jk} \equiv \frac{\sum_i b_i^{jk}}{\sum_i q_i^{jk}}. \tag{4.1}$$

It is not required by the institutional structure that the prices (4.1) satisfy the dimensionally allowed relation $p^{jk} = 1/p^{kj}$, though many sensible solution concepts may lead to solutions with this property. The allocation rule for agent i as a result of trades in all markets combines Eq. (3.5) and Eq. (3.6):

$$A_i^j = a_i^j + \sum_{k \ne j}\left(-q_i^{jk} + \frac{b_i^{jk}}{p^{jk}}\right) + \sum_{k \ne j}\left(q_i^{kj}p^{kj} - b_i^{kj}\right). \tag{4.2}$$

Since bids are consumables, there are no separate monetary state variables, and agents' holdings of each good change through both of its roles, as a sold item and as a money.

Note that failure of the double coincidence of wants a_{spec} reduces each agent to $2(m-1)$ DOF, the $\left\{q_i^{jk} \neq 0\right\}$ in the $(m-1)$ markets for his endowed good, and the $(m-1)$ $\left\{b_i^{jk} \neq 0\right\}$ in markets for other goods, for which the endowment is used as means of payment. The resulting total number of DOF is $2m(m-1)$, and the system leads to symmetric exchange solutions for specialists, which are constructable at any m, as derived in appendix 4.6.1. The efficiency of these allocations is less than unity, but by the smallest margin the one-period noncooperative solutions can achieve.

Market 1 is thus agent-permutation symmetric and robust in allowing nonzero-trade solutions under allocation constraints. If the costs of operating trading posts were considered, though, it would also be the most costly of the structures considered here at large m, because the costs to maintain $m(m-1)$ trading posts must be paid, even if agents can only use $2m(m-1)$ of the degrees of freedom they provide.

Market 2   (all-for-all, undirected)

$$\left[q_i^{jk}\right] = g^j \qquad \forall j, k$$
$$[N] \;= \text{various}$$
$$\left[b_i^{jk}\right] = g^k \qquad \forall j, k$$
$$\left[p^{jk}\right] = \frac{g^k}{g^j} \qquad \forall j, k$$

Features $m(m-1)/2$ markets. Payment in goods; no short sales, no credit. NE constructable, symmetric, but limited by allocation constraints for $m \geq 3$.

This market allows all-for-all exchange, like Market 1, but reduces the number of trading posts needed in a natural way. Markets are again indexed superscript jk, but there is now a unique trading post for direct exchange of any pair of goods.

The cost of this simplification is that bids and offers, rather than having separate roles in every market, become defined by context. All goods of type j delivered to post jk are interpreted as q-values, and all goods of type k at that post are interpreted as b-values. Since the name jk or kj of the post is arbitrary within this convention, this implies the identity $q_i^{jk} \equiv b_i^{kj}$. At general endowments a_{gen}, each agent is thus reduced to $m(m-1)$ strategic DOF, the $\{q_i^{jk}, b_i^{jk}\}$ in the symmetrized markets, and the total number of DOF is $m^2(m-1)$.

Price is computed just as in Eq. (4.1), with the context-dependent definition of the b and q, but now by definition $p^{jk} \equiv 1/p^{kj}$. There is a natural modification of the disaggregation rules for both goods, from Eqs. (3.5) and (3.6): each agent receives a fraction of the total both of the j and the k good equal to his contribution to the value at the jk post (this fraction is independent of which good is regarded as the money and measure of value). The value fraction for an agent i may be written

$$\frac{q_i^{jk} p^{jk} + b_i^{jk}}{\sum_{i'} \left(q_{i'}^{jk} p^{jk} + b_{i'}^{jk} \right)} = \frac{1}{2} \left(\frac{q_i^{jk}}{\sum_{i'} q_{i'}^{jk}} + \frac{b_i^{jk}}{\sum_{i'} b_{i'}^{jk}} \right), \tag{4.3}$$

and the allocation rule that follows from it (written with either market naming order) is

$$\begin{aligned} A_i^j &= a_i^j + \frac{1}{2} \sum_{k \neq j} \left(-q_i^{jk} + \frac{b_i^{jk}}{p^{jk}} \right) \\ &= a_i^j + \frac{1}{2} \sum_{k \neq j} \left(q_i^{kj} p^{kj} - b_i^{kj} \right) \\ &= a_i^j - \frac{1}{2} \sum_{k \neq j} \left(q_i^{jk} - q_i^{kj} \frac{Q^{jk}}{Q^{kj}} \right). \end{aligned} \tag{4.4}$$

In the first line of Eq. (4.5) good j is treated as the bought and sold consumable, while in the second line it is regarded as the means of payment for the other $k \neq j$ bought and sold consumables. In the last line (where $Q^{jk} \equiv \sum_i q_i^{jk}$), the order of jk is permuted so as to express all quantities as q, a convenience when maximizing utilities in appendix 4.6.

Under failure of the coincidence of wants a_{spec}, each agent still has $(m-1)$ DOF for a total of $m(m-1)$ DOF, because there are precisely $(m-1)$ markets for any single endowed good in exchange for other goods. The solutions are still symmetric and constructable at all m, and the collection of markets is half as costly as those in Market 1, in exchange for offering half the strategic freedoms. However, the clearing rule leads to large fractions of returned goods, so if there is no short sale, for $m \geq 3$ there is a shortage of either offers or means of payment to attain the interior solution. This is demonstrated in appendix 4.6.2. Thus agents would be better off spontaneously breaking the symmetry of solutions in Market 1 and abandoning one of the two markets for each good, but continuing to use the conventional clearing rules. While one might have expected that thinning of the markets in the directed case would affect final allocations, this turns out not to be the case in either the symmetric or fully broken solutions, since only the replication index affects the impact assessments.

Market 3   (commodity standard, cash payment)

$$\left[q_i^j\right] = g^j \ \forall j \neq m, \ q_i^m = 0$$
$$[N] = g^m$$
$$\left[b_i^j\right] = g^m \ \forall j \neq m, \ b_i^m = 0$$
$$\left[p^j\right] = \frac{g^m}{g^j} \ \forall j \neq m, \ p^m \ \text{undef}$$

$$g^m$$
$$g^1 \quad \cdots \quad g^{m-1}$$

Features $m - 1$ markets. Payment in a preselected good; no short sales, no credit. NE constructable, but approach the no-trade solution under allocation constraints.

This structure has $m - 1$ trading posts indexed simply by the good $j \neq m$ sold at them. Payment is in good m and, as we excluded goods-for-themselves markets in the previous cases, we do not introduce a market here exchanging m for m. At a_{gen} there are $2(m-1)$ strategic DOF per agent—the $\left\{q_i^{j \neq m}, b_i^{j \neq m}\right\}$— for a total of $2m(m-1)$ DOF. A version of this market is treated in [356], ch. 7, where the role of the mth good as money is given precedence over its consumable status.

Under failure of the coincidence of wants a_{spec}, the $m - 1$ agents of type $i \neq m$ are reduced to one offer q_i^i each, while agents of type m have $m - 1$ bids $\left\{b_m^{j \neq m}\right\}$. There are thus $2(m-1)$ total DOF. However, the solutions are highly asymmetric because only one agent type may bid in the commodity money. This asymmetry renders the exchange mechanism nearly useless; the strategic market game produces solutions that approach the no-trade allocation at large m. Because we have defined the efficiency of no-trade to be zero, the efficiency of the solutions to this game decays as $\mathcal{O}(1/m)$.

Market 4   (commodity standard, personal credit)

$$\left[q_i^j\right] = g^j \quad \forall j \neq m, \; q_i^m = 0$$
$$[N] = g^m$$
$$\left[b_i^j\right] = I_i(N) \; \forall j \neq m, \; b_i^m = 0$$
$$\left[p^j\right] = \frac{I_i(N)}{g^j} \; \forall j \neq m, \; p^m \text{ undef}$$

Features $m - 1$ markets for goods. Payment in promissory notes for a prese-lected good, with one clearinghouse for notes and that good. NE constructable at large m and survive under allocation constraints, but are not symmetric.

This structure has the same asymmetry as Market 3, but softens the impact of the failure of coincidence of wants by adding credit in the form of per-sonal promissory notes to deliver the mth good. All notes are given credit by the trading post pricing and allocation mechanisms (3.4–3.6) at face value. In other words, promissory notes are substitutable and the various dimensions $I_i(N), i \in 1, \ldots, mr$ may be regarded as a single dimension. With the addition of credit, bankruptcy rules are formally required to handle the possibility of default in the promissory notes. However, for the interior solutions which credit was introduced to render attainable, the bankruptcy constraint never becomes binding, because the consumption value of the commodity money ensures a net flow of good m to all of the type $i \neq m$ agents, enabling them to repay loans.

While a "money market" for the mth good is now definable, with bids in promissory notes for that good, we define the model not to include such a trading post. With this choice, each agent under generalist production a_{gen} has $2(m - 1)$ of the $\left\{q_i^{j \neq m}, b_i^{j \neq m}\right\}$ DOF, for a total of $2m(m - 1)$. The allocation rule for the mth good replaces Eq. (3.5) with the clearinghouse value

$$A_i^m = a_i^m + \sum_{j \neq m} C\left(q_i^j p^j - b_i^j\right). \tag{4.5}$$

(When this interior solution is impossible because a_i^m is too small, the bankruptcy penalties modify Eq. (4.5) and induce an endogenous rate of inter-est, which is the shadow price of the capacity constraint.)

The importance of credit is that at a_{spec}, each agent of type $i \neq m$ is reduced only to m DOF, the q_i^i for his own endowment and $m - 1$ bids $\left\{b_i^{j \neq m}\right\}$ (recall that agents had only 1 DOF in Market 3 where cash payment was required). Agents of type m retain the $m-1$ bids $\left\{b_m^{j\neq m}\right\}$ that they have in Market 3, for a total of $m^2 - 1$ DOF in the system.

Final allocations at a_{spec}, derived in appendix 4.6.3, while no longer converging to the no-trade solution at large m as in Market 3, are nonetheless still not symmetric. Although at $m \to \infty$ and $r \to \infty$ they converge to the competitive equilibrium, at large m and fixed r they converge at $\mathcal{O}\left((1/m)^0\right)$ to a relation of the form

$$\prod_j A_m^j \to \left(1 - \frac{1}{r}\right) e^{1/r} \prod_j A_{i\neq m}^j \to e^{-\frac{1}{r(r-1)}} \prod_j A_{CE}^j, \qquad (4.6)$$

where A_{CE}^j is the final allocation (the same here for all agents and all goods) that would be attained at a competitive equilibrium. At a level of resolution where there are many goods in the world produced by specialists, but relatively few truly equivalent producers of any one good (small r), the agents called on to provide the standard of value are penalized relative to the rest. Such a penalty arises because, whereas all other agents have some strategic freedom to impact the prices of their own goods, the provider of the numéraire loses this freedom. Though he has reduced purchasing power relative to other agents, in other respects he effectively becomes a price taker (as borne out by the symmetry of his final allocations A_m^j among j, a property of the CE allocations but not the other $\left\{A_{i\neq m}^j\right\}$ in the NE). The reduction in allocative efficiency due to the penalty on type-m agents is not compensated by the slight windfall given to the other types, so the efficiency of this market is the lowest of those that retain finite levels of trade at large m.

The practical relevance of the asymmetry in this market arises if one considers embedding its function into a larger game in which agents may *choose* to become specialist producers versus generalists. In such a game they may (on an even longer timescale) choose their desired market structure as well. If agents may strategically reallocate labor, a tragedy of the commons results. The vocation of money producer is strictly dominated by all other vocations. Therefore in an NE, even though the consumption utility without trade *and* without consumable good m becomes infinitely negative, it is the unique equilibrium. If, instead of being committed to a structurally unfair market, the rules of the larger game give agents "veto" power over the adoption of a market structure, Market 4 will be avoided in order to escape the labor allocation inefficiencies it creates.

The solutions in this case exist at all m, but they are formally noncon-
structable due to an unspecified degree of wash selling by each producer.
This formal ambiguity occupies an interval of relative size $1/m$ in price and
final allocation, though, and so it can practically always be placed below some
threshold of severity at large m. In practical terms, then, NE are "constructable"
in a limit of sufficiently many types.

Market 5   (personal credit with bankruptcy law)

$$\left[q_i^j \right] = g^j \quad \forall j$$
$$[N] = \text{free}$$
$$\left[b_i^j \right] = I_i(N) \; \forall j$$
$$\left[p^j \right] = \frac{I_i(N)}{g^j} \; \forall j$$

Features m markets for goods. Payment in personal promissory notes for an
arbitrary numéraire, credited at face value, with a court imposing bankruptcy
penalties. NE are not constructable.

One can attempt to patch up the asymmetry in Market 4 by adding a trading
post for good m, in effect a commodity money market. With this modification,
since bids for all goods are denominated in the same set of promissory notes
credited at face value, their denomination, and hence the numéraire, becomes
arbitrary up to its interpretation in the bankruptcy laws. Thus with the adoption
of a money market, the commodity that previously served as money returns to
being just another consumable good, at interior solutions.

Each agent naïvely has $2m$ DOF at a_{gen}, in the form of $\left\{ q_i^j, b_i^j \right\} \forall j$, giving
$2m^2$ total DOF for the system. However, correct counting of the strategic DOF
requires more careful treatment of the bankruptcy penalty as it applies to interior solutions.

The min operator in Eq. (3.8), having undefined derivative at zero argument,
is unsuited to evaluating the gradients required by Nash equilibria. The discontinuous derivative may be regularized for each agent by replacing Eq. (3.8)
with

$$\mathcal{U}_i \to \mathcal{U}_i + \kappa_i M_i \tag{4.7}$$

where M_i is defined in Eq. (3.6). Since there is no source of initial debts,
$m_i = 0, \forall i$. The discontinuous derivative is replaced in Eq. (4.7) with a set
$\{\kappa_i\}$ of Kuhn-Tucker multipliers, one for each agent i. This formulation of

bankruptcy has the interpretation of a game between each agent and the courts, in which the agent tries to maximize Eq. (4.7) with respect to the $\left\{q_i^j, b_i^j\right\}$, and the courts try to minimize it with respect to κ_i. Linear debt penalties differ from simple Kuhn-Tucker constraints in that the courts are only permitted the variation $0 \leq \kappa_i \leq \Pi$. (The κ_i are shadow prices associated with the constraints, and bankruptcy is a form of limited liability.)

At nonzero values of M_i, the derivative is manifestly that of Eq. (3.8), while at $M_i = 0$, the derivative of the penalty term with respect to M_i is κ_i. This gradient is set equal to the gradient of $\mathcal{U}_i$ to obtain the first-order conditions on the final allocations. Symmetric, interior solutions exist, and at these solutions no agent goes bankrupt. Rather, the $m_i = 0, \forall i$, and, by the accounting identity $\sum_i M_i = \sum_i m_i$, these satisfy exactly $M_i = 0, \forall i$, and $0 < \kappa_i < \Pi, \forall i$.

If the Kuhn-Tucker expression of the min were nothing more than a regularization method for derivatives, it would say that agents sample all b_i^j values, and then compare the relative merits of going bankrupt to buy a little more of good j to doing so for a little more of good j'. Obviously this is the wrong interpretation for interior values of κ_i, which are set by the utilities and not the legal value Π. Interior values are a device for comparing the relative prices of all pairs j and j' of goods. They thus represent a strategy evaluation in which bankruptcy is *not* considered, and the relative values of the goods are compared directly. In other words κ_i, like an ordinary binding Kuhn-Tucker or Lagrange multiplier, is one *negative* DOF per agent, leading to $-m$ DOF relative to the naïve count of $2m^2$ for the whole system. (This manner of counting Kuhn-Tucker multipliers as negative degrees of freedom is general.)

$2m^2 - m$ is still not the correct DOF count for this system, however. Promissory notes have an overall rescaling symmetry $b_i^j \rightarrow \Lambda b_i^j$, as long as the same Λ is applied by all agents. This scaling freedom corresponds to the arbitrariness of the numéraire familiar in competitive equilibria. It obviously does not affect a strategic ability of agents to change either allocations or utilities, and results only in an overall rescaling of prices. Therefore the correct number of total DOF is $2m^2 - m - 1 = (2m + 1)(m - 1)$. Catastrophically for the functioning of this market, however, this negative strategic degree of freedom is *distributed* over the agents, leading to two consequences. First, the negative degree of freedom resulting from symmetry is not fixed by a simple constraint such as a Kuhn-Tucker multiplier; all institutionally explicit constraints in the model have already been represented. Second and more important, and related to the fact that the negative degree of freedom is not made institutionally explicit, the presence of the rescaling freedom implies that *no choice process exists for agents* to arrive at a solution, even if they are fully rational, as long as we remain within the noncooperative-game framework.

The way to see the nonconstructibility of solutions is to recognize that, even knowing everything about all agent utilities and endowments, there is no way any agent can know the scale that other agents will use for all of *their* b_i^j, because he cannot know their moves in a noncooperative game. Since this scale factor is not constrained by the NE solution itself, there is no other information besides knowledge of other-player moves that could resolve this indeterminacy.

Were it not for the fact that agents have no way to find NE solutions, a continuum of such solutions indexed by the scale factor Λ exists, both at a_{gen} and at a_{spec}. In the latter case they even have the symmetry that the allocations of Market 4 lack. Allocation constraints remove $m - 1$ offer DOF $\left\{ q_i^{j \neq i} \right\}$ from each agent's strategies, or $m(m - 1)$ from the total, leaving $m^2 - 1$. These are the same DOF as in Market 4 except for two: agent m can now offer q_m^m in a market for his endowment, but this localized freedom is offset by the distributed constraint that overall rescaling by Λ has no consequences for equilibrium allocations.

Market 6   (personal credit monetized)

$$\left[q_i^j \right] = g^j \qquad \forall j$$
$$[N] = \text{free}$$
$$\left[b_i^j \right] = I_{CB}(N) \; \forall j$$
$$\left[p^j \right] = \frac{I_{CB}(N)}{g^j} \; \forall j$$

Features m markets for goods. Initial payment in personal promissory notes for an arbitrary numéraire, exchanged at a credit evaluator for central-bank promissory notes, at a computed rate of exchange. NE constructable at large m, symmetric, and robust under allocation constraints.

Market 5 attempted to recover symmetry and introduced a new, severe form of indeterminacy. The reason for this failure is that substituting unrefereed personal credit for a commodity standard replaces a localized constraint on agents of type m in Market 4 with a global scaling symmetry that is under the control of no one and not deducible by anyone. The institution that retains symmetry while restoring computability is effectively an exchange rate service, here considered as one function of a *central bank*. (In [391], Sorin modeled exactly the process used here, but rather than considering exchange rate computation to define a new institution, he described it as a modification to the clearing rule of the posts, which were then necessarily regarded together as a trading mechanism with a centralized clearinghouse or central bank that also calculates exchange rates.)

Agents again offer and bid in the mornings at markets for all m goods, in q_i^j and personal promissory notes. As in the previous model, the denomination of the notes is arbitrary. In the current model, however, the personal notes are not evaluated at face value, and the trading posts do not deliver goods or disbursements right away. Rather, they bring the notes along with a record of the received $\left\{ q_i^j \right\}$ to a central bank, which computes a set of *exchange rates* λ_i, and returns central bank promissory notes on behalf of i to the trading posts according to a formula

$$b_{CB(i)}^j = \lambda_i b_i^j. \tag{4.8}$$

These notes then become the effective deposit by agent i at post j. The dimensions of λ_i are thus

$$[\lambda_i] = \frac{I_{CB}(N)}{I_i(N)}. \tag{4.9}$$

Because they are notes not credited at face value, the b_i^j at different i are no longer directly interchangeable. They must therefore be regarded as separate goods with distinct dimensions, which we have illustrated graphically in the Market 6 diagram.

Equations (3.4–3.6) are then evaluated by the markets in the afternoon, as before, but with the bids for each agent i now represented in the uniformly denominated $\left\{ b_{CB(i)}^j \right\}$. Disbursements of central bank notes to the agents are made, and the central bank takes the agents to a clearinghouse in the evening. There, promissory notes are exchanged back to their originators at the rates λ_i defined earlier in the day.

The rule that the central bank uses to compute the λ_i is that all promissory notes will clear exactly at the end of the day, $M_i = 0, \forall i$. This "mechanical" institutional function, which deprives agents of the ability to set meaningful overall scales of their notes, also eliminates any need (or indeed, any role) for bankruptcy penalties. The $\{M_i\}$ are linear functions of the $\{\lambda_{i'}\}$, with coefficients $\left\{ M_i^{i'} \right\}$ that are functions of the $\left\{ q_i^j, b_i^j \right\}$. Assembling the constraints and the λ into column vectors, the condition of perfect clearing may be written

$$[M_i] \equiv \left[M_i^{i'} \right] [\lambda_{i'}] = [0]. \tag{4.10}$$

From Eq. (3.6) it is straightforward to compute the diagonal values

$$M_i^i = -\sum_j \left(1 - \frac{q_i^j}{Q^j}\right) b_i^j, \tag{4.11}$$

and the off-diagonal

$$M_i^{i' \neq i} = \sum_j \frac{q_i^j}{Q^j} b_{i'}^j. \tag{4.12}$$

It is then an elementary accounting check that

$$\sum_{i'} M_{i'}^i = 0, \ \forall i. \tag{4.13}$$

Thus $\left[M_i^{i'}\right]$ is degenerate, and so has at least one eigenvector $\left[\lambda_{i'}\right]$ of zero eigenvalue. (If more than one null eigenvector exists, this indicates that the bids and offers allow the market to break up into more than one independently valued subsystems of exchange.)

The null eigenvector(s) maps any $\left\{b_i^j\right\}$ that are consistent with an interior NE, up to a uniform but independent rescaling by each agent i, to the NE with a single consistent scale factor. Since $\left[\lambda_{i'}\right]$ is null, its overall scale is of course undetermined. This scale factor again corresponds to the ambiguity of the numéraire in general equilibrium. The bank may adopt any convention it likes to set a scale for $\left[\lambda_{i'}\right]$, and nothing about the final allocations will depend on this choice. Note that the central bank is *not* required to compute a general equilibrium solution, in the manner of a Walrasian auctioneer. Only the much simpler, linear note-clearing condition (4.10) is required, and this remains exact whether or not agents' bids are consistent with an NE.

The agents' strategies are now well defined, and the NE are constructable within the context of Nash optimization. Each agent is rational to compute his $\left\{b_i^j\right\}$ *as if* all other agents were generating $\left\{b_{i' \neq i}^j\right\}$ with the same assumed numéraire and scale, and *as if* all promissory notes were to be credited at face value. In general, of course, the scales assumed by different agents will have no relation. As long as each agent's bids have the correct ratios *internally*, the absolute scale factors they choose will not matter.

The scale freedom of the $\left\{b_i^j\right\}$, fixed in Market 5 by the Kuhn-Tucker multiplier but restored as a bidding freedom in Market 6, is not a new degree of freedom. It is fixed by the clearing rule (4.10) as a market service, rather than by threat from the courts. Thus one DOF per agent has been both added and subtracted, and in this respect the markets are the same. The only new feature in Market 6 is that the previously untraceable strategic symmetry—the overall scale—is now explicitly fixed by any choice of normalization made by the central bank, which counts as the required -1 DOF. The counting of DOF in both the a_{gen} and a_{spec} is thus the same as argued in Market 5. Further, all of the NE are the same. The only consequence of the institutional difference is to make such solutions identifiable within the standard paradigm of rational choice. It remains a feature of this market, as in the previous two, that the solutions retain a small indeterminacy in the degree of wash selling, which becomes harmless in the large-m limit. Appendix 4.6.4 shows that the solutions achieved by this market are the same as those in the all-for-all markets.

In the one-period setting of this chapter, with its single timescale and no strategic labor reallocation, we do not attempt to assign explicit costs according to the complexity of different markets. Nor do we attempt to compare these to the efficiency in money metric of the noncooperative equilibria that they generate. It is therefore convenient that the maximally distributed, barter-like Market 1, and the maximally centralized Market 6, generate solutions with the same symmetry and allocative efficiency. We may therefore compare directly, ceteris paribus, the trading post infrastructure, decision complexity, and information requirements in these two diametrically opposed, minimal models.

4.4.1   Foreign exchange or credit evaluation?

The evaluation service institutionalized here in a central bank has two interpretations, both relevant to economic life, but emphasizing different concepts. One could be called foreign exchange evaluation and the other credit evaluation. Both interpretations are forms of *monetization of personal credit*, which generalizes in a different way when issues of trust and visibility are introduced to solution concepts to compensate for incomplete rationality or incomplete information.

In Market 6, every agent effectively produces his own currency. The exchange rate evaluation occurs as if each were a country bringing goods and otherwise-valueless notes for trade to a set of international markets. The real goods offered and bid for, together with the distribution of the currency, can be used by a "world central bank" to determine exchange rates, at which no country is left holding another country's valueless notes at the end of the period. Values of real goods offered play an essential part in the relative valuation of currencies, a topic to which we return in more depth in chapter 6 where we consider the backing of fiat monies.

Alternatively, exchange rate evaluation makes sense as a form of *credit evaluation* in the absence of exogenous uncertainty, and it is under this characterization that we generalize it here. The function of credit evaluation in the monetization of credit is to exchange unreliable notes for reliable ones. The exchange rate is chosen to preclude only the strategic (and thus preventable) defaults, and as a consequence it enables trades that would not be possible with cash payment alone. When default can result from exogenous uncertainty in the world, as well as from strategic intentionality, this tradeoff is nontrivial and depends on some marginal valuation of more trade versus more default.

With or without uncertainty about the world, endogenous uncertainty can exist about the consistency of agent strategies. This form of uncertainty arises in Market 5 from the undeterminability of a reference scale for bids b_i^j made by different agents i. The purely endogenous component is special, though, in that it is *entirely* preventable with no sacrifice in trade, because it requires only a coordination mechanism. The mechanism for removing default solutions is the same for both forms of uncertainty: the imposition of exchange rates between personally and centrally generated credit. When uncertainty is introduced, its source will matter because an exchange rate generates an interest rate to balance default under exogenous uncertainty. The role of exchange in the model sequence presented here is that of a pure accounting tool to address a structural deficiency in market function.

4.4.2   The gauge structure of monetized credit

The relation of Markets 5 and 6 illustrates a new kind of symmetry different from those considered in chapter 3. It is a symmetry in the *space of strategic solutions*, as opposed to a symmetry in the scales of production, consumption, or time, or the discrete permutation symmetries that define market structures. For these markets, the space of bidding strategies is one dimension larger than the space of optimization conditions that agents use to choose their bids. As a result, there must be a continuous space of solutions that are identical with respect to allocation in the real-goods sector, but distinct from the perspective of agent choices. Markets 5 and 6 distinguish between a symmetry that is a *local* freedom of agent strategies, and one that is a *global* freedom left to the market as a whole, but which requires that agents first be coordinated. Both forms appear local to agents who act noncooperatively, but a true local symmetry permits solutions, whereas one that applies only to the market as a whole does not.

We may understand the distinction by considering how undetermined agent choices must propagate information to arrive at solutions. If *only* the global symmetry exists, the problem of coordination among the local elements to find any consistent set of bids can only be carried out by dynamics. This situation is familiar in statistical physics, where slight dynamical misalignments which convey information about the coordinated state are known as *Goldstone particles*. The problem of identifying a scale for prices from the dynamics of expectations has already been formulated as one of exchanging these particles [22].[3] The consequence of this fact for one-period models is that, if no time elapses to make dynamics definable, the coherent best solution cannot be formed, as has been shown in Market 5.

A physically different origin for degenerate (and therefore symmetric) solutions arises from what is called *gauge symmetry* in statistical physics. A gauge field is a globally defined excitation whose value serves as a reference for the scale of each of the locally defined symmetry transformations.

Gauge fields create a new class of *local* symmetries, which consist of changing the "gauged" value of the local variable, while adjusting the reference value (the "gauge") of the field together with it to indicate no change in the actual physical state. In the example of Market 6, such a so-called *gauge transformation* is the combination of

$$b_i^j \to e^{\eta_i} b_i^j, \quad \forall j \text{ at some } i \qquad (4.14)$$

with the corresponding adjustment that the central bank will make:

$$\lambda_i \to e^{-\eta_i} \lambda_i. \qquad (4.15)$$

Any agent is free to induce a gauge change independently of what the others do, and such a rescaling leads to no change in the market allocations (or indeed in any aspect of trading post function). A layer of paper remonetizing promissory notes could be added to any market with credit. However, for markets such as Market 4, in which optimal noncooperative bids can be determined directly from utilities, the additional paper degree of freedom would serve no purpose, and a constraint akin to Eq. (4.10) would simply remove it without adding any coordination or control function.

Gauge fields become functionally important when, as in Market 6, a global symmetry of the solutions can be absorbed as a degree of freedom in the gauge variation which does not affect allocations. Then the remaining, economically meaningful bidding degrees of freedom can be specified instantaneously and in a symmetric way by the gauge conditions.

In economics as in physics, a mechanism with gauge fields is different from one without. The difference affects both the instantaneous specification of a model's state space, as in the one-period models of this chapter, and the larger specification of a model's *dynamics* over multiple periods. An interesting issue when one comes to dynamics is that the evolution of gauge fields (financial instruments) and the underlying commodities is in general independently specified. While one must consider fluctuations about an optimal solution for this dynamics to have any consequence, such fluctuations are expected when one weakens ideal rationality to limited information or computational capacity (introduces "trembles" of whatever sort). Then the multiperiod solution states with financial instruments can be different from those without, even if under perfect rationality they would be specified to be the same at every instant.

4.4.3   Summary of complexity and symmetry in the one-period markets

Table 4.1 summarizes the various indices computed for the six market cases considered in section 4.4. We note a number of overlaps across columns in the table as institutions are added or changed, in either the specialist or generalist allocation situations.

Market 3 and Market 4 have the same DOF at a_{gen} because this is the case of "enough cash, properly distributed," in which the additional availability of credit is irrelevant to the Nash solutions. The models differ in their robustness against boundary solutions, but this does not affect the DOF count. It is, however, reflected in the collapse of the cash market under a_{spec} due to inability to overcome the Jevons failure, as reflected in the reduced DOF.

On the other hand, Markets 4–6 are indistinguishable for a_{spec}, and indeed all provide finite-trade solutions under allocation constraints. Their difference is in the computability of these solutions.

4.5   Conclusions

4.5.1   Relations of symmetry to efficiency

The one-period exchange mechanisms summarized in table 4.1 produce three qualitative types of solutions, which become more efficient as they become more symmetric, both under permutation of each individual's goods and under

Table 4.1
Summary of the properties of the one-period markets

Property	Market					
	1	2	3	4	5	6
Number of markets	$m(m-1)$	$m(m-1)/2$	$m-1$	$m-1$	m	m
a_{gen} DOF	$2m^2(m-1)$	$m^2(m-1)$	$2m(m-1)$	$2m(m-1)$	$(2m+1)(m-1)$	$(2m+1)(m-1)$
a_{spec} DOF	$2m(m-1)$	$m(m-1)$	$2(m-1)$	m^2-1	m^2-1	m^2-1
Symmetry	Yes	Yes	No	No	Yes	Yes
Constructability	any m	$m<3$	NT	large m	N/C	large m

Note: The first row is the number of trading posts, which would be input for costs if larger institution-choosing games were being considered. The second row is DOF for unconstrained bids and offers; the third row is DOF for the case of specialist producers. The fourth row indicates whether the NE have the same symmetry as the agents in the specialist case. In the last row, NT means degeneration to the no-trade solution, and N/C means not constructable. Large m denotes a limit not specifiable within the setting posed, but defined qualitatively in the solutions of appendix 4.6. The value qualifying as "large" in a larger game would depend on a tradeoff between costs of maintaining trading posts and either cardinality of the utility or the costs of bankruptcy.

permutation of individuals. There is an intrinsic asymmetry of endowments in the generalized Jevons failure a_{spec}, while the preferences are assumed to be completely symmetric. The efficiency of any market system considered here turns out to measure how effectively it erases the endowment asymmetry as a property of the allocations, and replaces it with the symmetry of the preferences, preferably without introducing any new asymmetry under permutation of agents. The difference in efficiency between any two market types, multiplied by the initial wealth rma of the system, may be thought of as a money measure of utility gain available to pay for any additional institutions required by the more efficient system. We will formally model this interpretation in chapter 5, where gains from trade must offset labor costs of the institutions which agents choose strategically.

If one assigns the pure no-trade solution as the consequence of strategic uncertainty of Market 5, this solution has efficiency $\eta_{NT} \equiv 0$. Barely better, the severely allocation-constrained solution of Market 3, in which total exchange is limited by the endowments of the cash holders, produce efficiencies $\eta \sim 1/m$. Market 2, for which symmetric interior solutions are limited by boundary constraints, is a more complex intermediate case in which efficiency should asymptotically approach a limit associated with trade by half the desired amount at large m.

In contrast, as soon as credit is introduced, most goods are traded, and efficiencies approach unity at large m and r. The least imprint of the endowment asymmetry on the final allocations is produced by Markets 1 and 6, which preserve the joint permutation symmetry of agents together with their endowed goods and attain the result (4.26): $\eta \sim 1 - 1/2m(r-1)^2$ (though the latter does so only at large m).

When the joint permutation symmetry of agents with their goods is violated by the institutional structure itself, as in Market 4, even though most goods are traded, the cost is a slightly reduced efficiency (4.52): $\eta \sim 1 - 1/2m(r-1)^2 - 1/2mr^2$. At large r, the reduction in welfare of the type-m agents, relative to the others, lowers efficiencies as much as the entire goods asymmetry for all agents combined in Markets 1 or 6.

4.5.2 The sequence from barter to credit evaluation

We wish to interpret the efficiency gains in the various markets as measures of the wealth that is made available to pay for the institutions that support trade. Relative to this measure of welfare gain, the multiplicity of institutions and their computational or informational complexity set the scales of what must be paid for. We formalize both of these ideas for a more limited class of market models starting in the next chapter. Here, making use of the rich taxonomy of markets even in a simple one-period setting, we argue qualitatively that different market types should be preferred according to the diversity and scale of trade desired by the underlying society. The complexity of production and consumption profiles may be partly exogenous to the economy, but it may also be affected by the opportunities to specialize which trade enables.

For sufficiently infrequent or specialized trade, we expect that only barter would exist. The choice of whether or not to form markets turns on whether the cost of sustaining even one post per good can be supported by the opportunity cost that is mitigated by a law of one price. If the volume of desired trades increases, but still involves only few types of goods and relatively little redundancy among their suppliers, then all-for-all markets could achieve the best noncooperative equilibria possible. They are robust and permit constructable equilibria at any m. For this social context, we would not attempt to explain the absence of centralized credit markets as developmental primitiveness or historical contingency. Such markets would not exist because they fail to make optimal noncooperative equilibria constructable when few types of goods m exist.

As the diversity of traded goods increases, however, the cost of the all-for-all trading posts grows quadratically in the number m. At the same time, the errors from misestimation of wash sales in the credit markets decline. Given any structure of costs per post and even admitting the maximal inefficiency from misestimation of wash selling, there will be some diversity above which all-for-all markets become unsustainable and centralized credit markets become the preferred institutional form.

These conclusions can be qualitatively drawn without reference to exogenous uncertainty or the other roles of credit evaluation, to money as a surrogate for trust, or to the heterogeneity of volumes and market types that affects real economies. If we add in these complicating factors, we could assess their importance by studying deviations from the market progression we have outlined here in the risk-free setting.

4.6   Appendix: Allocation-Constrained Solutions

We compute here the noncooperative equilibria for all of the nontrivial market models at a_{spec} endowments. Only solutions with the maximal symmetry respected by both the endowments and markets will be derived. These exist for all six models, but only for a subset, which we will note, are they unique. We will not attempt to prove nonexistence of solutions that spontaneously break the symmetry of the endowments or markets. However, in many cases, such as replica-asymmetric solutions in the all-for-all markets, it is elementary to show that these do not exist as long as preferences are convex and once-differentiable.

Because we are pursuing symmetric allocations, we will restrict utilities to the form (3.3). The cardinalization functions f_i will never matter. To factor these out of the optimization equations, we introduce the notation for the log derivatives

$$f_i^{(l)} \equiv \frac{d}{d \log \left(\prod_j A_i^j \right)} f_i \left(\prod_j A_i^j \right). \tag{4.16}$$

The *arguments* of the f_i will, however, be objects of recurring interest. This combination is the (measurable) function of consumables that determines the efficacy of markets, enabling us to compare both users within a single economy and market structures across economies. We use as a reference point the most symmetric outcome possible, and the one leading to the largest utility that all agents can simultaneously have. This is the (totally symmetric) allocation product produced by a competitive equilibrium,

$$\left. \prod_j A_i^j \right|_{CE} = \left(\frac{a}{m} \right)^m, \ \forall i. \tag{4.17}$$

In the derivations below, other allocations will be compared to the solution (4.17). We will find that at large m they differ by factors of the form

$$\frac{1+x}{e^x} < 1, \ \forall x \neq 0, \tag{4.18}$$

in which x will be various functions of the replication index.

4.6.1   Market 1

The final allocations are given as a function of the strategic variable choices by Eq. (4.2). Varying these, and adopting the notation $B^{jk} \equiv \sum_i b_i^{jk}$, $Q^{jk} \equiv \sum_i q_i^{jk}$, gives

$$\delta A_i^j = \sum_{k \neq j} \left(\frac{\delta b_i^{jk}}{p^{jk}} - \delta q_i^{jk} \right) \left(1 - \frac{b_i^{jk}}{B^{jk}} \right)$$
$$- \sum_{k \neq j} \left(\delta b_i^{kj} - p^{kj} \delta q_i^{kj} \right) \left(1 - \frac{q_i^{kj}}{Q^{kj}} \right). \qquad (4.19)$$

The parenthesized factors involving B^{jk} and Q^{jk} arise from the agents' own assessment of their impacts on prices. It it through these factors that the NE differ from the CE in all cases.

The condition of maximal utility for any agent i follows from Eq. (4.19) as

$$\frac{\delta \mathcal{U}_i}{f_i^{(l)}} = \sum_j \sum_{k \neq j} \left[\frac{1}{p^{jk} A_i^j} \left(1 - b_i^{jk} / B^{jk} \right) - \frac{1}{A_i^k} \left(1 - q_i^{jk} / Q^{jk} \right) \right] \left(\delta b_i^j - p^j \delta q_i^j \right).$$
$$(4.20)$$

The most symmetric solutions that can be generated by the markets are those in which all agents offer the same amount $q \equiv q_i^{ik}$ and bid the same amount $b \equiv b_i^{ki}$, for any $i \neq k$. The price at any trading post in terms of these is $p \equiv p^{jk} = b/q$, for any $j \neq k$. The only nonzero impact factors, respectively for bids and offers, are

$$\left(1 - \frac{b_i^{ki}}{B^{ki}} \right) = \left(1 - \frac{1}{r} \right),$$
$$\left(1 - \frac{q_i^{ik}}{Q^{ik}} \right) = \left(1 - \frac{1}{r} \right). \qquad (4.21)$$

The notation $\mathcal{A}^+$ may be introduced for the final allocation of any agent in terms of his endowed good, and $\mathcal{A}^-$ for his final allocation in any of the nonendowed goods; by symmetry all nonendowed goods take the same value. In terms of b and q, these are

$$\mathcal{A}^+ \equiv \frac{A_i^i}{a} = 1 - (m - 1) \frac{q + b}{a},$$
$$\mathcal{A}^- \equiv \frac{A_i^{j \neq i}}{a} = \frac{q + b}{a}. \qquad (4.22)$$

The intrinsic symmetry of the endowments, since it is respected by the market structure, implies that for symmetric solutions $p = 1 \Rightarrow b = q$. Substituted with the reduced notations (4.21–4.22) into Eq. (4.20), these fix the only undetermined ratio in the problem,

$$\frac{1}{\mathcal{A}^+} = \frac{\left(1 - \frac{1}{r}\right)}{\mathcal{A}^-}. \tag{4.23}$$

Eq. (4.23) is exactly solvable and unique for both $\mathcal{A}^+$ and $\mathcal{A}^-$ at all $m > 1$, but it is useful to expand the solution as a power series in $1/m$ for comparison to nonunique solutions of the markets that we will consider next:

$$\mathcal{A}^+ = \frac{1 + \frac{1}{r-1}}{m + \frac{1}{r-1}} = \frac{1}{m}\left[1 + \frac{1}{r - 1}\right] + \mathcal{O}\left(\frac{1}{m^2}\right),$$

$$\mathcal{A}^- = \frac{1}{m + \frac{1}{r-1}} = \frac{1}{m}\left[1 - \frac{1}{(r - 1)m}\right] + \mathcal{O}\left(\frac{1}{m^3}\right). \tag{4.24}$$

The consequence of correlating agent consumption levels with the goods that they produce as specialists is a reduction in the term $\prod_j A_i^j$. This term sets utility levels and determines allocative efficiency. At large m and any $r > 1$, it approaches the limit

$$\prod_j A_i^j \rightarrow \frac{\left(1 + \frac{1}{r-1}\right)}{\exp\left(\frac{1}{r-1}\right)}\left(\frac{a}{m}\right)^m, \quad \forall i. \tag{4.25}$$

The allocative efficiency (3.9) corresponding to Eq. (4.25) is then

$$\eta = \frac{\left(1 + \frac{1}{r-1}\right)^{1/m}}{\exp\left(\frac{1}{m(r-1)}\right)}. \tag{4.26}$$

This solution, generated by a redundant barter-like market structure, turns out to be the best that can be achieved in one-period exchange by agents who account for their own price impacts. Markets 1 and 2 are unique in making this solution constructable for any m, a feature that even the institutionally more complex credit markets do not attain. However, only Market 1 makes the solution accessible without short selling at finite $m \geq 3$.

4.6.2   Market 2

We begin with the expression for final allocations from Eq. (4.4), in which all submissions are treated as q_i^{jk}. The market index order rather than a q/b distinction is then used to identify which goods serve as bids and which as offers. Then the variation in final outcomes as a result of variation in bids and offers takes the simple form

$$\delta A_i^j = -\frac{1}{2} \sum_{k \neq j} \left(\delta q_i^{jk} - \frac{Q^{jk}}{Q^{kj}} \delta q_i^{kj} \right) \left(1 - \frac{q_i^{kj}}{Q^{kj}} \right), \qquad (4.27)$$

with Q^{jk} defined as for Market 1. The variation of any $\mathcal{U}_i$ is then

$$\frac{\delta \mathcal{U}_i}{f_i^{(l)}} = -\frac{1}{2} \sum_j \sum_{k \neq j} \left[\frac{1}{A_i^j} \left(1 - q_i^{kj}/Q^{kj} \right) - \frac{Q^{kj}}{Q^{jk} A_i^k} \left(1 - q_i^{jk}/Q^{jk} \right) \right] \delta q_i^{jk}. \quad (4.28)$$

Agents can offer only their endowed goods, and for symmetric solutions the volume offered will be the same for all goods. Therefore we may introduce an abbreviated notation $q \equiv q_i^{ik}$, for any k. This symmetry is the same as the $b = q$ property in Market 2, and it implies $Q^{kj}/Q^{jk} = 1$. The offer impact in the second line of Eq. (4.21) is as before, only now it includes the bid impact (up to the renaming of bids and offers at a post). The expressions for final allocations of the endowed and nonendowed goods are also much the same, with the only differences coming from factors of 2:

$$\mathcal{A}^+ \equiv \frac{A_i^i}{a} = 1 - (m-1)\frac{q}{2a},$$

$$\mathcal{A}^- \equiv \frac{q}{2a}. \qquad (4.29)$$

Eq. (4.23) again follows from maximization, so that the final allocations for all i are just those given by Eq. (4.24). The argument of the utility therefore remains as in Eq. (4.25).

We note that $q/2$ in Market 2 takes the same value as $q + b$ in Market 1. The interpretation is that each undirected market is "thicker" than its directed counterpart. The importance of thickness in Market 2 is that the best the agents can do under their allocation constraints is to reach a boundary solution approximating the NE at $m > 3$. Often this approximation is not close. By combining Eq. (4.29) with the second line of Eq. (4.24), we arrive at the total offer level

$$(m-1)\frac{q}{a} = \frac{2(m-1)}{m + \frac{1}{r-1}}. \qquad (4.30)$$

Eq (4.30) evaluates to a number greater than unity for $m \geq 3$. More than half of this required offer at market, of course, is returned to the agents by the clearing rule. However, as the absence of credit requires them to offer this quantity up front, the clearing rule has made the optimal solution inaccessible to them. This is an inefficiency not created by Market 1.

4.6.3   Market 4

The allocations (3.5) and (3.6) finally become simple with this market, and the notation for total bids and offers reduces to $B^j \equiv \sum_i b_i^j$, $Q^j \equiv \sum_i q_i^j$. The variation of the consumable goods takes the simple form

$$\delta A_i^j = - \left(\delta q_i^j - \frac{\delta b_i^j}{p^j} \right) \left(1 - \frac{b_i^j}{B^j} \right). \tag{4.31}$$

Market 4 also introduces money as a separate state variable for the first time, in the form of a final balance of promissory notes. The variation in this quantity is

$$\delta M_i = - \sum_j \left(\delta b_i^j - p^j \delta q_i^j \right) \left(1 - \frac{q_i^j}{Q^j} \right). \tag{4.32}$$

Using the bankruptcy-modified utility (3.8) within a range where the the min is identically zero, the optimization condition becomes

$$\frac{\delta U_i}{f_i^{(l)}} = \sum_{j \neq m} \left[\frac{1}{p^j A_i^j} \left(1 - b_i^j / B^j \right) - \frac{1}{A_i^m} \left(1 - q_i^j / Q^j \right) \right] \left(\delta b_i^j - p^j \delta q_i^j \right). \tag{4.33}$$

This market structure has the least symmetry of those in our taxonomy. It admits a single offer variable $q \equiv q_i^j$, and as in the previous markets it renders two bid variables strategically asymmetric: one $b^+ \equiv b_i^i$ for the endowed good, and another $b^- \equiv b_i^{j \neq i,m}$ for the nonendowed nonmoney goods $i \neq m$. In addition, Market 4 introduces a third bidding scale $b^0 \equiv b_m^{j \neq m}$ by the provider of the mth good for all other goods, which for him are not endowed. The total bids on any market may be denoted $mb \equiv B^j = b^+ + (m - 2) b^- + b^0$. In this notation the price of each nonmoney good is $p \equiv p^j = mb/q$, for any $j \neq m$.

The absence of a trading post for the quantity denominating the promissory notes removes an offer impact factor for agents of type m, separating goods into three categories: endowed, nonendowed, and the commodity money. It is convenient to define the nondimensional variables of the most symmetric solutions by momentarily letting i be the index of a non-m agent and his endowed good, and j any other nonmoney index, so that with $i \neq j \neq m$,

$$\left(1 - \frac{b_i^i}{B^i}\right) = \left(1 - \frac{b^+}{rmb}\right)$$

$$\left(1 - \frac{b_i^j}{B^j}\right) = \left(1 - \frac{b^-}{rmb}\right)$$

$$\left(1 - \frac{b_m^j}{B^j}\right) = \left(1 - \frac{b^0}{rmb}\right). \tag{4.34}$$

The offer impact is then relevant only for type i:

$$\left(1 - \frac{q_i^i}{Q^i}\right) = \left(1 - \frac{1}{r}\right). \tag{4.35}$$

The final allocations for agents of type i are named as before,

$$\mathcal{A}^+ \equiv \frac{A_i^i}{a} = 1 - \frac{q}{a}\left(1 - \frac{b^+}{mb}\right),$$

$$\mathcal{A}^- \equiv \frac{A_i^j}{a} = \frac{q}{a}\frac{b^-}{mb},$$

$$\mathcal{A}^m \equiv \frac{A_i^m}{a} = \frac{b^0}{a}. \tag{4.36}$$

Market 4 generates three levels of consumption for non-type-m agents. The allocations for agents of type m introduce two more scales, which we label as

$$\mathcal{M}^- \equiv \frac{A_m^j}{a} = \frac{q}{a}\frac{b^0}{mb},$$

$$\mathcal{M}^m \equiv \frac{A_m^m}{a} = 1 - (m-1)\frac{b^0}{a}. \tag{4.37}$$

The two nontrivial relations arising from Eq. (4.33) for type i are now

$$\frac{\left(1 - \frac{b^+}{rmb}\right)}{\left(1 - \frac{1}{r}\right)\mathcal{A}^+} = \frac{\left(1 - \frac{b^-}{rmb}\right)}{\mathcal{A}^-} = \frac{p}{\mathcal{A}^m}, \tag{4.38}$$

while the one relation for agents of type m is

$$\frac{\left(1 - \frac{b^0}{rmb}\right)}{\mathcal{M}^-} = \frac{p}{\mathcal{M}^m}. \tag{4.39}$$

In terms of these, the product $\prod_j A_i^j$ for the agents of any type $i \neq m$ evaluates to

$$\prod_j A_{i \neq m}^j = a^m \mathcal{A}^+ \left(\mathcal{A}^-\right)^{(m-2)} \mathcal{A}^m, \tag{4.40}$$

while $\prod_j A_m^j$ for the money providers evaluates to

$$\prod_j A_m^j = a^m \left(\mathcal{M}^-\right)^{(m-1)} \mathcal{M}^m. \tag{4.41}$$

It follows from the definition of p and Eqs. (4.36–4.37) that $p\mathcal{M}^- = \mathcal{A}^m$. Therefore the two type of allocations have the ratio

$$\prod_j \frac{A_{i \neq m}^j}{A_m^j} = \frac{\left(1 - \frac{b^+}{mb}\right)\left(1 - \frac{b^-}{rmb}\right)^{(m-2)}\left(1 - \frac{b^0}{rmb}\right)}{\left(1 - \frac{1}{r}\right)}$$

$$= \frac{\exp\left(-\frac{1}{r}\right)}{\left(1 - \frac{1}{r}\right)}\left[1 + \mathcal{O}\left(\frac{1}{m}\right)\right]. \tag{4.42}$$

The second expansion is appropriate at large m as long as $b^+/b, b^-/b, b^0/b \sim \mathcal{O}\left(m^0\right)$, which we will demonstrate in a moment.

Also following from the price definition and Eq. (4.39) is the relation

$$\frac{b^0}{b^-} = \left(1 + \frac{b^0}{rmb}\right), \tag{4.43}$$

which has a unique solution for b^0/b^- if $b^+/b \to 0$. Unique solutions therefore exist which involve no wash sales, and these can serve as a basis for the analysis of more general NE. The final allocation $\mathcal{M}^m$ (4.37) may also be computed in terms of the ratio b^0/rmb at general b values, as

$$1 - (m-1)\frac{b^0}{a} = \frac{1}{1 + (m-1)\left(1 - \frac{b^0}{rmb}\right)}. \tag{4.44}$$

Plugging this relation into Eq. (4.37) for $\mathcal{M}^-$, the offer constraint of no short sales $q \leq a$ implies the bound

$$0 \leq \frac{b^+}{b^-} \leq 1 + \frac{1}{r-1} + \mathcal{O}\left(\frac{1}{m}\right). \tag{4.45}$$

Together with the relation (4.44), this implies the asymptotically m-independent scaling of all components of b_i^j required to satisfy Eq. (4.42).

The nature of the NE parametrized by b^+/b is easy to understand, but implies a new form of indeterminacy for all solutions of this kind. It is clear that, given any interior NE with $b^+/b \to 0$ (which the above equations yield), it is strategically neutral for any single agent i to engage in wash sales. At $b^+/b \to 0$, he has offered less than his total endowment permits (the solution is interior in A_i^i). Therefore he may always offer some additional increment of q_i^i, and thereby increase his b_i^i, without incurring bankruptcy penalties. This remains true as long as his wash sales do not change the price.

Of course, if other agents knew he was going to thicken the market, it would change their own impact assessments, and so their bids would not remain the same, by Eq. (4.43). Thus the neutral curve for any agent given $b^+/b \to 0$ does not coincide at general m with the one-parameter family of NE obtainable by the group as they vary b^+ collectively. Since any b_i^i is subject to a neutral variation, nothing about the NE condition can fix it for any agent, and therefore he has no way to infer the value that will be chosen by other agents.

If we were to alter the solution concept, for instance by ranking the NE globally, the $b^+/b \to 0$ solution would be the least preferred. This is an algebraically tedious result to compute, but it introduces the notion of *salience* and cost-free signals to the solution concept, potentially allowing agents to guess a scale of bidding that will bring them into coordination. The reason the allocation products of NE are smaller than those of CE is that suppliers hoard their endowed good to some extent, because of a $(1 - 1/r)$ decrease in the marginal value of increasing offers, due to price impact. Any allowed increase in wash selling stabilizes prices to some degree, placing each agent in a situation slightly closer to that of a price taker, and so reduces the hoarding tendency and moves every agent's allocations closer to the symmetry of CE. Thus the maximum wash sale possible is the globally Pareto-superior NE. The tradeoff to Pareto superiority is that any agent who chooses that outcome is maximally vulnerable to bankruptcy, which is a more severe penalty than a slight reduction in consumption level. Therefore any other NE is risk-dominant over the maximal-wash-sale solution. Rather than pursue the question of salience in more refined solution concepts on the basis of this one market, we simply acknowledge the indeterminacy of the standard NE solution with the tools provided by bankruptcy institutions alone.

The problem of indeterminacy is regulated at large m by Eq. (4.45). No provider, through wash selling, can impact either the price or the total amount of his own bids by an amount larger than $1/m$. With vanishing price impact, the corrections by other agents also disappear, and so the neutral curve for each agent independently converges to coincidence with the collective change of b^+ in the NE. Therefore both choices become strategically null. The entire range of NE then corresponds to the allocations for type $i \neq m$ of

$$
\begin{aligned}
\mathcal{A}^+ &= \frac{1}{m}\left[1 + \frac{1}{r-1}\right] + \mathcal{O}\left(\frac{1}{m^2}\right), \\
\mathcal{A}^- &= \frac{1}{m}\left[1 - \frac{1}{(r-1)\,m}\right] + \mathcal{O}\left(\frac{1}{m^3}\right), \\
\mathcal{A}^m &= \frac{1}{m} + \mathcal{O}\left(\frac{1}{m^2}\right).
\end{aligned}
\tag{4.46}
$$

The corresponding solutions for type m are

$$
\begin{aligned}
\mathcal{M}^- &= \frac{1}{m}\left[1 - \frac{1}{r(r-1)\,m}\right] + \mathcal{O}\left(\frac{1}{m^3}\right), \\
\mathcal{M}^m &= \frac{1}{m} + \mathcal{O}\left(\frac{1}{m^2}\right).
\end{aligned}
\tag{4.47}
$$

At large m (but only there), for each agent it becomes rational to engage in any degree of wash sale within the bounds imposed by the NE. The product $A^j_{i \neq m}$ converges as $1/m$ toward

$$
\prod_j A^j_{i \neq m} \to \frac{\left(1 + \frac{1}{r-1}\right)}{\exp\left(\frac{1}{r-1}\right)} \left(\frac{a}{m}\right)^m.
\tag{4.48}
$$

This solution is the same as the solution for agents of type $i \neq m$ in Markets 1 and 2, except that in Market 2 the absence of short sales placed the equilibrium outside the boundary constraints.

The corresponding product $\prod_j A^j_m$ for the money providers converges in the limit as

$$
\prod_j A^j_m \to \frac{\left(1 - \frac{1}{r}\right)}{\exp\left(-\frac{1}{r}\right)} \prod_j A^j_{i \neq m} \to e^{-\frac{1}{r(r-1)}} \left(\frac{a}{m}\right)^m.
\tag{4.49}
$$

Their consumption level is smaller than that for the other types by the factor in Eq. (4.42), which is in turn smaller by a factor of the same basic form (4.18) than the CE solution.

The final allocation from this market is the only one in the one-period exchange taxonomy that falls off the hyperplane $\sum_j A_i^j = \sum_j a_i^j = a$. From Eq. (4.47) follows

$$\sum_j A_m^j = a\left[1 - \frac{1}{r(r-1)m} + \mathcal{O}\left(\frac{1}{m^2}\right)\right]. \tag{4.50}$$

Although we have not extended Eq. (4.46) to the order in $1/m$ needed to determine $A_{i\neq m}^j$, the symmetry of the solutions requires that

$$\sum_j A_{i\neq m}^j = a\left[1 + \frac{1}{r(r-1)m(m-1)} + \mathcal{O}\left(\frac{1}{m^3}\right)\right]. \tag{4.51}$$

These corrections to the type-$i \neq m$ allocations only perturb the efficiency at $\mathcal{O}\left(1/m^2\right)$. The order-unity reduction for type m versus the rest, in Eq. (4.49), perturbs the efficiency at $\mathcal{O}\left(1/m\right)$. As a result, the overall efficiency satisfies

$$\eta = \frac{\left(1 + \frac{1}{r-1}\right)^{1/m}}{\exp\left(\frac{1}{m(r-1)}\right)} - \frac{1}{m}\left[1 - \frac{\left(1 - \frac{1}{r}\right)}{\exp\left(-\frac{1}{r}\right)}\right] + \mathcal{O}\left(\frac{1}{m^2}\right). \tag{4.52}$$

The allocations become progressively less efficient as they become less symmetric.

4.6.4   Markets 5 and 6

The NE for both symmetric credit markets are identical, and it is more direct to compute them for the elementary Kuhn-Tucker form of the bankruptcy constraint in Market 5. We therefore derive these solutions for Market 5, disregarding the fact that agents cannot achieve them due to the scale ambiguity of bids. Since the rational solution concept in Market 6 is to assume a shared scale of bidding and continued bankruptcy limits, the strategic evaluation is the same, with the scale factor corrections between different agents' solutions merely supplied by the evaluation agency after the fact.

The variations of allocations and monies are the same in Market 5 as Eqs. (4.31–4.32). However, because the denomination of the promissory notes is now arbitrary relative to any of the consumables, the bankruptcy multiplier enters in a meaningful way into the Nash optimization (interior solutions for the consumables no longer make the bankruptcy constraint slack). The variation of the Kuhn-Tucker form (4.7) of the utility then becomes

$$\frac{\delta \mathcal{U}_i}{f_i^{(l)}} = \sum_j \left[\frac{1}{p^j A_i^j} \frac{\left(1 - b_i^j / B^j\right)}{\left(1 - q_i^j / Q^j\right)} - \frac{\kappa_i}{f_i^{(l)}} \right] \left(1 - \frac{q_i^j}{Q^j}\right) \left(\delta b_i^j - p^j \delta q_i^j\right), \quad (4.53)$$

where the magnitude of the penalty variable Π does not matter as long as the cardinalization of f_i makes $f_i^{(l)}$ sufficiently small.

There are now solutions entirely symmetric in the offer variable $q \equiv q_i^i$, and in terms of only two bid variables $b^+ \equiv b_i^i$, $b^- \equiv b_i^{j \neq i}$, for any i. The total bids on any post may be denoted almost as before, $mb \equiv B^j = b^+ + (m - 1) b^-$, and in that notation $p \equiv p^j = mb/q$, for any j.

The first two lines of Eq. (4.34), and of Eq. (4.35), again describe the only nonzero impact factors, and the final allocations $\mathcal{A}^+ \equiv A_i^i/a$ and $\mathcal{A}^- \equiv A_i^{j \neq i}/a$ again take the form in the first two lines of Eq. (4.36), in terms of the present definition of mb. The first equality of Eq. (4.38) remains true, as the only nontrivial relation. In these markets it defines a unique solution for $b^+/b \to 0$.

To obtain a bound on wash sales, one can introduce the parameter $\zeta \equiv b^-/b$, and show that

$$\frac{q}{a} \zeta = \frac{\left(1 - \frac{\zeta}{rm}\right)}{1 + \frac{\zeta}{r^2 m} \left(1 - \frac{1}{m}\right) / \left(1 - \frac{1}{r}\right)}$$

$$= 1 - \frac{\zeta}{(r - 1) m} + \mathcal{O}\left(\frac{1}{m^2}\right). \quad (4.54)$$

As before, $q/a \leq 1$ implies a bound on ζ at order $1 - 1/m$, showing that b^+/b lies in a range around unity of size $\leq \left(m^{-1}\right)$. Thus again, at large m but only there, the neutral curve of independent wash sales for each agent converges to the joint curve of b^+-parametrized NE, for which the allocations become degenerate.

To estimate the allocations simply, we observe that $b^+/b \to 0 \Rightarrow \zeta \to m/(m - 1)$. In this limit

$$\mathcal{A}^+ = \frac{1}{m} \left[1 + \frac{1}{r - 1}\right] + \mathcal{O}\left(\frac{1}{m^2}\right),$$

$$\mathcal{A}^- = \frac{1}{m} \left[1 - \frac{1}{(r - 1)(m - 1)}\right] + \mathcal{O}\left(\frac{1}{m^3}\right). \quad (4.55)$$

The allocations (4.55), at the indicated order for all allowed b^+/b, agree with Eq. (4.24) and the relevant lines of Eq. (4.46), for all agents i. The consumption level $\prod_j A_i^j$, and with it the efficiency, are thus the same as the result (4.25) produced by the all-for-all markets, in the large-m limit.

Notes

1 For an elegant treatment see Samuelson [313]. See also Russell [309, 310], who relates this duality of minimum systems—known as *Legendre duality*—to duality under a simplectic structure of goods and prices.

2 Attempts at measures of complexity for purely formal computational algorithms already suggest that distinct, mutually incommensurable notions of complexity may be needed to address different aspects of performance, and show that lack of formalization is often less of a problem in assessing relative complexity than are unclearly defined goals.

3 The use of this terminology in diffusive models, such as that of [22], requires slight clarification. The theorem known as *Goldstone's theorem*, which relates a global symmetry to a long-range propagating degree of freedom, was originally proved for the vacuum structure of zero-temperature quantum mechanics. The same kinds of symmetry can exist in classical reaction-diffusion systems, such as the stochastic process of [23]. In these systems, however, they are related to the existence of non-mean-regressing degrees of freedom that propagate as Brownian random walks, as described in [380].

5 Endogenizing the Choice of a Monetary System[1]

5.1 "Rules of the Game" within the Optimization Problem, and the Need for Multiple Timescales

In chapter 3 we introduced an essentially timeless model of preinstitutional society. Its continuously available production technologies and its preferences for consumption of goods or services provide an invariant background on which to compare economic functions. In chapter 4 we introduced trade as a single-timescale phenomenon overlaid on that background. Depending on the specific mechanism of trade, the timescale selected may affect economically significant observables. The mechanisms supporting trade in chapter 4 were exogenous to the economy, and the cost of the supports was not deducted from trade. In this chapter we introduce our first multi-timescale models of an economy. Longer timescales are associated with commitment to productive specialization, and to discounting and depreciation of durable goods. We compare an economy mediated by a durable commodity money with one with a fiat money implemented through a bureaucracy. The inefficiency costs associated with asymmetric strategic roles between money providers and producers of consumption goods are compared with explicit losses of material productivity due to labor costs to maintain a bureaucracy. We show how a stable trade system can emerge.

5.2 Material Capital and Institutional Capital

The concept of capital in a production economy is an essentially dynamical one. The material goods that make up the capital stock in an economy cost resources to produce. Once produced, they mediate the conversion of other resources from lower-value to higher-value forms, without themselves being consumed as part of the output stream of consumable resources. Capital stock generally decays or otherwise depreciates, but this is a qualitatively distinct process from being consumed as an input to production, and occurs on a timescale that is typically longer and—what is more important—variable with respect to the input ratios of normal factors in production.

The capital stock in an economy acts much like the stock of catalysts used to enable a chemical reaction. It necessarily participates in material conversion in fixed proportions to the reactants and products. Without it the conversion cannot take place, and the quantity of the catalyst determines the maximal rate of conversion, with the constant of proportionality set by the catalytic rate of transformation. Although its quantity matters because it participates in reactions, the natural lifetime of the catalyst is generally much longer than that of the resources whose conversion it mediates. In a framework such as general equilibrium, capital stock (including ideal, long-lived chemical catalysts) vanishes from the net input-output relation in an abstract "production function."

Everything that has been said here about physical capital in relation to production applies, equally well, to the institutions that support trade and lead to the extraction of surplus value through reallocation of goods in an exchange economy. The supports of trade cost resources to produce, and, like durable capital stocks or chemical catalysts, they vanish from the input-output relations recognized by general equilibrium. Without a process-based analysis, we are unable to provide a measure of the value of capital or trade that can offset the cost to provide its supporting institutions. We are left unable to do for capital and institutions what the economic optimization problem seeks to do for all other resources in the economy: to explain why they are produced and what factors set the scale at which they are used.

The growth theory of John von Neumann and David Gale, or the similar input-output analysis of Leontief, provided the appropriate process analysis to describe material capital in a production economy. In this chapter we will construct an equivalent process description for the institutional supports of trade. Much as von Neumann-Gale-Leontief input-output matrices quantitatively define the material conditions on which an abstract production function of general equilibrium is contingent, we will define quantitative market-clearing services on which Pareto-superior reallocation of goods is contingent.

We will focus on the problem of providing a *monetary system*, in the same way as the problem of describing local trading post mechanisms has been treated extensively in the previous chapter and elsewhere. A monetary system consists of a recognized money and a means for its adequate distribution.

Money acts as a substitute for trust in the models we will consider, and its quantity and therefore its value in trade are set either by the cost of its production if it is a commodity or by penalties imposed on default if it is government-issued fiat. Both of these are reducible ultimately to labor costs within the economy in the context of some production technologies. The tie between value in trade and labor costs is what makes provision of trading mechanisms a quantitative, as opposed to merely rule-based, sector of the economy, comparable to physical capital.

5.3   The Emergence and Eventual Separation of Money Systems from the Real-Goods Sector

The invention of a monetary system as an additional layer over the production technologies and consumption preferences that we take to define preinstitutional society is in one sense a singular event, comparable to the innovation of any other production technology. The monetary system introduces new conventions (recognition of money) and globally known constraints (related to limitations in money supply), which enable self-consistent choices of moves in underlying trading games. Here, as in chapter 4, we take the trading post mechanism to be preexisting, and we study the problem of creating coordination mechanisms as a choice of whether to employ an innovation.

However, in another sense money can be said to "emerge" from the underlying material economy, through a sequence of stages that we find historically attested and that may be understood in terms of the transfer of control from the informal society to the formal actions of government.[2] We will make explicit both the singular and the gradual nature of the emergence of monetary function by comparing two models: one of a durable commodity money and the other of a government-issued fiat.

At the lower stage, the value-in-trade of commodity money depends on its consumption value as a durable good; in general, that consumption value will also be augmented by a scarcity price arising from its store-of-value function during repeated trading. The dependence of the monetary function on material consumption value in this stage is reflected in a tight coupling of the money supply and velocity to the quantities and velocities of traded goods in the underlying production sector.

At the higher stage where control depends on centrally defined rules rather than on consumption utility distributed over the members of the society, two new institutions—a bureaucracy for the creation and collection of money, and a central bank to enable its distribution—decouple the means of payment from the time structure of repeated trading and thus from stocks and flows in the underlying economy. This decoupling is reflected in a money supply and velocity that are permitted to diverge from those of production goods as the trading period is made short. Money supply remains limited, but its limits now come from explicit penalties on default also enforced by the bureaucracy. Because enforcement is limited by the labor supply, trade in underlying goods remains regular under arbitrary variations in the trading period, even though flows in the financial sector now take on independent dynamics.

Our model of a fiat money is another attempt to introduce the conceptual distinction between distributed and centralized control in minimal form. It is more difficult to characterize the nature of minimality in this model than it was for the comparison of one-period markets in chapter 4, where we could directly compare symmetry groups and count strategic degrees of freedom.

Yet we believe that most features of the model are inevitable for the use of a fiat money system. The principal commitments are these:

1. If a fiat money is centrally produced, it is not globally available to agents. If its denomination is essentially arbitrary and requires being stabilized by the rules, we cannot even treat its distribution as a cumulative effect of history, as we can to some degree with a commodity money such as gold. Therefore fiat money requires some institution with the function of a central bank to enable its distribution, in a way that a commodity money does not.

2. If money is distributed through the mechanism of loans, this process introduces strategic default as a part of the feasible state space. Therefore, default must somehow be "trapped" as a condition and handled within the rules of the game. We have chosen to do this with a linear default penalty added directly to utility, and this choice is to some extent arbitrary. However, it does capture the separation between market functions and coercive functions, and a linear default penalty added to a concave utility captures the "public goods" aspect of default as a form of limited liability.

3. Clearly the provision of economic services comes at a cost; how shall we model such costs minimally? If we have already introduced linear penalties into the model, then a way to assign costs which assumes no further institutions, and uses only the parameters already required to define the play of the game, is to make costs linearly proportional to the capacity of the service that handles default. A direct and not-unrealistic way to implement such costs is to suppose that the service of handling default consumes an amount of the productive labor pool proportional to the service capacity.

Closing the model in this way leaves the costs of other trading mechanisms unchanged—the costs of the trading posts, which were also left implicit in chapter 4—and separates the optimization of the control system into one that can be studied in isolation.

5.4   Specialization in Production Defines a Common Coordination Problem

We continue to use the generalized Jevons failure of coincidence of wants to define a setting which is "preinstitutional" with respect to monetary coordination, though we will permit considerable complexity by assuming that production technologies and buy-sell trading posts are provided "free of charge" in the premonetary society.

While the fiat money model that we introduce here could be analyzed in a one-period setting like that used in chapter 4 (constituting a conversion of Market 4 from personal credit to bank credit), its performance can only be compared meaningfully to that of a commodity money in a setting of repeated trade.[3] Therefore we abandon the one-period setting in this chapter and introduce a hierarchical extensive-form game, in which a money system is chosen once at the beginning of the game and then mediates trade in a sequence of repeated rounds resembling those modeled in chapter 4. It is this extensive form that introduces a second timescale into the economic optimization problem.

In general, the production of money or of services such as contract enforcement required for the use of money will alter the distribution of other goods at the noncooperative equilibrium of the trading games. Therefore if the money choice is endogenous, the choice of specialist production cannot naturally be preassigned as it was in chapter 4. We therefore adopt a different separation of labor and production from that in the last chapter. The number of agents remains a property of the premonetary society, but the allocation of these agents among production functions is a strategic variable in the outer move of the extensive-form game, along with the choice of money system.

This modeling choice allows us to cast the extraction of surplus from specialist production as a standard social coordination problem, which may be solved in different ways by adopting either commodity or fiat monetary systems. This coordination problem, often assumed away in conventional economic models, has no satisfactory solution in the absence of any monetary system—to sharpen the problem, we model it as a no-trade situation—because specialist production requires a *long-term commitment*, leading to a generalized Jevons failure of the kind considered in chapter 4.

This way of representing precommitment to the acquisition of means of production (which could represent skill or sunk costs in capital) makes explicit the sense in which the introduction of money creates both new "rules of the game" for trade and new mechanisms of solution for preexisting strategies. The systematic comparison of the solutions created by distinct money systems is therefore a problem in mechanism design.

Absent money, agents in society still have the choice between generalist production (which we will refer to as *autarchy*) and committed specialist production. We suppose that generalist production is Pareto-inferior to specialist production with efficient trade, but that specialist production without trade is Pareto-inferior to generalist autarchic production. The general structure of optima limited to these classes of strategies is shown in figure 5.1. Without the ability to predict outcomes of trade, agents have no mechanism to attain Pareto-superior production and efficient allocation, and their strategy sets are effectively reduced to autarchy versus inefficient specialization under the Jevons failure. Finally, the introduction of a multiperiod setting allows us to characterize the relative independence of the money from the underlying commodities by studying the relative scaling in the two sectors as the time structure of the periods is varied.

5.4.1 Endogenous labor allocation: symmetric treatment in a nonsymmetric production sector

Chapter 4 emphasized the importance of symmetry for both equal treatment and efficiency. There we observed that the seemingly straightforward desire to *independently* give both agents and goods permutation-symmetric treatment required monies not drawn from within the sector of consumable goods. Moreover, the naïve way to introduce such monies—using promissory notes—caused the ambiguous scale of the numéraire to ramify to a strategic indeterminacy and a failure of market function. We will encounter a similar problem of symmetric treatment in this chapter, because, for both commodity and fiat monies, the specialists responsible for providing the money system necessarily participate in markets differently from producers of consumable commodities. In this chapter, making labor allocation strategic is what restores symmetric treatment of agents within a structurally asymmetric economy. In contrast to the last chapter, where we identified agent *types* with preassigned production functions, but then treated those production functions

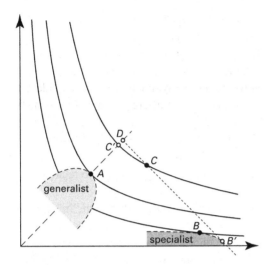

Figure 5.1

Qualitative features of the transition to specialization represented as regions in strategy space, and the valuation with or without trade mechanisms. Convex preferences in two goods are represented here by solid lines. Possible endowments achievable within the generalist or specialist production technologies are represented as shaded regions with dashed boundaries. Solid dots are outcomes realizable by certain combinations of production decision and trade technology, and open circles are reference points in the analysis. A is the best outcome one can achieve as a generalist, and B the (Pareto-inferior) best outcome as a specialist without trade. B' is the endowment that produces a best outcome (C) with the noncooperative equilibrium of some trading game, and D for reference is the competitive equilibrium at the same endowments. Utility in money metric, measured by integration along the Pareto set (diagonal dashed line) [378, 383], defines a natural measure of the relative commodity value of the different outcomes. The value of C, given by the expenditure function at the point C' (open circle on the Pareto set indifferent to C), stably dominates A but is dominated by D, capturing the gains to trade as well as inefficiencies associated with finite population size. (Other inefficiencies associated with costs of markets are not shown in this figure for simplicity.) In minimal models the endowment difference between B and B' is suppressed, as it depends sensitively on representations of both utility and specialist production at small arguments.

as permutation-symmetric in order to test the symmetry properties of the economy, here we will consider agents as providing a single undifferentiated input called *labor*, with all subsequent conversion of labor performed within the economy. Production of distinct nondurable consumables will continue to be treated as permutation-symmetric, for simplicity of solutions, but the multiperiod structure requires an inherent asymmetry between durable and nondurable consumables, so that the durable good may serve as a commodity money. With strategic labor allocation, permutation symmetry of the nondurable production functions is no longer needed to test for equal treatment under the rules of the economy, and is merely a convenience.

In this respect, the models of the current chapter resemble classical "labor theory of value" models. However, the discussions in chapters 3 and 4 provide a more appropriate interpretation for our use of symmetry than classical labor theories. We do not propose that actual labor is undifferentiated in the society,[4] and we capture an element of this by making the labor allocation a committed move covering a long period in the game. Rather, we use a model of society in which labor is an undifferentiated commodity as a benchmark against which to measure the symmetry properties of the economic system, and to relate these to sources of allocative inefficiency.

In the current chapter, we will pass quickly over small strategic indeterminacies, of types that were considered explicitly in previous chapters. One such indeterminacy in the strategic choice of labor allocation will be an uncertainty in how an agent should choose a specialization. Specifically, even if all agents know the optimal allocation of labor to each productive activity in the economy, this provides them no way to choose a particular specialization for *themselves*. In a large economy, even if each agent chose a profession by rolling an appropriate m-sided die, this uncertainty would only result in small deviations from optimality of the solutions. It would not render them undecidable, and the deviations themselves could be made arbitrarily small by a subsequent process of job switching.[5]

5.5   Definition of the Multiperiod Setting for Specialization and Trade

Time in our models has two characteristic scales, a long *episode* in which a money is adopted and labor is assigned to production functions, and a series of shorter *periods* for production, trade, and consumption. As in the one-period models, we define the substructure of a period on the model of a trading day. The general structure of the game is introduced below, and its refinements for the cases of gold or fiat monies are defined in respective sections.

5.5.1   Labor, production, primary goods, and capital

The society S comprises n interchangeable agents, so n defines the labor constraint. Primary production goods are broadly categorized only as durable or nondurable. We introduce m types of nondurable goods, which are distinct arguments of utility functions but are otherwise treated symmetrically with respect to permutation of types, and one durable good which we call "gold."

Unconsumed amounts of the nondurable goods vanish after each consumption round in the game, whereas gold may be carried forward across rounds. We will consider $m + 2$ primary production technologies, of which $m + 1$ output material goods and the remaining one provides enforcement of default penalties, in a manner defined below.[6] One type of primary production good is associated with each production technology. We set $n = mr$ for some positive integer r, so that optimizing production and trade involves redundancy in each productive activity and limits the price impact of any single agent's trading activities. A final quantity which is durable (meaning that it may be carried forward) but does not directly confer utility is fiat money. We do not model the production activities that create and disburse fiat explicitly, but we do define a specialization and "production function" for the enforcers of contracts transacted in fiat. Specialist production functions for each of the primary goods or for contract enforcement are mutually exclusive.

For expository convenience we refer to producers of each nondurable good as *farmers*, producers of gold as *prospectors*, and enforcers of fiat contracts as *bureaucrats*. The society optimization problem of labor allocation is shown in table 5.1, introducing notation for the numbers of agents who choose each allocation, and the rates of production of goods or contract enforcement per agent associated with each specialization. Mutual exclusion of the specialist productions implies that, if all nondurable goods receive the same labor allocations, $mv + v^0 + \bar{v} \leq n \equiv mr$, with equality if no agent chooses autarchy.

We treat gold as ideally durable (meaning that it is not worn out or lost) to simplify its properties in those cases where it is used as a money. To create a commodity value for it and to provide an exit pathway so that steady-state solutions exist, we introduce a separate, nonprimary good that we call *capital*

Table 5.1
Labor choices and their associated production functions

Labor specialization	Labor allocation	Good produced	Production rate
Farmer	v	Nondurable consumable	a
Prospector	v^0	Durable gold	e^0
Bureaucrat	$\bar{v}$	Contract enforcement	π

Note: v refers to the number of agents who elect to farm *each* nondurable good, while v^0 is the number of all prospectors and $\bar{v}$ the number of all bureaucrats. Production rates a of nondurable goods have elementary dimensions (bushels/day), and the extraction rate e^0 of gold is similar (ounces/day). The contract enforcement parameter π has a more complex definition in terms of disutility of default penalties, and is developed in the text below.

stock, into which gold may be converted when it is not being used as a money.[7] Capital stock is durable but carries across periods with depreciation, and yields utilitarian services in proportion to the amount agents hold in each period.

5.5.2   Definition of the extensive-form game

The extensive form of the game is shown in table 5.2. The long time period that we have called an *episode* begins with an initialization round in which agents adopt specializations and in doing so establish the parameters both of production and of the money system they will use. Following initialization, the agents play a repeated-stage game of production, trade, consumption, and carry-forward in short *periods* of length t_0.

5.5.3   Stocks and flows in production and consumption

The cost and the value of a money system adopted in the initialization round arise from its repeated use in the stage game. The scarcity constraint that relates utilities of services from gold used as a money to utilities of consumption of nondurables in the stage game motivates us to treat durables as *stocks* and nondurables in terms of *flows*. In the primary production sector, both stock quantities and flow rates remain well defined without reference to the trading period length t_0, so that the true scarcity constraint on the society over an episode is the product of the labor constraint with the time duration (hence "man-hours"). This constraint will turn out to determine the value-in-trade of real goods within either monetary system. A question of fundamental importance in the evaluation and comparison of money systems is whether properties of the monetary sector, such as supply and velocity of money, or measures of efficiency and cost of trade, depend on t_0, and if so, in what way?

Table 5.2
Extensive form of the repeated game

Game round	Simultaneous move by all agents
Initialization round	Choice of production function
Repeated rounds (t_0)	Production/conversion of gold to capital/salary
	Trade of nondurables and possibly gold for money
	Consumption/taxation and penalties if applicable
	Depreciation of capital and carry-forward

Note: Allocation of labor among productive specializations in the initialization round determines the conditions for trade in the subsequent repeated rounds. The utility of trade outcomes, summed over these rounds, implicitly determines the utility of the initial labor allocation.

Such questions are answered by considering classes of structurally equivalent models in which t_0, a, e^0, and other parameters defining production or utility are treated as having *dimension*, as introduced in the general discussion of chapter 3. Changes of t_0, a, e^0 are instances of *scale transformations*. Properties shared by classes of models, which take constant values either exactly or asymptotically in some limit such as $t_0 \to 0$, are properties of the whole equivalence classes of models under scale transformation, and not only of individual models. In particular, those which become independent of t_0 in the limit $t_0 \to 0$ are said to have a *continuum limit* with respect to modeling of time.

We consider it a fundamental principle of modeling to choose explicitly whether discreteness of time in models is meant to reflect an important feature of reality, or is merely a computational convenience that must eventually factor out of solutions. The use of continuum limits, defined as equivalence classes of discrete-time models, implements the distinction in a precise way.

5.5.4 Intertemporal utilities

We retain the utility of consumption for single trading rounds from previous chapters, here using the logarithmic form

$$\mathcal{U}_t = \Upsilon \left\{ s \log \left(\frac{C \rho_D}{e^0} \right) + \sum_{j=1}^{m} \log \left(\frac{A^j}{a} \right) \right\}. \tag{5.1}$$

The utility for the whole episode is simply the discounted sum of one-period utilities of consumption,

$$\mathcal{U} = \sum_{t=0}^{\infty} (\rho_D t_0) \, \beta^{t/t_0} \mathcal{U}_t. \tag{5.2}$$

The discrete-period discounting factor $1/\beta \equiv 1 + \rho_D t_0$ identifies ρ_D as the temporal discount rate, and β^{t/t_0} converges to the discount function $e^{-\rho_D t}$ with measure ρ_D in the continuum limit. With respect to the evaluation of Eq. (5.1), variables $A^j t_0$ designate agents' consumed quantities of nondurable goods, and C designates the quantities of capital stock rendering services, within each discrete period. These are optimization variables in the trading stage of the game. To express the scaling symmetry with respect to amount of production as well as length of the trading round, we render the per-period consumption $A^j t_0$ nondimensional by normalizing relative to a farmer's per-period productivity $a t_0$. C is rendered nondimensional with the prospector's extraction rate e^0

and the discount rate ρ_D.[8] In the game with fiat money we will use bankruptcy penalties to ensure that money payments are costly signals of commitment, and these will be modeled as direct impacts on utility. Therefore we introduce a parameter Υ to convert the dimensionless logarithm into a unit of measure for utility.

The final feature of the material economy which is common to all models is carry-forward of the durable capital stock. We introduce a variable σ_t (for each agent) in each repeated round, with $\sigma_t t_0$ designating the amount of gold converted to the agent's capital stock in that round. Conversion and depreciation both happen in the last move in each repeated round (see table 5.2), and the carry-forward equation is

$$C_{t+t_0} = (1 - \Delta t_0) C_t + \sigma_t t_0. \tag{5.3}$$

Δ is the depreciation rate, common to all agents.

5.5.5   Effective utilities for committed decisions

Perishability of the nondurable goods imposes a degree of independence between the repeated rounds of production, trade, and consumption. Both the gold and fiat money systems enable agents to optimize investment or carryover of durable goods against consumption of nondurables, leading to time-stationary solutions for all of the strategic variables chosen each round— although they achieve this in very different ways. The nested structure of the extensive form shown in table 5.2, together with stationarity of moves in the inner, repeated rounds, leads to the concepts of *committed moves* in the inner rounds which vary jointly—$\delta\sigma_t = \delta\sigma$, $\forall t$, etc. The joint variation of the committed moves is attributable to the production decisions in the first round. Their aggregated first-order conditions can then be rationalized by an *effective utility* for the allocation of labor among professions in this outer round of the game. We provide the derivation of the form of this effective utility in appendix 5.15. The result is that the sum (5.2) evaluates to

$$\mathcal{U}_{\text{comm}} = \frac{\Upsilon}{\beta} \left\{ \alpha^0 \log \left(\frac{\sigma}{e^0} \right) + \sum_{j=1}^{m} \log \left(\frac{A^j}{a} \right) \right\}, \tag{5.4}$$

where $\sigma = \Delta C$ is a representation for the capital stock in steady state. The coefficient s in Eq. (5.1) has been replaced by

$$\alpha^0 = \frac{s\Delta}{\rho_D + \Delta}, \tag{5.5}$$

which corrects the marginal utility of investment in capital to account for the combined effects of depreciation and discounting as the investment rate is varied.

The effective utility (5.4) for committed decisions may be converted by a monotone transformation to the *money-metric* form [404]

$$
\mathcal{U}_{\text{comm}}^{CD} = \left[\left(\frac{\sigma_i}{e^0} \right)^{\alpha^0} \left(\prod_{j=1}^{m} \frac{A_i^j}{a} \right) \right]^{\frac{1}{\alpha^0 + m}}, \tag{5.6}
$$

just as the Cobb-Douglas utility was expressed in money-metric form in defining the value of trade in chapter 3. Eq. (5.6) is the expenditure function at equilibrium prices corresponding to the utility level $\mathcal{U}_{\text{comm}}$ from repeated consumption at rates $\left\{ A_i^j \right\}$, σ_i.

The effective utility (5.4), like the original period utilities (5.1), has Cobb-Douglas form and so satisfies the Gorman conditions for aggregatability [404]. Therefore the sets of competitive equilibria for both utilities are linear spaces with the same equilibrium price systems at all points. The money-metric utility (5.6) is the basis for the efficiency measure relating the values of consumption resulting from autarchy to those from noncooperative equilibria of the two strategic market games with gold or fiat monies. By comparing either of these noncooperative equilibria to the competitive equilibrium, the money metric also permits a definition of the *efficiency* of extraction of economic surplus made possible by either money system [378].

5.6   The Monetary System Based on Durable Gold

The model of a preinstitutional society, including buy-sell trading posts for nondurable consumables, is converted to a model of an economy based on commodity money by denominating bids at the trading posts in gold and formalizing the constraint of cash up front.

To refine the notation for moves in the extensive-form game, from the single-agent definitions of section 5.5 to the multiagent setting, we expand the collection of production rates for nondurable consumables to a set $\left\{ a^j \right\}$ indexed by good j. In solutions we will consider only permutation-symmetric values $a^j = a$, $\forall j$. We expand the consumption variables A^j to include indices for the agent and the time period, $A_{i,t}^j$, and similarly for the capital stock variables $C_{i,t}$, and the rates at which agents convert gold to capital in each period, $\sigma_{i,t}$. The utilities (5.2) of whole histories of consumption take on agent indices $\mathcal{U}_i$, and the per-period utilities (5.1) become $\mathcal{U}_{i,t}$.

In each repeated stage of the extensive-form game, each agent begins by producing an "endowment" $a_{i,t}^j t_0$ of each consumable good, with $a_{i,t}^j = a^j$ if agent i has committed to producing good j as a specialist (farmer) in the initialization round, and zero otherwise. Agents specializing in gold extraction (prospectors) produce an endowment $e^0 t_0$ of money in a simultaneous move. The next activity in each repeated round is the conversion of an amount $\sigma_{i,t} t_0$ of each agent's gold to capital stock, which we return to describe when we consider money and capital stock utility. Following gold conversion, agents buy or sell each of the nondurable goods at a particular trading post for that good using the buy-sell model where a quantity $b_{i,t}^j$ of (gold) money is offered in payment and a quantity $q_{i,t}^j \le a_{i,t}^j t_0$ of good j is offered for sale. The post-trade allocations which appear as arguments to the utilities $\mathcal{U}_{i,t}$ are determined from the bids and offers (either of which may be zero) by the clearing relation

$$A_{i,t}^j t_0 = a_{i,t}^j t_0 - q_{i,t}^j + \frac{b_{i,t}^j}{p_t^j}. \tag{5.7}$$

As in previous chapters, $p_t^j \equiv \left(\sum_i b_{i,t}^j\right) / \left(\sum_i q_{i,t}^j\right) \equiv B_t^j / Q_t^j$. The use of gold money as payment at trading posts for nondurables provides a means for its distribution through the society, so we omit a trading post for gold.[9]

We define the consumption utility of services from capital stock appearing in $\mathcal{U}_{i,t}$ of Eq. (5.1) in each period t to depend on the amount $C_{i,t}$ held at the very beginning of the period, after depreciation from the previous round of the stage game but before augmentation by $\sigma_{i,t} t_0$ in the current round. Capital stock carries across periods according to Eq. (5.3).

5.6.1   Durable gold and the introduction of shadow prices

Gold money carries forward across periods, similarly to capital stock but independently of it and without depreciation. Following the same convention as for $C_{i,t}$, we introduce the notation $\mu_{i,t}$ for the quantity held by agent i at the very beginning of period t. Because we are excluding mechanisms of contract enforcement from the (nonbureaucratic) gold economy, we do not provide ways to borrow gold. Trading posts require "cash on the barrel," so the budget constraint for farmers is $\mu_{i,t} - \sigma_{i,t} t_0 - \sum_j b_{i,t}^j \ge 0$; for prospectors, who have an autonomous endowment, it is $\mu_{i,t} + \left(e^0 - \sigma_{i,t}\right) t_0 - \sum_j b_{i,t}^j \ge 0$. These constraints apply in each round of the stage game, and they are incorporated into the model by converting each period utility $\mathcal{U}_{i,t}$ to a Lagrangian with a Kuhn-Tucker multiplier $\lambda_{i,t} \in [0, \infty]$. The Lagrangian for the farmers becomes

$$\mathcal{U}_{i,t} = \Upsilon \left\{ s \log \left(\frac{C_{i,t} \rho_D}{e^0} \right) + \sum_{j=1}^{m} \log \left(\frac{A_{i,t}^j}{a^j} \right) \right\} + \lambda_{i,t} \left(\mu_{i,t} - \sigma_{i,t} t_0 - \sum_j b_{i,t}^j \right), \tag{5.8}$$

while that for prospectors is

$$\mathcal{U}_{i,t} = \Upsilon \left\{ s \log \left(\frac{C_{i,t} \rho_D}{e^0} \right) + \sum_{j=1}^{m} \log \left(\frac{A_{i,t}^j}{a^j} \right) \right\}$$
$$+ \lambda_{i,t} \left(\mu_{i,t} + \left(e^0 - \sigma_{i,t} \right) t_0 - \sum_j b_{i,t}^j \right). \tag{5.9}$$

The Kuhn-Tucker multipliers λ create the shadow prices for gold which augment its value from conversion to capital stock. They therefore distort per-period consumption from rates which would be optimal in the absence of a scarcity constraint. The service that gold provides as money, compensating for this distortion, is that the noncooperative equilibrium for the trading game approximates the competitive equilibrium at large r.

The last event that takes place in the stage game is the return of gold money from trading posts as proceeds for sales, in the amount $\sum_j q_{i,t}^j p_t^j$ to each agent i. Gold carries forward without depreciation, so the carry-forward relation for farmers is

$$\mu_{i,t+t_0} = \mu_{i,t} - \sigma_{i,t} t_0 - \sum_j b_{i,t}^j + \sum_j q_{i,t}^j p_t^j. \tag{5.10}$$

Since prospectors necessarily have $q_{i,t}^j \equiv 0$, $\forall j$, they simply carry forward whatever they have not spent or converted to capital stock,

$$\mu_{i,t+t_0} = \mu_{i,t} + \left(e^0 - \sigma_{i,t} \right) t_0 - \sum_j b_{i,t}^j. \tag{5.11}$$

We do not introduce a market for the trade of capital stock, because its primary purpose in the model is to regulate the long-period limit. Capital stock provides a consumption-based salvage value for gold, thus avoiding the Hahn paradox of unraveling of the chained equilibria, while also providing a regular exit pathway without requiring that gold itself depreciate. Since all agents hold gold and are capable of independently converting it to utilitarian capital, a further market for its exchange is not needed to serve these purposes, and would be a needless complication.

The first-order conditions following from this model lead to steady-state solutions for all bids, offers, conversion rates, and consumption values, which are computed in appendix 5.13.

5.7   Solution Properties for the Gold Economy

The stationary, optimal allocations in the stage game derived in appendix 5.13.1 follow the general pattern of solutions for a buy-sell strategic market game, developed in [94] and further elaborated in [356, 383]. They show how a closed system can consistently provide a commodity money of stable value at the same time as it supports trade of both durable and nondurable goods. Moreover, the allocations produced converge to those of the Pareto optima for the preferences of Eqs. (5.1, 5.2) as the time period $\rho_D t_0 \to 0$.

5.7.1   Labor allocation and stability of the money price

Gold prices of nondurable goods are set by the rate of money entry into the society, $e_0 \nu^0$, as a result of two optimizing conditions: (1) that all available gold is used in the markets in every period, and (2) that prospectors who use their entire period production of gold have utility comparable to that of producers of nondurable consumables. The stability of the money price of goods thus depends on the continual entry and exit of gold at some finite rate. However, as shown in Eq. (5.100) of appendix 5.15.1, the optimal fraction of social labor devoted to prospecting is given by $\nu^0/n = \alpha^0/(\alpha^0 + m)$. Hence the rate of injection of gold may be made arbitrarily small if capital stock is very durable and requires little replacement, the condition when $\Delta/\rho_D \to 0$.

Although the analyses in appendix 5.15.1 concern the deterministic optimization problem, they partly suggest the structure of stochastic extensions to the model, which bear on two important questions. One is the tradeoff between robustness and efficiency. The other is the empirically relevant way to think about backward induction in the limit of long, many-period episodes.

In the efficient limit $\Delta/\rho_D \to 0$ of the deterministic model, vanishingly small injections of gold are required to support trade. Thus vanishingly small labor (to support consumption of the utility of capital stock) is serving to stabilize the exchange price of gold. In this limit of vanishingly small stabilizing force per unit time, the importance of supply shocks to the price of nondurable goods will dominate even at low levels of stochasticity. The price of gold will then come to depend primarily on prices in the recent past and on distributional anomalies. In this context, the demand for new injections will be driven by scarcity shocks rather than by maintenance of a steady state between gold supply and depreciation.[10] As is typical of stochastic systems, there exists a tradeoff between the efficiency of the stock of gold in mediating exchange and the robustness of the predictability of prices.

The second important role of stochasticity is to remove the removable singularity at $\alpha \to 0$ that leads to the Hahn paradox, but which should actually be understood as a modeling artifact. In deterministic models the money price is well defined and independent of α^0 at all values $\alpha^0 > 0$. Yet in a model with $\alpha^0 \equiv 0$ it would be undefined, and the absence of a salvage value would unravel the backward induction through the periods, which enables gold to take a finite shadow price and serve as a store of value. Expectations or some other mechanism would need to be invoked to produce short-term price stability, as in [23]. If we bear in mind implicitly that stochastic effects are always present in the real economy, the singularity disappears. To emphasize that stability is a matter of degree but not of principle in the stochastic context, consider that $\alpha^0 \sim m$, on par with the *totality* of other consumable goods, defines a money price that would be stable under almost any realistic model of fluctuations. This stability diminishes, so that more of the short-term price stability comes to rely on expectations or other mechanisms, regularly as $\alpha^0 \to 0$. The principle we wish to emphasize is that *properties of a deterministic model that are not robust under stochastic extensions of the model are probably not economically meaningful.*

The final aspect of stability we note is that of the labor allocation move itself. The concavity of the utility functions automatically leads to a stable labor allocation problem in the gold economy. A simple equilibrium of supply and demand gives greater bidding strength to any specialist class that is in a minority relative to the marginal utility set by the corresponding good. Thus uncoordinated individual reallocations of labor from lower to higher consumption utilities can converge to the labor equilibrium. In the fiat economy model of the next section, we break concavity by introducing a linear default penalty, and this leads to a potential for instability because linear disutility of default is a *protection* if agents are driven to default at all. One of the technical challenges of defining a fiat economy is therefore to design a taxation protocol capable of avoiding this instability, making the fiat economy inherently more complex dynamically, as well as institutionally, than the gold economy.

5.7.2   The money value of money systems

The simple abstraction we have developed here of an economy mediated by commodity money, although a closed system constrained by its total labor, lacks representations of "waste" or other diversions of labor from primary productivity. Therefore the only form of cost it can represent, of a trade mechanism, is utility loss from non-Pareto-optimal allocation.[11]

In any strategic market game involving intertemporal utility and discounting, shadow prices will lead to a departure from Pareto-optimal allocation of agents' budgets to their consumption profiles. Agents will hoard goods they produce to compensate for small shadow prices on the budget constraint for bidding on others' goods (shown in Eqs. (5.34, 5.35) of appendix 5.13.2). These distortions are the counterparts, for this set of intertemporal models, to the variety of distortions resulting from asymmetry between monies and production goods demonstrated in chapter 4. In economies mediated by commodity money, shadow prices come from carry-forward across periods and the need for cash. We show in the next section that in fiat-mediated economies, separate periods are decoupled by the mechanism of central bank lending, and instead shadow prices come from liability for interest *within* periods, and for taxes that stabilize the money value.

This distortion from Pareto-optimal allocation is due to discounting $\rho_D t_0$ in the gold economy, and (we will see), through terms with identical functional forms, to taxation and money interest $\tau + \rho t_0$ in the fiat economy. The cost of this distortion is that, for any allocation Q_i of an individual at a noncooperative equilibrium of the strategic market game, the corresponding *inefficiency measure* $D(P \parallel Q_i) \propto (\rho_D t_0)^2 / m$, from Eq. (5.113). Upon comparing the two monetary systems, we find that prospectors in the gold economy share the consumption profile of *bureaucrats* in the fiat economy, while farmers are comparable between the two economies. The strategic distinction imposed by markets is therefore between the providers of the money supply and everyone else, as it was in the one-period models of chapter 4. It is not a distinction based on the durability versus nondurability of the goods.

5.8   The Monetary System Based on Fiat

Our preinstitutional society model is converted into a model of an economy based on fiat money by the addition of fiat itself as an economic quantity, of institutions for salary, lending, taxation, and more abstractly of contract enforcement, and of a variety of rules for the use of fiat which lead to constraints and other modifications of the utility functions of agents. A fiat economy is somewhat more complex than a gold economy in structure and in the precise specification of the extensive-form game, and therefore also in the range of solutions it permits.

5.8.1   Refinement of the general extensive-form game for the case of fiat

We begin with a refinement of the notation for utilitarian values introduced in section 5.5. At the same time, we introduce new variables associated with the use of fiat, and provide a more precise description of the substructure of the trading day.

The collection of production rates for nondurable consumables is generalized as it was in the treatment of the gold economy. In this case, because gold is not automatically distributed through the trading posts for nondurable consumables (bids now being denominated in fiat), an additional trading post for gold is introduced. To make the distinction of types easier to follow in the notation, we use overbars and indices k to distinguish bureaucrats, for whom the overall and per-period utilities become, respectively, $\bar{\mathcal{U}}_k$ and $\bar{\mathcal{U}}_{k,t}$.

Each repeated round of the stage game of production, trade, and consumption in the fiat economy now has the following sequential structure:

- Endowment or salary: In the first move of the round, each agent produces an "endowment" $a_{i,t}^j t_0$ of each consumable good, with $a_{i,t}^j = a^j$ if agent i has committed to producing good j as a specialist (farmer) in the initialization round, and zero otherwise. Each prospector extracts an endowment of gold equal to $e^0 t_0$, and no other agents receive endowments of gold. Simultaneously, each bureaucrat is paid a salary of fiat money in the amount $\bar{\mu} t_0$; no other agents are paid fiat.

- Borrowing: Fiat will be used as the means of payment for goods at market, and of taxes and interest at the end of each round, which will cause it to exit the economy. (For convenience, we will specify that all fiat is collected at the end of each round no matter what strategies agents employ; full collection is a property of optimal solutions, and we simplify the notation and analysis by ruling out fiat carry-forward across rounds.) Since only bureaucrats are paid salaries, other agents must borrow fiat if they are to participate in exchanges. We therefore introduce a central bank which lends fiat, and denote by $g_{i,t}$ the amount borrowed by any producer (farmer or prospector) i in period t, and by $\bar{g}_{k,t}$ the amount borrowed by any bureaucrat k. Borrowing takes place after the creation of endowments and salaries, but precedes all other moves in the stage game. The magnitudes of $g_{i,t}$ and $\bar{g}_{k,t}$ are not restricted by the rules of the game.

- Trading: Following endowment, salary, and borrowing, agents buy or sell any of the goods (nondurables or gold) at a particular trading post for each good using the same buy-sell model and cash-up-front constraint as in the last section, but with bids denominated in fiat. (We take trading post index $j = 0$ to refer to gold.) As with gold money, any agent's bids are limited to $\sum_j b_{i,t}^j \leq g_{i,t}$ for producer i or $\sum_j \bar{b}_{k,t}^j \leq \bar{\mu}t_0 + \bar{g}_{k,t}$ for bureaucrat k. Each trading post then clears at a price $p_t^j \equiv \left(\sum_i b_{i,t}^j + \sum_k \bar{b}_{k,t}^j \right) / \left(\sum_i q_{i,t}^j \right) \equiv B_t^j / Q_t^j$, and goods in the amount $b_{i,t}^j / p_t^j$, and proceeds of sale in the amount $q_{i,t}^j p_t^j$ are returned to each producer i. (Bureaucrats have no nondurable goods to offer, and for simplicity we rule out carry-forward and offering of gold by them—another property of optimal solutions—so they receive only purchased goods in quantity $\bar{b}_{k,t}^j / p_t^j$.)

- Conversion of gold to utilitarian capital: Because gold may be traded in this economy, all agents have a mechanism to acquire it. Therefore, following market clearing, any producer i may convert an amount $\sigma_{i,t} t_0$ of his current stock of gold to utilitarian capital. (To make our use of notation consistent, we use conversion rate $\bar{\sigma}_{k,t}$ to refer to bureaucrat k.) In the fiat economy, since gold is no longer used as a means of payment, conversion to capital stock *after* trading is equivalent to the sequence of conversion *before* trading that we invoked in the gold economy of section 5.6.

- Taxation and repayment of loans: Each loan $g_{i,t}$ or $\bar{g}_{k,t}$ is associated with a money interest $\rho t_0 g_{i,t}$ or $\rho t_0 \bar{g}_{k,t}$, along with the principal amount. Similarly, all bids at market attach to the bidder a proportional tax liability, $\tau \sum_j b_{i,t}^j$ for producers or $\tau \sum_j \bar{b}_{k,t}^j$ for bureaucrats. τ, a sales tax fraction, will actually be defined in the rules of the game as a *function* of the labor allocations $\{v^j, \bar{v}\}$. Since this function may be evaluated immediately upon the completion of the initialization round, it is therefore known to agents in all subsequent trading rounds. The form that leads to stable trade-optimizing solutions is complicated and defined in terms of an implicit function, so we defer the details to an appendix. To complete the definition of the stage game here, the sum of borrowed principal, interest, and tax is due to be repaid by each agent as the last move in each repeated round. Failure to pay the full amount leads to a *linear* subtraction from the period utility (enforced by the bureaucracy) proportional to the amount of underpayment. The linear form of default penalty has been considered in [356].[12]

The identification of an extensive-form game capable of endogenously stabilizing optimal trade is unfortunately somewhat cumbersome, and we have adopted shortcuts by writing certain properties of optimal solutions into the game rules when doing so leads to no important loss of generality. We introduce the last such simplification at this point. Both producers and bureaucrats will need to borrow fiat to support trade at general interior solutions to the game we have defined. Producers receive fiat income from trading posts with which to pay debts, while bureaucrats have no such income. We therefore regard *taxes* as the bureaucrat income, and credit the sum of tax liabilities, equal to $\tau \sum_j B^j$, to the collection of bureaucrats as income prior to the imposition of default penalties at the end of each round of the stage game. Since all fiat is collected, this credit is always possible within a closed system. The account credit given to bureaucrats may be thought of in the trading day's sequence given above as taking place after fiat is collected from the private sector, but before bureaucrats are held liable for repayment.

5.8.2   Budget constraints and penalties on default

The clearing rule for all trading posts (nondurables or gold) remains that of Eq. (5.7) above. For bureaucrats k in $\bar{U}_{k,t}$ we introduce the corresponding notation

$$\bar{A}^j_{k,t}t_0 = \frac{\bar{b}^j_{k,t}}{p^j_t}, \tag{5.12}$$

reflecting the fact that bureaucratic production leads to no endowments of consumables.

Money values determine constraints on both bidding and repayment obligations, and so we introduce an additional notation for them. Producer i's holding of fiat at the end of borrowing and trading is

$$M_{i,t} = g_{i,t} - \sum_{j=0}^{m} b^j_{i,t} + \sum_{j=0}^{m} q^j_{i,t} p^j_t, \tag{5.13}$$

while bureaucrat k's is

$$\bar{M}_{k,t} = \bar{\mu}t_0 + \bar{g}_{k,t} - \sum_{j=0}^{m} \bar{b}_{k,t}^j + \frac{\tau}{\bar{\nu}} \left(\sum_{j=0}^{m} B_t^j \right). \tag{5.14}$$

The tax payments which take the place of bureaucrat "proceeds" are evenly divided among the number $\bar{\nu}$ of individuals.

A quantity to be considered in the analysis will be the total money supply $\mathcal{M}_t$ in the period, which we define as the sum of salaries and borrowings

$$\mathcal{M}_t = \sum_{k} \left(\bar{\mu}t_0 + \bar{g}_{k,t} \right) + \sum_{i} g_{i,t}. \tag{5.15}$$

5.8.3   Default penalties as generators of shadow prices for fiat

We implement the budget constraint on bids at market with Kuhn-Tucker multipliers $\lambda_{i,t}, \bar{\lambda}_{k,t} \in [0, \infty]$ as in the gold economy, thus converting the producer and bureaucrat utilities into Lagrangians, with independent multipliers for each period. The budget constraint for producers is $g_{i,t} - \sum_{j=0}^{m} b_{i,t}^j \geq 0$, limited by borrowing alone, while for bureaucrats it is $\bar{\mu}t_0 + \bar{g}_{k,t} - \sum_{j=0}^{m} \bar{b}_{k,t}^j \geq 0$, from salary plus borrowing.

Since all agents pay back all fiat at the end of each round, the over- or underpayment of debts comes from $M_{i,t}$ or $\bar{M}_{k,t}$ and their respective tax and loan liabilities. For producer i the total liability is $g_{i,t}(1 + \rho t_0) + \tau \sum_{j=0}^{m} b_{i,t}^j$, and for bureaucrat k it is $\bar{g}_{k,t}(1 + \rho t_0) + \tau \sum_{j=0}^{m} \bar{b}_{k,t}^j$. Penalties on underpayment are imposed with a min function, added to the utilities in each period like the budget constraint multipliers. We introduce a parameter Π as the *intensity* of the default penalty, deferring until the next section the question of what value should be assigned to it. We may think of this trapping of Kuhn-Tucker multipliers and min functions, which convert a raw consumption utility to a complex constrained Lagrangian, as reflecting the conversion of an agent in the preinstitutional society into a member of the economy. Producer i is described by Lagrangian

$$\mathcal{U}_{i,t} \rightarrow \mathcal{U}_{i,t} + \lambda_{i,t} \left(g_{i,t} - \sum_{j=0}^{m} b_{i,t}^j \right)$$

$$+ \Pi \min \left[\left(M_{i,t} - g_{i,t}(1 + \rho t_0) - \tau \sum_{j=0}^{m} b_{i,t}^j \right), 0 \right], \tag{5.16}$$

and bureaucrat k by

$$\bar{\mathcal{U}}_{k,t} \rightarrow \bar{\mathcal{U}}_{k,t} + \bar{\lambda}_{k,t} \left(\bar{\mu} t_0 + \bar{g}_{k,t} - \sum_{j=0}^{m} \bar{b}_{k,t}^j \right)$$

$$+ \Pi \min \left[\left(\bar{M}_{k,t} - \bar{g}_{k,t} (1 + \rho t_0) - \tau \sum_{j=0}^{m} \bar{b}_{k,t}^j \right), 0 \right]. \quad (5.17)$$

When budget constraints are binding on solutions, their associated Kuhn-Tucker multipliers $\lambda_{i,t}, \bar{\lambda}_{k,t}$ are generally nonzero, representing shadow prices. The discontinuity of the min function defining the default penalty should generally be associated with a similar set of shadow prices, for interior solutions on which debt and taxes are binding constraints, but in which they are not yet sufficient to lead to intentional strategic default. To capture this feature, effectively *regularizing* the min function, we introduce a pair of *finite-range* Kuhn-Tucker multipliers $\eta_{i,t}, \bar{\eta}_{k,t} \in [0, \Pi]$. As shown in [383], all solutions to the optimization problem defined by Lagrangians (5.16, 5.17) are also solutions to the Lagrangians

$$\mathcal{U}_{i,t} \rightarrow \mathcal{U}_{i,t} + \left(\lambda_{i,t} + \eta_{i,t} \right) \left[g_{i,t} - \sum_{j=0}^{m} b_{i,t}^j \right]$$

$$+ \eta_{i,t} \left[\sum_{j=0}^{m} q_{i,t}^j p_t^j - g_{i,t} (1 + \rho t_0) - \tau \sum_{j=0}^{m} b_{i,t}^j \right] \equiv \mathcal{U}_{i,t}^{\text{econ}}, \quad (5.18)$$

$$\bar{\mathcal{U}}_{k,t} \rightarrow \bar{\mathcal{U}}_{k,t} + \left(\bar{\lambda}_{k,t} + \bar{\eta}_{k,t} \right) \left[\bar{\mu} t_0 + \bar{g}_{k,t} - \sum_{j=0}^{m} \bar{b}_{k,t}^j \right]$$

$$+ \bar{\eta}_{k,t} \left[\frac{\tau}{\bar{\nu}} \sum_{j=0}^{m} B_t^j - \bar{g}_{k,t} (1 + \rho t_0) - \tau \sum_{j=0}^{m} \bar{b}_{k,t}^j \right] \equiv \bar{\mathcal{U}}_{k,t}^{\text{econ}}, \quad (5.19)$$

in addition to which the latter provide a way to treat binding, nondefault solutions. We denote these the "economic-actor" utilities $\mathcal{U}_{i,t}^{\text{econ}}$ and $\bar{\mathcal{U}}_{k,t}^{\text{econ}}$ for the stage game. In Eqs. (5.18, 5.19), we have further rearranged linear combinations of the two Kuhn-Tucker multipliers so as to make the later analysis of first-order conditions more transparent. It is the sum of multipliers λ and η in the fiat economy that sets the scale for fiat as a numéraire. Because it has no consumption utility, the only price for fiat is its shadow price.

5.8.4   Labor allocation and the intensity of default penalties

We turn finally to the appropriate modeling of the intensity for the default penalty. We have introduced a parameter, π, into the definition of the economy to represent whatever technologies set the scale of the capacity to enforce default penalties. So far in the construction, however, the only representation of default that has arisen is the parameter Π in the utilities of agents *receiving* default penalties. Π is a constant of proportionality between an amount of default, denominated in money, and an amount of utility reduction. It is natural, since we have not yet specified the meaning of π, to let it take the same units as Π, and to serve likewise as a constant of proportionality between money and utility. Equivalence between the dimensions of π and Π will not be quite strong enough as a constraint to imply that these constants must simply be equal. To complete the derivation of the relationship the two constants must have, we argue that the capacity constraint, as defined in the macroeconomy by π and the supply of bureaucrat labor, must equal the aggregate demand for enforcement, coming from individual utilities and levels of default.

In order for the default penalty terms to mean what their functional forms suggest, the microeconomic constant Π must be defined so that the largest aggregate level of penalty enforcement that may arise for a given move profile by the agents is consistent with the level of enforcement that technology enables the bureaucrats to provide. The upper bound on the level of default that may arise from a given allocation of labor is attained when the whole money supply $\mathcal{M}_{\mathrm{eq}}$ goes into default. In this case the need for enforcement called out by the sum of the min functions in utilities equals $\mathcal{M}_{\mathrm{eq}}\Pi$. We will estimate $\mathcal{M}_{\mathrm{eq}}$ on dimensional grounds in the next section, and provide a detailed derivation in appendix 5.14. Here we consider the macroeconomic supply variable that must match this demand.

π must map a bureaucrat labor supply $\bar{\nu}$ to an amount of disutility. Since π, like Π, is a measure of utility per unit of money, another constant that maps $\bar{\nu}$ to a money level is needed to define a numéraire that sets a scale for π. The only parameter in the game definition that sets such a scale is the bureaucrat salary rate $\bar{\mu}$. However, $\bar{\mu}$ is a salary *rate*, while π requires an absolute amount of money to map labor to utility levels. Therefore a time constant is required. The time constant that relates overall utilities (5.2) to one-period utility rates (5.1) is the preference discount rate ρ_D. Therefore we *define* the meaning of the constant π through the combination of these other parameters, by declaring that $\pi\bar{\mu}/\rho_D$ is the level of total disutility a single bureaucrat has the capacity to inflict in serving default penalties. The requirement of equality between this supply and the aggregate demand then becomes

$$\mathcal{M}_{eq}\Pi \equiv \frac{\pi\,\bar{\mu}\,\bar{\nu}}{\rho_D}. \tag{5.20}$$

We will show that this condition closes the fiat system in a way that enables stable interior solutions whenever the constant π is sufficiently large.

5.9   Dimensional Analysis and General Properties of Solutions in the Fiat Economy

Optimal solutions for trade, in the stage game of our fiat economy model, follow the general pattern of solutions developed in the previous chapters for a buy-sell strategic market game. They are not noteworthy, except as confirmation that the fiat money system supports trade in the expected way. Therefore we relegate details of the analysis to appendix 5.14.

The relevant new features of the fiat money game are (1) the manner in which the penalties that discourage default depend on the endogenous labor allocation solution, and (2) the resulting money supply and size of the bureaucracy. Most of the algebraic detail resulting from solution of the first-order conditions is not needed to obtain the leading behavior of these quantities. These may be estimated directly from dimensional analysis, which we invoked as a general method in chapter 3. Here we use the case of the fiat economy to provide a worked example of a dimensional-analysis solution, both to illustrate the procedure and to show how, by extremely simple constructions, it can arrive at correct approximations to much more complicated functional forms. The detailed solutions to the first-order conditions are referenced back to their dimensional estimates in appendix 5.14.

5.9.1   Dimensions: notation and conventions

Square brackets around a variable denote the name of its dimension. For brevity we call the unit of time "days" and the numéraire of fiat "dollars." In this notation $[\Upsilon] \equiv$ util.[13]

Salaries have dimension $[\bar{\mu}] \equiv$ dollar/day. Ordinarily we would regard only these continuously measured quantities as the scalable quantities that are captured by dimensions. In this section, however, it will be easier to follow the reasoning based on scaling if we also regard the (discrete) size of the bureaucracy as a "dimensional" variable, and regard the dimensions of the salary rate as $[\bar{\mu}] \equiv$ dollar$/($day $\cdot$ bureaucrat$)$.

All pure rates in the problem have dimension $[\rho] = [\rho_D] = [\Delta] \equiv 1/$day. The existence of more than one quantity with dimensions $1/$day in the model poses a formal problem for dimensional analysis—any dimensionally consistent solution may be converted to another consistent solution by *any* (arbitrarily ill-behaved) function of the nondimensional ratios ρ/ρ_D, ρ/Δ, or ρ_D/Δ. Although in some cases the resulting ambiguity can render dimensional analysis effectively unusable, in many cases we may guess which pure rate to use in a dimensional estimate, if there is a clear distinction between which of ρ, ρ_D, or Δ controls the scaling of a given subset of the solution variables.

The penalties have dimension $[\Pi] = [\pi] \equiv$ util/dollar. Recall that Π is a derived quantity, not a fundamental parameter specifying the model. Therefore, we always treat π as the dimensionally controlling parameter.

5.9.2   Scaling predictions

We begin by considering the scaling of the money supply and the size of the bureaucracy. We noted in chapter 3 that one reason dimensional analysis can simplify complex problems is that dimensions retain their role as constraints across scales of aggregation in the economy. Our use of this feature in the consistency relation (5.20) is one approach to aggregating the microeconomy of agents to the macroeconomy of centralized supply variables.

Dimensionally $[\mathcal{M}] \equiv$ dollar, and its value must be determined by the parameters $\bar{\mu}$, π, and ρ that define the game structure, together with the size of the labor force $\bar{\nu}$, which is one of the solution variables. The only combination of these quantities that has the same dimensions as $[\mathcal{M}]$ is

$$[\mathcal{M}] = \left[\frac{\bar{\mu} \bar{\nu}}{\rho} \right] = \left(\frac{\text{dollar}}{\text{day} \cdot \text{bureaucrat}} \right) (\text{bureaucrats}) \left(\frac{1}{1/\text{day}} \right). \quad (5.21)$$

We therefore expect that, if the values given to any of $\bar{\mu}$, ρ, or $\bar{\nu}$ are changed, the money supply must likewise change. Moreover, the ratio of the new value for $\mathcal{M}$ to its old value, which we will call a *rescaling factor*, must depend on the rescaling factors of the parameters $\bar{\mu}$, ρ, or $\bar{\nu}$, in the form of a product as suggested by Eq. (5.21). The detailed derivation in appendix 5.14 confirms that $\mathcal{M} \approx \bar{\mu} \bar{\nu}/\rho$ is also the correct leading-order approximation as $t_0 \to 0$. Scaling relations of this form, which also furnish leading-order approximations, are denoted as $\mathcal{M} \sim \bar{\mu}\bar{v}/\rho$. We note as a corollary that the velocity of money, which is a rate and hence does depend on the trading period length (and not on the discount horizon), should scale as $\mathcal{M} \sim \bar{\mu}\bar{v}/\rho t_0$. From the scaling of $\mathcal{M}$ and Eq. (5.20) we obtain the scaling of Π, the microeconomic penalty variable, in terms of π, the globally defined technology parameter of the game:

$$\Pi \sim \pi \frac{\rho}{\rho_D}. \tag{5.22}$$

Since all agents and all goods are symmetric a priori with respect to permutation, the magnitude of any single agent's bid, on any single good, should be an equal fraction of the entire money supply, and thus

$$b \approx \frac{\mathcal{M}}{nm} \sim \frac{\bar{\mu}\bar{v}}{mn\rho}. \tag{5.23}$$

Again imposing consistency between the macro- and microeconomy, we may attempt to relate Eq. (5.23) to an independently estimated scale for b from the single-agent decision variables. The relevant scale factors are the penalty parameter Π in relation to the utility scale Υ, which yield a dimensional estimate

$$b \sim \frac{\Upsilon}{\Pi} \approx \frac{\Upsilon \rho_D}{\pi \rho}. \tag{5.24}$$

In the second approximation, we have used the consistency relation already imposed on penalty scales, which led to Eq. (5.22). Setting equal Eq. (5.23) and Eq. (5.24) we obtain a dimension- and symmetry-based estimate for the scaling of the fraction of society in the bureaucracy

$$\frac{\bar{v}}{n} \sim \frac{\Upsilon \rho_D}{\pi \bar{\mu}} m. \tag{5.25}$$

If we had had, from the start, only dimensions and no other information about the structure or symmetries of the game, we could have arrived at the scaling relation in Eq. (5.25) apart from the factor m. We followed the slightly longer sequence of analysis, relating micro- to macroeconomic variables and using symmetries, so that effectively we could treat discrete variables such as the number of goods (m) as scaling variables, and thus obtain the form (5.25) that closely approximates the exact solution.[14] Substituting Eq. (5.25) back into the scaling relation (5.21), we obtain the estimate for the money supply in terms of elementary model parameters, given in table 5.4.

Finally, we may use a similar line of reasoning, based on dimensions and scaling, to form a clearer understanding of the meaning of default penalties in relation to cardinal utility. The combination

$$[\pi\bar{\mu}] = \left(\frac{\text{util}}{\text{dollar}}\right) \left(\frac{\text{dollars}}{\text{day} \cdot \text{bureaucrat}}\right) = \left(\frac{\text{util}}{\text{day}}\right) / (\text{bureaucrat}). \quad (5.26)$$

Default penalties are only meaningful in combination with the numéraire, and we may think of Eq. (5.26) as the *disutility rate* that would result from a reduction in consumption of all goods in each period. Because, in this chapter, we have assumed the logarithmic form (5.1) for cardinal utility, a unit reduction in the logarithm corresponds to a reduction in consumption level by a *fraction* of order unity, relative to the total that agents could have achieved under best circumstances. (Historically, this would have been an appropriate minimal model of debtor's prison as punishment.) Then, if we recognize $\Upsilon\rho_D m$ as a utility rate per agent associated with consumption of all m goods, the ratio $\pi\bar{\mu}/\Upsilon\rho_D m$ has the interpretation of the number of individuals who can be "imprisoned" per bureaucrat enforcing the default laws.[15]

5.9.3 Comparison of dimensional estimates to econometric data

Dimensional analysis, and minimal models more generally, are coarse tools for quantitative estimation, though they become more useful for comparative analyses among multiple systems with common structure but different characteristic scales. We have used them here to illustrate the problem of endogenously stabilizing a money system based on an arbitrary currency, in a model where all flows are closed, and for that use they are appropriate.

However, we may push both tools outside their natural ranges of applicability, and we expect that the estimates they provide should compare to reality within factors that can be sensibly assigned to model simplifications. In that spirit we begin by considering Eq. (5.21) for the money supply. The size of the U.S. federal bureaucracy in 2003 was $\bar{\nu} \approx 2.7$ million employees [427]. Supposing a bureaucrat's salary to average $\bar{\mu} \approx \$40,000$ per year, and an average monetary rate of interest to be $\rho \approx 0.06$ per year, gives an estimated money supply of $\mathcal{M} \approx \$1.8$ trillion. For comparison, estimated M1 in 2003 was \$1.1 trillion. From Eq. (5.23) we may consider bm, any individual's spending constraint at any time, as a share of the national limitation in the money supply (irrespective of how many effectively symmetric goods m it buys). For a population of 288 million [427], and continuing within the dimensional estimate for $\mathcal{M}$, we obtain $bm \approx \$6,250$, comparable to consumer credit limits that for most Americans define their primary spending constraint. Dimensional estimates are therefore fairly successful at relating money supply to the rates of money injection and of interest, as they should be.

Our estimates of the size of the bureaucracy are more artificial, in one respect due to oversimplification of the dimensional analysis, in another to the use of Cobb-Douglas utilities and linear default penalties, which from an econometric perspective are arbitrary. We have interpreted the combination of model parameters $\pi\bar{\mu}/\Upsilon\rho_D m$ as a number of individuals per bureaucrat over which the bureaucracy can exercise strong coercive control. In a modern economy bankruptcy law rather than debtor's prison provides an interpretation for penalization. The number of total (business + personal) U.S. bankruptcies in year 1999 was 1,391,964 [426, table 736]. At the same time the number of police, legal, and judicial employees was about 1,473,000 [426, table 453].[16] The resulting crude measure of the strength of the bureaucracy becomes $\Upsilon\rho_D m/\pi\bar{\mu} \approx 1.47/1.39 \approx 1.06$. To treat this number as an interpretation for the estimate (5.25) for $\bar{v}/n$ would of course be unwarranted:[17] bankruptcy is an economic more than a directly utilitarian combination of protections and penalties, and at the same time only a minute part of enforcement labor services bankruptcies. The *existence* of such measures of force, however, gives meaning to models in which a coercive bureaucracy forces cardinal utility comparisons by agents, between decisions that determine private consumption rates and interventions imposed by the government.

The exercise of correcting the dimensional analysis to a form that would be consistent with realistic estimates for the coercive force of the government is informative, however. Eq. (5.25) reflects the assumption explicit in Eq. (5.20), that the bureaucracy stands ready to enforce quite severe penalties on default of the entire money supply. This is the best that a dimensional analysis can provide, because we have not modeled the threat capacity of law to prevent most strategic default by actively pursuing a few instances. Since at interior solutions none of the money supply is in default, the actual requirement for enforcement is something more like

$$\frac{\pi\bar{\mu}\bar{v}}{\rho_D} \to f\mathcal{M}_{eq}\Pi, \tag{5.27}$$

where $0 < f \ll 1$ is the fraction the bureaucracy actually needs to enforce. With Eq. (5.27), Eq. (5.25) becomes

$$\frac{\bar{v}}{n} \sim f\frac{\Upsilon\rho_D m}{\pi\bar{\mu}}. \tag{5.28}$$

Taking $\bar{v}/n \approx 1.47\,\text{million}/288\,\text{million} \approx 0.005$, we generate a value for $f \approx 1/200$.[18] The empirical evidence that threat or the trust of enforcement permit leveraging the money supply by factors such as $1/f$ is that economy-wide contractions or collapses often result from cascading defaults exacerbated by tightening margin requirements [150]. During good times, much trade is mediated by near monies and other forms of credit not fully policed by government or other institutions. When trust in these near monies collapses, the scale of trade supportable with fully margined securities is revealed to be considerably smaller.[19]

5.9.4   Efficiency of the fiat-mediated economy

Parallel analysis of the gold-mediated and fiat-mediated economies makes it possible to distinguish sources of allocative inefficiency, and from the distinctions to understand qualitative differences in the ways these systems encapsulate time periods. We may generally group into three types the deviations of the noncooperative equilibrium allocations in strategic market games from the allocations of competitive equilibria: (1) deviations that converge toward zero in the continuum (large-population) limit of agent numbers; (2) deviations that converge toward zero in the continuum (short-period) limit of the trading round; and (3) deviations resulting from the execution of a round of trade whatever its length and population number that cannot be removed by scaling.

Inefficiencies of the first kind are recognized, and are explicitly removed within general equilibrium theory by the assumption that trade equilibria are defined between *types* of agents, and not between finite numbers of distinct individuals. They appear in our market-clearing solutions through price impacts, and in the example solutions of this chapter we have mostly eliminated them by assuming the replication index $r \to \infty$.

Inefficiencies of the second kind are explicitly temporal in origin, and these appear as primary effects in the gold-mediated economy, and as secondary effects in the fiat economy. In both these models, scarcity constraints fill the role played by budget constraints in general equilibrium, establishing the relative marginal utilities of consumption. In games with time lags and discounting (whether monetary or utilitarian), the different value given to present and future consumption renders these marginal utilities unequal and thus not Pareto-optimal. Inefficiencies of this form may be removed in the continuum limit $t_0 \to 0$. They are therefore associated with other regular properties of the continuum limit, such as finite velocity of money, or a money supply that vanishes linearly in small t_0.

Inefficiencies of the third kind can arise either from costs per event of trade (as opposed to per volume), or from labor lost to primary production. These costs remain in the fiat economy as $t_0 \to 0$. (If we had explicitly modeled the costs of operating trading posts, they would have been a feature of the gold model as well.) Costs that do not vanish in the continuous-time limit are associated with other properties of the economy that diverge (formally) as $t_0 \to 0$, such as velocity of money, or the ratio between money supply and traded volume.

Whether a source of inefficiency will persist in continuum limits is determined by its scaling with t_0. As we show in appendix 5.17, the cost of contract enforcement is the leading loss of efficiency in the fiat model. It depends on the same shadow price terms as the allocative inefficiencies, but the labor cost is linear in t_0, while the utility lost to inefficiency is quadratic in t_0. Another way to say this is that, because in the fiat model the tax rate is a regular flow that scales in proportion to the labor allocation to the bureaucracy (a stock variable), these two cannot be made to vanish in a continuum limit. Beyond this explicit labor cost, the fiat model, like the gold model, also has a quadratic cost from inefficient allocation $\propto (\tau + \rho t_0)^2 / m$, which vanishes relative to the consumption utility rate as $t_0 \to 0$.

5.10   Summary Comparison of the Two Monetary Systems

We may summarize the results of this chapter by observing that the introduction of money necessarily turns one-period models into multiperiod models. Even in a setting where the "rules of the game"—that is, the technologies and norms for using money—are given, the *commitments* that make money useful are made on a longer timescale than the use of money in trade.

The principal function of money in these models has been to separate the trading decisions made on different time intervals, so that these influence each other only through the uniform interface of shadow prices.[20] When the money is a commodity, it separates periods through carry-forward. The store of value in a durable commodity enables much higher efficiencies from trade than was possible with only the use of perishable-commodity monies in the one-period Market 3 of chapter 4.

Fiat money has a fundamentally different structure, in that it creates many-period dynamics by concatenating one-period dynamics but not connecting them directly to one-another. Instead, it connects trade in each period to boundary conditions that are recreated within that period by institutionally centralized spending, loans, interest, and taxation. For this reason the many-period fiat models in this chapter are not so different in form, or in the efficiencies they can attain, from the credit-based markets in chapter 4.

In this chapter we have made a larger proportion of the real costs associated with evaluation explicit than was possible in the one-period setting. We have not tried to model the cost of verifying the quality of gold, which was historically an important burden on the function of gold-denominated markets and the reason for adoption of state-issued gold currencies that possess legal as well as commodity aspects. The fiat money model reflects certain costs of the monetary system that the gold model leaves implicit.

5.10.1   Shared essential functions of monies, and differences between commodity and bureaucracy implementations

Both money systems have been required to include mechanisms to inject money across the society, to provide a salvage value that defines its worth in trade for other goods and a signal of commitment, and to remove it from the system in order to permit stationary prices. Optimal trade further requires some form of decoupling of trading rounds, to yield stationary consumption of both durable and nondurable goods. Differences in the ways gold and fiat monies serve these functions determine their sources of cost, and the scaling of quantities in the financing system relative to the flows of real goods. Table 5.3 compares the sources of these fundamental functions and costs for the two systems, which result from the distinct structures of the two extensive-form games.[21]

- Mechanism to separate periods: In the economy mediated by commodity money, shadow prices came from carry-forward across periods and the need

Table 5.3

Comparison of money systems: structural properties

Money system	Mode of injection	Mode of extraction	Period budget supplied by	Constraint ensuring scarcity	Source of cost
Commodity gold	Direct production	Capital depreciation	Carry-forward	Cash on the barrel	Delayed consumption
Government fiat	Salary	Taxation and interest	Borrowing	Bankruptcy penalties	Lost primary production

Note: Cost, source of commitment, and salvage value of gold all stem from the labor cost of its extraction and ultimately from the consumption services of capital stock. The same services are provided by fiat money only through its participation in a cycle of salary and taxation that links contract enforcement by specialists to the valuation of an otherwise arbitrary currency.

for cash. In fiat-mediated economies, separate periods are decoupled by the mechanism of central bank lending, so that instead of resulting from a cash constraint, shadow prices arise out of the liability for interest *within* periods, together with the taxes that stabilize the money value.

- Scaling of money supply and velocity: The structural differences between gold and fiat monies lead to qualitatively different solutions for the money supply and velocity and for the efficiency of trade, as shown in table 5.4. In both systems the injection of money per period scales $\propto t_0$ and so defines a finite rate in the continuum limit. However, carry-forward makes gold money available across the society, resulting in a money supply also $\propto t_0$ and therefore a finite velocity, while central bank action is required to make fiat money available. Borrowing leads to a nonvanishing money supply as $t_0 \to 0$ and thus a divergent velocity of money.

- Sources of cost: Inefficiencies of trade exist in both systems and take the same functional forms of $\rho_D t_0$ for gold and $\tau + \rho t_0$ for fiat, where τ is a taxation rate and ρ a money rate of interest on loans defined for the fiat model. For gold, these allocative inefficiencies are the leading sources of lost surplus, while the fiat system also explicitly represents a loss of primary productivity $\propto (\tau + \rho t_0) \approx \bar{v}/n$ (the fractional size of the bureaucracy), which is expressed in terms of primitive model parameters in the table. The former term can be made to vanish as $t_0 \to 0$, while the latter, like the money supply, remains finite. The "extra" loss of efficiency in the fiat system arises because we have made the cost of contract enforcement explicit within the system, whereas it is unformalized and treated (presumably unrealistically) as free in the gold-denominated model.

Table 5.4

Comparison of money systems: solution properties

Money system	Supply $\mathcal{M}/n$	Injection per period per n	Velocity	Carry-forward	Borrowing	Inefficiency of trade
Commodity gold	$e^0 t_0$	$e^0 t_0 \times \alpha^0/m$	e^0	Used	Not used	$(\rho_D t_0)^2 / (2m)$
Government fiat	$(m\Upsilon/\pi) \times (\rho_D/\rho)$	$(m\Upsilon/\pi) \times \rho_D t_0$	$(m\Upsilon/\pi)/t_0 \times (\rho_D/\rho)$	Not used	Used	$(m\Upsilon/\pi) \times (\rho_D/\bar{\mu})$

Note: Only leading-order terms in $1/m$ are shown, to preserve readability; exact results are derived in the appendices to this chapter. Money supplies and injections per period are reported per agent, and velocity is defined as the quantity of money traded, divided by the period length. Inefficiency $\equiv (1 - \text{efficiency})$ is defined from appendix 5.16. The "enforcement" technology parameter π is defined by the interpretation of the combination $\pi\bar{\mu}/(m\Upsilon\rho_D)$ as the number of agents each bureaucrat could penalize for default by imposing a drastic loss of consumption, as explained in section 5.9.2.

5.11   Further Coment and Caveats

A central theme implicit in this chapter is the aspect of an administrative structure called for when fiat is introduced. In most societies, in many ways, the time horizon of the bureaucracy is longer than the time horizon of the politicians who are meant to be in control of the bureaucracy. Any attempt to capture this phenomenon requires at least three timescales.

Our basic concern has been to contrast gold and fiat and to show that the creation of the bureaucracy plays a central role in the introduction of fiat, but in maintaining a tight closed structure involving only two timescales we have only deconstructed the first stage of the eternal question underlying social systems, *Quis custodiet ipsos custodes*.[22] In understanding the choice of gold versus fiat, the roles of economics, bureaucracy, and politics and their differing timescales are centrally relevant.

5.12   Appendix: Summary of Notation for the Two-Timescale, Extensive-Form Games

This appendix provides a summary of notation used in the two repeated-period models. Parameters defining the game are listed first, followed by dynamical variables.

Table 5.5
Structural variables defining the extensive-form game

m	Number of types of consumption goods
$n \equiv mr$	Number of agents in the society; r is a replica number
t_0	Time interval for a cycle of production, trade, and consumption
$a^j \to a$	Allocation rate of consumption goods to farmers
e^0	Allocation rate of gold to prospectors
s	Utility weight of service from capital stock
α^0	Weight of service from capital stock in effective utility
$\bar{\mu}$	Bureaucrat salary rate
π	Penalty technology of the bureaucracy
Π	Penalty function of technology and labor allocation
Δ	Rate of decay of capital stock
ρ	Rate of interest on borrowing
τ	Fraction of gross receipts from sales demanded in taxes
Υ	Scale factor for utilities
ρ_D	Temporal utility discount rate
β	Per-period discount fraction

Note: Where we have used symmetry to set values equal among many agents as an aid for analytic solutions, the reduced notation is shown as well.

Table 5.6

Individual decision variables, and variables produced by the clearing rules

---

Individual decision variables (period notation → stationary notation)

$a_{i,t}^j$	Rate of self-production of a good by a farmer
$\sigma_{i,t}$	Gold converted to capital stock by a farmer or prospector
$\bar{\sigma}_{k,t}$	Gold converted to capital stock by a bureaucrat
$q_{i,t}^0 \to q^\sigma$	Gold offered by any prospector per period
$q_{i,t}^j \to q$	Self-produced consumption good offered by any farmer per period
$g_{i,t} \to g_0$	Borrowing by a prospector per period
$g_{i,t} \to g$	Borrowing by a farmer per period
$\bar{g}_{k,t} \to \bar{g}$	Borrowing by a bureaucrat per period
$b_{i,t}^j \to b_0$	Bid by prospector on any consumption good
$b_{i,t}^0 \to b^\sigma$	Bid by any farmer on gold
$b_{i,t}^j \to b$	Bid by any farmer on any other-produced consumption good
$\bar{b}_{k,t}^0 \to \bar{b}^\sigma$	Bid by any bureaucrat on gold
$\bar{b}_{k,t}^j \to \bar{b}$	Bid by any bureaucrat on any consumable good

---

Labor, price, and allocation variables (period notation → stationary notation)

$v_t^0 \to mr^0$	Number of prospectors at any time t
$v_t^j \to \hat{r}$	Number of farmers of any consumption good at any time t
$\bar{v}_t \to \bar{v} \equiv m\bar{r}$	Number of bureaucrats at any time t
$a_{i,t}^j t_0 \to a^j t_0, 0$	Endowment of nondurable goods to farmers per period
$Q_t^j \to Q$	Total quantity offered of a single consumable
$Q_t^0 \to Q^\sigma$	Total quantity of gold offered
$B_t^j \to B$	Total money bid (gold or fiat) on a single consumable
$B_t^0 \to B^\sigma$	Total fiat bid on gold
$p_t^j \to p$	Price of any consumption good at any time t
$p_t^0 \to p^\sigma$	Price of gold at any time t
$\lambda_{i,t} \to \lambda, \lambda_{k,t} \to \bar{\lambda}$	Kuhn-Tucker multipliers for budget constraints
$\eta_{i,t} \to \eta, \eta_{k,t} \to \bar{\eta}$	Kuhn-Tucker multipliers for default in the fiat model
$A_{i,t}^j \to A_0$	Prospector's final allocation rate of any consumption good
$A_{i,t}^j \to A_\parallel$	Farmer's final allocation rate of self-produced consumption good
$A_{i,t}^j \to A_\perp$	Farmer's final allocation rate of other-produced consumption good
$\bar{A}_{k,t}^j \to \bar{A}$	Bureaucrat's final allocation rate of consumption good
$\sigma_{i,t} \equiv A_{i,t}^0 \to \sigma_0 t_0$	Prospector's final allocation rate of gold in each period
$\sigma_{i,t} \equiv A_{i,t}^0 \to \sigma t_0$	Farmer's final allocation rate of gold in each period
$\sigma_{k,t} \equiv \bar{A}_{k,t}^0 \to \bar{\sigma} t_0$	Bureaucrat's final allocation rate of gold in each period
$C_{i,t} \to \sigma_0/\Delta$	Capital stock of prospectors
$C_{i,t} \to \sigma/\Delta$	Capital stock of farmers
$\bar{C}_{k,t} \to \bar{\sigma}/\Delta$	Capital stock of bureaucrats
$M_{i,t}$	Period-end money held by producers
$\bar{M}_{k,t}$	Period-end money held by bureaucrats
$\mathcal{M}_t \to \mathcal{M}_{eq}$	Money-metric budget of agent i for repeated strategies
φ_i	Arbitrary price normalization for general equilibrium solutions
$\mathcal{W}_i$	Money supply used in a period

Note: Reduced notation indicated as in table 5.5.

5.13   Appendix: Optimizing Solutions for the Gold Economy

Here we solve the first-order conditions for the general equilibrium model defined by the utilities, market-clearing conditions, and carry-forward relations in the gold-mediated economy. Appendix 5.12 summarizes the parameters and strategically optimized variables of the game, for time-stationary and type-symmetric solutions.

The gold economy has four important qualitative properties, which we wish to emphasize over and above the detailed algebraic forms: (1) in the repeated-stage game, solutions exist with stationary levels of production, trade, and consumption; (2) the Kuhn-Tucker multipliers from the budget constraint act on the carry-forward relation to impose a shadow price from future cash constraints on bids in the current period; (3) agents use all gold currently in their possession to bid on nondurable goods—for farmers carry-forward is possible only from the proceeds of sales, and for prospectors bids are paid for from new extraction each period; (4) agents never bid on the same good as they offer, and this asymmetry creates a slight distortion of the consumption profile from that of Pareto-optimal allocations.

These properties of the stage game break the independent permutation symmetry that is a prior property of both agents and types of goods, replacing the independent symmetries with a single symmetry under joint permutation of farmers with their produced-goods types. This violation of symmetry is a source of allocative inefficiency, and also arises in the fiat-denominated economy, as it did in the one-period economies of chapter 4.

5.13.1   First-order conditions for the spot markets

Utilities in the gold economy are functions only of the final allocation variables in the rounds of the stage game. We therefore begin by computing these as functions of the strategic decision variables produced by the clearing rules. The variation of the consumption level $A_{i,t}^j$ of Eq. (5.7), which results from variation of the underlying bids and offers, is

$$\delta A_{i,t}^j t_0 = -\left(\delta q_{i,t}^j - \frac{\delta b_{i,t}^j}{p_t^j}\right)\left(1 - \frac{b_{i,t}^j}{B_t^j}\right). \tag{5.29}$$

A consequence of finite replication index r (together with a finite number $m + 1$ of goods) is that variations in agent bids and offers impact the prices at which the goods on which they are bidding clear. Such "price impact factors" represent finite-economy hoarding effects, and cause the noncooperative equilibrium of strategic market games to differ from the competitive equilibrium at equivalent preferences, even in the absence of other inefficiencies such as nonzero discount factors or spot interest rates (fiat model only). Impact factors include $1 - b_{i,t}^j / B_t^j$ and $1 - \bar{b}_{k,t}^j / B_t^j$ affecting consumption in Eqs. (5.44, 5.45), and we will note other consequences of impact in the fiat model in appendix 5.14. In the interest of simplifying equations where no important loss of generality results, we suppress these terms by considering the infinite-replica limit $r \to \infty$, in which the price impacts differ from unity by terms $\mathcal{O}(1/r)$ or smaller.

The variation of a farmer's intertemporal utility (5.8), using the carry-forward relation (5.3) to accumulate the consequences of strategies over succeeding times, then becomes

$$
\delta \mathcal{U}_i = \sum_{t=0}^{\infty} \beta^{t/t_0} \left\{ \sum_j \frac{\Upsilon}{p_t^j A_{i,t}^j t_0} \left(\delta b_{i,t}^j - p_t^j \delta q_{i,t}^j \right) + \frac{\Upsilon s}{C_{i,t}} \sum_{t'=0}^{t-t_0} (1 - \Delta t_0)^{\frac{t-t'-t_0}{t_0}} \delta \sigma_{i,t'} t_0 \right.
$$
$$
- \lambda_{i,t} \left[\sum_j \left(\sum_{t'=0}^t \delta b_{i,t'}^j - \sum_{t'=0}^{t-t_0} p_{t'}^j \delta q_{i,t'}^j \right) + \sum_{t'=0}^t \delta \sigma_{i,t'} t_0 \right]
$$
$$
\left. + \left(\mu_{i,t} - \sigma_{i,t} t_0 - \sum_j b_{i,t}^j \right) \delta \lambda_{i,t} \right\}. \tag{5.30}
$$

The index of summation $j \in 1, \ldots, m$ because there is no trading post for gold.

The sum over periods t and t'—in which, respectively, decisions are made and later consumption takes place—may be rearranged, so that instead of grouping all decision variables that contribute to consumption in a given round, it groups all consequences of consumption that are affected by variation of a given decision variable. This rearrangement in Eq. (5.30) applies the "shadow of the future" to present decisions, resulting in the form

$$
\delta \mathcal{U}_i = \sum_{t=0}^{\infty} \beta^{t/t_0} \left\{ \sum_j \left(-\frac{\Upsilon}{p_t^j A_{i,t}^j t_0} + \sum_{t'=t+t_0}^{\infty} \beta^{\frac{t'-t}{t_0}} \lambda_{i,t'} \right) p_t^j \delta q_{i,t}^j \right.
$$
$$
+ \left(\frac{\Upsilon}{p_t^j A_{i,t}^j t_0} - \sum_{t'=t}^{\infty} \beta^{\frac{t'-t}{t_0}} \lambda_{i,t'} \right) \delta b_{i,t}^j
$$
$$
+ \left(\sum_{t'=t+t_0}^{\infty} \beta^{\frac{t'-t}{t_0}} (1 - \Delta t_0)^{\frac{t'-t-t_0}{t_0}} \frac{\Upsilon s}{C_{i,t'}} - \sum_{t'=t}^{\infty} \beta^{\frac{t'-t}{t_0}} \lambda_{i,t'} \right) \delta \sigma_{i,t'} t_0
$$
$$
\left. + \left(\mu_{i,t} - \sigma_{i,t} t_0 - \sum_j b_{i,t}^j \right) \delta \lambda_{i,t} \right\}. \tag{5.31}
$$

The sums of discounted $\lambda_{i,t'}$ are different for the q and b variations due to their different positions in the stage game relative to carry-forward. Both sums cannot be made to cancel against the marginal utility at the same j, forcing either $q_{i,t}^j$ or $b_{i,t}^j$ to be zero and enforcing a condition of no wash selling.[23] The shadow of the future looms one period larger on bids than it does on offers, introducing a hoarding effect which depends on Δt_0 and on β.

The variation of the utility of prospectors can be rearranged similarly to Eq. 5.31 for farmers, but takes a somewhat simpler form:

$$
\delta \mathcal{U}_i = \sum_{t=0}^{\infty} \beta^{t/t_0} \left\{ \sum_j \left(\frac{\Upsilon}{p_t^j A_{i,t}^j t_0} - \sum_{t'=t}^{\infty} \beta^{\frac{t'-t}{t_0}} \lambda_{i,t'} \right) \delta b_{i,t}^j \right.
$$

$$
+ \left(\sum_{t'=t+t_0}^{\infty} \beta^{\frac{t'-t}{t_0}} (1 - \Delta t_0)^{\frac{t'-t-t_0}{t_0}} \frac{\Upsilon s}{C_{i,t'}} - \sum_{t'=t}^{\infty} \beta^{\frac{t'-t}{t_0}} \lambda_{i,t'} \right) \delta \sigma_{i,t'} t_0
$$

$$
+ \left. \left(\mu_{i,t} + \left(e^0 - \sigma_{i,t} \right) t_0 - \sum_j b_{i,t}^j \right) \delta \lambda_{i,t} \right\}. \tag{5.32}
$$

5.13.2   Stationary, type-symmetric trade solutions

We search for and confirm the existence of solutions to the first-order conditions which are stationary in t and symmetric under permutations of agents of a given type, and under permutation of the types of goods j. For such stationary, symmetric solutions, it improves readability to replace the indexed decision variables with a simplified notation, indicating only the distinct values taken by each variable.

Such a reduced notation sets the offer levels $q_{i,t}^0 \equiv q^\sigma$ for prospectors, $q_{i,t}^j \equiv q$ for farmer i who produces a good of type j, and $q_{i,t}^j \equiv 0$ for goods of the types he does not produce. Similarly, bids are set to $b_{i,t}^j \equiv b_0$ from prospectors on goods $j \in 1, \ldots, m$ and zero otherwise, $b_{i,t}^0 \equiv b^\sigma$ from farmers on gold, and $b_{i,t}^j \equiv b$ for farmer i on goods *other than* the value $j \in 1, \ldots, m$ that he produces. Otherwise $b_{i,t}^j \equiv 0$. In the reduced notation, we must distinguish the carry-forward of gold with μ_0 for prospectors and μ for farmers.

For variables referring to final allocations, we let $A_{i,t}^j \to A_0$, $A_{\parallel}$, and $A_{\perp}$, respectively for prospectors, farmers consuming the good they produce, and farmers consuming goods produced by other types of specialists. Finally, to provide a notation for the labor allocation problem usable for both the gold and fiat economies, we set $\nu^0 \equiv mr^0$ and rename $\nu^j = \nu \to \hat{r}$ in all type-symmetric solutions, so that $n = mr = v^0 + \sum_j v^j \to m(r^0 + \hat{r})$. The full and condensed notations are summarized in table 5.6 of appendix 5.12.

We sum the geometric series of discount factors and solve for the Kuhn-Tucker multipliers λ in the above $\delta\mathcal{U}_i$, to relate consumption of nondurables and conversion of gold. Only nondurable goods are priced, and their prices are all equal, so the marginal utilities reduce to the set

$$\frac{1}{pA_0} = \frac{t_0}{b_0} = \frac{\alpha^0}{\sigma_0} \tag{5.33}$$

for prospectors,

$$\frac{1}{pA_\parallel} = \frac{t_0}{p(at_0 - q)} = \frac{1}{(1 + \rho_D t_0)} \frac{\alpha^0}{\sigma} \tag{5.34}$$

for farmers on their own goods, and

$$\frac{1}{pA_\perp} = \frac{t_0}{b} = \frac{\alpha^0}{\sigma} \tag{5.35}$$

for farmers on others' consumable goods. A new combination of the original game parameters has appeared,

$$\alpha^0 = \frac{s\beta\Delta t_0}{1 - \beta(1 - \Delta t_0)} = \frac{s\Delta}{\rho_D + \Delta}, \tag{5.36}$$

which sets the scale for marginal utilities of capital stock in the presence of intertemporal discounting. (Eq. (5.36) is reproduced as Eq. (5.5) in the main text.)

All Kuhn-Tucker multipliers are nonzero, so farmers either bid or convert all their gold every period, $\mu = \sigma t_0 + (m-1)b$, and prospectors carry nothing forward, $\mu_0 = 0$. Their extraction endowment covers bids and use in capital stock, $e^0 t_0 = \sigma_0 t_0 + mb_0$. Note that as a result the bids like the offers scale as t_0 rather than with a fixed money supply, so that the velocity of circulation goes to a constant as $t_0 \to 0$. From Eqs. (5.33–5.35), as $\rho_D t_0 \to 0$, bids and consumption become equivalent for all agents, implying that farmers carry forward the same quantity of gold as prospectors extract, and the money supply and velocity to $\mathcal{O}(1/m)$ are those shown in table 5.4 of the main text.

A general property of the buy-sell game in an intertemporal context is hoarding of endowed goods. Farmers hoard just to the point where the marginal utility of their less-than-Pareto-optimal offers matches the added shadow price on bids from future cash constraints. The result is that $A_\parallel/A_\perp = 1 + \rho_D t_0$. A similar distortion exists between prospectors and farmers, and at optimal solutions individuals will allocate labor among these professions just to the point where the scarcity price of consumable goods versus gold balances the different market inefficiencies suffered by the two types. The condition for equal utilities is the relation

$$(m + s) \log \frac{b_0}{b} = \log (1 + \rho_D t_0).$$ (5.37)

The absence of a gold market prevents prospectors from hoarding, so that their overall level of consumption is reduced to a utility equivalent to the suboptimal utility of hoarding farmers. All money is used each period and is returned to farmers from the posts to begin the next period, and therefore $pq = \mu \Rightarrow mb_0 r^0 / (r - r^0) = \sigma t_0$, implying that

$$m \frac{r^0}{r - r^0} \frac{b_0}{b} = \alpha^0.$$ (5.38)

5.13.3   Stabilization of the labor allocation problem

Because both consumables and goods are scarce, the bidding strength of prospectors versus farmers is inverse, through Eq. (5.38), to their numbers in the population. Equality of utilities (5.37) under labor tatônnement therefore defines a stable equilibrium. Combining solutions of Eq. (5.34) for q with Eq. (5.35) to remove the $1/\beta$, and making use of Eq. (5.38), sets the vector of consumption levels proportional (to ensure proper normalization) to a vector of bidding parameters, as

$$\left(\frac{A_0}{a}, \frac{A_\|}{a}, \frac{A_\perp}{a} \right) = \left(\frac{1}{m + \rho_D t_0 + \alpha^0} \right) \left(\frac{b_0}{b}, (1 + \rho_D t_0), 1 \right).$$ (5.39)

The budget constraint and equal marginal utilities of prospectors set $e^0 t_0 = (m + \alpha^0) b_0$, from which follows the gold investment distribution

$$\left(\frac{\sigma_0}{e^0}, \frac{\sigma}{e^0} \right) = \left(\frac{\alpha^0}{m + \alpha^0} \right) \left(1, \frac{b}{b_0} \right).$$ (5.40)

5.14   Appendix: Optimizing Solutions for the Fiat Economy

Here we solve the first-order conditions for the general equilibrium of the model of the fiat-mediated economy, parallel to the solutions for the gold economy derived in appendix 5.13.

The fiat economy has four important qualitative features, which we again emphasize over and above details of the algebraic solutions: (1) solutions with stationary levels of production, trade, and consumption exist; (2) all Kuhn-Tucker multipliers associated with both the budget and the default constraints are nonzero; (3) agents use all borrowed fiat to purchase the goods that they do not produce (so there is no wash selling); and (4) in optimal solutions the re-collection of fiat that we have written into the rules of the game is exactly sufficient to pay all debts without strategic default. The taxation rule, which is the government control parameter used to enable optimizing trade, is presented below in Eq. (5.71).

5.14.1 First-order conditions for the spot markets

For farmers, the bid and offer variables in the fiat economy are the same as those in the gold economy. Therefore the dependence of the final allocation of good j to producer i on these bid and offer variables is the same as in Eq. (5.29). The bureaucrats have no goods to offer in trade, so their only strategic variables are bids. For bureaucrat k the variation in the period-end allocation is

$$\delta \bar{A}^j_{k,t} t_0 = \frac{\delta \bar{b}^j_{k,t}}{p^j_t} \left(1 - \frac{\bar{b}^j_{k,t}}{B^j_t} \right). \tag{5.41}$$

For the fiat economy we must consider not only allocations of consumable goods at periods' ends, but also the magnitudes of default, if these are greater than zero. For a farmer or prospector i, the degree of default in fiat is

$$\delta \left[\sum_{j=0}^{m} \left(p^j_t q^j_{i,t} - \tau b^j_{i,t} \right) - g_{i,t} (1 + \rho t_0) \right]$$

$$= \sum_{j=0}^{m} \left[p^j_t \delta q^j_{i,t} \left(1 - \frac{q^j_{i,t}}{Q^j_t} \right) - \delta b^j_{i,t} \left(\tau - \frac{q^j_{i,t}}{Q^j_t} \right) - \delta g_{i,t} \rho t_0 \right]. \tag{5.42}$$

The variation for a bureaucrat k is slightly simpler:

$$\delta \left[\tau \sum_{j=0}^{m} \left(\frac{B^j_t}{\bar{v}} - \bar{b}^j_{k,t} \right) - \bar{g}_{k,t} (1 + \rho t_0) \right]$$

$$= - \left[\tau \sum_{j=0}^{m} \delta \bar{b}^j_{k,t} \left(1 - \frac{1}{\bar{v}} \right) + \delta \bar{g}_{k,t} (1 + \rho t_0) \right]. \tag{5.43}$$

If we now apply the variations (5.29, 5.42) in consumption and default to the nonbureaucrat utility form in Eq. (5.18), and recognize that the rate of conversion of gold to capital stock defines the final allocation rate for gold, $\sigma_{i,t} = A_{i,t}^0$, we obtain the first-order condition

$$
\begin{aligned}
\delta \mathcal{U}_{i,\text{econ}} = \sum_{t=0}^{\infty} (\rho_D t_0)\, \beta^{t/t_0} & \left\{ \left[\Upsilon s \sum_{t'=t+t_0}^{\infty} \frac{\beta^{\frac{t'-t}{t_0}} (1 - \Delta t_0)^{\frac{t'-t-t_0}{t_0}}}{p_t^0 C_{i,t'}} \left(1 - \frac{b_{i,t}^0}{B_t^0} \right) \right. \right. \\
& - \eta_{i,t} \left(1 - \frac{q_{i,t}^0}{Q_t^0} \right) \Bigg] \left(\delta b_{i,t}^0 - p_t^0 \delta q_{i,t}^0 \right) \\
& + \sum_{j=1}^{m} \left[\frac{\Upsilon}{p_t^j A_{i,t}^j t_0} \left(1 - \frac{b_{i,t}^j}{B_t^j} \right) - \eta_{i,t} \left(1 - \frac{q_{i,t}^j}{Q_t^j} \right) \right] \left(\delta b_{i,t}^j - p_t^j \delta q_{i,t}^j \right) \\
& - (\lambda_{i,t} + \tau \eta_{i,t}) \sum_{j=0}^{m} \delta b_{i,t}^j + (\lambda_{i,t} - \rho t_0 \eta_{i,t}) \delta g_{i,t} + \delta \lambda_{i,t} \left(g_{i,t} - \sum_{j=0}^{m} b_{i,t}^j \right) \\
& + \delta \eta_{i,t} \left[\sum_{j=0}^{m} (q_{i,t}^j p_t^j - b_{i,t}^j (1 + \tau)) - g_{i,t} \rho t_0 \right] \Bigg\}.
\end{aligned}
\tag{5.44}
$$

Applying the corresponding variations (5.41, 5.43) to the bureaucrat utility in Eq. (5.19), and using $\bar{\sigma}_{k,t} = \bar{A}_{k,t}^0$, gives

$$
\begin{aligned}
\delta \bar{\mathcal{U}}_{k,\text{econ}} = \sum_{t=0}^{\infty} (\rho_D t_0)\, \beta^{t/t_0} & \left\{ \left[\Upsilon s \sum_{t'=t+t_0}^{\infty} \frac{\beta^{\frac{t'-t}{t_0}} (1 - \Delta t_0)^{\frac{t'-t-t_0}{t_0}}}{p_t^0 \bar{C}_{k,t'}} \left(1 - \frac{\bar{b}_{k,t}^0}{B_t^0} \right) \right. \right. \\
& - \bar{\lambda}_{k,t} - \bar{\eta}_{k,t} \left(1 + \tau \left(1 - \frac{1}{\bar{\nu}} \right) \right) \Bigg] \delta \bar{b}_{k,t}^0 \\
& + \sum_{j=1}^{m} \left[\frac{\Upsilon}{p_t^j \bar{A}_{k,t}^j t_0} \left(1 - \frac{\bar{b}_{k,t}^j}{B_t^j} \right) - \bar{\lambda}_{k,t} - \bar{\eta}_{k,t} \left(1 + \tau \left(1 - \frac{1}{\bar{\nu}} \right) \right) \right] \delta \bar{b}_j^{k,t} \\
& + (\bar{\lambda}_{k,t} - \rho t_0 \bar{\eta}_{k,t}) \delta \bar{g}_{k,t} + \delta \bar{\lambda}_{k,t} \left(\bar{\mu} t_0 + \bar{g}_{k,t} - \sum_{j=0}^{m} \bar{b}_{k,t}^j \right) \\
& + \delta \bar{\eta}_{k,t} \left[\bar{\mu} t_0 + \sum_{j=0}^{m} \left(\frac{\tau}{\bar{\nu}} B_t^j - (1 + \tau) \bar{b}_{k,t}^j \right) - \bar{g}_{k,t} \rho t_0 \right] \Bigg\}.
\end{aligned}
\tag{5.45}
$$

The variations in $g_{i,t}$, $\bar{g}_{k,t}$, $\lambda_{i,t}$, and $\bar{\lambda}_{k,t}$ in both equations are permitted to range over unbounded intervals, so their coefficients must vanish. Hence the bidding constraint is always tight ($g_{i,t} = \sum_{j=0}^{m} b_{i,t}^{j}$, $\bar{\mu}t_0 + \bar{g}_{k,t} = \sum_{j=0}^{m} \bar{b}_{k,t}^{j}$), and we may also set $\lambda_{i,t} = \rho\eta_{i,t}$, $\bar{\lambda}_{k,t} = \rho\bar{\eta}_{k,t}$ in what follows. As $\eta_{i,t}$ and therefore $\lambda_{i,t}$ are nonzero, it is impossible for the $\delta b_{i,t}^{j}$ and $\delta q_{i,t}^{j}$ variations both to cancel in Eq. (5.44). Hence one of $b_{i,t}^{j}$ and $q_{i,t}^{j}$ takes the boundary condition 0 for any good j, leading (as in the gold economy) to the result that there is no wash selling in the private sector.

We seek and confirm the existence of stationary solutions, symmetric under permutation of agents of a given type, and under joint permutations of nondurable goods types with the agents who produce them. Again, a reduced notation renders solutions more readable. Offers are set equal to $q_{i,t}^{0} \equiv q^{\sigma}$ for prospectors, $q_{i,t}^{j} \equiv q$ for farmer i of a good of type j, and $q_{i,t}^{j} \equiv 0$ otherwise. Bids are set to $b_{i,t}^{j} \equiv b_0$ from prospectors on goods $j \in 1, \ldots, m$ and zero otherwise, $b_{i,t}^{0} \equiv b^{\sigma}$ from farmers on gold, and $b_{i,t}^{j} \equiv b$ for farmer i on goods *other than* the value $j \in 1, \ldots, m$ he produces, and zero otherwise. Bids from bureaucrats are $\bar{b}_{k,t}^{0} \equiv \bar{b}^{\sigma}$ on gold, and $\bar{b}_{k,t}^{j} \equiv \bar{b}$ on all nondurable goods. The Kuhn-Tucker multiplier for default by prospectors is denoted $\eta_{i,t} = \eta_0$, for farmers it is $\eta_{i,t} = \eta$, and for bureaucrats $\bar{\eta}_{k,t} = \bar{\eta}$. Finally, we denote $\bar{g}_{k,t} \equiv \bar{g}$ for stationary bureaucrat borrowing, $g_{i,t} \equiv g_0$ for i a prospector, or $g_{i,t} \equiv g$ for i a farmer.

Type symmetry presumes equal numbers of each type of farmer, which we denote $v_t^{j} = v \equiv \hat{r}, j \in 1, \ldots, m$, and we further introduce notations $v_t^{0} \equiv mr^{0}$, $\bar{v}_t \equiv m\bar{r}$, so that r^{0} and $\bar{r}$ are respectively the number of agents from each replica who become prospectors and bureaucrats. With this notation, $r^{0} + \hat{r} + \bar{r} \equiv r$ by definition. Total bids on gold are then denoted $B_t^{0} \equiv B^{\sigma} = m\hat{r}b^{\sigma} + m\bar{r}\bar{b}^{\sigma}$, and on nondurables $B_t^{j} \equiv B = mr^{0}b_0 + (m-1)\hat{r}b + m\bar{r}\bar{b}$. Offers of gold are $Q_t^{0} \equiv Q^{\sigma} = mr^{0}q^{\sigma}$, and of nondurables are $Q_t^{j} \equiv Q = \hat{r}q$. These notations are summarized in table 5.6 of appendix 5.12.

The price of gold, in the reduced notation, is then

$$p_t^{0} \equiv p^{\sigma} = \frac{B^{\sigma}}{Q^{\sigma}} = \frac{\hat{r}}{r^{0}}\frac{b^{\sigma}}{q^{\sigma}} + \frac{\bar{r}}{r^{0}}\frac{\bar{b}^{\sigma}}{q^{\sigma}}. \tag{5.46}$$

The price of the nondurables $j \in 1, \ldots, m$ is

$$p_t^{j} \equiv p = \frac{B}{Q} = (m-1)\frac{b}{q} + m\frac{r^{0}}{\hat{r}}\frac{b_0}{q} + m\frac{\bar{r}}{\hat{r}}\frac{\bar{b}}{q}. \tag{5.47}$$

Because of the way we have treated capital stock as a sink for gold, the final allocations of gold are denominated in terms of the investments in capital stock they produce: to prospectors $A_{i,t}^0 = e^0 - q^\sigma \equiv \sigma_0$, to farmers $A_{i,t}^0 = b^\sigma/p^\sigma \equiv \sigma$, and to bureaucrats $\bar{A}_{k,t}^0 = \bar{b}^\sigma/p^\sigma \equiv \bar{\sigma}$. As a result of summing the geometric series for depreciation of capital stock, in a solution with stationary conversion rates $\sigma_{i,t}$ or $\sigma_{k,t}$, the capital stock itself has the value $C_{i,t} = \sigma_0/\Delta$ for prospectors, $C_{i,t} = \sigma/\Delta$ for farmers, and $\bar{C}_{k,t} = \bar{\sigma}/\Delta$ for bureaucrats. We will show in appendix 5.15 how the variations in utilities (5.44, 5.45) involving $C_{i,t}$ and $\bar{C}_{k,t}$ then reduce to forms equivalent to those from Cobb-Douglas preferences, for the *stationary* values σ_0, σ, $\bar{\sigma}$. In this "effective" Cobb-Douglas utility, the exponent for all nondurable goods is $\alpha^j = 1, j \in 1, \ldots, m$, and for investment in gold is again α^0 defined by Eq. (5.36).

In type-symmetric solutions, we introduce a reduced notation $A_0, A_\parallel, A_\perp, \bar{A}$ for the four distinct values that final allocation rates can take. They refer respectively to the consumption levels of different types of agents in their own or others' produced goods. Final allocations of nondurable goods to prospectors are denoted

$$A_i^j t_0 \equiv A_0 t_0 = \frac{b_0}{p}, \tag{5.48}$$

to farmer i who produces good j they are

$$A_i^j t_0 \equiv A_\parallel t_0 = a t_0 - q, \tag{5.49}$$

and for farmers i of all types j that they do not produce,

$$A_i^j t_0 \equiv A_\perp t_0 = \frac{b}{p}. \tag{5.50}$$

Final allocation to all bureaucrats is the same for all nondurable goods, and is given by

$$\bar{A}_k^j t_0 \equiv \bar{A} t_0 = \frac{\bar{b}}{p}. \tag{5.51}$$

As in the gold economy's solutions in appendix 5.13, we again set the replication index $r \to \infty$ for the fiat model. In addition to removing terms $1 - b_{i,t}^j/B_t^j$ and $1 - \bar{b}_{k,t}^j/B_t^j$ from the final consumption level, this large-population limit also removes terms $1 - q_{i,t}^j/Q_t^j 0$ that affect the default level, and the term $\bar{\eta}_{k,t}/\bar{\nu}_t$ from Eq. (5.45) induced by the subsidy. (In this model, the limit $r \to \infty$ leaves r^0/r and $\bar{r}/r$ fixed.)

With these simplifications, the $q_{i,t}^0$ variation in Eq. (5.44) from prospectors requires

$$\frac{\Upsilon \alpha^0}{p^\sigma \sigma_0 t_0} = \frac{\Upsilon \alpha^0}{p^\sigma \left(e^0 t_0 - q^\sigma\right)} = \eta_0. \tag{5.52}$$

Their $b_{i,t}^j$ variations on $j \neq 0$ require

$$\frac{\Upsilon}{p A_0 t_0} = \frac{\Upsilon}{b_0} = \eta_0 \left(1 + \tau + \rho t_0\right). \tag{5.53}$$

The $b_{i,t}^0$ variation from farmers gives

$$\frac{\Upsilon \alpha^0}{p^\sigma \sigma t_0} = \frac{\Upsilon \alpha^0}{b^\sigma} = \eta \left(1 + \tau + \rho t_0\right). \tag{5.54}$$

Their $q_{i,t}^j$ variation requires

$$\frac{\Upsilon}{p A_\| t_0} = \frac{\Upsilon}{p \left(a t_0 - q\right)} = \eta, \tag{5.55}$$

and their $b_{i,t}^j$ variation on their nonendowed nondurable goods requires

$$\frac{\Upsilon}{p A_\perp t_0} = \frac{\Upsilon}{b} = \eta \left(1 + \tau + \rho t_0\right). \tag{5.56}$$

The $\bar{b}_{k,t}^0$ variation in Eq. (5.45) from bureaucrats gives

$$\frac{\Upsilon \alpha^0}{p^\sigma \bar{\sigma} t_0} = \frac{\Upsilon \alpha^0}{\bar{b}^\sigma} = \bar{\eta} \left(1 + \tau + \rho t_0\right), \tag{5.57}$$

while their $\bar{b}_{k,t}^j$ variations on $j \neq 0$ gives

$$\frac{\Upsilon}{p \bar{A} t_0} = \frac{\Upsilon}{\bar{b}} = \bar{\eta} \left(1 + \tau + \rho t_0\right). \tag{5.58}$$

The set of first-order conditions (5.52–5.58) establishes relations between the scale for utility, the stationary values of the strategic variables, and the various Kuhn-Tucker multipliers in terms of the parameters of the problem. These parameters include the taxation rate, for which we must now choose a functional form.

5.14.2   The taxation rule and interior solution

We consider here solutions in which the default constraint is tight but not violated. These are the solutions in the well-functioning economy where the laws support trade without creating incentives for agents either to allocate labor or to bid and offer at market in ways that will lead to default.

The one-period utilities of Eq. (5.18) for prospectors at $r \to \infty$ stationary solutions, in the reduced notation, are

$$\mathcal{U}_{i,\text{econ}}/\Upsilon \to s \log\left(\frac{\sigma_0 \rho_D}{e^0 \Delta}\right) + m \log\left(\frac{A_0}{a}\right), \tag{5.59}$$

while for farmers they are

$$\mathcal{U}_{i,\text{econ}}/\Upsilon \to s \log\left(\frac{\sigma \rho_D}{e^0 \Delta}\right) + \log\left(\frac{A_\parallel}{a}\right) + (m-1) \log\left(\frac{A_\perp}{a}\right). \tag{5.60}$$

The corresponding one-period utilities for bureaucrats from Eq. (5.19) become

$$\bar{\mathcal{U}}_{k,\text{econ}}/\Upsilon \to s \log\left(\frac{\bar{\sigma} \rho_D}{e^0 \Delta}\right) + m \log\left(\frac{\bar{A}}{a}\right). \tag{5.61}$$

The condition for an interior solution is that in the move where agents choose livelihoods, there is no incentive to change from the current choice; thus the utility levels given by Eqs. (5.59–5.61) must be equal.

Comparing the first-order conditions Eq. (5.52) and Eq. (5.54) to Eq. (5.56), we find that the relation $\sigma_0/\sigma = (1+\tau+\rho t_0) b_0/b = (1+\tau+\rho t_0) A_0/A_\perp$ must hold. Similarly from Eq. (5.55) and Eq. (5.56), we must have $A_\parallel/A_\perp = (1+\tau+\rho t_0)$. From Eqs. (5.54), (5.56–5.58), we find that $\bar{\sigma}/\sigma = \bar{b}^\sigma/b^\sigma = \bar{b}/b$ must hold. Combining these relations, the condition for neutrality between prospectors and farmers becomes

$$(m+s) \log \frac{b_0}{b} = (1-s) \log (1+\tau+\rho t_0). \tag{5.62}$$

The corresponding condition for neutrality between bureaucrats and farmers is

$$(m+s) \log \frac{\bar{b}}{b} = \log (1+\tau+\rho t_0). \tag{5.63}$$

A further useful relation comes from the requirement of equal marginal utilities given by Eq. (5.54) and Eq. (5.56), requiring that $b^\sigma/b = \alpha^0$. Corollary relations from the cash payment constraint are then $m b_0 = g_0$, $\left(\alpha^0 + m - 1\right) b = g$, $\left(\alpha^0 + m\right) \bar{b} = \bar{g} + \bar{\mu} t_0$.

We now consider the parameter values for which these first-order constraints on bids and borrowing are compatible with the full payment of obligations. The no-default condition for prospectors is that revenues must pay principal and interest on borrowings, plus tax on total bids (which equal the amount borrowed). Expressed as an inequality:

$$(1 + \tau + \rho t_0) g_0 \leq \frac{\hat{r}}{r^0} b^\sigma + \frac{\bar{r}}{r^0} \bar{b}^\sigma. \tag{5.64}$$

When equality holds (the bound is tight), this converts to

$$\frac{r^0 b_0}{\hat{r} b} = \left(\frac{\alpha^0}{m} \right) \frac{1}{1 + \tau + \rho t_0} \left(1 + \frac{\bar{r} \bar{b}}{\hat{r} b} \right). \tag{5.65}$$

Farmers must pay taxes on bids and interest on borrowings (for which they reclaim the principal spent on other farm goods through revenues from the trading posts), plus the principal they bid for gold (which they do not recover), out of revenues from bureaucrats and prospectors. As an inequality,

$$(\tau + \rho t_0) g + b^\sigma \leq \frac{r^0}{\hat{r}} m b_0 + \frac{\bar{r}}{\hat{r}} m \bar{b}. \tag{5.66}$$

When the bound is tight, together with Eq. (5.65), this reduces to

$$\frac{\bar{r} \bar{b}}{\hat{r} b} = (\tau + \rho t_0) \left[\frac{(\alpha^0 + m - 1)(1 + \tau + \rho t_0) + \alpha^0}{m(1 + \tau + \rho t_0) + \alpha^0} \right]. \tag{5.67}$$

Bureaucrats, on the other hand, reclaim taxes on their bids as part of revenue from taxation. Therefore they need only pay principal and interest on borrowings out of the taxes on private-sector bids (which consume all borrowings). The resulting no-default inequality is

$$(1 + \rho t_0) \bar{g} \leq \tau \left(\frac{\hat{r}}{\bar{r}} g + \frac{r^0}{\bar{r}} g_0 \right). \tag{5.68}$$

When combined with Eq. (5.64) and Eq. (5.66) and made tight, this yields a scale for bureaucrat bids

$$\bar{b} = \frac{\bar{\mu}}{\rho (\alpha^0 + m)} \cdot \frac{(1 + \rho t_0)(\tau + \rho t_0)}{(1 + \tau + \rho t_0)}. \tag{5.69}$$

By combining all three of these bidding levels with the levels of borrowing required to support them, we may obtain an expression for the total money supply. At an interior equilibrium, the money supply is given by the simple expression

$$\mathcal{M}_{eq} = \frac{\bar{\mu}\bar{v}}{\rho}\,(1 + \rho t_0)\,. \tag{5.70}$$

Note that, at $t_0 \to 0$, Eq. (5.70) converges to the dimensional-analysis estimate given in Eq. (5.21).

For the purpose of this model as a constructive proof that games with stable solutions exist, it is sufficient to choose a tax law that is convenient to express in terms of the population structure. From Eq. (5.67) and Eq. (5.63), the following relation, if satisfied functionally by τ, ensures optimal distribution at interior equilibria:

$$\frac{\bar{r}}{\hat{r}} = \frac{(\tau + \rho t_0)}{(1 + \tau + \rho t_0)^{1/(m+s)}} \left[\frac{(\alpha^0 + m - 1)(1 + \tau + \rho t_0) + \alpha^0}{m(1 + \tau + \rho t_0) + \alpha^0} \right]. \tag{5.71}$$

Eq. (5.71) is the implicit-function relation defining the taxation rule. In appendix 5.14.4 we will show that as $\rho t_0 \to 0$, this form ensures stability arbitrarily close to the no-default boundary.

Equality of all the no-default bounds gives allocations whose forms directly express the influences on marginal valuation. Writing these as sets of proportionality relations, the conditions on investment of gold into capital stock become

$$\left\{ \frac{\sigma_0}{e^0}, \frac{\sigma}{e^0}, \frac{\bar{\sigma}}{e^0} \right\} = \left(\frac{\alpha^0}{m + \alpha^0} \right) \frac{1}{1 + \tau + \rho t_0} \left\{ (1 + \tau + \rho t_0), \frac{b}{b_0}, \frac{\bar{b}}{b_0} \right\}, \tag{5.72}$$

while the consumption levels of nondurable goods become

$$\left\{ \frac{A_0}{a}, \frac{A_{\parallel}}{a}, \frac{A_{\perp}}{a}, \frac{\bar{A}}{a} \right\} = \left(\frac{1}{m + \alpha^0} \right) \frac{1}{1 + \tau + \rho t_0} \left\{ \frac{b_0}{b}, (1 + \tau + \rho t_0), 1, \frac{\bar{b}}{b} \right\}. \tag{5.73}$$

The relative amounts borrowed by different agent types also have direct expressions in terms of their relative bids, parameters, and the tax laws. For the ratio of bureaucrat to farmer borrowing,

$$\frac{\bar{g}}{g} = \frac{\bar{b}}{b} \left(\frac{\alpha^0 + m}{\alpha^0 + m - 1} \right) \frac{1}{(1 + \rho t_0)(1 + \rho t_0/\tau)}, \tag{5.74}$$

where we have used Eq. (5.63) for $\bar{b}/b$. For the ratio of prospector to farmer borrowing, the corresponding relation is

$$\frac{g_0}{g} = \frac{b_0}{b}\left(\frac{m}{\alpha^0 + m - 1}\right), \tag{5.75}$$

where we have used Eq. (5.62) for b_0/b.

5.14.3   Scaling of the penalty function

Note that the money supply (5.70) is proportional to $\bar{v}$. Since the borrowing and bids are comparable among all agents (at large m), the money supply per agent then scales as $\sim \mathcal{M}_{eq}/n$. Hence the scale for the largest possible penalty needed for default enforcement is $\sim \Pi\mathcal{M}_{eq}/n \sim \bar{v}/n$.

Agents optimize toward tight bounds on default by reallocating labor in the outer game into the private sector (this step could be implemented in a convergent tatônnement without explicit exogenous coordination). Reducing the bureaucracy reduces the money supply, driving the Kuhn-Tucker multipliers in equations (5.52–5.58) upward toward their limits Π.

From Eq. (5.62) and Eq. (5.63), the multipliers at any interior solution have ratios

$$\frac{\eta_0}{\bar{\eta}} = (1 + \tau + \rho t_0)^{\frac{s}{m+s}}, \tag{5.76}$$

$$\frac{\eta}{\bar{\eta}} = (1 + \tau + \rho t_0)^{\frac{1}{m+s}}. \tag{5.77}$$

Either prospectors or farmers will default first, and by choosing $s < 1$ (simply for definiteness in this example), we may take this to be the farmers. Farmers default when $\eta = \Pi$, giving the scale for the tax rate (evaluated at the interior function of population structure) at first default,

$$\frac{(\tau + \rho t_0)}{(1 + \tau + \rho t_0)^{1/(m+s)}} = \frac{\Upsilon\rho_D\left(\alpha^0 + m\right)}{\pi\bar{\mu}}. \tag{5.78}$$

An expression for the population structure at these solutions, not involving the tax rate explicitly, may be obtained by combining the various first-order conditions on bids and borrowing from the preceding section, as

$$\frac{\bar{r}g}{\hat{r}g + r^0 g_0} = \frac{\Upsilon\rho_D}{\pi\bar{\mu}}\left(\alpha^0 + m - 1\right). \tag{5.79}$$

This ratio approaches $\bar{r}/(r - \bar{r})$ at large m, by Eq. (5.75).

Alternatively, we can convert Eq. (5.79) to an expression for the sector borrowing, expressed in terms of the self-consistently determined tax rule, in a form that becomes simple in the limit of continuous-time trading, given by $\rho t_0 \to 0$, $\bar{\mu} t_0 \to 0$:

$$\frac{\bar{v}\bar{g}}{\mathcal{M}_{\text{eq}} - \bar{v}\bar{g}} \to \frac{\Upsilon \rho_D}{\pi \bar{\mu}} \left(\alpha^0 + m \right) (1 + \tau)^{\frac{1}{m+s}}. \tag{5.80}$$

At large m, this simplifies to the dimensional analysis result (5.25), but extends it to apply over the entire range $0 \le \bar{v} \le n$:

$$\frac{\bar{v}\bar{g}}{\mathcal{M}_{\text{eq}} - \bar{v}\bar{g}} \to \frac{\Upsilon \rho_D}{\pi \bar{\mu}} \left(\alpha^0 + m \right). \tag{5.81}$$

5.14.4   Stability of the labor allocation problem

Central bank lending—and with it the need to discourage runaway strategic default—create the potential for instability of the society's labor allocation. The difficulty is that a linear default penalty is, like real bankruptcy, a form of *protection*. If consumption utility is concave, a linear penalty is preferable to further-reduced consumption, for any agent whose marginal utility reaches the penalty intensity Π. If the group to default first are private producers, this protection creates an incentive to abandon the bureaucracy, leading to a spiral of decreased enforcement, smaller penalties Π, and ultimately the collapse of interior solutions.

The reason a proportional *sales tax* can overcome this instability is that bureaucrats reclaim the taxes on their own bids and need pay only interest on borrowed fiat, while producers in the private sector pay a fraction of the entire money supply per period in taxes. The leveraging effect when the velocity of money is large (finite $\mathcal{M}_t$ as $\rho t_0 \to 0$) makes it impossible for private producers to benefit relative to bureaucrats. Bureaucrats can always ultimately outborrow the private producers at a comparable or lesser penalty. The smaller rate at which the penalty on bureaucrats increases maintains the incentive to man the bureaucracy and keeps Π above a lower bound, which in turn prevents a spiral of strategic default, as we now demonstrate.

We consider what happens if Π is insufficient for Eq. (5.56) to hold b in the no-default region, as a result of the labor allocation in the outer game. Since this insufficiency of enforcement will be known to all agents, we compute the optimal allocation in the regime of strategic default by farmers (supposing $s < 1$ so that they default first), and we take as a conservative bound the condition of no-default for the other two types (even if they could improve utility slightly by defaulting). As long as the no-default solution by bureaucrats remains superior to the default condition by farmers, a labor allocation that leads to default by underpopulating the bureaucracy will not be an optimum of the outer game. We suppose that farmers deviate from the no-default condition by a small fraction ε. Specifically, rather than having $b/\bar{b}$ satisfy Eq. (5.63), we suppose that

$$b = (1 + \tau + \rho t_0)^{-1/(m+s)} \bar{b} (1 + \varepsilon).$$
(5.82)

Eq. (5.65) still holds, and the specialists can internally allocate $r^0/\hat{r}$ so that b_0/b satisfies Eq. (5.62). On this surface, the monetary amount of farmer default is

$$(\tau + \rho t_0) g + b^\sigma - \frac{r^0}{\hat{r}} mb_0 - \frac{\bar{r}}{\hat{r}} m\bar{b} = \varepsilon \frac{\bar{r}}{\hat{r}} \left(m + \frac{\alpha^0}{1 + \tau + \rho t_0} \right) \bar{b}.$$
(5.83)

At the same time, the overall scale for borrowing is set by the bureaucrat no-default condition, which changes from Eq. (5.69) to

$$\bar{b} = \frac{\bar{\mu}}{\rho} \cdot \frac{(1 + \rho t_0)(\tau + \rho t_0)}{(1 + \tau + \rho t_0)(\alpha^0 + m) - (\tau \varepsilon / \rho t_0)\left(m + \frac{\alpha^0}{1+\tau+\rho t_0}\right)}.$$
(5.84)

Bureaucrats need only pay interest on borrowings, allowing them to escalate the scale of bidding by $1/\rho t_0$ relative to the degree of farmer default.[24] From the utilities (5.16, 5.17), with the former only in default, using the penalty definition (5.20) and equilibrium money supply (5.70), and approximating $\log(1 + \varepsilon) \approx \varepsilon$, the approximate utility difference resulting from farmer-only default is

$$\mathcal{U}_{i,\text{econ}}/\Upsilon - \bar{\mathcal{U}}_{k,\text{econ}}/\Upsilon \approx \varepsilon \left[s + m - \left(\frac{\pi \bar{\mu}}{\Upsilon \rho_D} \right) \frac{(\tau + \rho t_0) \bar{r}/\hat{r}}{\frac{(1+\tau+\rho t_0)(m+\alpha^0)}{m+\alpha^0/(1+\tau+\rho t_0)} - \frac{\tau \varepsilon}{\rho t_0}} \right].$$
(5.85)

Using $\pi \bar{\mu}/\Upsilon \rho_D$ to approximate the tax function at first default through Eq. (5.78), we simplify Eq. (5.85) to

$$\mathcal{U}_{i,\text{econ}}/\Upsilon - \bar{\mathcal{U}}_{k,\text{econ}}/\Upsilon \approx \varepsilon \left[s + m - \left(\frac{\bar{r}}{\hat{r}} \right) \frac{(\alpha^0 + m)(1 + \tau + \rho t_0)^{1/(m+s)}}{\frac{(1+\tau+\rho t_0)(m+\alpha^0)}{m+\alpha^0/(1+\tau+\rho t_0)} - \frac{\tau \varepsilon}{\rho t_0}} \right].$$
(5.86)

At nonzero ρt_0, for $\bar{r} < \hat{r}$, there is generally a range of $\varepsilon > 0$ for which farmers benefit from excess consumption, inducing strategic default and with it defection from bureaucracy to the private sector in the outer optimization, relative to $\varepsilon = 0$. Such a situation illustrates the potential instability described above. However, τ and the equilibrium allocation change only by $\mathcal{O}(\varepsilon)$ from equilibrium values, and Π does not change at all under these rules. Meanwhile, at any nonzero ε there is a bound on ρt_0 below which Eq. (5.86) becomes negative due to the pole in $\tau \varepsilon / \rho t_0$ in the fraction, making farmers worse off by default than nondefaulting bureaucrats. This is true even though we have not supposed that the bureaucrats have fully optimized their own consumption by a small amount of default $\propto \varepsilon$ allowed to them. When farmers are worse off, the equilibrium of the outer game must have a population allocation closer to the interior (no-default) solution. Thus at sufficiently small ρt_0 we may place the equilibrium of labor allocation arbitrarily close to the no-default boundary, and $\varepsilon \propto \rho t_0 \to 0$ in the continuum trading limit.

5.15   Appendix: Money-Metric Utilities for Committed Decisions

The adoption of a money system effectively commits a society to a specific labor allocation and trade strategies, by making those the rational strategies within the setting of each trading period, for as long as they use that money system. Both the labor allocation and the per-period trading strategies are noncooperative equilibria of a strategic market game, and are generally different from the strategies that would lead to any Pareto-optimal allocation. We may think of the comparative statics between money systems as inducing a joint change in all of the one-period strategies, corresponding to the change in stationary solutions that would result from change of the underlying game. Likewise, among the full set of variations that define the first-order conditions for optimization, we may consider a subset that preserve the property of time stationarity and permutation symmetry, corresponding to variation in the reduced notations introduced in the previous two appendices.

The per-period preferences induce preferences for these variations in the reduced notation, which correspond to joint *committed variations* of the individual strategic moves over the full sequence of periods. Preferences for committed variations may be described by a utility function that we call an *effective utility*, the form of which is generally not the same as that in the intertemporal model. However, for the goods space and preferences modeled here, it will be possible to show that the effective utility remains of Cobb-Douglas form, and indeed its only change from the form of the single-period utilities will be that the Cobb-Douglas weight s in the period utilities (5.1) is replaced by the parameter α^0 of Eq. (5.5). The shift from s to α^0 for the durable commodity, which is not matched by any shift of the Cobb-Douglas parameter for nondurable goods, factors in the repeated service delivered by durable goods, jointly with both their decay and with discounting.

The time-stationary allocations which are the arguments of the effective utility are identical to the time-stationary subset of possible allocation histories in the underlying intertemporal game, and the Pareto optima of the effective utility are exactly those of the original multiperiod utility. Because the effective utility, like the per-period utilities (5.1), will have Cobb-Douglas form, it satisfies the Gorman conditions for aggregatability [404] discussed in chapter 3. Recall that in aggregatable economies, the entire Pareto set is identified with a single price system, and the associated money measure of any utility level is the expenditure function for that level at equilibrium prices, known as the *direct money-metric utility*. Thus, for committed repeated moves, as for moves in the one-period setting, the money-metric cardinalization of the effective utility assigns a natural and unique valuation to all stationary consumption profiles. Also as in the one-period setting, the ratio of money-metric value at a noncooperative equilibrium to that of any of the Pareto optima measures the efficiency of any trade process that could produce the final allocation from an initially completely asymmetric endowment point [378, 383].

5.15.1   Effective preferences for repeated decisions

We construct the effective utility from the multiperiod utility (5.2) considering only the consumption term and omitting Kuhn-Tucker multipliers or other terms associated with constraint or penalties (such as arise in the model for a fiat economy). These extra Lagrangian terms are always zero at the interior noncooperative equilibria we have derived, and the purpose for the effective utility is to define a money metric for consumption, not to produce the stationary solutions from its first-order conditions.

For any agent i, combining Eqs. (5.2, 5.1) gives the discounted utility

$$
\mathcal{U}_i = \sum_{t=0}^{\infty} (\rho_D t_0)\, \beta^{t/t_0} \Upsilon \left\{ s \log \left(\frac{C_{i,t}\rho_D}{e^0} \right) + \sum_{j=1}^{m} \log \left(\frac{A_{i,t}^j}{a^j} \right) \right\}. \tag{5.87}
$$

As in the previous two appendices, we denote by r^j the number of agents producing nondurable good j in steady state, and by mr^0 the number producing gold. However, for the variations considered in this appendix, it will not matter to which of these types i belongs. Recursively applying Eq. (5.3), we may express i's capital stock as a function of depreciated conversions, from any initial value $C_{i,0}$,

$$C_{i,t} = (1 - \Delta t_0)^{t/t_0} C_{i,0} + \sum_{t'=0}^{t-t_0} (1 - \Delta t_0)^{\frac{t-t_0-t'}{t_0}} \sigma_{i,t'} t_0. \qquad (5.88)$$

The variation of Eq. (5.87) as a function of its per-period consumption variables is

$$\delta \mathcal{U}_i = \sum_{t=0}^{\infty} (\rho_D t_0) \, \beta^{t/t_0} \Upsilon \left\{ s\beta \delta \sigma_{i,t} t_0 \sum_{\tau=0}^{\infty} \frac{[\beta(1-\Delta t_0)]^{\tau/t_0}}{C_{i,t+t_0+\tau}} + \sum_{j=1}^{m} \frac{\delta A_{i,t}^j}{A_{i,t}^j} \right\}. \qquad (5.89)$$

Expanding about any stationary solutions $A_{i,t}^j \equiv A_i^j$, $\sigma_{i,t} = \sigma_i$ of the kinds derived in appendices 5.13 or 5.14, in which $C_{i,t} = \sigma_i/\Delta, \forall t$, Eq. (5.89) becomes

$$\delta \mathcal{U}_i = \sum_{t=0}^{\infty} (\rho_D t_0) \, \beta^{t/t_0} \Upsilon \left\{ \alpha^0 \frac{\delta \sigma_{i,t}}{\sigma_i} + \sum_{j=1}^{m} \frac{\delta A_{i,t}^j}{A_i^j} \right\}, \qquad (5.90)$$

where α^0 is the quantity defined in Eq. (5.36).

Commitment to a repeated strategy sets $\delta A_{i,t}^j \equiv \delta A_i^j$, $\delta \sigma_{i,t} \equiv \delta \sigma_i, \forall t$. The resulting utility change under committed variation,

$$\delta \mathcal{U}_{i,\text{comm}} = \frac{\Upsilon \rho_D t_0}{1 - \beta} \left\{ \alpha^0 \frac{\delta \sigma_i}{\sigma_i} + \sum_{j=1}^{m} \frac{\delta A_i^j}{A_i^j} \right\}, \qquad (5.91)$$

is the variation of the *effective utility* for a committed strategy

$$\mathcal{U}_{i,\text{comm}} = \frac{\Upsilon}{\beta} \left\{ \alpha^0 \log \left(\frac{\sigma_i}{e^0} \right) + \sum_{j=1}^{m} \log \left(\frac{A_i^j}{a} \right) \right\}, \qquad (5.92)$$

reproduced in the text as Eq. (5.4).

Following the development of chapter 3, Eq. (5.92) is equivalent, under monotone transformation, to the Cobb-Douglas utility

$$\mathcal{U}_{i,\text{comm}}^{CD} = \left[\left(\frac{\sigma_i}{e^0} \right)^{\alpha^0} \left(\prod_{j=1}^{m} \frac{A_i^j}{a} \right) \right]^{\frac{1}{m+\alpha^0}}. \qquad (5.93)$$

If we wish to find the Pareto optima of a society with utilities of this form, we must know the constraints on the arguments $\{\sigma_i\}$, $\left\{ A_i^j \right\}$. Conversion of gold to capital stock is limited by the whole-society production rate, determined by labor mr^0 and the production function e^0, so at full utilization,

$$\sum_i \sigma_i = mr^0 e^0. \tag{5.94}$$

Similarly, consumption of nondurables is limited by farming labor r^j allocated to each type, and by the production rates that we have set equal to a for all types,

$$\sum_i A_i^j = r^j a. \tag{5.95}$$

The first-order conditions for a Pareto optimum of trade under these whole-society endowments take the usual form for an economy with Cobb-Douglas utilities,

$$\left(p^0, p^{j \neq 0}\right) = \frac{\varphi_i}{m + \alpha^0} \left(\frac{\alpha^0}{\sigma_i}, \frac{1}{A_i^j}\right). \tag{5.96}$$

In Eq. (5.96) we have introduced the arbitrary price normalization φ_i of general equilibrium, in terms of which the budget for agent i in any period is

$$\left(p^0 \sigma_i + \sum_{j=1}^m p^j A_i^j\right) t_0 = \varphi_i t_0. \tag{5.97}$$

The rate of wealth input to the society as a function of its labor allocation is

$$\sum_i \varphi_i = p^0 mr^0 e^0 + \sum_{j=1}^m p^j ar^j. \tag{5.98}$$

At any Pareto optimum of trade, therefore, the gold conversion and consumption levels are proportional to labor input, as

$$\left(\frac{\sigma_i}{e^0}, \frac{A_i^j}{a}\right) = \frac{\varphi_i}{\sum_{i'} \varphi_{i'}} \left(mr^0, r^j\right). \tag{5.99}$$

The individual values φ_i distinguish among Pareto optima, according to the wealth distribution over individuals. However, the allocation of wealth to consumption by any individual has the same proportions at all equilibria, as for all Gorman-aggregatable economies [378].

Independently of variations in their budget allocations, agents can individually alter the labor allocation, subject to the constraint of a fixed size of the society: $\sum_j \delta r^j + \delta\left(mr^0\right) = 0$. Enforcing this constraint on Eq. (5.91),[25] and using

Eq. (5.99) to relate variations in A_i^j and σ_i to r^j and mr^0, gives the property of prices and labor allocations at any Pareto optimum of these preferences subject to a fixed labor force and production technology:

$$p^0 e^0 = p^j a \;\Rightarrow\; mr^0 = \alpha^0 r^j, \; j \in 1, \ldots, m. \tag{5.100}$$

If we normalize prices by the condition $p^0 e^0 = 1$,[26] the society wealth (5.98) on the Pareto set becomes

$$\sum_{i'} \varphi_{i'} = mr. \tag{5.101}$$

The money metric for this repeated game, then, in which total available labor is the prior constraint that commits all repeated trade decisions, is therefore a *labor metric*. We may, thus, speak precisely about the sense in which this model defines a labor measure of value.

5.15.2   Direct money-metric utility for repeated strategies

As was shown in chapter 3, the direct money-metric utility [404] for any agent i at equilibrium prices is the expenditure function of an equilibrium consumption bundle indifferent to i's actual bundle $\left(\sigma_i, A_i^j\right)$. With the labor normalization for prices (5.101), the equilibrium-price direct money-metric utility corresponding to Eq. (5.93) is

$$\varphi_i \equiv \mathcal{U}_{i,\text{comm}}^{DMM} = \left(\frac{\sigma_i}{e^0} + \sum_{j=1}^m \frac{A_i^j}{a} \right) e^{-D(\mathcal{P} \| \mathcal{Q}_i)}. \tag{5.102}$$

We repeat here for convenience the definition of the Kullback-Leibler divergence [63],

$$D\left(\mathcal{P} \,\|\, \mathcal{Q}_i\right) \equiv \mathcal{P} \log \frac{\mathcal{P}}{\mathcal{Q}_i} \tag{5.103}$$

of the actual distribution of i's budget over the consumables,

$$\mathcal{Q}_i \equiv \frac{1}{\sigma_i/e^0 + \sum_{j=1}^m A_i^j/a} \left(\frac{\sigma_i}{e^0}, \frac{A_i^1}{a}, \ldots, \frac{A_i^m}{a} \right), \tag{5.104}$$

from a reference distribution which is the one adopted by any agent in the Pareto set:

$$\mathcal{P} \equiv \frac{1}{\alpha^0 + m} \left(\alpha^0, 1, \ldots, 1 \right). \tag{5.105}$$

Recall that $D\left(\mathcal{P} \,\|\, \mathcal{Q}_i\right)$ is positive semidefinite and Hausdorf, vanishing only for $\mathcal{Q}_i = \mathcal{P}$.

At any allocation of the economy, the sum over agents i of utilities (5.102) gives an intrinsic money measure of that part of the Pareto set assigning positive allocations to all agents, but falling outside the indifference surfaces which for each agent i pass through i's consumption bundle $\left(C_i, \left\{A_i^j\right\}\right)$. This sum is the part of the Pareto set "captured" by trade, relative to the initial endowments, and therefore has the interpretation of the economic surplus extracted collectively by the agents if they can pass from a point on the boundary of the allocation space (all agent utilities $\mathcal{U}_{i,\text{comm}}^{DMM} = 0$) to the allocation under consideration. The maximum possible for the sum, equal to total labor mr, is attained everywhere in the Pareto set and serves as a reference for optimal welfare. The ratio

$$\frac{1}{mr} \sum_i \mathcal{U}_{i,\text{comm}}^{DMM} = \sum_i \mathcal{W}_i e^{-D(\mathcal{P}\|\mathcal{Q}_i)} \tag{5.106}$$

is the labor-metric measure of the *efficiency* of any allocation produced by a stationary labor and trade strategy. $\mathcal{W}_i$ in Eq. (5.106) are the weight functions

$$\mathcal{W}_i \equiv \frac{1}{mr}\left(\frac{\sigma_i}{e^0} + \sum_{j=1}^{m} \frac{A_i^j}{a}\right) \tag{5.107}$$

measuring the fraction of the total labor which generated i's consumption bundle. These weights satisfy $\sum_i \mathcal{W}_i = 1$ for all outcomes in which every agent adopts one of the primary production technologies. Note that Eq. (5.106) is a function only of *rates* of consumption relative to rates of production, but that Eq. (5.107) converts these ratios into the fractions of a stock variable (population) provisioning any individual i.

5.16 Appendix: Efficiency in the Gold Economy

Drawing on the solutions of appendix 5.13, we now compute the weight functions and labor distributions for farmers and prospectors. Define a parameter

$$\xi \equiv \frac{b}{b_0}\left(\frac{m + \rho_D t_0 + \alpha^0}{m + \alpha^0}\right) \tag{5.108}$$

which will control distortions from allocative efficiency due to aggregate effects of discounting and depreciation. The forms with which it appears in distributions in this appendix will closely resemble those in which a slightly different distortion parameter x will appear in the solutions of appendix 5.17.

The Pareto-optimal consumption profile for the utilities (5.92) is given by Eq. (5.105). Solving progressively from Eq. (5.39), the ratio of distributions of wealth that determines the Kullback-Leibler divergence of farmers from Pareto optima is

$$\frac{\mathcal{Q}}{\mathcal{P}} = \frac{m + \alpha^0}{m + \rho_D t_0 + \alpha^0 \xi} (\xi, 1, \ldots, 1, (1 + \rho_D t_0), 1, \ldots, 1), \qquad (5.109)$$

where $(1 + \rho_D t_0)$ appears in the jth entry corresponding to the good a particular farmer produces. A farmer's weight, evaluating Eq. (5.107), is

$$\mathcal{W} = \frac{1}{mr} \left\{ \frac{m + \rho_D t_0}{m + \rho_D t_0 + \alpha^0} + \left(\frac{r^0}{r - r^0} \right) \frac{m}{m + \alpha^0} \right\}. \qquad (5.110)$$

The labor distribution ratio for prospectors is

$$\frac{\mathcal{Q}_0}{\mathcal{P}} = \frac{m + \alpha^0}{m + \alpha^0 \xi} (\xi, 1, \ldots, 1), \qquad (5.111)$$

and a prospector's weight is

$$\mathcal{W}_0 = \frac{1}{mr} \left\{ \left(\frac{r - r^0}{r^0} \right) \frac{\alpha^0}{m + \rho_D t_0 + \alpha^0} + \frac{\alpha^0}{m + \alpha^0} \right\}. \qquad (5.112)$$

We may check immediately that $m (r - r^0) \mathcal{W} + mr^0 \mathcal{W}_0 = 1$, saying simply that all labor is utilized in production of consumable goods. The distributions $\mathcal{Q}$ and $\mathcal{Q}_0$ differ from $\mathcal{P}$ by terms $\sim \rho_D t_0, (\xi - 1)$.

To extract an efficiency measure from these weights and distributions, using Eq. (5.106) in an algebraically simple limit, we suppose $\alpha^0/m \ll 1$. This limit, in which durables have high price elasticity of demand, can be achieved at large m, small salvage value s, or durable capital stock $\Delta/\rho_D \ll 1$. In this case $\mathcal{W} = 1 - \mathcal{O}(\alpha^0/m)$, $\mathcal{W}_0 = \mathcal{O}(\alpha^0/m)$, and $D(\mathcal{P} \parallel \mathcal{Q}_0) = \mathcal{O}(\alpha^0(\rho_D t_0)^2/m^3)$. The efficiency is then $\exp\{-D(\mathcal{P} \parallel \mathcal{Q})\} + \mathcal{O}(\alpha^0/m)$, where

$$D(\mathcal{P} \parallel \mathcal{Q}) = \frac{1}{m + \alpha^0} \log \left[\frac{(1 + \rho_D t_0/(m + \alpha^0))^{m + \alpha^0}}{1 + \rho_D t_0} \right]$$

$$\times \left\{ 1 + \mathcal{O}(\alpha^0/m^2) \right\}$$

$$\to \frac{1}{m + \alpha^0} \log \left(\frac{e^{\rho_D t_0}}{1 + \rho_D t_0} \right) \times \left\{ 1 + \mathcal{O}(\alpha^0/m^2) \right\} \quad (5.113)$$

at large $m + \alpha^0$. Translating the efficiency measure (5.113), at leading order in α^0/m, into an amount of lost labor whose disutility would equal the disutility of imperfect trade, yields

$$mr\left(1 - e^{-D(\mathcal{P}\|\mathcal{Q})}\right) \to r\log\left(\frac{e^{\rho_D t_0}}{1 + \rho_D t_0}\right) \approx \frac{r}{2}(\rho_D t_0)^2. \tag{5.114}$$

Expression (5.114) equals mr times the *inefficiency* of the gold-mediated economy appearing in table. 5.4. Eq. (5.114) shows that the utilitarian cost to each set of agents sufficient to make up a full suite of specialist production, from the imprinting of the discount horizon onto a monetary interest rate, is equivalent to having lost the output of $\sim (\rho_D t_0)^2/2$ agents' worth of labor deployed with the same durable capital stock but without interest.

5.17   Appendix: Conversion of the Consumption Profile to Efficiencies in the Fiat Economy

In the fiat economy, suboptimal efficiency relative to a competitive equilibrium results both from budget distributions different from Eq. (5.105) due to hoarding, and from a $\sum_i \mathcal{W}_i$ strictly less than unity because not all labor is allocated to primary production of consumables.

The distributions (5.72, 5.73) derived in appendix 5.14 are simple functions of a variable

$$x \equiv \frac{b}{b_0}, \tag{5.115}$$

which corresponds to the quantity ξ of Eq. (5.108) in appendix 5.16. The ratio of distributions determining the divergence from ideal allocation for prospectors is

$$\frac{\mathcal{Q}^0}{\mathcal{P}} = \frac{m + \alpha^0}{m + \alpha^0(1 + \tau + \rho t_0)x}\left((1 + \tau + \rho t_0)x, 1, \dots, 1\right). \tag{5.116}$$

For farmers it is

$$\frac{\mathcal{Q}}{\mathcal{P}} = \frac{m + \alpha^0}{m + \tau + \rho t_0 + \alpha^0 x}\left(x, 1, \dots, 1, (1 + \tau + \rho t_0), 1, \dots, 1\right). \tag{5.117}$$

Here $(1 + \tau + \rho t_0)$ appears in the jth entry corresponding to the good produced; recall that in appendix 5.16 the corresponding quantity was $(1 + \rho_D t_0)$. For bureaucrats the ratio of distributions is

$$\frac{\bar{\mathcal{Q}}}{\mathcal{P}} = \frac{m + \alpha^0}{m + \alpha^0 x}\left(x, 1, \dots, 1,\right). \tag{5.118}$$

The corresponding weight functions for the three types are

$$\mathcal{W}^0 = \frac{1}{mr} \left(\frac{b_0}{b} \frac{1}{1 + \tau + \rho t_0} \right) \frac{m + \alpha^0 (1 + \tau + \rho t_0) x}{m + \alpha^0}, \tag{5.119}$$

$$\mathcal{W} = \frac{1}{mr} \left(\frac{1}{1 + \tau + \rho t_0} \right) \frac{m + \tau + \rho t_0 + \alpha^0 x}{m + \alpha^0}, \tag{5.120}$$

$$\bar{\mathcal{W}} = \frac{1}{mr} \left(\frac{\bar{b}}{b} \frac{1}{1 + \tau + \rho t_0} \right) \frac{m + \alpha^0 x}{m + \alpha^0}. \tag{5.121}$$

It follows from the no-default conditions (5.42, 5.43) that now $mr^0\mathcal{W}^0 + m\hat{r}\mathcal{W} + m\bar{r}\bar{\mathcal{W}} = (1 - \bar{r}/r)$—that is, labor is not fully utilized in the production of consumable goods. The distributions (5.117, 5.118) correspond, respectively, to Eqs. (5.109, 5.111) for the gold economy, under the replacements $\xi \to x$ and $\rho_D t_0 \to \tau + \rho t_0$. In this sense, bureaucrats in the fiat model replace prospectors of the gold economy as the providers of the money supply, while farmers in both models have equivalent profiles. The reason the bureaucrat in the fiat model allocates goods as the prospector does in the gold economy is that neither has a money-market trading post. In the fiat model, Eq. (5.116) for prospectors is a new form because prospectors produce the only non-permutation-symmetric good.

It follows from exactly the arguments of appendix 5.16 that at small $\tau + \rho t_0$, the inefficiencies resulting from misallocation by all agents are $\mathcal{O}\left((\tau + \rho t_0)^2, (x - 1)^2\right)$. Meanwhile, from Eqs. (5.75, 5.79) we may extract the leading source of lost efficiency in the fiat model, which comes not from allocative distortions but from labor lost to primary production, $m (r - \bar{r}) / mr$. This fraction of lost labor,

$$\frac{\bar{r}}{r} \approx \frac{\alpha^0 + m - 1}{\alpha^0 + m} (\tau + \rho t_0), \tag{5.122}$$

equal to $\bar{v}/n$, remains finite as $\rho t_0 \to 0$ and is linear rather than quadratic in the small quantity τ. It therefore dominates the inefficiencies due to hoarding. Making use of Eq. (5.25), this term is reported in table. 5.4.

Notes

1 Much of the work in this chapter is based on a publication by Smith and Shubik [384].

2 By treating the one-period trading mechanism as an invariant, along with the preinstitutional society, we may isolate these stages of emergence of money and compare them as stages in the evolution of control.

3 Recall that the commodity-money-mediated Market 3 of chapter 4 converges to a no-trade solution in the one-period setting.

4 The problem of realistically representing the constraints on the use of labor is a major reason to model institutions explicitly. In general equilibrium theory, where institutions are epiphenomenal—at most serving as transparent representations through which individual preferences are expressed—the problem of optimizing production is, equivalently, either instantaneous or timeless. A severe difficulty with many forms of economic change in reality is that most people rely on the institutional frameworks of society to create jobs through which their labor can be converted into a means of survival.

5 More formally, random asynchronous job switching.

6 For brevity we will often refer to this service as "contract enforcement." However, its important property, which is the scale of the labor force it requires, is set directly and solely by the model of default.

7 Because it is not the purpose of these models to consider the emergence of material production technologies, we do not use capital stock in a von Neumann-Gale-Leontief model, but the definition of capital stock that we adopt could be extended to such a use if desired.

8 Once quantities are regarded as having dimensions, dimensional homogeneity requires that only nondimensional combinations may appear as arguments to transcendental functions such as the logarithm.

9 In anticipation of the next model, we note that such a post will be required in a fiat money economy to make the services from gold a consumable good available to the agents who are not prospectors.

10 In physics terminology for a corresponding phenomenon, in this stochastic domain money becomes a *Goldstone boson* [22].

11 Appendix 5.15.2 derives a result first introduced in appendix 3.7 of chapter 3: For each agent, this cost depends on the positive-semidefinite and Hausdorf Kullback-Leibler divergence, or relative entropy $D(\mathcal{P} \parallel \mathcal{Q}_i)$, of the agent's budget distribution $\mathcal{Q}_i$ from a Pareto-optimal allocation $\mathcal{P}$. Although infrequently encountered in economics, the Kullback-Leibler divergence is widely used as a pseudo-distance to measure the difference between two probability distributions, and its development in the fields of probability and information theory is extensive [63].

12 The linearity is by no means necessary, but is convenient for the calculation here.

13 The use of default penalties, like the use of expected utility or a variety of other extensions of the deterministic general equilibrium formulation, inevitably assigns meaning to cardinal utilities and not just to their ordinal forms. Here we accept that inevitability, and derive its consequences for scaling.

14 It is not required that only continuous-valued variables may be assigned dimensions, as we have done in this construction. Dimensional analyses may be constructed to capture any scale invariances that a problem has, including those in which large, discrete population-counting variables such as m, n, $\bar{\nu}$, etc., approximate a continuum and thus induce a scaling symmetry. Because such counting variables play a minor role in the constructions of this chapter, we have not pursued such a more-involved construction of dimensions.

15 We note that our stock-flow distinction remains well defined under this interpretation and its associated dimensional analysis. $\Upsilon \rho_D m$ is dimensionally a *utility rate*, while $\pi \bar{\mu}$ is a rate at which penalties are imposed. Their ratio, $\pi \bar{\mu} / \Upsilon \rho_D m$, is therefore a "stock variable" corresponding to a number of private citizens over whom each bureaucrat can exercise control.

16 Note that this estimate of the explicitly legal component is comparable to the federal bureaucracy quoted in the preceding estimate for the money supply, within a factor of 2.

17 In Eq. (5.25), doing so would also generate the result of a bureaucracy equal in size to the population, but this is an artifact of the dimensional estimate. The corresponding number in the exact game solution is given in Eq. (5.81) in appendix 5.14. It provides for a solution $\bar{\nu} < n$ at

all values of $\Upsilon \rho_D m / \pi \bar{\mu}$, which by any of these estimates for bureaucracy size would yield $\bar{\nu}/n \approx 0.5-0.6$.

18 Note that this is just the fraction of the society in bankruptcy, from which the estimate used for bureaucracy size cancels.

19 Here again a realistic comparison would need to take into account the difference in velocity of money in financial and banking sectors from the velocity in markets directly mediating production and commerce.

20 Thus we see that, with respect to dynamics, the principal function of money and the price system is to define a separating hyperplane between decisions, much as the price system separates production and consumption in the timeless context of general equilibrium [212].

21 In comparing the two closed systems we note that even if the lending of gold were permitted, without invoking the standard deus ex machina of a small-country international trade model that permits the outflow or influx of gold, the model with gold is unable to vary the money supply in the flexible manner that is feasible with fiat.

22 Latin, "Who will guard the guardians themselves."

23 A wash sale involves both buying and selling the same commodity by a single individual, thus giving the impression of a higher volume of trade than is justified by actual demand and supply.

24 Note that when this bid-up is severe, Π will also be insufficient to prevent bureaucrat default. The point is that the amount bureaucrats borrow in a default equilibrium is only $\mathcal{O}(\varepsilon)$ larger than the no-default limit that is our bound.

25 We do not write the Lagrangian multiplier here to simplify the presentation. It takes the standard form for a capacity constraint.

26 The straightforward normalization $\rho_D t_0 / (1 - \beta) = 1/\beta$, corresponding to the infinite sum of discounted values of one producer's gold in each period of the game, differs from unity only because we have scaled utilities with $\rho_D t_0$ rather than $1 - \beta$, using Euler's formula to normalize the utility weights to one at $t_0 \to 0$.

6 The Economy: Time, Size, and Complexity

6.1 Comments on Changes in Paradigm

The first five chapters have been devoted to reformulating a preinstitutional static theory of general equilibrium to consider the economy in terms of process where markets and other economic institutions exist embedded within and interacting on different timescales with the polity and society. This embedding of the economy within the framework of government and society provides both a natural formal and informal control system. The government provides the formal rules with the laws and their enforcement, and the society and polity on different timescales provide the pressures on the government on rule formation and the direct pressures on the economy to conform to custom as well as law. The price system where it exists provides a perception device in which the pressures of disequilibrium are signaled by the shadow prices that develop both on commodities and on loans and other financial instruments.

From the emphasis on static equilibrium in an institution-free environment, the first steps are taken here in a sequence of three developments beyond general equilibrium needed to comprehend economic dynamics. They are:

1. The production and exchange economy in a process setting;

2. The economy with innovation: Schumpeter revisited;

3. From innovation to evolution.

We deal here with the first in some detail, leaving the other two to a later discussion in chapter 8 readdressing the problems of complexity, control, and prediction.

6.2   The Production and Exchange Economy in a Dynamic Setting

The simple transformation to a fully defined multistage economy immediately exposes the difficulties with the forward-looking features of the noncooperative equilibrium solution and calls for the need for coordination. The literature on repeated games (Mailath and Samuelson [237] or Fudenberg and Levine [146], for example) illustrates many inadequacies and redundancies in the unqualified concept of the noncooperative equilibrium. Do individuals look ahead and compute infinite-horizon strategies that are exceptionally consistent, or do they use simpler rules of thumb such as a local backward-looking optimal response strategy? As soon as one writes down some form of difference or differential equation to describe process, it is easy to spell out time paths with virtually any trajectory including cycles, bubbles, inflations, and deflations of any magnitude. There is a formal mathematical literature on cycles dating from at least Harrod [176] and Domar [86]. The mathematical literature on growth theory includes Ramsey [301], von Neumann [410], Phelps [290] (on the golden rule), and many others. Hicks [186] provides simple difference equation models with easy macroeconomic interpretations that display growth, decline, and cyclic behavior in more or less elementary mathematical models.

A way of coping with these situations appears to lie more in the realm of political economy, with government providing a control mechanism, than in refining the concept of a noncooperative equilibrium. An example of the need to exploit the interface with other disciplines is provided by the concept of a coordinated equilibrium point suggested by Aumann [19]. A simple example is provided by the matrix (often called "battle of the sexes") shown in table 6.1.

A married couple wants to go to the movies. He prefers the strategy pair $(1, 1)$ whose outcome is to go to movie A while she prefers $(2, 2)$ with movie B, but both want to go together. How can they decide? The correlated equilibrium has them flip a single coin deciding between $(1, 1)$ and $(2, 2)$ giving them an expectation of $(2, 2)$, as contrasted with the mixed-strategy equilibrium where each randomizes, $(1/4, 3/4)$ for him and $(3/4, 1/4)$ for her, and they obtain an expectation of $(3/4, 3/4)$, symmetric but mutually unsatisfactory. In this

Table 6.1
Battle of the sexes

	1	2
1	3,1	0,0
2	0,0	1,3

example with a context of husband and wife the mathematics is impeccable, and the explanation of where the coordinating device comes from is provided for by context.[1] But for the abstract game illustrated in table 6.1 there is no correlating device provided within the theory. Society, at a financial, political, or sociopsychological resource cost, provides the coordinating devices.

One can argue that the nature of dynamics might best be immediately reflected in agent-based models with the agents projecting into the future in a very limited manner. Even in the most advanced of corporate planning, beyond a five-year horizon long-range planning appears to consist more of moral imperatives and broad statements of intention and desire than calculation and computation. Yet the rational-agent model has served microeconomics as a basic approximation, and scholars such as Friedman [145], Lucas [233], and others have advocated and applied this model to the macroeconomy.

We believe that the dichotomy made between the model of rational behavior and other behavioristic theories is a false one. In simple enough environments, with a short enough timescale and a conscious short-term goal such as minimizing this year's tax payment, "rational man" may be a good approximation. But in human affairs for extremely short times in a local environment, action tends to be instinctive. For times involving a few hours in a formally structured relatively local environment such as a workplace or closed network, the rational decision maker provides a reasonable approximation of behavior. However, in a long-term and broad environment characterized by high complexity with an intermix of considerations arising from the economy, polity, and society, the decision maker is at best a creature of habit, values, and the environment. He or she may well utilize rules of thumb and convention to simplify the high levels of complexity and uncertainty.

6.2.1   Social and political process and jointly owned goods

Even were we to imagine a society with no innovation or evolution but with consumption, production, and jointly owned goods, we would be required to solve two different types of coordination and control process. They are the production and distribution of private goods and of jointly owned goods. Chapters 3, 4, and 5 have been directed toward building the control apparatus for a production and exchange economy without considering the broad array of joint enterprises and public goods extant in organized economies of any complexity. We do not deal directly with public goods in this volume beyond interpreting bureaucracy as a very special public good—i.e., the jointly owned and designed good of a society that provides it with a self-policing capability that can withstand considerable stress. However, we note that joint enterprises are soon called for in many evolving forms, including communal enterprises, cooperatives, partnerships, and corporations. In section 6.6 below we note that natural problems of scale can easily call forth the need for joint forms of ownership and the needs for financing in even elementary situations.

6.2.2   Pareto optimality, welfare functions, and political process

In chapters 3, 4, and 5 we developed and stressed a physical-process-oriented notation and milked the usage of aggregating, symmetry, conservation, and the quasi-linearity of a money in an economic control system because we believe that these tools provide insight into the control structure. In particular, at the cost of what may appear to be a cumbersome notation, stress was laid on the careful distinction between stocks and flows and on the operational aspects of services, perishables, and capital goods. In our simplifications we have resurrected older, somewhat ill-defined concepts such as a social welfare function and money measure in a modern garb because we believe that as approximations they are productive and can be justified methodologically. In particular when all individuals have identical preferences, a social welfare function can be defined and efficiency can be measured. This is important because although Pareto optimality can be well defined in a no-process or cost-free-process world, when the enforcement and coordination mechanism itself absorbs resources Pareto optimality must be replaced with optima in a cost-reduced feasible set. A comparison of mechanisms within an appropriate domain is called for.

In fact the distribution of public goods is primarily a sociopolitical and only secondarily an economic process. Direct representative government, indirect representation, and a host of other mechanisms guide both the procurement and allocation of these goods. Jointly owned accumulations of capital assets such as public utilities and privately held corporations lie somewhat closer to the simple world of individually owner-fungible chattels than do many complex public goods.

In this volume there is no opportunity to deal with either the theory or applications of voting beyond noting that voting methods are simultaneously mass perception, control, and evaluation devices. These features are stressed in the perceptive theorizing of Owen and Shapley [280] and the work of Balinski and Laraki [24], who argue that an approach to political choice via grading all candidates avoids many of the paradoxes in various voting schemes.

6.2.3   The bureaucratic production function

In chapter 5 we built and analyzed two models of a society with a government bureaucracy[2] that in actual economies may account for anywhere between 10 and 30 percent of the work force (as can be seen in the statistics from the International Monetary Fund or in part in the *Statistical Abstract of the United States*). The size depends heavily on whether and how one aggregates national and other political-subdivision bureaucracies such as state, city, and town employees. Government expenditures may run anywhere from approximately 15 to 50 percent of GDP or possibly slightly more. As we merely used an abstract bureaucratic production function to illustrate the linkage among governmental costs, the size of the bureaucracy, and governmental control and enforcement of the laws, we did not go into any serious estimates of the nature of the "black box" of bureaucracy. We believe, however, that an empirical understanding of even a highly simplified estimate of the bureaucratic production function is called for. There is a fair amount of empirical work, as is exemplified by Rauch and Edwards [302], indicating the role of bureaucracy as of considerable importance in understanding the economic performance differences manifested when the bureaucratic, legal, and social structure of different countries are taken into account.

Beyond observing the importance of the accounting conventions, the commercial code, the bankruptcy laws, and the laws of contract, we do not expand further the remarks on this work. The work of Shleifer and Vishny [319] and colleagues on financial structure is highly pertinent as an empirical start in the formulation of the structure of the bureaucratic production function and its interaction with the economy.

6.3   The Economic Control Problem Restated

The control apparatus we constructed in chapter 5 was presented primarily in economic terms, contrasting the economy with gold miners with the economy with bureaucracy controlling and enforcing paper money. The richness of the political, legal, and educational system may well provide for, and be influenced by, the honesty and efficiency of the bureaucracy; but these are factors shaping institutions playing out on different timescales than most of what we call either micro- or macroeconomic analysis.

The distinguished macroeconomist Jim Tobin regarded macroeconomic analysis as utilizing a short-run closed general equilibrium model of the

.

economy open in the longer run to the polity and society, so that many key parameters and institutional structures required reestimation or restructuring frequently to take into account the changes due to feedbacks on an evolving economy from the polity, the society, and technology. For periods ranging from a few months to a few years, nevertheless, the economy could be usefully regarded as a closed general equilibrium system for the answering of some economic questions. Although this insight can be easily expressed verbally, the making of the formal connections between the evolving system and the static analysis calls for the structure of fully defined process models with a parsimonious representation of how the economy connects to its polity and society.

In an 1891 address, the great mathematical economist F. Y. Edgeworth [107] posed the problem that has illustrated the gap between pure abstraction and application for many years:

It is worth while to consider why the path of applied economics is so slippery; and how it is possible to combine an enthusiastic admiration of theory with the coldest hesitation in practice. The explanation may be partially given in the words of a distinguished logician who has well and quaintly said, that if a malign spirit sought to annihilate to whole fabric of useful knowledge with the least effort and change, it would by no means be necessary that he should abrogate the laws of nature. The links of the chain of causation need not be corroded. Like effects shall still follow like causes; only like causes shall no longer occur in collocation. Every case is to be singular; every species, like the fabled Phoenix, to be unique. Now most of our practical problems have this character of singularity; every burning question is a Phoenix in the sense of being sui generis.

We are in accord with Edgeworth but do not interpret this as a counsel of despair. Instead it says to us that general theory is no substitute for knowing your business. In application the perceptors need microdetail. As in military theorizing, the selection of goals and grand strategy when applied must be in concord with tactics, and tactics require the appreciation of detail. The cries of the practical businessman against the theorist need to be considered seriously by the theorist.

We argue that the act of converting a timeless static equilibrium model into a *playable game* forces us to open the elegant but lifeless static model to its environment. Little details like default rules, inheritance rules, accounting rules emerge even at a minimalist level as necessities in constructing a minimally viable organization. There may be a vast array of minimal organizations reflecting the ecological richness of an economy embedded in a polity and society. But these all still obey the general laws.

The criterion of minimality can be well defined and is at the essence of economics. Any item removed from a minimal model will prevent the performance of some function it is meant to perform. Thus minimality is associated with the level of complexity reflected by the functions.

In our introduction of a bureaucracy, central bank, and money we have changed the paradigm of a closed, static preinstitutional economy. Money provides the lifeblood of the economy and the bureaucracy; government and other institutions provide the control mechanism for the economy generated by the polity and society.

Money and credit provide not only the possibility for a decentralized system but a part of the need for various levels of coordination and control. They provide the sufficient conditions for the functioning of a loosely coupled system. Any system that remains robust under change must, perforce, be loosely coupled.

In this chapter as a specific example we develop and analyze an overlapping generations (OLG) model with publicly owned capital stock such as an irrigation system, community silos, or a power plant or other utility to demonstrate how the needs for financing arise from the basic physical dynamics. The problems encountered are related to but different from those of chapter 5. We note that the utilization of a fiat monetary system may be both more flexible and more dangerous than the gold economy.

This chapter provides a proof in principle that one can take a relatively explicit OLG microeconomic model with production, capital stock, and a financial structure and explore its properties analytically; but even at this relatively simple level such an exploitation requires numerical analysis to illustrate the implications of the dynamics given by the laws of motion. Nevertheless the fundamental question to be answered is: can we illustrate formally the roles of finance in controlling and improving the efficiency of a simple dynamic economy? The answer is yes, but at the cost of considerable simplification.

We suggest that our abstraction reflects the economic history of the development of nineteenth-century agricultural finance in the western United States.

6.3.1   The problem of buffering structure from scale

We may abstract the problem introduced in the OLG model of this chapter, and developed further in our analysis of money velocity and the quantity theory in subsequent chapters, as that of buffering the *structure* of an economy from fluctuations or shocks in its *scale*. Beyond the inputs of institutional mechanism, structure includes such output properties as prices including interest rates, velocities of trade and of money, consumption levels, and sources of uncertainty such as default rates. Stability of these structural outputs may be essential for even the most limited bounded-rational planning, as it underpins the role of money as a store of value and provides a basis for longer-term commitments such as labor specialization. Yet, even within the institutional structure of a stable economy, the institutions may be capable of functioning at a range of scales, and some scale fluctuation may be necessary for the economy to serve its purposes. Population, endowment inputs (including labor), consumption demands, or requirements for liquidity may all fluctuate as a result of natural events, seasonality, life cycles, or the temporal fine structure of clearing.

In a suboptimal economy, fluctuations in scale may drive fluctuations in structure as a result of institutional limitations, even when such structural fluctuations are deleterious and would be suppressed or altered if they could be controlled independently. An optimal economy places control of structure under control mechanisms independent of scale, so that the coupling between the two can be driven by policy objectives and suppressed altogether if desired. The OLG models of this chapter show an intrinsic scale fluctuation driven by the lifetime of a large and long-lived capital stock. In a society where population, endowments, and consumption demands are all time-stationary, and in which there is no uncertainty, the need to recycle capital stock creates asymmetric and temporally cyclic demands for some goods, which may lead to price or consumption cycles. The contrast of different financing mechanisms shows how these may transmit the investment cycle into not only differing degrees but different patterns of fluctuations in price and allocation.

6.3.2   An aside on bureaucracy

Initially in the formal models presented below we had intended to include the roles of intermediaries and bureaucrats as active agents, but as we have covered the public bureaucrats in chapter 5 and as our prime purpose here is to illustrate the influence of different time lags in economic activity, even though we believe that the role of private bureaucracies is of considerable importance we omit it in order to concentrate the implications on financing of the lags and to contrast the results with the static treatment of an OLG model most closely associated with GE.

6.4   Power, Prediction, and Control

The basic difference between prediction and control of the economy is that the first is concerned with the details of the dynamics and the path prediction of the variables under consideration. In contrast, those interested in control are less concerned with the specifics of a time path and more concerned with keeping the dynamics within an acceptable boundary.

The analogy with medicine (and the difference between medical research and medical practice) is clear. Rather than provide macroeconomics a sound microeconomic basis, it is perhaps more important to provide microeconomics a stronger and richer basis than the general equilibrium paradigm while maintaining the rigor and precision it provided. In applied medicine, the theoretical fine points of understanding why a cure works do not need investigation unless unaccounted-for side effects appear or the cure stops working. In applied macroeconomics, undoubtedly theoretical argument of every variety may serve to bolster the decision making, but the mere fact that it is easy to assemble two teams of economic experts with highly divergent views on almost any important macroeconomic topic is sufficient to indicate that macroeconomic advice is part of an evolutionary process, where the advice aims to provide tradeoffs among social preferences, technical and political feasibility, and economic insight.

We reemphasize that control is not prediction; it uses prediction to improve its efficacy in cutting out segments of the feasible set of actions available to the economic actors, but the tradeoff between power and perception is ever-present. Flexibility and decisiveness must be balanced against the perceptions of economic, bureaucratic, political, and social feasibility.

6.5   On the Time Structure of Assets and Individuals

The time structure of society's assets and population feature as important factors in considering the basic constraints on dynamics. All of our previous formal models have been based on perishable consumables and individuals who live as long as the economy exists; but societies—especially rich ones—abound with longer-term assets that outlast a single generation. These physical facts, even in most simplified and abstract form, place considerable constraints on the dynamics and call forth a financial structure consistent with their features. Thus as is well known the development of the overlapping generations model by Allais [7, pp. 238–241] and Samuelson [312] was a critical development in economic thought, as was the life cycle model proposed by Modigliani and Blumberg [266]. These facts of life combined with lives and production aspects of capital stock provide sufficient economic structure that, when embedded in a polity, they remove much of the arbitrary aspects of the financial system. The choices are broad, and a myriad of institutional arrangements may be feasible each of which may depend on history and random events; but all still obey the basic economic laws. The application of the laws, however, requires detailed institutional knowledge. It is worth noting that Maurice Allais, in the 1940s, hand-computed a macro-microeconomic OLG model with production, banking, and a government sector, taking well over 100 pages in an appendix of his book. This appears to be one of the earliest mathematical economics model where the importance of institutions and assets was taken into account in a process and control description.

6.5.1   The roles of experimental and operational gaming

Before laying out an economic model accounting for the features noted above, we make some further comments on the importance of experimental gaming in the development of basic knowledge about the economic process.

As already noted, the value to setting up a playable game cannot be underestimated in defining models of economic and financial control. In a directly operational mode this has been manifested in the form of institution design as evinced in the work of Charles Plott [291] and others. Experience in both operational and experimental gaming shows that critical details that are easily overlooked in untested formal models appear with great regularity. The playable game provides the test for a fully defined structure.

A second set of uses is directly aimed at testing economic and social scientific theories of behavior.

Evidence from Smith [387], Gode and Sunder [164], Siegel and Fouraker [369], Fouraker, Shubik, and Siegel [135], Huber, Shubik, and Sunder [190], and many others appears to point out that, while basic economic theory is reasonably well borne out in highly simplified situations, behavioristic features involving learning, cognition, and memory limitations appear quickly with any level of complexity; and much gaming is devoted to investigating the play for heuristic rules of behavior and for learning and the evolution of competition or coordination in various contexts. In our work we explicitly do not deal with the many important questions of behavioral dynamics, as we believe that for the eventual understanding of economic dynamics there is still much to be learned from adding the basic limiting conditions that must be present in structures that support economic dynamics. They reemphasize our central theme, that the opening up of the tight nonprocess model of GE indicates where the parameters must go in order to build a loosely coupled system.

6.6 A Production and Exchange OLG Economy

The models developed below illustrate the need to introduce new financing and control features in a system where there are two or more generations with overlapping finite lives. When construction time, length of lifetime of the asset, and consumption timing all differ, efficiency considerations call forth somewhat sophisticated finance.

6.6.1 Construction of a playable overlapping-generations strategic market game

Our view of economic process models is that there are myriads of plausible models and in virtually any area of investigation there are multiple choices. However, these can be judiciously pruned in concert with the questions being asked. In the listing below we present a large shopping list of features pertaining to OLG models and indicate by an asterisk or a comment the modeling choices we have made.

1. Time segment: (a) $[T_1, T_2]$, (b) $[T_1, \infty)$*, or (c) $(-\infty, \infty)$
2. Number of types of legal persons: (a) natural persons alone, (b) natural and corporate persons*. The latter are directly or indirectly fully owned by the former.
3. Life span of natural persons: They live T_1 years. *We select $T_1 = 2$.*
4. Life span of corporations: They live T_2 years; but if they are extant at the end of a finite game they (including the government) are liquidated on the day of final settlement. *We select $T_2 = 3$.*
5. Agents: (a) representative* or (b) individual agents* or (c) both. *When there is no exogenous uncertainty, the distinction between representative agents and type-symmetric individual agents may not matter.*
6. Price formation: The economy may be modeled as (a) sell-all, (b) buy-sell, or (c) a bid-offer strategic market game.

7. Number of types of goods and services: They are: (a) labor/leisure*;
   (b) services; (c) perishable consumables*; (d) storable consumables; (e)
   reproducible durables*; (f) nonreproducible durables or land.

8. Depreciation rates: There are many; *but as an extreme-case simplification,
   rather than dealing with various discount rates we give all entities specific
   lives (the one-hoss shay phenomenon)*.

9. Length of production time: For simplicity we may assume that the length
   of production for all producible items is 1 period. *We note, however, that for
   many services such as supermarkets and electric plants one may build the
   durable, after which it supplies services for may years and new construction
   may not be needed for many periods. This is central to our models*.

10. The role of the banks: *We model a dummy inside bank that makes loans
    or accepts deposits of gold at a fixed rate of interest ρ, or an outside bank
    that stands ready to make one-period loans of fiat. The interest rate ρ is
    determined by policy objectives of the banks and properties of solutions
    determined by the markets.*

11. The default condition is given as part of the rules of the game. For sim-
    plicity it is introduced as a quasi-linear term that connects money with
    utility.

12. Type of money: (a) barley, (b) gold*, (c) fiat*. An official government
    money is specified. All trades are made in government money. All bor-
    rowing and lending are via the bank. *We consider both gold and fiat in
    different models.*

13. Initial conditions consist of a vector of initial physical resources and finan-
    cial instruments owned by all the n natural persons together with a set of
    production transformation sets that are owned by the k existing firms (here
    $k = 1$). We assume that there is a vector of estimated or predicted initial
    first-period prices that exists for all real and financial assets. This enables
    us to place an estimated monetary value on the initial bundle of assets.

14. Terminal conditions: In full generality, terminal conditions should be full
    algorithms dependent on the path down the tree. *We make a great simplifi-
    cation by defining models for which terminal conditions do not propagate
    more than a finite number of individual life cycles into the interior solu-
    tions of the OLG, so that steady state solutions we compute in the interior
    are independent of a large class of changes in detail of the terminal con-
    ditions.*

15. The process of liquidation: At the end of the game this would require that all nonreal corporate legal persons be liquidated at **the day of final settlement.** The order of settlement is that all firms pay back their loans, and if they have negative money this is flowed through to the real persons. The firms are then liquidated at the initial prices assigned in the first period. Any profits or losses of the central bank are flowed through; all real and financial assets are then liquidated at the initial prices. At this point the real persons must settle their accounts. *These complications are avoided in studying the steady state.*

16. The behavior of the firms: Firms can be modeled as (a) strategic dummies*, (b) price-taking agents, (c) power strategic players. *Here there is only a communal enterprise that mechanically converts nonconsumable inputs into consumable service streams. The proceeds from the sale of these streams are distributed in the manner of dividends or partnership shares. The conversion efficiency or payout is a parameter of the system. Here for simplicity we assume it is 100 percent.*

17. The definition of short-term profits is another free parameter of the system as it is in accounting systems. We define short-term profits as the revenues from sales minus the direct costs of the directly relevant inputs.

18. Inheritance conditions: There are many mixed monetary and nonmonetary ways these can be defined. *We want the inheritance conditions to reflect the condition "I want the next generation to be as well off as I am." To define minimal models that introduce the fewest new ad hoc parameters, we will use only the utility functions already defined for agents, and we will introduce intergenerational transfers only when these are needed to overcome constraints of the production functions that would lead to zero consumption of some essential quantities and thus to singular solutions.*

19. Preferences and utility: The utility function, together with complete preferences, is a severe and difficult abstraction to justify; but for many purposes, without enormous complication it appears to be about as good a crude economic approximation as one can produce.[3] Edgeworth included a quasi-concave term for concern for others, and one can consider his "coefficient of concern" (conventionally denoted θ) with $\theta = 1$ to be the equivalent of concern that your children should have at least the chance you had. For purposes of our producing a model for the financing of a capital good that can be explicitly analyzed, we select a specific simple form for the utility function, as is noted below.

6.7   Production and Exchange OLG Economies with Gold, Fiat, and Inheritance

The first model below is a continuation of the model with gold as currency presented in chapter 5 where we considered the microstructure of production, trade, and consumption within a single generation, modeled with a large number of symmetric periods. Here we consider multiple timescales created by lifetimes of institutions or capital goods with sunk costs, which may be longer than a generation for agents. The relation of periods in the lifecycle of goods to the lifecycle periods or generations of agents may also be heterogeneous, creating a mismatch with agent preferences in situations where the latter are time-symmetric. The stress on the market system comes from the need to smooth over such mismatches between material constraints and agent preferences. A further source of stress that we introduce comes from nonconvexity in the production process, particularly in the form of capacity constraints to exploit higher-efficiency production methods. Thresholds for feasible production together with long lifetimes are common characteristics of goods produced by firms or publicly held utilities.

6.7.1   Introduction to particular OLG models

The time structure we consider is shown in figure 6.1.

We abstract to two types of production functions: one for nondurable consumables which we consider in aggregate and refer to as "food," and the other for a durable that we call "gold," which may be used as money but is also an input to production. As in chapter 5, the choice of a production function remains a commitment over an agent's lifetime, so agents have two types, again termed *farmers* and *prospectors*.

6.7.1.1   Time structure for capital stock as a "one-hoss shay"   Capital stock introduces the new longer timescale into the model. A minimal model of agents is a standard two-period OLG model, for which initial conditions must be specified but which may be indefinitely repeated thereafter.[4] We term the two periods "young" and "old" for any generation of agents.

We suppose that a production/retirement cycle for capital stock requires three periods, and we distinguish the generations that are young in each period with superscript $\tau \in \{0, 1, 2\}$, where period 0 is the period in which capital stock is built. We consider an endless sequence of cycles of capital stock production and retirement. Capital stock consumes a finite quantity of gold when

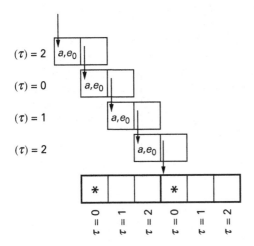

Figure 6.1

Structure of the overlapping generations model with episodic construction of capital stock. Boxes represent periods. Columns represent time, indexed τ, and rows indicate birth time, indexed (τ). Cascading two-period rows indicate generations of farmers or prospectors, with the endowment indicated by the parameters a or e_0 in the boxes representing the young period. Three-period heavy boxes at the bottom indicate the service cycle of capital stock, with the period of production indicated by *. Vertical arrows show the times at which intergenerational transfers of gold may be made by farmers.

it is constructed, delivers utilitarian services at a fixed rate over its life, and disappears entirely at the end of its third period. (It is a "one-hoss shay" rather than a smoothly depreciating asset.) It therefore provides the mechanism by which nondepreciating gold exits the system.[5]

6.7.1.2 Production with thresholds We wish to consider the general class of cases in which efficiency gains from scale are possible, but a threshold unit size is required to capture them. This problem is similar to the problem of exploiting the gains from specialization considered in chapter 5, but in an OLG setting.

Publicly owned (government or large-scale corporate) works are often of this kind, including dams, power plants, mass production assemblies, etc. Typically a unit capacity C exists for a minimal unit, and these units can then be replicated in integer numbers. We avoid the complexities of integer programming as far as possible by focusing on the threshold for production of the first unit, and considering production thereafter to be linear in the invested amount.

Figure 6.2 shows a rationale for this model of production. Three production functions are shown on a log-log scale. For a society large enough to far

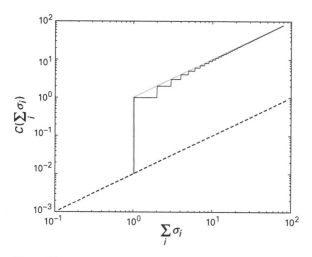

Figure 6.2

Three production functions. The dashed line represents the low-yield proportional production, with $\varepsilon = 1/100$, as used in the later numerics. The solid black line is the granular production we might consider realistic, with a fixed unit size, resulting in a stairstep. The gray line is our model, which keeps the first step—the most important, in relation to the low-yield fallback—but replaces the subsequent steps with a linear production function for ease of handling. The range shown for labor below the capacity constraint—between 10^{-1} and 10^{0}—is the range of stress that we model in numerical simulations.

exceed the capacity C for investment, the steps of integer production are minor perturbations. For a society that cannot reach the capacity at any allocation of labor, only linear production with a reduced efficiency ε can be attained. This low-yielding production serves the same function as a fallback position that autarchy served in chapter 5.

Our interest is in the intermediate range, where the society under a strained labor allocation can meet the capacity constraint, but sufficient strain makes this no more favorable for some class of agents than autarchy. Our model of production (the gray curve in figure 6.2) treats production above capacity C with the same linear form as autarchy, but higher efficiency. This upper-semicontinuous function permits an invariant utility when agents can meet the threshold at the noncooperative equilibrium of the OLG game, because all production and consumption are homogeneous of order one in population size. At an expanding population equilibrium, the extra production provides enough to sustain a constant living standard.

6.7.1.3   Production efficiency for the low-yield capital stock   The utility value of capital stock is determined by its rate of delivery of a service, which we denote S. We measure the service in the same units as the gold invested to build the capital stock, to avoid introducing a distinct type of unit. The important feature of capital stock is that, once built, the rate of services it yields is constant over three periods until its service life ends and it must be replaced. Therefore, for each amount of capital stock shown in this and later sections, the total service stream delivered multiplies that amount by three.

We represent the quantity of capital stock built as an upper-semicontinuous function of the investment level, and we distinguish low-yielding from high-yielding production by labeling these functions $C_<$ and $C_>$, respectively.

The amount of capital stock formed with the low-yielding production process corresponds to the linear functional form

$$C_<\left(\sum_i \sigma_i\right) \equiv \varepsilon \sum_i \sigma_i, \tag{6.1}$$

where $\sum_i \sigma_i$ represents the investments of all agents who can invest in period $\tau = 0$. The sum takes the value $\sum_i \sigma_i = n\,(\sigma_0 + \sigma_1) + n_0\,(\hat{\sigma}_0 + \hat{\sigma}_1)$, where

$\sigma_i \equiv$ investment by farmers,
$\hat{\sigma}_i \equiv$ investment by prospectors.

There is considerable notation associated with the model; we define the new symbols as they are introduced, but for convenience a full listing is given in appendix 6.12.

6.7.1.4   Production efficiency for the high-yield capital stock with threshold   The amount of capital stock formed with the high-yielding production process defines the function $C_>$ in terms of a threshold function c,

$$C_>\left(\sum_i \sigma_i\right) \equiv c\left(\sum_i \sigma_i\right), \tag{6.2}$$

where $c(y)$ approximates the discrete threshold function

$$c(y) \approx y\,\Theta(y - C). \tag{6.3}$$

In Eq. (6.3) Θ is the Heaviside function and C the threshold to produce the first unit.[6] The nature of this approximation, and the relation to the low-yield production process, are shown in figure 6.3 and discussed in appendix 6.13.

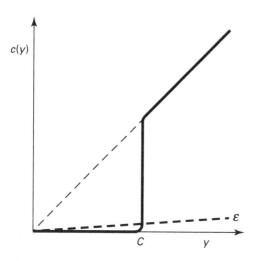

Figure 6.3

Low-yielding (heavy-dashed) and high-yielding (heavy solid) production functions. The low-yielding function $C_<(y) = \varepsilon y$, while the high-yielding function has form $c(y) \approx y\,\Theta(y - C)$, with derivatives at transitions smoothed to make optimization criteria well-defined.

6.7.1.5   Time-symmetric and type-symmetric consumption utilities   All agents are given identical functional forms of consumption utility for both food and the services delivered by capital stock. The endowment a for food to farmers and the endowment e_0 for gold to prospectors set the scales for consumption. A fully specified consumption bundle is a quantity A or S of food or services, a subscript index i for the agent, superscript (τ) for the generation in which the agent was born, and further subscript 0 or 1 to indicate whether the agent is in the young or the old period of life. A Cobb-Douglas consumption utility[7] for agent i then becomes

$$
\mathcal{U}_i^{(\tau)} = \log\left(\frac{A_{i0}^{(\tau)} A_{i1}^{(\tau)}}{(a/2)^2}\right) + s\log\left(\frac{S_{i0}^{(\tau)} S_{i1}^{(\tau)}}{e_0^2}\right) + \theta s\log\left(\frac{S_{i0}^{(\tau+1)} S_{i1}^{(\tau+1)}}{e_0^2}\right),
\tag{6.4}
$$

where:

$A_{i0}^{(\tau)}$ = food consumption of the focal generation-τ agent i when young,

$A_{i1}^{(\tau)}$ = food consumption of the focal generation-τ agent i when old,

$S_{i0}^{(\tau)}$ = services consumption of the focal generation-τ agent i when young,

$S_{i1}^{(\tau)}$ = services consumption of the focal generation-τ agent i when old,
$S_{i0}^{(\tau+1)}$ = services consumption of the equivalent offspring generation-$(\tau + 1)$
to agent i, when young,
$S_{i1}^{(\tau+1)}$ = services consumption of the equivalent offspring generation-$(\tau + 1)$
to agent i, when old.

Our parameter θ is one exemplar of Edgeworth's "coefficient of concern" of one generation for the next. It is mediated by the *particular* concern about the offspring generation's consumption of services from capital stock, which we choose because the agents can avert shortages either by intergenerational transfers or by borrowing.

We will quickly suppress the agent index i and pass to a notation that refers only to agent type. Because the period subscript (0 or 1) will carry an important distinction, in this chapter we will distinguish the strategic variables and consumption bundles of farmers from those of prospectors by using carets over all prospector variables. The buy-sell game will define market clearing, with notation b for bids, q for quantities offered, and p for clearing prices. In models with markets for both gold and food, bids, quantities, and prices in the gold market will be explicitly subscripted b_G, q_G, and p_G.

The life cycle of capital stock is chosen longer than that of agents, so that some generations of agents cannot directly finance the capital stock's construction or own shares in the services it provides. The important *catalytic* function of the constructed capital good is that it converts durable gold from a good with no inherent consumption value into an entity delivering a stream of services with direct utility of consumption. It is the episodic nature of this *conversion* opportunity that may leave some generations of agents with a surplus of gold and a deficit of services rendered by gold, while other generations encounter a lumped demand for gold which leads to underconsumption of other goods.

6.7.1.6 A comment on logarithmic utilities

In this chapter as in the preceding we use logarithmic utilities of consumption as minimal models. Logarithmic utility reflects homothetic preferences and leads to price elasticities of unity, which rule out modeling certain classes of price response to scarcity. In the models below, this simplification has the desirable feature of separating the types of agents and thus simplifying analysis and solution of models where our interest is in demonstrating the nature of the financing. Apart from these simplifications, the qualitative differences among market systems that we demonstrate should not depend sensitively on our use of logarithmic utility.

6.7.1.7   Population structure is not a strategic variable, but may be optimized by adaptive adjustment   The abstraction that stress on market systems and allocative efficiencies is created by a mismatch between the timescales and cycles of physical assets and the needs of agents entails the assumptions that agents cannot freely shift production in response to cyclical exogenous constraints. We simplify this abstraction into a minimal form by supposing that numbers n of farmers and n_0 of prospectors, in each of the two generations, are slowly changing variables even relative to the cycle of capital stock, so that stationary solutions to strategic market games can be computed treating these quantities as fixed parameters. We take the total number of agents $2 (n + n_0)$ as a fully fixed constraint, and consider the adjustment of the allocation of labor n/n_0 to be a slow process that equalizes some aggregation of utilities across the three generations of farmers with the same aggregation across the three generations of prospectors. (In the examples solved below, we will take this aggregation to be simply the arithmetic mean.) The process of adjusting the labor allocation is not modeled explicitly as the strategic variables are, and the selection of the utility-equalizing value using stationary solutions for the strategic variables is therefore akin to a problem in comparative statics. Informally, we consider this a proxy for slow processes of cultural adaptation that are outside the scope of our models.

6.7.2   The competitive rational-expectations equilibrium allocation and utilities

The temporal structure of OLG models exposes the difficulties in extending the competitive equilibrium definition, because given the finiteness of expected life many contracts implicit in GE are ruled out (although, as Samuelson noted [312], the presence of money helps to restore some contracts). Furthermore the formulation of full dynamics calls for a treatment of initial and terminal conditions that introduce many degrees of freedom that have to be accounted for in well-defining the models. An easy but not always satisfactory way to treat the infinite horizons consistently with the spirit of GE is to account for initial and terminal conditions by a "rational-expectations assumption" which solves only for dynamic equilibrium but leaves unanalyzed the influence of transient states.

For the examples below, we suppose that complete markets exist both within and across the two periods of any individual's life cycle and the three periods of existence of the capital stock. That is, young farmers purchase forward contracts for food in their old periods, at prices equal to the spot market prices in those periods, in which both young and old prospectors also trade.

The assumption that complete contracts must include forward contracts requires that, in an OLG setting with a definite starting period, it is necessary to suppose that agents who are already old in that period have initial allocations of gold, or forward contracts for food, in amounts that are consistent with the rational-expectations equilibrium values inferred for later periods.

6.7.2.1   Consumption levels, population structure, and utility level   Suppose that the society is either large enough or small enough that, at the equilibrium allocations of labor, we are in the linear regime of either the high-yield or the low-yield production function. In a competitive equilibrium among agents with identical preferences, relative prices between food and the services from capital stock are the same for all agents, and only their budgets have the potential to distinguish them. However, we consider the labor allocation n_0/n as also identified by the criterion that all agent utilities be identical (so that changing professions over long times is never advantageous to either type of agent), making the market value of all agents' endowments equal.[8] Therefore we do not notationally distinguish consumption levels A or S either across periods or between farmers and prospectors, and solve the equilibrium for the values which are common to all of these.

With total production na of food per period, all equilibrium consumption levels are

$$A_0^{(\tau)} = A_1^{(\tau)} = \frac{na}{2\,(n+n_0)}. \tag{6.5}$$

With production $n_0 e_0$ of gold per period, and a durable capital stock that consumes $3n_0 e_0$ units to produce but then yields an equal level of services for *three* periods, the service consumption level per period per agent becomes

$$S_0^{(\tau)} = S_1^{(\tau)} = \frac{3n_0 e_0}{2\,(n+n_0)}. \tag{6.6}$$

At these symmetric allocations, the utility of any agent given by Eq. (6.4), with high-yielding production, becomes

$$\mathcal{U}^{(\tau)} = 2\log\left(\frac{1}{1+n_0/n}\right) + 2s\,(1+\theta)\log\left(\frac{3}{2}\frac{n_0/n}{1+n_0/n}\right). \tag{6.7}$$

Since the service stream delivered over an entire cycle, when measured in units of invested gold, is three times the actual quantity of the scarce resource (gold) produced by prospector labor, it is $S^{(\tau)}/3$, rather than $S^{(\tau)}$, which appears in marginal rates of substitution. (That is, the factor $3/2$ in the logarithm of Eq. (6.7) leads to a constant summand in utility for all agents, which does not affect the optimization problem.) The equilibrium price system defined by the marginal rates of substitution is therefore

$$p_{\tau,\text{CE}} = \frac{S^{(\tau)}/3}{s\,(1+\theta)\,A^{(\tau)}} = \frac{n_0 e_0}{s\,(1+\theta)\,na}. \tag{6.8}$$

The competitive equilibrium labor allocation, obtained by varying Eq. (6.7) with respect to n_0/n, becomes

$$\frac{n_0}{n} \xrightarrow{\text{CE}} s\,(1+\theta), \tag{6.9}$$

giving $p_{\tau,\text{CE}} = e_0/a$.

6.8   Three Economic Systems: Informal Intergenerational Transfer, Gold Banking, and Fiat with Government as a Reserve Buyer of Gold

We now consider the way that economies with this common OLG model of agent preferences and threshold-limited production, but different levels of institutional structure, meet the needs of distribution of food, concentration of gold for investment, and distribution of services. We will use total population as a control variable that determines the stress on the system as measured by the shadow price of the capacity constraint. For each model a noncooperative equilibrium exists for populations at or above a (model-dependent) critical size N_C. At $N = N_C$, and the utility-equalizing allocation n_0/n of the noncooperative equilibrium, the total prospector gold endowment over three generations meets the threshold for high-efficiency production: $3n_0 e_0 = C$. All of these noncooperative equilibria require critical populations N_C larger than the competitive-equilibrium value (6.9), which provides one measure of their inefficiency.

In each case, for $N < N_C$, the capacity constraint develops a nonzero shadow price, which quantifies the stress on the system. The rate at which the economy can allow $N/N_C < 1$ to decrease relative to the rise of the shadow price provides a measure of the robustness of its functions of distribution.

6.8.1   Synopses of the three cases

6.8.1.1   Case 1: food markets denominated in gold money, with intergenerational transfers of gold   We model an "informal" economy without financial support as one with trading post markets for food denominated in gold, and individual bequests of gold by agents in their old period to furnish an initial

endowment of gold for agents of the same type in the next generation in their young period. These bequests are the only mechanism of intergenerational transfer (IGT). The prospector endowment of gold flows primarily through the food markets to accumulate in period $\tau = 0$ when it is needed for capital stock construction. The internalization of offspring utilities of consumption of services from capital stock is sufficient to produce interior solutions in which those farmers who require gold to purchase shares in period $\tau = 0$ receive nonzero IGTs from the previous generation. Stress from an insufficient population leads to asymmetric contribution from farmers and prospectors to meet the capacity constraint, and strong divergence of the utilities of different prospector generations despite producing only mild divergence of food prices if the overall budget share from gold remains small.

6.8.1.2   Case 2: an inside bank for gold in place of intergenerational transfers   The concentration of stress on a single period of agents, and its resulting impact on the investment levels and on divergent consumption bundles of agents born in different generations, can be mitigated by introducing an inside bank, which provides a repository and pass-through institution to redistribute gold. In place of IGTs that propagate gold forward in time through the capital cycle, bank loans couple consumption between the young and old periods *within each generation*. A limited intergenerational flow of gold occurs through the payment of interest on loans and deposits. However, the need of an inside bank to balance interest payments of debtors and creditors creates a complicated coupling among the roles of gold as an input to production, a medium of exchange, and an interperiod (and hence indirectly through the food markets) intergenerational store of value. This coupling is expressed in a counterintuitive requirement for a nonzero interest rate (indeed the maximal rate in the model) in the unstressed noncooperative equilibrium, and a dependence of prices on this interest rate that moves them away from the competitive equilibrium value and contributes part of the non-CE allocation of labor in the population.

6.8.1.3   Case 3: a central bank for fiat and a reserve buyer for gold   The role of gold as a durable consumable can be decoupled from the function of the money system by introducing fiat exchange, which places all producers on an equal footing with respect to purchasing and interest. In the particular model we present here, multiple functions must be introduced, because the replacement of gold as a medium of exchange requires the introduction of both a gold market and of a reserve buyer for gold in periods when there is no demand in the open market of noncooperative agents. We combine these functions in a model of a policy-guided central bank, which provides loans in fiat money, collects interest, provides gold demand in slack periods, and restores stored gold when it is needed for production. The introduction of a fiat exchange system creates multiple control parameters by which the central bank may influence policy objectives. We show, however, that no single value for these parameters is generally utility-improving or price-stabilizing; rather the parameters must generally be tuned to the particular configuration of population constraints and shadow prices faced by the society.

6.8.2 The markets used to allocate food, gold, and services in all models

6.8.2.1 A notation for agent-symmetric solutions within each type We look for noncooperative equilibria in which all agents of a given type make the same bids and offers, and have the same consumption levels. We denote the bid and offer variables for farmers by $\left(b_0^{(\tau)}, q^{(\tau)}\right)$ in the young period, and by $b_1^{(\tau)}$ in the old period. Their bids on gold in the young and old periods are denoted $\left(b_{G0}^{(\tau)}, b_{G1}^{(\tau)}\right)$. Their consumption levels of food and services are $\left(A_0^{(\tau)}, S_0^{(\tau)}\right)$ in the young period and $\left(A_1^{(\tau)}, S_1^{(\tau)}\right)$ in the old period. The clearing price for food in period τ is denoted p_τ.

The corresponding quantities for prospectors are $\left(\hat{b}_0^{(\tau)}, \hat{b}_1^{(\tau)}, \hat{b}_{G,0}^{(\tau)}, \hat{q}_G^{(\tau)} \hat{b}_{G,1}^{(\tau)}, \hat{A}_0^{(\tau)}, \hat{S}_0^{(\tau)}, \hat{A}_1^{(\tau)}, \hat{S}_1^{(\tau)}\right)$. The gold clearing price is $p_{G\tau}$. The prospector variables replace an offer q of food with an offer $\hat{q}_G$ of gold in cases where gold markets exist.

6.8.2.2 Price formation and market clearing The clearing price for food markets relates to bids of both types, and to offers, as

$$p_\tau = \frac{nb_1^{(\tau-1)} + n_0\left(\hat{b}_1^{(\tau-1)} + \hat{b}_0^{(\tau)}\right)}{nq^{(\tau)}}. \tag{6.10}$$

The comparable clearing price for gold (in models with a gold market) is expressed as

$$p_{G,\tau} = \frac{nb_{G,1}^{(\tau-1)} + n_0\left(\hat{b}_{G,1}^{(\tau-1)} + \hat{b}_{G,0}^{(\tau)}\right)}{n\hat{q}_G^{(\tau)}}. \tag{6.11}$$

The consumption level of food for farmers is

$$A_0^{(\tau)} = a - q^{(\tau)} + \frac{b_0^{(\tau)}}{p_\tau}$$

$$A_1^{(\tau)} = \frac{b_1^{(\tau)}}{p_{\tau+1}}, \tag{6.12}$$

and the level for prospectors is

$$\hat{A}_0^{(\tau)} = \frac{\hat{b}_0^{(\tau)}}{p_\tau}$$

$$\hat{A}_1^{(\tau)} = \frac{\hat{b}_1^{(\tau)}}{p_{\tau+1}}. \tag{6.13}$$

6.8.2.3   Private share rights and publicly held utilities for services   In the following models, we will solve separately for the noncooperative equilibria with investments in either low-yielding or high-yielding capital stock. Agents who are alive in the period when capital stock is built can purchase proportional shares in the stream of services. When these agents die, the part of the service stream no longer consumed by them becomes a publicly held utility, which we distribute equally among the remaining agents.

Letting C stand for either $C_<$ or $C_>$ as in section 6.7.1.3, according to the production function under consideration, the service consumption levels measured in units of invested gold, for the three generations of agents and their two periods, are given by

$$S_0^{(0)} = S_1^{(0)} = \frac{\sigma_0}{\sum_i \sigma_i} C\left(\sum_i \sigma_i\right); \quad \hat{S}_0^{(0)} = \hat{S}_1^{(0)} = \frac{\hat{\sigma}_0}{\sum_i \sigma_i} C\left(\sum_i \sigma_i\right)$$

$$S_0^{(1)} = \hat{S}_0^{(1)} = \frac{1}{n+n_0} \frac{\sum_i \sigma_i - (n\sigma_0 + n_0\hat{\sigma}_0)}{\sum_i \sigma_i} C\left(\sum_i \sigma_i\right); \quad S_1^{(1)} = \hat{S}_1^{(1)} = \frac{1}{N} C\left(\sum_i \sigma_i\right)$$

$$S_0^{(2)} = \hat{S}_0^{(2)} = \frac{1}{N} C\left(\sum_i \sigma_i\right); \quad S_1^{(2)} = \frac{\sigma_1}{\sum_i \sigma_i} C\left(\sum_i \sigma_i\right); \quad \hat{S}_1^{(2)} = \frac{\hat{\sigma}_1}{\sum_i \sigma_i} C\left(\sum_i \sigma_i\right).$$

$$\tag{6.14}$$

In the first and third lines, for generations $\tau = 0$ and $\tau = 2$, the factors $\sigma_0, \hat{\sigma}_0$ and $\sigma_1, \hat{\sigma}_1$ represent explicit ownership rights of the focal agent, from investments in the $\tau = 0$ period. The expressions for $S_0^{(1)}, \hat{S}_0^{(1)}$ in the second line represent the proportional publicly held service allocation of all explicit (farmer and prospector) rights from $\tau = 2$ agents who have died. The important feature

of the sum $\sum_i \sigma_i - \left(n\sigma_0 + n_0\hat{\sigma}_0\right)$ in the numerator is that it contains only decision variables from the generation $\tau = 2$. Therefore, while it affects the con-
sumption levels of $\tau = 1$, which appear in the utilities $\mathcal{U}_i^{(0)}$, those consumption
levels do not depend on the $\tau = 0$ decision variables except at higher order in
$1/N$ (hence, on finite replicates), which terms we omit. Note that in the linear
ranges of either production function, the factors of $C\left(\sum_i \sigma_i\right)$ and $\sum_i \sigma_i$ cancel,
leaving only simple linear functions of σ_0 or σ_1.

6.8.2.4   Budget conditions and budget constraints   If we take $\mu_0^{(\tau)}$ to be
the initial budget from exogenous variables, whether endowment or intergenerational transfers, then a general Lagrangian for the budget constraint that can
encompass all three models may be written

$$\mathcal{L}_{\text{Common}}^{(\tau)} = \mathcal{U}^{(\tau)} + \eta_0^{(\tau)}\left(\mu_0^{(\tau)} + g_0^{(\tau)} - \sigma_0\delta_{\tau,0} - b_0^{(\tau)} - b_{G,0}^{(\tau)}\right)$$
$$+ \eta_1^{(\tau)}\left(\mu_1^{(\tau)} - g_1^{(\tau)} - \sigma_1\delta_{\tau,2} - b_1^{(\tau)} - \kappa^\tau\right), \qquad (6.15)$$

with hatted variables used if the agent is a prospector. Here g are amounts
borrowed from a bank (in either gold or fiat), with negative values representing
lending to the bank. In models where the institutions entailed by the use of
some variable are not included, that variable is set to zero. We provide the
general form here so that we may write in one place the relations between
marginal utility of consumption and the Kuhn-Tucker multipliers $\eta_0^{(\tau)}, \eta_1^{(\tau)}$ for
the budget constraint, in those first-order conditions that are common to all
agent types in all models.

The second-period initial budget for the two types is given in terms of the
first-period budget, expenditures, and proceeds of sale for farmers and prospectors respectively by

$$\mu_1^{(\tau)} = \mu_0^{(\tau)} + g_0^{(\tau)} - \sigma_0\delta_{\tau,0} - b_0^{(\tau)} - b_{G,0}^{(\tau)} + q^{(\tau)}p_\tau$$
$$\hat{\mu}_1^{(\tau)} = \hat{\mu}_0^{(\tau)} + \hat{g}_0^{(\tau)} - \sigma_0\delta_{\tau,0} - \hat{b}_0^{(\tau)} - \hat{b}_{G,0}^{(\tau)} + \hat{q}_G^{(\tau)}p_{G,\tau}. \qquad (6.16)$$

**6.8.3   Representation of a jointly binding capacity constraint with
an effective Kuhn-Tucker multiplier and associated shadow
price**

Constraints on individual strategic variables are readily implemented with
Kuhn-Tucker multipliers, which have the interpretation of shadow prices. The
jointly binding capacity constraint, that investment must reach a threshold

before high-yielding production is possible, is not in general similarly representable by such a multiplier, because the threshold is not under the strategic control of any single agent. Often in such cases an additional market would be required in reality, to propagate real price signals to individuals.

In these models, we exploit a property of logarithmic utilities that permits us to represent the jointly binding capacity constraint in terms of a single Kuhn-Tucker multiplier Λ which is common to the optimization problems of all agents, which has the interpretation of a shadow price. Our approach is to first regularize the threshold behavior of the production function to a smooth but nonconvex and sharply curved function. The strongly nonlinear dependence of the derivative of this function on the investment level in a neighborhood of the capacity threshold value, together with logarithmic dependence of utility on the consumption level, permits us to treat the log derivative of the nonconvex production function as a Kuhn-Tucker multiplier. The detailed construction is presented in appendix 6.13.

6.8.4   Common first-order conditions and their consequences for consumption

6.8.4.1   Farmer bid and offer variables   The common terms in the first-order condition for farmers in all models are

$$
0 = \delta \mathcal{L}^{(\tau)} = \left[\frac{1}{A_0^{(\tau)} p_\tau} - \eta_1^{(\tau)} \right] \left(\delta b_0^{(\tau)} - p_\tau \delta q^{(\tau)} \right) - \eta_0^{(\tau)} \delta b_0^{(\tau)} + \left[\frac{1}{b_1^{(\tau)}} - \eta_1^{(\tau)} \right] \delta b_1^{(\tau)}
$$
$$
+ \left[\frac{2s}{\sigma_0} + 2(1+\theta)\Lambda - \left(\eta_0^{(\tau)} + \eta_1^{(\tau)} \right) \right] \delta \sigma_0 \delta_{\tau,0}
$$
$$
+ \left[\frac{s}{\sigma_1} + (1+2\theta)\Lambda - \eta_1^{(\tau)} \right] \delta \sigma_1 \delta_{\tau,2}, \tag{6.17}
$$

where Λ is the effective Kuhn-Tucker multiplier for the capacity constraining on high-yielding production, derived in appendix 6.13.

(In Eq. (6.17) and all subsequent equations, $\delta_{\tau,0}$ is the Kronecker δ-function, which takes value 1 when $\tau = 0$ and zero otherwise, and $\delta_{\tau,2}$ is the corresponding Kronecker δ-function with respect to $\tau = 2$.) Because the utility (6.4) does not saturate, farmers will always consume a part of their food, and the first and third conditions in Eq. (6.17) therefore give

$$
A_0^{(\tau)} p_\tau = b_1^{(\tau)}. \tag{6.18}
$$

To provide a complete analysis we must consider the (unlikely) possibility that farmers engage in wash selling in their young period, as we did for models in previous chapters. The equation that determines the value of $\eta_0^{(\tau)}$, which excludes wash sales if it is positive in Eq. (6.17), is

$$\frac{2s}{\sigma_0} + 2(1+\theta)\Lambda - \frac{1}{b_1^{(0)}} = \eta_0^{(0)}. \tag{6.19}$$

We provide a systematic analysis covering all cases in appendix 6.14. There we show that wash selling may be excluded from all solutions derived below, either because it cannot occur or because it cannot affect prices or allocations, so that any solution with wash sales can be replaced by an equivalent solution without them.

6.8.4.2 Prospector bids on food   Prospectors bid on food in both periods, and generations ($\tau = 2$) or ($\tau = 0$) will invest in capital stock in period $\tau = 0$. The common terms in their first-order conditions including budget constraints are

$$0 = \delta\mathcal{L}^{(\tau)} = \left[\frac{1}{\hat{b}_0^{(\tau)}} - \left(\hat{\eta}_0^{(\tau)} + \hat{\eta}_1^{(\tau)}\right)\right]\delta\hat{b}_0^{(\tau)} + \left[\frac{1}{\hat{b}_1^{(\tau)}} - \hat{\eta}_1^{(\tau)}\right]\delta\hat{b}_1^{(\tau)}$$
$$+ \left[\frac{2s}{\hat{\sigma}_0} + 2(1+\theta)\Lambda - \left(\hat{\eta}_0^{(\tau)} + \hat{\eta}_1^{(\tau)}\right)\right]\delta\hat{\sigma}_0\delta_{\tau,0}$$
$$+ \left[\frac{s}{\hat{\sigma}_1} + (1+2\theta)\Lambda - \hat{\eta}_1^{(\tau)}\right]\delta\hat{\sigma}_1\delta_{\tau,2}. \tag{6.20}$$

The general relation between bids in the two periods is

$$\frac{1}{\hat{b}_0^{(\tau)}} - \frac{1}{\hat{b}_1^{(\tau)}} = \hat{\eta}_0^{(\tau)}. \tag{6.21}$$

Situations in which prospectors carry gold over between periods, requiring $\hat{\eta}_0^{(\tau)} = 0$, are distinguished from those in which the periods are related through lending at interest, requiring $\hat{\eta}_0^{(\tau)}\rho\hat{\eta}_1^{(\tau)} = \rho/\hat{b}_1^{(\tau)}$, and the relation between bids and total budget is then given by Eq. (6.21) in either case.

6.8.5   The model with intergenerational transfers and without banking

In this model, the Lagrangian $\mathcal{L}^{(\tau)} = \mathcal{L}_{\text{Common}}^{(\tau)}$ of Eq. (6.15). The defining feature of the model is the introduction of intergenerational transfers $\kappa^{(\tau)}$ from each generation (τ) of farmers to their successor generation. The IGTs appear in the budget conditions as

$$\kappa^{(\tau-1)} = \mu_0^{(\tau)}$$
$$\mu_0^{(\tau)} - b_0^{(\tau)} - \sigma_0 \delta_{\tau,0} = \mu_1^{(\tau)}$$
$$\mu_1^{(\tau)} + q^{(\tau)} p_\tau = b_1^{(\tau)} + \sigma_1 \delta_{\tau,2} + \kappa^{(\tau)}. \tag{6.22}$$

The first-order conditions and their consequences in this economy are derived in detail in appendix 6.15. We summarize the major properties of the model here in a series of figures.

Analytic results for the labor allocation in the unstressed equilibrium give $n_0/n \to s(1+\theta)/6$. Pinning $3n_0 e_0 = C$ at the lower limit of this equilibrium, we arrive at a critical lower population for $N = 2(n+n_0)$ of

$$N_C \equiv \frac{2C}{3e_0}\left(1 + \frac{n}{n_0}\right) = \frac{2C}{3e_0}\left(1 + \frac{6}{s(1+\theta)}\right), \tag{6.23}$$

roughly six times larger for $s \ll 1$ than the corresponding CE critical population.

The stress level on the price system, represented as the shadow price value of the capacity constraint, Λe_0, is shown versus the population below its threshold level N/N_C in figure 6.4.

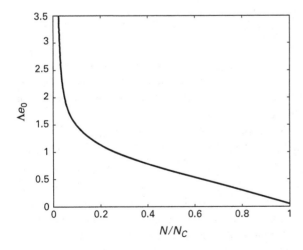

Figure 6.4
Stress level as measured by the shadow price $\Lambda e_0 \in [0, 3.5]$, as a function of $N/N_C \leq 1$.

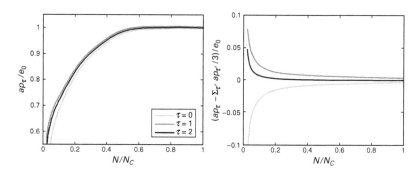

Figure 6.5

Absolute prices ap_τ/e_0 for periods 0, 1, 2. The left panel is absolute; the right panel is relative to the mean: $\left(ap_\tau - \sum_{\tau'} ap_{\tau'}/3\right)/e_0$ for periods 0, 1, 2.

The response of food prices to $N/N_C < 1$ is shown, both in absolute terms and with the three-period mean subtracted, in figure 6.5. In the unstressed equilibrium, prices approximate the CE value $ap_\tau/e_0 \to 1$ to $\mathcal{O}(s)$.

The relation of investment to the market value of food in the competitive equilibrium is just that of the optimal labor allocation: $n_0 e_0/(nap_{CE} + n_0 e_0) = n_0/(n + n_0) \approx s(1+\theta)$ for $s \ll 1$. In the numerical solutions we show $\theta = 1/2$, leading to a CE investment level of $3se_0/2$. In the unstressed noncooperative equilibrium, prospector investment levels $\hat{\sigma}_0 \approx se_0$, and $\hat{\sigma}_1 \approx se_0/2$ for $s \ll 1$. In the farmer sector, where generation $\tau = 0$ depends on IGTs from the $\tau = 2$ generation, which are discounted by θ, the unstressed equilibrium investment levels are $\sigma_1 = e_0 s/2$ and $\sigma_0 = \kappa^{(2)} = e_0 s\theta$.

The distribution of investments needed to meet the constraint $n(\sigma_0 + \sigma_1) + n_0(\hat{\sigma}_0 + \hat{\sigma}_1) = C = 3n_0 e_0$ in noncooperative equilibria with shadow prices is shown in figure 6.6. With decrease of $N/N_C < 1$, an increasing fraction of investment is met by prospectors.

While three-period average utility has been set equal for farmers and prospectors as the condition that determines the labor allocation n_0/n, the utilities within individual periods may still differ. Measures of this difference such as variance over the three generations may be used as a measure of the failure of allocative efficiency by the IGT mechanism, or the minimum single-generation utility may be used as a fragility threshold in a coalitional-form solution concept: if it falls below the noncooperative equilibrium utility for low-efficiency production, this generation has no incentive to remain within the coalition that cooperates to produce high-yielding capital stock.

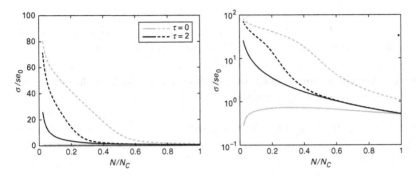

Figure 6.6
Investment levels: or who is contributing most to meet the capacity constraint for the jointly constructed good. Values σ are normalized by se_0. The lighter lines represent period 0; darker lines are period 2. Solid lines are farmers, dashed lines are prospectors. The left panel is linear; the right panel is the same data on a log scale.

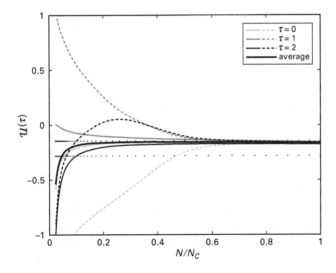

Figure 6.7
Utilities for generations 0, 1, 2 are indicated by line styles. Dashed lines mark prospectors, solid lines are farmers. Heavy black is the average, which is equal for both types. The upper black dotted level is the CE utility, and the lower black dotted level is the CE minus the correction for autarchic production $2(1+\theta)\log(0.01)$.

Figure 6.7 shows the absolute utility levels versus $N/N_C \leq 1$. The utility levels of the CE with high-yielding and with low-yielding production are shown for comparison. The generation-($\tau = 0$) prospectors suffer utilities far below autarchy for $N/N_C < 0.4$. The lower limit for population shown is $N/N_C \sim 1/50$, so still twice the sacrifice in total rate of capital services encountered in going from high-yielding production to autarchy.

6.8.6   An inside bank as a pass-through entity for gold, in place of intergenerational transfers

In the banking model agents of both types borrow or lend gold at a fixed rate of interest ρ to couple the expenditures between their own young and old periods, rather than across generations as in the IGT economy. Since the purpose behind banking is to optimize utilities, the bank will return all gold to the market economy within each cycle of generations. Since it is an inside bank, it has no other source of gold, and thus cannot return more than it receives. The condition that gold flow balance within each production cycle therefore closes the system.

The bank has no remaining degrees of freedom if it is constrained to balance gold flows. However, unlike in chapter 5, we are not modeling the costs of banking, so the bank is not required to make a profit in order to function. In this sense the bank is a strategic dummy, implicitly representing a banker who is equivalent to an unpaid bureaucrat.

The model introduces loan variables $\left(g_0^{(\tau)}, g_1^{(\tau)}\right)$ for farmers and $\left(\hat{g}_0^{(\tau)}, \hat{g}_1^{(\tau)}\right)$ for prospectors in each period, along with their associated Kuhn-Tucker multipliers $\Lambda_B^{(\tau)}$ and $\hat{\Lambda}_B^{(\tau)}$. The Λ_B values are varied on a finite interval to implement the linear bankruptcy constraint of previous sections. We give values for these shadow prices of the bankruptcy constraint at interior solutions, but will assume that the penalty is strong enough that strategic default is always excluded, and will therefore not introduce a separate notation for the strength of the penalty. The sign convention will be that positive g denotes borrowing by agents from the bank, while negative $\hat{g}$ denotes lending to the bank.

The Lagrangians for farmers are then expansions of the common terms from Eq. (6.15) of the form

$$\mathcal{L}^{(\tau)} = \mathcal{L}_{\text{Common}}^{(\tau)} - \Lambda_B \left[(1 + \rho) g_0^{(\tau)} + g_1^{(\tau)} \right], \tag{6.24}$$

with an equivalent with hatted variables for prospectors. The same constraint term works for both borrowing and lending, ensuring that the amount withdrawn can never exceed the discounted negative of the amount deposited.

The corresponding budget sequences for farmers and prospectors, respectively, become

$$0 = \mu_0^{(\tau)}$$
$$\mu_0^{(\tau)} + g_0^{(\tau)} - b_0^{(\tau)} - \sigma_0 \delta_{\tau,0} = \mu_1^{(\tau)}$$
$$\mu_1^{(\tau)} + q^{(\tau)} p_\tau = b_1^{(\tau)} + \sigma_1 \delta_{\tau,2} + g_1^{(\tau)}, \qquad (6.25)$$
$$e_0 = \hat{\mu}_0^{(\tau)}$$
$$\hat{\mu}_0^{(\tau)} - \hat{b}_0^{(\tau)} - \hat{\sigma}_0 \delta_{\tau,0} - \left(-\hat{g}_0^{(\tau)}\right) = \hat{\mu}_1^{(\tau)}$$
$$\hat{\mu}_1^{(\tau)} + \hat{g}_1^{(\tau)} = \hat{b}_1^{(\tau)} + \hat{\sigma}_1 \delta_{\tau,2}. \qquad (6.26)$$

6.8.6.1 Solution properties, and a review of the problem of achieving high-yielding production below the critical population size A full analysis of the first-order conditions and budget conditions, and their solutions, is given in appendix 6.16. There we show that the full return of gold from the banks to the individual sector is not compatible with the first-order conditions governing farmer investment, at arbitrary combinations of interest rate ρ and population composition n_0/n. The two conditions can be met only for a function ρ which approaches unity at $\Lambda e_0 = 0$, and *decreases* with increasing Λe_0, shown in figure 6.10. To understand the meaning and consequence of this interest rate, we review the problem of achieving high-yielding production in a society whose population N is below the critical value N_C required to invest the required gold without a shadow price.

The unstressed, noncooperative equilibrium with low-yield production is always a joint solution (autarchy) to this strategic market game at all populations $N \leq N_C$. If we consider the comparative statics of this class of solutions with fixed n_0/n as population is increased, we find a class of solutions homogeneous of order one in population size, bids, and investment levels, with a fixed interest rate $\rho = 1$. At $N = N_C$, the utility level undergoes a discontinuous jump $2(1 + \theta) \log(1/\epsilon)$ as low-yield production is replaced with high-yield production at the same investment level.

For $N \geq 2C/3e_0$, however, agents may also lower the interest rate, reallocate labor until $n_0 = 2C/3e_0$, invest at a higher absolute rate with most investments made by the expanded prospector sector, and adopt a noncooperative equilibrium in which the marginal utility of scarce food and uneven consumption of services is balanced by the shadow price of the capacity constraint. As $N \to N_C$ from below, n_0 remains fixed at $2C/3e_0$, the excess gold per capita declines, prospector deposits and interest payments on them decline as well, and farmer investment levels for services in the young and old periods are driven to be nearly equal by cash flow constraints. This solution—$\sigma_0 = \sigma_1 + \mathcal{O}(s)$—is also a property of the competitive equilibrium, but not of any of the noncooperative equilibria we construct in this chapter, because the returns on investment and hence the first-order conditions differ for σ_0 and σ_1. In order to make the optimal investment levels converge, the discount factor to interest payments $1 + \rho$ must approach 2, returning the economy to the value $\rho = 1$ of the unstressed equilibrium. This sequence provides a continuous interpolating path between low-yield and high-yield production, as the population size is increased to its critical value.

6.8.6.2   Consumption, prices, and critical population size   For $s \ll 1$, utility levels are dominated by food consumption. Because prospectors borrow in both periods to buy food, their consumption becomes uneven (by the factor $1 + \rho$) in the old versus the young periods. Their young-period consumption is governed by their endowment and remains high, while their old-period consumption is further augmented by interest that they *earn*.

Since farmers always borrow and prospectors always lend, food prices ap_τ/e_0 must compensate the farmers for the interest factor $(1 + \rho)$ by which the gold value of prospector consumption is inflated. For logarithmic utilities of the form (6.4), this compensation gives the scaling of prices

$$\frac{ap_\tau}{e_0} \rightarrow \sqrt{1 + \rho} \tag{6.27}$$

for $s \ll 1$. Therefore in the unstressed equilibrium, $ap_\tau/e_0 \rightarrow \sqrt{2} + \mathcal{O}(s)$, a large distortion from the CE value of unity.

The corresponding critical population size, derived in appendix 6.16, becomes

$$N_C \equiv \frac{2C}{3e_0}\left(1 + \frac{n}{n_0}\right) = \frac{2C}{3e_0}\left(1 + \frac{3}{\sqrt{2s}}\right). \tag{6.28}$$

Numerical solutions for absolute and relative price levels, investment levels by each type and period, stress level Λe_0 and interest rate ρ, and single-period absolute utility levels, for comparison to those in the IGT economy without banking, are shown in figures 6.8–6.11.

6.8.6.3   Gold requirements of the bank   The gold requirements of the bank in order to meet net withdrawals with a minimum balance of zero are shown in figure 6.12. To interpret the per-capita version, refer to figure 6.8 showing that at the lower end of the N/N_C range, $ap_\tau/e_0 \sim 1$. A (gold stock) / $(n + n_0)\,e_0 \sim$ 0.3 means that gold stored in the bank to buffer prices equals almost $1/3$ the

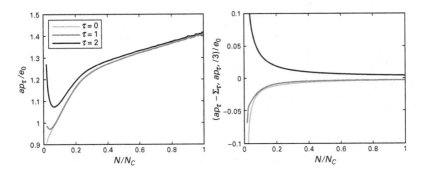

Figure 6.8

Absolute prices ap_τ/e_0 for periods 0, 1, 2. The left panel is absolute; the right panel is relative to the mean: $\left(ap_\tau - \sum_{\tau'} ap_{\tau'}/3\right)/e_0$ for periods 0, 1, 2. Relative prices are shown on the same scale as for figure 6.5 (absolute prices approach $\sqrt{2}$ in the unstressed equilibrium, rather than unity as in the IGT economy or the competitive equilibrium). Note that for banking $ap_2 > ap_1 > ap_0$, and we can confirm with the analytic expressions (6.90) that this must be the case. For IGTs the order was $ap_1 > ap_2 > ap_0$.

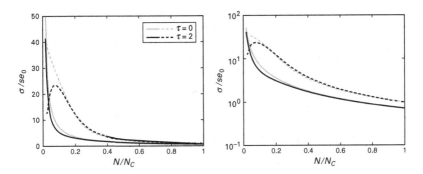

Figure 6.9

Investment levels: or who is providing the public good. Values σ are normalized by se_0. Solid lines are farmers, dashed are prospectors. The left panel is linear; the right panel is the same data on a log scale. The pairings in the unstressed equilibrium are now different than for the IGT economy, with both-period farmers grouping together and both-period prospectors grouping together. Here the cause is that the interest rate $\rho \to 1$ in the unstressed equilibrium causes $1 + \rho$ to cancel the factor-of-2 differences that would otherwise distinguish σ_0 from σ_1.

total value of the food markets. (At the lower limit shown here, $n/n_0 \sim 5$, so $\sim 5/6$ of the economy's value is still represented by the food market. However, this condition is still stressed relative to the unstressed equilibrium value $n/n_0 \sim 50$.)

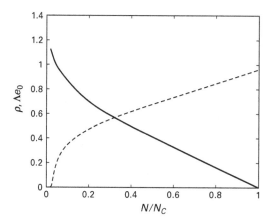

Figure 6.10

Interest rate ρ (dashed line), and stress level (solid line) as measured by the shadow price Λe_0, as a function of $N/N_C \leq 1$. Note that now $\Lambda e_0 \in [0, \sim 1]$, so banking permits a lower shadow price for the capacity constraint at comparable N/N_C.

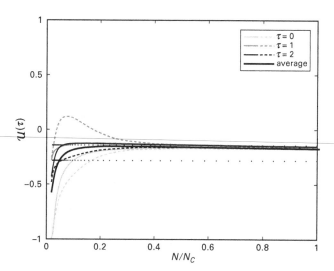

Figure 6.11

Utilities for generations 0, 1, 2, with active regulation. Solid lines are farmers; dashed lines are prospectors. Heavy black is the average, again set equal for the two types. The upper black dotted level is the CE utility, and the lower black dotted level is the CE minus the correction for autarchic production $2(1 + \theta)\log(0.01)$. Axes are the same as those in figure 6.7 for comparison.

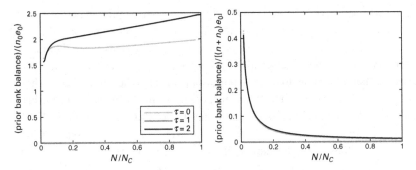

Figure 6.12

Prior gold balances of the bank in the three periods, normalized by $n_0 e_0$ (left) or by $(n + n_0) e_0$ (right), as a function of N/N_C. (Recall that n_0 is fixed by the capacity constraint $C = 3n_0 e_0$.) Line styles indicate prior balances coming into periods $\tau = 0, 1, 2$. (Prior balance for $\tau = 1$ is zero, and coincides with the lower boundary of the figure.)

The combination of price distortions, and the requirement that significant amounts of gold be held out of circulation, show the main weaknesses of banking with a commodity money that is also an input to production, and motivate the features of a fiat banking model considered next.

6.9   An Economy with a Central Bank that Lends Fiat and Serves as a Reserve Buyer for Gold

Our third OLG model changes the means of payment from gold to fiat money issued by a central bank.

6.9.1   Institutional structure of a fiat OLG economy

The removal of gold as a means of payment requires the introduction of a gold market, which we make a buy-sell market equivalent to the food market. This move immediately converts prospectors into a class of *producers* on an equal economic footing with farmers, and leads to prices in the unstressed noncooperative equilibrium that converge to those in the CE. Fiat is introduced into the economy through loans which are recollected with interest at rate ρ.

The removal of gold as a means of payment also eliminates a form of cross-generation transmission through the food markets, removing demand for gold from the open markets in the two periods when it cannot be used to invest in capital stock. Therefore in addition to being a lender of fiat, the central bank must become a buyer of gold in two periods, and a net supplier in period $\tau = 0$. Its role as a gold buyer defines the numéraire for fiat. At the same time, the government's freedom to dictate offer prices for gold in periods when there is no open-market demand, together with the interest rate, provide control degrees of freedom that may be set to achieve policy objectives of the central bank. These degrees of freedom are not all independent. As in the inside-gold-banking model of the last section, we suppose that the central bank returns all gold to the private sector within each production cycle, and we also assume that it balances the flow of fiat to stabilize its price. The result of these constraints is that the central bank is left with two independent control variables that it may set freely within finite intervals.

6.9.1.1   The period structure for a model with gold markets and fiat money   The natural use of the existing OLG period structure makes gold markets parallel to food markets in their operation. Bids and offers are placed in one period; purchases and proceeds are distributed as the initial values of goods and money for the next period. Under this market structure, ($\tau = 0$) farmers— who were not yet born in the previous period $\tau = 2$—have no way to secure delivery of gold in time for them to invest in capital stock. Since all investors will still be alive in their young period, these farmers also have no publicly held service stream from which to draw. This situation results in zero consumption and singular ($-\infty$) utilities, unless we reintroduce intergenerational transfers, which are now no longer money but simply durable property. The reintroduction of IGTs restores the relation between investments and IGTs in the farmer sector which are the first two lines of Eq. (6.61), except for a factor $(1 + \rho)$ because the money must be borrowed to buy gold.

6.9.1.2   The use of control variables in the fiat economy   The fiat economy admits a regular $\rho \to 0$ limit of solutions for the unstressed equilibrium.

Maintaining $\rho \ll 1$ for all values of N/N_C is not optimal policy for a benevolent central bank. If interest rates are set to zero for populations below the critical size, the model solution becomes identical to that of the prefinancial IGT economy shown in figure 6.7. The stresses lead to price reductions and severe dispersion of utilities for agents in different generations. The following sections show that a policy objective of minimizing dispersion of utility between the generations of prospectors leads to a schedule for interest rates and payments that remains closer to the competitive equilibrium for smaller populations $N < N_C$ than either of the previous two models.

6.9.2 Farmer budgets, preferences, and first-order conditions

Because fiat rather than gold is the money in this economy, two separate budgets coexist, for gold and for money. Parallel to the notations $\left(\mu_0^{(\tau)}, \mu_1^{(\tau)}\right)$ for beginning young-period and old-period money budgets, we introduce notations $\left(\gamma_0^{(\tau)}, \gamma_1^{(\tau)}\right)$ for beginning young-period and old-period gold stocks. Intergenerational transfers (which in most periods may be zero) provide the young-period endowment of gold for farmers, and the old-period gold stock may be augmented with gold purchases. Gold in either period may be used for investment, and in the old period part of it may also provide an IGT to the next generation. The equations for gold stocks of farmers are

$$\kappa^{(\tau-1)} = \gamma_0^{(\tau)}$$
$$\gamma_0^{(\tau)} - \sigma_0 \delta_{\tau,0} = \gamma_1^{(\tau)} \geq 0$$
$$\gamma_1^{(\tau)} + \frac{b_{G0}^{(\tau)}}{p_{G\tau}} - \sigma_1 \delta_{\tau,2} - \kappa^{(\tau)} \geq 0. \tag{6.29}$$

The Lagrangian for farmers contains the common terms (6.15) as well as a constraint term for repayment of young-period borrowing (now denominated in fiat), as well as two new constraint terms for gold stocks, which we enforce with Kuhn-Tucker multipliers $\eta_{G0}^{(\tau)}$ and $\eta_{G1}^{(\tau)}$, both on the interval $[0, \infty)$:

$$\mathcal{L}^{(\tau)} = \mathcal{L}_{\text{Common}}^{(\tau)} - \Lambda_B^{(\tau)} \left[(1+\rho) g_0^{(\tau)} + g_1^{(\tau)} \right]$$
$$+ \left(\gamma_0^{(\tau)} - \sigma_0 \delta_{\tau,0} \right) \eta_{G0}^{(\tau)} + \left(\gamma_1^{(\tau)} + \frac{b_{G0}^{(\tau)}}{p_{G\tau}} - \sigma_1 \delta_{\tau,2} - \kappa^{(\tau)} \right) \eta_{G1}^{(\tau)}. \tag{6.30}$$

The loans, bids, and repayments that determine the forms of the money balances in the budget terms of the common Lagrangian (6.15), for the farmers in this economy, become

$$0 = \mu_0^{(\tau)}$$
$$\mu_0^{(\tau)} + g_0^{(\tau)} - b_0^{(\tau)} - b_{G0}^{(\tau)} = \mu_1^{(\tau)} \geq 0$$
$$\mu_1^{(\tau)} + q^{(\tau)} p_\tau - b_1^{(\tau)} + g_1^{(\tau)} \geq 0. \tag{6.31}$$

Bids may now be made for gold as well as for food, but investments in capital stock are now made from the gold supply (6.29) rather than from the money budget (6.31).

The terms in the farmer first-order conditions that follow from these preference and budget expressions (suppressing the variations in Kuhn-Tucker multipliers which simply enforce the inequality constraints), are then

$$
\begin{aligned}
0 = \delta \mathcal{L}^{(\tau)} =& \left[\frac{1}{A_0^{(\tau)} p_\tau} - \eta_1^{(\tau)}\right]\left(\delta b_0^{(\tau)} - p_\tau \delta q^{(\tau)}\right) - \eta_0^{(\tau)} \delta b_0^{(\tau)} + \left[\frac{1}{b_1^{(\tau)}} - \eta_1^{(\tau)}\right]\delta b_1^{(\tau)} \\
&+ \left[\eta_0^{(\tau)} + \eta_1^{(\tau)} - (1+\rho)\Lambda_B^{(\tau)}\right]\delta g_0^{(\tau)} + \left[\eta_1^{(\tau)} - \Lambda_B^{(\tau)}\right]\delta g_1^{(\tau)} \\
&+ \left[\frac{2s}{\sigma_0} + 2(1+\theta)\Lambda - \left(\eta_{G0}^{(\tau)} + \eta_{G1}^{(\tau)}\right)\right]\delta \sigma_0 \delta_{\tau,0} \\
&+ \left[\frac{s}{\sigma_1} + (1+2\theta)\Lambda - \eta_{G1}^{(\tau)}\right]\delta \sigma_1 \delta_{\tau,2} \\
&+ \left[\frac{2\theta s}{\kappa^{(\tau)}} + 2\theta\Lambda - \eta_{G1}^{(\tau)}\right]\delta \kappa^{(\tau)} \delta_{\tau,2} \\
&+ \left[\frac{\eta_{G1}^{(\tau)}}{p_{G\tau}} - \left(\eta_0^{(\tau)} + \eta_1^{(\tau)}\right)\right]\delta b_{G0}^{(\tau)}.
\end{aligned}
\tag{6.32}
$$

6.9.3   Prospector budgets, preferences, and first-order conditions

For prospectors, the endowment e_0 from their production function, rather than intergenerational transfers, furnishes their initial stock of gold, and they may offer part or all of this (a quantity $\hat{q}_G^{(\tau)}$) for sale on the gold market to provide money for food, as well as investing it in capital stock. The equations for the prospectors' gold stocks, denoted $\left(\hat{\gamma}_0^{(\tau)}, \hat{\gamma}_1^{(\tau)}\right)$, are then

$$
e_0 = \hat{\gamma}_0^{(\tau)}
$$
$$
\hat{\gamma}_0^{(\tau)} - \hat{\sigma}_0 \delta_{\tau,0} - \hat{q}_G^{(\tau)} = \hat{\gamma}_1^{(\tau)} \geq 0
$$
$$
\hat{\gamma}_1^{(\tau)} - \sigma_1 \delta_{\tau,2} \geq 0.
\tag{6.33}
$$

The prospector Lagrangian is directly parallel to Eq. (6.30) for farmers (with hatted variables in $\mathcal{L}_{\mathrm{Common}}^{(\tau)}$), and with modified gold stock constraint terms enforced with Kuhn-Tucker multipliers $\hat{\eta}_{G0}^{(\tau)}$ and $\hat{\eta}_{G0}^{(\tau)}$:

$$
\begin{aligned}
\hat{\mathcal{L}}^{(\tau)} =& \mathcal{L}_{\mathrm{Common}}^{(\tau)} - \hat{\Lambda}_B^{(\tau)}\left[(1+\rho)\hat{g}_0^{(\tau)} + \hat{g}_1^{(\tau)}\right] \\
&+ \left(\hat{\gamma}_0^{(\tau)} - \hat{\sigma}_0 \delta_{\tau,0} - \hat{q}_G^{(\tau)}\right)\hat{\eta}_{G0}^{(\tau)} + \left(\hat{\gamma}_1^{(\tau)} - \hat{\sigma}_1 \delta_{\tau,2}\right)\hat{\eta}_{G1}^{(\tau)}.
\end{aligned}
\tag{6.34}
$$

The loans, bids, and repayments that determine the forms of the money balances in the budget terms of the common Lagrangian (6.15), for the prospectors in this economy, then become

$$0 = \hat{\mu}_0^{(\tau)}$$
$$\hat{\mu}_0^{(\tau)} + \hat{g}_0^{(\tau)} - \hat{b}_0^{(\tau)} = \hat{\mu}_1^{(\tau)} \geq 0$$
$$\hat{\mu}_1^{(\tau)} + \hat{q}_G^{(\tau)} p_{G\tau} - \hat{b}_1^{(\tau)} + \hat{g}_1^{(\tau)} \geq 0. \tag{6.35}$$

The terms in the prospector first-order conditions that follow from these preference and budget expressions (again suppressing the variations in Kuhn-Tucker multipliers which enforce the inequality constraints), are then

$$
\begin{aligned}
0 = \delta\hat{\mathcal{L}}^{(\tau)} = {} & \left[\frac{1}{\hat{b}_0^{(\tau)}} - \left(\hat{\eta}_0^{(\tau)} + \hat{\eta}_1^{(\tau)}\right)\right]\delta\hat{b}_0^{(\tau)} + \left[\frac{1}{\hat{b}_1^{(\tau)}} - \hat{\eta}_1^{(\tau)}\right]\delta\hat{b}_1^{(\tau)} \\
& + \left[\hat{\eta}_0^{(\tau)} + \hat{\eta}_1^{(\tau)} - (1+\rho)\hat{\Lambda}_B^{(\tau)}\right]\delta\hat{b}_0^{(\tau)} + \left[\hat{\eta}_1^{(\tau)} - \hat{\Lambda}_B^{(\tau)}\right]\delta\hat{b}_1^{(\tau)} \\
& + \left[\frac{2s}{\hat{\sigma}_0} + 2(1+\theta)\Lambda - \left(\hat{\eta}_{G0}^{(\tau)} + \hat{\eta}_{G1}^{(\tau)}\right)\right]\delta\hat{\sigma}_0\delta_{\tau,0} \\
& + \left[\frac{s}{\hat{\sigma}_1} + (1+2\theta)\Lambda - \hat{\eta}_{G1}^{(\tau)}\right]\delta\hat{\sigma}_1\delta_{\tau,2} \\
& + \left[\hat{\eta}_1^{(\tau)}p_{G\tau} - \left(\hat{\eta}_{G0}^{(\tau)} + \hat{\eta}_{G1}^{(\tau)}\right)\right]\delta\hat{q}^{(\tau)}. \tag{6.36}
\end{aligned}
$$

6.9.4 Price formation and the central bank as a reserve buyer for gold

Food clears according to the price formation rule (6.10). If an analogous rule to Eq. (6.11) were adopted, which we write here as

$$
p_{G,\tau}^{\text{private only}} = \frac{nb_{G,1}^{(\tau-1)} + n_0\left(\hat{b}_{G,1}^{(\tau-1)} + \hat{b}_{G,0}^{(\tau)}\right)}{nq_G^{(\tau)}}, \tag{6.37}
$$

receiving bids only from private individuals, then a price of zero would result in periods $\tau = 0, 1$, because in these generations no individual has a salvage value for gold in his old period, when it would be delivered from the markets. The ($\tau = 0, 1$) prospectors would then have no source of income, and interior solutions would be unattainable.

The solution we adopt here to this market failure is to make the central bank a reserve buyer and seller of gold. Denoting the bank's bids and offers by $B_G^{(\tau)}$ and $Q_G^{(\tau)}$, respectively, we modify the price formation rule (6.11) to the form

$$p_{G,\tau} = \frac{nb_{G,1}^{(\tau-1)} + n_0\left(\hat{b}_{G,1}^{(\tau-1)} + \hat{b}_{G,0}^{(\tau)}\right) + B_G^{(\tau)}}{nq_G^{(\tau)} + Q_G^{(\tau)}}. \tag{6.38}$$

Participation by the central bank in the open gold markets does two things. First, it defines the numéraire of fiat, which would be left undetermined by the mere existence of a nonzero interest rate. Second, it gives the central bank several control variables, by which it may achieve policy objectives for distribution and welfare in the society.

To identify the control variables as well as to make a minimal model, we constrain the central bank's policies to be drawn from those which return all purchased gold to the economy within each three-period cycle, and which balance all payments of fiat aggregated over gold purchases and sales and interest payments. The former constraint may be seen as a social welfare condition: since gold has value as an input to production, and since the central bank (a strategic dummy) does not take profits or pay for labor, net extraction of gold would constitute waste of part of the endowment. The latter constraint ensures stable fiat prices for food and gold (no net fiat injected into the private economy) while enabling solutions without strategic default (no net fiat extraction required to avoid default).

We may finally require that the bank not engage in wash selling either as a buyer or a seller of gold. Any allocation that can be achieved by a solution with wash selling can be achieved by another solution without it, which differs only by additive constants in the accounts of gold and fiat held by the bank. Excluding wash selling results in bank moves that return all gold to the private economy in (at least) one round when the bank is a net seller, giving the lowest level of reserved gold in that class of solutions. (Solutions of the model will show that the bank is a buyer in two periods and a seller only in period $\tau = 2$.)

The four strategic parameters available to the central bank are the interest rate ρ, its two bid levels $B_G^{(0)}$ and $B_G^{(1)}$, and the offer level $Q_G^{(2)}$. Of these, the offer $Q_G^{(2)}$ is constrained by the requirement to recycle gold, and one combination of the bids and ρ is constrained by the requirement to recycle all fiat.

6.9.4.1 The central bank's policy objective: minimizing the cross-generation dispersion of prospector utilities

We demonstrate the use of the two remaining unconstrained variables as control parameters by choosing the policy objective of the bank to be minimization of the cross-generation variance of prospector utilities,[9]

$$\text{var}\left(\left\{\mathcal{U}_{\text{Pros}}^{(\tau)}\right\}\right) \equiv \frac{1}{3}\sum_{\tau}\left(\mathcal{U}_{\text{Pros}}^{(\tau)}\right)^2 - \left(\frac{1}{3}\sum_{\tau}\mathcal{U}_{\text{Pros}}^{(\tau)}\right)^2. \tag{6.39}$$

Any feasible policy objective could, of course, be implemented by the central bank. The motivation to minimize the variance (6.39) is that it extends the presumptive region of validity of the joint high-production noncooperative equilibrium. While we have not considered the problem of strategic labor reallocation at the level of individuals, the justification for the joint noncooperative equilibrium clearly becomes questionable if one generation of one profession systematically has very disparate and very low utility. To avoid secession of such a generation, a more fully specified game might require other constraints against individual labor reallocation.

In whatever domain the central bank can maintain all population utilities above the level of the joint noncooperative equilibrium with autarchy, there is no utility improvement for any single generation or profession to secede, and the high-production noncooperative equilibrium stands on its own without further qualification.

6.9.5   Properties of the fiat economy without and with active control from the central bank

The first-order conditions, budget conditions, price cycle, and consequences of central bank purchases and sales are solved in appendix 6.17.

The availability of control in the fiat economy enables both higher mean utilities and lower prospector utility variance than either the IGT or gold-banking economies at almost all values of n_0/n. The noncooperative equilibrium with zero interest rate, as noted above, is identical to that for the preinstitutional IGT economy. Since the optimal interest rate $\rho \to 0$ as the shadow price on the capacity constraint $\Lambda e_0 \to 0$, the fiat economy has the same critical population size (6.23) as the preinstitutional IGT economy. With decreasing population size $N/N_C < 1$, increasing interest is required to redirect money flows, and most bids for gold are made in period $\tau = 0$, causing a rise in gold prices p_{G0}.

6.9.5.1   How interest rate and bid structure serve to reduce variance of prospector utilities   Figure 6.13 illustrates the effects of interest rates, and the relative bids offered by the government when it is the sole buyer of gold, on utility levels. When $\rho = 0$, gold prices become constant over periods, the

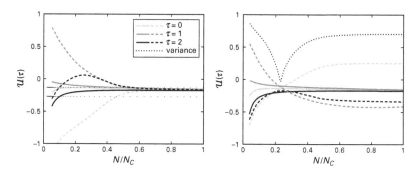

Figure 6.13

The use of interest to reduce variance in the prospector utilities. At left, generation-(0, 1, 2) utilities for farmers (solid) and prospectors (dashed) at $\rho = 0$ for a range of $N/N_C < 1$. Divergence of prospector utilities creates an incentive for some generations to leave the economy, because they are worse off than they would be under autarchy. At right, generation-(0, 1, 2) utilities in the same range of $N/N_C < 1$ for values $\rho = 0.069$, $\alpha = -0.522$, which minimize variance of the three-generation prospector utilities at a particular value N/N_C. The dotted curve is $1 + 8 \times \log(\text{variance})$, used for illustration to show the extent of reduction.

prospector gold offers and investment levels (6.102, 6.103) become those of the IGT equilibrium, central bank bids in fiat (6.108) substitute for prospector bids in the IGT gold-denominated markets, and farmer consumption and intergenerational transfers become those of the preinstitutional IGT model. In this limit the solution to the fiat model converges to that of the IGT model. In particular, under increasing shadow price Λe_0 with decreasing $N/N_C < 1$, uneven per-period demand for gold causes prospector utilities to diverge.

If instead parameters $\rho = 0.069$, $\alpha = -0.522$ (defined below in Eq. (6.120)) are chosen, different-generation utilities become very different in the $\Lambda e_0 \to 0$ equilibrium, but at a particular value $N/N_C < 1$ they compensate for uneven gold demand to bring different generations' utilities together.

Figure 6.14 illustrates the use of full control over interest rates and the offer prices in periods (1, 2), by choosing values (ρ, θ) as functions of N/N_C to minimize the cross-generation variance of the prospector utilities at each value of $N/N_C < 1$. In the absence of control ($\rho = 0$), gold prices remain stable but food prices decline in all periods with decreasing N/N_C. Prospector utilities diverge sharply, making ($\tau = 0$) prospectors worse off than they would be under autarchy for $N/N_C < 0.425$. If the government raises interest rates and bids appropriately, a rising price of gold in period $\tau = 0$ stabilizes all prospector utilities, and also food prices.

The variance-minimizing contour of ρ and θ is shown in figure 6.15, together with the shadow price that it generates as a function of N/N_C.

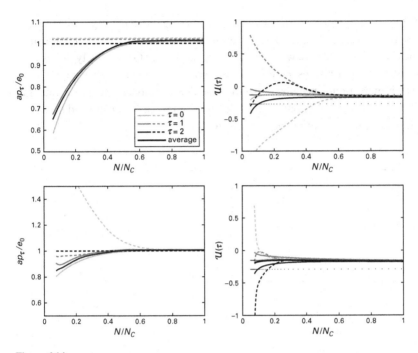

Figure 6.14
The use of tuned values of ρ and α to minimize variance of prospector utilities at each value of $N/N_C < 1$. Left panels: food (solid) and gold (dashed) prices; right panels: single-generation farmer (solid) and prospector (dashed) utilities. Top panels: with $\rho = 0$; bottom panels: with ρ and α along the variance-minimizing contour.

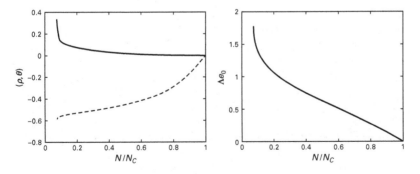

Figure 6.15
Left: ρ (solid) and α (dashed) values that minimize cross-generation variance of prospector utilities; right: stress level measured as the shadow price value of the prospector endowment Λe_0, both as functions of $N/N_C < 1$. This control contour was used to produce the utilities and prices in the lower panels of Figure 6.14.

6.9.5.2   Properties of the variance-minimizing fiat economy   The remaining price and investment-level plots in the fiat economy, for comparison to the other cases, are shown in figures 6.16 and 6.17. Qualitatively, the investment levels closely resemble those of figure 6.6 for the IGT economy, even when interest rates become nonzero. Note that the largest value of ρ found in figure 6.15 is $\rho \sim 0.5$, only half of the interest rate at the unstressed noncooperative equilibrium of the gold-banking economy.

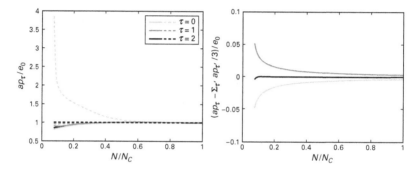

Figure 6.16

Absolute and relative food (solid) and gold (dashed) prices for the fiat model, using full control. Only food price divergence is shown relative to the mean in the right panel to reduce clutter; gold price divergence is dominated by period $\tau = 0$, as shown in the left panel.

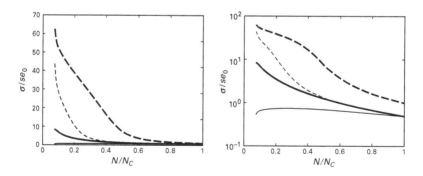

Figure 6.17

Investment levels for farmers (solid) and prospectors (dashed). The darker lines represent σ_0; lighter lines are σ_1. The left panel uses a linear scale, the right panel a log scale.

6.10   Summary and Comparisons

The noncooperative equilibria are inefficient relative to the competitive rational-expectations equilibrium. This is expressed both in lower average utilities (true by the definition of efficiencies) and also in a larger critical size of the population required to meet the capacity constraint in an unstressed equilibrium (no shadow price for the capacity constraint).

The critical population size and the market value of the food endowment relative to the gold endowment are shown in table 6.2.

Gold banking buffers prices and equalizes utilities for the three generations significantly more effectively than intergenerational transfers, and for $\theta \leq \sqrt{2} - 1/2 \approx 0.9$, it leads to lower critical population size. However, since the mean utility at the critical size is lower than the utility maintained with a nonzero shadow price, the lower value of N_C simply means that this inefficient noncooperative equilibrium obtains for a larger range of absolute population size than in the other models. It is also a property of this model that, for small populations, a significant fraction of the wealth of the economy is stored in the bank in some periods to buffer prices.

In a real society, the relation of a population to the critical value for its noncooperative equilibrium with each money supply is not the relevant variable for comparison of financing systems. Rather, it is the absolute population size relative to the size of the gold supply required to meet the capacity constraint. In figure 6.18 we illustrate the interaction of N_C and utility levels by plotting mean utility versus N normalized relative to the critical population $(N_C)_{CE}$ at the *competitive equilibrium*. The fiat and IGT economies have the

Table 6.2
N_C values and relative wealth values ap_τ/e_0p_{G2} for various types of economy

	CE	Fiat	Bank	IGT
N_C	$\frac{C}{e_0}\left(\frac{2}{3}+\frac{2}{3(1+\theta)s}\right)$	$\frac{C}{e_0}\left(\frac{2}{3}+\frac{4}{(1+2\theta)s}\right)$	$\frac{C}{e_0}\left(\frac{2}{3}+\frac{\sqrt{2}}{s}\right)$	$\frac{C}{e_0}\left(\frac{2}{3}+\frac{4}{(1+2\theta)s}\right)$
ap_τ/e_0p_{G2}	1	1	$\sqrt{1+\rho}\to\sqrt{2}$	1

Note: CE = competitive equilibrium; Bank = unstressed noncooperative equilibria with banking and balanced interest payments; IGT = intergenerational transfers without banking. In all models except the fiat economy, gold may be taken as numéraire, in which case $p_{G2} \equiv 1$. In the fiat economy, this factor removes the numéraire dependence from ap_τ. p_τ values differ only by $\mathcal{O}(s)$ in this regime, so which τ is chosen does not matter. The CE price system is drawn from Eqs. (6.8) and (6.9).

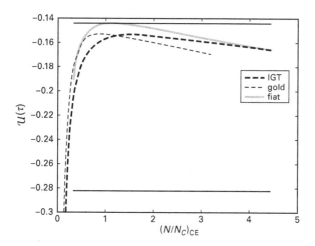

Figure 6.18

Cross-generation average utilities (by construction the same for farmers as for prospectors) in the three models, as a function of N now measured in absolute size relative to $(N_C)_{CE}$ of the competitive equilibrium, rather than relative to the N_C specific to each economy. The fiat economy produces the highest maximal utility, converging to the CE value when the actual population is close to the CE critical value (1 on the abscissa).

same critical sizes and unstressed noncooperative equilibria, but over the range $N < N_C$ the controlled fiat economy yields higher utility, closely approaching the CE utility when $N \sim (N_C)_{CE}$.

Mean utilities only present one aspect of social welfare. It must also be remembered, from the contrast between figures 6.11 and 6.7, that the gold-banking economy maintains much lower cross-generation variance of utilities at comparable N/N_C, as well as having a lower critical population size N_C. Therefore, if the possibility of secession of some producers from the economy is considered, the superior average welfare of the gold-banking economy over the preinstitutional IGT economy for $N/(N_C)_{CE} < 1$ actually extends to a more robust solution at much larger values of N.

6.11   Concluding Comments

Process models of the economy are by definition institutional because they require carriers of process that are abstractions of institutions. Basic game theory considerations tell us that the proliferation of reasonable models is hyperastronomical in size. However, by adding the time structure of individuals and goods to a closed T-period economy, we can obtain enough special structure to build models that reflect many of the specific features that abound in an economy with physical assets and individuals existing on many different timescales. Many of these combinations call for the creation of the vast array of special financial instruments designed to cope with timing and coordination. These mismatches must and can be overcome by a well-designed financial system. The system is open to its environment and requires considerable parametric specification, where each choice provides a somewhat institutionally different mechanism, fitted ad hoc to the micro-micro detail of the part of the economy under scrutiny. Yet all models obey the economic optimization structure reflecting Edgeworth's inaugural observations.

The transition from a general economic model illustrating static equilibrium to economic dynamics calls for the invention of financial institutions and instruments to guide the economy in motion. The optimization problem does not disappear, but it is manifested in economy and efficacy of the institutions and instruments called forth to provide an economic way to handle the needs of the economic dynamics.

Our models presented here were designed to provide illustrations of the physical richness of a durable asset-laden economy and some of the financial arrangements called forth to supply the needed financial engineering. It is fairly evident on considering this relatively simple example that even elementary sensitivity analysis, let alone further complexity, calls for simulation and computational methods beyond the type of analytical methods employed here and on other low-dimensional economic models.

At the start of this chapter we noted that we wished to indicate the new layers of complexity introduced into the dynamics by considering production and exchange. The problems of durable capital stock and the time differentials that occur naturally in a specialized economy call for an important role for financial institutions and instruments to facilitate the transfer of funds involving saving and investment and inheritance, but once in place their existence offers possibilities of social and politico-economic control over the outcomes. It can be easily argued that contrasting the role of the gold miners is a caricature in our simplifications in the models here, but even with these gross simplifications the implications of differentials between gold and fiat and the added feature of inheritance can be illustrated, as is indicated in sections 6.7 to 6.10.

6.12   Appendix: Notations Used in the Chapter

Table 6.3

Parameters defining model properties and parameters optimized outside the strategic context, either by adaptive adjustment or by optimizing policy objectives

n_0	Number of prospectors of each generation
n	Number of farmers of each generation
$N = 2\,(n_0 + n)$	Total number of agents alive at any point
N_C	Critical population size for high-yielding production without shadow price
$\mathcal{C}$	Threshold of investment to achieve high-yielding production
ε	Ratio of low-yielding to high-yielding production, per unit gold
τ	Subscript indexing a period of time
(τ)	Superscript indexing a generation of agents
ρ	Interest rate on either gold or fiat money
θ	Edgeworth's "coefficient of concern"
a	Food endowment to farmers
e_0	Gold endowment to prospectors

Table 6.4

Strategic variables in the models

$\mathcal{U}^{(\tau)}$	Consumption utility for an agent of generation (τ)
$\mathcal{L}^{(\tau)}$	Lagrangian for an agent of generation (τ)
$A_i^{(\tau)}$	Food consumption of a farmer in (young/old) period i
$\hat{A}_i^{(\tau)}$	Food consumption of a prospector in (young/old) period i
$S_i^{(\tau)}$	Services consumed by a farmer in (young/old) period i
$\hat{S}_i^{(\tau)}$	Services consumed by a prospector in (young/old) period i
$b_i^{(\tau)}$	Bids by a farmer on food in (young/old) period i
$\hat{b}_i^{(\tau)}$	Bids by a prospector on food in (young/old) period i
$q^{(\tau)}$	Quantity of food offered by a young farmer in period τ
p_τ	Price of food in period τ
$b_{Gi}^{(\tau)}$	Bids by a farmer on gold in (young/old) period i
$\hat{q}_G^{(\tau)}$	Quantity of gold offered by a young prospector in period τ
$Q_G^{(\tau)}$	Quantity of gold offered by a central bank as seller
$B_G^{(\tau)}$	Bids on gold by a central bank as buyer
α	Parameter representing relation of $B_G^{(0)}$ to $B_G^{(1)}$
$p_{G,\tau}$	Price of gold in period τ
σ_0	Investment by young ($\tau = 0$) farmers
σ_1	Investment by old ($\tau = 2$) farmers
$\hat{\sigma}_0$	Investment by young ($\tau = 0$) prospectors
$\hat{\sigma}_1$	Investment by old ($\tau = 2$) prospectors
$g_i^{(\tau)}$	Loan or deposit (gold or fiat) by a farmer in (young/old) period i
$\hat{g}_i^{(\tau)}$	Loan or deposit (gold or fiat) by a prospector in (young/old) period i
$\kappa^{(\tau)}$	Intergenerational transfer by a farmer from generation (τ)

Table 6.4

(Continued)

$\mu_i^{(\tau)}$	Starting money budget of a farmer in (young/old) period i
$\hat{\mu}_i^{(\tau)}$	Starting money budget of a prospector in (young/old) period i
$\eta_i^{(\tau)}$	Kuhn-Tucker multiplier for farmer budget constraint in (young/old) period i
$\hat{\eta}_i^{(\tau)}$	Kuhn-Tucker multiplier for prospector budget constraint in (young/old) period i
Λ	Kuhn-Tucker multiplier for the capacity constraint on high-yielding production
$\gamma_i^{(\tau)}$	Starting gold stock of a farmer in period i (fiat model)
$\hat{\gamma}_i^{(\tau)}$	Starting gold stock of a prospector in period i (fiat model)
$\eta_{G,i}^{(\tau)}$	Kuhn-Tucker multiplier for farmer gold stock in period i (fiat model)
$\hat{\eta}_{G,i}^{(\tau)}$	Kuhn-Tucker multiplier for prospector gold stock in period i (fiat model)

6.13   Appendix: Regularizing the Threshold Constraint on Capacity with Logarithmic Utilities

Consider the optimization problem for an economy with one consumption good, the demand for which by each agent i we denote S_i, and which we think of as services from capital stock in the manner defined in chapter 5. Here, however, rather than considering the capital stock and its delivery of services to be disaggregated, we suppose that the capital stock is produced in a single package and that its services are distributed in proportion to shares in the package that agents own. We suppose that each agent i has a utility of demand

$$\mathcal{U}_i(S_i) = s \log S_i. \tag{6.40}$$

We will begin with the general notation for a strictly concave utility, to indicate its role in the calculation, and then use the logarithmic form to propose a specific simplified representation for the optimization problem.

Suppose that capital stock is built with contributions from agents, which we denote σ_i. The contributions must come entirely from endowments e_i that the agents receive, so that they maximize the Lagrangian

$$\mathcal{L}_i(\sigma_i, \eta_i) = \mathcal{U}_i(S_i) + \eta_i(e_i - \sigma_i) \tag{6.41}$$

in which $\eta_i \in [0, \infty]$ is the Kuhn-Tucker multiplier enforcing $e_i - \sigma_i \geq 0$.

We must now specify how the set of service streams $\{S_i\}$ is determined from the set of contributions $\{\sigma_i\}$. The integer programming problem that we wish to solve is a threshold problem: qualitatively, if the sum of investments $\sum_i \sigma_i$ exceeds some threshold capacity C, then the total output is $\sum_i \sigma_i$; otherwise it is zero. Because both the value and the derivative of this function are discontinuous at $\sum_i \sigma_i = C$, we replace the discontinuous function with a strongly nonconvex but twice-differentiable function

$$c\left(\sum_i \sigma_i\right),$$

of the form indicated in figure 6.3.

The service streams are then allocated in the proportions of the buy-sell clearing rule for markets:

$$S_i = \frac{\sigma_i}{\sum_{i'} \sigma_{i'}} c\left(\sum_{i'} \sigma_{i'}\right). \tag{6.42}$$

The first-order condition for any agent's optimization problem is

$$\frac{d\mathcal{U}_i}{dS_i} \frac{dS_i}{d\sigma_i} - \eta_i = 0, \tag{6.43}$$

in which

$$\frac{dS_i}{d\sigma_i} = \frac{c\left(\sum_{i'} \sigma_{i'}\right)}{\sum_{i'} \sigma_{i'}} \left(1 - \frac{\sigma_i}{\sum_{i'} \sigma_{i'}}\right) + S_i \left.\frac{d\log c(y)}{dy}\right|_{y=\sum_{i'} \sigma_{i'}}. \tag{6.44}$$

The important property of $d\log c(y)/dy$ is that it is a function only of the total contributions by all agents, and it runs from a minimum of $1/C$ for $\sum_i \sigma_i > C$ to a maximum of ∞ for $\sum_i \sigma_i$ slightly less than C. By making the "corner" of the transition in the function c very sharp, we may compress the interval of this transition as much as desired.

In the special case (6.40) that the utility is logarithmic, the marginal utility $d\mathcal{U}_i/dS_i = s/S_i$, and we may rewrite the first-order condition (6.43) as

$$\frac{d\mathcal{U}_i(\sigma_i)}{d\sigma_i} + \Lambda - \eta_i \approx 0. \tag{6.45}$$

In Eq. (6.45) we have used $S_i \approx \sigma_i$ as an upper-semicontinuous function in Eq. (6.42) to replace the argument of $\mathcal{U}_i$, we have ignored terms at order $\sigma_i / \sum_{i'} \sigma_{i'}$ in Eq. (6.44) as a large-population approximation, and we have introduced a lumped representation

$$\Lambda \equiv \frac{d\mathcal{U}_i}{dS_i} S_i \left.\frac{d\log c(y)}{dy}\right|_{y=\sum_{i'} \sigma_{i'}}$$

$$= s \left.\frac{d\log c(y)}{dy}\right|_{y=\sum_{i'} \sigma_{i'}}, \tag{6.46}$$

making use of the logarithmic utility. Note that Λ is a function only of the total contribution $\sum_{i'} \sigma_{i'}$ but not otherwise of σ_i.

The result is that we may solve the original optimization problem by maximizing (over $\{\sigma_i\}$) and minimizing (over $\{\eta_i\}$ and Λ) the expression

$$\mathcal{L} \equiv \sum_i [\mathcal{U}_i(\sigma_i) + \eta_i (e_i - \sigma_i)] + \Lambda \left(\sum_i \sigma_i - C \right), \tag{6.47}$$

treating Λ as a Kuhn-Tucker multiplier shared among all the agents.

This solution is chosen for simplicity in the case of logarithmic utility, and it retains this form even when $\mathcal{U}_i$ has more complex dependence on σ_i, as occurs in the inheritance model of this chapter. The generalization of this method of regularizing threshold functions to more complicated utilities, or to utilities with different functional forms for different agents, is straightforward, though the solution that results will no longer have the general form of a simple Kuhn-Tucker multiplier.

6.14   Appendix: The Exclusion of Wash Selling in the OLG Models

It is possible simply to rule out wash selling from the rules of the game, but it is cleaner to model the economy as treating agent types symmetrically, so that all constraints that differentiate their types originate in their choices of production function. In these models it will be possible to show that wash selling does not arise, as a property of solutions.

The first line of Eq. (6.17) shows that $b_0^{(\tau)}$ will be zero if either $\eta_0^{(\tau)} > 0$ or the initial budget $\mu_0^{(\tau)} = 0$ (there is nothing to spend). Wash selling does not occur if either of these conditions can be established.

6.14.1   No wash selling in banking models

Borrowing at interperiod interest rate ρ from any kind of bank (gold or fiat) will produce a Kuhn-Tucker multiplier from the default constraint that will always set

$$\eta_0^{(\tau)} = \rho \eta_1^{(\tau)} > 0, \tag{6.48}$$

so wash selling will not arise in models with banking.

6.14.2   No wash selling in models with intergenerational transfers and without banking

The case with intergenerational transfers (IGT) among farmers, but without banking, is more complicated but still tractable. ($\tau = 1$) farmers cannot invest and their consumption level is not directly influenced by IGTs, so the ($\tau = 0$) first-order conditions set transfer $\kappa^{(0)} = 0$. Hence the ($\tau = 1$) budget $\mu_0^{(1)} = 0$ also, and so $b_0^{(0)} = 0$.

6.14.2.1   No transfers from generation ($\tau = 0$)   For $\tau = 0$ and transfer $\kappa^{(2)}$ from the previous generation, it is possible to show that as long as $\theta < 1$, the transfer in the unstressed equilibrium is always smaller than the minimum for $\eta_0^{(0)}$ in Eq. (6.19), excluding wash sales in this limit. While we do not offer an analytic argument, the numerical solutions presented in this chapter show that as the capacity constraint binds, $\eta_0^{(0)}$ increases monotonically with the shadow price Λe_0, becoming linear at large Λe_0. (This result is not surprising, as a shadow price for the capacity constraint lowers all investment levels relative to their unstressed-equilibrium values, but does not similarly force food consumption downward.) Therefore wash sales are excluded from all solutions in the farmer ($\tau = 0$) generation.

6.14.2.2   No transfers for a large range of shadow prices from generation ($\tau = 1$)   For ($\tau = 2$) farmers, the first-order condition from the offspring-regarding utility at generation ($\tau = 1$), which determines whether transfers $\kappa^{(1)} > 0$, is complicated because these transfers may be partly used by ($\tau = 2$) farmers for investment. It is again possible to show that for a very large range of stresses including the unstressed equilibrium, the first-order condition never permits $\kappa^{(1)} > 0$, so the budget constraint sets $b_0^{(2)} = 0$. However, allocations consistent with $\kappa^{(1)} > 0$ do fall within the configuration space for sufficiently large Λe_0, and the fact that all investment for generation $\tau = 2$ occurs in the second period requires $\eta_0^{(2)} = 0$ if any nonbinding level of wash selling is chosen. The required parameter range for $\kappa^{(1)} > 0$ is never encountered in the solutions we present, however, so for these wash selling is excluded by the budget.

6.14.2.3   Any solution at ($\tau = 2$) with wash sales may be replaced by an equivalent solution without wash sales   We note for completeness one precise sense in which the degree of wash sales has no effect on any macrovariables and thus does not matter. We consider the case that, whatever the degree of wash selling, it is the same for all agents.[10]

The budget for ($\tau = 2$) farmers in the IGT model is

$$\kappa^{(1)} + \left(q^{(2)}p_2 - b_0^{(2)}\right) = b_1^{(2)} + \sigma_1 + \kappa^{(2)}. \tag{6.49}$$

The quantity in parentheses on the left-hand side does not depend on strategic variables of the ($\tau = 2$) farmers, so the entire left-hand side is for them a boundary condition. The first-order conditions (given in section 6.15.2.2) then make the right-hand side a monotonic equation in $b_1^{(2)}$, which is solved uniquely for $\Lambda b_1^{(2)}$ in terms of $\Lambda \left[\kappa^{(1)} + \left(q^{(2)}p_2 - b_0^{(2)}\right)\right]$. Thus the ($\tau = 2$)-old-period expenditures are fixed, independent of wash selling.

But the first-order condition (6.18) may then be used to write the price level as

$$ap_2 = \left(q^{(2)}p_2 - b_0^{(2)}\right) + b_1^{(2)}. \tag{6.50}$$

The term in parentheses is an input, and $b_1^{(2)}$ is a wash-sale-independent function of the inputs, so the price p_2 is also independent of wash sales. At fixed prices, $q^{(2)}$ becomes an affine function of $b_0^{(2)}$ with coefficients determined only by $\kappa^{(1)} + \left(q^{(2)}p_2 - b_0^{(2)}\right)$, which then also leaves all consumption levels and budgets invariant.

Since nothing depends on wash selling, and since it is not disfavored by the first-order conditions, we could exclude it by a secondary criterion of simplicity and identifiability by agents. It is one of two boundary cases ($b_0^{(2)} = 0$ or $b_0^{(2)} = \kappa^{(1)}$), and of these it is the simpler because it does not depend on $\kappa^{(1)}$.[11]

6.15   Appendix: Analysis of the OLG Model with Intergenerational Transfers but without Banking

For the OLG model with intergenerational transfers but without banking, we analyze the prospector sector first because the logarithmic utility separates prospectors' decision variables from the rest of the economy except through the shadow price of the capacity constraint and the labor allocation required to equalize three-period average utilities between farmers and prospectors.

6.15.1   Prospector sector

The prospector first-order conditions are given in Eq. (6.20).

The prospectors get all endowments in the young period and must spend in both periods, so they must have carry-forward, which means that their $\eta_0^{(\tau)} \equiv 0$, and they are governed by Eq. (6.51) with $k = 2$. If we disallow IGTs for them, then their total wealth is just the endowment e_0 for every generation, and the results become very simple.

The solutions to a variety of first-order conditions of the form (6.20) are given in terms of the net worths of individual endowments by solutions to a closely related set of quadratic equations. Therefore we introduce the notation for a function

$$\varphi_z^{(k)}(s;y) \equiv \frac{k + zs + (z + 2\theta)y}{2(z + 2\theta)y}\left[1 - \sqrt{1 - \frac{4k(z + 2\theta)y}{(k + zs + (z + 2\theta)y)^2}}\right]. \quad (6.51)$$

The sign convention for the square roots is that $\varphi_0^{(k)}(s;y) \equiv 1$, $\forall k, s, y$. Next, $y \to 0$ will define the unstressed noncooperative equilibrium for each model ($\Lambda e_0 \to 0$, or nonbinding capacity constraint), so we note that

$$\varphi_z^{(k)}(s;0) = \frac{k}{k + zs}. \quad (6.52)$$

For the case of prospectors in the no-banking IGT model, their bids on food are given by

$$\hat{b}_0^{(\tau)} = \hat{b}_1^{(\tau)} = \frac{e_0}{2}\varphi_{\tau-1}^{(2)}(s; \Lambda e_0). \quad (6.53)$$

The investment levels $\hat{\sigma}_0$, $\hat{\sigma}_1$ are then given by the general budget relation

$$e_0 = \hat{b}_0^{(\tau)} + \hat{b}_1^{(\tau)} + \hat{\sigma}_0\delta_{\tau,0} + \hat{\sigma}_1\delta_{\tau,2}. \quad (6.54)$$

6.15.2 Farmer sector

For the farmers we give forms for the marginal utilities and budget constraints individually for each generation, because the offspring-regarding term presents different difficulties of evaluation in each generation. The general method of solution begins with recognizing that the lack of an investment opportunity for $\tau = 1$ gives $\kappa^{(0)} = 0$ directly from the ($\tau = 0$) first-order conditions. This creates a break point for IGTs in the cycle, from which we can recursively solve the remainder of the allocation variables from any sequence of prices (p_0, p_1, p_2). The prices are determined by matching gold inflow to markets with farmer investment by which gold exits the system.

6.15.2.1 $\tau = 0$ The extension of the consumption-first-order condition (6.17) to include the IGT variable $\kappa^{(0)}$ is

$$0 = \delta\mathcal{L}^{(0)} = \left[\frac{1}{A_0^{(0)} p_0} - \eta_1^{(0)}\right]\left(\delta b_0^{(0)} - p_0\delta q^{(0)}\right) - \eta_0^{(0)}\delta b_0^{(0)} + \left[\frac{1}{b_1^{(0)}} - \eta_1^{(0)}\right]\delta b_1^{(0)}$$
$$+ \left[\frac{2s}{\sigma_0} + 2\left(1 + \theta\right)\Lambda - \left(\eta_0^{(0)} + \eta_1^{(0)}\right)\right]\delta\sigma_0 - \eta_1^{(0)}\delta\kappa^{(0)}. \qquad (6.55)$$

We start with an educated guess that $\eta_0^{(0)} > 0$, which we will return to and verify at the end. This requires both $b_0^{(0)} = 0$ and $\sigma_0 = \kappa^{(2)}$ from the IGT cycle. It also sets $\kappa_0^{(0)} = 0$, making the bid and offer variables

$$\Lambda b_1^{(0)} = \frac{\Lambda a p_0}{2}, \qquad (6.56)$$

$$\frac{q^{(0)}}{a} = \frac{1}{2}. \qquad (6.57)$$

6.15.2.2 $\tau = 2$ Working backward in time, the condition $\sigma_0 = \kappa^{(2)}$ enables $(\tau = 2)$ farmers to evaluate all first-order conditions, for their own consumption and the offspring-regarding term for $(\tau = 0)$ farmers. These take the form

$$0 = \delta\mathcal{L}^{(2)} = \left[\frac{1}{A_0^{(2)} p_2} - \eta_1^{(2)}\right]\left(\delta b_0^{(2)} - p_2\delta q^{(2)}\right) - \eta_0^{(2)}\delta b_0^{(2)} + \left[\frac{1}{b_1^{(2)}} - \eta_1^{(2)}\right]\delta b_1^{(2)}$$
$$+ \left[\frac{s}{\sigma_1} + \left(1 + 2\theta\right)\Lambda - \eta_1^{(2)}\right]\delta\sigma_1 + \left[\frac{2\theta s}{\kappa^{(2)}} + 2\theta\Lambda - \eta_1^{(2)}\right]\delta\kappa^{(2)}. \qquad (6.58)$$

Note in passing that for the value $\theta = 1/2$ used in numerical solutions, the first-order conditions for σ_1 and $\kappa^{(2)}$ in the unstressed equilibrium are the same. Therefore $(\tau = 2)$ farmers invest the same amount as they transfer to their $(\tau = 0)$ offspring for investment. In the $s \ll 1$ limit, where prices $ap_\tau \to 1$, this is equal to the investment level of $(\tau = 2)$ prospectors, and half that of $(\tau = 0)$ prospectors. These relations may be seen in figure 6.6.

From the first-order conditions and the budget constraint, the relation between any received transfers $\kappa^{(1)}$, the market value of the endowment ap_2, and the expenditures is

$$\kappa^{(1)} + ap_2 = 2b_1^{(2)} + \sigma_1 + \kappa^{(2)}. \qquad (6.59)$$

We may express this as a relation between the worth of the farmer endowment and the received transfers scaled by the shadow price of the capacity constraint, $\Lambda a p_2 + \Lambda \kappa^{(1)}$, and the similarly scaled bids $\Lambda b_1^{(2)}$, in the form of a cubic equation in $\Lambda b_1^{(2)}$:

$$\Lambda b_1^{(2)} \left[2 + \frac{s}{1 - (1 + 2\theta) \, \Lambda b_1^{(2)}} + \frac{2\theta s}{1 - 2\theta \, \Lambda b_1^{(2)}} \right] = \Lambda a p_2 + \Lambda \kappa^{(1)}. \quad (6.60)$$

For numerical solution in the IGT model and also the banking model (presented next), we treat $\Lambda b_1^{(2)}$ as an implicit function of prices and transfers through Eq. (6.60), meaning that we will take $\Lambda b_1^{(2)}$ as an independent variable and express other quantities as functions of it, leaving the inverse functions implicit. The key to a constructive solution—a consequence of the separation between farmer and prospector sectors provided by logarithmic utilities—is that prospector bids and investment are functions of the absolute stress level in the economy Λe_0 only, while price levels, and farmer bids and investments, are matched to these scales through their dependence on the bid level $\Lambda b_1^{(2)}$, on population n_0/n, and on explicit prospector bids.

For use in all following sections, introduce the notation $x \equiv \Lambda b_1^{(2)}$. If we can simultaneously solve for x and $\Lambda \kappa^{(1)}$ in terms of prices, then we will have the ($\tau = 2$) bid, and we can compute the following cascade of offer, investment, and transfer variables:

$$\Lambda \sigma_1 = \frac{sx}{1 - (1 + 2\theta) x}$$

$$\Lambda \sigma_0 = \Lambda \kappa^{(2)} = \frac{2\theta sx}{1 - 2\theta x}$$

$$\frac{q^{(2)}}{a} (\Lambda a p_2) = x \left[1 + \frac{s}{1 - (1 + 2\theta) x} + \frac{2\theta s}{1 - 2\theta x} \right] - \Lambda \kappa^{(1)}. \quad (6.61)$$

We will require a simultaneous solution in general, because x and $\Lambda \kappa^{(1)}$ are not independently identified. To resolve their dependence, we must analyze the previous period.

6.15.2.3 $\tau = 1$ Because ($\tau = 2$) farmers may now make investments that depend on $\kappa^{(1)}$ if $\kappa^{(1)} > 0$, but because their level of use is no longer expressed in a simple constraint, the first-order condition for the offspring-regarding terms of ($\tau = 1$) farmers is defined implicitly in terms of this partial use.

The full first-order conditions, including this implicit dependence, may be written

$$0 = \delta \mathcal{L}^{(1)} = \left[\frac{1}{A_0^{(1)} p_1} - \eta_1^{(1)}\right]\left(\delta b_0^{(1)} - p_1 \delta q^{(1)}\right) - \eta_0^{(1)} \delta b_0^{(1)} + \left[\frac{1}{b_1^{(1)}} - \eta_1^{(1)}\right]\delta b_1^{(1)}$$
$$+ \left[\left(\frac{\theta s}{\sigma_1} + \theta \Lambda\right)\frac{d\sigma_1}{d\kappa^{(1)}} - \eta_1^{(1)}\right]\delta \kappa^{(1)}. \tag{6.62}$$

Before considering the value of $\kappa^{(1)}$, the result $\kappa^{(0)} = 0$ that we already have from $\tau = 0$ gives the bid and offer relations to prices

$$\Lambda b_1^{(1)} = \frac{1}{2}\left(\Lambda a p_1 - \Lambda \kappa^{(1)}\right),$$
$$\frac{q^{(1)}}{a}(\Lambda a p_1) = \frac{1}{2}\left(\Lambda a p_1 + \Lambda \kappa^{(1)}\right). \tag{6.63}$$

Now return to $\kappa^{(1)}$. If, on the first-order condition for $b_1^{(1)}$, the resulting coefficient

$$\left(\frac{\theta s}{\sigma_1} + \theta \Lambda\right)\frac{d\sigma_1}{d\kappa^{(1)}} - \frac{2}{a p_1 - \kappa^{(1)}}$$

of $\delta \kappa^{(1)}$ in Eq. (6.62) cannot be made nonnegative, then $\kappa^{(1)} \to 0$. Otherwise, vanishing of this coefficient determines the interior value for $\kappa^{(1)}$. The alternative between these two cases can be written

$$\Lambda \kappa^{(1)} = \max \left\{0, \Lambda a p_1 - \frac{2}{\theta}\left[\left(\frac{s}{\Lambda \sigma_1} + 1\right)\frac{d\sigma_1}{d\kappa^{(1)}}\right]^{-1}\right\}. \tag{6.64}$$

The expression (6.64) can be evaluated, because in the range where $\kappa^{(1)} > 0$ an analytic form can be written for the sensitivity

$$\left(\frac{s}{\Lambda \sigma_1} + 1\right)\frac{d\sigma_1}{d\kappa^{(1)}} = \frac{s(1 - 2\theta x)/x}{s + 2[1 - (1 + 2\theta)x]^2\left[1 + \theta s/(1 - 2\theta x)^2\right]}. \tag{6.65}$$

This is a nonmonotonic function that starts at ∞ (when $x = 0$), rapidly decreases to $\mathcal{O}(s)$, and then increases (passing through a weak interior maximum) to value 1 at $x \to 1/(1 + 2\theta)$. The small-x branch of solutions is never the relevant one to Eqs. (6.60, 6.64), and the large-x branch will only make Eq. (6.64) positive for $x \sim 1/(1 + 2\theta) - \mathcal{O}(s)$. From the second term in brackets on the left-hand side of Eq. (6.60), we may recognize that this is the extreme range of stressing where σ_1 accounts for a fraction of $ap_2 + \kappa^{(1)}$ comparable to the fraction from $b_1^{(2)}$.

Once the value of $x = \Lambda b_1^{(2)}$ is found from any pair of values $(\Lambda ap_2, \Lambda ap_1)$, jointly with the value of $\Lambda \kappa^{(1)}$ from Eq. (6.64), all other quantities in the three periods are determined. Included in these (if we also supply Λp_0) is an expression for $\eta_0^{(0)}$, which we may verify is nonzero. Numerical checks show that the coefficient of $\delta \kappa^{(1)}/e_0$ in Eq. (6.62) remains within a few tenths of -2 over the range $\Lambda e_0 \in [0, 3.5]$.

Note that there is a strong nonequivalence in the roles of prices. Only the expression (6.56) for $b_1^{(0)}$ depends on p_0, and that through a constant relation. (Likewise $q^{(0)}$ is simply a constant.) All other quantities—even σ_0—are explicitly functions only of the pair of prices $(\Lambda ap_2, \Lambda ap_1)$.

6.15.3   The price cycle

Once we have excluded wash selling, for any relative numbers n_0 of prospectors and n of farmers, the amount of gold bid in each of the markets is straightforward to express from Eq. (6.53):

$$q^{(\tau)}p_\tau = b_1^{(\tau-1)} + \frac{n_0}{n}\frac{e_0}{2}\left(\varphi_{\tau-1}^{(2)}(s; \Lambda e_0) + \varphi_{\tau-2}^{(2)}(s; \Lambda e_0)\right). \qquad (6.66)$$

The first term is from old farmers, the second is from young prospectors, and the third is from old prospectors. (In the following equations, where no ambiguity results, we will adopt the shorthand φ_τ for $\varphi_z^{(2)}(s; \Lambda e_0)$ to improve readability.)

The expression (6.66) for inputs may be combined with the general budget relation for expenditures, which takes the form

$$\kappa^{(\tau-1)} + q^{(\tau)}p_\tau = b_1^{(\tau)} + \sigma_1 \delta_{\tau,2} + \sigma_0 \delta_{\tau,0} + \kappa^{(\tau)}. \qquad (6.67)$$

Adding the bids in all three periods from Eq. (6.66), canceling the explicit $b_1^{(\tau)}$ terms that appear on both sides, and using the budgets (6.67) to resolve the remaining $q^{(\tau)}p_\tau$ terms, we arrive at a relation between aggregate prospector bids and farmer investments:

$$\frac{n_0}{n}(\Lambda e_0)(1 + \varphi_1 + \varphi_2) = \Lambda(\sigma_1 + \sigma_0) = \Lambda\left(\sigma_1 + \kappa^{(2)}\right)$$

$$= \Lambda b_1^{(2)}\left[\frac{s}{1 - (1+2\theta)\Lambda b_1^{(2)}} + \frac{2\theta s}{1 - 2\theta \Lambda b_1^{(2)}}\right]$$

$$= x\left[\frac{s}{1 - (1+2\theta)x} + \frac{2\theta s}{1 - 2\theta x}\right]. \qquad (6.68)$$

(Recall, using Eq. (6.53), that prospectors invest $n_0 e_0 (2 - \varphi_1 - \varphi_2)$, resulting in a total of $3 n_0 e_0$ over the economy.)

The following rearrangements of the bid and budget equations then produce explicit relations among the three price levels:

$$\Lambda \left(a p_1 - a p_2 \right) = \frac{n_0}{n} \Lambda e_0 \varphi_2$$

$$\Lambda \left(a p_2 + \kappa^{(1)} \right) = \Lambda a p_0 + \frac{n_0}{n} \Lambda e_0$$

$$(\text{recall Eq. (6.60))} = x \left[2 + \frac{s}{1 - (1 + 2\theta) x} + \frac{2\theta s}{1 - 2\theta x} \right]$$

$$(\text{now use Eq. (6.68))} = 2x + \frac{n_0}{n} \left(\Lambda e_0 \right) \left(1 + \varphi_1 + \varphi_2 \right)$$

$$(\text{subtract } l2 \text{ from } l4)$$

$$\Lambda a p_0 = 2x + \frac{n_0}{n} \left(\Lambda e_0 \right) \left(\varphi_1 + \varphi_2 \right). \tag{6.69}$$

The foregoing equations are solved numerically as follows: To any pair of values of $(x, \Lambda e_0)$, Eq. (6.68) assigns a value of n_0 / n. From this, the first line of Eq. (6.69) assigns the difference $\Lambda a p_2 - \Lambda a p_1$, and the last line assigns $\Lambda a p_0$. In the range where $\kappa^{(1)} = 0$, the third line assigns a value for $\Lambda a p_2$, fully determining the system. We need only search for the contour of equal utilities to specify the other variables as functions of n_0 / n. We will show numerically that over the range $\Lambda e_0 \leq 3.5$, the first-order conditions remain far from permitting $\kappa^{(1)} > 0$, so the foregoing assignments are consistent and exact.

6.15.3.1   Utility differences

The utility differences have fewer terms than the absolute utility magnitudes, because the allocations of publicly held services are the same to both types in the periods where they occur. Therefore we first identify the utility difference expressions that will select a particular contour of $(x, \Lambda e_0)$ values from the two-dimensional space.

The differences from the consumption utilities for food, using Eqs. (6.18, 6.53), may be written as a general function of τ, as

$$\mathcal{U}_{\text{Farm,food}}^{(\tau)} - \mathcal{U}_{\text{Pros,food}}^{(\tau)} = 2 \log \left(\frac{2 b_1^{(\tau)}}{e_0 \varphi_{\tau-1}} \right). \tag{6.70}$$

The difference in utilities from consumption of services by the agents themselves is

$$\mathcal{U}_{\text{Farm,self}}^{(\tau)} - \mathcal{U}_{\text{Pros,self}}^{(\tau)} = (\tau - 1) s \log \left(\frac{\sigma_0 \delta_{\tau,0} + \sigma_1 \delta_{\tau,2}}{e_0 (1 - \varphi_{\tau-1})} \right), \tag{6.71}$$

where all expressions $\tau - 1$ are understood to be evaluated cyclically.

The difference in utility of services consumed by offspring are cycled in τ and scaled by θ:

$$\mathcal{U}^{(\tau)}_{\text{Farm,offspr}} - \mathcal{U}^{(\tau)}_{\text{Pros,offspr}} = \theta \left(\mathcal{U}^{(\tau+1)}_{\text{Farm,self}} - \mathcal{U}^{(\tau+1)}_{\text{Pros,self}} \right). \tag{6.72}$$

It may be clearer to write these for each period independently, filling in evaluations for bid variables using the preceding relations. An evaluation that emphasizes the role of prices is

$$\mathcal{U}^{(0)}_{\text{Farm,food}} - \mathcal{U}^{(0)}_{\text{Pros,food}} = 2\log\left(\frac{ap_0}{e_0}\right) + 2\log\left(\frac{1}{\varphi_2}\right)$$

$$\mathcal{U}^{(1)}_{\text{Farm,food}} - \mathcal{U}^{(1)}_{\text{Pros,food}} = 2\log\left(\frac{ap_1 - \kappa^{(1)}}{e_0}\right)$$

$$\mathcal{U}^{(2)}_{\text{Farm,food}} - \mathcal{U}^{(2)}_{\text{Pros,food}} = 2\log\left(\frac{ap_2 + \kappa^{(1)}}{e_0\varphi_1}\right) - 2\log\left(\frac{ap_2 + \kappa^{(1)}}{2b_1^{(2)}}\right)$$

$$= 2\log\left(\frac{ap_2 + \kappa^{(1)}}{e_0}\right) + 2\log\left(\frac{1}{\varphi_1}\right)$$

$$- 2\log\left(\frac{2 + \frac{s}{1-(1+2\theta)x} + \frac{2\theta s}{1-2\theta x}}{2}\right). \tag{6.73}$$

The difference for services consumed by self becomes

$$\mathcal{U}^{(0)}_{\text{Farm,self}} - \mathcal{U}^{(0)}_{\text{Pros,self}} = 2s\log\left(\frac{\sigma_0}{e_0\,(1 - \varphi_2)}\right) = 2s\log\left(\frac{\kappa^{(2)}}{e_0\,(1 - \varphi_2)}\right)$$

$$= 2s\log\left(\frac{ap_2 + \kappa^{(1)}}{e_0}\right) + 2s\log\left(\frac{s}{1 - \varphi_2}\right)$$

$$- 2s\log\left(\frac{(1 - 2\theta x)\left[2 + \frac{s}{1-(1+2\theta)x} + \frac{2\theta s}{1-2\theta x}\right]}{2\theta}\right)$$

$$\mathcal{U}^{(1)}_{\text{Farm,self}} - \mathcal{U}^{(1)}_{\text{Pros,self}} = 0$$

$$\mathcal{U}^{(2)}_{\text{Farm,self}} - \mathcal{U}^{(2)}_{\text{Pros,self}} = s\log\left(\frac{\sigma_1}{e_0\,(1 - \varphi_1)}\right). \tag{6.74}$$

A numerical analysis from the condition that the equally weighted sum $\sum_\tau \mathcal{U}_{\text{Farm}}^{(2)} - \mathcal{U}_{\text{Pros}}^{(2)} = 0$ gives the shadow price, food price, and investment levels is shown in the main text of this chapter.

To convert the expressions for utility differences into absolute utility magnitudes, it is easiest to use the prospector variables. The prospector utility of food consumption is

$$\mathcal{U}_{\text{Pros,food}}^{(\tau)} = \log\left(\frac{(e_0\varphi_\tau - 1)^2}{ap_\tau\, ap_{\tau+1}}\right). \tag{6.75}$$

The prospector investment levels are given in Eq. (6.54), and the service levels derived from them for the three periods are given in Eq. (6.14). From these values for both the focal agent and the offspring generation, we obtain the utility levels plotted in figure 6.7.

6.16   Appendix: Analysis of the OLG Model with an Inside Bank for Gold

The first-order conditions for the banking model follow from the Lagrangian (6.24). The reason this model brings prices in the unstressed noncooperative equilibrium close to those in the competitive equilibrium is that now all agents face a similar relation between their bids and the market value of their endowments, apart from interest payments. Therefore solutions for farmers and prospectors are structurally more similar than in the IGT economy.

6.16.1   Farmer sector

The first-order conditions for farmers are

$$
\begin{aligned}
0 = \delta\mathcal{L}^{(\tau)} = {}& \left[\frac{1}{A_0^{(\tau)}p_\tau} - \eta_1^{(\tau)}\right]\left(\delta b_0^{(\tau)} - p_\tau \delta q^{(\tau)}\right) - \eta_0^{(\tau)}\delta b_0^{(\tau)} + \left[\frac{1}{b_1^{(\tau)}} - \eta_1^{(\tau)}\right]\delta b_1^{(\tau)} \\
&+ \left[\frac{2s}{\sigma_0} + 2(1+\theta)\Lambda - \left(\eta_0^{(\tau)} + \eta_1^{(\tau)}\right)\right]\delta\sigma_0\delta_{\tau,0} \\
&+ \left[\frac{s}{\sigma_1} + (1+2\theta)\Lambda - \eta_1^{(\tau)}\right]\delta\sigma_1\delta_{\tau,2} \\
&+ \left[\left(\eta_0^{(\tau)} + \eta_1^{(\tau)}\right) - \Lambda_B^{(\tau)}(1+\rho)\right]\delta g_0^{(\tau)} + \left[\Lambda_B^{(\tau)} - \eta_1^{(\tau)}\right]\left(-\delta g_1^{(\tau)}\right).
\end{aligned}
\tag{6.76}
$$

The option to lend or borrow sets $\Lambda_B^{(\tau)} = \eta_1^{(\tau)} > 0$, and this in turn sets $\eta_0^{(\tau)} = \rho \eta_1^{(\tau)}$ for all τ. There is no wash selling ($b_0^{(\tau)} = 0$), and the remaining expenses satisfy the budget relations

$$g_0^{(\tau)} = \sigma_0 \delta_{\tau,0}$$
$$A_0^{(\tau)} p_\tau = b_1^{(\tau)} + \sigma_1 \delta_{\tau,2} + (1 + \rho) g_0^{(\tau)}. \tag{6.77}$$

The other first-order condition we will use is the general relation Eq. (6.18).

We will show below that the interest rate in the unstressed equilibrium goes to $\rho \to 1 + \mathcal{O}(s)$. Note that in Eq. (6.76) this value for ρ makes the first-order conditions for σ_0 and σ_1 the same, leading to the same investment level in both generations $\tau = 0, 2$. We will see a similar equality between generations for prospectors, but prospectors will invest at the higher level because they can lend rather than borrow. This difference (nominally a factor of 2) will be partly compensated (to a factor of $\sqrt{2}$) because the unstressed-equilibrium price levels $ap_\tau/e_0 \to \sqrt{2}$ rather than 1 as in the CE and the IGT economy. All these limits are met in numerical simulations in figure 6.9.

The budget and first-order conditions lead to a relation between bids, investment, and prices of the form

$$ap_\tau = 2b_1^{(\tau)} + (1 + \rho) \sigma_0 \delta_{\tau,0} + \sigma_1 \delta_{\tau,2}. \tag{6.78}$$

The first-order conditions between σ and b variables also lead to quadratic relations between b and ap levels comparable to those for prospectors in both the IGT and banking models. They are

$$b_1^{(0)} = \frac{ap_0}{2} \varphi_2^{(2)} \left(s; \frac{\Lambda ap_0}{(1 + \rho)} \right)$$
$$b_1^{(1)} = \frac{ap_1}{2}$$
$$b_1^{(2)} = \frac{ap_2}{2} \varphi_1^{(2)} (s; \Lambda ap_2). \tag{6.79}$$

6.16.2 Prospector sector

The first-order conditions for the prospectors are

$$0 = \delta \mathcal{L}^{(\tau)} = \left[\frac{1}{b_0^{(\tau)}} - \left(\eta_0^{(\tau)} + \eta_1^{(\tau)} \right) \right] \delta b_0^{(\tau)} + \left[\frac{1}{b_1^{(\tau)}} - \eta_1^{(\tau)} \right] \delta b_1^{(\tau)}$$
$$+ \left[\frac{2s}{\sigma_0} + 2 (1 + \theta) \Lambda - \left(\eta_0^{(\tau)} + \eta_1^{(\tau)} \right) \right] \delta \sigma_0 \delta_{\tau,0}$$

$$+ \left[\frac{s}{\sigma_1} + (1 + 2\theta)\, \Lambda - \eta_1^{(\tau)} \right] \delta \sigma_1 \delta_{\tau,2}$$
$$+ \left[\left(\eta_0^{(\tau)} + \eta_1^{(\tau)} \right) - \Lambda_B (1 + \rho) \right] \delta g_0^{(\tau)} + \left[\Lambda_B - \eta_1^{(\tau)} \right] \left(-\delta g_1^{(\tau)} \right).$$

$$(6.80)$$

Two general conditions that follow immediately are $\eta_0^{(\tau)} = \rho \eta_1^{(\tau)}$ and $b_1^{(\tau)} = (1 + \rho)\, b_0^{(\tau)}$.

The budget relation is

$$e_0 = b_0^{(\tau)} - g_0^{(\tau)} + \sigma_0 \delta_{\tau,0}$$
$$- (1 + \rho)\, g_0^{(\tau)} = g_1^{(\tau)} = b_1^{(\tau)} + \sigma_1 \delta_{\tau,2}, \qquad (6.81)$$

which converts into an expression counterpart to Eq. (6.78), of the form

$$e_0 = 2 b_0^{(\tau)} + \sigma_0 \delta_{\tau,0} + \frac{\sigma_1}{(1 + \rho)} \delta_{\tau,2}. \qquad (6.82)$$

From these, the same algebra used for the IGT economy produces three relations for the bids in terms of the endowment

$$b_0^{(0)} = \frac{b_1^{(0)}}{(1 + \rho)} = \frac{e_0}{2} \varphi_2^{(2)}(s; \Lambda e_0)$$
$$b_0^{(1)} = \frac{b_1^{(1)}}{(1 + \rho)} = \frac{e_0}{2}$$
$$b_0^{(2)} = \frac{b_1^{(2)}}{(1 + \rho)} = \frac{e_0}{2} \varphi_1^{(2)}(s; (1 + \rho)\, \Lambda e_0). \qquad (6.83)$$

These equations can be compared to Eq. (6.53) for the IGT economy. The relative forms are the same, but all positions of e_0 for prospectors are scaled by $(1 + \rho)$ relative to their counterparts for ap_τ.

If we want a single expression that covers all three periods, we may write

$$b_0^{(\tau)} = \frac{b_1^{(\tau)}}{(1 + \rho)} = \frac{e_0}{2} \varphi_{\tau-1}^{(2)}\left(s; (1 + \rho \delta_{\tau,2})\, \Lambda e_0\right). \qquad (6.84)$$

6.16.3   The price cycle

The three equations that relate bids to prices in the banking model, taking the place of Eq. (6.66) for the IGT model, are

$$(1+\rho)\sigma_0 + b_1^{(0)} = q^{(0)}p_0 = b_1^{(2)} + \frac{n_0}{n}\frac{e_0}{2}(\varphi_2 + (1+\rho)\varphi_1)$$

$$b_1^{(1)} = q^{(1)}p_1 = b_1^{(0)} + \frac{n_0}{n}\frac{e_0}{2}(1 + (1+\rho)\varphi_2)$$

$$\sigma_1 + b_1^{(2)} = q^{(2)}p_2 = b_1^{(1)} + \frac{n_0}{n}\frac{e_0}{2}(\varphi_1 + (1+\rho)), \qquad (6.85)$$

where all φ here are shorthand references to the prospector functions in Eq. (6.84).

Again adding all three equations, and canceling the b variables which appear on both sides, gives the relation of total prospector bids to the farmer level of investment, counterpart to Eq. (6.68) of the IGT economy:

$$(1+\rho)\sigma_0 + \sigma_1 = \frac{n_0}{n}e_0\left(1 + \frac{\rho}{2}\right)(1 + \varphi_1 + \varphi_2). \qquad (6.86)$$

Price levels in this loop are fixed when we demand that interest payments on loans and deposits balance. Equality between total borrowing and total lending reads

$$\sigma_0 = \frac{n_0}{n}\frac{e_0}{2}[\varphi_2 + 1 + (2 - \varphi_1)]$$

$$= \frac{n_0}{n}\frac{e_0}{2}(3 - \varphi_1 + \varphi_2), \qquad (6.87)$$

where the expressions on the right-hand side in the first line refer to the prospector investments that draw interest in periods 0, 1, 2, respectively.

The condition (6.87) for balance of interest payments will not generally be compatible with the form for σ_0 from the first line of Eq. (6.79), at the price levels generated by balanced interest payments. Hence they will violate the first-order condition in the second line of Eq. (6.76). The contours of compatibility of these two conditions in $(x, \Lambda e_0)$ space can be determined numerically, and they are isoclines along which the utility differences between farmers and prospectors vary monotonically. Therefore, in numerical solutions, we must first assign compatible ρ values throughout this space, and then show how ρ varies as a function of $N/N_C \leq 1$ along the contour of equal utilities. Examples showing the contours associated with these two distinct constraints are given in figure 6.19.

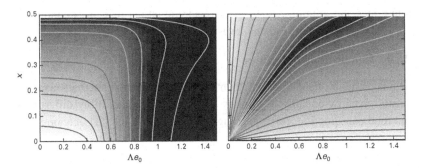

Figure 6.19

Gray-scale plots (with contours) of ρ (left) and $\mathcal{U}_{\text{Farm}}^{(\tau)} - \mathcal{U}_{\text{Pros}}^{(\tau)}$ (right). (Utility differences are plotted in log of absolute value so that the zero crossing shows as a sharp valley.) See that the isocontours of ρ with the associated values of n_0/n that balance interest and satisfy the first-order conditions are circle-like arcs around the origin, while the iso-utility contours are rays from the origin that cut across these arcs.

Subtracting Eq. (6.87) from Eq. (6.86) gives the relation between $x \equiv \Lambda b_1^{(2)}$ and Λe_0 that specifies n_0/n:

$$\sigma_1 = \frac{sx}{1 - (1 + 2\theta)x} = \frac{n_0}{n}\frac{e_0}{2}[(1 + \varphi_1 + \varphi_2) - 2(1 + \rho)(1 - \varphi_1)]. \quad (6.88)$$

Note that, at any Λe_0, Eq. (6.88) sets a limit on the interest rates that could be compatible of

$$\rho \le \frac{3\varphi_1 + \varphi_2 - 1}{2(1 - \varphi_1)}, \quad (6.89)$$

and this in turn limits the range of stresses Λe_0 over which this model has stationary solutions with $\rho \ge 0$, to $3\varphi_1 + \varphi_2 \ge 1$.

From these conditions it is possible to assign all price levels as functions of x and Λe_0, in the banking counterpart to the IGT price cycle of Eq. (6.69),

$$\Lambda ap_2 = 2\Lambda b_1^{(2)} + \Lambda \sigma_1$$

$$= x\left(2 + \frac{s}{1 - (1 + 2\theta)x}\right)$$

$$\Lambda ap_1 = 2\left(\Lambda b_1^{(2)} + \Lambda \sigma_1\right) - \frac{n_0}{n}(\Lambda e_0)[\varphi_1 + (1 + \rho)]$$

$$= x\left(2 + \frac{2s}{1 - (1 + 2\theta)x}\right) - \frac{n_0}{n}(\Lambda e_0)[\varphi_1 + (1 + \rho)]$$

$$\Lambda ap_0 = \Lambda ap_2 - \frac{n_0}{n}(\Lambda e_0)\left[1 + \frac{\rho}{2}(1 - \varphi_1 + \varphi_2)\right]. \quad (6.90)$$

From prices, the solutions (6.79) to the quadratic farmer first-order conditions then assign all remaining bid and investment levels.

6.16.4 Equalization of utilities

The final contour of solutions parametrized by either Λe_0 or alternatively n_0/n is again given by equality of utilities. The banking model utility differences from food consumption, corresponding to Eq. (6.73) for the IGT economy, are given by[12]

$$
\begin{aligned}
\mathcal{U}^{(0)}_{\text{Farm,food}} - \mathcal{U}^{(0)}_{\text{Pros,food}} &= 2\log\left(\frac{ap_0}{e_0}\right) + 2\log\left(\frac{\varphi_2^{(2)}\left(s;\frac{\Lambda ap_0}{(1+\rho)}\right)}{\varphi_2^{(2)}(s;\Lambda e_0)}\right) - \log(1+\rho) \\
&= 2\log\left(\frac{\frac{\Lambda ap_0}{(1+\rho)}\varphi_2^{(2)}\left(s;\frac{\Lambda ap_0}{(1+\rho)}\right)}{\Lambda e_0\,\varphi_2^{(2)}(s;\Lambda e_0)}\right) + \log(1+\rho) \\
\mathcal{U}^{(1)}_{\text{Farm,food}} - \mathcal{U}^{(1)}_{\text{Pros,food}} &= 2\log\left(\frac{ap_1}{e_0}\right) - \log(1+\rho) \\
&= 2\log\left(\frac{\Lambda ap_1/\sqrt{1+\rho}}{\sqrt{1+\rho}\,\Lambda e_0}\right) + \log(1+\rho) \\
\mathcal{U}^{(2)}_{\text{Farm,food}} - \mathcal{U}^{(2)}_{\text{Pros,food}} &= 2\log\left(\frac{ap_2}{e_0}\right) + 2\log\left(\frac{\varphi_1^{(2)}(s;\Lambda ap_2)}{\varphi_1^{(2)}(s;(1+\rho)\,\Lambda e_0)}\right) - \log(1+\rho) \\
&= 2\log\left(\frac{\Lambda ap_2\,\varphi_1^{(2)}(s;\Lambda ap_2)}{(1+\rho)\,\Lambda e_0\,\varphi_1^{(2)}(s;(1+\rho)\,\Lambda e_0)}\right) + \log(1+\rho).
\end{aligned}
\tag{6.91}
$$

The utility differences from an agent's own consumption of services, counterpart to Eq. (6.74) for the IGT economy, are given by

$$
\begin{aligned}
\mathcal{U}^{(0)}_{\text{Farm,self}} - \mathcal{U}^{(0)}_{\text{Pros,self}} &= 2s\left[\log\left(\frac{ap_0}{e_0}\right) + \log\left(\frac{1-\varphi_2^{(2)}\left(s;\frac{\Lambda ap_0}{(1+\rho)}\right)}{1-\varphi_2^{(2)}(s;\Lambda e_0)}\right) - \log(1+\rho)\right] \\
&= 2s\log\left(\frac{\frac{\Lambda ap_0}{(1+\rho)}\left(1-\varphi_2^{(2)}\left(s;\frac{\Lambda ap_0}{(1+\rho)}\right)\right)}{\Lambda e_0\left(1-\varphi_2^{(2)}(s;\Lambda e_0)\right)}\right) \\
\mathcal{U}^{(1)}_{\text{Farm,self}} - \mathcal{U}^{(1)}_{\text{Pros,self}} &= 0
\end{aligned}
$$

$$\mathcal{U}_{\text{Farm,self}}^{(2)} - \mathcal{U}_{\text{Pros,self}}^{(2)} = s\left[\log\left(\frac{ap_2}{e_0}\right) + \log\left(\frac{1 - \varphi_1^{(2)}(s; \Lambda ap_2)}{1 - \varphi_1^{(2)}(s; (1+\rho)\Lambda e_0)}\right) - \log(1+\rho)\right]$$

$$= s\log\left(\frac{\Lambda ap_2\left[1 - \varphi_1^{(2)}(s; \Lambda ap_2)\right]}{(1+\rho)\Lambda e_0\left[1 - \varphi_1^{(2)}(s; (1+\rho)\Lambda e_0)\right]}\right). \qquad (6.92)$$

The offspring term continues to satisfy Eq. (6.72). Its role in the banking economy is much simpler than in the IGT economy, as it acts only through the shadow price of the capacity constraint.

Numerical solutions for absolute and relative price levels, investment levels by each type and period, stress level Λe_0 and interest rate ρ, and single-period absolute utility levels are shown in figures 6.8–6.11 of the main text.

6.16.5 The distinctive response of interest rates to shadow price on the capacity constraint in the gold-banking model

An inside bank that returns all deposits is a highly constrained entity, which may be required to adopt particular interest rates at zero and nonzero shadow prices in order to satisfy its constraints. In particular, the first-order conditions for consumption of services for agents who invest in generations ($\tau = 0$) and ($\tau = 2$), to be met, may require particular ratios of consumption levels σ_0/σ_1, or $\hat{\sigma}_0/\hat{\sigma}_1$, while the fact that these investments (for farmers) are limited by bidding levels for food may require other particular levels. The interest rate is the only device the bank has available to bring these two conditions into compatibility and ensure its balance of deposits and withdrawals. We therefore consider here in detail the set of constraints that determine interest rates, and the way these depend on the shadow price of the capacity constraint.

6.16.5.1 Contribution from the first-order conditions Comparison of the second and third lines in the first-order condition for farmers (6.76), together with the relation between the Kuhn-Tucker multipliers $\eta_0^{(\tau)} = \rho\eta_1^{(\tau)}$ which will hold in any economy with lending at interest, leads us to expect the coarse scaling $\sigma_0 \sim 2\sigma_1/(1+\rho)$. The greater marginal utility of investment σ_0 in the young period is weighed against the requirement to borrow gold to supply it.

The full relations, obtained from Eqs. (6.78, 6.79), are

$$(1+\rho)\sigma_0 = ap_0\left[1 - \varphi_2^{(2)}\left(s; \frac{\Lambda ap_0}{(1+\rho)}\right)\right] \to ap_0 s(1 + \mathcal{O}(s))$$

$$\sigma_1 = ap_2\left[1 - \varphi_1^{(2)}(s; \Lambda ap_2)\right] \to \frac{ap_2 s}{2}(1 + \mathcal{O}(s)). \qquad (6.93)$$

The first expression on the right-hand side of each line is a closed form; the second expression is the leading small-s approximation when the corresponding $\Lambda a p_\tau \to 0$. At interest rates $\rho \ll 1$, the first-order conditions favor twice the investment level in σ_0 as in σ_1.

6.16.5.2   Accounting identities and balance of interest payments   The requirement to balance interest payments, in the context of the income/expense accounting relation for farmers, places an independent set of constraints on σ_0 and σ_1.

We may rearrange the sum (6.86) of income and expenses for farmers into the young-period and old-period bids by prospectors, as

$$(1 + \rho)\,\sigma_0 + \sigma_1 = \frac{n_0}{n}\frac{e_0}{2}\left[(1 + \varphi_1 + \varphi_2) + (1 + \rho)\,(1 + \varphi_1 + \varphi_2)\right], \quad (6.94)$$

in which the expressions φ_τ refer to the prospector allocations given in Eq. (6.83).

The equation (6.87) of total farmer loans with total prospector deposits, necessary to balance interest payments, may be similarly rearranged as

$$\sigma_0 = \frac{n_0}{n}\frac{e_0}{2}\left[(1 + \varphi_1 + \varphi_2) + 2\,(1 - \varphi_1)\right]. \quad (6.95)$$

The remainder of the prospector payments that support farmer investment, Eq. (6.88), which is simply the difference of the previous two equations, then becomes

$$\sigma_1 = \frac{n_0}{n}\frac{e_0}{2}\left[(1 + \varphi_1 + \varphi_2) - 2\,(1 + \rho)\,(1 - \varphi_1)\right]. \quad (6.96)$$

By the prospector first-order conditions (6.80), their bids on food in the old and young periods always have the ratio $(1 + \rho)$. Moreover, in the unstressed ($\Lambda e_0 \to 0$) equilibrium, almost all of the prospector endowment is used to buy food; that is, the factors $(1 - \varphi_1) \approx s/2 \ll 1$ in Eqs. (6.95, 6.96). This condition produces $\sigma_0 \sim \sigma_1$, so that σ_0 (with interest) is both paid for by *old*-period prospector bids and in turn provides the interest stream to produce them, while σ_1 is paid for with *young*-period prospector bids, nearly equal in quantity to σ_0.

However, this condition, together with the property that when $s \ll 1$, inter-period fluctuations in food prices are $\mathcal{O}(s)$, then drives $(1 + \rho) \to 2$ in Eq. (6.93), giving the consequence of the first-order conditions.

6.16.5.3   Interest rates decrease from the unstressed-equilibrium value $\rho = 1$ with increasing shadow price   It is not obvious a priori whether interest rates should increase or decrease as the shadow price on the capacity constraint increases from zero due to insufficient population. Since the relative value of present to future consumption is inverse to the interest rate, the way interest rates respond to shadow prices will depend on the way payment streams respond. In the fiat-banking model considered next, interest rates will increase from a value $\rho = 0$ in the unstressed equilibrium as Λe_0 increases. But in this model, interest rates *decrease* from their value $\rho = 1$ in the unstressed equilibrium as Λe_0 increases. Here we summarize how that response is produced by the intersection of the first-order conditions and balance-of-payment constraints.

It is important to remember that, while the formation of a shadow price on the capacity constraint for capital stock represents a stress relative to the $\Lambda e_0 = 0$ noncooperative equilibrium, it corresponds to the situation $N < N_C$, in which there is a *surfeit* of gold per capita relative to the unstressed equilibrium. Therefore, although all prospector bids on food decrease per capita as described by Eq. (6.94), as prospectors supply a larger relative share of investments, their deposits in the bank decrease *less quickly* than their bids on food, according to Eqs. (6.95, 6.96). At an interest rate ρ that balances total interest payments, the farmer investment σ_0 on which interest is paid therefore declines more slowly than the investment σ_1 on which interest is not paid. Moreover, the term $(1 - \varphi_1)$ responsible for the difference in bid levels increases with increasing Λe_0, while the common term $(1 + \varphi_1 + \varphi_2)$ decreases. When, at finite Λe_0, these two contributions pass through the ratio $2 : 1$, it is possible to satisfy both the first-order conditions and the accounting identity with $\rho \to 0$, even if food prices remain similar across periods.

6.16.6   Analytic solutions for limits in the unstressed noncooperative equilibria

Once it is recognized that these constraints determine the dependence of ρ on Λe_0, closed-form solutions are easy to obtain at $s \ll 1$ for the population composition required for $\Lambda e_0 \to 0$, and hence for the critical population size for high-yielding production.

Utility levels are dominated by food consumption at $s \ll 1$, and at $\Lambda e_0 \to 0$ all φ terms cancel in Eq. (6.91), casting the condition of equal utility in the same functional form for all generations (τ). Therefore all gold-denominated food prices converge to the same value $ap_\tau / e_0 \to \sqrt{1 + \rho}$, reproduced in Eq. (6.27).

Using the general budget relation (6.78), and the particular evaluation from the first line of Eq. (6.79) to express σ_0 in terms of ap_0, the interest-balance condition (6.87) at $s \ll 1$ and $\Lambda e_0 \to 0$ gives the ratio of prospectors to farmers

$$\frac{n_0}{n} \to \frac{2s}{3(1+\rho)} \frac{ap_0}{e_0}. \tag{6.97}$$

As explained in the previous subsection, a similar but independent expression is obtained for σ_1 in terms of ap_2, using Eq. (6.78) and the second line of Eq. (6.79). If these two relations are inserted in the remaining accounting identity (6.88) between total bids and investment, together with the approximation at $s \ll 1$ that all ap_τ take the same value at $\Lambda e_0 \to 0$, we find that the required interest rate in the unstressed equilibrium is $\rho \to 1 + \mathcal{O}(s)$. Eq. (6.27) then gives $ap_\tau / e_0 \to \sqrt{2}$, which in Eq. (6.97) goes to

$$\frac{n_0}{n} \to \frac{\sqrt{2}s}{3}. \tag{6.98}$$

The resulting critical population size for the unstressed equilibrium to support investment $3n_0 e_0 = \mathcal{C}$ is given as Eq. (6.28).

6.16.7   How much gold does the bank need?

If we require that the bank lend physical gold, we may track the amount that it must hold at the beginning of the period, in order to supply net demands by the agents. The details of required bank reserves can of course depend on the fine structure of sequencing of deposits and withdrawals in each period. The simplest choice (and one consistent with the interpretation of periods as entire stages of life) is to not assume a detailed structure of lags between withdrawals and deposits of various kinds, and to model deposits and withdrawals within a period as being cleared in a single meeting of all agents with the bank in that period. This is always possible, because prospectors hold all gold they deposit from their endowments coming into the period, and farmers hold all gold they may owe from clearing of the previous period's food market.

Total deposits in the bank, both lending by prospectors and repayment of principal and interest by farmers, may be computed in each period as

$$\frac{(\text{Deposits})_0}{n_0 e_0} = \frac{1}{2} \varphi_2^{(2)}(s; \Lambda e_0)$$

$$\frac{(\text{Deposits})_1}{n_0 e_0} = \frac{1}{2} + (1+\rho) \frac{\sigma_0}{e_0} \frac{n}{n_0}$$

$$\frac{(\text{Deposits})_2}{n_0 e_0} = 1 - \frac{1}{2} \varphi_1^{(2)}(s; (1+\rho)\Lambda e_0). \tag{6.99}$$

Withdrawals in each period are

$$\frac{(\text{Withdrawals})_0}{n_0 e_0} = (1+\rho)\left[1 - \frac{1}{2}\varphi_1^{(2)}(s;(1+\rho)\Lambda e_0)\right] + \frac{\sigma_0}{e_0}\frac{n}{n_0}$$

$$\frac{(\text{Withdrawals})_1}{n_0 e_0} = (1+\rho)\frac{1}{2}\varphi_2^{(2)}(s;\Lambda e_0)$$

$$\frac{(\text{Withdrawals})_2}{n_0 e_0} = (1+\rho)\frac{1}{2}. \tag{6.100}$$

The bank balance at the end of each period is the prior balance net of deposits and withdrawals, and we choose the maximum balance so that the minimum over the cycle is zero. Recall that the capacity constraint is $\mathcal{C} = 3n_0 e_0$, so $(\text{Deposits})_\tau/\mathcal{C} = (1/3)(\text{Deposits})_\tau/n_0 e_0$, and similarly for withdrawals and balances. We will see from the solutions that in the unstressed equilibrium, the bank needs to hold approximately $(2.5/3)\mathcal{C}$ at the beginning of period $\tau = 2$, and in the small population limit where $\rho \to 0$, this requirement falls below $(2/3)\mathcal{C}$ for the value of $\theta = 1/2$.

Numerical solutions for the prior balance of the bank in all three periods are shown in figure 6.12. The absolute gold reserve required diminishes weakly with N/N_C as interest rate diminishes, because it is determined mostly by the scale of capital stock. Bank reserves per capita therefore increase roughly as N_C/N.

6.17 Appendix: Solutions for the Economy with Fiat Banking and Control through Purchase and Sale of Gold

6.17.1 Solutions to the first-order conditions

In the fiat economy, the relation of the gold endowment for investment becomes much more symmetrical with the role of the food endowment for single-period consumption than it is in an economy with gold money. As in the previous examples, logarithmic utility leads to convenient simplifications of the optimization for the prospectors, so we begin with them. Because the numéraire of fiat is now an arbitrary choice of the central bank, all prices will be referenced to a single price that fixes this numéraire, which we take to be the $\tau = 2$ price for gold: p_{G2}.

6.17.1.1 Prospector sector The accounting identity for the fiat value of the prospector endowment of gold is

$$e_0 p_{G\tau} = \hat{q}_G^{(\tau)}p_{G\tau} + \left(\hat{\sigma}_0\delta_{\tau,0} + \hat{\sigma}_1\delta_{\tau,2}\right)p_{G\tau}$$

$$= 2\hat{b}_1^{(\tau)} + \left(\hat{\sigma}_0\delta_{\tau,0} + \hat{\sigma}_1\delta_{\tau,2}\right)p_{G\tau}. \tag{6.101}$$

In the second line we have used the budget relations (6.36), along with the fact that the first-order conditions with lending at interest give $\hat{b}_1^{(\tau)} = (1 + \rho) \hat{b}_0^{(\tau)}$, as they did for the banking model in Eq. (6.84).

Then the first-order conditions for prospectors relate their bids on food to total gold price levels in each period as

$$(1 + \rho) \hat{b}_0^{(\tau)} = \hat{b}_1^{(\tau)} = \frac{e_0}{2} p_{G\tau} \varphi_{\tau-1}^{(2)}(s; \Lambda e_0), \tag{6.102}$$

the investment levels are given by

$$\hat{\sigma}_0 = e_0 \left(1 - \varphi_2^{(2)}(s; \Lambda e_0) \right)$$
$$\hat{\sigma}_1 = e_0 \left(1 - \varphi_1^{(2)}(s; \Lambda e_0) \right), \tag{6.103}$$

and therefore the offered quantities satisfy

$$\hat{q}_G^{(\tau)} = e_0 \varphi_{\tau-1}^{(2)}(s; \Lambda e_0). \tag{6.104}$$

These inputs form the basis for all other price formation rules, given any shadow price valuation of the gold endowment Λe_0.

6.17.1.2   Farmer sector   The first-order conditions for investment relative to old-period bids on food take the same form as they did in the IGT economy,

$$\Lambda \sigma_1 = \frac{sx}{1 - (1 + 2\theta) x}$$
$$\Lambda \sigma_0 = \Lambda \kappa^{(2)} = \frac{2\theta sx}{1 - 2\theta x}, \tag{6.105}$$

in terms of a collection of variables that we abbreviate

$$x \equiv \frac{\Lambda b_1^{(2)}}{(1 + \rho) p_{G2}}. \tag{6.106}$$

(Definition (6.106) differs from the x in Eq. (6.61) in the IGT model by the factor $(1 + \rho)$, and by pricing specifically relative to period-$(\tau = 2)$ gold through the factor p_{G2}.)

6.17.1.3   Bank action   Only $(\tau = 2)$ farmers in their young period can bid on gold in time for its delivery to serve either their own investments or their transfers to support the investments of their $(\tau = 0)$ offspring. Therefore we may write the gold price formation rule (6.38) more explicitly in the form

$$\frac{n}{n_0} b_{G0}^{(2)} \delta_{\tau,2} + \frac{B_G^{(\tau)}}{n_0} = \left(\hat{q}^{(\tau)} + \frac{Q_G^{(\tau)}}{n_0} \right) p_{G\tau}. \tag{6.107}$$

All other bids outside period $\tau = 2$ must come from the central bank. Using the expression (6.104) for offers of gold in these periods, and descaling with p_{G2} to remove the numéraire of fiat, we arrive at two of the central bank's control variables expressed in terms of their effect on interperiod ratios of gold prices, as

$$\frac{B_G^{(\tau)}}{n_0 e_0 p_{G2}} = \frac{p_{G\tau}}{p_{G2}} \varphi_{\tau-1}^{(2)}(s; \Lambda e_0), \tag{6.108}$$

for $\tau = 0, 1$.

The exclusion of wash selling means that offers are not made in these periods, so that the central bank offers gold only in period $\tau = 2$. Full return of gold then requires

$$\frac{Q_G^{(2)}}{n_0} = q^{(0)} + q^{(1)}$$

$$= e_0 \left(\varphi_2^{(2)}(s; \Lambda e_0) + 1 \right). \tag{6.109}$$

Evaluating the price expression (6.107) at $\tau = 2$, and using Eq. (6.109) for $Q_G^{(2)}/n_0$ together with the fact that $B_G^{(\tau)} = 0$ by exclusion of wash sales, gives a relation between the total offered quantity (which depends only on e_0 and Λ), the labor allocation n_0/n, and the farmer bid level set by $b_{G0}^{(2)}$, in the form

$$\frac{\sigma_1 + \sigma_0}{e_0} = \frac{\sigma_1 + \kappa^{(2)}}{e_0} = \frac{b_{G0}^{(2)}}{e_0 p_{G2}} = \frac{n_0}{n} \left(1 + \varphi_1^{(2)}(s; \Lambda e_0) + \varphi_2^{(2)}(s; \Lambda e_0) \right)$$

$$= \frac{sx}{\Lambda e_0} \left(\frac{1}{1 - (1 + 2\theta)x} + \frac{2\theta}{1 - 2\theta x} \right). \tag{6.110}$$

The expressions on the first line involve only relative quantities of gold, and ensure that the total investment from farmers and prospectors equals $3n_0 e_0$ (by Eq. (6.103)). The relation to x—the farmer bid level in ($\tau = 2$) gold prices in the second line—follows from the farmer first-order conditions.

In numerical solutions, we will sweep the variables Λe_0 appearing in the first line and x appearing in the second line of Eq. (6.110), and for each pair, determine the consistent value for n_0/n to appear in later relations.

6.17.2   Price cycles

6.17.2.1   Cyclic accounting identities for fiat and gold   The farmer budget equation that cycles fiat among periods in the food markets is

$$
\begin{aligned}
q^{(\tau)} p_\tau &= b_1^{(\tau)} + (1+\rho)\, b_{G0}^{(\tau)} \\
&= b_1^{(\tau-1)} + \frac{n_0}{n} \left(\hat{b}_1^{(\tau-1)} + \hat{b}_0^{(\tau)} \right) \\
&= b_1^{(\tau-1)} + \frac{n_0}{n} \left((1+\rho)\, \hat{b}_0^{(\tau-1)} + \hat{b}_1^{(\tau)} \right).
\end{aligned}
\tag{6.111}
$$

The first line includes the bids (along with interest on bids from the first period) that farmers pay from proceeds of sales, and the second (and equivalently, third) line lists the source of money from the pricing rule (6.10).

Summing Eq. (6.111) over τ, and canceling the factors $b_1^{(\tau)}$ that appear on both sides of the equality, gives the accounting relation between farmer income and expenses

$$
(1+\rho)\, \frac{n}{n_0} b_{G0}^{(2)} = (2+\rho) \sum_\tau \hat{b}_0^{(\tau)}.
\tag{6.112}
$$

The only farmer expenses that are not recycled are the bid on gold in period $\tau = 2$ and the interest paid on it.

Summing, instead, the price formation rule (6.107) over τ, and then using relations (6.104) and (6.102) for prospector gold offers and food bids, gives a relation between central bank bids and offers, prospector food bids set by e_0 and Λ, and the farmer bidding scale set by $b_{G0}^{(2)}$,

$$
\frac{n}{n_0} b_{G0}^{(2)} + \sum_\tau \frac{B_G^{(\tau)}}{n_0} = \sum_\tau \hat{q}^{(\tau)} p_{G\tau} + \sum_\tau \frac{Q_G^{(\tau)} p_{G\tau}}{n_0}
$$

$$
= (1+\rho) \sum_\tau 2\hat{b}_0^{(2)} + \frac{Q_G^{(2)} p_{G2}}{n_0}.
\tag{6.113}
$$

The difference of Eq. (6.113) from Eq. (6.112), multiplied by n_0, is the cycle identity for fiat,

$$
\rho \left(n b_{G0}^{(2)} + n_0 \sum_\tau \hat{b}_0^{(2)} \right) + Q_G^{(2)} p_{G2} = \sum_\tau B_G^{(\tau)}.
\tag{6.114}
$$

The left-hand side includes all expenditures by agents; the first term is interest on borrowing, the second is payment for gold in period $\tau = 2$. The right-hand side includes all fiat expenditures by the central bank, in bids for gold. This equation is predicated on the repayment of interest in full without strategic bankruptcy, which will imply one constraint on the interest rate in relation to the bid levels $B_G^{(\tau)}$, which is derived below.

6.17.2.2   The food price cycle

The relation between endowment and price for farmers in the food sector, parallel to Eq. (6.101) for prospectors in the gold sector, becomes

$$
\begin{aligned}
ap_\tau &= A_0^{(\tau)} p_\tau + q^{(\tau)} p_\tau \\
&= 2b_1^{(\tau)} + (1+\rho)\, b_{G0}^{(\tau)},
\end{aligned} \tag{6.115}
$$

where one first-order condition is used to evaluate $A_0^{(\tau)} p_\tau$ and Eq. (6.111) is used to evaluate $q^{(\tau)} p_\tau$.

Combining these expense relations with Eq. (6.111) for inputs gives an expression for the food price cycle

$$
\begin{aligned}
ap_\tau + (1+\rho)\, b_{G0}^{(\tau)} &= ap_{\tau-1} - (1+\rho)\, b_{G0}^{(\tau-1)} + 2\frac{n_0}{n}\left(\hat{b}_1^{(\tau-1)} + \frac{\hat{b}_1^{(\tau)}}{1+\rho} \right) \\
&= ap_{\tau-1} - (1+\rho)\, b_{G0}^{(\tau-1)} + \frac{n_0}{n} e_0 \left(p_{G\tau-1}\varphi_{\tau-2} + \frac{p_{G\tau}\varphi_{\tau-1}}{1+\rho} \right).
\end{aligned} \tag{6.116}
$$

The starting level for the cycle may be taken as the value of ap_2 determined from x appearing in Eq. (6.110), Eq. (6.115), and the first-order conditions (6.105):

$$
\frac{\Delta ap_2}{(1+\rho)\, p_{G2}} = x\left\{ 2 + \frac{s}{1-(1+2\theta)x} + \frac{2\theta s}{1-2\theta x} \right\}. \tag{6.117}
$$

6.17.2.3   Central bank bid variables and control over gold prices

Eq. (6.110), together with the farmer income/expense balance (6.112) and the expression (6.102) for $\hat{b}_1^{(\tau)}$, gives a relation between interperiod ratios of gold prices (or equivalently, their control through central bank bids) and interest rates of

$$
\sum_\tau \left(\frac{p_{G\tau}}{p_{G2}} - \frac{(1+\rho)^2}{(1+\rho/2)} \right) \varphi_{\tau-1}^{(2)}(s; \Delta e_0) = 0. \tag{6.118}
$$

Separating $\tau = 2$, in which in which the central bank does not bid, from the other two periods, we obtain a constraint on one linear combination of bids:

$$\rho \frac{3 + 2\rho}{2 + \rho} \varphi_1^{(2)}(s; \Lambda e_0) = \sum_{\tau = 0,1} \left(\frac{p_{G\tau}}{p_{G2}} - \frac{(1 + \rho)^2}{(1 + \rho/2)} \right) \varphi_{\tau-1}^{(2)}(s; \Lambda e_0)$$

$$= \sum_{\tau = 0,1} \left(\frac{B_G^{(\tau)}}{n_0 e_0 p_{G2}} - \frac{(1 + \rho)^2}{(1 + \rho/2)} \varphi_{\tau-1}^{(2)}(s; \Lambda e_0) \right),$$

(6.119)

where the second line uses Eq. (6.108). The central bank cannot, thus, set all gold prices equal and at the same time require full repayment of fiat, except in the limit $\rho \to 0$.

We will introduce an "angle" α to express the two-period bids relative to the interest rate, as

$$\frac{B_G^{(0)}}{n_0 e_0 p_{G2}} - \frac{(1 + \rho)^2}{(1 + \rho/2)} \varphi_2^{(2)}(s; \Lambda e_0) = \left(\frac{\cos \alpha}{\cos \alpha + \sin \alpha} \right) \rho \frac{3 + 2\rho}{2 + \rho} \varphi_1^{(2)}(s; \Lambda e_0)$$

$$\frac{B^{(1)}}{n_0 e_0 p_{G2}} - \frac{(1 + \rho)^2}{(1 + \rho/2)} = \left(\frac{\sin \alpha}{\cos \alpha + \sin \alpha} \right) \rho \frac{3 + 2\rho}{2 + \rho} \varphi_1^{(2)}(s; \Lambda e_0).$$

(6.120)

Within the interior of the interval $\alpha \in [-\pi/4, 5\pi/4]$, either of the bids $B^{(0)}$, $B^{(1)}$ may be taken to zero. The range $\alpha < 0$ places maximum bids in $B^{(0)}$; the range $\alpha > \pi/2$ places maximum bids in $B^{(1)}$. In numerical solutions, we will sample over the variables ρ and α to minimize the prospector utility variance (6.39) at the values of x and Λe_0 that equate cycle-averaged utilities of farmers and prospectors, and are compatible with a given value of n_0/n through Eq. (6.110).

Notes

1 Mas-Colell and Hart [250] have shown that under reasonable conditions for the repeated game the correlated equilibrium will emerge. In sequential experimental games, simple alternations have been observed after a few moves.

2 In much political rhetoric it often appears as if the bureaucratic structure only pertains to government. In fact in a world with many corporations with hundreds of thousands of employees, the presence of bureaucracies characterizes both the public and the private sectors.

3 We need to seek some form of sensitivity analysis to help to justify this simplification that is difficult in the extreme to measure. This is discussed further in sections 10.2.1 and 10.2.2.

4 While initial conditions are required for a well-defined game, we typically regard them as an aggregate representation for the legacy of a long past. For the models we will introduce,

even though agent generations repeat indefinitely, for a wide range of terminal conditions, cross-generation interactions truncate over a finite number (here, zero or one) of generations. Therefore, the precise statement of the role of terminal boundary conditions is that among a wide range of specifications (all those that do not involve divergent salvage values for any gold held by agents in the last period), differences do not affect strategic choices sufficiently prior to the last generation.

5 It may be still physically present but in a form that makes its reclaim uneconomic.

6 The Heaviside function $\Theta(x) \equiv 0$ if $x < 0$ and $\Theta(x) \equiv 1$ if $x \geq 0$.

7 Originally the Cobb-Douglas function was introduced as a production function with two inputs (land and labor) and exponents for these inputs that sum to unity. It has become common to refer to the same functional form, when used in utilities, as a "Cobb-Douglas" form, to relax the restriction that the coefficients sum to unity (since the result of this relaxation is at most monotone transformation), and to include in the "Cobb-Douglas" appellation all cardinal utilities that share the same homothetic preferences as the original power-law Cobb-Douglas form.

8 This is equivalent to the reduction to a labor-equivalent metric of utility developed in chapter 5.

9 Here we are not concerned with the best estimator for the variance but simply with the second moment around the mean, so we normalize with $1/3$ rather than with $1/2$.

10 This assumption maintains the framework of type-symmetric solutions assumed for all other analyses of this volume. The first-order conditions never exclude type-symmetric solutions, so at most we are failing to look for a high-dimensional set of nonsymmetric solutions which we haven't proved do not exist.

11 This analysis has been for the infinite-replicates limit. We note, however, that in other chapters with finite rather than infinite replicates in same buy-sell game, wash selling was *weakly but explicitly* excluded (at $\mathcal{O}(1/N)$) by the first-order conditions.

12 In the second lines of each of the following equations, we group terms to emphasize the uniform way in which factors of $1 + \rho$ interact with wealth levels measured either as $\Lambda a p_\tau$ (for farmers) or e_0 (for prospectors).

7 Building Theories of Economic Process

7.1 Steps toward Economic Process

In the previous chapters, we have provided proofs of principle for representing institutions as the carriers of process, using strategic market game models highly related in form to those of general equilibrium, but with extra constraints imposed by the institutions sufficient to carry process. Nevertheless, except in chapter 6 we have avoided explicit treatment of dynamics. Structure may limit equations of motion, but it does not fully specify enough to identify game models consistent with those of general equilibrium without further consideration of intent and behavior.

In this chapter we turn explicitly to the problem of constraining dynamics, and begin by considering, in varying degrees of brevity, modeling structures that have been constructed to provide a true dynamics that meet the criterion that they supply a time path out of equilibrium to a stationary state as well as the proof of the existence of a stationary state or growth path.

Before considering dynamics, we note that problems with general equilibrium models of an economy are encountered even with static analysis. There is a considerable distinction between nonconstructive proof of existence and computability of equilibria. Fortunately the work of Lemke [217] adapted by Scarf [316] and others following him has provided a basis for computation.

True dynamics poses many other problems involving not only motivation, learning, communication, and information flow, but also the nature of the context within which the economic behavior takes place.

In economics, the unifying power of general equilibrium analysis comes from the fact that *it is not a model, but rather a collection of principles for building models*. It suggests a uniform configuration space based on goods, services, and extended in some cases to time periods or uncertainty, utilizing

more or less standard representations of ordinal and cardinal utilities and production functions, and the dual structure responsible for prices. Models may
be invented within this framework to illustrate particular points or to capture
aspects of particular systems, and they may be taken or left without entailing
judgments about the validity of the superordinate framework. In this regard the
general equilibrium framework behaves much like a *theory* in one of the natural sciences, and its models behave like representations of particular systems
as those instantiate the theory. To the extent that this analogy is appropriate, we
might say that general equilibrium is a theory of economic constraint imposed
by exchange and production on optimal choice. It is presented at a level of
abstraction in which there is no indication of how it may involve aspects of
trust and information in trade and control and ownership in production.

7.2   A Change in Emphasis and a Change in Paradigm

We propose that the next steps toward an economic dynamics require both a
change in emphasis and a change in paradigm.

The level of generality of general equilibrium theory, while appropriate for
proof of the existence of equilibria, requires more structure to be specified for
the development of dynamics. Full process models must be provided.

7.2.1   Capital stock and production

In considering dynamics one must weigh the intermix of both the structure and
behavior that are observed. Although we acknowledge the roles of both, our
emphasis is on structure. We concentrate primarily on the constraints imposed
by the production structure and the financial structure. As much as we can,
we finesse details from socioeconomic and psychoeconomic behavior, though
not because we do not regard them as important. They are critical and supply
the rich sources that enable us to provide many plausible but not adequately
tested or solved equations of behavior. The two most popular hypotheses of
behavior leading to equations amenable to some general analysis or simulation
have local optimizers or rational-expectations optimizers. Yet even with the
rational-expectations models, proof of convergence of a given process to an
equilibrium is hardly ever provided.[1]

We conjecture that given the mutation rate of sociopolitical systems [205,
236], about the closest one will come to reasonably robust equations of motion
are those situations where the economic motive is high and conscious and

where the sociopolitico-economic structure can be deemed to be reasonably stable for the time horizon appropriate to the problem at hand.

7.2.1.1 The approach to dynamics via sequential learning behavior   We recognize that the study of learning behavior in sequential games is highly important; but in our estimate, in spite of considerable work, there is still a morass of pure game theory with incomplete knowledge of rules and nonsymmetric information, where little is known about the sensitivity of the mathematical results to the sociopsychological, psychological, and ad hoc contextual aspects of these models. This is the domain where experimental gaming can be of service. A hope lies in those situations where a reasonably stable context can be postulated and there is a mass of small agents whose optimization can be regarded by each as a one-person game against "Nature, or the market or the economy."

Our approach is presented not as a substitute for behavioral economics but as complementary with it. We stress that, for many economic problems of importance, an understanding of the general principles of how to build process models indicates how to provide constraints on the feasible motions.

7.2.1.2   The approach to dynamics via the time structure of production
We argue that there is a structure underlying economic dynamics that requires a larger list of basic elements beyond that required for static GE. In particular an appropriate general set of SMGs requires explicit considerations of the roles of control, guidance, and ownership in a far more specific manner than is provided in GE. We deal with the basic ingredients of a dynamic economy below in table 11.2.

7.2.2   The further change in paradigm: ownership and control

In chapter 1 the first basic shift in modeling was to incorporate government as a significant player. As we move toward dynamics we note that not only is GE not dynamic but it is clearly noninstitutional and abstracts away considerations of control. The shadow firms are pro forma profit maximizers. Dividends are a needed convenience to balance books when profits are nonzero. Ownership and control problems are irrelevant to the structure, as is evinced by the introduction of implicitly nonvoting shares (see [344]).

In the (nevertheless masterful) abstraction of the various authors of GE theory, at the cost of a nonconstructive existence proof approach, items such as perception, innovation and public goods, finances and private and government control were fully abstracted. A natural change from GE to an abstract but fully process class of models is given by strategic market games. They offer the means to incorporate these features while maintaining contact with the general structure now extended to process models. In particular, the results of individuals such as Geanakoplos and Mas-Colell [154] showing enormous indeterminacy in trying to erect a monetary and financial system on the general equilibrium structure were no surprise whatsoever. The indeterminacy disappears in the complete specification of the microeconomic details for the myriads of process models called forth by a loosely coupled control system.

7.3   Control, Coordination, and Competition

In chapters 5 and 6 the emphasis became far more institutionally oriented than previously, even if the institutions performing the extra functions were minimal. With the addition of a government bank and bureaucracy, the financial and political control and guidance systems that had been abstracted from the GE system reentered explicitly in an SMG version with bureaucracy in chapter 5. As we showed, the resource and political organization cost of a fiat or symbolic monetary system becomes substantial when the overall system is to become self-policing to a sufficiently high degree.

In order to proceed from a classical preinstitutional economy, we organize the remainder of this chapter as follows:

First we consider a highly simplified transformation matrix indicating the basic actors and physical and financial instruments that serve as the basic building blocks of a politicoeconomic system. This system is called for because the dynamics requires that the strategic relationship between ownership and control be made explicit.

We then consider briefly each of the items selected as building blocks independently to justify their inclusion as basic items in a simple dynamic system.

The transformation matrix is too coarse-grained to have production usefully described. In section 7.6 it is connected with some specific linear dynamic models.

We raise some essentially ontological and linguistic problems in the precise definition of several economic concepts and consider applications to several explicit problems. We regard this work as somewhat far from a traditional economic approach and highly preliminary, but believe that eventually this type of examination of basic economic concepts is called for and is of operational worth, especially in the confrontation between economic thought and legal interpretation. This approach is utilized in the text to discuss the catalytic properties of capital, but further discussion is relegated to appendix 7.13 for the reader interested in this type of application.

7.4   A Transformation Matrix and Linear Dynamics

In a previous publication [356], a transformation matrix of the basic building blocks of an economy was suggested. Upon further reflection we present here a somewhat modified version of this and connect it to the development of linear dynamic models of the economy where true dynamics is first to be encountered, in the sense that these models include time paths for all states of the system. Previously it was suggested that combinations of eight basic instruments were sufficient to serve as a basis on which to construct all variations of economic and financial instruments. Upon further reflection we have somewhat modified this. Many definitions depend on the fineness of the time grid selected. We also attempt to make a clearer distinction between point consumption and essentially continuous consumption and distinguish reproducible versus nonreproducible assets.

The matrix conforms to our requirements of minimal complexity. It is restricted to relationships involving only two periods of time and relationships involving only one or two agents. A reasonable unit of time for much empirical work is a calendar year. Given this time interval, a durable may be defined as a good lasting more than one period. This simple matrix linking only two periods fails to pick up an economy with a historical time profile in its real assets and financial contracts. It also fails to portray the dynamics of uncertainty overlaid on the profile of the assets; but it serves as the basis from which to add these complexities.

The inclusion of uncertainty adds considerable complexity to the nature of the transformations, and more time periods can be brought in by multiplication of one-period transformations; but this is not sufficiently complex to pick up the differences in life spans of economic agents and goods, the importance of which has already been indicated in the analysis in chapter 6.

7.4.1   On agents

We note above that contracts depend on two agents. The modeler concerned with economic dynamics at a high level of abstraction requires at least two if not three types of agent. In particular we introduce natural persons and other legal persons as a representation of government and other corporations as basic entities. Corporate persons are nonnatural persons that are recognized as legal persons. For many purposes it may be desirable to distinguish government from other corporate persons. Simple contracts are written between any two agents of these types.

The natural persons appear in two roles: both as owner-agents and as a basic natural resource. The rules of the game determine whether this asset can be traded.

The treatment of the natural person as a primitive unit in an economic theory with preferences and ownership rights is reasonably natural. The treatment of either government or other nonperson legal entities as primitive units, while it is often done, requires considerable care as in each case they are complex institutional black boxes. As such they give rise to many of the current paradoxes in political economy, such as: What are the goals of a central bank or a government? Are firms expected to be profit maximizers? What dividends should they pay?

7.4.2   On real assets and contracts

The ten primitive assets intimated above are described below.

1. Natural persons viewed as the asset behind the service of labor,

2. Perishable point consumption goods; many foods for example,

3. Storable point consumption goods; preserved foods, many office and household supplies,

4. Continuous services such as water, electricity, heat, communication service products,

5. Producible goods such as buildings, household durables, transportation vehicles,

6. Land,

7. Nonreproducible natural resources,

8. Labor,

9. Fiat money,

10. Ownership paper.

A minimal contract is of the form: "Agent i supplies agent j with a quantity of primitive resource a at time t in return for agent j supplying agent i with a quantity of primitive resource b at time $t + 1$." If we limit ourselves to contracts that are always intermediated with money, there are $(10 \cdot 9)/2 = 45$ possible types.

Several simple contracts are noted:

- A service contract: "Agent i supplies agent j with a flow of services at time t in return for agent j supplying agent i with a quantity of fiat money at time $t + 1$."
- A futures contract: "Agent i supplies agent j with a quantity of fiat money at time t in return for agent j supplying agent i with a quantity of wheat at time $t + 1$."
- A debt contract: "Agent i supplies agent j with a quantity of fiat money at time t in return for agent j supplying agent i with a quantity of fiat money at time $t + 1$."

The transformation matrix is of size 20×22, where the extra column is required to indicate when an item existing at time t ceases to exist or is transformed into nothing at time $t + 1$. If we limit ourselves to contracts always involving money, the size of the matrix is reduced considerably.

We do not display the matrix, but note that its structure is easy to describe. At this level of simplicity the ten basic units each map into the same item category one period later, except for services which disappear and those durables at the end of their lives at time t which also disappear at time $t + 1$. Each minimal contract maps into the item to be delivered. This holds under the implicit assumption of no uncertainty or strategic default. At a higher level of complexity this is no longer true.

7.5 Linear Production Spaces

The models in chapters 5 and 6 have illustrated the transition from preinstitutional preferences to heavily institutionalized optimization problems in which increasingly many of the strategic variables appear only in constraint terms and not directly in the utility. The problem of defining the institutional constraints on dynamics is much higher-dimensional, but it remains possible to identify domains in which the structure and role of constraints can be studied systematically. Here we consider the space of linear transformations among demand bundles defined at a sequence of times. This collection of models includes those introduced by Ramsey, von Neumann, and Leontief, as well as the transformation matrix with which we opened the chapter. Linear production space models may be used in three ways. They may be embedded within the general equilibrium and strategic market game paradigms,[2] deriving prices from utilities subject to production constraints. Alternatively, the price system defined by input/output ratios may be regarded as the primitive, and utilities derived which are consistent with it. Finally, utilities may be bypassed entirely if we wish to focus on the limits of feasible dynamical trajectories imposed by production constraints.

7.5.1   Definition of linear transformations on multiperiod demand spaces

Consider intertemporal models defined on a space of demands indexed by time $(x_0, x_1, \ldots)$, in which each x_t is a (column) vector of quantities of m distinct goods $[x_{i,t}]$ with $i \in 1, \ldots, m$. The sequence of periods $\{t\}$ considered may be finite or it may be infinite. Corresponding to the goods at all times, there may be a set of vectors of endowments $(e_0, e_1, \ldots)$ which we regard as coming into the economy from outside within each period.

Suppose that all of the goods have quantities that may not be negative. Then if we wish to consider optimization problems involving these demand spaces, we may restrict model solutions to lie within this space by introducing a set of (row) vectors of Kuhn-Tucker multipliers $(\eta_0^T, \eta_1^T, \ldots)$, with each $\eta_t^T \equiv [\eta_{i,t}]^T$ and all $\eta_{i,t} \in [0, \infty)$.

The space of linear transformations of the intertemporal demands was introduced by von Neumann as a linear model of production [359]. The most general linear space is generated by a *set* of pairs of matrices conventionally denoted $\{(A_t, B_{t+1})\}$, in which the columns of each A_t represent inputs to production in period t, and their respective columns in B_{t+1} give the outputs in period $t + 1$. We will suppose here that all coefficients in the A and B matrices are nonnegative, but we do not otherwise restrict their form. In particular, at any t, A_t and B_{t+1} may be $m \times k$ matrices with $k \neq m$. Allowing these matrices to differ at different t indices represents changing processes of production.

The columns of the input and output matrices may be used at arbitrary levels which we denote by column vectors $(j_0, j_1, \ldots)$. For any such vector of utilization rates, the relation between the endowments and the demands at a time t is

$$x_t = e_t + B_t j_{t-1} - A_t j_t. \tag{7.1}$$

7.5.2   Various uses of linear production models

7.5.2.1   General equilibrium
An immediate use for linear production models is found within the conventional structure of general equilibrium. If we suppose that an intertemporal utility $\mathcal{U}(x_0, x_1, \ldots)$ exists, then we may form a Lagrangian

$$\mathcal{L}(x_0, x_1, \ldots; \eta_0, \eta_1, \ldots) = \mathcal{U}(x_0, x_1, \ldots) + \sum_t \eta_t^T x_t, \tag{7.2}$$

in which the demands $\{x_t\}$ are functions (7.1) of the $\{j_t\}$, which become the optimization variables.

7.5.2.2 Strategic market games With the utility and constraint structures in place, linear production may be added to any of the intertemporal strategic market games of the forms we have derived in the preceding chapters.

7.5.2.3 The original von Neumann model The original von Neumann model, in contrast with the one-dimensional treatment of Ramsey, dispensed with the high-dimensional assumption of an intertemporal utility, and proceeded directly to the optimization problem for production. It assumed constant production technologies $A_t = A$, $B_t = B$, $\forall t$, and considered the producer's optimization problem. If a set of prices $\{p_t\}$ and a discount factor β are given, one can consider the optimization of the discounted net present value

$$W \equiv \sum_t \beta^{t-1} p_t^T x_t, \tag{7.3}$$

or a variety of other objective functions [359].

7.5.2.4 Relations to the transformation matrix introduced at the beginning of the chapter A particular subset of the von Neumann transformations is the one that fully consumes all assets in each time period. This is possible if the columns of A span the goods space, ensuring that we can find at least one assignment for the vector j_t at each t for which

$$A j_t = x_t. \tag{7.4}$$

Then, starting from initial endowments e_0, we may recursively define a vector of the demands produced at each time

$$x_{t+1} = e_{t+1} + B j_t, \tag{7.5}$$

in which each x_t is understood to be evaluated before it is fully consumed to produce x_{t+1}.

In the particular case where A has an inverse, Eq. (7.5) simplifies to

$$x_{t+1} = e_{t+1} + B A^{-1} x_t. \tag{7.6}$$

The matrix BA^{-1} in the von Neumann model provides a way to arrive at transformations to the next period. In the case that multiple solutions j_t to Eq. (7.4) may be found at each time (because the matrix A has excess, linearly dependent rows), the space of demand histories (7.5) at each time forms a convex polyhedron, whose coefficients identify the subspace of the n^2-dimensional space of matrices compatible with the underlying linear production model.

7.5.2.5   From von Neumann to Leontief   Wassily Leontief's input-output methods [218] are less general, and may be understood as a projection of the von Neumann real-goods input/output matrices via a price system to input/output matrices for money.

The projection to money flows removes the use of transformation matrices one step further from the requirements of utility modeling in a direction that permits empirical calibration, at the cost that prices become hidden parameters within the accounting rather than either dynamic entities or even explicit constraints on optimization. In the Leontief input-output interpretation of a matrix such as BA^{-1} from Eq. (7.6), instead of regarding components $x_{i,t}$ as quantities of distinct goods, they are regarded as expenditures from different sectors. The sectors may be industrial, geographic, political, or more complex combinations of these. They may in principle be disaggregated to the level of individual firms,[3] in which case the particular elements $\left(BA^{-1}\right)_{ij} x_{j,t}$ have the interpretation of expenditure flows from one industry to another. In this finely resolved limit, such flows may correspond to the money value of a few or even one good traded between pairs of firms or households.

Since the quantities updated in Eq. (7.6) are denominated in money, the endowments e_t become inputs to different sectors from outside the domain of the input/output analysis, and a further accounting identity is imposed on the matrix BA^{-1}. Expenditure results in a closed flow of money among the sectors, leading to the accounting identity that[4]

$$\sum_i x_{i,t+1} = \sum_i e_{i,t+1} + \sum_i x_{i,t}.$$

Therefore BA^{-1} must have the property that its rows sum to the unit vector, or

$$\sum_i \left(BA^{-1}\right)_{ij} = 1, \ \forall j. \tag{7.7}$$

What is achieved with these many assumptions, usually along with an assumption of stationarity of the input-output matrices, is the ability to deduce long-range constraints of money flow throughout an economy.

7.5.2.6   A comment on models, accounting, and data gathering   Do data precede theory, or is it vice versa? The answer is both. The models serve as data organizers. Among the important influences of the development of the Keynesian revolution was its role in the creation of macroeconomic statistics, and the linear models have stressed microeconomic statistics. The interfacing of the financial control sector with the microeconomic structure of physical assets is still heavily a work in process. When one takes into account the costs involved, even in a highly computerized world with data banks, a natural locus for this development lies heavily in the melding of accounting and data gathering with both the needs of enterprises and the development of economics.[5]

7.6   Money, Credit Capital, and Liquidity

7.6.1   The catalytic function of capital

Even so simple a transformation as the persistence of an economic good through time may be an active process. Therefore in a system for modeling economic dynamics, it may be appropriate to require the modeling environment to continuously enforce contingencies, such as the persistence of a stock on the continuous delivery of flows. A simple physical example is the requirement of refrigeration for ice cream if it is to persist as a good delivering a certain kind of consumption. Nowadays the refrigeration itself is a service delivered by a machine, which in its turn requires the input of electric power, as well as a protected space and occasional maintenance, and ultimately disposal.

A rich type space is possible for goods that require or deliver services and in turn may be consumed or may become factors in production of other goods. We sketch in this section one way that a type space might be formalized to support a consistent imposition of constraints on a wide array of models. Our choice of formalization is a natural generalization of linear input/output models, with particular emphasis on the ability to incorporate topological concepts such as continuity in the passage of time. As an example to illustrate formal denotations, we consider only one such class, which we denote **Capital Goods**.[6] We might identify interesting subclasses of **Capital Goods**, like refrigerators, by a service they deliver (cold preservation) and another that they require (electric power), either to provide their service outputs or even to persist.

Suppose that X is the name assigned to an instance of an input service (e.g., a type and amount of power) and Y the name of an output service (a temperature and volume of cold preservation), and that we introduce a notation $\chi\,(X, Y, \tau)$ to refer to the subclass of **Capital Goods** for which these are input and output. We have also characterized the class by a remaining "service lifetime" τ, measured from the present, after which it will be transformed into a different good (for instance, a dead refrigerator requiring disposal).

It is conventional in general equilibrium economic modeling to represent any collection of goods (for instance, the collection owned by some agent) as a vector, whose basis elements are measures of each type of good, and whose scalar coefficients are real numbers multiplying the basis elements. Just as our types can have dimension, we can regard them as basis elements in a vector space describing the physical state of the world, only now there are distinct kinds of basis elements for stocks and flows. We may represent all states in terms of stocks in a discrete-time model, as long as the scaling of stocks representing accumulations of flows respects time continuity.

We may then capture the interesting transformation properties of capital goods by representing their action on the class $\chi\,(X, Y, \tau)$, hence on all of its subclasses and instances, in conjunction with the consumption of service X and the production of service Y. The transformation on the basis elements, represented as a map of vectors, induces the transformation on a general goods space by multiplication with appropriate real coefficients.

Over any short period Δt, the modeling environment is required to perform the replacement

$$(X\Delta t) + \chi\,(X, Y, \tau) \rightarrow (Y\Delta t) + \chi\,(X, Y, \tau - \Delta t), \qquad (7.8)$$

(and if it cannot do so, due to the unavailability of X, to transform the capital good or its service in some specified way). Eq. (7.8) says that an amount of accumulated power $X\Delta t$ (dimensionally, an energy), and a refrigerator of service lifetime τ, are transformed into an amount of cold preservation (volume and time) $Y\Delta t$ and an older refrigerator of service lifetime $\tau - \Delta t$, and that this transformation is the only admissible representation of the passage of time for this class of goods. This is a surrogate for the "mechanical" action of the world that functions beneath the level of economic choice, though the particular functions may result from production enabled by the economy.

If $\chi\,(X, Y, \tau - \Delta t)$ differs significantly from $\chi\,(X, Y, \tau)$, the good may be said to depreciate. If we consider a multiple s giving some number of refrigerators of the kind represented by $\chi\,(X, Y, \tau)$, that collection of capital goods similarly transforms $sX\Delta t$ into $sY\Delta t$ per interval Δt, so both sides of Eq. (7.8) are multiplied by s. The type space is thus made into a vector field, with $\chi\,(X, Y, \tau)$, X, Y, etc. as its basis elements, and s as scalar "coordinates."

If, relative to the timescales of interest, $\tau \rightarrow \infty$, Eq. (7.8) describes the continuous conversion of services $X \rightarrow Y$, contingent on the presence of a good in the class $\chi\,(X, Y, \tau)$ capable of that conversion. The stipulation that this transformation apply for *any* sufficiently short Δt identifies X and Y as services, and aging as a process consistent with a continuous topology for time. Such a continuous but contingent conversion of services is the defining characteristic of *catalysis*. A model that specifies the possible classes $\{\chi\,(X, Y, \tau)\}$ of capital goods, and procedures and costs for the creation of each, defines the physical constraints on transformation of services in an economy. As services can equal the time rate of change of inventories of stocks, this conversion amounts to a process model for production as well.

The discussion here is not only aimed at considering the catalytic aspects of capital stock; it also contains our attempt to frame a linguistic approach to the examination of basic economic phenomena. We believe that for greater precision and clarity, not only is a mathematical approach required but, as many of the phenomena are hard to define, let alone measure, a linguistic approach is also called for. Appendix 7.13 offers a brief tour of this approach applied to several further phenomena relevant to our modeling of capital, but we believe that they are still a work in process and we are not totally satisfied with the development.

7.7 Strategic Process Analysis

The general equilibrium model of a production and exchange economy was studied, abstracting out both financial instruments and commodity and service flows. The mathematization of the models of Arrow [13], Debreu [12, 79], and McKenzie concentrated on prices and quantities of goods and services in the physical economy, supposing that the physical transformation properties we have described above could be both modeled transparently and evaluated into an indefinite future from the time of contracting. The legal constraints on money and financial instruments were irrelevant for those purposes.

In a world with complete contracts and without transaction costs, the financial structure would not matter to the equilibrium analysis. There could be vast domains of indeterminacy involving trade in the financial assets. However, once the microeconomic details of process have been spelled out and it is realized that every process consumes resources, it is natural to assign resource consumption to the construction and maintenance of markets, monies, and laws [384]; thus the need to specify transaction costs is not merely an institutional detail but a logical necessity of process description. Furthermore if the resource consumption is relatively small in comparison with production processes, this implies that slight changes in relative costs could cause large changes in utilization.

The counterpart of the physical process language we have suggested above, for strategic action, is provided by game theory. Games may be specified in so-called *extensive, strategic, and coalitional forms* [354]. The first gives an explicit description of the sequence of possible events and all strategic contingencies, and is readily integrated with physical process models. The second provides a compressed (hence nonunique) description of the structure of independent strategic actions and the payoffs that accrue to them. The third assumes negotiations, side payments, enforcement, or other mechanisms for forming coalition strategies from individual strategies, and is appropriate to a meta-analysis of a complete process specification, or for the formation of upper and lower bounds on the requirements of money and financial services in cases where the external influences on coalition formation cannot be well estimated.

7.7.1   Levels of game-theoretic analysis

As the real economy is in a sense a playable game and not an abstract problem of equilibration, it is natural to require the same in models. A specification of trade mechanisms at the strategic level results in the *strategic market games* [356]. They are more fully defined than the general equilibrium models, providing a full specification of information conditions and payoffs in all states of the game. They are more institutional in the sense that items such as price formation must be specified. These games can be simulated or utilized in gaming experiments as well as being analyzed for their noncooperative equilibria.

A simple consideration of the price formation mechanisms shows that for procedures as simple as department store pricing or English auctions or the pricing of specialty steel, it is possible to specify millions of different models and it is scientifically difficult to select the appropriate sensitivity analysis. The local laws of motion require institutional detail. There is, however, a next step to escape from nonprocess statics, which is to utilize the strategic form of the game in the formal mathematical specification of what we have called a *minimal institution*, a model that is sufficiently rich to display the basic properties of the instruments and institutions involved, yet which cannot be further simplified without losing the properties being considered. It has been argued elsewhere [356] that there are only three minimal price formation mechanisms.[7] These have the technical property that the strategic and extensive forms of the game coincide. These minimal strategic representations can be reasonably well analyzed mathematically without having to become enmeshed in institutional detail.[8]

The structural analysis of chapter 4, and similar related work [356, 361, 383, 384], shows the effects of differences in market structure and money type on the costs and outcomes of noncooperative strategic equilibria. Here we attempt to capture some aspects of the flexible and sensitive evaluation and control structure of the web or skein of financial instruments, in a partly aggregate representation. Attempts to formalize these issues without a structured process description have led to descriptions whose meaning and application are somewhat unclear, as is suggested below.

7.8   Velocity, Loose Coupling, and Transients

We have advocated a physical model-building methodology in this book. It is reasonable to ask whether this methodology helps to provide any extra insight into classical problems that have been under debate for many years. We select three classical items: *"real bills only,"* the *equation of exchange or PQ = MV*, and the *quantity theory of money*, because in some sense the compact equation (or identity?), whether implicit in Smith or Hume or Newcomb or Fisher or von Mises or Friedman, is an exemplar of the clash between verbal description and the essay in the development of economic thought and its reduction to symbols and formal mathematization.

There is a delicate balance between the qualitative and quantitative in economic modeling. Political economy in particular requires a complex mixture of hard and soft facts.

7.8.1   A preamble to analysis

Prior to our analysis we stress that, for the most part, we have left out of this chapter four items central to economic dynamics but not immediately required for the critique below. They are:

1. The critical role of both exogenous and endogenous uncertainty;
2. The logical necessity for bankruptcy and default rules;
3. The importance of transient influences in redirecting the dynamics;
4. The questions of behavioral economics and finance.

These are all considered in chapters 8 and 9, but some brief observation are called for here.

Uncertainty is a central unpleasant fact of economic life, and any rationalizations that offer us an easy way out of facing up to the processes of politico-economic prediction are welcomed by both the analyst and policymaker. A central task of good political economy is not prediction but the control and amelioration of the havoc caused by difficult-to-predict trajectories.

Bankruptcy and default are logical necessities in defining the economic arena, and the possibility of even partially strategic default links expected money wagers directly with preferences.

Merely solving dynamic models for equilibrium states may easily obliterate the importance of the transient states in changing the path of the economy. Acts such as innovation (considered in chapter 8), both in their rationale and their consequences, are highly dependent on transients.

For the most part in this work we have adhered to the highly restricted view of the economic agent employed in much conventional theory. To wit: the expected profit-maximizing firm and the utility-maximizing natural person. We have never met a utility function we liked; but we believe that the highly restricted view has been a fruitful approximation. This model of the economic agent is only one of the many behavioral types that could be postulated. A false dichotomy can be easily made of the differences between the classical economic agent and the new behavioral player. In some parts of their theorizing Keynes and other macroeconomists have suggested behavioral models of the consumer other than the classical utilitarian ones. Such selections depend on two features: empirical evidence and Occam's razor. Keep the models as simple as possible, unless there are strong reasons to do otherwise.

7.8.2   Some relevant aspects of our methodology

In our approach to mathematical process models in the application to political economy, we believe that the framing of good questions is critical. The specification of relevant ad hoc detail is still more or less an art form. We apply our methodology to the items selected. A brief list of our considerations includes:

1. The selection of numériare,
2. The physical properties of the money,
3. The specification of minimal units (grid size, coarse or fine graining),
4. The laws of conservation,
5. The presence of linear measures,
6. The ability to assign dimensions to the symbols specified,
7. The role of aggregation and index problems,
8. Measures of efficiency,
9. The specification of types of agents,
10. Few, finitely many, or a continuum of agents,

11. Initial conditions,

12. Terminal conditions,

13. Ensuring that the state space is well defined (default conditions, other bounds, such as reserve requirements),

14. Specification of the equations of motion,

15. Grid size for time (discrete or continuous, or both),

16. Event- or clock-driven updating (or both),

17. The specification of time lags,

18. The presence of strategic and exogenous uncertainty,

19. Knowledge and information conditions,

20. Behavioral assumptions,

21. Sensitivity analysis.

The list is not meant to be complete, but it highlights most of the key items that must be checked before a formal mathematical model can be accepted as a representation of the observable aspects of the political economy it is meant to represent. Almost all of the behavioral aspects of the model are in items 19 and 20. Without these assumptions, the description of the economic situation itself does not provide the extra assumptions to specify equations of motion, no matter how crude or informal.

7.8.2.1 "Real bills only" A history of the role of *real bills* in classical economics is given in Schumpeter's monumental history of economic thought [327]. An excellent brief summary is provided by Roy Greene [171] and, more recently, an extensive perceptive overview has been provided by Thomas Sargent [315].

In essence two schools—the banking school and the currency school—were distinguished, with the banking school advocating the extension of credit beyond 100 percent metallic reserves while the currency school advocated no further extension.

No attempt is made here to dive into a historical consideration of this controversy on the nature of the size of the money and credit supplies and the velocity of money. We note that to this day there are still problems in making precise distinctions in the functioning of payment systems concerning the boundaries between *clearance functions* and *short-term circulating loans*.

The clearance mechanisms of a modern economy as illustrated by institutions such as the Clearing House Interbank Payments System (CHIPS) and the Federal Reserve's Automated Clearing House (ACH) are devoted to taking care of the mechanics of final payments or settlements of trade where the terms have been fully and finally agreed on.

In essence to the practical person, as a good first-order approximation all risk has been removed from the transaction at the level of clearing, and all that remains is the mechanistic settlement of all accounts; but even here, even though the amount of time allocated to final clearance may be small and the amount of uncertainty that remains is miniscule, they are not zero, even though they may be deemed so by approximation. How to model such a situation requires that the nature of the approximation be made explicit.

Depending on time and place, many transactions in an organized economy may easily involve two, three, four, or even more parties. The bill of exchange has two parties at each end. Reinsurers may also be involved in laying off special risks.

Adam Smith [375, p. 288], in his discussion of banking, suggested concerning the issue of bank money:

> What a bank can with propriety advance to a merchant or undertaker of any kind, is not either the whole capital with which he trades, or even any considerable part of that capital; but that part of it only that he would otherwise be obliged to keep by him unenjoyed and in ready money for answering occasional demands.
> ...
> When a bank discounts to a merchant a real bill of exchange drawn by a real creditor upon a real debtor, and which, as soon as it comes due is really paid by that debtor; it only advances to him a part of the value which he would otherwise be obliged to keep by him unenjoyed and in ready money for answering occasional demands.

These perceptive words omitting the precise specification of time and essentially squeezing out the amount of uncertainty present by the use of the word "real" have provided a happy hunting ground for the economic modeler trying to produce mathematical models that fit the facts.

Who finances and insures the residual risk for the minute gaps of time involved in clearing, and who finances the longer but still relatively brief lengths of time in the financing of working capital for retailers and the longer times for producers? These all call for highly detailed ad hoc models requiring the explicit selection of items such as: What is the fineness of the time grid at which the sequencing of payments made can be ordered in time or else must be regarded as simultaneous? What is the minimal time period for which interest-bearing loans can be made, and who makes them?

Applying our methodology to Smith's characterization, we observe immediately that it is straightforward to produce *sufficient conditions* for a formal strategic market game with the following assumptions made explicit. Up to a good first-order approximation:

1. The time period considered is τ_1 days or less,

2. The minimal loan length is τ_2 days,

3. There is no exogenous uncertainty,

4. The banker's assessment of the possibility of default is essentially zero,

5. The bank's paper is universally accepted on par with government money,

6. The firm's paper is accepted only by the banks,

7. The agents are competent trustworthy retailers and reputable banks,

8. Initial and terminal conditions are expected to be more or less normal,

9. The markets are thick enough,

10. The firms are profit maximizers,

11. The model is open partial equilibrium,

12. The velocity of money is essentially constant.

If all of the items above hold, the bank requires no contingent reserves whatsoever and Adam Smith's implicit model can be mathematized easily; but they are empirically challengeable assumptions, and as they are weakened and various forms of uncertainty become important, the need for reserves will grow. Depending parametrically on the intensities attached to these assumptions, cases can be made out for anywhere between 0 and 100 percent reserves. Three hundred years of experience indicates that reasonable safety probably lies somewhere between 5 and 15 percent for commercial banking.

It is straightforward to construct experimental games with the assumptions above treated parametrically.

7.9   The Equation of Exchange or $PQ = MV$ and the Quantity Theory

In reality, of course it is very rarely possible to establish such precise mathematical relations as theory demands. Both the advocates and opponents of the quantity theory must content themselves with asserting or denying that an increase or reduction in the relative quantity of money will cause a corresponding change in the commodity price level and a reverse change in the value of money.
—Wicksell [416, p. 143]

The attempt to quantify and mathematize the models underlying the verbal debate over the centuries, starting with the increasing rise of paper money and central banks, leads naturally to the examination of the quantity theory and the equation of exchange as the starting point from whence a host of dynamic monetary models can be constructed.

Originally our intention was to consider the equation of exchange and the quantity theory separately. However, they are so closely intertwined that considering them together is more appropriate.

This volume does not pretend to be a work in the history of economic theory; if it were so, one could argue about the equation often referred to as the equation of exchange or the quantity theory equation and ascribe its origins to Bernardo Davanzati, John Locke, Jean Bodin, David Hume, or Simon Newcomb. The mathematician and astronomer Newcomb [274, p. 328], appears to have been the first to write down the specific equation he called "the equation of societal circulation"[9] that is associated with the quantity theory of money. Following Irving Fisher [130, p. 26], economists have attempted to formalize the control function of the money supply in several variants of this stylized equation $PQ = MV$, which was perhaps originally intended to resemble a thermodynamic equation of state. Here P is supposed to represent some kind of aggregate price, Q the time rate of flow of goods traded at average price P, M the amount of money used in trade, and V its average time rate of turnover; that is, how many trades are mediated by each unit of money per unit time. V is conventionally termed the *velocity of money*, and has units of $(\text{time})^{-1}$.[10]

Whereas money is abstracted away in the general equilibrium analysis, and only allocation of physical resources matters, the quantity equation intuitively captures the constraining capability of the money supply. In typical economic period-based models of trade, cash in advance requires that money be circulated at most once per period, meaning that the process description sets an upper limit on V of one turnover per period. Thus limitations in M imply limits in either the price or the quantity traded per period. Closely related to velocity and frequently measured in commercial practice is the number of inventory turns per annum, which is similarly utilized to gauge potential profitability in industries with thin selling margins.

Yet in much of macroeconomic thought it has been noted that the velocity of money may vary. Is this variation important? If so, why does it matter? Among the factors influencing velocity that Fisher lists are: habit, technology, rate of interest, and cyclical effects. They are an intermix of technology, habit, and conscious economic behavior. The key question is how much the variation of velocity is due to strategic behavior.

7.9.1 A brief review of the Newcomb-Fisher equation and some of its cousins

"When I use a word," Humpty Dumpty said, in rather a scornful tone, "It means just what I choose it to mean—neither more nor less."

"The question is," said Alice, "whether you can make words mean so many different things."

"The question is," said Humpty Dumpty, "which is to be master,—that's all."

...

"That's a great deal to make one word mean," Alice said in a thoughtful tone.

"When I make a word do a lot of work like that," said Humpty Dumpty, "I always pay it extra."

—Through the Looking-Glass

Although more than one word, the equation of exchange qualifies as hardworking under Humpty Dumpty's rubric. There are many different combinations and variants of the basic equation. There may be many asset quantities Q_i with different prices P_i that may have different trade turnover rates V_i, and at the same time there may be supplies of several different monies which in different measures can mediate the various kinds of trade. The number of monies and near monies may not be constant through time.

7.9.1.1 The number of monies and near monies
At the time of writing this, in the United States the money supply is defined at three levels, called M1, M2, and M3.

M1 has four components: (1) currency,[11] (2) travelers checks, (3) deposits, and (4) other checkable deposits such as NOW accounts. Thus at least we need to consider four instruments in the aggregate description.

M2 includes M1 with the addition of: (1) money market funds, (2) retail savings deposits, (3) thrift institutions, (4) small-time deposits.

M3 includes M2 and: (1) large-time deposits, (2) repurchase agreements, (3) Eurodollars, and (4) money market funds, for institutions only.

We note that the United States thus uses a 12-component definition of the money supply. A crude statistic on the orders of magnitude involved is

Table 7.1

Gross national product (GNP) and money supplies
M1, M2, and M3, for the United States in the years
shown, in billions of dollars

	1980	1990	2000
GNP	2775	5832	9848
M1	408	824	1085
M2	1600	3277	4927
M3	1996	4152	7090

indicated in table 7.1, which shows the three money supplies and gross national
product for 1980, 1990, and 2000 measured in billions of dollars.

7.9.1.2   What causes flows?   Even these crude numbers raise deep problems in conceptualization and measurement in economic theory and practice. In particular the turnover in the New York Stock Exchange in 2002
was 10492/9603 or over 109 percent of total valuation, and turnover at the
NASDAQ was higher, yet the equilibrium models of economic theory can at
best account for only a fraction of such trade, and at the high level of abstraction of general equilibrium theory without overlapping generations the equilibrium may involve no transactions of shares at all.

The gap between financial reality and the economic theory of rational
investor behavior is so large that a new emphasis on physically accurately
defined process models, examined for both equilibrium and disequilibrium
behavior, is called for. It must provide at least a conceptual framework and
some crude estimates of how much of the actual trade could be accounted for
by models invoking "rational expectations," and how much would require some
form of disequilibrium solution concept involving a yet-to-be-determined
blend of behavioral factors involving growth, innovation, and inductive behavior. At this point in the development of economics as a science we are far from
having an adequate theory of economic dynamics, but with care it appears
to be feasible to demonstrate the extreme limitations of equilibrium analysis
in the financial markets. Doing so, however, requires not only the utilization
of the methods of physics and game theory, but the recognition that the very
essence of the financial system is that of a delicate fast-acting multiagent perception and control mechanism over an economy in perpetual disequilibrium.
This is reconsidered in chapters 8 and 9.

7.9.1.3   The dimensions of $PQ = MV$ We begin with the dimensional analysis of the simplest model we can construct, a one-commodity, one-money world. Let:

M = the amount of money in circulation. Call its dimension $\{M\}$;

Q = the flow of aggregate commodity through the market. Call its dimension $\{QT^{-1}\}$;

P = the average price of the goods. It has a dimension of $\{MQ^{-1}\}$;

V has been commonly called the velocity of money. But as Newcomb more precisely observed, its dimensionality is forced by the other terms in the equation of exchange. Given

$$PQ = MV,$$

we obtain

$$\{MQ^{-1}\}\{QT^{-1}\} = \{M\}\{V\}$$

or

$$\{T^{-1}\} = \{V\}.$$

If the dimensions are to match, then V must be considered as the turnover rate of money, and MV is the properly designated "velocity."

In accounting usage turnover refers to the number of times an asset is replaced during a specified period.

In basic analysis of retail establishments this relationship between the stock of inventory and how fast it flows out is often utilized as an indicator of the health of the firm.

In financial markets the turnover analysis of the number of shares traded per period as a percentage of total issue is an important measure of activity and is probably best interpreted as a function of differences in estimation and perception rather than as an equilibrium measurement.

7.9.1.4 $PQ \equiv MV$ as an accounting identity   The equation can be interpreted merely as an accounting identity. At the end of some specified period— for example, a year—the product of observed prices P and quantities Q sold in a world that uses a fixed stock M of a single currency (gold, barley, or fiat, or records where each has a fixed line of personal credit denominated in the official unit of account) may be used to calculate V and interpret it as the scalar measure of the average number of times the money supply had to turn over to support the volume of trade noted by PQ.

If the interval is, say, $[0, T]$ and we divide it into k equal segments where $\Delta t = T/k$ is the smallest unit of time recognized in the system, then we might rewrite the basic identity as an average if the sequence has temporal structure:

$$\frac{1}{k} \sum_{t=0}^{T-\Delta t} P_t Q_t \equiv MV.$$

If we wish to consider time as continuous, the same average becomes

$$\frac{1}{T} \int_{t=0}^{T} dt\, P(t)\, Q(t) \equiv MV.$$

In either of these forms, or even embellished to include many real goods and monies explicitly, in general no equations of motion are provided explicitly, although Dubey, Sahi, and Shubik [99] have provided the analysis of a strategic market game model where turnover can be made arbitrarily large.

Many of the various discussions leave open the possibility that the equation of exchange needs to be formally structured as part of a larger closed system where both the supply and demand for money and near monies are accounted for. Other views are that it should be reserved for open model building. A statement by Friedman emphasizes this point of view, as discussed in the next section.

7.9.1.5   The quantity theory and the demand for money   The Cambridge equation version of the original equation of exchange can can be specified as

$$m = kPQ$$

In contrast with the original form that stresses overall transaction, this version is an equation for the demand for money by the individual, where k is the percentage of total purchases that an individual wishes to retain in cash, m is the amount of money this will amount to, and PQ is defined as before. Note, by comparison to the previous dimensional analysis, that this "equation" cannot be dimensionally consistent without further commentary. If m is regarded as a fraction of *income*, then it, like PQ, has dimensions of (money/time). If, instead, m is regarded as a pure quantity (such as the balance maintained in a demand deposit account or in cash), then k must have units of a characteristic timescale, if we are to keep the measurement of Q as a measure of quantity traded *per unit time*.

In a book of essays he edited, Friedman [143] states:

> The purpose is rather to set down a particular "model" of a quantity theory in an attempt to convey the flavor of the oral tradition which nurtured the remaining essays in this volume.
>
> 1. The quantity theory is in the first instance a theory of the demand for money. It is not a theory of output, or of money income, or of the price level. Any statement about these variables requires combining the quantity theory with some specifications about the conditions of supply of money and perhaps other variables as well.
> 2. . . .
> 3. The analysis of the demand for money on the part of the ultimate wealth-owning units in the society can be made formally with that of the demand for a consumption service. . . . The substantive differences from the analysis of the demand for a consumption service are the necessity of taking account of intertemporal rates of substitution . . . and of casting the budget constraint in terms of wealth.

Friedman goes on to consider the differences between the consumer and producer demands for money; however, the theorist concerned with a fully defined formal model is left to induce just what is the precise point. The article is about an assertion being made that with a sketch of an open theory of monetary demand based on classical demand theory informally modified to take care of the infinite horizon, demand will be $h(0)$ for a fiat money. This is with no treatment of uncertainty. In the fascinating essays on inflation and hyperinflation that follow, the stories are replete with exogenous uncertainty, default, and bankruptcy that play no role in Friedman's sketch of theory. Wicksell's observations from the 1930s, quoted above, still seem to hold.

We believe that as long as a reasonable host of simplifications is made to the modeling, a case can be made for a set of institutionally oversimplified well-defined mathematical models that display the $h(0)$ property. These models include some formal dynamic programming models of cash-in-advance economies by Lucas [231] and associates and some of the strategic market models of Karatzas, Sudderth, and Shubik [199].

7.9.2   Keynes and a complete model of the economy

Patinkin in his survey *Keynes' Monetary Thought* [287, p. 18] observed, "Indeed there are many who see Keynes' trilogy as The Saga of Man's Struggle for Freedom from the Quantity Theory." Although Keynes was originally involved in the Cambridge equation in his three books on money [202, 203], he finally escaped from the tyranny of old ideas and attempted, with a minimum of formal mathematics, to formulate a dynamic monetary structure for an overall economy using to some extent what could be classified as ad hoc assumptions (and what would, in modern terms, be labeled as behavioral assumptions), such as the consumption function or liquidity preference, that implicitly bypassed assumptions concerning the individual and aggregate utility functions and how individuals forecast.

"It is better to be roughly right than precisely wrong," wrote Keynes. Even a brief glance at *The General Theory* shows a great clash between Keynes the theorist and Keynes the great practitioner and man of the world who used every ad hoc simplification and characterization of a world filled with uncertainty, inept and obtuse politicians, bureaucrats and towering bureaucracies in order to move mountains here and now.

The level of organizational complexity Keynes was advocating was and to a great extent still is beyond comfortable mathematical characterization and analysis. To the modern theorist interested in spelling out dynamic models that encompass uncertainty, prediction, coordination, and control, Keynes offers the insights associated with a loosely coupled dynamic control system with critical time lags and frictions. He does not offer a relevant model for these times, but more importantly, Keynes the theorist pointed the way of escape from the tightly coupled equilibrium systems, opening up a new view of how to model disequilibrium dynamics; as summarized by Patinkin, "I have interpreted the General Theory not as a static theory of unemployment equilibrium, but as a dynamic theory of unemployment disequilibrium" [287, p. 113].

In our view the Keynes books represented an attempt, albeit primarily verbal, to sketch out a full set of equations of motion, where the stress was on interdependent fates but also independent behaviors and the disequilibrium process. The emphasis was more on process than equilibrium. The *General Theory*, in particular, provided an explicit emphasis on the coordination problem that is one of the central problems in the performance of a decentralized system. This problem is one the most basic items that underlies much of the research in modern noncooperative dynamic game theory and mechanism design.

7.10   The New Quantity Theory? Cash-in-Advance and Strategic Market Games

Robert Lucas utilizing cash-in-advance models and Karatzas, Shubik, and Sudderth [199] using strategic market game models both employed dynamic programming models, with somewhat different goals. Lucas and associates were primarily interested in macroeconomic theory and eventually policy problems; their school has had significant, even if controversial, impact on macroeconomic thought in the late twentieth and early twenty-first centuries. Karatzas, Shubik, and Sudderth were concerned with basic microeconomic theory and possible testing using experimental gaming. It is argued here that the simple versions of these models directly conform with the quantity theory, though this may not hold true as the models are made more complicated.

For expository reasons we select the simplest sell-all strategic market game model (see chapter 4) to illustrate the connection with the quantity theory.

7.10.1   A simple sell-all economy without banking

The cash-in-advance assumption employed by Lucas et al. enables the modeler to hook money into a one-aggregate-commodity model in a reasonably natural way, especially in an economy where all or almost all trade is monetized. The sell-all assumption does this as well, but with a somewhat different modeling motivation. It calls for both money and goods in advance, as it requires a price formation mechanism where price is formed by strategic action.

The macro models have tended to utilize a price-taking representative agent, whereas the strategic market games models have frequently utilized the individual agent. When there is no exogenous uncertainty present, the representative-agent solution and the type-symmetric noncooperative equilibrium individual-agent formulations, in essence, yield the same equilibrium.[12]

We first consider an extremely simple infinite-horizon model with a continuum of agents bidding for a single perishable commodity every period while attempting to maximize

$$\sum_{t=1}^{\infty} \beta^{t-1} \varphi(x_t^\alpha),$$

where β with $0 < \beta < 1$ is the discount factor and x_t^α is the consumption of a small agent α at time t. All agents α are endowed at the beginning of every period with an amount $Q_t^\alpha = Q$. Each starts each period with the ownership claim to the quantity Q. It is convenient to adopt the notation $d\alpha$ for the measure over agents, with $\int_\alpha d\alpha \equiv 1$, so that $Q\,d\alpha$ is a density, and Q is both the quantity held by each agent and the aggregate amount in the society:

$$\int_\alpha d\alpha\, Q_t^\alpha = Q.$$

Each also has at the start of the first period $M_t^\alpha = M$ units of money, where

$$\int_\alpha d\alpha\, M_t^\alpha = M.$$

By "sell-all" we mean that all individual owners are required to put up their individual stock of Q for sale. They will obtain the income from its sale after the market clears, and as there is no further market making in the period and no banking, this is effectively the same as cash-in-advance.[13]

A *strategy* by an individual α is a vector $(b_1^\alpha, b_2^\alpha, \ldots, b_t^\alpha, \ldots)$ where b_t^α is the amount of money bid by α in period t for goods.

Equations of motion:

Price formation is given by

$$p_t = \frac{\int d\alpha\, b_t^\alpha}{Q},$$

and the resulting consumption levels are $x_t^\alpha = b_t^\alpha / p_t$.
Wealth update is given by

$$m_t^\alpha = m_{t-1}^\alpha - b_t^\alpha + p_t Q$$
$$\text{for } t > 1 \text{ and } m_1^\alpha = M.$$

Optimization:

$$\max_{0 \le b_t^\alpha \le m_t^\alpha} \sum_{t=1}^\infty \beta^{t-1} \varphi(x_t^\alpha)$$

or if $W(m)$ stands for the value of the dynamic program, we may write

$$W(m) = \max_{0 \le b \le m} \left[\varphi\left(\frac{b}{p}\right) + \beta W(m - b + pQ) \right].$$

The solution yields $m = M$, and as there is only one market session per period, if V is the turnover of capital per period then

$$V = \frac{\int d\alpha\, m^\alpha}{M} = \frac{M}{M} = 1.$$

Thus $PQ = MV$ or the equation of exchange emerges with a velocity of one in this instance.

7.10.1.1   The addition of uncertainty   If we complicate the model and add uncertainty to the amount of the perishable supplied to each individual each period, then the representative-agent and the individual-agent models diverge (see also Bewley [32]). The Lucas asset model has the market price absorb all of the randomization, all money is utilized, $V = 1$ always, and hence as quantity varies, price varies. In contrast, in Karatzas, Shubik, and Sudderth as the random term is i.i.d. for each individual, the solution yields a constant price with an overall fixed wealth distribution, where the uncertainty is reflected in the variability of the individual wealth distribution. Once more the equation of exchange emerges and can be interpreted in Cambridge form in the sense that, although the bid b^α is the independent *move* of α that helps to determine price, the *optimal policy* is how much to save, which is a function of the individual's wealth.[14] The system is $h(0)$.

The Bellman equation becomes

$$W(m,q) = \max_{0 \le b \le m} \left[\varphi\left(\frac{b}{p}\right) + \beta W(m - b + pQ, Q + y) \right],$$

where y is a random variable such that $-Q \le y$.

7.10.2   The addition of an outside bank and default laws

The two models above had no banking system. Hence the interest rate is only implicit as no borrowing or lending takes place. Individuals save by hoarding. In considering a role for a rate of interest and in keeping with simplicity, we can add a central bank or a commercial bank or a money market. If we wish to vary the money supply without invoking a fractional reserve commercial banking system, we can do so by limiting ourselves to introducing a central bank. In our first model, in this simple stationary-state economy the addition of any of these institutions makes no difference. There is no need to vary the money supply that is given initially as M. In the second model the individuals who are hoarding would be delighted to have a banking system paying a positive money rate of interest and lending money if need be. But in such a system, if the bank is the controller of the money supply, the rate of interest is one of its control variables. If a constant price level is one of its goals, then in an economy with exogenous uncertainty the Fisher equation emerges with ρ determined by $1 + \rho = 1/\beta$. When uncertainty holds, the Fisher equation is no longer true and has to be replaced by a somewhat more complex relationship to provide an expectation of zero inflation [152].

As soon as borrowing or lending takes place, the logic of being able to completely define the state space for the class of models with lending requires that default and bankruptcy laws be specified in order to cover the states where an individual is unable to meet his or her obligations. The Bellman equation becomes:

$$W(m,q) = \max_{0 \leq b \leq m+\hat{c}} \left[\varphi\left(\frac{b}{p}\right) + \delta\beta W((m-b)(1+\rho) + pQ, Q+y) \right.$$

$$\left. + (1-\delta)\beta W(0, Q+y) \right],$$

where $\rho \geq 0$ is the exogenously set money interest rate selected by the outside bank, φ must now be defined for negative values, and δ has the value of 1 if $(m-b) \geq 0$ and 0 otherwise.

The key element to note is that the perception of the lender has appeared in the term $\hat{c}$; it represents the lending limit that the central bank is willing to extend to a borrower. This is where bank evaluation and "haircuts" enter.

The details of the solution are given elsewhere, but the important feature to note in terms of this monetary model is that the economy is no longer $h(0)$ on prices. If the price level drops too much, strategic bankruptcy becomes profitable.[15] In essence the bankruptcy laws have become a public good controlling the level of default that the country can live with. Neither the fixed level of credit called for by the banking school nor the flexible credit called for by the real bills extension of credit will achieve optimality even in an economy using fiat, if strategic bankruptcy is attractive even without exogenous uncertainty but the extra flexibility of real bills will enable a higher "second-best"[16] to be obtained. In order to adequately model the spirit of 100 percent reserves lending with fiat money, one had to impose a reserve level B on the central bank. If these reserves are specified as relatively low relative to the bankruptcy conditions, they can yield a worse second-best solution than is achieved by relaxing this constraint. This is demonstrated in chapters 11 and 12 of [356].

7.10.2.1   The role of bankruptcy   It is worth noting that Newcomb [274, p. 332] was aware that bankruptcy could play a role. He recast his equation (identity) as

$$K \times P = V \times R + B,$$

where the B is the loss from bankruptcy. In modern symbolism we prefer to stress this as an identity or

$$K \times P \equiv V \times R + B.$$

7.10.3   Real capital: the next level of needed complication

In the development of a viable theory of money and financial institutions, the *sine qua non* (almost all the Latin we remember) is the introduction of durable capital. This is not only a fact of modern economic life; it contrasts starkly the difference between the liquidity to the individual of long-term physical and financial assets. The importance of different financing of long-term assets has already been illustrated in chapter 6. Here we note the critical new properties that are emerging. The explicit differentials in the time structure of real and financial assets are going to play a major role in the duration of transient behavior of the system for virtually any dynamic model of the economy. In the increasing differentiation of the division of labor called for by the growth of the complexity of the financial sector, the differentiaton between the financiers and investment bankers and the remainder of the population is that their key roles are as evaluators or perception devices that direct the transient flows of financial capital to the private sector. The central banks are the perceptors and evaluators for the economy as a whole. Who controls the perceptors is a choice jointly arrived at by the polity as a whole.

Keynes noted in the *Tract on Monetary Reform* [204, p. 80] that "The long run is a misleading guide to current affairs. In the long run we are all dead." When long-run real assets are considered, the need to deal with transients comes further to the fore.

7.11   Models Built around *PQ*=*MV* Matter More than Money

How much money matters appears to be heavily determined by place, time, and specific politicoeconomic structure. All of these items are vastly different now from when Wicksell, Keynes, and their contemporaries were writing. They are also different from when Friedman, Tobin, and other more modern macroeconomists were writing. Given financial innovation and political change, "here and now" probably does not have a time span of as much as twenty years. If this is the case, what are the invariants in economic theory and practice? We suggest here that the ability to build and analyze a vast array of basic models consistent with an underlying theory of economic motivation, and to connect them with the world of here and now, is what is called for. This suggests that although there may be a basic microeconomic theory for all seasons at a relatively high level of abstraction, its instantiations in macroeconomics and finance are not invariant.

The interpretations of $PQ = MV$ have been quintessentially macroeconomic. To the microeconomist the equation is either an accounting identity or one equation in an incompletely built model. There are many ways of constructing a complete closed model incorporating it within a variety of causal patterns. Depending on these constructions, the importance of causality and the weapons of control can go in any direction the modeler desires. The variants can yield a pure quantity theory or Wicksellian or Keynesian models, as well as other variants adding the embellishments to the appropriately Delphic utterance of $PQ = MV$.

The empirical demonstration of which of these models best fits the current economy has to overcome the critique that these extremely low-dimensional models suppressing so many factors cannot claim to be more than unverified theory and do not offer more to policy than the essay form of writings such as those of Hyman Minsky [263]. The encyclopedic book of Woodford [424] offers broad coverage on the construction of policy rules based on modifications of a Wicksellian model. It is not our purpose to enter into the debate on the policy advice based on modern macroeconomics, as currently important as that may be. Instead, we seek to connect with these macroeconomic models from a strictly strategic microeconomic viewpoint in order to be able to better understand at what points in the construction of minimal complexity models more complexity must be added to cover new phenomena not manifested in the simpler models.

7.12   Comments on Income Distribution and Complexity

7.12.1   Income distributions and the role of constraint

Empirical observation suggests that the equal income condition implicit with a representative-agent, rational-expectations model rarely if ever applies to dynamical economies. The distribution of wealth and income in previous economies and current industrialized nations around the world [55] is nonsymmetric. It has been known since Pareto [285] that a significant fraction of the wealth in these economies is held by a small number of individuals (or families). The income accruing primarily from ownership of wealth (as capital) appears to obey a power law, and the income for wage earners may be exponentially or log-normally distributed [275, 392]. Although many examples of such distribution are known, there still is no fully conceptual and quantitatively adequate explanation. A remarkable feature of all these distributions is that they maximize the Shannon entropy [63] of the wealth or income distribution, subject to constraints [91, 260] on some function of wealth or income (its value, variance, or logarithm, for the various cases).

It may be a qualitatively robust result [275, 392] that the two distinct regions of wealth and income distribution are associated with additive and multiplicative randomization, suggesting a correspondence with wage versus capital dynamics. If this is so, there is persistent competition between the accumulation of wealth as capital, driven at least in part by innovation, and its distribution in the less flexible domain of wage labor. As long as such competition persists, the shadow price of money from constraints on trade is always nonzero.

7.12.2   Steady-state economies?

In suggesting the universality of power law distributions and wealth constraints, however, it is important to remember that all the economies studied have existed within the industrial age, a period of continual real earnings growth, roughly matched in physical terms by growth in per capita energy consumption [286, 414; see also U.S. Department of Energy Report "Internal Energy Outlook 2005," Report # DOE/EIA-0484(2005), available at http://www.eia.doe.gov/oiaf/ieo]. Some intriguing studies originating in biological allometric scaling [268] suggest that, despite the structural differences between economies and biological organisms, biological reproduction may respect universal constraints related to energy consumption, even when that energy is consumed industrially and mediated economically.

An interesting possibility is that economic growth is essentially an energetic phenomenon, in which case it cannot persist indefinitely on earth.[17] It may be that the competition between capital investment and wages would persist in a steady-state economy, as a result of a "red-queen effect" of persistent innovation [403]. Alternatively, it may be that the wealth constraints exhibited by industrial economies now are only reflections of innovation made possible by energetic growth and would disappear in steady-state economies, leading to characteristic exponential wealth distributions associated with simple optimizing trade under uncertainty [199]. Predictions about the future of wealth distributions are thus good (and falsifiable) tests of our understanding of the dynamics and constraints of money and capital.

7.12.3   Indexing the complexity of an economy

A crude analogy can be made between the evolution from the one-celled organism to the progressively more complicated multicellular animal and that from simple hunter-gatherer economies to the complex economies of today. New connections are established and new functions appear. In particular with the growth of the division of labor, of separate functions for many different types of corporation and partnerships, and the proliferation of anonymous mass markets, the need for coordination and evaluation has grown enormously. The standardization and utilization of many financial instruments over the last century has brought the role of finance to the fore as the control, organizing, and perception device over the economy as a whole.

This process of innovation is clearly structured, and at some stages it is hierarchical. Markets and monies to some extent coevolve, but the transition from commodity monies toward pure fiat monies and to government debt has only occurred in the context of sophisticated markets, and what we would regard as modern frameworks for enforcing laws. Corporations and stocks and bonds are only required when large-scale production is combined with autonomy of capital ownership from the state, and successive layers of ownership paper and derivatives arise to disaggregate ever finer components of risk, as the cost of producing and monitoring such instruments comes down.

The financial sector of a modern economy is invariably its highest-velocity sector, and the one most susceptible to fluctuations in usage patterns. Presumably this is because the value added by financial instruments comes primarily from information, while the cost of financial transactions is small. Small information value may be gained per transaction, but a small commitment of credit suffices to cover a large transaction volume because of the high velocity of the financial markets. A certain technological sophistication is required to handle such large-volume, large-value-in-trade, small-value-added transactions at acceptable cost. We may thus ask whether, among the many measures of complexity posited [155], the position of an economy in the hierarchy of financial control is an index to its complexity.

7.12.4   Simplicity, complexity, the quantity theory, and dynamics

Much of this chapter has been devoted to a reconsideration of the quantity theory of money in its old and new versions. Until the 1940s the useful mathematization of economic dynamics was essentially out of the question. At the cost of great simplifications starting with von Neumann's seminal structure, the interest in growth models has flourished.[18] The introduction over the last forty years of dynamic programming methods has brought the possibility of precision but at the cost of the curse of extremely low-dimensional models. Even with this disadvantage, the underlying validity of the quantity theory emerges in the most stripped-down models. However, as state and decision variables are added and introduce new complexities, the quantity theory is of highly diminished worth. There is need for ad hoc dynamic modeling that reflects the many different relevant time lags and exploits the roles of durable assets and differential expertise in evaluation and control in an economy with many financial agents.

7.13   Appendix: A Particular Class of Dynamical Models: Event-Driven Depreciation and Time-Driven Depreciation

We have noted that durable goods depreciate, with the implication that capital goods—serving the role of catalysts—will not generally be ideally preserved factors of production. At the simplest level, capital goods may depreciate in two qualitatively distinct ways. Their depreciation may be driven simply by temporal aging, or it may be driven only in proportion to the level at which they are employed. The two important distinctions between these forms of depreciation are these:

1. Usage levels are discretionary and thus potentially subject to economic control, whereas the passage of time is a law of nature not subject to control.

2. Because usage levels are discretionary, they may be loosely (or not at all) correlated among distinct goods, subject only to constraints on availability in the form illustrated by the Kuhn-Tucker multipliers in Eq. (7.2). In contrast, the passage of time is uniform and may thus lead to correlations in the depreciation or other properties of durable goods including capital.

7.13.1   A more detailed treatment of a subset of cases in the original paradigm of the transformation matrix

To incorporate features such as depreciation within the von Neumann formulation of the linear production space, it may be necessary to enlarge the goods space considerably. Goods must be distinguished not only by major qualitative features, but also by measures of age which advance to represent depreciation. This enlargement is not arbitrary, because the age structure and life cycle of goods places a topology on the space. One way to efficiently use this topology is to represent transition matrices in terms of typical joint transformations involving inputs or outputs, and aging that may be coupled either to time or to usage level.

Here we consider two examples of durable goods, to illustrate the different contingency structures typical of durable consumables versus capital goods that enable production. Following the distinction of stocks from flows in chapter 5, we are particularly concerned with the scaling properties of short-time limits of the transformation process. We argue below that two simplifying features emerge in utility maximization problems that have well-defined continuous-time limits: linear-separable goods and (at least short-term) exponential discounting.

7.13.1.1 Storable consumable goods *Durable or storable consumables* persist through time unless they are consumed, whether this consumption is represented in an argument of utility or as an input to production. They may reflect the passage of time both through their own aging, and—important for the contingency structure of intertemporal dynamics—because they may require continuous inputs of services in order to persist.

We continue to represent a vector of goods x_t in any period t as a set of scalars $\{x_{i,t}\}$ multiplying basis vectors indexed by goods type i and period t. Rather than write these basis vectors as columns with a single entry of 1 at index i, we give them explicit names which refer to continuous ranges of age. For a consumable good, we may label the basis vector $\Xi(X,\tau)$,[19] in which for convenience we include not only the age τ as part of the label, but also X corresponding to the name of some service that may be required for this good to persist.[20]

In a world where we distinguish stocks from flows, X is itself the name for a basis vector corresponding to a specific rate of flow of a specific service or other input. Calling X a flow translates into the requirement that, in a period model with length Δt, the stock basis element associated with one period's-worth of consumption of X has label $X\Delta t$.

Then the action of the transformation matrix on any state that contains scalar multiples of good Ξ and service $X\Delta t$ may be written

$$X\Delta t + \Xi(X,\tau) \rightarrow \Xi(X,\tau + \Delta t). \tag{7.9}$$

The entries $X\Delta t$ and $\Xi(X,\tau)$ represent index positions in the columns of the input matrix A, while $\Xi(X,\tau + \Delta t)$ is the index mapped to in the corresponding column of the output matrix B. In the discrete-period model, a good whose aging rate does not depend on its level of use is converted to the "adjacent" good of age $\tau + \Delta t$.

7.13.1.2   Capital goods that age in relation to time   A large category, viewed from the mechanical perspective of the von Neumann economy, subsumes those capital goods that convert inputs to outputs and that age proportionally to time, together with natural persons. Let $\chi(X,Y,\tau)$[21] stand for the basis vector for such a good which takes flows of input X and converts them to flows of output Y. Then in a discrete-period model with period length Δt the action of the transformation matrix becomes

$$X\Delta t + \chi(X,Y,\tau) \to Y\Delta t + \chi(X,Y,\tau+\Delta t), \qquad (7.10)$$

reproduced as Eq. (7.8) in the main text.

A capital good may be incompletely utilized or completely utilized. We may represent this freedom by including a continuous class of *production technologies* in the same spirit as we have introduced a continuously indexed space of goods. A capital good that may be utilized at any of a range of levels without changing its efficiency or the amount of the good itself required for production, and which ages in proportion to time irrespective of its level of use, is defined by the family of production functions represented as

$$\lambda X\Delta t + \chi(X,Y,\tau) \to \lambda Y\Delta t + \chi(X,Y,\tau+\Delta t). \qquad (7.11)$$

Here λ is the one-parameter index of the family. The scale-independence of efficiency requires that X and Y both be homogeneous of order one in the same scale factor, whereas χ itself is homogeneous of order zero.

Capital goods with limited output capacity will generally impose a range $\lambda \in [0, C]$ for some capacity limit C. Natural persons (in the simplest case) are capital goods with a specific requirement C, reflecting their needs (food, shelter), and their outputs (labor/leisure), which are more or less tightly coupled to the passage of time, and cannot be varied either up or down by large factors.

7.13.1.3   Capital goods that age in proportion to use   We may handle the age structure of goods that depreciate in proportion to use simply by altering the transformation rule on their indices. Under a rescaling of X and Y by λ, instead of Eq. (7.11), we require that the class of production technologies satisfy the scaling

$$\lambda X\Delta t + \chi(X,Y,\tau) \to \lambda Y\Delta t + \chi(X,Y,\tau+\lambda\Delta t). \qquad (7.12)$$

Note that these scaling relations among members of a family of production functions define independent columns in the matrices A and B, and do not correspond to simply changing the level of utilization of these production technologies.[22]

7.13.2   Continuous-time limits in utility

We consider next the consequence of well-defined flow variables and continuous-time limits for the structure of utilities and of discounting. Two strong assumptions that simplify utility analyses for both general equilibrium and strategic market games are those of a linear-separable good and of geometric discounting. The assumptions lead to powerful simplifications such as strong aggregatability and time-stationarity, but they are commonly regarded as restrictive and not-general. We note here that the existence of continuous-time limits for utilities of flow variables implies linear separability as well as a limited form of geometric discounting. We interpret the existence of such limits not as properties that may automatically be assumed for individuals or firms, but as properties brought into existence by the creation of one-price, continuously available markets. Whether or not a continuous utility of flows was an inherent property of agents in the preinstitutional society, any model of optimization in the presence of continuously available markets forces upon us the question of what constitutes rational, consistent valuation of the stocks and flows traded in such markets.

7.13.2.1   The general form of linear separability for debt service   In the models of chapter 5, where we were chiefly concerned with continuous production and consumption, we considered utilities that depended only on rates of consumption of flows. Letting $(x_0, x_1, \ldots)$ stand generically for the (scalar or vector) scales of these rates of consumption, and $X \Delta t$ be the corresponding (one-component or many-component) basis vectors, the intertemporal utility could generally be written

$$\mathcal{U}(x_0, x_1, \ldots) = \sum_{t=0}^{\infty} U_t(x_t X \Delta t). \qquad (7.13)$$

Here we do not assume any particular form of discounting, so that discount factors are absorbed in the definition of the one-period utility functions U_t.

We wish to consider the possibility that utilities depend not only on rates of consumption of flows, but potentially also on stocks of goods held in each period. Let a sequence $(g_0, g_1, \ldots)$ represent the amounts held of a bundle of stocks, and G their corresponding basis vectors, which for convenience we suppose to be the same at each time. Then the most general utility that depends only on spot levels of consumption and on goods held takes the form

$$\mathcal{U}(x_0, x_1, \ldots; g_0, g_1, \ldots) = \sum_{t=0}^{\infty} U_t(x_t X \Delta t; g_t G). \qquad (7.14)$$

We now ask what functional forms for the period utilities U_t are consistent with the existence of a continuum limit $\Delta t \to 0$ representing the same preferences and consumption levels. The existence of such a limit first rules out nonconvergent expansions in Δt, so we may suppose that U_t converges to its Taylor series expansion. Exponents of $x_t X \Delta t$ less than unity lead to a divergence of $\mathcal{U}$ as $\Delta t \to 0$, while exponents larger than unity vanish in the expansion. Therefore we are left only with the forms

$$\mathcal{U}(x_0, x_1, \ldots; g_0, g_1, \ldots) = \sum_{t=0}^{\infty} x_t X \Delta t u_t(g_t G)$$

$$= \Delta t \sum_{t=0}^{\infty} x_t X u_t(g_t G)$$

$$\to \int_{t=0}^{\infty} dt\, x_t X u_t(g_t G), \qquad (7.15)$$

for some functions u_t depending only on the stocks held.

The continuum-limit utility is now linear in each of the service rate levels x_t, though potentially still nonlinear in the stock variables $\{g_t\}$. For problems that depend only on ordinal utility, however, we may remove any *single* coefficient of the vector $X u_t(g_t G)$ by a monotone transformation of $\mathcal{U}$, leaving the corresponding component of x_t linear-separable for all agents.

7.13.2.2   The particular case of intertemporal loan markets

Suppose that among the markets in the system, one is an intertemporal loan market for money, and suppose that it is both liquid and available in every period. That is, unpaid interest can be covered with revolving loans, and agents have the freedom to repay principal and all outstanding debt service in any period. What is a consistent utilitarian valuation of this debt service, if we require that the utility have a regular continuum limit?

Let the linear-separable good $x_{i,t}^j$ in each agent's utility be the one-period debt service,[23] which we may write $x_{i,t}^j = \rho_{i,t} P_{i,t}$ for outstanding principal $P_{i,t}$ held by agent i in period t, on the assumption of one-price markets. $P_{i,t}$ is a stock variable (hence one of the goods), and because $x_{i,t}$ is linear-separable, the interest rate ρ_t that determines the amount of debt service owed must equal the marginal utility of $P_{i,t}$ to each agent i. Note that $P_{i,t}$ can, through constraint terms, affect the utility over many periods, so this marginal utility could be quite complicated.

If the functions $\{u_{i,t}(g_{i,t}G)\}$ converge continuously in $g_{i,t}$ as $\Delta t \to 0$, then the monotone transformation that makes any successive period's debt service $x_{i,t}, x_{i,t+1}, \ldots$ linear-separable varies smoothly in t in the continuum limit, and if the sum $\mathcal{U}_i$ has continuous first derivative under a shift $t \to t + \Delta t$ as $\Delta t \to 0$, then the interest rate ρ_t will be smoothly varying in t as well. Therefore discounting is locally exponential in time over sufficiently short intervals, although the interest rate itself may be smoothly varying.

7.13.2.3 An example from Markowitz portfolio theory

It is common in mathematical economics to construct models that illustrate a particular relation without requiring that they be consistent with other models selected to illustrate different points. Many models chosen to illustrate the relation of money to constraints (including many in our own chapters) adopt utilities in which money is the linear-separable good. Yet in the preceding section, we have argued that embedding economic decisions consistently in a material world which imposes topologies such as continuity of time may render some other quantity as linear-separable—and may argue specifically against this role for money. The linear-separable quantity may even be a flow such as debt service rather than a stock. To show that such utilities already arise commonly in widely used economic models, we consider an example from finance.

The dividend-discount model of Markowitz portfolio theory is a standard model for quasi-linear utility which illustrates many aspects of scaling, and in which debt service arises naturally as the unique linear-separable quantity. This model illustrates that not all variables must be smooth to admit continuous-time limits in which the scaling arguments of the previous section apply, and in which debt service converges to a well-defined flow variable. In particular, the dividend stream may be given the limiting form of a Wiener process (the continuous-time limit of a discrete random walk), and the foregoing arguments all apply. (The moments of the Wiener process become the smooth arguments of an expected utility.)

The basic quantities in the model are shares of some stochastic dividend-paying asset, and money. We suppose contracts are defined so that, for any exchange, the change δM in money, δN in shares owned, and δD in debt service owed are related as

$$\delta M = -p_N \delta N + \frac{1}{r\delta t}\delta D. \tag{7.16}$$

Here p_N and $r\delta t$ are prices that apply at the moment of exchange. Although we have written $r\delta t$ as a product of an interest rate with the period length, since we permit r to change with time in a way that we have not yet specified, no specific scaling with δt is implied by this notation (*yet*).

The dynamics of the system that includes the dividend process and contractual obligations, in each of a sequence of periods t, changes the agent's money wealth as

$$(\Delta W)_t \equiv N d_t - D_t + \phi_t[M_t], \tag{7.17}$$

where d_t is the payout of the dividend process in the period, D_t is the debt service owed (whose repayment we supposed to be enforced by mechanisms that we do not digress to formalize within this example), and $\phi_t[M_t]$ is all other contributions to wealth within the period that result from holding money M_t.

The wealth changes $(\Delta W)_t$ have the property of flow variables insofar as the cumulative wealth change in a sequence of periods is a sum of $(\Delta W)_t$ values within the periods. Therefore we may use $\sum_t (\Delta W)_t$ as an ordinal utility that respects this additive property. A monotone transform of the wealth change, suited to the average over Gaussian fluctuations that was the original constant absolute risk aversion (CARA) model of Markowitz portfolio theory, yields the exponential form

$$u_{\text{card}} \equiv -\exp\left\{ -\sum_t (\Delta W)_t/v \right\}, \tag{7.18}$$

in which v is a measure of an agent's risk tolerance.[24]

A deterministic utility for general equilibrium modeling is formed by averaging u_{card} over the multivariate distribution for fluctuations of the dividend process, here for convenience assumed independent in different periods. The result is the *certainty equivalent of wealth*, which general equilibrium uses only for its property as an ordinal utility

$$u_{\text{ord}} = -\exp\left\{ -\sum_t \left[N_t \bar{d}_t \left(1 - \frac{N_t \bar{d}_t}{2v} \sigma_t^2 \right) - D_t + \phi_t[M_t] \right] / v \right\}. \tag{7.19}$$

Here $\bar{d}_t$ is the mean dividend yield in period t and the variance is written $\left\langle (d_t - \bar{d}_t)^2 \right\rangle \equiv \bar{d}_t^2 \sigma_t^2$.

7.13.3   Markets and monies

The cultural and legal concept that creates an economy from people and physical goods and processes is a system of *ownership rights*. Private ownership is the simplest system to formalize, because it associates with every good or process an agent with rights to dispose of it. However, the nominal simplicity of private ownership rights displaces the complexity of social coordination onto the system of *contracts* that enables agents to transfer ownership. The two most severely violated assumptions of general equilibrium economics are of the existence of *complete* and *costlessly formable and enforceable* contracts. The failure of complete contracts leads to the economic notion of "externalities," consequences of economic activity that are not part of the bargaining process during contract formation. The task of providing and enforcing contracts at acceptable cost is served by economic and legal institutions. We will consider only two here: markets and monies.

Trade is intrinsically a joint strategic act by two or more agents, or a single agent against an anonymous market. If the agents are asymmetric, like a government in relation to one of its citizens, the joint act of trading may be consistent with the notion of agency, because the government may act unilaterally while the citizen's act is contingent. Voluntary trade among equals involves a breach of the notion of individual agency, because each agent's action is contingent on the other's. Markets work around this breach by disaggregating the joint action into independently performed individual actions, such as bidding and offering. Agents unilaterally relinquish either ownership or control to markets, and in exchange markets implement prespecified algorithms for converting bids and offers into *clearing contracts* among two or more agents, to which the agents are then bound by law or custom. The unique restriction on markets is that they fulfill the prespecified algorithm for any possible instance of agent bids and offers, making possible the rational evaluation of unilateral action by agents. Section 7.7 addressed the formalization of these strategic disaggregation mechanisms.

The one element common to all market functions is the submission of *bids* [356], and with these the notion of "money-ness" as a new, quintessentially economic dimension arises. Markets per se only overcome the problem of creating joint strategies; they potentially leave unaddressed the problems of search for suitable trading partners, overlap of the offered and desired goods of buyers and sellers (known as the "double-coincidence of wants" [195]), and exchange ratios defining acceptable prices to both parties. The goods that historically have become monies overcome these problems.

As a type (not yet implying dimensionality), a *money* is accepted as a bid in most or all markets in an economy, giving a starlike shape to a graph of goods in trade. Near monies, such as bank credit, may be acceptable in a large subset of markets. Universal acceptance simplifies problems of search, and overcomes the failure of the double coincidence of wants. A formal type specification of a money or near money might include as arguments the set of markets in which it is accepted for bids.

The other general features of monies are *divisibility* and *interconvertibility*. Salt, tea, gold, and government-issued paper monies are all by their nature arbitrarily divisible, and all have served as monies at various times. Those that qualify as monies in an economy are also substitutable in some ratio as bids, in all markets that accept them. The operation of bidding at market, together with divisibility, operationalizes "money" as a dimension, while the conversion rate permits the specification of each type as a particular *unit of money* (e.g., **ounces of gold** or **U.S. dollars** as types). As the regulatory problems of bimetallism illustrate, exchange rates between units of money must generally be determined by the dynamics of an economy, so in a formal system the only requirement is that *the operations of subdivision and unit conversion commute at any instant of time*. Thus, the price (conversion rate) for ounces of gold to dollars must be independent of the amount converted if both are to qualify as units of money.

The criteria of money-ness are often only approximately fulfilled, as are the recognized functions of money as medium of exchange, store of value, or numéraire in exchange. Thus only one good may qualify as an ideal money in a model economy, with other goods inheriting approximate function as monies through divisibility and market-determined conversion rates (as in the "money markets" for short-term debt obligations).

7.13.4   Bonds and stocks

Intertemporal loans may be secured with collateral or debt obligations, a purely legal form of contingent constraint on the future strategy set of the borrower. Such loans make possible a limited transfer of wealth, whether because default penalties have limited severity or because the transfer of ownership of complete goods between agents limits liquidity. They are thus often suited to small-scale borrowing by individuals, but not to the large-scale aggregations of wealth needed to create firms. Bonds and stocks are introduced to overcome these limitations, as well as to separate certain divisible rights of ownership from the decision making that controls the use of capital, and to separate components of risk in different kinds of contingent claims.

General dynamical modeling of bonds and stocks requires the introduction of the **corporation** as a type of agent, different from the utilitarian individual.

Corporations have agency in order to own and dispose of property, but they differ from *natural persons* in that corporations are *owned* by other agents. Rather than having open-ended strategies only circumscribed by law (the most that is realistic in the modeling of natural persons), or utility functions, corporations must be supplied with explicitly defined strategic options and a process that converts strategic acts of the owners into strategic acts of the corporation (similar to "methods" in object-oriented programming [37]). It is natural to let the strategy-generating process be a game played by the owner-agents, but we do not pursue further formalization here.

Stocks are a type of contract that assigns ownership rights of a corporation to a collection of agents. The sale of stocks bestows on the buyers new strategic choices created by the game that controls the corporation, among which may be the liquidation of the corporation and sale of its assets in some predefined market. Stocks generally also assign a *contingent claim* to proceeds in the event of liquidation, though these may be contingent not only on the context of the liquidation but also on the payment of debts.

Bonds are a different type of contract for a contingent claim, without ownership rights. They may also promise interest as a service and repayment of a principal or "face value," and introduce default on either obligation as a condition requiring liquidation. Because bond obligations are limited while the liquidation value of stock is not, bonds obtain their value by assigning first priority to repayment of their obligations in the event of liquidation.

Bonds thus minimize downside risk while limiting upside reward, while stocks do the complement. Both of these instruments are readily formally specified as types, though the specification is more complex than those we present here. An important property of bonds is that the principal and interest obligations of a bond issue, which are generally denominated in money, are essentially arbitrarily divisible.[25] Short-term bonds, whose face value is a stock variable like money itself, readily take on properties of monies, and are key components in money markets. Longer-term bonds, whose interest streams (flows) must be valued against their purchase prices (stocks), may qualify as near monies in nonstochastic environments, but progressively lose this association as interest rate fluctuations cause the value of a determined interest stream to vary.

We have omitted the treatment of risk in this minimal survey of types, which is a subject in itself, both for physical quantities and for utilities. We note, however, that the legal definition of economic rights is based on realized outcomes, and therefore contingent though not generally predictive.

7.13.5   Applications of a physically structured economics: some examples

A modern capitalist economy is often referred to as a "market economy," but a market and the existence of efficient prices associated with it are a creation of humans. The simplest markets were for fungible chattels such as food, clothing, and individual tools. As economies have become more complex, new markets evolved or were consciously invented for real estate, shares in corporations, futures, and trading in rights such as pollution rights.

The "natural" ability of a market to produce a globally efficient outcome is not a general property in a complex highly interconnected world with many public goods and externalities. Markets, voting and taxation, and subsidies are socially created devices aimed at defining and achieving social optima in a manner that is as decentralized and as efficient as possible.

In a modern economy with externalities such as pollution of many kinds and public goods such as roads, space exploration, government bureaucracies, museums, research establishments, laws, and law enforcement, even an elementary investigation calls for a sorting of factors and a dimensional analysis that requires a basic understanding of both the societal and physical properties of the system. The description, nature, and measurability of the interlinked factors are critical.

Problems such as devising an optimal energy policy, devising policies for the control of global warming, the coordination of a space program, or promotion of the level and direction of innovation are examples of the type that require a physics- and operations-research-like investigation before society can devise markets, voting, and other transfer mechanisms to measure social efficiency and to provide optimal mechanisms. All of these have in common that they are large complex societal problems involving complex relationships among many factors which do not fit with any comfort into conventional markets. They call for the creation of optimal combinations of old and new markets, and also of voting and transfer procedures. There are only a handful of basic ways in which resources can be transferred among individuals [350]. When one imposes the desideratum of a broad level of freedom of individual choice together with some limiting criteria on efficiency and degree of equity or symmetry in the outcomes, the need for a detailed understanding of the physical structure and its measurement becomes a necessary preliminary to the human shaping of the incentive and distribution mechanisms.

An example of a case in which significantly structured physical process models might provide a better coarse-grained foundation for economic analysis than anything that presently exists is the seemingly ordinary—but currently unsolved—economic problem of estimating the demand elasticities for energy and consumables that depend on energy under new stresses that can be predicted to arise within the next century. A collision of commitments and investments in human demographics and habits that have accumulated over the past 250 years in a context of low-cost fossil energies and externalized environmental impacts, with tightening constraints on both, will force a restructuring of energy generation and use systems that will be difficult to execute smoothly.

The complexity of the problem, and the difficulty of solving it within current economic methodology, stem from the pervasive role of energy use in creating the material capital and social development of societies. Entrenched patterns of population distribution, manufacturing, and agriculture, as well as specialization of talents and tastes of individuals, have formed around low-cost transportation, materials extraction and conversion, and agro-ecological intervention with pesticides, fertilizers, and machinery. Society has developed in forms that are fragile to both environmental and energy shocks, at the same time as climate stresses from energy use are increasing the frequency and severity of such shocks, as the costs of energy conventionally used to cope with them are increasing and as population growth further stresses production systems and reduces the margin of safety for fluctuations in their output.

A standard economic approach to predicting paths of change is a cost-benefit analysis for replacement of infrastructure associated with energy generation and use (of which a good example is the Stern report, available at http://www.hm-treasury.gov.uk/independent_reviews/stern_review_economics_climate_change/sternreview_index.cfm). Elasticities of demand are hoped to be estimable from current prices, on the assumption that markets have efficiently incorporated producer constraints and consumer preferences. However, it is an elementary result of neoclassical theory that the current externalization of environmental impacts produces price systems that are not on the efficient frontier [304]. To the extent that discounting of the future, as reflected in the interest rate, does not capture the real structure of cognitive and social discounting more fully represented in law and regulation as well as the price system, the value and depreciation of physical infrastructure built from irreplaceable low-cost carbon energy will also not be correctly priced. Hence a cost-benefit analysis based on prices generated by current markets will systematically fail to differentiate demand elasticities governed by physical constraints from those governed by social history and habit.

An underpinning of physical constraints in economic models should not be expected to provide all the unknown factors influencing production and demand aggregation, which are implicitly treated as a black box by methods that assume current market prices. Rather, it should be expected to impose those constraints that are well understood, within a larger domain of substantial ignorance about other factors, and to permit partial disaggregation of the price system into the components governed by different classes of constraints. Such disaggregation is particularly appropriate for the analysis of energy systems, because energy consumption is a fundamental physical constraint in the production, maintenance, and disposal of systems for energy capture, often limited by established and relatively inelastic technologies and sometimes by physical laws. These constraints may be contrasted to more flexible patterns in population distribution or in the distribution over agricultural practices, and the role of the price system in coupling the sectors may be partially understood without making all the assumptions of aggregation entailed in taking current prices as given.

Notes

1 In some instances it can be illustrated by simulation [262].

2 Von Neumann's original accomplishment was to prove the existence of a vector of utilization rates that would maximize an aggregate measure of growth in a complicated production setting involving inputs and outputs of many goods, without recourse to utility or mediation by price systems. One may, alternatively, introduce consumption utilities for goods which compete with production, and use the von Neumann input/output matrices to define the constraint space against which utilities are maximized. Such production models offer a richer space of constraints than scalar convex functions. Dual to any optimizing solution, one may then derive the price system that will support that schedule of inputs to production and outputs to consumption.

3 The data collection requirements for any extensive degree of coverage at this degree of disaggregation often become prohibitive in practice.

4 Here we assume that money remains fully utilized. Within Leontief's simplifying assumption, even savings deposits in banks have offsetting outlays in the form of loans.

5 A corporation may need three to four sets of books, one for the tax authorities, one for the stockholders, one for corporate general control, and possibly one for production.

6 Class names will be denoted in boldface, as might be done for an object-oriented computer language, to reflect their role in defining and organizing the language.

7 We revisit this discussion below in section 11.5. It can be argued that, under appropriate simplifying assumptions, this number can be reduced to two.

8 In contrast with *strategic market games*, we may use an approach based on *market games* and cooperative or coalitional game theory, presenting a higher level of abstraction than general equilibrium theory. It is explicitly normative in the sense that it assumes joint optimality as an expected property of any solution. Market games utilize the concept of totally balanced games [334, 337]. This approach enables us to explore the properties of a price system beyond the conventional feature of decentralized decision making, and is covered in [359].

9 In his symbolism $V \times R = K \times P$. He also took great care to distinguish quantities from flows.

10 A better appellation would use $\dot{Q}$ for the flow of goods, emphasizing that it is a rate, and make MV the "velocity of money," as its dimensions would then be an amount of money per unit time. However, the terminology is established, and to avoid further confusion we will follow convention.

11 This component in M1 includes only currency outside of the Federal Reserve and Treasury.

12 This is false when default conditions are relevant, or when numbers are few or when the law of one price is not assumed.

13 See Quint and Shubik [298], ch. 6, for details on a finer division of the single period.

14 Explicit examples are provided in [199].

15 The bankruptcy law connects fiat with preferences. Consider just two types. If the amount and distribution of fiat are low, there are instances when one type will be motivated to go bankrupt and the other will not. If we increase the amount of money by a factor of k to all, at some point it will not be optimal to go bankrupt.

16 A dreadfully sloppy but occasionally useful imprecise phrase used to indicate a constrained optimum.

17 In recent times it has become increasingly common to call for economic attention to nongrowth scenarios [67, 68].

18 For a brief review see [359].

19 Ξ is for *Consumable*.

20 A stone doorstop might be left unguarded in sun, rain, or snow, whereas ice cream must be kept refrigerated and gold must be guarded.

21 χ is for *Capital*.

22 By contrasting Eq. (7.12) with Eq. (7.11) we wish to capture the distinction between the head of an axe and the hull of a ship. For its essential purpose, the axe head degrades in proportion to the number of trees chopped. The hull of a ship, in contrast, reflecting to an equal degree the nature of its main function, corrodes with the passage of time, whether it is at anchor or under way. Natural persons share the property of inelastic time requirements for consumption, but we wish to emphasize that they are not the only elements in a von Neumann economy that could have this property.

23 Following the index conventions of chapter 5, subscript i indicates the agent and superscript j refers to a particular good, which is debt service in the intertemporal money market.

24 For simplicity, we will suppose here that ν does not depend either on t or on the period length δt.

25 Sometimes mutual funds that invest in bonds are required for very small-scale aggregation and disaggregation.

8 Uncertainty and Velocity

8.1 On Time, Dynamics, and Uncertainty

For the element of Time, which is the center of the chief difficulty of almost every economic problem, is itself absolutely continuous: Nature knows no absolute partition of time into long periods and short; but the two shade into one another by imperceptible gradations, and what is a short period for one problem, is a long period for another.
—Alfred Marshall, preface to first edition (1890) of *Principles of Economics* [245]

Marshall wrote before the understanding of quantum mechanics, and in particular before the full broad appreciation of the central role of risk in much of economic practice and theory. His magisterial sweep blending the short and long run is undoubtedly true and challenges those who try to generalize on "how short is short"; but as he well knew, the art of economic analysis lies in carving out good ad hoc models that can be claimed as having application to reasonably broad topics. Those who indulge in simulations know that even if time is deemed to be continuous, it well may be compressible or expandable. The common phrases such as "the day seemed like an eternity" during a panic or "the two weeks went like a flash" after a successful vacation may have meaning, and there are some phenomena more fruitfully studied with event time rather than clock time.

In this chapter the two features of uncertainty and the variability of velocity are considered. Both of these are fundamental to considering the more subtle features of a monetary economy. They are interlinked, and both add further complex features to the information, perception, and control mechanism of modern monetary systems.

8.2   The Central Role of Risk

There has been an explosive development in the study of both the qualitative and quantitative properties of risk. The power of careful modeling and sophisticated stochastic analysis has already shown itself in the context of the stock market and other financial markets, but as the various qualitative aspects of risk are being uncovered and well defined, the scope of a useful econophysics stretches far beyond the dynamics of paper traded on paper in the stock market, to starting to unravel the structures at the interface where the neural system and broad control mechanism of the economy as a whole meets the physical entities over which various agents battle for control. Conventional microeconomic theory has stressed production and consumption; applied macroeconomics has implicitly assumed a control role for government through fiscal and monetary policies; but the change now in the making is in the development of a general disequilibrium microeconomics with the intertwining of production, consumption, and finance, in ways that may even exceed the visions of writers such as Simmel [370], Schumpeter [325], von Mises [408], Hayek [181], or Keynes [235]. In particular the advent of worldwide cheap, almost instant communication combined with the computational powers of computer systems and the growth of a cadre of mathematicians, physicists, and probability theorists may have provided the weaponry to destroy the powers of many of the activities of any central bank and much of the power of current economic regulation and tax laws. The nature of the dynamics of competition is that every measure invokes a countermeasure.

8.2.1   Exogenous and endogenous risk

8.2.1.1   Risk exogenous to the economy   In the economy we are confronted with many aspects of political risk such as war, revolution, social unrest, and change in regime. Natural disasters such as floods, famines, earthquakes, and fires are ever present. Medical risks including plagues, pollution, and epidemics and a host of personal health inflictions befall all of us. Robbery, assault, and terrorism are present in one form or another.

Most of the items noted above can be insured against, and special insurance industries have the appropriate statistics to be able to do a reasonably good job of assessing risk and assigning more or less appropriate premia. Items such as the risk of death by auto accident have specific probability models associated with them, with causal models developed.

Some risks are deemed uninsurable by private means; if the disaster is big enough, even the government may not be able to provide much relief.

8.2.1.2   Endogenous risk   Many risks are encountered and identified in the financial structure of a modern economy. A brief list is noted:

Interest change risk,

Foreign exchange (FX) risk,

Default risk,

Redemption risk,

Inflation risk,

Market risk.

In the world of derivative instruments there is a veritable fancy butcher shop activity in defining different types of risk, cutting them out of the original instruments and institutions, and packaging and treating them separately. Thus an industry concerned with adding adjectives to the noun "risk" has been constructed.

As finer and finer distinctions are made concerning the multiple functions of financial instruments, the different functions of a single instrument can be stripped from it and sold or insured separately from the actual instrument. The purposes in doing so may be to enhance the credit rating of the instrument, to avoid taxes or other legislation, or to partition the liquidity of the original instrument.

8.2.2   Behavior and risk distributions

Fire and automobile insurance are based to a good first-order approximation on mass statistics on individual habitual behavior and can be regarded as providing reasonably solid predictions of behavior. The same cannot be said for the economy as a whole and the financial markets in particular. Measures have been constructed such as value at risk (VaR) [196], and methods for predicting the value of options such as the Black-Scholes formula [34] have been developed, utilizing a lognormal distribution in price movements. Yet empirical evidence in stock and commodity markets seems to indicate the presence of power laws and "fat-tailed" distributions. Economic theory does not provide a clean theoretical basis for the presence of the endogenous risk, but empirically the evidence is that the change in variation of price is not lognormal. When more than five or six events are observed whose probability is predicted as a

20σ occurrence by the reigning theory, one has to worry about the reigning theory (see [241, p. 93]).

The interface of science, habit, law, and politics cannot be ignored. Mere observation is not going to immediately overthrow a procedure accepted by practitioners, with routines designed to be used easily by them and with the blessings of a court system that will accept the application of a procedure such as the Black-Scholes calculations as proof that a guardian of other people's money has fulfilled his or her fiduciary responsibilities. It takes a few disasters or other blatant failures before an entrenched procedure is replaced.

8.2.2.1   Aggregation and index construction as a form of endogenous risk
A natural endogenous form of risk enters the economy in the act of aggregating or consolidating information for use.

All aggregations and indices represent compression of information, and this loss of detail creates uncertainty. In essence any index has a certain level of fineness or graining. Those who see more perceptively or who understand what dimensions have been left out may gain from their insight. But society as a whole and the economy in particular are required to estimate, digest, classify, and simplify the enormous flow of information that would otherwise overwhelm their operation.

8.2.2.2   Why index theory is so important   Few humans handle high-dimensional uncertainty with any ease in their decision making. As populations increase and society grows more complex, the need to provide compact descriptions grows. One-dimensional measures such as the inflation rate, unemployment rate, consumer price index (CPI), or the growth rate provide examples. The indices are useful and needed.

A simple example of the potential for the politics of index choice is given when adjustments in pension payouts are linked with the CPI. A change in the index might call for billions to be spent in extra pension payments. An opportunity to adjust the bundle of goods on which the index is based, or to modify the method of calculation, offers a way to change the outcome.

The selection of indices that are consistent with the basic theory of consumer choice through time poses a mathematical problem. The early textbooks devoted considerable time to examining the virtues and failing of popular indices such as those of Paasche and Laspeyres. Sidney Afriat produced an elegant analysis [4] providing the basic mathematical properties required for an adequate index consistent with the strong law of revealed preferences.

8.2.2.3 Strategic uncertainty Above we have noted endogenous uncertainty generated by aggregation. We must also cover game-theoretic uncertainty caused by the independent actions of many individual in situations whose outcomes are dependent on the actions of all. This problem in the social sciences may be regarded as worse than the classical n-body problem in physics. At best, solutions of the equations of motion are to be expected only for special cases.

8.2.2.4 Individuals, risk, and three roles In a complex developed economy, for all individuals there are probably three different styles of behavior present in each individual. As a consumer, the individual may be more or less regular and reasonably rational, reasonably well informed except about new complex or rarely acquired items. As a worker, the individual in an economic society is more or less competent, understanding his or her occupation in a cultural setting of a market economy that justifies more or less conscious economic behavior. When the individual has to deal with aspects of life other than more or less regular consumption and production, the informational and behavioral bases for decision change considerably. Behavior in regard to religious, societal, and political beliefs does not fit so easily into the economic rubric. Neither do long run economic decisions which may be made infrequently and with a low basis of professional knowledge. It is here that the fiduciary role of those who control the financial system is central to the economy. Most members of a society have neither the interest nor the ability to become even semiprofessional financiers. Yet what to do with savings is a problem faced by all but the poor. The innovative work of Robert Shiller has been addressed both to scholarship on and advocacy for new financial instruments to tackle long-term societal problems [341]. The problems in implementation are more political, legal, bureaucratic, and social than due to the lack of theory.

8.2.3 Matching and random-sequence markets

Lucas and colleagues, Karatzas, Shubik, and Sudderth [199], and others have all used variants of the standard Bellman equation set up with a fixed clock that tends to play down and make it difficult to study the differences in velocity and flexibility of financial instruments in a model economy. In order to study these differences, we must find a way to model the micro-microeconomic details of trade in minutes or even microseconds.

The work of Doyne Farmer [69, 122, 124–128, 160, 191, 225, 226, 377] and associates provides examples of the stock market viewed as a continuous double-auction market. Bak, Paczuski, and Shubik [23] constructed simple models of a stock market and suggested that the large variations may be due to a crowd effect, where agents imitate each other's behavior. The variations over different timescales can be related to each other in a systematic way, similar to the Lévy stable distribution proposed by Mandelbrot to describe real market indices. In the simplest, least realistic case, exact results for the statistics of the variations are derived by mapping onto a model of diffusing and annihilating particles. When the relative number of rational traders is small, "bubbles" often occur in which the market price moves outside the range justified by fundamental market analysis, as was noted first in a somewhat different model of De Long et al. [76, 77]. When the number of rational traders is larger, the market price is generally locked within the price range they define.

Separate from the new financial literature on near-instant trading is a large economic literature on search and matching. Although the mathematical structure of the binary search and matching and allocation models is clean and well defined, there are at least two underlying themes. One might be regarded as being close to economic anthropology. Instead of taking markets as a primitive concept, the economist can view the stochastic search and binary matching models as possibly casting light on the emergence of formal markets. Other models such as the variants of the assignment games, the Böhm-Bawerk horse market [338], and the marriage matching problem [148] provide a cooperative-game-theoretic analysis.

8.3   Uncertainty and a Loosely Coupled System

Probably the key function of a modern financial system is to provide for loosely coupled dynamics in an uncertain environment. In a world with random events constantly bombarding the economy, even if the system as a whole were tending toward some equilibrium it would be incessantly knocked off course.

The existence of liquid money earning no interest fits in with Keynes's comments on precautionary and speculative calls for cash. They both appear naturally in process models involving random variables and expectations.

In a complex evolving economy, is the concept of equilibrium operationally worth embellishing? The purely formalistic control theorist with no interest whatsoever in application can announce broad expansions of the application of the concept of equilibrium by enlarging the state space over which action takes place, thereby including more and more history in the decision process. Unless accompanied with empirical justification, such an approach is not particularly operationally helpful. Each dimensional enlargement without empirical justification may easily add spurious generality.

8.4 Bubbles and Socioeconomic Dynamics?

A loosely coupled system provides the opportunity for a dynamics exhibiting great instabilities. Is there or will there be a general economic theory of bubbles and panics?

An informal, plausible but debatable verbal sketch of a possible dynamics sufficient to produce a housing bubble such as the one experienced in 2008 in the United States is suggested, prior to a formal model below. The dynamics could depend on differentials in expertise, the spread of raw data in the system, the differences in the ability of the various agents to decode the data into operationally useful information, and the perverse incentives in the system.

We consider as the initial conditions a housing market with prices that have been rising sufficiently for a few periods that the purchasers of houses include not only those who intend to live in them or professional traders and brokers, but also amateurs willing to buy and flip houses.

The supply of new housing comes from builders and professional speculators helping to finance them.

The banking system together with minimal guarantees from the government lends liberally and fails to perform the level of due diligence it might have done in a previous, more conservative era where it might have retained and serviced the mortgages booked, using permanent salaried employees to do so.

The banking system changes involve the shift caused by being able to quickly sell the mortgages to investment bankers capable of packaging them into tranches of mortgage-backed securities. This change provides a "hot potato" incentive for the banks. By being able to pass through the mortgages quickly, the banks cut exposure to local adverse consequences. It therefore pays to increase the volume of mortgages booked and flowed through. The task of maximizing the volume of mortgages sold is more suited to commission-paid sales people than to more conservative strictly salaried personnel.

The banks generate a higher volume of riskier mortgages where there is a perverse incentive in sales commissions, and as they can be flowed though quickly the due diligence constraint on the bank is lessened.

The tranches cut up by the financial institutions creating the mortgage-backed securities can even be enhanced in credit rating by financial reinsurance. With a sufficiently high rating, the instrument is attractive to pension funds and to investment officers with large positive cash flows who are not at the same level of sophistication as producers and raters of the mortgage-backed security. After enough weak mortgages have been written and the market is more or less saturated with the high-risk mortgages, the price growth diminishes and the weaker mortgages of both the poor and the amateur speculators default, triggering a decrease in demand and a downward spiral. The key elements are:

- Perverse incentives in selling mortgages,

- Liberal support encouraging home ownership among the less well off and less financially educated,

- Lowering of due diligence by the banks who flow through risk,

- The ability to package and enhance the ratings of the mortgage tranches,

- The presence of a high demand by portfolio managers such as pension funds where the pressure on employees of lesser skill than the sellers to "beat the market average" are large,

- Finally saturation followed by bankruptcies and an overall change in expectations.

The foregoing elements emphasize preference and incentive in a structured environment. However, merely mechanical aspects of market function should not be overlooked, as they may create inherent instabilities or limit the options agents have to respond in their own interest, even when their appraisal of risk becomes realistic. We consider such mechanical aspects, and also the influence of the *selection process* on the multiplicity of dynamical trajectories and equilibria, in the next subsection.

8.4.1   Multiple equilibria and self-fulfilling prophecies in unstable markets with limited buyers and sellers

We formalize only a small part of this complex problem, emphasizing the role of dynamics in determining the meaning, multiplicity, and determinacy of equilibria, and addressing the central question: in what sense can it be rational for agents to enter a market attempting to profit, when the market is susceptible to correlated-failure mechanics, and when agents create failure somewhat independently of fundamentals by trying to mitigate the risk of that very failure?

8.4.1.1   A mechanism assembled from heterogeneous, coarse-grained abstractions at many scales   A formal model of dynamics as complex as the failure of markets for mortgage-backed securities, and their influence in both real estate markets and wider credit markets, would require intermediate abstractions of a range of heterogeneous subprocesses. The acknowledgment of their heterogeneity is an admission that a market failure is not a simple game, but an output from a mechanism assembled from a substructure of game-theoretically different choices and constraints. Yet intermediate levels of abstraction are possible because the subchoices are not an idiosyncratic tangle: for example, repurchase markets require basic rules for lending, rules for collateral valuation, and procedures to determine haircuts, each of these arising from its own context of legal and accounting practices as well as its contribution to the market's function. These abstractions can be characterized coarsely in terms of function, and the need for the basic functions would persist even though they might be realized through different micromechanisms. Such categories of subprocesses are thus abstracted in much the same way we have proposed for minimal institutions. A fully developed formal model is an operations research problem that goes beyond the scope of this discussion, but we note some intermediate elements that have been recognized in literature, before formalizing a single one of them.

- *Timescales and the term structure of liabilities:* Working capital for intermediaries such as dealer banks [105] can be obtained from combinations of stocks, long-term bonds, and short-term debt instruments such as overnight loans (uncollateralized) or repurchase agreements (collateralized). The portfolio of liabilities issued by an intermediary such as a dealer bank, or the portfolio held by an intermediary higher in the chain such as a commercial or investment bank, can have large consequences for the feedbacks and stability properties of asset and credit markets. Cúrdia and Woodford [66] have suggested that the composition of even the central bank balance sheet, as well as interest rates, or aggregate reserve requirements on commercial banks, be examined as an instrument of regulatory policy.

- *Recursive rules that mechanistically generate stability or instability:* Widespread adoption of uniform rules such as mark-to-market collateral valuation can create correlated and destabilizing positive feedbacks when they are part of loops of debt-financed purchases [229], as when dealer banks use repurchase agreements (repos) to pass ownership of mortgage-backed securities through to investment or commercial banks. The use of a collateral valuation rule based on a publicly available signal such as market price may seem desirable by criteria of uniformity and responsiveness to market conditions (and legal defensibility). However, transient dealer-bank demand funded with borrowed money can increase market price and, through mark-to-market valuation, the value of the collateral for existing repos, increasing available funds and further inflating prices. The complement positive feedback operates in periods of price decline, and if it becomes sufficiently rapid can lead to fire sales [320]. If positive-feedback-inducing rules are updated overnight in markets with slowly changing sets of buyers and sellers, the aggregate effect can be exponential amplification of supply or demand excesses, which may either be abstracted as generic null models for time series, or further coarse-grained and treated as aggregate instantaneous correlated offers to buy or sell. Highly homogeneous conventions such as mark-to-market backed by legal precedent can combine with (and be exacerbated by) uncodified but still widespread conventions for updating haircuts or other reserve requirements [150] in response to changes in perceived risk of default.

- *Liquidity in relation to stability:* A second role for abstraction of destabilizing elements is found in the formalization of liquidity. A market might be called liquid if it can absorb the effects of any single correlated destabilizing feedback loop such as collateral or haircut responses without entering a self-reinforcing trajectory of price increase or decrease.

- *Inherent partitioning of roles between small and large players:* Minsky has argued [263] that a general pattern of business cycles achieves both undesirable features—inflationary pressures and also excess indebtedness and a failure to regulate loan quality—because the activity and roles of players are partitioned in time over the cycle. While leverage is increased during expansionary phases, large numbers of "innovative" loans are distributed through the economy, with innovation driven partly by the provision of new services and partly by an incentive to evade regulation. Since these small loans cannot be recalled during the contracting phase when reserves must be restored and markets stabilized against fire-sale conditions, only the government or a similar large oligopolistic player (such as banks in the federal reserve system under central bank pressure) can move the required large amounts of money in the required short times, although at the expense of borrowing or printing currency. The reserves infused into the system from government debt during the contraction fund inflation during the subsequent expansion, but the support (or feasibility) of regulation that might be created by recessions and bailouts does not propagate to the subsequent booms to meaningfully keep pace with market "innovation." The aggregate effect might be called a *decision ratchet*, in that the noninterchangeable roles of small agents during the expansion and the government or centrally coordinated banks during the recession lead to a one-way flow of money from centrally acquired debt to broadly distributed inflationary pressure.

- *Number and determinacy of equilibria:* A final, outermost level of coarse-graining concerns the number and determinacy of equilibria, and whether the full employment of a market sector is advantageous to investors. The disbursement of investor capital deposited in commercial banks to interest-bearing loans such as mortgages involves all the problems of "creation of liquidity" that arise when the use of money requires commitment on a longer term than the the fluctuating demands for currency by the depositors can accommodate directly. The incentive to keep money fully utilized, and the way in which doing so links contracts that provide liquidity to risks of failure by bank runs, were clearly described by Bagehot [21] during the rise of fractional-reserve banking in England in the nineteenth century. The new element introduced in modern complex financial markets is the layer of credit instruments—mortgage-backed securities, repurchase agreements—interposed between depositors and borrowers, and the way these credit instruments seek to provide some degree of liquidity to intermediaries such as dealer banks, whose nominal service is evaluation of the quality of loans and loan-backed portfolios. When markets are fully utilized and valuation of the loans and intermediate instruments is maintained by stable market prices, these ensure full utilization of money. However, when valuation rules lead to value collapses and market failures, the ultimate distribution of capital that results may be Pareto-inferior to having remained out of the markets, and the layer of intermediate credit instruments may be destroyed. In a formal model we consider the problem of identifying the number and stability of equilibria when stabilizing and destabilizing elements are both at work in the sector, and, indirectly, what this problem implies about the concept of equilibrium.

Problems of multiple equilibria and correlated dynamics that select—potentially arbitrarily—among them arise in many contexts, and no single model will provide a literal representation of more than a few closely related cases. We have discussed the case of collateral and leverage cycles at greatest length because it illustrates many other important points about dynamics and mechanism besides ambiguity of equilibrium. Other cases that are equally diverse, but have been considered to reflect similar economic phenomena, include bank runs [83, 84] and currency attacks [267]. The classic papers on these problems have used a much higher level of abstraction, without intermediate layers of mechanism, as direct noncooperative strategic choices among many parallel agents. However, their solutions, expressed in terms of rule-bound representative agents perhaps distinguished only in having different values of noisy signals, are equally well suited to correlated behavior mediated by institutional rules that lead to herding behavior. Parallels between classic individual-initiated bank runs and modern financial crises in which banks or firms may run on other banks or firms, and in which the annihilation of credit may involve instruments circulating mostly within the banking sector, are explained in [168].

We therefore switch now to a canonical model of bank runs, which is among the simplest, oldest, and best-known models in this class. For the solution method we present below—exploration among related rules with adoption proportional to their success—the interpretation of herding behavior mediated by a cluster of similar but nonidentical trading and lending rules remains sensible.

8.4.1.2   Why problems of multiple/indeterminate equilibria arise naturally from the "creation" of liquidity   The classic formal model capturing (a subset of) Bagehot's insights [21] about the problem of "creating liquidity" is the bank run model of Diamond and Dybvig [83]. The premise of the model is that an investment opportunity requires commitment of capital which then becomes unavailable to meet short-term demands for cash (to meet needs arising from outside the model). For whatever reason,[1] a complete set of Arrow-Debreu securities does not exist to cover short-term, unforeseen and idiosyncratic demands of would-be investors for cash. The resulting investment program is suboptimal, in that investors with sudden needs for cash forfeit a large return from investment, even though in principle a price system exists at which other agents would sell claims on portions of their investment (at lower marginal utilities of return) to insure the idiosyncratic demand.

In this model, a bank demand deposit contract with a positive rate of return fills the function left uncovered by Arrow-Debreu securities, but the deposit contract introduces a new risk (bank runs). Stated abstractly, the demand deposit contract *creates liquidity contingent on conditions*. Since, in aggregate, the long term of commitment to investment cannot be "converted" to the short term of available money, the demand deposit contract uses aggregation scale and the law of large numbers—under the crucial assumption that individual depositors are small and that their demands are uncorrelated—to distribute demands in the same manner as an insurance contract would. The liquidity "created" in the part of the state space with uncorrelated demands, however, is more than lost in the part of the space with totally correlated demands, where all returns from investment are lost and money is reallocated in an uneven distribution that is Pareto-inferior to the original allocation. The risk of loss can lead to a Nash equilibrium in precisely this part of the state space, which is the bank run. The equilibrium condition selects correlated demand behavior among the agents even if there is no exogenous source of correlation.

Although Diamond and Dybvig's formulation [83] is a general equilibrium exposition and accepts many of the interpretations of that framework, its institutional model serves much more broadly to capture conceptual relations between timescales, liquidity, and risk among multiple indeterminate equilibria. In reality Arrow-Debreu securities may be unavailable for a wide range of reasons,[2] while demand deposit contracts are flexible and widely used alternatives. The essential observation—that a mismatch of timescales and uncertainty about future needs for cash cannot be eliminated, but can at most be moved from one part of the state space to another by aggregation—creates the link between an incentive to keep money fully utilized, and the risk of self-fulfilling correlated suboptimal equilibria. This is the essential similarity that links bank runs to other kinds of market failure, such as collapse of credit markets coupled to correlated selling of assets.

An important feature of the Diamond-Dybvig model is that the bank run equilibrium *need not* occur. It is essentially arbitrary whether, in a given instance, agents settle on correlated withdrawals and suffer a bank run, or withdraw only if they have real needs and benefit from the Pareto-superior insured equilibrium. This essential uncertainty also affects the timing of market collapses in situations such as the 2008 mortgage-backed-securities markets. Precisely because it was not clear when (or to some parties, *whether*) markets would collapse, some investors judged it rational to continue to hold mortgage-backed securities, while others continued to carry the debt obligation from repurchase agreements on these. Both such parties suffer losses when valuations collapse, credit is withdrawn but currency is not sufficient to repay loans, and markets become highly illiquid.

8.4.1.3 Mechanism-induced sources of coordination in multiscale heterogeneous economies such as loan markets

In classic bank run models (and in many historical cases), the decision to run is an individual strategic choice. Depositors see lines outside the bank door and follow suit. In the 2008 failure of mortgage-backed-securities markets, the correlated sell-off was at least partly an outcome of correlated collateral devaluation, mediated by institutional rules, and effectively amplifying small fluctuations over short times. The important point of similarity with a classic bank run is that, although the saturation of natural buyers and the resulting market fragility may be fundamental features, the small fluctuations amplified by the unstable collateral/short-term loan feedbacks are essentially arbitrary and unpredictable. Although they are endogenously generated, their origin is sufficiently cryptic that they can present a significant uncertainty to dealer banks or commercial banks attempting to keep money fully utilized, and so needing to decide when to exit or to remain in markets.

A further difference is the way in which the creation or destruction of credit is coupled to the distribution of primary monies in modern markets. A pure fractional-reserve banking system can lend gold or government fiat while offering demand deposits as long as only a subset of depositors need money at any time (or as long as central bank lending can buffer excess fluctuations, as the Bank of England did for London banks in the 1800s [21]). In a more complex system, bank or business credit (checks or other negotiable instruments) may be issued against reserves, expanding effective money supply, but the extra instruments may become valueless if the bank fails, together with whatever distribution of fiat results. In a modern complex securities market, not only may government fiat be redistributed to mortgage borrowers from depositors (or from the central bank or treasury), but large sectors of securities or loan contracts may be brought into existence and then made valueless or nullified if markets collapse. We consider the consequences of this distinction for velocity below.

8.4.1.4   Measures of liquidity in inherently unstable systems   For many purposes, liquidity is treated as almost a dimension along which markets may vary continuously. This is certainly common when using market impact, price diffusion, or mean regression of midpoint prices in financial markets [69, 125, 126, 160, 191, 225, 377]. Bubbles, panics, bank runs of various sorts, and other problems in the control of money and credit supply offer another formulation in which liquidity may be thought of as a property that is either present or absent, and identified in terms of a computable threshold. The essential observation is that markets will generally be subject to both stabilizing and destabilizing forces, the former often due to uncorrelated stochastic elements, the latter often due to correlation among participants created by optimizing behavior. A market is liquid if the stabilizing forces are sufficiently stronger than the destabilizing forces to produce a basin of attraction, in which prices can fluctuate dynamically without spiraling outward to a market failure or other boundary solution.

An example of a destabilizing mechanism which may be identified in rules of practice (so that one need not speculate on rules of behavior) is the interaction of mark-to-market collateral pricing with the financing of new acquisitions by repurchase agreements (repos). Mark-to-market may be adopted as a standard collateral valuation rule for a class of securities such as mortgage-backed securities, because it provides predictability to dealer banks and a standard of legal defensibility for fair lending practices by the investment banks that lend to them. Repo-based financing—putting aside for the moment the dynamics of haircuts, and considering only the dependence on collateral levels during times when haircuts are stable—delivers a pool of cash for new purchases that defines the leverage of dealer banks' initial investment capital. Increases in the available cash pool have an inflationary effect on new purchases of securities, but under mark-to-market valuation this price increase feeds back to increase the amount that can be borrowed against existing securities transferred through repos. The converse happens during contractions of available cash, which deflate prices, increase collateral requirements, and further reduce available cash. The two rules, one adopted for uniformity and the other as a mechanism to expand credit, therefore jointly form a self-amplifying or positive-feedback loop, which acting alone will drive prices into inflating or deflating spirals.

The internal dynamics of mark-to-market and repo financing do not generally act alone, but interact with the production of new securities and the entry and exit of traders in the markets. To the extent that the latter processes are uncorrelated or responsive to constraints outside the markets, they should stabilize prices and returns on invested capital.

The distinction between liquid and illiquid securities markets is then defined according to whether the stabilizing effects of entry, exit, and supply variations are larger or smaller than the self-amplifying effects of mark-to-market valuation and repo financing. In a minimal model (which we do not develop here), stabilizing influences could take the form of a mean-regressing random walk in inventory and available capital. The characteristic decay time from this effect would create a quantitative threshold above which the feedback of internal financing (the strength of which is determined by haircuts) becomes destabilizing, and the markets illiquid.

8.4.1.5 On multiple equilibria associated with liquidity failure   An important feature of catastrophic market failures as distinct from mere reevaluations of oversupplied securities is that insolvency can be driven by liquidity failures in which prices diverge widely from measures of "value" of underlying securities, such as expected discounted future interest payments. A liquidity failure requires only that a large fraction of participants take the sell side of markets. The idea that doing so can be rational even though all sellers accept lowered prices involves elements of either time or incomplete information in an essential way; sitting out a fire sale is only a genuine risk if a seller cannot wait for future opportunities to sell the security at a better price, or if long-term estimates of fundamental values are likely to be revised. Fire sale conditions thus have the same element of self-fulfilling prophecy as bank runs: they may do real economic damage even though they are not inevitable, and even though the coordinating signal needed to generate the fire sale is the attempt by agents to escape precisely the damage that they collectively create.

Self-fulfilling prophecy creates the two fundamental questions that define bank runs and structurally similar market failures:

- If all agents act rationally at each time given their present information, how many equilibria can the market system have? Can a high-yielding equilibrium with full investment coexist, under the same incentives and information, with a low-yielding equilibrium created by self-fulfilling beliefs by agents that they may lose value in a fire sale?

- If two such equilibria can exist, can it ever then be rational for agents to enter the markets in the first place, and how does a rational expectation of gain from a good equilibrium relate to the fact that it is only the agents' own actions that may generate a bad equilibrium, which they did not judge "likely" at the time they entered the markets?

Two opposite answers to these questions have been given for a class of models of bank runs, currency attacks, and similar coordination problems. The first, a general equilibrium analysis by Diamond and Dybvig [83, 84], argued for the presence of two Nash equilibria, representing a high-yield coordinated equilibrium and a bank run, respectively. The essential features of the Diamond-Dybvig model are that agents have an investment opportunity that yields a payoff $R > 1$ per unit input, only if they leave the money invested for two periods. This condition represents inherent illiquidity of the investment. Some agents learn, however, after the initial opportunity to invest, that they must withdraw after the first period, in which case the investment returns only the original input value (so no strict loss is assumed for early withdrawal). The signal that agents must withdraw early is "private information" available only to them, and not insurable with contingent contracts. Therefore agents who invest individually and then learn that they must withdraw early lose the entire excess return $(R - 1)$.

Diamond and Dybvig then add to this single-agent problem a bank that offers demand deposits, and acts as a proxy investor for the agents' aggregate deposits. The demand deposit contract offers a return $r > 1$ for withdrawals after the first period, *subject to availability of funds*. The bank withdraws from investment whatever funds are demanded to pay depositors, at unit return, leaving the remainder (if any) invested to yield return R. The return R on the deposits that are not withdrawn is then paid out to depositors who withdraw after the second period. Because first-period demanders withdraw a multiple $r > 1$ of the amount they deposited, the return to those who wait through the second period is less than R times their own deposits; this is the price they pay to insure the *ex ante* risk of having needed to withdraw early themselves.

The optimal value r^* for r is self-consistent if only the agents who *must* withdraw in the first period do so. All agents have the option to withdraw early, however, and since a multiplier $r > 1$ of the maximum available funds in the first period has been promised, not everyone can be paid in an early withdrawal. If the demands to withdraw exceed the total available funds, a random ordering of agents is generated, and the first agents in the queue are paid the promised amount r; later agents are paid nothing. If such a run occurs which exhausts all funds, agents who wait until the second period are assured zero payout; hence they are better off participating in the run and receiving a probability $1/r$ to be paid than waiting, making the run a Nash equilibrium. The efficiency of the high-yielding outcome is monotone-increasing in r on the interval $0 \leq r < r^*$, while the efficiency of the bank run is monotone-decreasing at all r, so the creation of liquidity is inherently linked to the risk of bank runs.

The main results of the Diamond-Dybvig analysis are:

1. *Under general equilibrium assumptions that all agents respond identically taking prices as given*, that the high-yielding equilibrium could achieve the same efficiency as a complete set of Arrow-Debreu securities without requiring the publicly verifiable information implicit in the GE insurance contracts;

2. That agents may be rational to enter demand deposit contracts that promise to pay more than the quantity of their reserves and so are subject to runs,

if the probability of a bank run is sufficiently small, though Diamond and Dybvig did not address the way this probability is determined or estimated by agents;

3. That adding insurance to bank deposits (backed by a central bank or government) could stabilize the high-yielding equilibrium and eliminate the bank run equilibrium.

A second analysis, by Morris and Shin [267], retained the two-stage structure of Diamond and Dybvig but embedded it in a larger extensive-form game for which they sought a *correlated* noncooperative equilibrium. Agents were given a signal about the number of individuals who must withdraw early, with the crucial feature that each agent receives an independent signal with some error from the actual population state. Morris and Shin showed that, for a small error distribution, no strategy dominates a simple threshold strategy, in which an agent withdraws early if his idiosyncratic signal exceeds the threshold and waits if the signal is below the threshold. Thus the two equilibria of Diamond and Dybvig disappear, even without exogenous deposit insurance. A curious feature of the Morris-Shin correlated equilibrium is that it remains the unique equilibrium for any *nonzero* noise, no matter how small, but that the solution is undefined at zero noise (exact signals of the population state), so noise is a singular perturbation about the noise-free model. The singularity of the noise-free model is reminiscent of the removable singularity encountered in our discussion of the Hahn paradox in chapter 5. In deterministic multiperiod models, any salvage value stabilizes the trade value of fiat money over an arbitrarily long time, but a strictly zero salvage value renders the trade value undefined.

The sensitive dependence of the outcomes of the Diamond-Dybvig and Morris-Shin analysis on what seem like small details of information conditions, and the singular-perturbation nature of noise in the Morris-Shin equilibrium, suggest that neither model is a robust analysis of the number and determinacy of equilibria. We argue that a more empirically appropriate interpretation of problems in this category requires a notion of *fragility* of correlated equilibria. In certain (typically large-noise) regimes of the signal about the population state, the Morris-Shin equilibrium is unique and is robust against small changes in assumptions of the model. However, in an *open interval* about zero noise, the regulating role of the signal is fragile, and this is the content of the apparently removable singularity at zero noise. In the fragile regime, fluctuations may become more important than the regulator, and the multiple, indeterminate equilibria of Diamond and Dybvig may be restored. The analog for the

Hahn paradox is that a final salvage value stabilizes the exchange rate for fiat over sufficiently short terms, but that over long *but still finite* terms in models with stochasticity, exchange value is determined by fluctuations in the recent past, as in the model of [22]. A similar result for evolutionary updating in repeated games is derived in [380].

8.4.1.6 Formalization A full analysis of the following formalization of these ideas is provided in [385]. Here we present the structure of the game and summarize the key features of an adaptive solution concept that captures the transition between robust unique equilibria and multiple equilibria with endogenous uncertainty of bank runs.

A three-stage extensive-form game linking liquidity creation to risk of coordination failure is shown in figure 8.1. A large number of identical agents, which we model as a continuum indexed on the unit interval, are each given an endowment of one unit of a capital good. In banking models, these are savers who own gold or government fiat money. In real estate security markets they may be dealer banks with their initial capital. In the first move of the game, they deposit with an institution that invests on their behalf and agrees to return an amount $r > 1$ in the event of withdrawal after one period. In the original Diamond-Dybvig model this represents demand deposits in a bank; in the real

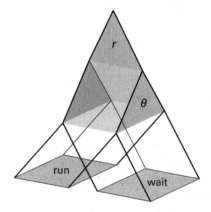

Figure 8.1

An extensive-form game for bank runs. In the first ply, the agents move, declaring a payout for early withdrawals $r \in [1, R]$. In the second ply, nature moves, selecting a fraction of Type 1 agents $\theta \in [0, 1]$, and randomly assigning agents within the two groups. (Filled wedges indicate continuous decision variables.) In the third ply, which is the subgame, agents of Type 2 make a binary decision to run or wait.

estate securities context it may represent in aggregate the set of investment banks that accept mortgage-backed securities as collateral, while agreeing to charge interest rates that provide a rate of return r to the dealer banks, which is the spread between the payment stream from the underlying securities and interest charged by the investment banks, multiplied by the leverage (determined, in turn, by the haircut). The securities have a long amortization period, and since the loans cannot be recalled or the properties repossessed without significant loss, the securities are of low value to any agents not able to wait for the full repayment stream. Under an attempt to sell a large fraction of them short of maturity, the price drop may nullify the payment stream from interest rate spreads. Here we give this the most conservative representation, following [84], as a return of the initial capital; a loss of capital could also be modeled but is not necessary to the result below.

In the second (continuous-valued) stage, nature selects a random subset of agents with measure $\theta \in [0, 1]$ who become *Type 1* agents that must withdraw in the first period. The remainder, called *Type 2*, have the option to remain invested until the second period. Type 1 agents may be dealer banks who, by their own choice or under constraint from their investment bank lenders, do not renew repurchase agreements or default on them, leading to the sale of the collateral securities (by either party) to recover the loan amounts. If the market is liquid, this sale may be performed without devaluing the remaining securities (e.g., through mark-to-market feedbacks), which return their full payoff R. If, however, enough agents choose to sell short of maturity, the loss of principal negates any received interest payments, and the late sellers receive nothing. In the third (discrete) move, the Type 2 agents decide whether to withdraw from the investment in the first period, potentially contributing to a run, or to wait until maturity.

To study correlated equilibria of this game, after the second move we permit each Type 2 agent to poll K randomly selected individuals, who honestly report their type. The fraction k/K of Type 1 agents in the poll becomes a sample estimator $\tilde{\theta}$ for the actual fraction θ of Type 1 agents in the population. The binomially distributed sample estimators become Morris and Shin's idiosyncratic, noisy signal about the population state.

Morris and Shin [267] show, for a uniform distribution $p(\theta)$, that no strategy dominates a simple threshold strategy in which all agents choose the same optimal threshold θ^* and withdraw early if their sample estimators $\tilde{\theta}$ exceed θ^*. This equilibrium remains unique even if the variance in the conditional distribution $p\left(\tilde{\theta} \mid \theta\right)$ goes to zero, corresponding in the model above to $K \to \infty$. However, at $\tilde{\theta} \equiv \theta$ the strategy becomes undefined.

In [385] we analyze an alternative, *local and exploratory* solution algorithm, based on evolutionary updating. Instead of a homogeneous population that precomputes solutions with self-consistent expectations, the population consists of subpopulations. All agents use threshold strategies, but the agents in each subpopulation differ in the values of their threshold parameters θ^*. Under repeated play, subpopulations are rewarded in proportion to their expected payoff, and their numbers (either of individuals or of invested capital) increase or decrease by this amount, thus changing the average threshold in the population. For the binomially distributed sample estimators $\left(\tilde{\theta} \mid \theta\right)$ and a suitable distribution of subpopulations, the aggregate population response may be made arbitrarily similar to the response of a homogeneous population using the mean threshold strategy with a slightly wider distribution of sample estimators.

By the *fundamental theorem of evolutionary game theory* [187], the Nash equilibria of the noncooperative game are also rest points of the replicator dynamic, as the mutation rate (responsible for dispersion of the population strategy) is taken to zero. Away from rest points, the mean threshold has a nonzero velocity, because thresholds slightly higher or lower are superior responses to the aggregate population behavior. The signs of the resulting velocities of the mean $d\langle\theta^*\rangle/dt$ as a function of the promised payout r and the instantaneous mean $\langle\theta^*\rangle$, in the replicator dynamic for three prior distributions $p(\theta)$, are shown in figure 8.2.

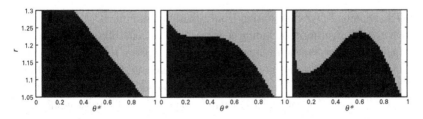

Figure 8.2

Signs of the evolutionary velocity $d\langle\theta^*\rangle/dt$ for the three prior distributions described in the main text. Black is positive velocity; gray is negative. Left panel: the uniform distribution in which each r has a unique stable fixed point θ^*. Middle panel: Gaussian $p(\theta)$ with standard deviation $\approx$ 0.152 which is the critical value for onset of bistability. Right panel: Gaussian $p(\theta)$ with standard deviation $= 0.1$ showing two stable fixed points and one unstable fixed point over the range $r \in [1.12, 1.24]$.

The first plot of $d\langle\theta^*\rangle/dt$ as a function of $\langle\theta^*\rangle$ and the return r is for a uniform density $p(\theta)$. The second is for a Gaussian density with mean $\langle\theta\rangle = 0.5$ and standard deviation 0.152, and the third is for a Gaussian with mean $\langle\theta\rangle = 0.5$ and standard deviation 0.1. For any value of r negotiated in the first move of the extensive-form game, the rest point is the boundary between gray (negative velocity) and black (positive velocity). Stable rest points are those with gray to the right of black. The figure shows that, for the uniform density $p(\theta)$ at any r, a unique stable rest point θ^* exists. This is the Morris-Shin threshold strategy. However, for Gaussian $p(\theta)$ with standard deviation 0.152, a threshold value $r \approx 1.225$ leads to neutral stability of this rest point, and for Gaussian $p(\theta)$ with standard deviation 0.1 a bistable regime develops. The upper and lower stable rest points are the two equilibria of Diamond and Dybvig, and the intermediate rest point is repelling. Optimizing the *ex ante* expected payoff along any of these (r, θ^*) fixed-point contours then selects the correlated-equilibrium value for r.

In [267] we also show that a stochastic replicator dynamic creates a probability for rare transitions between the stable and unstable rest points, allowing us to estimate within the model the likelihood of the bank run equilibrium, along with its properties. In the example shown here, the bank run equilibrium may indeed be made sufficiently rare under indefinitely repeated play that it is rational for agents to invest in this market.

8.4.1.7   Key points from the model   The interpretations of the model that we believe are general across a range of coordination problems are the following:

- The Diamond-Dybvig intuition from general equilibrium—that multiple *ex post* Nash equilibria including a Pareto-inferior equilibrium can be self-induced by agents who *ex ante* expect returns superior to remaining outside the markets—is consistent with a range of local and constructive solutions. When multiple equilibria exist, they may be *metastable*, meaning that rare constellations of agent choices may move a population from one equilibrium to another.

- The Morris-Shin insight also applies: that a source of dispersion that distributes population responses brings into existence a class of unique, stable threshold strategies. The *need* for dispersion, however, keeps even the Morris-Shin equilibrium that corresponds to the good (correlated) Diamond-Dybvig equilibrium from achieving the efficiency of Arrow-Debreu insurance. The need to distribute the population response in order to stabilize the threshold strategy requires both the mean threshold and the returns to agents in the conservative tail to produce suboptimal payoffs.

- The same need for dispersion that causes threshold solutions to fall short of general equilibrium efficiency also limits the range of situations over which they can provide stability. For highly disperse signals, all of the prior densities $p(\theta)$ in our example have unique stable threshold solutions at each r. In the range of very narrow sample-estimator distributions $p(\theta^* \mid \theta)$, however—in this case, narrow compared to the standard deviation of the prior density $p(\theta)$—the transition from unique stability to multivalued and metastable equilibria emerges.

- In the domain of unique equilibria, the properties of almost all repeats of the game are determined by the population structure and payoffs in small neighborhoods of the rest point. When multiple equilibria emerge, not only neighborhoods of both rest points but also a neighborhood around the *least-improbable transition trajectory* between them determine the distribution of population outcomes. A new class of relevant questions about this distribution, including the characteristic persistence times in each equilibrium, emerges. We characterize this as the regime where the dispersion of the sample estimators has become a "fragile regulator," and the late-time properties of the outcome are determined by the sampling, exploration, and reward dynamics of the population.

8.5   The Role of Velocity

A conventional macroeconomic definition of the velocity of money is: Velocity is a ratio of nominal GDP to a measure of the money supply (M1, M2, or M3). As noted in chapter 7, it can be thought of as the rate of turnover in the money supply—that is, the number of times one dollar is used to purchase final goods and services included in GDP. How good is this definition of velocity of money and how useful a concept is the velocity of money, and for what? This section is devoted to these considerations.

The intermix of lags in technology, habits, bureaucracy, law, and custom impose time lags in decision making (try filling in tax forms, completing probate, getting a passport or visa). Strategic decision making has to adjust to these facts of life, and the resulting time lags may control much of the dynamics and account for the growth of financial, legal, accounting, and other intermediaries. Much of two-party trade involves at least five parties: the two principals, two brokers or traders, and as a fifth an actual institution providing the market mechanism (such as a stock market) with or without a separated clearing facility. With the growth of financial intermediaries and government and industrial bureaucracies, the time lags are a far cry from face-to-face exchange. The time lags involving money delivery, the delivery of other financial instruments, and their creation and destruction as well as timing of delivery of physical goods and services contribute considerably to the guidance of economic dynamics.

8.5.1   Technological, habitual, and strategic velocities

We suggest that empirical models of the transaction velocities call for at least seven sources of supply and demand if one wishes to disaggregate sufficiently to see the highly different time lags and exposure to—or lack of—fungibility, marketability, and liquidity of physical and financial assets in the early twenty-first century in the United States and elsewhere. The major functions of credit generating, insurance, and risk assessment remain invariant in time and place in any economy, but the institutional agents delivering the instruments to perform the functions are in continuous flux.

In the United States at the time of this writing it is desirable to know the demand for and supply of money and near monies for:

1. Individual natural legal persons;

2. Business and industry;

3. Government without the central bank;

4. The central bank;[3]

5. Commercial banks;

6. Other saving institutions;

7. Investment banking and venture capital.

We believe that the proportions of behavior dominated by habit, technology, and strategic optimization vary considerably among all. Given tastes, habits, and technology as relatively fixed in a period of a year or less, the interesting economic analysis devolves on the strategic leeways in the supply and demand for the means of payment. In a closed economy utilizing gold only as a means of payment (as shown in chapter 5), the models are precise and clear. They are less so in a fiat money world with many near monies and high levels of communication that provide the possibility for the formation of payment subsystems ranging down to organized barter swaps.

A brief heuristic overview of the seven types of agent is noted:

1. For the *natural-person agents* their strategy space is relatively passive. Much of daily life is still dominated by habit. They can save in a bank or under the mattress, venture into a mutual or pension fund, shift the dates of some payments and withdraw deposits, or in some instances opt for default; but in essence, for the most part, they do not have the knowledge or the time to be active investors. Owners of houses and consumer durables may have a considerable percentage of their wealth tied up in durables. They are more or less passive players stirred into action by items such as panics or job loss or windfalls. When faced with massive economic failure, they may take to the streets and seek political cures, be they riots, dictatorships, or peaceful change in government.

2. The *nonfinancial firms* own considerable assets that must be financed by stocks, bonds, and other loans. They are, for the most part, conscious (primarily fiduciary) economic agents, often limited in speed of maneuver by their bureaucracy. If they succeed, their financing problems must include where to park their cash. This may involve building up their own war chests, paying dividends, lowering other debt, or shrinking shares outstanding. They have no choice but to be active economic agents. The small innovators have to look to themselves, to their own families and friends, or to the venture capitalists for financing or attempt innovative finance such as crowd funding.

3. The major money players in the new economies are the *governments and financial institutions*. The governments (central and local), relative to the individuals, are oligopolistic agents. Depending on how one aggregates, the government sectors may account for anywhere between 15 and 50 percent of GDP. The sources of funds are primarily taxation, with some earning from the central bank, other government monopolies, and some sales such as leases or land.

4. The *commercial banks* are more or less profit maximizers whose main function is to run the transactions technology, with considerable service to natural persons and short-term financing for firms; but with the growth of financial supermarkets the name of the function and the institution providing the function may vary considerably, such as having a broker acting as a retail consumer bank.

5. Other *savings institutions* are insurance companies, pension funds, mutual funds, and money market funds, where all the managements have as their

sources of capital relatively uninformed individuals with neither the time nor ability to handle their own investments directly. The managements either are—or present themselves as—experts in the selection of savings with the appropriate risk profiles. They are faced with the classical matching book problem [342, 390] when one lends for times longer than the time lengths for which one has borrowed.

6. The *investment bankers and venture capitalists* in much of the twentieth century were partnerships essentially, with many rich partners both active and sleeping with much of their own money at risk. In corporate form their sources of funds are the issue of stock and borrowing (other people's money). Their uses of funds are in evaluation, communication, and deal-making leading to private placements where they eventually guide the few successes to initial public offerings. All of their activities are disequilibrium activities.

8.5.2   A comment on the need for precision

An apparently quite reasonable answer to a question such as "What is Say's Law?" is "Supply creates its own demand." When one tries to translate this simple observation into mathematics, the subtlcty and the vagueness of language emerges. Questions of time lags and causality emerge in profusion. In economics, almost always a fully mathematized model is too simple for some of its users; but the precision provides clarification. It helps one identify where the basic differences in perception of the modelers lie.

Our stress is that the paradigm shift proposed by Keynes was clearly set up to capture the shift from a tightly coupled system yielding to analysis, to a far more analytically complex loosely coupled system. Unfortunately the analysis of such systems even today is highly restricted. An ingenious article by Hicks [185] simultaneously was a masterpiece of exposition and aided the acceptance of Keynes's work, yet it virtually assassinated the central theme of Keynes's escape into disequilibrium. It did so by bringing it back to a structure where equilibrium analysis could be managed and loose couplings and transients were conveniently downplayed.

Since the 1930s, however, the understanding of the economies as control and perception systems has changed enormously. Especially given that the economies are much larger and more complex than before by any measure, the full melding of information, communication, computation, money, and finance is critical to understanding control. This calls for the interaction of essay, mathematical model, and ad hoc simulation and operational gaming in the generation of operational advice on economic control.

8.6   The Meanings of Liquidity

Before we consider velocity further, we need to reconsider the meaning of liquidity in terms of our methodology. From current use and colloquial comment we know that prior to considering an item's liquidity we need to check its marketability.

For an item to be marketable there must be no legal or other societal institutions that block bringing it to a market, if such a market exists. It has been well known since at least Edgeworth [109] that a market is not a single locale but a thick enough interconnected network of professional traders set up to trade some sufficiently standardized form of contract or fungible commodity so that quality validation and nonstandard boilerplate legal considerations are not required for a trade.

The colloquial definition of "liquidity" understood by most practitioners is: An item is liquid if there exists a market in which it can be sold more or less immediately at a price more or less the same as the price of the last sale of a similar item. As noted in section 8.4.1.4, this may be a matter of degree or it may be a discrete criterion for the stability of markets and their ability to remain within bounded trading domains.

In order to make this meaning precise, we suggest that liquidity is generally defined with respect to the following conditions and parameters:

Players: Players are buyers with a means of payment and sellers with a positive supply of some item such that there is an active supply and demand over a common range.

Expectations: The change in expectations between periods has minor influence on the size of supply and demand between t and $t + 1$. Furthermore individual expectations are not heavily correlated.

Parameters:

- The necessary accounting time units and size of $\Delta t = t_i - t_{i-1}$ (relative to an integer index i over events) are specified.
- A second time parameter k may be called for, subdividing the Δt into minimal transactions time segments. For example, what is the minimum time required to buy, then sell, the asset and be in a position to reuse the funds?
- The size of the minimal tradable quantity Q is specified.
- The populations n_1 and n_2 of traders are large enough to constitute a thick market.

Some of the problems that arise in constructing these types of models are illustrated below, considering the financing of a play of roulette, a repo, and the purchase of a consumer good.

The mechanism and intermediaries: The market mechanism such as a continuous double-auction market operates within the Δt required to describe a one-shot bid-offer game. When more "realistic" market mechanisms are described, a host of small changes and special details appear, and in those changes a wedge of a few basis points here or there provides a comfortable living for an intermediary.

8.7   The Turnover of Money in Various Transactions

Ever since the emergence of a formal financial system in renaissance Florence, the velocity of money in interbank trade has been systematically higher than that in the real-goods sector.[4] A narrative can be composed to the effect that this would be expected: the concentration of money under decision-making power in banks is larger than it is for most private traders; the exchange of money for debt contracts or the clearance of money among accounts can be faster than exchanges involving real goods which must be delivered. More subtly, because one role of banks is as perceptors and aggregators of information from many complex trading sectors, banks experience more frequent demands to rebalance accounts, to provide liquidity, or to hedge against future fluctuations in supply or demand for credit.

The narrative, however, does not provide a way to address many quantitative questions, which would provide tests of its validity. The velocity in interbank and various other financial trade is neither equal to, nor infinitely larger than, velocity in various real-goods sectors, but rather is larger by a considerable factor. What institutional or social/behavioral conditions determine this factor? Money trade in financial markets is often regarded as a signal of estimates of valuation by traders informed in differing degrees about a variety of securities; the market aggregates this information to supposedly generate a price signal that is more reliable when averaged over market trade than the information available to any individual trader. From a mechanism design perspective, then, what determines the cost of such signals? Is it correct to assign a price to information in the same manner as one assigns a price to goods (perhaps using a game-theoretic construction similar to the one in chapter 5 that generates a money-metric value of market clearing rules), and how then is the price formed? What is the predicted velocity required to carry a certain rate of information about valuations? How is information itself to be measured? If traders act under budget or credit constraints, what are the consequent informational inefficiencies of financial markets? How much of financial velocity is determined by technological advances that reduce clearing time and transaction costs, and how much is determined by behavioral limits? For each of these questions, the quantitative answer will likely differ among financial sectors as it does among real-goods exchange sectors. These differences and the sector weights therefore enter into any prediction or estimate for average velocity.

Formulation of these questions for actual markets, in a way that can be econometrically calibrated, is a complex problem of operations research. Here we consider three economic activities, to suggest elements of the game-theoretic, institutional finance, and material constraints that affect velocity.

8.7.1 The turnover of money playing roulette

The turnover in the financial markets appears to be far faster than in the industrial or consumer markets, and in general more complex than the turnover of money at a roulette table. However, the operations research formulation of the turnover of money or chips at a roulette table is instructive in laying out many of the problems in defining and measuring the turnover of money for any financial instrument.

The financial instrument
A single play at one turn of the roulette may be regarded as the purchase and immediate execution of a lottery ticket. This has a minimal time k associated with it.

The market institution
The institution is the table generally run by one croupier set in the gambling hall of a casino or hotel-casino. The croupier is supplemented by general supervision and service staff watching for cheats and drunks and bringing drinks to the table. Financially these provide the information for assigning the overheads and variable cost to running the table, where the accounting unit may be $\Delta t =$ one day.

Financing the play
In general the tables do not use cash. The individual player buys chips and pays for them in cash, by check, by credit card, or sometimes by personal IOU. After play if the player has finished gambling she cashes out her terminal supply of chips and otherwise is required to settle accounts.

House reserves
In general there is no formal statement of the size of the house reserves. It is implicitly assumed by all players that the house has sufficient cash or bank credit to honor any redemption with cash or check.

Upper bound on turnover
How fast can the chips turn over? One full spin of the wheel also involves time for individuals to place their bets and to have the winners paid. Including breaks, this appears to be in the range of 25 to 60 times an hour.

Goals of the players
In spite of a house take with 0 and 00 of over 5 percent, the roulette tables flourish, and the economists and psychologists have their hands full in trying to explain the motivations to play roulette. If an individual plays for 2 hours for entertainment and has a maximum amount of investment of, say, $300 worth of chips and is playing at a $5 minimum bet table with 30 games an hour, her expected loss for the two hours of entertainment is $15.789, not much different from a movie.

Velocity of chips or money?
If the house permitted only cash at the table, it is clear that we would be discussing the velocity of a component of M1. But in the two-hour interval the player plays, her money has become part of the reserves of the casino. The turnover of the chips does reflect the "action" at the table but not the turnover of money. In a like manner, intracorporate trade is recorded in accounting transfers but no cash flows are noted.

8.7.2   The turnover of money buying repos

A repurchase agreement (repo) is a form of collateralized loan in which an instrument such as a Treasury note is sold to a bank overnight with a contract to repurchase it next day. The market for repos in the U.S. has been estimated at a turnover of $2,194 billion per diem in face value in 2013.[5]

It appears that the repo has been a key instrument in obtaining leverage in recent years, although in its elemental form the repo is noted in a parliamentary interchange reported by Bagehot [21, appendix] in 1858:

> 1171. But you sometimes lend money upon bills deposited with you by bill-brokers? —Yes.
>
> 1172. And you occasionally call in that money and re-deliver these securities? —Yes; but that we do to a very small extent.
>
> 1173. Is not that the equivalent to the rediscount of bills? —No, the discount of a bill and the lending money on bills are very different things. When we discount a bill, that bill becomes our property; it is in our control and we keep it and lock it up until it falls due; but when brokers come to us and want to borrow, say 50,000*l.* on a deposit of bills, and we let them have the money and afterwards return those bills to them and we get back our money, surely that is not a rediscount?
>
> —Evidence given by Mr. Alderman Salomons 1858.

The essential structure and financial function of the repo are independent of the underlying instrument used as security, as any bond will do; but depending on the bonds sold, the "haircut" that they are given will differ. Thus a Treasury gets a $2\frac{1}{2}$ percent haircut. If you put up a middle-tranche mortgage-backed security, it might get a 25 percent haircut. But even then (leaving out trading costs) an individual with $1,000 with an account at a bank could with a single phone call buy $4,000 of a mortgage-backed security whose ownership under the repurchase agreement would be assigned to the bank for "overnight" until on the next day the repo is closed out. The repo may be renewed by the bank indefinitely on a daily basis. The key features are the ability of the bank to assess the safety level of the haircut and the ability of the seller to evaluate the risk-reward aspects of the security. The seller of the repo may be a dealer in government securities or a hedge fund, and the buyer a large bank of a still larger holding company where legal and other constraints forbid the bank to make such an investment directly by itself. If the borrower goes bankrupt, as the security pledged is owned by the creditor it does not appear in the settlement proceedings of the bankruptcy and is now owned completely by the bank.

In practice, institutional features such as the accounting and bankruptcy seniority rules also enter.

Specifically, the six shared characteristics of repo markets and secured lending trades that are required at the agent level are:

1. Principal amount,

2. Interest rate,

3. Collateral type,

4. Size of haircut,

5. Tenor, and

6. Nature of the counterparty.

Gorton [168] and Gorton and Metrick [167] provide a discussion and analysis of the 2008 housing bubble covering the crucial role of the repo market.

8.7.3   The turnover of money in consumer goods

The third example involves the exchange of real goods for money, although there may be cash, checks, credit cards, debit cards, and food stamps involved. The features considered are:

The nature of the final good,

The market institutions involved,

Financing the transaction,

Reserves requirements,

The upper bound on turnover,

The goals of the players [149].

The variants here are legion, including a purchase of bread once a day in the morning for cash in a French town, or a weekly purchase of a longlasting loaf paying by credit card in much of the United States.

8.7.4   Velocity and change in velocity

If we could measure velocity and changes in velocity accurately, why should we care about it and what would we learn?

It appears that financial velocity is much faster than the velocity encountered when finished goods are traded. The fundamental difference appears to be that in ultimate purchase of a final short-lived consumer good, the evaluation problem is solved with the purchase and the good does not return to the market; with longer-term goods such as automobiles and houses, future resale prices may be of some concern. However in the exchange of financial instruments there is a constant readjustment of valuation and a redistribution of ownership claims and bets, as the system is meant to be the immediate evaluator and reevaluator of all exogenous and endogenous forces impinging on the economy.

8.7.5   An aside on velocity, bankruptcy, and the creation and destruction of money

It is often not appreciated that in bankruptcy fiat money is not destroyed; it is reallocated. Credit is destroyed, but if one calls credit "money," then definitional problems in the concept of the velocity of money appear. The nature of short-term credit is such that it is, in general, a contract that is used once. It may be replaced in a rollover by a similar but nevertheless different contract. It is meaningful to talk of the turnover of a long-term marketable bond that may be sold and resold many times with no contractual change in the instrument. A repo "dies after dawn" and is replaced, frequently automatically but with the chance that the replacement will not be forthcoming.

8.8   A Heuristic Discussion of Firms, Financial Assets, and Real Assets

Many mathematical economists have wondered about the plethora of degrees of freedom that seem to appear when one tries to introduce money into a general equilibrium structure. As is usually the case, a paradox is no paradox when examined from the appropriate point of view. In attempting to describe the general equilibrium structure as a playable game with a monetary economy, one is subject to the immediate critique that a playable strategic market game is specially constructed and could have been done in an astronomically large number of ways. That criticism is completely correct and completely misses the positive message that the game sends. The message provides the link between static economics on one side and economic dynamics and biology on the other side. With the plethora of degrees of freedom, it becomes feasible to construct hosts of ad hoc micro-microeconomic models that fit special niches and are able to adjust with varying flexibility to the micro and the macro dynamics to which they are exposed.

A good industry specialist trying to forecast the dynamics of a firm and its viability will investigate real and financial assets and liabilities as well as management and software. A checklist includes:

1. Labor,
2. Land,
3. Buildings,
4. Machinery,
5. Raw materials,
6. Goods in process,
7. Office supplies,
8. Cash and receivables,
9. Short-term debt,
10. Long-term debt,
11. Financial assets,
12. Software, and off-balance-sheet assets such as derivatives,
13. Management.

Each of these items may have a time profile attached to it, such as the ages and length of service of management and the age structure of machinery.

Cautious accounting calls for leaving the worth attributed to organization and quality of management off the balance sheets; but one of the key tasks of a good analyst is to attach estimates to the worth of this off-balance-sheet asset.

A little contemplation of the description in these terms of a family restaurant, an automobile rental firm, a large oil company, a bank, a hedge fund, or a funeral parlor immediately calls for a taxonomy of dynamic models at least as diverse as an animal kingdom stretching from whales to ants or mites.

The sizes in terms of both personnel and assets, the flexibility of the institutions and their complexity differ so considerably that it is unlikely that a single taxonomy might be constructed easily when one is trying to develop an economic dynamics. This is not counter to general economic theory; it merely places two sets of empirical constraints on it. It implicitly suggests that an understanding of the dynamics of a specific firm in the steel industry requires that one knows considerable physical and financial detail about both the firm and its industry. Yet that alone is not sufficient to describe the dynamics. The description of the structure of the game requires an appropriate representation of the institutions; but in order to attempt to describe their dynamics of play one also requires a description of their management, its goals and its decision-making procedures.

In general the larger institutions are all run by committees of fiduciaries using "other people's money" (OPM) and buried in a Byzantine mixture of tax laws, regulation, and accounting conventions that place considerable constraints on the manifestation of economic behavior.

Among the smaller firms there are many individually or family-owned establishments where, to some extent as a function of specific skills, knowledge, and education, the management resembles the individually owned one-aggregate-product firm of many economic textbooks since Marshall.

Significant in numbers but not in total revenue terms, there are firms with a single or few employees such as many restaurants or art galleries or small specialty retail stores. Here, before the dynamics can be considered, is the domain in which behavioral economics may have a chance to flourish. The model of *homo oeconomicus* that might fit the managers and large active stockholders of middling and large firms hardly applies. The experience and professional training levels and motivation for the family restaurant or small art gallery or gift shop call for a different dynamics than that of the major corporation. The failure rates within the first two years indicate that the population of owners is far closer to nonprofessional consumers than to professional managers, from the retirees who dream of their own little restaurant to the multimillionaire's wife who runs her art gallery for pleasure.

The basic theme here is not that the economic paradigm is of no value, but that its value depends on social, political, technological, and economic facts that provide the structure of economic dynamics. These need to be supplemented by a behavioral understanding that there are many plausible models of the human decision-maker whose efficacies vary in context. In the attempts to unify macro- and microeconomics it is equally easy to be overwhelmed by detail or to ruthlessly abstract away all detail to the point that key questions cannot be answered in the oversimplification; for example the representative-agent models rule out questions concerning any aspect of wealth distribution.

Utilizing as an approximation an expected discounted-profit-optimizing fiduciary management, one can at least obtain an answer to a question such as how likely a candidate for a takeover a firm is going to be. This is in essence the answer to how liquid the firm is in the market for corporations. It is clear that this relates immediately to the possibility that the firm is worth more broken up than it is as an entity. This represents an arbitrage possibility among different markets: the market for corporations, the stock market, and the market for real assets.

Other questions of macro significance in a fragile economy are the leverage of debts in the structure of the earnings and its implication in the probability of bankruptcy and inadequate reserves. Bagehot's great book in the nineteenth century already spelled out the profits to be had and the risks generated by leverage.

Except more or less as parables, low-dimensional dynamic programming solutions are of little help in providing applied advice for the running of a financially controlled dynamic economy. The very instruments, markets, and institutions that supply the financial community with its critical role of analysis and information generation as well as evaluation and control are not present in the limited mathematical representation that is not designed to handle the cascades of inequalities and boundary conditions that characterize much of the motion in a financially sophisticated economy.

8.9   The Concept of "Enough Money"

In discussion of the economics of production and exchange, the question "Does the economy have 'enough money'?" is frequently asked. This concept can be made mathematically precise for an equilibrium model; but the answer to the question splits into three pieces, one of which is purely mathematical and the other two of which are heavily institutional. The first covers GE statics and the other two dynamics and exogenous uncertainty. They depend on the way in which the economy has been modeled as a set of rules designed to be explicit about the price formation processes.

8.9.1   Enough money with complete markets

In essence the general equilibrium system with its focus on the wealth constraints on all individuals calls for the mathematics of the equations of wealth, whereas strategic market games with their specification of cash flow constraints call for the mathematics of inequalities. Without going into the full technical detail, the heuristic argument is as follows. In a mass anonymous market with a single universally acceptable means of payment, a jointly recognizable and accepted money may be utilized as a substitute for trust. However, if cash payments are required, unless credit or clearing arrangements are considered the cash payments impose cash flow constraints on the optimization. These take the form of inequalities. The concept of "enough money well distributed" [356] is that none of these inequalities are binding on any agent in the economy. The analysis of enough money is completely well defined mathematically, but requires the full specification of the price formation mechanism and the individual strategy sets.

8.9.2   How much money is enough for an economy?

In an economy without innovation or any other uncertainty and an omniscient passive central bank that issues central bank money against IOU notes that at equilibrium it knows can and will be paid back,[6] enough money is an amount required to obtain an interior solution [345]. In a living dynamic economy with uncertainty, the concept of the correct amount of money needs to be associated with the use of reserves of the government money, the laws of bankruptcy and default, and the public's willingness to accept a positive default as the cost of innovation.

The overall question, conceptually definable as how much money is required in an economy for all goods transactions, has been under consideration since Sir William Petty, as has been noted by Marshall [246, p. 47], who states:

> Petty thought that the money "sufficient for the nation is so much as will pay half a year's rent for all the lands of England and a quarter's rent of the Housing, for a week's expense of all the people, and about a quarter of the value of all exported commodities." ...
> Locke estimated that "one fifth of wages and one fourth of the landowner's income and one twentieth part of the broker's yearly returns in ready money will be enough to drive the trade of any country." Cantillon (A.D. 1775) after a long and subtle study, concludes that the value needed is a ninth of the total produce of the country, or, what he takes to be the same thing, a third of the rent of land. Adam Smith has more of the skepticism of the modern age and says: "it is impossible to determine the proportion" though "it has been computed by various authors at a fifth, at a tenth, at a twentieth and at a thirtieth part of the whole value of the annual product."

In essence, although enough money is precisely defined in some extremely impoverished models, in application it is enormously difficult to define and approximate given the proliferation of near monies.

8.10   It Is Not the Velocity of Money but the Creation and Destruction of Near Monies that Counts

The discourse on the velocity of money may be conceptually misleading to our understanding if it concentrates primarily on the turnover of government currency. Given that M is a multidimensional measure with many short-term instruments, the change is less in the velocity of individual instruments than it is in the quickened destruction and creation of new instruments, and it is the quantity of credit in the aggregate that grows or shrinks.

The variation in the turnover of government money diverts attention from the enormous swings in the creation and destruction of other means for transacting and settling trade. The magic of the creation and destruction of billions in the nominal unit of currency is almost always not in the currency itself, but in the near monies. As computational and communication methods improve, so do the opportunities for subgroups to invent, use, and police much of their own means of payment.

The term "velocity" in financial affairs is an unfortunate one. The analogy with physics does not hold for debt instrument near monies. In physics, regardless of the speed with which a ball is thrown, it remains a ball. In finance the process involves recontracting for a variety of legally new even if apparently identical instruments [390].

Notes

1 In the general equilibrium framework of [83] the parable of "private information" is adopted.

2 These may include concepts such as private information, or prohibitive costs in a framework such as our chapter 5 where economic services compete with production. Other causes may include time delays for clearing, undersupply or maldistribution of currency, or refusal to extend credit for any number of reasons.

3 In the United States this should include the Treasury.

4 See chapter 5 of Padgett and Powell [281]. At the beginning of mercantile banking in Tuscany, families were the analogues of banks. Often, marriages served as the equivalent of quick interbank communication, essentially calling forth the flow of bills of exchange with interfamily monetary settlement. While not referring to this as velocity directly, this chapter implicitly shows the high velocity made possible by the bill-of-exchange mechanism, which required only a netting in cash periodically.

5 reported by ICAP http://www.icap.com/investor-relations/monthly-volume-data.aspx

6 If an individual has the strategic freedom to decide whether or not to honor her IOU, an enforcement mechanism is required. That is why the bankruptcy laws and their enforcement must be supplied in any economy that uses credit, regardless of whether the recognized means of payment is government fiat or gold.

9 Innovation and Breaking the Circular Flow

9.1 Preamble

This chapter has a basic theme that even the simplest venture into innovation takes us into the realms of disequilibrium where the study of behavior in transient states of any length is unavoidable, even if one sticks to the mantra of the rational economic agent.

If one is to solve and perform a sensitivity analysis on the models we build, the explosion of complexity implied by high dimensions forces us to utilize low-dimensional models. It is our belief that a low-dimensional model that is presented as a representation of an actual economy must be viewed as dealing with parable and metaphor intermixed with applied macroeconomics. For this reason, although our approach overlaps in some techniques with models in the Lucas school, our goals are somewhat different. They are devoted to studying process mechanisms and showing the unavoidable consequences of extending the general equilibrium paradigm to dynamics. This involves step by step the invention of a variety of minimal financial, legal, and governmental institutions to perform the myriads of needed functions to guide a dynamic economy. Even with the gross behavioral simplifications of rational expectations, these models can provide answers or at least raise precise questions in economic theory such as those noted in chapter 7 in relation to the mysteries of "bills only" or to the many interpretations of "Say's Law." They can do so because precision is provided in specifying conditions on degrees of freedom, unit size, symmetry, and laws of conservation. These are all critical to understanding the relationship between money and credit and innovation.

The cost of the precision we advocate is that even the simplest of illustrative examples may involve fine micro-microeconomic distinctions and considerable tedious calculation, as seen below.

Possibly the most important point we illustrate is that innovation, even at its simplest, when there are many individuals in a monetary economy, in general requires *the breaking of the circular flow of capital*. This, furthermore, raises *ownership problems*. Who controls and supplies the financial capital to fund the innovation?

In order to appreciate fully the role of finance in innovation, it is highly instructive to understand first the problems faced by Robinson Crusoe in a world where all items are physical and money and credit do not exist. This contrasts with the multiagent economy with financial institutions, where the availability of money and credit not only adds to efficiency but provides a mechanism for financial control of physical processes.

9.1.1   A caveat on closed dynamic general equilibrium models

Our stress on using closed models is heavily directed toward the unification of physical and financial economics and to understanding at the most elemental level the conceptual difficulties in modeling production, destruction, and control of various forms of money and credit. Direct applications to economic history we believe to be highly speculative, especially if the low-dimensional models are representative-agent and hardly model the financial sector. The perceptive review of Peter Temin [398] is in accord with our view on the limits of the application of the rational-expectations, low-dimensional representative-agent models.

9.2   The Last Modification from Equilibrium to Disequilibrium

Schumpeter and Keynes dealt with dynamics and disequilibrium. In order to understand fully how either of them relate to general equilibrium, a complete closed model that also specifies equations of motion must be constructed.

In this and several related publications [298, 356, 357, 359] a progressively more complex cascade of models has been examined. The underlying thesis is that the general equilibrium model in all of its austere abstract unreality has provided a critically basic useful model for much of economic analysis. Its very assumptions usefully highlighted and clarified the nature of the enormous gap between reality and the price-decentralized ideal world of the perfect markets with bloodless isolated maximizers. This world is blessed with no public goods, no fully defined institutions, and no need for government. Once one tries to set up such models as full process models, the institutions of the economy emerge as carriers of process. There is a multitude of institutions that can be designed to provide any function. Selecting among them often calls for reaching into the micro-microeconomic and/or sociopsychological aspects of design (such as perception or cognition). Many of the plethora of models are plausible, and viable variations abound. Yet understanding the potential dynamics of a monetary system depends far less on the myriads of models than on getting at least one coherent, consistent, and fully closed system right, so that the cash flows, the creation and destruction of the monies involved, the mechanisms of the markets and payment systems, the time lags and unit sizes are all spelled out. Even though the model may be a metaphor, the physics of its equations of motion may be made complete without having to resort to helicopters or handwaves. The very unreality of such a model aids in highlighting where the realities lie.

Until this point the critical role of innovation has been completely left out. Chapter 8 was a needed preliminary to being able to tackle innovation, finally considering uncertainty with incomplete markets and clearing some of the underbrush involving near monies, liquidity, and the velocity of financial instruments and physical resources.

The specific "value-added" to the topics of innovation, control, and ownership attempted here is to start to bridge the mathematical gap between general equilibrium theory and Schumpeter's writings on innovation. This calls for introducing finance. In the past twenty to thirty years there have been considerable writing and empirical work on innovation and the economic and behavioral questions it raises; see for example Arthur [16], Dosi et al. [90], Bechtel et al. [26], Baumol [25], Lamoreaux and Sokoloff [299], Day, Eliasson, and Wihlborg [73], Nelson [272], Nelson and Winter [273], Shubik [358], and in particular the essay of Day [73]. Other micro innovation treatments are exemplified by Aghion [5] and Boldrin and Levine [35], and a useful coverage of recent literature is given by Thompson [399]. Mariana Mazzucato [253] devotes a book to stressing the historical role of the state in financing innovation. She documents many instances.

The work here in chapters 9 and 10 is meant to be complementary with these but aimed specifically at trying to characterize mathematically, via dynamic programming and other formulations of strategic market games, the monetary aspects of innovation, eventually including ownership and financial control and coordination features of a market economy within a society represented minimally by the presence of a governmental agent and a commercial banking system. Allied with this approach to the specifics of "breaking the circular flow of capital" have been the recent works of Dosi et al. [88, 89]

and Caiani et al. [46]. They present somewhat richer models than we do, but are highly complementary with those here. They use simulation methods and a macroeconomic approach showing the relationship with both Keynes [235] and Minsky [263].

9.2.1   Types of innovation

The study of innovation cannot be approached monolithically. There are at least four distinct types of innovation, namely:

* Radically new product innovation,
* Engineering variation of current products,
* Distribution, network, information, and communication innovation,
* Organization, cost reduction, or other process innovation influencing efficiency.

In terms of uncertainty they are highly different. The most difficult to handle by conventional economic analysis are radical product and network innovations. Both the production procedures and the demand acceptance are unknown. There is often little if any precedent. The subjective probabilities for success, if any, may be cooked up by stretched analogy with other products and networks that have succeeded or failed, and can only be quantified for the purpose of the construction of imaginary or pro forma financial statements used to persuade potential investors. They are also often subject to "winner take all increasing returns," as suggested by the insightful work of Arthur.

More or less standard product variation fits reasonably well into the current theory of oligopolistic competition. The large firms selling, say, refrigerators have products that are close to being identical. It is the job of marketing and the production engineers to have a spice shelf full of technically known modifications or additions that can help to differentiate the product. Costs and demand can be reasonably estimated for such innovations. Innovation can also fit into a modified model of a competitive market, as has been shown by Boldrin and Levine [35]. The cost innovation discussed here can be considered in competitive markets, especially when one takes into account that the appropriation by others of new ideas, industrial secrets, and expertise is by no means instantaneous.

By far the most prevalent form of innovation in many economies is process innovation involving organization and frequently reducing costs of production by orders of magnitude. New inventions call for expensive prototypes. Even if the market for the new product is clearly present, over the first few years, especially with mass market possibilities, there is a considerable focus on unit cost reduction. The prototype is highly expensive, and the first batch for sale, though cheaper than the prototype, is usually produced at nowhere near the intended cost. It appears to be far easier to quantify a gaming experiment with cost innovation and provide a reasonable scenario than to construct an experimental game to illustrate radical product innovation. Here we restrict our concern to cost reduction innovation in a competitive environment.

9.2.2 Some behavioral considerations

Much of the work in mathematical economics and in game theory has been based explicitly or implicitly on an abstract *homo oeconomicus* or von Neumann man. This individual has perfect recall and an ability to compute everything. In actuality there are many different behavioral types that are worth considering. (See [358] for a discussion.)

Here for simplicity we will restrict attention to the von Neumann player.[1]

9.2.3 Property rights, information, and appropriation

The modeling and analysis of innovation is replete with difficulties. In much of the mythology of purely competitive markets, adjustments usually take place immediately. In fact, in a dynamic system profits are made by innovators having the lead, given the myriads of time lags in the diffusion of information and expertise. The time it takes for an industrial secret to leak, and the delays and barriers caused by legal, accounting, and tax considerations, are all considerable.

Virtually everything is permeable at some point. Thus patent protection must be looked at as a time delay device and other barriers to entry as delay devices. Law cases are often brought merely as time delay instruments.

In Crusoe's world none of these details exist. At the level of abstraction here, these items, often critical to any serious deal, are abstracted away. We also avoid the introduction of taxes and subsidies that are a part of everyday life. In finance many of the profits lie in taking care of the details that arise out of equilibrium.

9.2.4 Physical and financial assets, innovation, and equilibrium?

We address specifically cost innovation and the breaking of the circular flow of funds. Also considered are some of the inevitable problems of the interaction between ownership and control. The models here are based directly on several essays, one dealing with equilibrium in a closed monetary economy without innovation [200], the second concerned with the physical-good aspects of innovation in a Robinson Crusoe economy [364], the third an essay of Shubik and Sudderth on innovation in a monetary economy and further work [365]. Section 9.7 notes the basic structure of the monetary economy and its dynamic equilibria without innovation. In particular the role of the money interest rate as a control variable emerges in this relatively simple financial setting. We then present a more or less straight exercise in operations research where, in a nonmarket, nonmonetary setting, Robinson Crusoe has to evaluate how to give up physical assets needed to be consumed in a risky innovation.

In our deconstruction of the investment decision there are five features that merit individual analysis:

1. Equilibrium in a closed monetary economy prior to the knowledge that innovation is feasible;

2. Innovation in a Robinson Crusoe setting, involving only physical assets;

3. Innovation in a closed competitive monetary economy with only short-term assets available, investigating the need for the expansion of money and credit;

4. The roles of long-term capital assets, locus of control, evaluation, and funding for innovation; and

5. The implications of continuing innovation for the distribution of firm size and investment.

We immediately comment on the first two items but limit our analysis here to the third and fourth items in order to make explicit the monetary flows and their control. We comment on the last two features of innovation in sections 9.7 and 9.8, but we recognize that there is far more to be done to deal with the central aspects of control and valuation in a competitive innovating economy.[2]

9.3   Robinson Crusoe without Markets or Money

The study of Robinson Crusoe deciding whether or not to innovate enables us to see clearly how, when we switch from an isolated technical problem to innovation in a monetary economy, the role of finance and evaluation by those who control resources becomes central.

The examples provided here originally appeared in [364] and [365]. Consider a model in which a single agent, Robinson Crusoe, produces a good for his personal consumption. Suppose he begins with $q \geq 0$ units of the good, puts i units into production, and consumes the remaining $x = q - i$, thereby receiving $u(q - i)$ in utility. The agent begins the next period with $f(i)$ units of the good and the game continues. (Both the utility function u and the production function f are assumed to be concave and nondecreasing on $[0, \infty)$, with $f(0) = 0$.) The value of the game $V(q)$ to Robinson Crusoe is the supremum over all strategies of the payoff function

$$\sum_{n=1}^{\infty} \beta^{n-1} u(x_n),$$

where x_n is the amount of the good consumed in period n and $\beta \in (0, 1)$ is a discount factor. For this model without the possibility of innovation, the value function V satisfies the Bellman equation

$$V(q) = \sup_{0 \leq i \leq q} [u(q - i) + \beta V(f(i))].$$

Assume that there is an input i_1 such that $f'(i_1) = 1/\beta$. (This is certainly the case if $f'(0) = \infty$ and $\lim_{i \to \infty} f'(i) = 0$, as is often assumed.) Let $q_1 = f(i_1)$.

THEOREM 1   (Karatzas et al. [200]) If the initial value of the good is q_1, then an optimal strategy is to input i_1 in every period. Consequently,

$$V(q_1) = \frac{1}{1 - \beta} \cdot u(q_1 - i_1).$$

9.3.1   Innovation by Robinson Crusoe

Assume now that our single agent with goods q is allowed to input i for production and invest j in innovation, where $0 \leq i \leq q$, $0 \leq j \leq q - i$. The agent consumes the remainder $q - i - j$. The innovation is successful with probability $\xi(j)$, resulting in an improved production function $g = (1 + \theta)f$, where $\theta > 0$. The innovation fails and the production function is unchanged with probability $1 - \xi(j)$. Let V_1 be the value function for the game with production function f without innovation, as in the previous section, and let V_2 be the value function for the game with the improved production function g. Then the value function V of the game with innovation satisfies

$$V(q) = \sup_{\substack{0 \leq i \leq q \\ 0 \leq j \leq q - i}} [u(q - i - j) + \beta \{\xi(j) V_2(f(i)) + (1 - \xi(j)) V_1(f(i))\}].$$

Let $\psi(i,j)$ be the function of i and j occurring inside the supremum. For an interior optimum we must have the Euler equations:

$$\frac{\partial \psi}{\partial i} = \frac{\partial \psi}{\partial j} = 0.$$

To find a solution to Crusoe's innovation problem, we must calculate the values of V_1 and V_2 where the quantity of goods is the amount $f(i)$ yet to be determined. Theorem 1 only gives an expression for the value at one equilibrium point, which is different for the two production functions f and g. This situation is a mathematical reflection of Schumpeter's insight that the circular flow must be broken.

The next two sections treat special cases where the value function can be found for all values of q and the innovation problem can then be solved explicitly.

9.3.2   A risk-neutral Crusoe

If the agent is risk-neutral, then there is a simple description of the optimal strategy at every value of q.

THEOREM 2   Assume that $u(x) = x$ for all x. Then an optimal strategy is to input q if $q \leq i_1$ and to input i_1 if $q > i_1$. For $q \geq i_1$, the value of the game is

$$V(q) = q - i_1 + \frac{\beta}{1 - \beta} \cdot (q_1 - i_1).$$

Proof. A player with goods $q > q' \geq 0$ can always consume $q - q'$ and then play from q'. Hence,

$$V(q) \geq q - q' + V(q').$$

Consider now $q \leq i_1$, and a strategy that inputs $i < q$. The best possible return from such a strategy is

$$q - i + \beta V(f(i)).$$

But an input of q gives a best return of

$$\begin{aligned} \beta V(f(q)) &\geq \beta \cdot [f(q) - f(i) + V(f(i))] \\ &\geq \beta \cdot \left[f'(q)\,(q - i) + V(f(i)) \right] \\ &\geq q - i + \beta \cdot V(f(i)) \end{aligned}$$

since $f'(q) \geq f'(i_1) = 1/\beta$. So it is optimal to input q when $q \leq i_1$.

Now suppose that $q > i_1$. Since $u' = 1$, the Euler equation reduces to $f'(i) = 1/\beta$ or $i = i_1$. The appropriate transversality condition is trivially satisfied since $q_n = q_1$ for all $n \geq 1$. It is easy to check that the strategy is interior and therefore optimal. $\square$

Consider next the innovation problem of the previous section for our risk-neutral agent with $u(x) = x$.

Assume that $f'(i_1) = 1/\beta$ and $g'(i_2) = 1/\beta$. Then by Theorem 2, $V_1'(q) = V_2'(q) = 1$ for $q \geq \max\{i_1, i_2\}$. Thus if $f(i) \geq \max\{i_1, i_2\}$, we have

$$\frac{\partial \psi(i,j)}{\partial i} = -1 + \beta \{\xi(j)f'(i) + (1 - \xi(j))f'(i)\}$$

$$= -1 + \beta f'(i),$$

$$\frac{\partial \psi(i,j)}{\partial j} = -1 + \beta \xi'(j)\{V_2(f(i)) - V_1(f(i))\}.$$

Hence, in this case, the solutions to the Euler equations are

$$i^* = (f')^{-1}(1/\beta) = i_1 \text{ and } j^* = (\xi')^{-1}\left(1/\beta\left[V_2(f(i^*)) - V_1(f(i^*))\right]\right).$$

To illustrate the solution, we calculate it below for a very simple example. We will revisit essentially the same example for several other models.

9.3.2.1   A numerical example   Assume that the initial production function is $f(i) = 2\sqrt{i}$ and $\theta = .1$ so that, after a successful innovation, the production function is $g = 2.2\sqrt{i}$. Set $\beta = .95$.
Solve

$$f'(i_1) = 1/\beta \qquad \text{and} \qquad g'(i_2) = 1/\beta$$

to get

$$i_1 = .9025, \qquad i_2 = 1.092$$

and

$$q_1 = f(i_1) = 1.9, \qquad q_2 = g(i_2) = 2.299.$$

For $q \geq i_2 > i_1$, it follows from Theorem 2 that

$$V_2(q) - V_1(q) = \frac{i_1 - i_2}{1 - \beta} + \frac{\beta}{1 - \beta}(q_2 - q_1) = 3.791.$$

Assume now that the probability of successful innovation from investing j is $\xi(j) = j/(1+j)$. As noted above, the first Euler equation has the solution $i^* = i_1 = .9025$ so that $f(i^*) = f(i_1) = q_1 = 1.9$. Since $1.9 > i_2 > i_1$,

$$V_2(f(i^*)) - V_1(f(i^*)) = 3.791$$

and the solution to the second Euler equation is $j^* = (\xi')^{-1}(1/(.95)$ $(3.791)) = .8977$. Thus $\xi(j^*) = .8977/1.8977 = .473$ is the probability that the innovation is successful.

We can use the formula from Theorem 2 to calculate

$$V_2(f(i^*)) = V_2(1.9) = 23.741,$$

and

$$V_1(f(i^*)) = V_1(1.9) = 19.95.$$

These values together with the values for i^* and j^* can be substituted in the formula for the value of the game with innovation to get $V(q) = q + 18.86$ for $q \geq i^* + j^*$. The value of the game without innovation can also be calculated as $V_1(q) = q + 18.05$, which shows the value of the possibility of innovation in this instance.

9.3.3   A risk-averse Robinson Crusoe with proportional production

Many of the interesting features of investment call for the consideration of risk-averse individuals. In general, it is not possible to achieve the sort of instant adjustment to a stationary state that can be obtained with a risk-neutral Robinson Crusoe. However, analytic solutions are available when the utility function has constant elasticity and production is directly proportional to the input.

In this section we take $u(x) = \log x$ and $f(i) = \alpha i$, where α is a positive constant. (The full class of constant-elasticity utilities is considered in a nice article of Levhari and Srinivasan [219].) Thus the Bellman equation is

$$V(q) = \sup_{0 \leq i \leq q} \left[\log(q - i) + \beta V(\alpha i) \right].$$

The Euler equation for an interior solution $i = i(q)$ takes the form

$$\frac{1}{q - i(q)} = \frac{\beta \alpha}{\alpha i(q) - i(\alpha i(q))}.$$

The solution is $i(q) = \beta q$ and does not depend on α. Thus the optimal plan is for Crusoe to input βq for production whenever he holds q units of the good. Under this plan Crusoe's successive positions are

$$q_1 = q, \; q_2 = (\alpha \beta) q, \; \ldots, \; q_n = (\alpha \beta)^{n-1} q, \; \ldots,$$

and the optimal return is

$$V(q) = \sum_{n=1}^{\infty} \beta^{n-1} \log{(q_n - \beta q_n)} = \sum_{n=1}^{\infty} \beta^{n-1} \log{\left((\alpha\beta)^{n-1}(1-\beta)q\right)}.$$

Using properties of the log function and geometric series, we can rewrite the return as

$$V(q) = \frac{\log q}{1-\beta} + \frac{\log(1-\beta)}{1-\beta} + \frac{\beta}{(1-\beta)^2}\left[\log\alpha + \log\beta\right].$$

9.3.3.1 Innovation by a risk-averse Robinson Crusoe Consider now the situation of an agent who begins with the utility $u(x) = \log x$ and production function $f(i) = \alpha i$ as in the previous section, and contemplates the possibility of an innovation leading to an improved production function $g(i) = (1+\theta)\alpha i$. As in section 9.3.1, let V_1 and V_2 be the original value function and the value function after a successful innovation. Then the value function $V_1(q)$ is given by the formula of the previous section, and $V_2(q)$ is given by the same formula with the constant α multiplied by $1+\theta$. Thus

$$V_2(q) = V_1(q) + \frac{\beta}{(1-\beta)^2}\log{(1+\theta)},$$

and the final term above represents the value to Crusoe of having the improved production function. The value function V for the game with innovation can now be written as

$$V(q) = \sup_{\substack{0\leq i\leq q \\ 0\leq j\leq q-i}} \left[\log{(q-i-j)} + \beta\left\{\xi(j)V_2(\alpha i) + (1-\xi(j))V_1(\alpha i)\right\}\right]$$

$$= \sup_{\substack{0\leq i\leq q \\ 0\leq j\leq q-i}} \left[\log{(q-i-j)} + \beta\left\{V_1(\alpha i) + \xi(j)\frac{\beta}{(1-\beta)^2}\log{(1+\theta)}\right\}\right].$$

The Euler equations for an interior solution $i = i(q)$, $j = j(q)$ can be obtained by letting $\psi(i,j)$ be the function inside the supremum and setting its two partial derivatives equal to zero. Here is the result:

$$\frac{1}{q-i-j} = \frac{\beta}{(1-\beta)}\frac{1}{i} = \frac{\beta^2}{(1-\beta)^2}\log{(1+\theta)}\xi'(j).$$

The first equation can be solved for i to get

$$i = \beta(q-j).$$

This expression for i can then be substituted back in to obtain

$$\xi'(j) = \frac{1-\beta}{\beta^2 \log (1 + \theta)} \cdot \frac{1}{q - j}.$$

This equation can be solved explicitly if, as in section 9.3.2.1, $\xi(j) = j/(j+1)$. In this case, the equation above for j becomes a quadratic. Using $\beta = .95$, $\theta = .1$ as in section 9.3.2.1, and setting $q = 2$, the positive root of this quadratic equation is $j^* = .57$ and, for this value, the chance of a successful innovation is $.57/1.57 = .36$.

9.3.4   A comment on saving and assets

We have so far modeled Crusoe without durable assets. Prior to introducing money, this is done to illustrate the simple point that without durables Crusoe's wealth is limited to his immediate production. Hence his ability to innovate calls for his cutting back on immediate consumption. If he is able to store durables, there may be no need to diminish consumption. An ideal durable may be regarded as a catalyst with zero storage costs such that $x_t \rightarrow x_{t+1}$. The concept of utility or end use consumption involves flows rather than stocks. Durable assets may provide a flow of consumption or production services over time. If Crusoe's island contains a deserted town he might derive little if any direct consumption value from its presence, but it could supply assets for innovation.

In the model of the next section, Crusoe has both a durable and a nondurable asset. The consumption value of the durable asset is represented by a parameter γ, which may be extremely small. However, the asset can be used to increase the probability of success of the innovation.

In a modern economy the predominant form of real asset is a production asset such as a steel plant or bank or computer center that yields no direct consumption value. Furthermore consumer assets such as houses, automobiles, and appliances yield a stream of daily services that are relatively small in comparison with their asset value in a multistage dynamic economy.

9.3.5   Crusoe innovates using a long-term asset

Suppose that in addition to his holdings of q units of a nondurable good, Crusoe also has r units of a durable good that yield a utility of γr in each period, where γ is a positive constant.

If only the nondurable good is used for production, then his optimal reward $V_1(q,r)$ will satisfy

$$V_1(q,r) = \sup_{0 \le i \le q}\ [u(q-i) + \gamma r + \beta V_1(f(i),r)]$$

$$= V_1(q) + \frac{\gamma r}{1 - \beta}.$$

Here $V_1(q)$ is the value of the previous sections in which Crusoe held only one good and had production function f.

Likewise if Crusoe has a production function $g(i) = (1+\theta)f(i)$, then his optimal reward is

$$V_2(q,r) = V_2(q) + \frac{\gamma r}{1 - \beta},$$

where $V_2(q)$ is the corresponding value when he holds only q.

Now assume that Crusoe can invest any quantity $j \in [0,r]$ of the durable good in an attempt at innovation. As in section 9.3.1 the investment of j is successful with the probability $\xi(j)$, resulting in the improved production function $g(i) = (1+\theta)f(i)$. With probability $1 - \xi(j)$ the innovation fails and the production function is unchanged. The optimal reward will take the form

$$V(q,r) = \sup_{\substack{0 \le i \le q \\ 0 \le j \le r}}\ [u(q-i) + \gamma\,(r-j) + \beta\,\{\xi(j)\,V_2(f(i),r-j)$$

$$+ (1 - \xi(j))\,V_1(f(i),r-j)\}].$$

Let $\psi(i,j)$ denote the expression occurring inside the supremum. It can be rewritten as

$$\psi(i,j) = u(q-i) + \frac{\gamma\,(r-j)}{1 - \beta} + \beta\,\{\xi(j)\,[V_2(f(i)) - V_1(f(i))] + V_1(f(i))\}.$$

9.3.5.1   A numerical example with a long-term asset

As in the example of section 9.3.2, let $u(x) = x, f(i) = 2\sqrt{i}, \theta = .1, \beta = .95$, and $\xi(j) = j/(j+1)$. Also set $\gamma = .1$. It follows from the calculation in section 9.3.2.1 that, for $q, f(i)$, and r sufficiently large,

$$\psi(i,j) = q - i + 2\,(r-j) + .95\left\{\xi(j)\,(3.791) + V_1\left(2\sqrt{i}\right)\right\}.$$

Setting

$$\frac{\partial \psi}{\partial i} = \frac{\partial \psi}{\partial j} = 0,$$

we find that the optimal values are

$$i^* = i_1 = .9025, \qquad j^* = \xi'^{-1}\,(2/(.95)(3.791)) = .34$$

with the success probability $\xi(.34) = .34/1.34 = .25$.

9.3.5.2   A comment on continuous time   It is well known that it is difficult to obtain closed-form solutions to dynamic programming models. Approximations are called for. There are two reasons that make the consideration of continuous-time models attractive. The first, important to economic theory, is that it lays emphasis on the distinctions between stocks and flows, and the second is that the recursive difference structure may be reduced to differential equations that may be more easily solved or have solutions approximated.[3]

9.4   Real Assets, Monies, and Terminal Conditions

Before discussing explicit models, we make some general observations on basic distinctions needed in both the real-goods and the financial economy.

In all instances we may wish to construct a model that is a playable game. If this criterion is used, as experiments must terminate we need to specify terminal conditions. There is no need to specify terminal conditions for perishables as they are not left over; but salvage values are required for reproducibles and durables.

9.4.1   Tomatoes, barley, gold, and fiat

Taxonomies are influenced by the selection of scale; thus with the time unit for trade set at a week, a ripe tomato is a perishable and unsuited for use as a transactions money. Barley, gold, and fiat all are suitable, but their physical properties make a difference. All are durables and require that a salvage value be assigned to each at the end of the game. Table 9.1 shows these differences.

MOP stands for means of payment. Barley being a storable perishable can be consumed, providing a counterexample to the proposition that one cannot eat money. However, the individual has the strategic choice to eat it or not, depending on the salvage value attached to it. In contrast gold is not edible and the society as a whole will be forced to have it left over. Gold can provide a stream of consumption services and MOP services; but at any point in time it can provide only one or the other, not both. Fiat, in contrast, as paper gold provides no consumption services but does provide MOP services.

Table 9.1

Aging and utilitarian value of durable goods affects their roles as means of payment

	MOP	Depreciation	Consumption Value
Barley	Yes	Yes	If asset eaten
Gold	Yes	No	Service stream
Fiat	Yes	None	None

The physical economy has perishables, storable consumables, and depreciating and nondepreciating durables. There are many variants of dynamic models that can be formed from these ingredients. We select only a few of the simplest that are sufficient to illustrate the basic aspects of innovation.

9.5   The Closed Economy as a Sensing, Evaluating, and Control Mechanism

Prior to considering the formal closed models with innovation, we cover several general items that supply context. A detailed sketch of the whole closed system is presented in figure 9.1; it is somewhat simplified in figure 9.2 prior to the formal analysis.

Figure 9.1 shows differentiated economic units with some enforcement and evaluation included. The figure diagrams the way credit evaluation, clearinghouses, the banks, central bank, and law courts fit into the information and enforcement structure. Institutional reality has many variations and it is easy to argue with the particular "wiring" presented here; but the purpose of this diagram is to give a *Fingerspitzengefühl* or intuitive feeling of what the many realities look like.

Compared with the abstracted figure 9.2, additional institutions appear. They are the clearinghouse, the credit evaluation agency (implicitly including the accountants), and the courthouse. In much economic theory expertise is ignored primarily because it is too hard to deal with. In old-fashioned securities analysis and accounting, due diligence and expertise are central, but they are often ignored in much of economic and finance theory because it is implicitly assumed that the risky economic instruments being dealt with can be regarded as lottery tickets that have already been correctly evaluated. We follow this extreme approximation because it is good enough for our prime purpose, which is consideration of the breaking of the circular flow of capital. Even at this level of abstraction the phenomenon may still occur.

9.5.1   On money, credit, banks, and central banks

In institutional fact the definition and measurement of the money supply is difficult at best, as noted in chapter 8. Here we utilize a ruthless simplification in order to highlight the distinction between money and credit and to be able to stress an upper bound on economic control via government money. Consider money to be paper gold, or some form of blue chip in which payments are made. Credit is a contract between two entities A and B, in which individual A delivers money at time t_1 in return for an IOU or a promise from B to

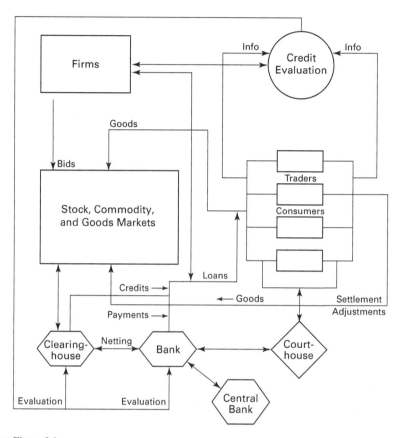

Figure 9.1
The overall closed control mechanism.

repay an amount of money to A at time t_2. Either A or B may be a natural person or a legal person such as a firm, a bill broker, a bank, a credit-granting clearinghouse, or a central bank.

9.5.2   Where does the money go?

Drive for show, but putt for dough!
—Golf saying

We may consider several ways to vary the money supply. The first and simplest is to permit the central bank to print money. We utilize this simplistic mechanism here in our simplest model.

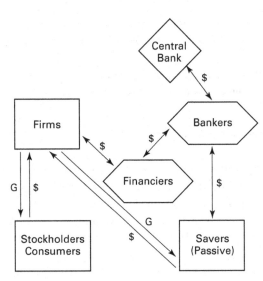

Figure 9.2
Who controls what? (G stands for the flow of goods, $ for the flow of money.)

Another way to vary the money supply is to have all individuals accept the IOU notes of commercial banks as money. Say they are red chips, in contrast with the central bank's blue chips and the consumers' IOUs that are nonnegotiable.

As we wish to maintain as high a level of simplification as possible in this chapter in order to illustrate the breaking of the circular flow for the first model, we select a minimalistic structure for the banking system. It is considered a single entity and is called the central bank. It has funds above its reserves[4] that it can lend.[5] The commercial banking system is considered in chapter 10.

9.5.3   An aside on accounting

Before considering the formal models, an accounting problem must be noted. Much microeconomic theory does not define short-term profits, and accounting timing differences do not matter in a stationary equilibrium. Unfortunately when one is concerned with disequilibrium conditions in a dynamic economic process, the accounting conventions must be selected.

We have to enlarge the notation used for Robinson Crusoe to take into account the introduction of a money and markets.

If we use cash accounting, the firm's profits for periods n and $n + 1$ differ from matching accounting where the full carrying costs of inputs are charged against their associated outputs.

Furthermore accounting conventions concerning the distinctions between assets and flows and the amortizing of assets become relevant.

9.6   The Separation of Management and Ownership

The next level of complexity beyond the owner-manager firm utilizes two types of agents, managers of the firms and stockholder-owners. In our simplest example the economy can be interpreted as a fully defined game of strategy where there are many independent small firms; by assumption we limit the solution to a type-symmetric noncooperative equilibrium, so that all agents of any type, even though independent, will employ a strategy common to their type. In illustrating some of the basic aspects of financing and control of innovation, the individual-agent models show microeconomic uncertainty where innovation is individual choice. After attempting to innovate, these firms will divide into two classes—the successful and the failed agents—at which point the system will not be in a stationary equilibrium. It requires proof to establish that a type-symmetric stationary equilibrium will eventually emerge.

The individual-agent model is sufficient to illustrate the wealth distribution aspects of microeconomic uncertainty. We utilize the individual-agent model observing that both it and the representative-agent model are extreme cases of a better (and more complex) model where the exogenous uncertainty can be correlated generally among the agents.

9.6.1   Managerial optimization

Unfortunately, the conditions in which consumer optimization and firm profit maximization coincide lose their generality once the separating hyperplane theorem fails. Instead of a pristine mathematical economic theorem establishing perfect decentralization by static price signals, other conditions must be found.

There is a vast literature approaching the goals and strategies of management from many angles. This includes agency theory, industrial organization studies involving asymmetric information, sociopsychological and sociological studies of group behavior, as well as legal and historical views of management behavior.

Among the suggested goals of management have been the maximization of expected long-term profit; the maximization of short-term profit; the maximization of a company's earnings before the deduction of interest, tax, and amortization expenses; and the maximization of sales or market share subject to an earnings constraint. In any of this ad hoc listing there is no generally accepted justification for the discount factor utilized by the firm's controllers, and little justification of the time horizon involved beyond the convenience of a good enough heuristic approximation that includes risk estimate, insurance, and time discount in one package. A 5-year payback period for almost any investment decision and a horizon of at most 5 to 10 years for any numerical form of long-range planning appear to set the scope for pro forma calculations.

In the twenty-first century, management control of most of the corporations with over a thousand employees appears to be the rule in the United States. Here, and more so elsewhere, there are also some large family-controlled firms.

We suspect that management behavior is directed toward taking care of an admixture of many constituencies including workers, unions, low, middle and upper management, suppliers, customers, politicians, stockholders, and short- and long-term debt holders. In many instances the maximization of profits of stockholders is well down on the list of priorities of a controlling management, even if presented as a high priority in the rhetoric.

For our prime purpose, in illustrating the breaking of the circular flow of money during innovation we need a behavioral condition for management. We cut the Gordian knot involved in selecting one among the many competing descriptions by selecting expected profit maximization.[6]

9.7 A Closed Economy Prior to Innovation: The Circular Flow of Money Illustrated

The model presented here is based on work by Karatzas, Shubik, and Sudderth [200] on an economy with money, credit, and an outside bank in a world initially without innovation; this is then extended to the economy with innovation, and the disequilibrium aspects of innovation on the money supply are considered.

9.7.1 A closed economy with producers, consumers, monied individuals, and a central bank

In the remainder of this chapter the focus turns to monetary and financial control in a closed economy.

The underlying model is that of a "cash-in-advance" market economy with a continuum of firms $\phi \in J = [0, 1]$ that produce goods all of which must be put up for sale, and a continuum of stockholder agents $\alpha \in I = [0, 1]$ who own the firms and purchase these goods for consumption. The agents hold cash and bid for the goods in each of a countable number of periods $n = 1, 2, \ldots$. The firms hold no cash and must borrow from a single outside bank to purchase goods as input for production in every period. The bank is modeled as a strategic dummy that accepts deposits and offers loans at a fixed interest rate ρ.[7]

The initial period begins with the sale of goods that have been produced previously. Their quantity is a given in the initial conditions. There is a continuum of *agents* $\alpha \in I = [0, 1]$, each of whom holds cash and bids in every period to buy goods for consumption or may save by depositing in the bank. There is a continuum of *firms* $\phi \in J = [0, 1]$, each of which produces goods for sale in the market. The firms hold no cash, and must borrow from a central bank to purchase goods as input for production; they are owned by the above agents, who hold equal shares in all the firms and receive as income the profits earned by the firms in each period. For this reason we call these agents *owner agents*.

In addition to the owner agents, there may be a continuum of *saver or monied agents* $\gamma \in K = [0, 1]$, each of whom holds cash, bids in every period to buy goods for consumption, and subsists entirely on her savings. These agents can be thought of as "retirees" or private capitalists.[8] We return to a more detailed interpretation of these agents later. Figure 9.2 shows the structure of the economy with firms, owners, savers, and a central bank. In our first innovation model we leave out independent savers; they are implicitly aggregated into a single owner-consumer-saver agent.

The six boxes give a simple intuitive insight into the spreading out of ownership and control in a modern enterprise economy. The firms are in general corporate; they do not own themselves. They have (at some ultimate level) natural-person stockholders who are also consumers. Directly or indirectly they depend on at least four sets of decision makers for debt (and some equity or options) financing. They are the passive savers, the financiers, the commercial banks, and the central bank. Without having to elaborate further it should be evident that in any dynamic setting the coordination problem is considerable. In the mathematics and first innovation model below we grossly simplify the financial sector, ignoring the financiers, collapsing the commercial banks and central bank into one, and having the passive savers save in the aggregate bank while the firms borrow only from this bank.

Each firm ϕ begins every period n with goods q_n^ϕ that are to be sold in the market. The total amount of goods offered for sale is thus

$$Q_n = \int d\phi \, q_n^\phi.$$

Each firm ϕ also borrows cash $b_n^{\text{firm},\phi}$ from a central bank, with $0 \le b_n^{\text{firm},\phi} \le \left(p_n q_n^\phi \right) / (1 + \rho)$, where p_n is the price of the good in period n (as defined below) and $\rho > 0$ is the interest rate. The firm spends the cash $b_n^{\text{firm},\phi}$ to purchase the amount of goods

$$i_n^\phi = \frac{b_n^{\text{firm},\phi}}{p_n}$$

as input for production, and begins the next period with an amount of goods

$$q_{n+1}^\phi = f\left(i_n^\phi \right) + y.$$

Here $f(\cdot)$ is a *production function* which satisfies the usual assumptions, and $y \ge 0$ is a constant, deterministic endowment. During period n each firm ϕ earns the (net) profit

$$\pi_n^\phi = p_n q_n^\phi - (1 + \rho) b_n^{\text{firm},\phi},$$

since it must pay back its loan with interest. The goal of the firm is to maximize its total discounted profits[9]

$$\sum_{n=1}^{\infty} \left(\frac{1}{1+\rho} \right)^{n-1} \pi_n^\phi.$$

In a given period n, the total amount of goods offered for sale by all the firms, and the total profits generated by all the firms, are

$$Q_n = \int d\phi \, q_n^\phi \quad \text{and} \quad \Pi_n = \int d\phi \, \pi_n^\phi,$$

respectively. The profits Π_n are distributed to the owner agents in equal shares at the end of the period.

The owner agents are now considered. A typical *owner agent* α holds money $m_n^{\text{own},\alpha}$ at the beginning of period n. The agent bids an amount of money $b_n^{\text{own},\alpha}$ with $0 \le b_n^{\text{own},\alpha} \le m_n^{\text{own},\alpha} + \Pi_n / (1 + \rho)$, which buys him an amount $c_n^{\text{own},\alpha} = b_n^{\text{own},\alpha} / p_n$ of goods. Any extra money an owner agent has is deposited and earns an interest of ρ. The agent begins the next period with cash

$$m_{n+1}^{\text{own},\alpha} = (1 + \rho) \left(m_n^{\text{own},\alpha} - b_n^{\text{own},\alpha} \right) + \Pi_n.$$

Each agent α seeks to maximize his total discounted utility

$$\sum_{n=1}^{\infty} \beta^{n-1} u\left(c_n^{\text{own},\alpha}\right),$$

where $0 < \beta < 1$ is a given discount factor.

Also considered is a typical *saver agent* γ, who holds $m_n^{\text{save},\gamma}$ in cash at the start of period n. The saver bids an amount $b_n^{\text{save},\gamma}$ of cash with $0 \le b_n^{\text{save},\gamma} \le m_n^{\text{save},\gamma}$, which buys him a quantity $c_n^{\text{save},\gamma} = b_n^{\text{save},\gamma}/p_n$ of goods, and starts the next period with

$$m_{n+1}^{\text{save},\gamma} = (1+\rho)\left(m_n^{\text{save},\gamma} - b_n^{\text{save},\gamma}\right)$$

in cash. If $v(\cdot)$ is his utility function, with the same properties as $u(\cdot)$, the saver agent's objective is to maximize the total discounted utility

$$\sum_{n=1}^{\infty} \beta^{n-1} v\left(c_n^{\text{save},\gamma}\right).$$

The total amounts of money bid in period n by the owner agents, the firms, and the saver agents are

$$B_n^{\text{own}} = \int d\alpha\, b_n^{\text{own},\alpha}, \qquad B_n^{\text{firm}} = \int d\phi\, b_n^{\text{firm},\phi}, \qquad \text{and} \qquad B_n^{\text{save}} = \int d\gamma\, b_n^{\text{save},\gamma},$$

respectively. The price p_n is formed as the total bid over the total production

$$p_n = \frac{B_n^{\text{own}} + B_n^{\text{firm}} + B_n^{\text{save}}}{Q_n} \qquad p_n = \frac{A_n + B_n + \Gamma_n}{Q_n}.$$

An equilibrium is constructed as follows. Suppose that all owner agents begin with cash $M_1^{\text{own}} = m^{\text{own}} > 0$, all saver agents begin with cash $M_1^{\text{save}} = m^{\text{save}} \ge 0$, and all firms begin with goods $Q_1 = q > 0$. Thus, the total amount of cash $M_1 = M_1^{\text{own}} + M_1^{\text{save}}$ across agents is equal to

$$m = m^{\text{own}} + m^{\text{save}},$$

and the proportion of money held by the saver agents is

$$\nu = \frac{m^{\text{save}}}{m} = \frac{m^{\text{save}}}{m^{\text{own}} + m^{\text{save}}}, \qquad \text{with} \qquad 0 \le \nu < 1.$$

Suppose that the bids of the agents and firms are

$$b_1^{\text{own}} = b^{\text{own}} m, \qquad b_1^{\text{firm}} = b^{\text{firm}} m, \qquad b_1^{\text{save}} = b^{\text{save}} m,$$

that is, proportional to the total amount of cash, so that the price is also proportional to this amount:

$$p_1 = p(m) = \frac{\left(b^{\text{own}} + b^{\text{firm}} + b^{\text{save}}\right) m}{q}.$$

Then the profit of each firm is

$$\Pi_1 = p_1 q - (1 + \rho) b_1^{\text{firm}} = \left(b^{\text{own}} + b^{\text{save}} - \rho b^{\text{own}}\right) m,$$

the cash of each owner agent at the beginning of the next period is

$$M_2^{\text{own}} = (1 + \rho) \left(m^{\text{own}} - b^{\text{own}} m\right) + \Pi_1,$$

and the cash held by each saver agent is

$$M_2^{\text{save}} = (1 + \rho) \left(m^{\text{save}} - b^{\text{save}} m\right).$$

Thus, the total amount of cash held by all agents at the beginning of the next period is

$$M_2 = M_2^{\text{own}} + M_2^{\text{save}} = \left(1 + \rho - \rho \left(b^{\text{own}} + b^{\text{firm}} + b^{\text{save}}\right)\right) m = \tau m,$$

introducing the notation

$$\tau = 1 + \rho - \rho \left(b^{\text{own}} + b^{\text{firm}} + b^{\text{save}}\right).$$

Define

$$r = \frac{(1 + \rho)(1 - \beta)}{\rho}. \tag{9.1}$$

The following theorem has been established.

THEOREM 3   There are two cases.

1. Suppose that $f'(0+) < (1 + \rho)/\beta$. Then there is an equilibrium for which, in every period: each firm bids $b^{\text{firm}*} = 0$, inputs 0, and produces y; each owner agent bids the proportion $b^{\text{own}*} = r - (1 - \beta) v$ of the total money supply and consumes $\left(1 - \frac{\rho v}{1 + \rho}\right) y$; whereas each saver agent bids the proportion $b^{\text{save}*} = (1 - \beta) v$ of the total money supply and consumes $\left(\frac{\rho v}{1 + \rho}\right) y$.

2. Suppose that $f'(0+) \geq (1 + \rho)/\beta$ so that there exists i_4 with $f'(i_4) = (1 + \rho)/\beta$. Then there is an equilibrium for which, in every period: each firm inputs i_4, produces $q_4 = f(i_4) + y$, and bids the amount

$b_n^{\text{firm}} = b^{\text{firm}*} M_n$; each owner agent bids $b_n^{\text{own}} = b^{\text{own}*} M_n$; and each saver agent bids $b_n^{\text{save}} = b^{\text{save}*} M_n$. Here

$$b^{\text{own}*} + b^{\text{firm}*} + b^{\text{save}*} = r, \qquad b^{\text{firm}*} = \frac{r}{q_4} \cdot i_4, \qquad b^{\text{save}*} = (1 - \beta) \nu$$

$$(9.2)$$

and $M_n = M_n^{\text{own}} + M_n^{\text{save}}$ is the amount of cash held across agents in period n.

Furthermore, in each period n: every owner agent consumes the amount $c^{\text{own}*} = \left(1 - \frac{\rho \nu}{1 + \rho}\right) q_4 - i_4$; every saver agent consumes the amount $c^{\text{save}*} = \left(\frac{\rho \nu}{1 + \rho}\right) q_4$; whereas every firm makes $\pi^* M_n$ in profits, with $\pi^* = r - (1 + \rho) b^*$.

The proof is given in [200]. It is shown that the consumption and total discounted utility of the owner agents are decreasing functions of ρ in case 2 of the theorem; such agents prefer as *low* an interest rate as possible. Similarly, the firms also prefer an interest rate as close to zero as possible, in order to maximize their profits. But the situation of the saver agents is subtler: under certain configurations of the various parameters of the model (endowment variable, discount factor, production function) they prefer as *high* an interest rate as possible; whereas under other configurations they settle on an interest rate $\rho^* \in (0, \infty)$ that uniquely maximizes their welfare. Let

$$\tau^* = 1 + \rho - \rho \left(b^{\text{own}*} + b^{\text{firm}*} + b^{\text{save}*}\right).$$

Given the passive or dummy central bank, the money and prices inflate (or deflate) at rate τ^* in the equilibrium of Theorem 3. Also, in both cases we have $b^{\text{own}*} + b^{\text{firm}*} + b^{\text{save}*} = r$, so that the Fisher equation $\tau^* = \beta (1 + \rho)$ when there is no exogenous uncertainty. This is not true when there is exogenous uncertainty, as has been established elsewhere [153].

Remark 9.1   We observe that formally setting $\nu = 0$ in Theorem 3, we obtain an economy with only producer firms and owner/consumer agents.[10] This is useful in illustrating the basic problems with the circular flow and money supply with innovation in a simplest context.

9.7.2   Money, politics, the interest rate, and pensioners

Although in the work on innovation we omit including pensioners as a separate group, it is important to note that in a monetary economy the presence of a group living off their savings appears naturally, depending on the parameters of the system. There is no natural rate of interest; it must reflect a political decision as to whose ox will be gored.

9.8   Innovation in an Asset-Poor Economy

In the model in section 9.7 all goods are aggregated into a single perishable consumable that is utilized in consumption or production or consumed in innovation. There is no capital stock, such as steel mills. There is no "fat" in the economy; innovation resources come directly out of consumption resources.

9.8.1   The meaning of an asset-poor economy

In actuality any advanced economy is rich with real durable assets, with a time profile of durables of many ages that are consumed in production. Gross domestic product may be split into consumption and investment. If we consider around 70 percent in consumption and 30 percent gross investment, 5–15 percent depreciation, then we note that at market prices the values of real assets such as steel mills, automobile factories, houses, automobiles, machinery, and other consumer durables[11] are priced probably between 4 and 10 times the value of the consumption stream, considering depreciation schedules. None of these items are meaningfully placed directly in the (consumption) utility functions of the individuals. Furthermore it is the services of consumer durables that are ultimately valued, not the durables themselves. This is even truer of items such as steel mills. In our models here so far we have not reflected the presence of this large mass of assets owned by individuals, the size of which is such that the loss or exchange of a small percentage while pursuing innovation will hardly change the consumption of the owners of large amounts of real assets. We return to this point in chapter 10.

In a poor country the amount of available assets relative to consumption will be much smaller than in a rich economy. Here we consider the extreme simplifying case where innovation must come directly out of consumption. This makes it easier to be specific about the breaking of the circular flow of capital and to observe the match between real assets and money.

In essence, innovation is the execution of an idea for a new process to rearrange and employ existing assets in a different manner.[12] It is a breaking of equilibrium that in a rich country calls for an alternative use for productive assets but does not directly cut down heavily on current consumption. In contrast in an asset-poor economy, sacrifice of immediate consumption is required.

9.8.2   Innovation in an asset-poor economy: breaking the circular flow

In [364, 365] the general equations used in determining innovation together with the general existence proof are presented for the case represented below in Eq. (9.10). Although general existence proofs provide the critical first step in understanding the models, the ability to actually solve the equations describing a specific model in full detail and to provide a basic economic interpretation is highly desirable. For this reason we present some simple examples.

In the following examples we represent innovation as replacing the production function f of a static one-good economy with some other function converting the same good from an input to an output, but at lower cost or with less-constrained capacity. When innovation becomes possible, even in the simplest case of a single producer/consumer without money or markets, a shock to the system causing a disequilibrium between investment and consumption is generally introduced, and the system may take an extended time to recover to a new equilibrium. This disequilibrium will generally extend to money, prices, and savings in more complex economies. We demonstrate and contrast two approaches to obtaining tractable models in the presence of such disequilibria. One approach, well suited to intertemporal models in which periods represent extended time intervals, is to consider capacity constraints, thereby making production a threshold function with corner solutions. The dynamic programming solution to models of this variety can in general have transients of any duration. The inelasticity of output at corner solutions, with their corresponding flexibility of shadow prices, has the effect of separating consumption decisions in different periods. By choosing the following simple example, we limit the transient to one period. Suppose i is the input to production at the beginning of the period, and $f(i)$ the output which may be consumed or carried forward. A linear production function with an upper output capacity C is[13]

$$f(i) = \begin{cases} 3i \; ; i \le C \\ 3C \; ; i > C \end{cases}. \tag{9.3}$$

An alternative approach is to retain differentiable production functions and accept the multiperiod Bellman equations that result, but to use a continuous-time limit to reduce these potentially complicated difference equations to tractable ordinary differential equations. Examples of games with similar structure to the discrete-period games presented here, but in which the extended-time relaxation structure is explicitly solved, are developed in a separate publication as noted above [363]. Details of the response to innovation will depend on which approach is taken, but many broad features of the breaking and recovery of the circular flow can be recognized to coincide among the diverse models.

9.8.3   Innovation for cost efficiency: Robinson Crusoe revisited

As a benchmark we consider Robinson Crusoe as an innovator. In all discrete-period models we suppose that Crusoe's valuation for a consumption level c is

$$u(c) \equiv 100c - \frac{1}{2}c^2. \tag{9.4}$$

We consider "cost innovation," in which the successful innovator replaces the pre-innovation production function (9.3) with a more efficient production function

$$\tilde{f}^{(\text{cost})}(i) = \begin{cases} 3i(1+\theta) \; ; \; i \le C/(1+\theta) \\ 3C \qquad \; ; \; i > C/(1+\theta) \end{cases}. \tag{9.5}$$

The meaning is that capacity for the number of units stays the same, but unit cost of output drops in terms of input.

Let $V^{(\varnothing)}$ be the value function for a stock s of goods carried into the next period if innovation fails, and $V^{(\text{cost})}$ the corresponding value function if it succeeds. These satisfy the Bellman equations without uncertainty (the opportunity to innovate occurs only in a single period and never again):

$$V^{(\varnothing)}(s) = \sup_{0 \le i \le s} \left\{ u(s-i) + \beta V^{(\varnothing)}(f(i)) \right\}$$

$$V^{(\text{cost})}(s) = \sup_{0 \le i \le s} \left\{ u(s-i) + \beta V^{(\text{cost})}\left(\tilde{f}^{(\text{cost})}(i) \right) \right\}. \tag{9.6}$$

To solve Bellman equations with piecewise-linear production functions, it is convenient to write the derivatives of f and $\tilde{f}^{(\text{cost})}$ as variables Λ and $\tilde{\Lambda}^{(\text{cost})}$, which undergo all their change at the corner values ($i = C$ or $i = C/(1+\theta)$, respectively), in the same manner as we have handled piecewise-linear bankruptcy constraints in previous chapters. With this convention,

$$\frac{df(i)}{di} \equiv \Lambda, \qquad \text{where} \qquad \Lambda \in [0,3], \tag{9.7}$$

$$\frac{d\tilde{f}^{(\text{cost})}(i)}{di} \equiv \tilde{\Lambda}^{(\text{cost})}, \qquad \text{where} \qquad \tilde{\Lambda}^{(\text{cost})} \in [0, 3(1+\theta)]. \tag{9.8}$$

At corner solutions, the derivatives $du(s-i)/ds$ determining dV/ds in Eq. (9.6), and $-du(s-i)/di$ determining the argument i of the supremum, are the same value. It follows that at the supremum for a steady-state solution, $\Lambda = 1/\beta$ or $\tilde{\Lambda}^{(\text{cost})} = 1/\beta$ respectively, so Eqs. (9.7, 9.8) give the admissible range of β for such solutions. The steady-state corner solutions have $s = f(\mathcal{C}) = 3\mathcal{C}$ or $s = \tilde{f}^{(\text{cost})}(\mathcal{C}/(1+\theta)) = 3\mathcal{C}$ respectively, and the resulting gradients of the value functions are given by

$$V^{\varnothing'}(3\mathcal{C}) = u'(2\mathcal{C})$$

$$V^{(\text{cost})'}(3\mathcal{C}) = u'(3\mathcal{C} - \mathcal{C}/(1+\theta)). \tag{9.9}$$

Suppose now that the opportunity to innovate can be represented by a binary lottery ticket that can be obtained by utilizing j units of input material. The ticket is such that with probability $\xi(j)$ the innovation succeeds and with probability $1 - \xi(j)$ it fails.[14] Failure leaves the innovator with the original production function f. In the examples below we will use $j = 5$, $\mathcal{C} = 25$, and $\xi(j) = 1/2$.

Consider the value function V in the current period when the choice whether or not to innovate is made. If innovation is selected, V satisfies the Bellman equation

$$V(s) = \sup_{\substack{0 \le i \le s \\ 0 \le j \le s - i}} \left\{ u(s - i - j) + \beta \left[(1 - \xi(j)) V^{(\varnothing)}(f(i)) + \xi(j) V^{(\text{cost})} \left(\tilde{f}^{(\text{cost})}(i) \right) \right] \right\}. \tag{9.10}$$

The first-order condition that identifies the supremum is

$$u'(s - i - j) = \beta \left[(1 - \xi(j)) V^{\varnothing'}(f(i)) \Lambda + \xi(j) V^{(\text{cost})'} \left(\tilde{f}^{(\text{cost})}(i) \right) \tilde{\Lambda}^{(\text{cost})} \right]. \tag{9.11}$$

We suppose finally that prior to the period of innovation, Crusoe is at the steady-state corner solution with consumption $c = 2\mathcal{C}$, investment $i = \mathcal{C}$, and hence output coming into the focal period $s = 3\mathcal{C}$. For sufficiently small $1/\beta$, corner solutions again exist with $i = \mathcal{C}$, even though a fraction $\theta/(1+\theta)$ of the investment is "wasted" in the event that innovation succeeds.

If Crusoe chooses not to innovate, his value remains the same as $V^{\varnothing}$, given by

$$\begin{aligned} V^{\varnothing}(3\mathcal{C}) &= \frac{u(2\mathcal{C})}{1 - \beta} \\ &= 21 \times u(50) \\ &= 21 \times 3750 = 78750. \end{aligned} \tag{9.12}$$

If we set the efficiency gain $\theta = 1$ and the discount factor $\beta = 1/1.05$, the value (9.10) from choosing to attempt innovation evaluates to

$$
\begin{aligned}
V(3C) &= u(2C - j) + \frac{\beta}{1 - \beta}\left[(1 - \xi(j))\,u(2C) + \xi(j)\,u\left(3C - \frac{C.}{1 + \theta}\right)\right] \\
&= V^{\emptyset}(3C) - [u(2C) - u(2C - j)] \\
&\quad + \frac{\beta}{1 - \beta}\xi(j)\left[u\left(3C - \frac{C}{1 + \theta}\right) - u(2C)\right] \\
&\to V^{\emptyset}(3C) - [u(50) - u(45)] + 10\,[u(62.5) - u(50)] \\
&= V^{\emptyset}(3C) - 262.50 + 10 \times 546.875 \\
&= V^{\emptyset}(3C) + 5206.25 \\
&= 83956.25.
\end{aligned}
\tag{9.13}
$$

The fourth line of Eq. (9.13) separates the cost and benefit terms of innovation. The cost term is always a one-period effect, whereas the benefit term is the discounted geometric sum weighted by $\xi(j)$. We observe that with these parameters it pays the "uni-cell" nonmonetary Crusoe to innovate. Increase of cost j, decrease of β, or decrease of $\xi(j)$, by sufficient factors, could make innovation unfavorable.

9.8.4   Consumer-owners and firms in a monetary economy

We now replace our fantasy of Robinson Crusoe by another fantasy, a small firm that maximizes expected profits with the owner/manager as the sole power in a competitive money-utilizing economy. The real resource base per capita is somewhat different from Crusoe's, and the small firms are in an economy that uses fiat money.

We may consider several variants of this basic model. The most natural for the ideal small business economy is that the owner maximizes her utility and the actions of the firm appear merely as a constraint on her optimization. This may hold reasonably for firms with less than 20 or 30 employees.

Even in a small-firm economy we may consider a separation of ownership and management. Firms of the size of 100–1,000 employees may have professional managers and stockholders. With size the structure becomes more impersonal. An extreme simplification that reflects this separation has a manager-run firm that maximizes expected profits and pays out the profits to the owners who maximize their individual preferences. Firms with over 100,000 employees have to have some layers of professional management, although there are many institutional instances where the founding entrepreneur or family still occupies the top and controls the firm, such as the Mars Company in the United States.

In a mass economy such as the United States in the early twenty-first century, we may envision the existence of a set of mutual funds basically acting as administrative pass-through devices providing passive owners with some insurance obtained by diversification and professional bookkeeping and accounting, but at the implicit cost of removing much of the operationally anonymous ownership even further from the firms they own, with an intermediary whose aggregated portfolio is such that many of its clients do not even know which firms they own in part.

If the firm acts as a fiduciary for its stockholders, it may be considered as risk-neutral, but the owners may be risk-averse. Decisions will depend on the locus of control and will, in general, have outcomes varying with this locus. The firm that has control over its own policy may regard the owners or stockholders as merely a boundary condition.

The basic structure of this model is that the owner-managed firms borrow to finance their production and choose an investment level of goods in order to maximize discounted profits, which are then turned over, via a set of passive flow-through mutual funds, as income to the consumers in their role as owners.

In addition to exhibiting the breaks in the circular flow of money and goods, a fundamental question for the minimal model is whether a central bank (or some other controller or creator of credit) is required to stand ready to vary the money supply (lacking which innovation is precluded), or whether the necessity of such a role depends on the utility functions for money and goods. The latter appears to be true.

Prior to considering this in detail, we consider some points in infinite-horizon modeling.

9.8.4.1   The bite-one's-tail and the cash-consuming economy and a comment on transversality conditions

There are several ways in which we can consider how a finite model of an economy approaches the infinite-horizon model. Basically the transversality conditions needed in the study of multistage models state that the books must balance at the end. We concentrate on two variants[15] that can be named colloquially the "bite-one's-tail" and the "cash-consuming economy." Heuristically we may look at the presence of fiat money as an asset in a simple production-and-exchange economy of finite length. We keep to the analogy of an experimental game, first with only one period of strategic play, $T = 1$; then we consider the game with arbitrary length as $T \to \infty$. If the quantities are bounded, different finite terminal conditions such as the two noted here will lead to the same physical infinite-horizon equilibrium treatment, as eventually the factor β^T will reduce any bounded term to insignificance.

9.8.4.2 Bite-one's-tail The initial conditions have the firms with an initial endowment of $i_0 =$ the amount of goods in process that will yield $q_1 = f(i_0)$ for sale in a "sell-all" game.

The firms also start with a debt of $(1 + \rho_0) a_0$ that they have to pay back at the start of period $T = 1$ after selling their goods q_1.

The firms then pay out their period 1 profits to the owners

$$\Pi_1 = p_1 q_1 - (1 + \rho_0) a_0$$
$$= p_1 f\left(\frac{a_0}{\rho_0}\right) - (1 + \rho_0) a_0.$$

The firms have no money and must finance any future production by borrowing from a central bank or a money market.

The consumers begin activity at $T = 1$ holding $m_1 = (1 + \rho) m_0$ units of money that have been paid to them by the referee (government or central bank). The consumers each have no goods initially but must buy consumption goods from the market. The consumers have preferences represented by a utility function of the form

$$U(x_1, m_2) = u(x_1) + \beta v(m_2).$$

The last term is not an assumed general utility for money, but the valuation or expectation attached at the final settlement to the salvage value of any assets left over at $T + 1$. The β may be regarded as a natural discount factor.

A strategy by a firm in this game is to optimize Π by borrowing sufficiently to make an optimal bid a_1. A strategy by a consumer is to offer a bid b_1 and an amount g_1 to deposit in savings or lend directly. If the latter, then there would be a money market and

$$1 + \rho_1 = \frac{\int a_1}{\int g_1}.$$

The price of the good would be

$$p_1 = \frac{\int a_1 + \int b_1}{\int q_1}.$$

If instead of a money market there is a single outside central bank, then it announces the rate ρ_1 at which it will borrow or lend. The firms borrow a_1 each and the consumer-owners deposit g_1 each and bid b_1. The price of the good, as before, will be

$$p_1 = \frac{\int a_1 + \int b_1}{\int f(i_0)},$$

and the amount of the good bought by the consumers for consumption and the firms for production will be

$$x_1 = \frac{\int_\alpha b_1^\alpha}{p_1} \text{ and } i_1 = \frac{\int_\alpha a_1^\alpha}{p_1},$$

where α is an infinitesimal agent.[16]

Turning to period $T = 2$ which is the day of settlement, we note that

$$m_2 = (m_1 - b_1)(1 + \rho) + \Pi_1$$
$$\text{where } \Pi_1 = p_1 q_1 - (1 + \rho) a_0.$$

For completeness we require the existence of a salvage value for leftover money and goods.

We need to consider which goods should have a salvage value. One convention might be all durables. Another is only durables that need not be carried forward; another attributes salvage value to all items that can reach $T + 1$.

In the models above, the only item that must be carried forward is fiat money, but a salvage value for leftover inventory will prompt manufacture.

If we permit firms and individuals to roll over their loans until $T + 1$, then the final day of reckoning is the only time at which the settlement involving default is called for. It is not sufficient to attach a value to leftover money, but one also requires a specification of the negative worth of an unpaid debt. For simplicity we can attach a separate term with a parameter μ^*. A simple example illustrates the structure.

Let $f(i) = 2i$ with a capacity constraint at 2 and $u(x) = 2\sqrt{x}$, with initial values of $a_0 = 1$, $m_1 = 2$; terminal salvage value for a unit of goods is p_0, while the terminal value for a unit money is given by

$$v(m_{T+1}) = \mu^* m_{T+1}.$$

We observe that for the parameter values $m = 2$, $\beta = .5$, $\rho = 1$, $\mu^* = 1$ we have $p_t = i_t = x_t = a_t = b_t = 1$ and $q_t = 2$.

The firm optimizes

$$\Pi = \sum_{t=1}^{\infty} \beta^{t-1} \left[2 i_{t-1} p_t - (1+\rho) i_{t-1} p_{t-1} \right],$$

where in the infinite horizon the terminal term in the T-period final horizon game is irrelevant to the optimization.

The consumer-owners in the finite horizon approach the infinite economy as

$$U = \lim_{T \to \infty} \sum_{t=1}^{T} 2 \sqrt{\frac{b_t}{p_t}} + \beta^T \mu_{\text{person}} \left(m_2 + p_2 f(i_1) \right),$$

but with the terminal conditions equal to the initial conditions they are stationary for any T.

9.8.4.3   The cash-consuming economy   In the cash-consuming economy, we consider that all of the aspects of the model are the same except for the terminal conditions and the role of the central bank. We consider that the central bank announces a fixed rate of interest at which it will lend or accept deposits

$$1 + \rho = \frac{1}{\beta} + \varepsilon(T).$$

For the model with $T = 1$ we have

$$m_1 = 2$$
$$m_2 = (m_1 - b_1 + \Pi_1)(1+\rho) + \Pi_2,$$

where

$$\Pi_1 = p_1 q_1 - (1+\rho) a_0.$$

Because money is valueless at the end, it pays any small individual to borrow from the central bank so that her net indebtedness at settlement time $T+1$ is zero. Borrowing is a negative operator through time as it enables one to buy now and pay later.

Utilizing a modified version of the example, we note that with $f(i) = 2i$ and $u(x) = 2\sqrt{x}$, the firm optimizes

$$\Pi = 2 \left(\frac{a}{p} \right) p - (1+\rho) ap, \text{ giving}$$
$$2 = (1+\rho) a, \text{ or}$$
$$a = \frac{2}{1+\rho}$$

for our example of a stationary economy

$$a = \frac{2}{2 + \varepsilon(T)},$$

and the owners optimize

$$U = 2\sqrt{\frac{b_1}{p_1}} + \beta \mu_{\text{person}} (m_2 + p_2 f(i_1)).$$

Suppose $\rho = 1 + \varepsilon(T)$ and $m = 2$; then $p = 1$, $\mu^* = 1$.

As $T \to \infty$ we may have $\varepsilon(T) \to 0$ on an open set, but the physical steady state is maintained although prices are in constant motion. For a small enough ε for any finite length T the two solutions appear to be identical, but the second better reflects the financial dynamics.

The salvage conditions have two parameters (μ^*, p_2^*) that can be interpreted as the common expectations by the agents of the future worth of money and the good. Thus the full optimizations for the firms and consumer-owners are for the firms

$$\sup_{a_1} \left(\Pi_1 + \beta_{\text{firm}} \Pi_2 \right),$$

and for the consumers

$$\sup_{b_1, g_1} \left[u(x_1) + \beta v(m_2) \right].$$

9.8.5   OLG or dynasty?

Here utilizing a dynasty model of the population, the limit interest rate for a fully stationary state is $1 + \rho = 1/\beta$; but had we considered overlapping generations (OLG) the stationary state rate of interest would be zero, and for many purposes (such as the study of the life cycle) the OLG model may be deemed to be better than the dynasty model.

9.9   An Experimental-Game Example of Innovation Financing

An extremely simple example is constructed in order to well-define a model with innovation and the breaking of the circular flow of money. It is best to consider this example as an experimental game because it poses the problem of fully defining all the rules needed to present the model as a playable game.

Our concern is with the integration of a monetary control mechanism over a mutating economy. We are concerned with minimally complex models that can illustrate a given phenomenon in a closed monetary economy. In an attempt to conform with the modeling requirements of consistency, completeness, conservation, dimensional analysis, and scaling we are required to specify many institutional features that are easy to overlook but whose functions appear as logical necessities.

The nature of institutions performing the same necessary function may differ, giving us many choices of a sufficient structure. In essence logical consistency must be satisfied along with technological adequacy.

Although in the highly simplified model below because we limit our investigation to only one random variable and are able to consider an eventual stationary equilibrium state, we believe and expect to show that with additional considerations such as an opportunity to innovate each period in a monetarily controlled evolving economy, paths are historic, the transients are eternal, and equilibrium in a conventional sense does not exist.[17]

9.9.1   Innovation with central bank finance and fiat money only

The model presented here is simplified as much as possible in favor of monetary control as all trade is monetized and must be paid for in fiat. There are only three types of agents: governments and firms which are corporate entities, and ultimate owner-consumers who are natural persons.

Consider an example where the only source for extra money to finance innovation is a central bank.

9.9.1.1   The central bank   Before we consider the creation of credit by commercial banks or financiers, we may restrict ourselves to a "cash-on-the-barrelhead" economy with one form of money, gold or fiat. We select fiat as the central bank money. We consider the central bank as the only agent with the power to supply and remove money from the economy. To start with, however, we consider the central bank as passive.

$\rho_1 = 1$ is the central bank rate of interest on the deposits of the consumers or firms.[18]

$\rho_2 = 1$ is the central bank rate of interest for loans to the consumers or firms. The bank makes loans or accepts deposits at the will of the firms and consumers.

$\mu^* = $ the bankruptcy penalty per unit of unpaid debt.

9.9.1.2   The consumer-owners as savers   Let

$$u(x) = 100x - .5x^2$$

be the one-period utility function for the consumer where $0 \leq x \leq 100$.

The full-game payoff for a consumer is

$$U(m_1) = \sum_{t=1}^{T} \beta^{t-1} \left(100x_t - .5x_t^2 + \mu^* m_t^- \right) + v(m_{T+1}),$$

where m_t^- signifies a negative monetary balance at the start of time t and μ^* is society's (or the bankruptcy court's) evaluation of the marginal utility of negative money.[19]

If $m_t < 0$ at the start of time t and no rollover of debt is permitted, then a penalty of size $\mu^* m_t$ is levied and m_t is reset to $m_t = 0$ and the agent may borrow again.

The worth of fiat or debt at the final settlement day is $v(m_{T+1})$:

$$v(m_{T+1}) = \begin{cases} \beta^T \mu^* m_{T+1} & \text{if } m_{T+1} < 0 \\ \beta^T \mu^{**} m_{T+1} & \text{if } m_{T+1} \geq 0 \end{cases}.$$

At the end of the game, for full specification we must specify how any positive amounts of fiat left over are to be evaluated in the payoff. There are several conventions possible; we select the following rule: The amount of fiat handed out to any agent at the start must be returned by the agent at final settlement. This may be interpreted as though the central bank had given the consumers an interest-free loan of size m_1 that must be returned at settlement. Any short-fall results in a deduction of score, while any positive residual is rewarded as indicated above.

The range $\mu^* - \mu^{**}$ may be regarded as a collar on the valuation of money, where μ^* may be regarded as the highest marginal value of money to be expected and μ^{**} is the lowest marginal value to be expected. In an experimental game these can be clearly enunciated by the referee. In an economy the first can be regarded as a bankruptcy penalty announced by government and the second as an expectation of the future worth, or purchasing power, or an intuitively selected aggregate measure that the individual may wish to select, such as Friedman's "permanent income" valuation.

m_t = the amount of money at the start of period t after the clearinghouse has settled all accounts,
$\bar{m}_t$ = the amount of money at the end of period t.

Thus generally $m_t = \bar{m}_{t-1}+$ dividends $+$ interest earned $-$ interest owed, and $\bar{m}_t = m_t -$ bids $-$ deposits $+$ loans.

Consider initial conditions for the quadratic example in which the initial stationary state has the consumer at, say, $x = 40$ and $p = 60$.

Let $m_1 = 4,800$ be the amount of money held by the consumers at the start of period 1. (Initial holdings of fiat money may be considered as including dividend and interest payments from all sources from last period's earnings paid immediately at the start of the new period via a completely efficient clearinghouse.)

We consider:

$\beta = 1/2$ as the utility discount,
$p_t =$ the market price of the input/output good at time t,
$b_t^\alpha =$ the monetary bid of the consumer α at time t for consumption goods,
$x_t^\alpha =$ the amount consumed by the consumer α at time t.[20]

9.9.1.3 The firms For simplicity in both exposition and computation, we employ a simple linear production function with a limited capacity. Let the measure of all firms be 1.

$i =$ the input of goods for production. Production takes one period.

$$f(i) = \begin{cases} 2i \text{ if } i \le 40 \\ 80 \text{ if } i > 40 \end{cases}, \text{ where each firm's profit is measured independently.}$$

$\Pi^\phi =$ the firm ϕ's per-period profit at time t. It is given by $p_t q_t - a_{t-1}(1+\rho)$.
$a_{t-1} =$ the monetary bid of the firms for input goods in the previous period and

$$i_t = \frac{a_t}{p_t} \text{ and } q_t = f(i_{t-1}) = 2i_{t-1},$$

where

$$p_t = \frac{\int a_t^\phi + \int b_t^\alpha}{\int q_t^\phi}.$$

We observe that without innovation we can avoid intricate computation for the optimization problem of the firm and replace it with either

$$i = \begin{cases} i = 0 \text{ if expected profit is negative} \\ i = 40 \text{ if expected profit is nonnegative} \end{cases}.$$

This follows from the linearity of the profit function that is linear until it hits the capacity constraint.

The initial holdings of a firm are $(0, 40)$. It has no money and 40 units of goods in process.

By inspection one may verify that the steady-state solution for the system is as follows:

$b = 40 \times 60 = 2{,}400$

$a = 2{,}400$

$p = 60$

$q = 80$

$i = 40.$

In particular a firm's profit for period 1 and all subsequent periods is

$$\Pi_1 = pq - pi\,(1 + \rho)$$
$$= 60 \times 80 - 60 \times 40 \times 2 = 0.$$

The firms earn 0 and the consumers gain

$$U(4800) = \left(\frac{1 - \beta^{T+1}}{1 - \beta} \right) (100 \times 40 - .5 \times 1600)$$

$$= \left(\frac{1 - \left(\frac{1}{2}\right)^{T+1}}{\frac{1}{2}} \right) 3200 \text{ as } T \to \infty$$

which gives 6,400.

9.9.2   Breaking the flow

Innovation has not yet been discussed. It calls for a diversion of resources in at least one period and possibly in more later. For simplicity we assume that innovation takes one period and requires j units of input. $j = $ the amount of input needed for innovation. jp_1 may be viewed as the cost of a lottery ticket.

Suppose $j = 2$. Further consider that the probability of success is $\xi = 1/2$ and for failure is $(1 - \xi) = 1/2$. A successful invention cuts the input needs by 75 percent or to $1/4$. Thus after innovation half of the population of firms has had a considerable cost improvement and the other is as before, but both have paid for their lottery ticket. Initially 40 units were available to the consumers and the firms made no profit. Hence the value to the firms of the steady state is 0 to each.

We assume the firms have the single choice to innovate or not in the first period. They will need to borrow $2p_1$ to do so, and they will start to make payments on the loan in period 2.

If the firms decide to innovate, after the random move 1/2 of the firms succeed and 1/2 fail, hence 80 units go to market. The firms together need 25 for the next input and the price falls to 45, with the consumers buying 55. All the firms lose and make negative profits in period 2 of

$$45 \times 80 - 62 \times 40 (1+\rho) - Z_2$$
$$= -17 \times 80 - Z_2 = -1360 - Z_2$$

as, although the sale price has dropped, with matching accounting the cost of input from last period is at its highest. Then in period 3 full stationarity gives

$$45 [80 - 10 (1+\rho)] - Z_t$$
$$= 3600 - 900 - Z_t$$
$$= 2700 - Z_t$$

per period where Z_t is the payment in period t for the financing of the innovation loan to buy 2 units of the good for innovation purposes.

9.9.2.1   A problem in accrual and amortization   Our key concern is with the dynamics of the money supply during and after innovation. This is where the comments on breaking the circular flow of capital need to be operationalized. Schumpeter [326, p. 111] verbalized the problem of innovation thus: "If innovation is financed by credit creation, the shifting of factors is effected not by the withdrawal of funds—'canceling the old order'—from the old firms, but by the reduction of the purchasing power of existing funds."

In our model here the purchasing power of the consumers has gone down. The central bank has increased the money supply to the firms enough to enable them to displace consumer demand by 2 units. The amount of extra money required is $p_2 \times j = 62 \times 2 = 124$. At this point a problem in accounting and loan structure must be addressed. Should the loan appear on the income or the capital account or in part on both? At the extremes we have $Z_2 = 2p_2 (1+\rho)$ and $Z_t = 0$ for all $t > 2$. This treats all of the investment as a short-term loan immediately to be paid back. At the other extreme we may have all $Z_t = 2\rho p_t$ for all $t \geq 2$; the loan is amortized by a stream of interest payments. It is as though firms have a perpetual loan for which they need only service the debt each period. Reality usually lies between the short-term loan and the perpetuity with finite amortization.

For specificity we assume that the loan requires constant interest payment each period after the first, or $Z_t = 2\rho p_t = 124$ for all $t \geq 2$.

At the first period there will be 38 units of good available for the consumers and 42 for the firms. The price will be 62 and the upper bound on the profits for all firms together in period 1 will be

$$\Pi_1 = [80 \times 62 - 40 \times 60 \times 2]$$
$$= 4960 - 4800 = 160.$$

In period 2 the firms will know the outcome of their attempt at innovation; as noted above, all will lose money in period 2 due to lower prices and high input costs. From period 3 onward, profits are made; thus total profits are

$$\Pi = \frac{1}{2} \left[160 + \frac{1}{2} (-1360) + \left(\frac{1}{2} \right)^2 (2700 \times 2) \right]$$
$$+ \frac{1}{2} \left[160 + \frac{1}{2} (-1360) + \left(\frac{1}{2} \right)^2 (0) \right] - \sum_{t=2}^{\infty} Z_t$$
$$= 160 - 680 + 675 - \frac{1}{2} \times 2 \times 2 \times 62 = 31.$$

Several modeling issues remain. They concern limited liability, bankruptcy, and conservation of money.

9.9.2.2   A problem with limited liability   If a firm fails to innovate after trying, it is forced to go bankrupt as it is unable to pay back or even service its loan. This difficulty can be cured by unlimited liability, which is manifested in having the firms flow though the negative as well as positive profits. Paradoxically the consumers can pay back the debt for many periods, and this keeps useful capacity in production.

9.9.2.3   Bankruptcy and debtor in possession   An alternative solution to the problem of bankruptcy is to allow limited liability of the owners, permit bankruptcy at time t, and reset $m_t = 0$ wiping out the debt, leaving all unsuccessful firms making zero profits but providing the appropriate capacity. This reflects the Marshallian concept of the marginal firm in production that obtains no rents; thus it makes no profits as all income is paid out for factors of production. In bankruptcy this leaves the debtor in possession. The firm continues as a legal entity.

9.9.2.4   The central bank and cash flows   If the loan is serviced, then there is a cash flow of 124 every period out of the private economy to the central bank; but this implies that in a stationary physical state, given a fixed velocity and in spite of $1 + \rho = 1/\beta$, unless there is a counterflow the price level must be falling. However, if the consumers save enough this could be reversed.

In considering the debt to the bank of 124 units of money we must distinguish between debt service and repayment of capital.

The solution values from the model are summarized in table 9.2, where "Inc" is sales income and "Int" is loan interest payments; Π_1 is the profit of a successful firm. Thus a winner has a steady income of $2,576$ per period and a loser loses -124. The firms as a group earn $1,226$ per period.

9.9.2.5   A final stationary state?   The money supply has gone from a start at 4,800 to 4,924 in period 1, but at the price of 45 in period 2 only 3,600 is needed and the consumers could deposit $1,324$ in the bank, causing an influx of fiat. Suppose that they roll over this deposit until $T + 1$; then at settlement we have

$$\mu^{**}\beta^T m_{T+1} = 1 \times \left(\frac{1}{2}\right)^T \left[2^{T-2} \times 1324 + k\right].$$

As $T \to \infty$ this approaches $1324/4 = 331$, where k is anything else left over without an exponential growth.[21]

Paradoxically with $\mu^* = \mu^{**} = 1$ we have a solution following the contours with a bonus of 331 to the players at the end. The cash flow is shown in table 9.3.

Rather than presenting the depositors with the windfall, all or part could be taxed away.

Table 9.2

Exchange properties of the circular flow model

t	Π_1	Π_2	Inc	Exp	Int	p	Profit	x	$i+j$
0	0	0	4800	2400	0	60	0	40	40
1	160	160	4960	2480	0	62	160	38	42
2	-1360	-1360	3600	4960	124	45	-1360	55	25
3	2576	-124	3600	1125	124	45	2700	55	25
4	2576	-124	3600	1125	124	45	2700	55	25

Table 9.3

Cash flow time series

Period	1	2	3	4	5
Cash	4800	4924	3600	3600	3600

9.9.3   An aside on measurable utility

In our examples above, if we imagine that when the managers are the decision makers the owners all hold one big mutual fund, then from a decision-making point of view they face no uncertainty at all. They are presented with the old stationary economy if the managers choose not to innovate and a single well-defined different economy if they choose to do so; thus the demand function reflects only marginal utilities, not risk.[22] When this is the situation, the shape of the utility function is limited to any concavity-preserving function independent of lotteries. Unless we believe in an axiom linking risk aversion with changes in marginal utility [297, 335], the full range of risk aversion functions is consistent with the riskless demand.

Without carrying out any elaborate calculations, it follows immediately that we can display a robust set of examples where the owners would always reject innovation were they in control even though their expected consumption increases when the firm forces innovation on them.

9.9.3.1   Stockholders or debt owners?   With only one aggregte consumer-owner, the natural person is also the direct or ultimate[23] debt holder, and we can cook up examples where the firms' debt/equity ratios can be varied with no change in the investor-bondholder's earnings consistent with Modigliani and Miller's observations, as long as the bankruptcy conditions needed to fully define the game out of equilibrium do not become active. As long as behavior takes place away from the bankruptcy constraint, one cannot distinguish debt from equity. This provides a nice example of pitfalls in the tradeoff between verbal description and mathematical formulation.

9.9.4   An aside on gold or fiat

In chapter 4 we showed in detail basic control differences in the utilization of gold or fiat as a money. Concerning the difficulties in the properties of matter, to a good first approximation both fiat and gold can be used for transactions, but although fiat has no alternative use, gold does. In a stationary equilibrium with complete markets, fiat is more efficient as it releases gold for alternative use.

9.10   The Important Role of Experimental Gaming

We have suggested that we have doubts concerning the value of low-dimensional representative-agent models in applied economics; but we believe that they are of considerable importance in developing a scientifically sound economic theory.

There is a basic clash between the in vitro aspects of experimental gaming and the contextual richness of the in vivo problems they are meant to represent. The appropriate question concerning the workhorse model of the economic agent is to ask how much it explains experimentally in very simple reasonably controlled situations, and all of our models provide such a test bed. In particular these comments on innovation generate many testable hypotheses concerning complexity and terminal conditions.

9.10.1   Long- or short-term finance for innovation?

A modeling decision is required concerning how to finance innovation. At this point it is natural to introduce the long-term loan. In general, even though the expected future discounted flow of profits may be sufficient to repay the loan with interest, it is often unlikely that this will be feasible in the one period of a short-term loan. We could consider a sequence of rollovers of one-period loans, as has occurred in a more sophisticated manner with the use of repos [168] or other instruments; but this will depend on the micro-microeconomics of risk sharing. Above we considered the instance where the costs of innovation are charged to the capital account and only the servicing of the loan is attributed to the income account. The easiest long-term loan to handle is the perpetuity loan of infinite duration that permits payments involving just the servicing of the loan. Finite amortization may influence the decision making.

Even without adding the complexity of a different profile for the time preference among consumers, the need for financing of innovation is sufficient to justify the need for long-term loans. The reason is simple. Although an investment needed to cover a profitable risky innovation will more than repay the investor when adding the discounted cash flows associated with it, the profile of the profits may be such that it is not possible to repay the loan in the single period required by a one-period non-rollover loan under all circumstances. At the very least we must assume that a loan rollover is always available. If there is uncertainty intervening each period, then the interaction between possible default and loan length becomes of concern.

9.10.2   Finite amortization

We utilize the infinite horizon here for loans because our point is to show that there is some tractable model with long-term financing and a "consol"-style loan that can be handled conventionally. Finite amortization in discrete-period models can readily be defined, but it can rapidly become complicated to solve. In general, if a loan spans more than one period, it will take on a natural repayment term that depends on the parameters of production and consumption, as these interact with the discrete-period structure. If periods are defined that model repeated, equal intervals of real time, the repayment schedule may lead to a complex cascade of difference equations to be solved self-consistently with matching conditions in the period when the loan is fully repaid. If a type-symmetric model has only solutions in which agents partition into multiple types that use different strategies, the combination of multiple difference equations with matching conditions as the different loans are repaid can rapidly lead to a collection of cases that is opaque at best and intractable in general.[24] We suggest that finite term structure of long-term debt is better handled with continuous time [363]. However, with discrete time we do handle the upper and lower bounds on amortization. They are given by the perpetuity and the one-period loans.

9.11   An Observation on Government Control and Its Degrees of Freedom

In introducing the role of government in a monetary economy, considerable care needs to be taken in counting and accounting for the number of degrees of freedom being introduced into the set of strategies that are attributable to governmental power. A brief listing of some of the potential weapons of government control includes taxation, subsidies, the fixing of interest rates at which it might borrow or lend, manipulation of the money supply, reserve ratios, bankruptcy and default laws and routines, limits on national debt, and the issue of bonds and notes. All of these provide many dimensions for government action, and when approached without context provided, they supply the extra degrees of freedom that enable government as a player to do almost anything. In fact sociopolitical reality provides bounds and tradeoffs on all of them and thus restricts the powers of government. Several policies that appear to be equivalent from the viewpoint of economics may be differentiated on the basis of political acceptability.

Here, so far, we have explicitly limited government participation to a passive role in borrowing or lending on request or on flowing through funds.

9.11.1   A comment on consumer-created credit

The understanding of money and financial institutions calls for a delicate mix of abstract theory combined with institutional understanding. At a high level of abstraction the concept of every individual issuing her own currency cannot be dismissed. There is a literature on the idea of everyone being a banker [33, 311, 391]—i.e., of an economy where every agent writes his or her own IOU notes and they are accepted as a universal means of exchange. While this is logically feasible, nevertheless with highly implausible information, communication, and enforcement conditions together with free perfect memory accounting one can actually construct and run an experimental game where all players create their own currency and verify that under these stringent conditions the generation of individual currency can produce efficient trade [189]. As a model of reality it leaves much to be desired. It can be beaten onto a bed of Procrustes to produce this explanation if one's goal is to exhibit a logical possibility regardless of any sense of context and transaction costs. We omit this model here, but note that in a limited context individuals can and do produce their own means of payment, especially when bank lending is tight, and thereby weaken the power of both the commercial banks and a central bank. In particular with modern technology if two or three large corporations have a considerable amount of trade among themselves over many periods it may be in their self-interest to establish a computerized netting system to settle gross trades.

9.12   Ongoing Innovation Opportunities

In this consideration of the financing of innovation we have confined our observations to one simple random event at the start. There is no difficulty in extending the Robinson Crusoe model directly. No more conceptual difficulties of basic importance appear. When a monetary economy is considered this is not so.

Even when we utilize gross simplifications, the conditions needed to establish the convergence of both real resources and financial arrangements from nonequilibrium initial conditions to an equilibrium do not exist in any generality. With an innovation choice in each period influenced by chance, the turbulence will increase considerably, and the characterization of even the simplest market with innovation with a random element in each period will lead to a path-dependent nonsymmetric distribution of firm size and stochastic increasing returns of the variety indicated by Brian Arthur [14].

Under serial innovation opportunities, individual trajectories will generally become unpredictable simply due to stochasticity. This alone does not imply that predictability is lost in the system, only that if it remains it shifts to other properties such as moments of distributions over trajectories. The most important factor determining whether an increase in the number of goods and the number of serial innovation opportunities increases or decreases predictability is the *correlation* between the current state of a player and the opportunities available to him. If the two are largely uncorrelated, distributions over trajectories may converge rapidly to highly reproducible forms (whether stationary or time-dependent). In that case, while an individual's fate may vary over instantiations of the innovation outcome process, if the individual's decisions depend only on instruments that diversify over the trajectories of others, the economy as a whole may remain stable and amenable to rational expectations. If states and opportunities are highly correlated, the economy as a whole may take on unpredictable trajectories.

9.12.1   A comment on prices of long-term assets

In an actual economy there is a time profile of assets whose prices will be influenced at various levels up to being completely obsolete. Thus wide fluctuations in individual wealth are to be expected.

9.12.2   An aside on continuous time

A continuous-time model developed in a separate publication [363] employs a stopping rule: if Crusoe does not possess enough stock to invest in innovation, he passes the round and does not attempt it. This feature, combined with the fact that *any* nonzero production rate permits a recovery to the asymptotic production level, allows the number of agents who would ever achieve zero production and become stuck there to approach measure zero in the continuous-time limit. Therefore a lower bound of goods at which production approaches zero is a reflecting boundary, near which individuals may be unable to innovate but in which they do not become trapped. A different class of processes with states from which individuals cannot escape may also be considered. The latter are known as *absorbing states*,[25] and the class of statistics that can be computed for them includes distributions of absorption times or measures of agents who absorb in each state if more than one exists [119]. Stochastic population processes with many similar properties to those of a random portfolio affected by innovation have been developed in mathematical population genetics [118, 129, 215].

9.13   Summary Remarks

Our basic goal was to produce an adequate mathematical model that could reflect formally the meaning of Schumpeter's breaking of the circular flow of capital in a closed economy; and to show not only that the variation of the money and/or credit supply is a necessary (but insufficient) requirement, but that there are several other basic features that static or even dynamic conventional equilibrium models cannot capture. In particular nine other items are noted. The first three have been covered in this chapter, and the remaining six are addressed in chapter 10. The items are:

1. The concept of innovation and comparative statics,

2. Robinson Crusoe and the parallel worlds of goods and finance,

3. The problems posed concerning convergence that are critical even with only one random event,

4. Financing and control of innovation,

5. Financing and two-way causality,

6. Bankruptcy as the delimiter of risk in a loosely coupled system,

7. Bankruptcy and the money supply as public goods controlling mutation,

8. That failure involves the destruction of credit not government money,

9. That the locus of innovation finance may be public or private.

Innovation utilizes existing resources. It involves developing and employing a process that previously was unknown or not deemed feasible. This is modeled here by considering an economy, essentially in a stationary state, where in each period there is a small ϵ probability that a new process is seen sufficiently clearly that it is deemed to be worth considering as a candidate for investment. Thus it is possible that for many periods the contemplation of an innovation remains below a threshold for consideration. Once there is a realization of the ϵ probability event, the perceptual conditions for innovation are met and the stationary equilibrium may be broken. Perhaps a better term for the initial stationary equilibrium is a "$1/\epsilon$-stationary equilibrium." This indicates that the expected time the stationary state may last unchallenged is $1/\epsilon$.

An understanding of Robinson Crusoe's innovation opportunities provides a clear preliminary way to understand the roles of real resources and ownership control prior to seeing the strategic decoupling offered by money and the financial system in a complex economy [200].

Even if the system were in equilibrium originally, innovation has to disturb the equilibrium, and even with only one shock to the system the time to attain a new equilibrium is ad hoc depending on the specific structure of production and consumption.

We reiterate:

- Innovation is a physical process; it may take place without involving finance.

- When there is a financial system present in an economy, two sets of adjustment processes are set in motion. Even under relatively simple circumstances (such as only one commodity and money), even if the existence of an adjustment process can be proved (see [365] for proof), the adjustment to equilibrium may be of arbitrary length.

- In general, conservation of money rules out the ability of profit-maximizing firms to increase profits with innovation unless the money supply is increased.

- The ability to increase the money supply confers power over the decision to innovate.

- In particular it is easy to construct instances where a firm that is maximizing expected profits will not act in the best interests of the stockholders even if an open stock market exists. In practice the highly imperfect management decision-making with managers or dominant stockholders in control and the law court's availability appear to be an evolving economy's "good enough" solution.

Notes

1 As this is easily formulated as an experimental game with innovation, one could test the divergence in performance between human nonexperts and the "rational" noncooperative players of our theory.

2 One of our goals is to provide some sufficiently tractable examples that can serve as a basis for experimental games.

3 In a separate publication [363] we have considered this approach.

4 Central bank reserves in a fiat money economy are a creation of law and possibly economic theology. Mathematically they are just societal rules of the game or an algorithm stating how the central bank can create money. They specify its strategy set. In actuality the strategy set is also bounded by political pressures.

5 In general central banks do not accept deposits from natural persons, but for modeling simplicity here we permit them to do so.

6 The optimization may or may not be corrected for any inflation discount beyond selecting $1 + \rho = 1/\beta$ in order to stack our assumptions in favor of rational-expectation models. When the

payoff function is linear, producer durables are either short-lived or with no depreciation, and taxes or simple inflation correction may not make a difference to behavior.

7 We may regard the bank as an aggregate abstraction of the commercial and central banking system with the profits made being either held in reserve (+ or −) or spent on buying resources to support the bureaucracy, or paid out as a subsidy to some part of the population.

8 In a less draconian abstraction the difference between retirees and capitalists is not merely age but expertise. The role of competence in finance involving record keeping, calculation, perception, and evaluation cannot be overstressed.

9 In institutional fact the large firm has a considerable constituency of customers, employees, the government, and others as well as the owners.

10 Of course, the proportion ν has to be strictly less than one; for otherwise there is no one to engage in productive activity, own the firms, or receive their profits, and the model unravels.

11 Depreciation times are given in [356]. Here we exclude the capital value of gold and land, which legally are nondepreciating assets.

12 Bankruptcy in a basic way is similar to innovation in the sense that it may involve a nonequilibrium redeployment of assets.

13 In numerically explicit examples we will take the capacity threshold $C = 25$.

14 We make $\xi(j)$ a function of j to reflect the possible dependence of the outcome on investment level while leaving the form of the outcome the same for simplicity. If a continuous range of j values were admitted, a first-order condition for investment level would be required. In examples here we permit only $j = 0$ or one nonzero value to avoid complexity.

15 Some variations include the following:
Suppose individual i starts with m_i and the firm with 0 units of money. The game ends at T and all accounts are settled at $T + 1$.

Case 1a: Money has no value at $T + 1$. By backward induction a no-trade equilibrium is obtained. If goods in process delivered as goods at $T + 1$ have some positive salvage in money, the referee has a definitional problem. Does this increase the firm's payoff to the detriment of the owners?

Case 1b: Money has no value at $T + 1$ but an outside bank offers to lend at fixed interest rate $\rho > 0$ (or possibly $\rho = \rho(T)$ and as $T \to \infty$ then $\rho(T) \to 0$ on the open set). All debt must be paid back by $T + 1$ or a penalty in proportion to debt is suffered.

Case 2a: Money has a specific value at the end (say the marginal value at the first period) discounted by β^T.

Case 2b: Money has a specific value, but first all must return their initial bundle to the government, then anything left over ($\pm$) obtains the terminal valuation.

Now we go to the limit as $T \to \infty$.
    When does the value of the limit games equal the value of games at the limit? And how are these distinctions reflected in the economics?
    We note that the presence of overlapping generations kills the "natural discount" story and possibly brings out the importance of inheritance.

16 We do not carry the extra index α as its presence should be clear from context.

17 At best we can hope for a stochastic definition such as a fixed point in a function space.

18 The interest rate of $\rho = 1$ is picked on purpose to kill the preinnovation equilibrium profits of the firm and to raise problems with the treatment of bankruptcy. Any lower rate would yield profits to the firms.

19 For simplicity we may consider a linear default penalty, but it could be replaced by a more complex rule as long as the penalty remains high enough.

20 When it is clear from context we omit individual-agent superscripts.

21 $k = m_0 + 2p_1\rho$ or the initial money supplied plus the capital for investment retired.

22 The utility function $u(x) = 100x - .5x^2$ could have equally well been written as $\varphi(u(x))$ where φ is a concavity-preserving transformation. $u(x)$ likwise is defined only up to φ unless $v(m)$ is linear. If so φ is defined up to a linear transformation. In the two examples with $T \to \infty$, the first has $v(m)$ linear, the second does not.

23 If he is a depositor in the central bank or other intermediary that flows through his deposit as a loan, he is an indirect holder of the firms' debts.

24 An alternative approach with discrete periods, when type-nonsymmetric solutions arise, would be to let period lengths vary in such a way that one full repayment occurs within each period, so that repayment and matching conditions are handled at period boundaries as in the model of section 9.8.4. The number of periods required would then equal the number of distinct combinations of repayment states taken by players in the economy. While possible in principle, defining the correct length-dependent production functions and consumption utilities raises a different set of technical difficulties, suggesting that in application to an operational problem an ad hoc approach is called for.

Our approach to minimizing technical overhead and distractions, while illustrating the essential problem of rational optimization in type-nonsymmetric solutions with amortized repayment, is to make the period length arbitrarily short compared to amortization schedules, scaling production functions and consumption utilities appropriately so that a consistent continuous-time limit is defined.

In the dynamics of innovation one should consider both efficiency and capacity increased. The more efficient firms may wish to enlarge capacity to take advantage of cost effectiveness. A model similar to a combination of cost and capacity innovation, with these properties, is defined and solved elsewhere [363]. The absence of an intrinsic timescale removes much of the complexity of difference equations, and leaves matching conditions only at the repayment events defined by the repayment timescales that emerge from the dynamics of different kinds of agents interacting strategically through a common price system.

25 See [343] for an early example of an absorbing state associated with bankruptcy.

10 Innovation and Evolution: Growth and Control

10.1 Preamble

In connecting Walras and modern general equilibrium theory with Keynes and Schumpeter we have confined ourselves to one-ply games with a government and a central bank and initial and terminal conditions specified. One can take the fundamental first step in going from no-process to full-process models with only one strategic move per player and minimal information. A case can be made for considering the noncooperative equilibrium as a reasonable solution concept. With a few reasonable restrictions, there are not that many behavioral solutions that can be suggested for a one-shot game. Pandora's box is opened at two-ply or more. Then the whole world of learning, teaching signaling, nonsymmetric information and habit, herd and rule-of-thumb behavior must all be specified in order to be able to take the description of the institutional carriers of process[1] and add behavioral rules that lead to specifying the equations of motion.

In chapter 9, although we have broad misgivings about the application of the rational-expectations solution concept to growth models with even a reasonable amount of complexity, we solved several examples, in part to be able to formulate fully experimental games that could be used to test the behavioral validity of rational expectations, but even more importantly to show that a one-shot Schumpeterian breaking of the circular flow of capital could be completely mathematized within an initial and terminal equilibrium framework, and acheived with minimal control by the government.

Disequilibrium and the full force of evolution emerges with period-by-period strategic ability to innovate (see section 9.12). Here our concern is more with government guidance, the mechanisms, instruments, and institutions and their control functions, rather than with the computation of another rational-expectations solution.

There is such a plethora of reasonable but complex models that can be specified and so few hard facts on behavior that the full development and analysis of a completely specified dynamic model is heavily dependent upon both context and specific questions to be answered.

The era of the large macroeconomic many-equation structural model of the economy with many parameters reestimated frequently appears to have passed, but technology has changed, and economic knowledge and computational and simulation ability have increased. The early advocates of the large mechanistic simulation such as Jay Forester of MIT [134] or the vast databank-organizing simulation such as Guy Orcutt of Yale [279] advocated have gone and are, for the most part, forgotten, but the data gathering and processing and the feasibility of manipulating large models have completely changed in the last 40 years. We have reserved most of our comments, recommendations, and obiter dicta concerning practice and the intersection between theory and practice to chapter 13; here we make an exception concerning simulation and experimental gaming.

10.1.1   Science, policy, and truth in packaging

Neither these authors nor anyone else has achieved the dynamic theory of economic behavior; but it is well worth the theorist's time to simplify assumptions about both structure and behavior to obtain as low-dimensional a context and parameter-free a representation of structure and behavior as she deems plausible and to analyze the implications of such a model. One may then wish to switch roles and behave as an advisor or advocate claiming that the low-dimensional analysis provides the best advice available. The politics and sociology of the melding of science and policy advice may be such that this is about all that is feasible; however, we suggest a politically naive alternative.

The coordination problem is central to many aspects of a complex economy, as it is to any complex evolving organism. The government as a whole as well as the central bank in particular must provide much of the coordination and conflict resolution for the economy. We propose the creation of an operational gaming section in any national central bank. This would be done in concert with the economics research departments of universities and policy and research institutions. Several economic models varying in size from large such as the Ray Fair macroeconomic model [120] down to smaller specialized models devised to answer only one or two specific questions would be utilized and reformulated as parts of an overall playable game open to modification during the game. This would provide a structured debate aimed at examining jointly the political, bureaucratic, and economic feasibility of proposed policies.

A large war game may use small formal operations research models such as a damage exchange model between submarines and destroyers to predict tactical outcomes that feed back to the strategic game. An economic game might use a formal small model to calculate the first-order outcomes of a change in taxation.

In a central-bank-hosted econo-political exercise (EPE) the players would consist of bank and other government bureaucrats, selected politicians, and business executives. There would be three playing teams and the referee team. The playing teams would be the central bank, an aggregate of other government agents concerned with fiscal problems, and the private business sector. The consumers' demand and many other aspects of the overall economy would be parts of the simulation. The largest model and the smaller ones would bear a relationship to each other similar to that between the special operations research models and the overall game in a major war game, such as those employed in the politico-military exercises at the Naval War College in the United States and in other military establishments. There the key aspects of the game are decisions of the teams, possibly rejected by the referee team as implausible, then modified and accepted in joint discussion and utilized as inputs into the overall simulation. Thus the game combines an operational debate evaluating intangibles with a period-by-period formal simulation where not just the technical parameters are being updated but the assumptions and concepts behind the game are being challenged. The design calls for the utilization of financial historians much in the same way that the military gaming scenarios employ military historians [82].

The gaming facility responsible for producing these operational "war games" would provide a link between operational applications and research in the sense that as a product incidental to the operational purpose there is an implicit or explicit ongoing critique of the formal economic models and simulations involved.

A major weakness with this proposal is its political feasibility. It is not axiomatic that a political stakeholder welcomes operational clarification.

10.2   Aspects of an Innovating Economy

The last chapter on innovation stressed the breaking of the circular flow of funds and an attempt to vary the money supply via a passive central bank. This chapter notes some of the problems that appear with innovation in a financial system that has commercial banks, a national debt, and other loci of control.

In particular, items to be covered are:

1. Utility and/or wealth optimization,
2. The role of many assets and side payments,
3. Financing and control of innovation,
4. Financing and two-way causality,
5. Bankruptcy as the delimiter of risk in a loosely coupled system,
6. Bankruptcy and the money supply as public goods controlling mutation,
7. Failure as involving the destruction of credit, not government money,
8. The locus of innovation finance whether public or private.

10.2.1   Utility and/or wealth optimization

The utility function was devised, developed, and replaced by the map of preferences in the study of consumption under certainty. One of the earlier and elegant developments of mathematical economics was the theory of consumer choice. Glued together with a theory of production, cleverly closed, this produced general equilibrium theory. The utility function went out of fashion with theorists, who observed that consumer choice under certainty utilized only ordinal properties of preference. This apparent great generality dies, however, when we are dealing with decision making under uncertainty.

The axiomatization of measurable utility introduced by von Neumann and Morgenstern in 1944 [411] was not at first well received by the profession, as is evinced in the commentary by Baumol [40], but in the next two decades, especially with the development of a theory of finance, it became a centerpiece. Interest was renewed in the work of Bernoulli, and Menger [258] considered problems with and solutions to the Bernoulli paradox and the utility of money, from which some open questions remain to this day.

The measurement of the utility of money began to be used in finance within the development of a set of partial equilibrium models in an open economy with no concern with the details of consumer choice. Since the 1970s there has been a development both in macro- and microeconomics of the use of dynamic programming and rational expectations. Bewley [31], Lucas [232], Shubik and Whitt [366], Stokey and Lucas [394], and Karatzas, Shubik, and Sudderth [199] provide examples. In both the macro- and microeconomic applications noted, essentially for reasons of mathematical tractability the commodity set was aggregated into a single aggregate commodity, thereby obliterating the structure's suitability for the study of any of the details of consumption, but stressing its use for the study of income and wealth measured in terms of money.

We suggest that the picture of the consumer painted in Hicks [184] or in Debreu [79] is a mathematical picture of consumers who have to ration their wealth over consumption goods, and certainly is not descriptive of the entrepreneurs or financiers with plutomania whose mantra may be "the player who dies with the most chips wins," or the many fiduciaries whose performances are measured in money returns.

At the level of abstraction adhered to in this book, the assumption that the natural persons within a society all have the same preferences is a useful approximation. It is reasonable to consider several different segments of a wealth-utility function that determine behavior as a function of wealth. Table 10.1 based on the study of Edward Nathan Wolff [421] displays the distribution of income and wealth in the United States in 2010.

Those with incomes in the bottom two quintiles have essentially a hand-to-mouth existence. As the income flows in, it is spent on consumption. The net wealth of households at an income level of around $30,000 or less a year, such as it is, is in real consumer goods such as clothing, furniture, consumer durables, automobiles, and housing. The financial wealth of these families is negligible, and for many negative.[2]

As the family's income rises, the utilization of income for subsistence consumption starts to weaken. More goods and better-quality goods may enter into consumption, and the holding of real consumption assets grows. The rented

Table 10.1

Wealth and income in the United States, 2010

W or I	M Inc (2009)	M N W	M F W
Top 1%	$1,318,200	$16,439,400	$15,171,600
Top 20%	$226,200	$2,061,600	$1,719,800
Bottom 80%	$72,000	$216,900	$100,700
Bottom 60%	$41,000	$61,000	$12,200
Bottom 40%	$17,300	−$10,600	−$14,800

Note: W or I = Wealth or Income; M Inc = Mean Income; M N W = Mean Net Wealth; M F W = Mean Financial Wealth.

apartment may be replaced by the house. As income continues to rise, financial saving in the form of savings accounts and holdings in money market or mutual funds starts to appear. Somewhere between incomes of say $1,000,000 and $20,000,000 the disconnect between marginal income and consumption becomes more or less complete.[3] The extra money is no longer consumption money but is primarily investment money (after status and ego money uses have been accounted for). At the lower end of the income scale we have the poorer consumers who devote their total income and time to consumption. At the upper end of the scale some extra income may be spent to aid in the mechanics of consumption, delegated to interior decorators, caterers, chauffeurs, servants, and others; but the bulk is primarily for investment.

In order to formalize this heuristic sketch we need to take into account the considerations noted below.

10.2.1.1   Goods, services, financial instruments, and wealth   As we sweep over income levels, the consumers are concerned with:

• Consumables and services,

• Consumer durables,

• Simple financial instruments such as mutual fund shares, land, possibly gold,

• More complex financial assets and structures,

• Political and social power and prestige.

10.2.1.2   The economics of pure consumer choice without uncertainty
Pure consumer choice à la Hicks [184] has the economic agent purchase the services of perishables and consumer durables subject to an income constraint. In the presentation the distinction between stocks and flows is hardly made. Suppose:

M_1 is a set of consumables,
$|M_1| = m_1$ is the number of consumables,
M_2 is a set of consumer durables,
$|M_2| = m_2$ is the number of consumer durables,
$u(x_1, \ldots, x_{m_1}; \dot{y}_1, \ldots, \dot{y}_{m_2})$ is the utility of consumption,
$(a_1, \ldots, a_{m_1}; b_1, \ldots, b_{m_2})$ are initial resources,
$(p_1, \ldots, p_{m_1})$ are prices of consumables,
$(\hat{p}_1, \ldots, \hat{p}_{m_2})$ are prices of services of consumer durables,
$(\tilde{p}_1, \ldots, \tilde{p}_{m_2})$ are prices of consumer durables,
x_j is the consumption of a consumable j,
$\dot{y}_j$ is the consumption of the services of a durable j.

The consumer optimization is given by

$$\max u(x_1,\ldots,x_{m_1};\dot{y}_1,\ldots,\dot{y}_{m_2})$$

subject to

$$\sum_{i=1}^{m_1} p_i(a_i - x_i) + \sum_{j=1}^{m_2}(\tilde{p}_j b_j - \hat{p}_j y_j) \le 0. \tag{10.1}$$

One of the crowning joys of the 1930s–1940s exposition of consumer choice was to observe that the optimization subject to wealth constraint did not need to involve a utility function. It was often stated that the utility function could be defined up to an arbitrary ordinal transformation. However, if one were to enlarge the domain of choice to include contingent commodities, then under the von Neumann axioms it could be defined only up to an arbitrary linear transformation.

Even without the extra axiom on gambles, if convexity of the utility function were lost the market would endogenously introduce gambling.

10.2.1.3   Finance and the von Neumann utility
Uncertainty is the key to the von Neumann treatment of utility. He enlarged the choice set and added one extra axiom beyond the axioms for a preference ordering to give a utility function defined up to a linear transformation. The axiom was the equivalence of a certainty outcome to a lottery ticket. Given $a \succ b \succ c$, there exists a probability η such that $\eta a + (1 - \eta)c \sim b$. Given this condition, the utility function u is determined up to two parameters such that $\alpha u + \beta$ will also serve as a representation of the utility function.[4] If there is a natural zero point, such as the worth of no trade, the modeler may select $\beta = 0$ and the utility is defined up to an affine transformation. If interpersonal comparisons are possible then the α may be fixed.[5]

An individual is deemed to be risk-neutral if

$$\eta a + (1 - \eta)c = b$$

implies that

$$\eta u(a) + (1 - \eta)u(c) = u(b). \tag{10.2}$$

The development of much of finance such as portfolio theory, the analysis of options, and the construction of derivatives has taken place in a world where lottery tickets are the primary reality. Implicitly in studying any market the economic reality of the actual corporation together with its management and physical product is replaced by a lottery ticket measured in money. Due diligence, securities evaluation, and other aspects of evaluation are abstracted away from the financial analysis. Depending on the question being asked, this may be deemed to be an excellent or highly inadequate abstraction.

In finance the stress is on the utility of wealth of the individual measured essentially in terms of money. Thus "how much is X worth" is answered by adding up all assets deemed to be liquid, then adding the other assets, with estimates or guesstimates of the orderly liquidation worth of the other assets, with haircuts given to reflect any market imperfections.

In utilizing the overall utility function for wealth one must take care to avoid a post hoc ergo propter hoc fallacy, confusing the induced valuation of producer assets at an equilibrium solution with the intrinsic valuation by individual consumers who can neither eat nor evaluate steel mills. Investment bankers and deal makers may do this evaluation as part of the ongoing money game. The major study of finance is within the development of an open and not full feedback model; thus in those models the influence of the government on the utility for money may be regarded as exogenously given, and previous prices are hard evidence but not sufficient alone to provide the behavioral basis for the formation of expectations.

10.2.1.4   The rich consumer-investor   At the lower end of the wealth scale consumer choice is concerned with hand-to-mouth existence, with finance appearing as a more or less tight constraint on the procurement of consumption goods and services. This contrasts with the richer end where consumption goods and services are merely part of the real goods allocation and monetary wealth. By conservation, all goods have to be somewhere. The steel plants, the industrial farms, hotels, the buildings and factories have owners who do not derive direct utility from the vast array of large durable assets.

In a modern society the government may own anywhere between 10 and 50 percent of the physical infrastructure such as roads, land, public buildings. Few individuals own large assets in a direct manner. They own the public or private shares of the institutions that own the assets.

10.2.2   The utility-wealth function

Nowadays people know the price of everything and the value of nothing.
—Oscar Wilde, *The Picture of Dorian Gray*

Wilde's rhetoric is closer to the basic problems in finance than he conceived. In a complex society the evaluation of the worth of many assets and their prices may require considerable skill and perception.

If we view the utility-wealth function that the individual is meant to optimize as the sum over all expected consumption streams until death, then at any point we are forced to include current valuations of his long-term physical and financial assets. The discussion presented here is related to but different in detail and emphasis from the Friedman permanent income hypothesis (see [144] and others).

The study of finance is about equities, debt, and hybrid instruments such as corporate shares, bonds, and derivatives and how they connect with real means of production, durable assets, and other financial instruments and are evaluated in terms of money. In contrast consumption theory is usually discussed over a high-dimensional commodity space, and the mapping into one dimension which is meant to represent a utility function is of little interest in the study of most questions in consumer choice. Finance theory tends to deal just with a single-good "money" and complex lottery tickets involving valuations of institutions and processes in terms of money bets.

If we look at a rich individual both consuming and investing, it is reasonable to deal with two representations. The first deals with consumption preferences, emphasizing choice among consumption goods and services subject to an investment decision constraint which may easily be lower than either the wealth or the income constraint. The second representation deals with a utility-of-wealth function for investment that has, in essence, allocated consumption to a separate anaylsis connected to it by the lower bound reflected in the implicit or explicit decision on what to spend this year.[6] The financial decision payoff function is reasonably represented by a one-dimensional utility for wealth.

For many operational questions in finance and consumption theory it is most convenient to use the two different representations.

The individual or family is at least two agents, and this unit illustrates the roles of aggregation, disaggregation, and money faced by a single decision maker. Depending on the aggregation used, the goods and services space may vary from a few dozen to a few thousand dimensions. When running a house, going to a movie, or buying groceries, several alternative goods and services are considered. When buying a major consumer durable such as a new car or a house the problem may be framed as: Can we afford it (or do we have enough money)? The investment and ownership side of the family is primarily represented in money.

If we try to model the behavior of the rich, we need to consider context and usually select a different representation for production and consumption, with a money representation dominating production and the acquisition of the ownership of direct or indirect production assets.

A way to investigate some of the implications of an asset-rich economy is to consider as a first-order approximation that most individuals have a utility-wealth function that consists of a concave function up to some level of wealth followed by an unbounded linear utility function, where the concave segment represents the level of wealth at which one is still concerned about consumption. Beyond that point the additional wealth is for chips at the investment table.

10.2.3   Fiduciary behavior and utility

We know that the vast majority of financial decisions are made by fiduciaries. The fiduciaries are legal but not natural persons. They are for the most part clearly owned by natural persons.[7] The social psychology of formal group decision making is a topic that is not completely terra incognita, but even with agency theory what the firm maximizes has many answers. Minimal complexity and ease in analysis call for expected discounted profits as a goal, or the "utility function" of the firm. There are some questions for which this may be a reasonable approximation, but, as has already been noted in chapter 5, large bureaucracies may have many other goals.

10.2.4   Risk-neutral rich and fiduciaries and the risk-averse others

Even if all natural persons were considered as having the same preferences, in an economy with considerable uncertainty the rich and the fiduciaries may be expected in aggregate to assume most of the investment risk and to earn accordingly. However, in a complex economy with an information processing division of labor in finance as well as an industrial division of labor, this nonsymmetry could be even larger. Those not in the financial world may be unaware of many of the risks that are there. Furthermore there are many risks they may be aware of but do not understand. The nonprofessional does not have the training, skills, perceptions, or time to perceive and evaluate risk. The rich professionals not only buy and sell the risky assets, but expend much of their energy in minimizing the risk to themselves by selling off the parts they deem to be too dangerous to those who may be less perceptive than themselves. This is all part of the politicoeconomic valuation process.

10.2.5   An aside on quasi–side payment cooperative games

Side payment cooperative-game theory offers a way to study phenomena such as cartels or mergers and acquisitions among oligopolistic players. The use of the characteristic function to consider oligopolistic structures and solutions such as the core was first considered [346] as early as 1956. No further analysis to this approach is given here;[8] but the central observation is made that in an economy with innovation, a nonsymmetric, oligopolistic form of industry is to be expected from the dynamics. This combined with the presence of many nonconsumption real assets and their financial instrument representations leads naturally to a quasi-cooperative structure in deal making in the oligopolistic "market" for firms.

10.3   Innovation in an Asset-Rich Economy

In chapter 9 we treated innovation in an asset-poor economy. Like many of the studies employing dynamic programming, we utilized a single aggregate consumption/production good. A far more felicitous but more difficult model requires the presence of producer durables to reflect the real wealth of a developed economy.

10.3.1   A discussion on an asset-rich economy

We could extend the example provided of the asset-poor economy in chapter 9 by adding extra durable commodities in the form of land and producer goods as part of production. Rather than provide an extra calculated example, a verbal sketch is given to stress the new feature and why it is worth considering.

In the previous model Crusoe had to expose himself to considerable loss in consumption in order to risk innovation. There was only one real commodity that served both as the input of the production processes and the only output available for both production and consumption in the society. A richer array of assets could change his risk.

Embellishing the classical land, labor, and capital trinity, we assume the existence of:

- A consumption good C;
- Labor E (which splits into labor and leisure);
- Land L which is an infinitely lived nonreproducible asset that plays a catalyst role in production;
- Reproducible capital goods[9] that do not appear in the utility function directly. Depending on ownership and use, they are more or less categorized as (a) producer durables and (b) consumer durables. For the purposes of illustrating the point, just the addition of land and labor is sufficient.

10.3.1.1   Consumption   We assume that Crusoe has preferences $u(c, \dot{e}, \bar{l})$ for the consumption good and the services of leisure and land, where:

c is the consumption of an individual,
$\dot{e}$ is the amount of leisure, and
$\bar{l}$ is the value derived from consumption use of land.

Historically in the opening up of new terrain, the new land was primarily owned by the emperor, monarch, nobility, or other forms of government and eventually was awarded or sold to the public.

Even if Crusoe were deemed to own his island, except for the land in immediate use such as his hut and cultivated area it is difficult to attribute consumption worth to his nondirect utilization of the other land.[10]

Crusoe, being his own monarch with unutilized land, may attribute no direct worth to it, but if it along with other productive assets that may be present on the island serve as the prime inputs to his new activities, they then assume production worth and may require that he risk few if any consumption assets beyond his own labor.[11]

If we go beyond Crusoe to the competitive economy, the presence of many producer assets and land and other basic resources employed in active processes justifies a positive price for them. Governments such as the United States may still hold a substantial amount of the land and natural resources as the monopolist, referee, and participant in the economy.

As the implementation of an innovation is, in essence, the utilization of a new process with the existing resources, the resources required are culled out of the economy to be put to a higher expected utilization. In a rich economy almost all of the resource reallocation can fall on production goods and labor services and not current consumption. In economic activity, the context of the polity is always present; thus, for example, in virtually any society in wartime the political conditions and the financing possibilities may be more favorable to production and innovation than in peacetime. The choice is made decisively for guns and weapons innovation rather than butter.

10.3.2   Financing and control of innovation

The need to finance innovation may not only require borrowing but may involve elements of control and valuation. In figure 9.2 of chapter 9 an economy with six actors was shown:

- Nonfinancial firms,
- Stockholders,

- Savers,
- Commercial bankers,
- Financiers or financial firms,
- The central bank and government.

In an economy with a given configuration of physical resources, the financing of an innovation can take place in many different ways depending not merely on the physical and financial resources available but on the structure of their control.

A large corporation such as a General Electric is in a sufficiently powerful position to be self-financing. A more or less unknown startup, depending on the nature of the innovation involved, may have its principals borrow from friends and family or try to obtain financing from a venture capitalist or other financial institution. Depending on the nature of the innovation, government funding may be available.

The key observation is that the financing of new businesses and innovation requires not merely the availability of funds but the availability of a group or institution with the requisite knowledge and evaluation abilities. The nature of the market involved is far different from the ideal exchange of the stock market.

In the stock market anonymity is, in essence, the rule, and the two evaluations involved in a trade are independent and have been performed (if at all) before coming to the market. The existence of a previous market price permits the institution of the stock market to serve at any instant as an exchange device, not as a microeconomic evaluator. At best it can be regarded as outputting a consensus evaluation of the average opinion, with the time series of price changes conveying information on the dynamics. With every improvement in technology, the stock market as a clearing device becomes less expensive to operate.

In contrast there are always at least two and possibly several parties face to face in an essentially quasi-cooperative game involved in the financing of a non-self-financed innovation, where evaluation is of the essence and transaction costs are, of necessity, high. The distinction is not unlike that between a marketable derivative where all the boilerplate has been standardized and all units agreed on and the hand-tailored derivatives that are personalized contracts with little or no marketability.

10.3.3   Financing and two-way causality

The availability of a perceived-to-be-worthwhile new process to be developed may bring forth a demand for extra credit or money; however, the financing of innovation may also be generated by the availability of extra money or credit looking for an opportunity to sponsor a desired innovation; thus causality may go in both directions. The history of innovation during wartime and the bubble behavior in Silicon Valley provide examples. Consider margarine, aircraft, radar, the atomic bomb, the computer.

10.3.4   Bankruptcy as the delimiter of risk in a loosely coupled system

In general, in any loosely coupled economy we have already noted that bankruptcy laws are a logical necessity needed to account for the possibility of failure. If innovation fails and individuals are bankrupted, their remaining resources may be redistributed to cover fully or in part their contractual obligations.

As has been observed elsewhere [356], bankruptcy settlements by the very nature of their role are neither a pure market phenomenon nor are they unique. They are a joint product of their societies and polities as well as their economies; but they are even far more. They are a key factor in the dynamic ecology of an ongoing socioeconomy, as is indicated immediately below.

10.3.5   Bankruptcy and the money supply as public goods controlling mutation

As soon as exogenous uncertainty is present in an economy, there is a confounding of the phenomenon of strategic bankruptcy with misfortune.

The concept of an optimal bankruptcy code under exogenous uncertainty must contain within it a consideration of the willingness of a society as a whole to absorb the losses caused by what *ex post* turned out to be a misallocation of resources. In essence, given uncertainty the severity of the bankruptcy penalties influence the willingness of individuals to take risk; thus it is a control factor of the intensity of economic mutation. From the viewpoint of society as a whole, the bankruptcy laws are a public good.

In general, optimal bankruptcy laws will not be unique, as has been noted in chapter 12 of [356]. The pressures of the political and social structure in any specific society may favor the debtors or the creditors as a matter of social and political choice.

10.3.6   Failure involves the destruction of credit, not government money

In many uses in everyday life, the distinction between bank money and fiat or government money comes only at the level of details affecting the individual such as portability, divisibility, cognizability, anonymity, speed of transfer, and other aspects of a transactions technology that may be of considerable importance in some contexts but are often not of high conscious import in everyday life.

Especially in times of politicoeconomic uncertainty, the possibility of default becomes nontrivial. A key distinction can be made between what happens to credit instruments and to government money under (nonsovereign) bankruptcy. In a default it is only credit instruments that are destroyed. Neither real goods nor government money are destroyed; they get redistributed. The distinction between bank money and government money becomes painfully clear.

It is in extremis under hyperinflation or revolution that the context changes to the point that fiat money may be wiped out and the virtues of gold reappear.

10.3.7   The locus of innovation finance may be public or private

Necessity is the mother of invention.
—Origin unknown

Historically both private and public resources have been involved in innovation. Items such as global exploration, then space exploration, were heavily government enterprises to start with, and the private sector followed. This is also true for items such as the Internet.

Although it may fly against the sensibilities of many, war appears to provide a considerable impetus to invention. In the United States, though the cotton gin is held up as an example of great individual enterprise, it appears to be one of the earliest candidates for government subsidy. Another important innovation emerging from the Civil War was the standardization of manufactured parts so that it became considerably easier to repair items such as damaged rifles [188]. Later in the United States the roles of the Office of Naval Research (ONR) and the Advanced Research Projects Agency (ARPA) were considerable. Over the years basic research has been sponsored by emperors and governments. In modern times in parts of Europe and the United States, development and implementation are claimed to be primarily the domain of private industry. However, while the individual inventor may tinker in his garage, the financing of innovation basic research, especially in times of war, involves government sponsorship; and as indicated by the work of Richard Day, Gunnar Eliasson, and Clas Wihlborg, a government may play the role of both the initial direct sponsor and the architect of the privatization of the industry [73].

10.4   Increasing Returns and Innovation

Our prime concern is with the financing of innovation, not with the specific details of innovation itself. But innovation is closely interlinked with both increasing returns and disequilibrium. This brief section merely notes a few of the developments involving increasing returns. Marshall describes what may be considered as increasing returns via scope [247]: as the infrastructure builds up, so do districts with many competitors in the same trade. For the treatment of corporate scale and scope see Panzar and Willig [283, 284] and Chandler [54]. Arrow [11] describes a different form of increasing returns from learning. The elementary textbooks from at least the 1940s came complete with graphs of U-shaped average cost curves that essentially signaled the presence of set-up costs that were spread over increasing production.

The Phelps [290] and Solow [389] growth models utilizing a production function of the form $ax^\alpha y^{1-\alpha}$ for multistage macroeconomic models added an exogenous growth term k^t to reflect the increasing productivity of labor.

The work of Brian Arthur [14] treats stochastic increasing returns and the possibility of path dependence as characteristic of an innovating economy. In oligopolistic competition that characterizes much of mass production, stochastic increasing returns of the variety indicated by Arthur appear to be highly relevant.

With a random event occurring each period, the turbulence may be large, and the characterization of even the simplest market with innovation with a random element in each period will lead to a path-dependent nonsymmetric distribution of firm size.

More recently Paul Krugman [288] has considered trade and geography and offered a view of trade theory blending a macroeconomic theory of an intertwined industrial and occupational distribution characterized by economies of scale in production and a preference for diversity in consumption. Paul Romer [307] offers a long-run competitive-growth model where the driver of innovation is the endogenous growth of intellectual capital stock in a multiplicative manner.

These models appear to assume implicitly that the financing of development is more or less a minor side issue to economic growth. We believe that in context, all of the work noted briefly above represents different relevant contributions to understanding increasing returns; but in all instances an understanding is needed of the battle for the allocation of funds, both private and public. It is key to the appreciation of the locus of the sources for control, perception, and evaluation that critically affect innovation.

10.5   Unpacking the Commercial and Investment Banks: Context and Control

The devil is in the details.
—Origin unclear

In chapter 9 many functions of three banking institutions are packed into one: these are the central banks, the commercial banks, and the investment banks.[12]

10.5.1   A sketch of an approach

In the packing together of functions in chapter 9 there was only one means of payment, the "blue chips" of the central bank. We now add the "red chips" of the commercial banks as a means of payment.[13,14]

The understanding of institutional detail in financial structure is critical in application but only merits explicit mathematical modeling with the appropriate detail if there is a specific important question that cannot be answered adequately otherwise. The speed of change in institutions and instruments is such that form is ephemeral,[15] but basic functions remain, and as complexity increases, new functions are added. Here we discuss some of the basic questions about the relationship between central and commercial banking as well as commenting on investment banking, and we discuss the building blocks for a formal model for illustration.

We advocate treating different financial instruments as though they are different colors of poker chips in order to give them a simple physical reality. The red chips and the white chips are created together in pairs. The blue chips are "paper gold" mined, issued, or hoarded in central banks and treasuries in many different institutional ways blessed by the various laws of the nations. In treating different monies and credit this way and encountering the difficulties in trying to do so, it becomes easier to see what is left out in dealing with the proliferation of credit in a complex economy.

By splitting banking into two pieces, the central bank and the commercial banking system, we are able to describe in a fairly natural way the earnings from lending and the various control mechanisms between the commercial banks and the central bank that provide flexibility in the money supply in return for being able to earn commercial bank profits. This is in contrast to an alternative of a monolithic central bank with owned outlets and the attendant bureaucratic costs.

Among the functions handled by a commercial banking system are the provision of consumer transactions and producer working capital needs, information gathering, and evaluation services over an area on which to base lending decisions as well as providing the host of bookkeeping and managerial services that accompany these activities.[16] The system provides an alternative to having a centralized central banking system's branches provide the services.

Given the changes in transactions and clearance technology and law, the delivery of the functions associated with commercial banks is in a state of flux.

The commercial banking system poses many ad hoc problems in mechanism design. The control of variation in money supply alone is sufficient to illustrate why competition in the commercial banking system is not a simple problem in enterprise economics such as competition among restaurants or shoe stores or even supermarkets.

10.5.2   National debt and taxes

We note below in section 10.8 that in modern biology much consideration is given to the concepts of modularity, flexibility, and robustness in an uncertain environment. These have their analogues in the financial control system.

In chapter 9 a minimal model of government influence on the money supply was sketched in the construction of a playable game. Throughout this volume our approach has tended to introduce new features one item at a time and to consider increasing complexity.

For this sketch of a system with commercial banks we introduce several new instruments and institutions in order not only to consider the variation of the money supply but to illustrate the links between monetary and fiscal problems and to illustrate that from the viewpoint of mechanism design the additional complexity in adding fiscal instruments may make the monetary control problem considerably easier.

The presence of both taxation and a national debt provide a mechanism to construct a capacitance in a monetary flow system of any size, as taxes provide a flow of money from the private or essentially nongovernment sector to the government while the payments on the national debt provide a flow in the opposite direction. Adjustments of net flows change the money supply. In his advocacy for a central bank, Alexander Hamilton [255, pp. 40–44] understood the control aspects of both the bank and a national debt.

In actuality the time structure of a national debt provides flexibility in adjusting a whole profile of maturity-dependent interest rates, thus increasing flexibility in the fine tuning of time-dependent rates while also imposing new inflexibility in creating a need for retirement or refinancing of bonds due for repayment. For simplicity in analysis or the construction of a game, we may suppose the national debt to be in perpetuities with a single interest rate based on a perpetuity's face value. All have the opportunity buy or sell the perpetuities that constitute the national debt.

At the level of detail required to fully define a playable game we have a modeling choice: Are bonds bought and sold for blue chips, red chips, or both, or are there special conditions that the central bank rules may apply? As one of the roles of the central bank here is to enable the banking system to adjust the money supply smoothly, a natural policy for the central bank is to permit the purchase and sale of the national debt in blue or red chips, using the mix of its payments as a factor in the control over the reserve money.
Let:

x_t^α = bid for consols by consumers;
x_t^K = bid for consols by banks;
x_t^{CB} = bid for consols by the central bank.

Let:

y_t^α = offer of consols by consumers;
y_t^K = offer of consols by banks;
y_t^{CB} = offer of consols by the central bank.

The price of consols will be

$$p_t^* = \frac{x_t^\alpha + x_t^K + x_t^{CB}}{y_t^\alpha + y_t^K + y_t^{CB}}.$$

Moving the price of consols moves their effective yield to

$$\rho_t^* = \rho^* \frac{p^*}{p_t^*}.$$

The ability to move this interest rate depends on the relative size of government purchases and sales in comparison to those of the other agents which individually may be small.

10.5.2.1   A reprise on a continuum of agents   We have used the technical term "a continuum of agents" to remind us that from the viewpoint of strictly formal modeling if we wish to prove that the agents are small enough to become (posted, previous) price takers, we require that each agent be of measure zero. At this level of modeling this level of precision is usually not required. There are many ways in which one can consider white noise, or many other market imperfections, such that for all intents and purposes the assumption that all agents are price takers is reasonable without a discourse on measure theory. In much experimental gaming the presence of around 10 to 20 agents appears to be adequate for the players to ignore their individual influence on price.

If measures are used, it is probably desirable to note that the relative measures of the different agents are considerably different. In the United States currently there is only 1 central bank; $5,000$–$6,000$ commercial banks; around $340,000$ manufacturing establishments; and a population of around 318 million. The sizes of the banks and manufacturing establishments are heavily skewed, as are the incomes of individuals.

10.5.3   Why commercial banks?

In any process model where consumers have no direct utility for money but are given both a per-period and terminal boundary condition penalizing any individual for default and there is a final settlement at $t = T + 1$, the terminal conditions will determine a range on a price of money at $t = T + 1$. Any point in the range will provide a basis for a backward induction that together with the per-period default conditions suffice to determine the ratios of price to marginal utility of consumption $u'(c)$ across periods. In a competitive equilibrium the path of the dynamics is interior; it presses neither the bounding conditions of default nor the money supply in any period. In disequilibrium the money supply and the courts provide the (porous)[17] barriers that permit the value of money to fluctuate.

The importance of the boundary conditions is signaled in their shadow prices, and two vital roles of the commercial banks are to sense the pressures and act to relieve them.

Consider a structure with a single central bank and many (say k) commercial banks. We introduce two kinds of money. One kind of money (the "blue chips") is exchanged only between the central bank and the commercial banks.[18] This is "heavy money," and we think of it as the central bank's currency. Neither commercial banks nor firms and consumers can either create or destroy it. The central bank is an outside bank with respect to this model but with a larger set of instruments comprising its given strategy than in the models of section 9.8.4. These include the existence of taxes and a national debt.

A second kind of money (the "red chips") is exchanged between the commercial banks and the firms and consumers. We think of this as the commercial banks' money. For additional simplicity we may assume that only red chips circulate outside the banks. In this analogy we may consider that in the game the banks all issue their own banknotes that circulate. Immediately we are faced with operational and historical detail. In the United States in the nineteenth century many banks issued their own notes, and, depending on the distance from the point of circulation and the evaluation of the reputation of the specific bank, an array of discounts appeared. With the growth of the use of checks the pattern of payments changed considerably. With better interbank communication and accounting, more and more of bank money becomes a virtual money existing only as a set of ciphers in a network of bank accounts moved electronically.

In a game stressing the physical existence of bank money, given that all banks are required to have blue chip reserves we may assume that all individually issued red chips are identical in value; but if a red chip is identified with and can only be destroyed by the bank that issued it, there are k different bank monies. These can only be regarded as one money if there is a set of rules and an enforcement mechanism over the commercial banking system that enforces fungibility among all red chips. This requires both bank failure and consumer insurance laws. Suppose that one of the many ways of selecting this structure were in place. Our achievement over the models in chapter 9 has been to separate out the consumer transactions and producer short-term circulating capital functions, assigning them to the commercial banks. The central bank may retain its role as an investment bank. In order to separate out private invesment bankers, yet another complication would be required.

The commercial banks may be considered to be owned by the consumers in equal shares, and they distribute their profits to the consumer-owners in red chips.

10.5.3.1 A sketch of model structure and behavior The boundary conditions and the terminal settlement condition lead to a shadow price and extraction of all money (both blue and red chips) from the economy at a definite time $t = T + 1$.

In essence the terminal conditions are exogenous. The rational-expectations assumption provides a behavioral assertion that apparently endogenizes them and links (in a not necessarily unique manner) initial and terminal conditions for a stationary state, but even this "proof by assumption" is not sufficient to provide equations of motion that lead to an equilibrium.

The model employs a separation of ownership from control. Commercial banks are profit-maximizing institutions that flow profits back to their owners much as firms do. The banks are controlled by the central bank's rules on reserve requirements and other constraints specified below.

Consumers and firms optimize their purchases subject to no-default conditions within each period. The shadow price of default therefore creates a flexible relation between price levels and marginal utilities of consumption $u'(c)$, leading to price dynamics like those created by a threshold utility of money in section 9.8.4.

Commercial banks do not break the circular flow of funds in response to innovation or other shocks. Borrowing for innovation requires a separate entity willing to lend long. This could be an investment bank or a development bank. For simplicity here we may consider a development bank that is part of government.

10.5.3.2   The structure of a class of models   The main features of a class of models, and some variables associated with each, are the following:

1. Time is discrete with periods $t = 0, 1, \ldots, T$. A terminal period $t = T + 1$ is used to provide a modified "bite-your-tail" boundary condition where all initial monetary endowments must be returned.

2. Each commercial bank maintains a quantity of blue chips r^* with the central bank which are *required reserves*. If it holds less than this amount the bank is not permitted to function. The reserves held at the beginning of period t are denoted r_t^K. Reserves held with the central bank neither earn nor pay interest.[19] A commercial bank may have paid in capital of $r^{**} \geq r^*$.

3. At the beginning of any period, a commercial bank may deposit in or borrow blue chips from the central bank to increase its reserves, or it may draw down any reserves above its required minimum reserves; it may return capital or buy government bonds. Central bank loans accrue interest at a rate ρ^{CB}, which is time-independent. We denote by d_t^K the quantity of blue chips borrowed by a commercial bank at the beginning of period t ($d_t^K < 0$

is a deposit in the central bank). The bank's reserves entering period t are then $r_t + d_t^K$, which are required to be at least r^*. The reserve ratio determined by the central bank is ϕ, permitting a commercial bank to issue ϕ units of red chips for 1 unit of blue chips held in reserve.

4. All red chips available for payments at the beginning of each period are held by consumers and the central bank. We denote their quantities by n_t^α and n_t^{CB}.

5. The *interest* on red chip loans between the commercial banks and the firms and consumers, which we denote by ρ_t^K, is dynamically determined. We establish an interest rate by introducing a buy-sell trading post between red chips and firms' or consumers' IOU notes in the morning. Either commercial banks or consumers may offer red chips, and banks, firms, and consumers may bid in IOU notes payable in red or blue chips, but denominated in blue chips at the end of the period. The trading post clears using the standard quantity price formation rule. (Notation is provided below.)

6. Consumers may carry red chips from one period to the next, but firms (which deliver all their remaining red chips as profits to the consumer-owners at the end of each period) must borrow red chips in order to purchase inputs to production. Once the morning trading post for red chips has cleared, firms and consumers bid for the firms' previous-period output of consumable goods $f(i_{t-1})$ in a sell-all trading post as in section 9.8.4. Firms purchase inputs to production denoted i_t in period t, and consumers purchase quantities c_t of goods for consumption.

7. After the goods market has cleared, firms pay their debts of IOU notes (in red chips) to the commercial banks, and then distribute their profits to the consumer-owners. Firms are pure pass-through entities, meaning that any unpaid IOU notes are also passed to consumer-owners.

8. Once manufacturing firms' and banks' profits have been distributed, consumers pay their debts of IOU notes (in red chips, including any unpaid IOU notes from the firms) to the commercial banks. A default penalty is imposed for any IOU notes in excess of the chips they have to pay.

9. At the start of next period, there is trade in national debt and the natural persons pay an income tax. No tax is paid by the firms or banks.

10. At settlement day the commercial banks are liquidated. r^* must be returned and an addition to or subtraction from the final payoff is based on the amount $r_{T+1} - r^*$.

	Money Market Clearing	Goods Market Clearing	Consumers/Bank Clear Debts	
Central Bank				
Commercial Banks $\downarrow d^K$	$q^K \ b^K$		$b^K \uparrow q^K(1+\rho)$	$\uparrow d^K(1+\rho^C)$
Money Market	$b^K/(1+\rho)$			
Firms	$q^g \ b^\phi \ b^d$ $\quad b^d/(1+\rho)$			
Goods Market		$f(i) \ a \quad a/p \uparrow f(i)p \ b^d \ \pi$		π^K
Consumers	$b^g(1+\rho)$	$b \uparrow \ b/p$		
Bids Clearing			$b^g \ q^g(1+\rho)$	

Figure 10.1

Structure of exchanges within a single period of the central/commercial banking system model. Flows of blue and red chips are indicated with dashed and dark gray arrows, respectively. IOU notes (all of which are bids) are in black. Consumable goods flows are in light gray. Each box indicates the clearing of one market. Quantities indicated where repayment is required are those that involve no default (to simplify notation) in type-symmetric noncooperative equilibria. The arrow on blue chip flows indicates the direction if $d^K > 0$, but deposits with $d^K < 0$ and flow in the opposite sense are also possible.

A diagram with the structure of the trading day for this model is shown in figure 10.1.

10.5.3.3 The trading post for red chips and IOUs We note that by utilizing unlimited liability this model rules out both bankruptcy of the firms and bank failure and hence is not suitable for considering panic or runs as was done in the model in chapter 8.

The following list defines the bid and offer variables, and which agents control them:

b_t^α = the bid for bank money by a consumer α;
b_t^ϕ = the bid for bank money by a firm ϕ;
q_t^K = the offer of bank money by a bank K.

The interest rate ρ_t for red chip loans in period t is then formed as

$$\left(1 + \rho_t^K\right) \equiv \frac{b_t^\alpha + b_t^\phi}{q_t^K}. \tag{10.3}$$

In a type-symmetric solution, the quantities of red chips received by each group in the beginning of the period are:[20]

$b_t^d / (1 + \rho_t)$ by the firms;
$b_t^g / (1 + \rho_t) - q_t^g$ by the consumers.

The quantities of red chips paid out by each type of agent at the period's end is[21]

$b_t^K - q_t^K (1 + \rho_t)$ by the commercial bank;
b_t^d by the firms;
$b_t^g - q_t^g (1 + \rho_t)$ by the consumers.

10.5.3.4   Initial and terminal conditions   As initial conditions, we provide each firm with a quantity i_0 of goods in production, and nothing else. Each consumer begins with a quantity m_0^α of red chips, and equal ownership claims to the firms and banks held in a mutual fund that flows through all profits. Each commercial bank begins with a quantity $r_0^K = r^{**} \geq r^*$ of blue chips held as its capital.

The only terminal condition is the default penalty for $r_{T+1}^K < 0$. Commercial banks are defined to maximize discounted profits, which they can do by increasing the size of loans or buying government bonds. Therefore they have an incentive to increase their reserves by borrowing from the central bank, or to draw down their reserves to avoid paying interest on borrowings. A nonzero shadow price therefore forms at $t = T + 1$, setting $r_{T+1}^K = 0$.

10.5.3.5   Commercial bank profits and changing the money supply   In this model, commercial banks choose their bids or offers in the red chip markets to maximize discounted profits. The three quantities that control profit maximization under reserve ratio restrictions are the amount of reserves held, given by

$$r_t + d_t^K, \tag{10.4}$$

the net quantity of red chips in circulation in the period, given by

$$n_t + q_t^K - \frac{b_t^K}{1 + \rho_t}, \tag{10.5}$$

and the net income at period's end, if no agents default, given by

$$\rho_t \left(q_t^K - \frac{b_t^K}{1 + \rho_t} \right). \tag{10.6}$$

Commercial banks either pay or accrue interest if they borrow or deposit blue chips at the central bank, so their reserves between periods update as

$$r_{t+1} = r_t - d_t^K \rho^C. \tag{10.7}$$

One needs to specify whether the central bank will permit a commercial bank to pay the interest due to the central bank on its borrowing of reserves using only blue chips, or will also accept earned profits in red chips. If the former, then by conservation the banks may eventually run out of blue chips unless borrowing is unbounded. It is details such as these that make the full definition of a closed complete model hardly worth doing unless the model is to be used as an experimental game or as a representation of an explicit empirical system. An economic historian might argue with much justification that custom and the opaque aspects of the law overrule trying to incorporate this level of microdetail into a general model.

10.5.3.6 Properties of solutions   If all agents other than the central bank are optimizers, then no-arbitrage conditions require that

$$\rho_t^* = \rho_t^K \geq \frac{\rho^{CB}}{\phi}.$$

The central bank interest rate and reserve ratio are control parameters, and the other two rates are determined in part by competition. By the device of having the national debt in position, the central bank has an easy way to flood the economy with commercial bank credit by buying some of its debt. Again more microdetail is required. The central bank's loan facility, by the rules of the game, permits the commercial banks to borrow to increase their reserves. They cannot borrow to buy bonds. If this were not so, at least temporarily a widow's cruise would be opened. The central bank could permit, at least for some period, the commercial banks to purchase bonds with red chips, thereby immediately giving them an instant profit of

$$\frac{\rho^*}{\phi} - \rho_t^{CB}$$

per unit of bond sold. The pressures would be for the interest rates to eventually equalize; however, if the central bank/treasury is also issuing bonds at the same time, it controls both an input and output variable and can thereby have considerable influence on the adjustment speeds of the interest rates. Furthermore if the level of income taxes can be changed, another opportunity is provided for control of profit levels.

Distribution of profits: As the profits of the banking system are flowed through, this device for a speedy injection of purchasing power per se creates no questions of equity. In the models sketched above, all consumers were lumped into a symmetric ownership of all sources of income. The question of equity might arise via a skewed ownership structure.

Exogenous uncertainty and wealth shares: Ignoring obvious differences in talent and specialization among the population, the presence of uninsured, not fully correlated uncertainty, is sufficient to produce a considerable skewing of wealth [199]. The income distribution feature is obliterated in a representative-agent model unless there are many representative agents.

The development bank: The class of models sketched above need a specification as to who lends long in a situation involving risk. Once more there are several different institutions that are sufficient to perform the necessary task. An easy-to-select and historically justified institution is the development bank; another is the independent investment banker. In either instance the determination of the price of the loan depends on the perception and assessment of the risk interest rate and the structure of the market, which appears to be both oligopolistic in structure and possibly subject to increasing returns to scale. A potential for instability exists in the use of leveraged short-term borrowing instruments such as repos, as has been noted in section 8.4.1.1.

Other behavior: It cannot be overstressed that all through this volume we have utilized a variant of noncooperative equilibrium behavior not because we believe in it, but because it provides a useful connection to much of the generally accepted literature. It gains some appeal when the role of many small agents is made clear; but even then many open questions remain. From our point of view there are many highly different solution concepts all of which, *in the appropriate context*, are able to complete the equations of motion for specialized models. We do not believe that one behavioral solution concept fits all contexts. Much investigation remains to be done in comparing different solution concepts on several test beds reflecting different contexts.

10.5.4   Investment banks

Critical to innovation are the investment banks, but these unlike the commercial banks are consumers and distributors, not producers,[22] of the means of payment. They may create new instruments such as a whole cascade of common and preferred stock and other mezzanine financial instruments; thus their various methods of financing may influence liquidity and in the United States may add briefly (and sometimes violently) to the M2 money supply (for example the repo). Even so, to some extent the nomenclature of "investment bank" rather than a term such as "investment house" is misleading.

Although we do not develop formal models of investment banking here, we note that investment banks are critical to the control aspects of innovation, and they along with direct government actions provide much of the direct control of the forces of innovation.

Public mythology and the understanding of causal factors in innovation are only loosely connected. The symbolism of Silicon Valley with gunslinger entrepreneurs, Wild West individualists, and garage inventors is far more congenial to the ethos of a country such as the United States than are its beliefs in ONR, ARPA, and Los Alamos, let alone the sponsorship of invention under empires and dictatorships and the universal stimulus of war.

10.6   A Comment on Monied Individuals: Retirees or Active Capitalists?

In section 9.7.1 we considered a class of individuals whose only asset was money. Because the solution supported the fiat as both a means of payment and a store of value, these individuals were able live off their money. In our example in section 9.8.4, looking only at central bank financing we omitted them for simplicity.

The introduction of a class of agents living off money provides for a basic reconsideration of the role of finance in the economy. In particular their interest in influencing a government-set rate of interest may be diametrically opposed to the desires of the producers.

Is a retired surgeon with $10,000,000 the economic equivalent of a professional money lender or investment banker or hedge fund operator with $10,000,000? Almost always the answer is no. Information, evaluation, and expertise and specialization of the financial functions are in essence an evolutionary aspect of the overall body economic. The essential difference between a merely rich amateur investor and a professional is perception, expertise, knowledge, and a network of professional connections. The professional investor is part of the perception and general sensory system of the economy, dealing in the perception and evaluation of risk in an economy in motion. The rich retiree is better off investing indirectly though a professional investor, be it a bank, investment bank, or other financial professional, unless she has a network of connections of her own that enable her to invest directly in a family's or friend's business.

The remarks above imply that at least we should split the savers into two parts, passive savers and active financiers. The first deposit only in the commercial banks, pension funds, or mutual funds, while the second are involved in evaluation and deal directly with the firms and the markets for firms and their stocks.

Finance is micro-microeconomics. It deals with information, perception, and evaluation as well as the retail and wholesale aspects of the transactions, saving, and investment technologies. The level of aggregation of institutional structure employed in formal models depends heavily on the basic questions being answered. Aggregations such as monied individuals or a banking system cover many functions. In our models the stress is on breaking out some of the basic functions attributed to the institution.

A natural model that we do not develop here but that merits noting, at least, would involve both investment bankers and the savers in our society: in particular the retirees and pension funds whose fiduciaries supply the funds to the investment bankers as part of the needed division of labor in the perceptual and due diligence part of the investment process in a complex economy.

10.7   A Comment on Monetary and Fiscal Policy

It has been customary in applied macroeconomics to make a distinction between monetary and fiscal policy. Tobin [400], Okun [277], Nordhaus [276], and many others have observed that both are a part of the policy of the same player. From the purely economic viewpoint this is clear, and policy coordination is called for, but the distinction between them may be justified by the history of political and bureaucratic happenstance. In the context of day-by-day political and bureaucratic behavior, the boundary constraints on the various governmental policy weapons are such that they do not offer independent choice.

The long debate on the level of political freedom that should be bestowed on a central bank represents a concern as to how to design a powerful bureaucracy with the strategic freedom to function under less political pressure on a far longer time horizon than those of fiscal policymakers answerable to their

political masters on a day-by-day basis. The answers to the problems posed
here are given in the process of an ongoing political-legal-societal-economic
debate that is somewhat institutionally different in various societies. Pure economic methodology provides no direct answers to sociopolitical questions; at
best it can give economic advice to all the constituencies. This provides some
boundary conditions, but little more.

10.7.1   Money as a flexible measure

In the earlier parts of this book we have stressed the relationship between
some of the methods of physics and economics. Here, as we stress aspects of
innovation and a complex financial control structure, we appear to be veer-
ing toward connections with biology. Whereas physics employs a standard
meter that for most purposes is a fixed measure, all participants in the economy
know that their central measure—money—is in motion relative to preferences,
though hopefully by "not too much." It is designed to provide measurement
in a loosely coupled system where virtually any construction links money to
preferences via ever-moving prices and more slowly shifting default laws and
depreciating assets.

The miracle, in our estimation, is how well, given the complexity of the
system, it appears to have worked. Bewley [30, p. 284] terms the constant
marginal utility of money the formalization of the "permanent income hypothesis" of Friedman.

The breaking of the circular flow calls for violation of the constant utility
of money for a transient of indefinite length; and with intermittent innovation
the system has to be in perpetual irregular motion. This sets the context for
a central bank's attempt to keep a purchasing power or marginal value for its
money within bounds.

10.7.2   Many monies and the weakening of control

In spite of the difficulties and complexity, we have suggested that, at least in
principle, it is possible to specify a full mathematical model of the control
problem of a government in a simplified economy containing only one source
of government money and one source of credit; but with the advances in communication and computation the monetary system becomes ever more porous,
and the clear control mechanisms of yesterday become museum specimens of
today. The era of the powerful national central bank is over, and the economic
guidance and control mechanisms are undergoing a sea change.

10.8   Fluctuation, Uncertainty, and Robustness

In the remainder of this chapter we sketch some analogical connections among biology, ecology, and economics. The more one views the economic system as a dynamic evolving entity, the more the biological analogy appears relevant to the proliferation of forms designed to cope with viability in an uncertain environment. A reader skipping this section will not lose the continuity of the overall work, but will miss some of the signposts concerning future interdisciplinary developments.

We have shown in chapter 9 how deterministic models can suffer large structural instabilities when even single instances of innovation are introduced as new elements that the economy must absorb. A simple extrapolation of this result might suggest that economies undergoing constant innovation would be structurally chaotic, or that our models would produce such chaos even when we do not see it in actual economies most of the time.

There are two reasons, learned from experience in evolutionary biology, to believe that real instability in economies will not be continuous but a matter of occasional *punctuation* [169], and that at least in principle we understand the origin of this phenomenon and have some tools with which to model it. First, selection for robustness will often produce modular and buffered systems that concentrate change within rare large events against backgrounds of quiescence. Second, the presence of noise, which provides a constant signal on which selection for robustness can act, may produce systems whose buffering also lends stability against the disrupting effect of innovations.

10.8.1   Fluctuations, modularity, robustness, and canalization

The economy, like the polity, society, and biosphere within which it occupies a nested hierarchy, is a loosely coupled system of components, each experiencing continual stochastic shocks and disturbances. The response of a multicomponent system to stochastic perturbation may be either unstable or stable, depending on details of the component interactions (which may not be apparent). However, if the system is to function reliably, we expect that only architectures that remain stable enough of the time will emerge from filters that select for reliability.[23] Modeling the process of selection for robustness, and characterizing robust architectures, is still a frontier of theory in evolutionary dynamics, and will likely remain technically challenging for economics as well. However, a number of general principles relating robust architecture to perturbations and selection are widely used by evolutionary theorists.

Herbert Simon, who studied robust organization in a range of economic, social, biological, and engineered systems, put forth a well-known argument [372, 373] that hierarchical, complex organizations may only be robust if their architecture is *modular*.[24] Modular architectures are those in which components or processes are partitioned into subsystems (the "modules"), with dense or strong linkage among components within each module, and less dense or weaker linkage among components in different modules. The dynamics within modules is largely autonomous, and in a stochastic setting is responsible for identifying and eliminating many errors without reliance on signals from the environment. The weaker coupling between modules limits propagation of errors, but for the same reason limits the flow of controlling information, requiring autonomous stability of most intramodular processes. Conventional examples in Simon's writing include the assembly of complex multicomponent instruments such as (old-fashioned mechanical) wristwatches or the Alexandrian empire.

Modularity may be a "found" property of the material or social substrate, along which an evolving system naturally aligns because this makes its error correction problem easiest, as has been argued for metabolism [43]. However, modularity may also be actively evolved through selection both for robustness *and* (perhaps surprisingly) for adaptability. A theory in biology known as *facilitated variation* [158, 159] asserts that biological systems often show modular architecture, in which the weak links across module boundaries have evolved to become standardized interfaces for control or coordination. Thus, not only do they erect barriers against error propagation, but they provide predictable signaling systems which may be used to change intermodular interactions without disrupting intramodular stability and functions. In systems showing facilitated variation, modular stability enhances robustness, at the same time as standardized interfaces support adaptation. Interface standardization may also ease the prediction problem for systems that depend on internal models for their regulatory functions [60], because viable evolutionary change is concentrated at the few links on module boundaries. Examples of deliberate engineering for modularity, in the spirit of facilitated variation, are widespread in computer science, and include the separation of hardware from operating-system layers, the transfer control protocol/internet protocol (TCP/IP), and the widespread shift from procedural to object-oriented programming languages.[25]

A particular evolutionary process recognized by biologists, in which external cues become anticipated and incorporated into internal regulatory systems, is known as *canalization* [412]. Canalization is one process by which systems can become more modular and less sensitive to their environments, though canalization produces a form of robustness that does not necessarily serve greater adaptability unless specific sensors are added at the interface to the environment.

A system that has evolved robustness, whether through canalization or by exploiting some other (preexisting or actively evolved) form of modularity, becomes a capacitor for shocks [213, 214]. Because it can absorb more error than a system not similarly selected for robustness, it can also fail to express changes in function which might otherwise provide feedback enabling selection to eliminate the errors.[26] Therefore such systems may show long-term steady-state behavior punctuated by rare but large transitions, not necessarily triggered by outsized causes. Such punctuated intervals need not be equilibria in either the mechanical physicists' or the neoclassical economists' sense; they may be internally active dynamical steady states.

10.8.2   Evolution designs using the robust components

When we observe evolved natural systems, whether molecular, organismal, social, or institutional, we may fall into the illusion of a collection of inherently rigid mechanical components assembled into a Newtonian clockwork. This illusion is harmless as long as we can take for granted that both the natural system and our designed interventions draw from a common stock of devices already filtered by selection for robustness.

The risk in using deterministic models to describe evolved natural systems is that the model interactions may not respect the actual structure of perturbations or the selection that has happened in response to them, making it difficult to distinguish model instabilities that reflect inappropriate model choice from those that predict instabilities in real systems.

In molecular biology, some progress has been made toward showing the explicit role of stochasticity in selecting system components. In some cases stochasticity is a negative effect, away from which selection directs the system, as in the case of "kinetic funnels" or chaperones[27] in protein folding [201, 278]. In other cases, stochasticity may be actively employed as part of system function. Examples include stochastic resonance (first proposed as a mechanism for sensitivity enhancement in auditory systems) [28, 197], or the employment of large spaces of correlated fluctuations to increase discriminatory resolution and reliability (proposed for optimal molecular recognition) [323, 324].

10.8.3   Robustness evolved to absorb fluctuations may also absorb innovations

The same mechanisms that may insulate the components of a system evolved for robustness from random shocks may also enable them to absorb effects of innovation without structural instability—up to a point. Examples in biology include developmental regulatory networks apparently evolved for robustness against environmental noise, which secondarily produce phenotypes that are robust against many mutations causing large changes in the coupling parameters between the regulatory components themselves [407].

Ultimately, sufficient change in system components (whether through shocks or through innovation) must change system function. In systems buffered as a result of selection for robustness, these changes appear as destabilizing transitions or tipping points [318]. As for noise-induced structural changes, instabilities triggered by innovation may not indicate that the triggering events are especially large. They may simply reflect watershed events that result from saturation of underlying buffers.

A pattern that is widely recognized in both engineered and natural systems [47] is the tuning of buffers to actively compensate for certain classes of shocks, in which the active compensation renders them more sensitive to shocks for which they are not designed.[28] It has been argued that the resulting robust yet fragile system performance reflects a principle that the absolute capacity of a system's components to absorb external change is fixed; only the distribution of that capacity over the spectrum of events may be altered by design or natural selection.

The concept of a fixed capacity to respond to variation has been quantified for some classes of combinatorial search and optimization problems in a set of "no free lunch" theorems [422, 423]. These theorems apply to discrete problems such as search for Boolean variable assignments simultaneously satisfying complex networks of constraints, in which the problem instances are related by elements within some permutation group. A solution algorithm, which must be defined for all instances in the problem set, may be viewed as an active system designed to identify and remove the permutation degrees of freedom by which instances differ, as it reduces each problem instance to a standard solution form such as a satisfying variable assignment. The no-free-lunch theorems show that, under a uniform probability measure to sample problem instances over the permutation group, no algorithm can have performance better than the average on all problem instances. That is, the best that can be achieved is to match the properties of the solution method to a known class of problem instances, at the cost that the method will perform worse than the average on instances outside the class.

10.8.4 Liquidity as an example

Liquidity may furnish an example in the economy of a property adopted to handle uncertainty but also capable of enabling innovation. We derived in chapter 9 an example of Schumpeter's problem of "breaking the circular flow of funds" created by the introduction of new methods in production. In an optimal deterministic system, all money is fully utilized, and the adoption of new production methods creates a transient problem of reallocating money (or providing new money) to new sectors whose solution is undefined within the equilibrium paradigm. As Keynes suggested, in a monetary economy there may be both precautionary and speculative reasons for holding money. As is shown in inventory theory [32, 317], agents may keep stocks of money untouched to cope with ordinary uncertainties such as clearing or unforeseen demand shocks, and they may also hold stocks of money to spend on targets of opportunity in the form of new products or methods of production. To the extent that we model liquidity as a deliberate underutilization of money, we explicitly acknowledge that economic process falls outside the paradigm of equilibrium under perfect knowledge and complete contracts. (A system with complete contracts would by assumption contain correctly priced insurance to enable transactions under all states of the world.) It may not be surprising, then, that attempts to characterize liquidity within equilibrium demand models such as Hicks's IS/LM model [185] fail to capture dissimilarities between liquidity and ordinary goods or services, at the same time as noncooperative equilibrium models with incomplete markets may show instability under innovation that would be absorbed in nonequilibrium models requiring liquidity as a buffer.

10.8.4.1 A note on mark-to-market The characterization of liquidity as a buffer for market "noise" is only one approach to formalization or operationalization that we might pursue. The adoption of mark-to-market rules to define collateral value creates a new functional role for liquidity as the concept applies to market clearing. A practical measure of the liquidity of a market (which may be contingent on the degree of leverage of the associated securities) is that ordinary fluctuations in demand for securities do not lead to price fluctuations large enough to feed back through the collateral valuation to create self-fulfilling price spirals.

10.9 How Many Derived Layers Will a Production and Exchange Economy Support?

Innovation in finance, as in production, is a perpetual feature of capitalist economies, and a pressure toward it appears to be a constant in human society, at least in the industrial era. Commentators such as Minsky have argued [263] that financial innovation is inherently destabilizing, and it certainly gives the appearance in current society of generating an evolutionary arms race between bankers and regulators. We are therefore led to ask whether there is a natural limit to the number of layers of derivative complexity, or of regulatory complexity, that may evolve on top of a given production and exchange economy. We do not propose that we (or anyone else) can provide a definitive answer to this question for economies, but we may find precedents for it in the evolution of biological complexity.

10.9.1   Metabolic primary production as an analogue to production and exchange

The rough analogue to production and exchange in the economy is metabolism in biology. Like the extraction of consumer's surplus from aggregate production technologies and scarce resources, metabolic primary production is the aggregate output of a network of processes balanced both within organisms and among organisms within ecosystems. A remarkable fact is that innovations in the core process of primary production—carbon fixation—appear to have occurred entirely within the first 1.5 billion years of life, before the rise of biologically produced molecular oxygen [42, 43, 381]. Over this entire interval, life was not only unicellular but composed exclusively of bacteria and archaea—that is, even the composite *eukaryotic* cell architecture shared by one-celled protists and all plants and animals had not yet evolved. The most complex aggregates under the control of single genotypes were colonies of unicells, and the most complex ecosystems were microbial communities. The history of innovation in carbon fixation therefore played out entirely within an era of comparatively low, and slowly changing, regulation.

10.9.2   The major transitions in evolution and the distinctive separation of productive from regulatory innovation

The second-largest transition in evolution, after the emergence of cellular life, came with the saturation of the earth's chemical buffers with biotically produced oxygen [216]. In rapid succession, eukaryotic cells and then multicellular organisms emerged, land was colonized by colonial unicells, animals, and plants, and major cycles of carbon, water, and continental weathering were altered. It is difficult to make precise estimates of the change in primary production through this period [254, 293], but the estimated increase in power density of cells enabled by molecular oxygen is at least tenfold. The change enabled by this increase in power density [216] was reflected in innovations in both organism and ecosystem architecture, but more fundamentally it introduced an era of innovation in regulation, which continues into the present.

We are careful to emphasize that innovations in regulation—manifested as developmental complexity and diversification in organisms [71, 113–116] and network complexity in trophic ecosystems [106]—were largely driven by increases in the *magnitude* of primary production. Indeed, a strong argument can be made [117] that the best-known elaboration of regulatory systems— the early-Cambrian radiation of taxonomic groups—was tightly coupled to increases in available energy, as the oxidation state of the ocean and benthic muds shifted rapidly through a period of disequilibrium. However, these changes in magnitude were not due to innovations in *mechanisms* of core processes such as carbon fixation.[29] Rather, the rise of oxygen seems to have marked (more likely, to have actively created) a boundary, dividing an earlier period of innovation in the most fundamental mechanisms of primary production from a later period where increases in production rate generated more complex regulatory systems within organisms, and more complex life cycles, predations, digestive, fermentative, and respiratory metabolisms, symbioses, and other protocols that coordinate the interactions between organisms within ecosystems.

Thus, in at least one realized example, innovations in both the extent and mechanisms of regulation did not require parallel innovations in the diversification of primary production, though they almost certainly required increases in its rate.

10.9.3   The importance of friction in setting limits of complexity

The completion of the first-round human genome project [61] and other related projects brought several surprises—the protein-coding parts of human and chimp genomes (the "gene" parts of the genomes) are roughly 99 percent identical [330];[30] several vegetables as well as some mollusks have more genes than humans (human est. 23,000; rice est. 28,236; tomato est. 31,760 [62]; maize est. 32,000 [322]; sea urchin est. 23,300; pufferfish est. 27,918); and similar violations of expectations. It is now widely appreciated that the manifest differences in organisms long characterized as "genetic" are largely differences in developmental regulation [87]. As is apparent for human and chimp, these regulatory changes appear to depend on no absolute increase in metabolic power.

At the level of ecosystems a similar observation may be made. It is difficult to compare net primary productivity (NPP) for ancient and modern systems, but for some isolated systems such as reefs attempts have been made [110, 282]. Whereas the species inhabitants of paleo-reefs may differ widely from the current inhabitants, NPP values for the two are estimated to be broadly similar.

Two further figures bearing on the relation between primary production and regulation may be worth noting. First, in general the genomes of bacteria and archaea consist mostly of sequences coding for proteins, the directly functional machinery of the cell. Some of these proteins are regulatory in nature, but the amount of genetic material used for regulation at the expense of protein synthesis remains small across the range of bacterial genome sizes. With eukaryotes—the protists, animals, plants, and fungi that emerged following the rise of oxygen—this basic relation changes. Genome size increases in direct proportion to cell size, while the part used for protein coding increases much more slowly.[31] For reference, in humans roughly 1.5 percent of the genome codes for protein [61]. How much of the remainder will eventually be found to participate either directly or indirectly in regulation is currently unknown, but many diverse and extensively used classes of regulatory domains within the noncoding regions are already recognized [87]. Second, among the protein-coding part of the genome, estimates are that a fully self-sufficient metabolism could be supported by about 700 genes [162]. The smallest free-living self-sufficient bacteria possess about 1,500 genes [80]. Moreover, if we kept only those genes within an ecosystem that contribute to the core reactions of primary production, they would be largely the same gene set. For comparison, the common intestinal bacterium *E. coli* has about 5,000 genes, and a human has about 23,000.[32] Essentially all of this excess, and the great majority of the gene inventory in the biosphere, contributes to development, complex physiology, specializations or plasticity of organism phenotype that enable coupling to ecological neighbors, life cycle complexity, or direct active regulation. A further allotment of genetic material to regulatory functions arises through control loci or the production of RNA outside the protein-coding regions [87]. By any measure, the vast majority of genomes and genetic activity in the biosphere serve some form of developmental complexity or regulation not directly within the chemical pathways of primary production.

Thus, while structurally major changes to very low-level developmental and physiological regulatory networks appear to have required increases in power density, many of the differences in regulation that have been the focus of evolutionary biologists from Darwin into the early twentieth century appear to have been energetically nearly "free of additional cost." If such an observation generalizes to the economy, it would suggest that incremental limits to economic complexity may come from dynamic instability in the arms race between financial innovation and regulatory control, but that the underlying production mechanisms impose no obvious limits to complexity as long as the costs of regulatory mechanisms can be kept sufficiently small.

At the same time, a word of caution is in order. Whether before the rise of oxygen, in the early Cambrian, or in the present, the biosphere has never contained all carbon on earth. Even in the modern age of photosynthesis, natural systems only alter the conversion rate of energy from sunlight to heat by about 0.1 percent of the planetary ambient rate. Some problem of balancing growth against decay appears to limit NPP across all these periods, and while this limit has not strongly constrained the innovation of regulatory strategies, it also has not been much shifted by them, at least since the Cambrian and the subsequent colonization of continents. Therefore, while the fraction of biological activity devoted to regulation can apparently exceed the fraction in primary production by a large factor, it does not follow that the total magnitude of either system can expand without limit. Since the economy falls within the biosphere on a finite planet, it seems that such limits are inevitable.

It appears that in the economy the presence of transaction costs and other frictions are at least as severe as in biology.

10.10   Body Economic or Ecology Economic?

The participants in an economy are heterogeneous, partly autonomous but also coordinated, limited in the flexibility of their roles, and constantly subject to constraints from both institutional rules and the collective effects of behavior by other participants. While we conventionally model economic action with severely simplified games involving a few categories of agents and one or a few atomic players representing firms or the government, a richer description could attempt to posit an extensive-form game involving anywhere from tens to hundreds of millions of agents, with complex information conditions and a mix of noncooperative and coalitional-form solution concepts. The play of such a game at many points is hierarchically ordered with tight constraints on player strategies, and suggests a coarse-graining into large aggregates subsuming many individuals' autonomy.

The temptation is considerable to digress even further into the opening vistas in biology and ecology, but we limit ourselves to noting briefly a few further germane items:

- Professions of economic actors may resemble cell types in a multicellular organism in the sense that both are specialized for a range of functions. The body versions include:

  1. *Perception and evaluation:* These include sense organs, the somatosensory nervous system, the brain and central nervous system. The human brain accounts for about 2 percent of body mass, but consumes 20 percent of whole-body O_2.

  2. *Maintenance of the internal chemical environment:* The highest energy demand comes from the liver. It is comparable to metabolic demand from the brain in humans, and two or more times larger than the brain in other mammals. (In other mammals, the brain is smaller in proportion to body size, whereas the liver is comparable.)

  3. *Transport:* This includes blood circulation, breathing, peristalsis in the gut, etc. The heart accounts for about 10 percent of whole-body O_2 consumption.

  4. *Motion and mechanical action on the environment:* In humans, this comes primarily from skeletal muscles, which collectively account for about 20 percent of whole-body O_2 consumption.

  There is probably considerable freedom and ambiguity in assigning function to a particular tissue type as we go further down the list.

- Cells in an organism are, for the most part, subject to tighter control than most agents in an economy. The very limited "autonomy" that many cells have as their developmental programs become set defines one sense in which the organism provides a less apt analogy for the economy than would an ecological community.

- Importantly, most cells in an organism (the "soma") do not reproduce beyond a certain stage in development, and therefore are not directly subject to Darwinian selection as a population. Because mathematically selection is equivalent to Bayesian updating [331], one might say that these cell populations do not "learn" over generational time, in the same parallel sense that populations of organisms do "learn" (as a synonym for adaptation) when all individuals have the opportunity to reproduce.[33]

- The Darwinian character of competition among agents in an economy has been heavily emphasized (for instance by Friedman)[34] and may act either on the agents as repositories of information or skills or on their portfolios which are effectively a different class of entities within the economy. To the extent that economies as wholes are made up of competing agents, but are not themselves vertically oriented entities undergoing competitive selection and replication, economies resemble ecosystems more than they resemble organisms. Firms are perhaps better analogues to organisms, in the sense that their status as entities is legally defined, they may be formed, may divest branches, or may close at discrete events, and their internal vertical integration through lines of command and control is (at least in stylized accounts) put up as an alternative to the negotiated-contract interaction protocols of markets.

- The way that selection can act at multiple levels to produce both stability and adaptedness has sometimes led to blurring of distinctions between organisms and ecosystems. Ecosystems, like organisms, can sometimes actively maintain homeostasis against external perturbations, functioning analogously to the way the body acts to maintain a stable internal state, though not necessarily employing analogous regulatory architectures to do so. Observations of this kind have led to characterizations of ecosystems as "super-organisms," in efforts to capture their status as elementary entities [230]. We regard this as an error, though one that must be stated carefully. The fundamental distinction between ecosystems and organisms is that organisms instantiate forms of *individuality* in their architecture and dynamics, whereas ecosystems employ less hierarchical and more parallel threads of coevolutionary and community dynamics. Although individuality is a complex concept instantiated in multiple forms and possibly at multiple levels within a single system [183], it is nonetheless a distinctive shift in regulatory architecture from that of a community. The wish to emphasize the status of ecosystems as primitive entities in their own right is not to be criticized in the Gaia approach. It should be properly addressed by a shift in thinking in evolutionary biology that would take individuality less for granted and acknowledge its complexity as a constructed mode of organization, and at the same time recognize the fundamental and integrated status of other levels of organization such as ecosystems as well. An interesting case in which the distinction between organism and ecosystem may genuinely blur concepts is the case of eusocial insects, in which colonies possess many but not all features of organism-level organization [227].

- The in-principle formalization of economies as 10^8–10^{10}-player games allows us to make contact with both organism and ecosystem organization at two points. Gathered together in [380] are a variety of standard observations that general fitness functions for evolutionary dynamics can be expanded in hierarchies of k-player normal-form games, for $k \in 1, \ldots, \infty$. It can further be argued that the general framework provided by this game expansion should be understood as formalizing development in its most general sense (thus including processes such as niche construction) [380]. The use of games to describe the way the fitness function is generated, both for selection within organismal development and among organisms in a population, is fairly common, and can provide a disciplined way to think about social evolution [139]. The further refinement from normal-form to extensive-form games gives a process underpinning to the way the fitness function is constructed from more elementary moves [65, 380], including such functions as message passing to coordinate multistage developmental processes. The refinement from normal-form to extensive-form games provides an important general mechanism to characterize lateral or oblique transmission (in parallel with the "vertical" transmission by descent).

  The use of extensive-form games to characterize the interplay of development and ecological interactions with reproduction and selection dynamics begins to capture the complexity of serious evolutionary thinking, and the diversity of cases that are worth distinguishing. It demands explicit descriptions of processes, either the unfolding of events and interactions that take place between events of reproduction, or the processes of matching and change in population composition that change the information content between generations. The ambiguity in what concept an "agent" or "player" represents, which admits interpretations both as an individual within an ecosystem and as a component such as a chromosome within an individual, and the ambiguity that the extensive-form game admits, between processes that occur within ontogeny and complex interactions that take place in populations, are valid reflections of the reuse of mechanisms in real systems, which tend to cross-cut categories and sharpen the needs for conceptual clarity in their use.

- Many of the themes that we briefly note in this section, when developed in depth, lead to a reconceptualization of the nature of the living state in a much broader range of terms than has traditionally been used. While all of the operative concepts are resident in extant biological, chemical, or physical sciences, the need to conceptually integrate them is compelled particularly in efforts to understand the emergence of life on Earth from an earlier lifeless planetary state. A fuller treatment of the problem of the origin of life, and its dependence on a theory of the nature of the living state, is pursued in [382].

Among the most important revisions argued there is the need for a comprehensive theory of stability and total, asymptotic error correction in systems which develop complex, multilevel order that is inherently an order of *processes*. Total error correction is a concept formalized in communication theory [333] and optimal control theory [18], and also in statistical physics [165] (though only sometimes in this language). In the context of biology it leads to a distinction between such processes as Darwinian selection on populations as *mechanisms supporting* error correction, and the closure of error correction itself. It is argued that a theory of total biological error correction must also account for the context of population processes originating in scales ranging from chemistry to ecology, which determine the "paths of least resistance" along which the optimal control problem of evolution possesses solutions.

10.10.1   Envoi

In the near-poetic area around ecology, biology, economics, and organization theory which we have here briefly explored, much is in a high state of flux, definitions are incomplete, taxonomies are shaky, and analogies and metaphors abound. We considered styling the representative of a human as "a portrait of the artist as a 2^{42}-person game," with the actors being the human cells and the organs institutions; but decided to provide a somewhat more sober overview indicating that the time is drawing close when these highly diverse disciplines will have much to contribute to a joint understanding.[35]

Notes

1 Including the specification of initial conditions.

2 Even with the poor, social custom clashes with utilitarian economics. Among the nearly destitute, weddings and funerals provide an opportunity for conspicuous consumption that the individuals can ill afford from the viewpoint of mere economics.

3 There are some special consumption sinks for the centimillionaire or billionaire such as high-end art collection or running one's own space program, buying a major sports team, or becoming a philanthropist. Buying political office or satisfying one's need for revenge in the style of the Count of Monte Cristo can be sinks for conspicuous consumption.

4 As von Neumann himself stressed, axioms such as this must have their basis in observations of the physical world, hence they should be testable. Although intuitively attractive, the whole concept of the existence of an individual utility function is fraught with difficulties and has not yielded much in the way of satisfactory experimental results.

5 A completely different way to approach measurable utility was proposed by Lloyd Shapley. The measure is developed utilizing axioms describing individual ability to perceive preference differences among pairs of objects. An individual can state that her preference for item a over b is greater than, less than, or equal to her preference for c over d. The two scales are clearly different and require a further axiom in order to match that is, in all probability, empirically false [297].

6 The bound may well be loose in the sense of some decision rule such as "Stay within 10 percent of last year's budget"; but unless the question being asked of the theory requires that details of consumption be relevant to investment, there is no need to provide them to consider investment.

7 Although it requires considerable legal consideration to define the operational meaning of the ownership of government, the religious bodies, educational institutions, and other social institutions.

8 Chapter 20 of [359] was devoted to considering this possibility.

9 The tension between physical production economics and financial and ownership economics is illustrated in the different uses of the word "capital."

10 Other than the possibly real joys of looking at an undeveloped uninhabited landscape.

11 Leaving out Man Friday.

12 In chapters 8 and 9 of [359] a long list of functions of these institutions was given. The set of functions reinforce each other, yet a central minimal function of two of these institutions is the variation of the money supply. In the ideal world of complete markets run by the perfect clearinghouse this disappears. How close to this ideal a modern economy can approach is not evident. But even the slightest friction makes the limit unattainable.

13 We could further divide a commercial bank's money into banknotes and checks and pure ciphers, but at this point we stay with "red chips."

14 This could include the signed, legalized IOU notes of the borrowers as "white chips" that may serve as a local or global money depending on the size of the acceptance network.

15 Although names for highly changed institutions may remain the same, such as "bank."

16 Any good modern text on financial institutions such as Ang [9] or Elton et al. [111] provides a listing. A discussion is also given in [359], ch. 8, p. 217.

17 We use the adjective "porous" to indicate that depending on the timescale the boundary conditions may change as part of "the games within the game," where the rules for financial motion are set by political control and that, in turn, may be subjected to social pressure.

18 This provides a considerable simplification that was also utilized in chapter 3 of volume 1 of Schumpeter's discussion of business cycles [326].

19 These are societal rules and there is no logical reason to rule out interest payments.

20 We rule out wash selling by consumers as it can be shown that with a continuum of agents it will not occur. Examples were derived in chapter 4.

21 Some entries in these lists can of course be negative. The entries indicated are gross "receipts" or "payments" when they are positive. If they are negative, then the converse.

22 Even here the clash between law, custom, and reputation appears. If an individual's IOU is accepted endorsed to others at face value, she has, for practical purposes, created a near money.

23 Selection for robustness, of course, may co-occur with selection for other properties such as adaptability, and the two forces may or may not be aligned. We discuss the particular interaction between robustness and adaptability further below.

24 In a somewhat different way, Marvin Minsky's *The Society of Mind* [264] can be interpreted as stressing modularity.

25 The first high-level languages in wide industrial use were all procedural. These included FORTRAN and C. Procedural languages act directly on memory stores in the form of variables with assigned values, in a way that offers only limited protection against interference by the procedures in one section of code with structures of data or even assigned values that other sections of code depend on having preserved. In object-oriented languages (of which almost all heavily used modern programming languages are instances), both data and procedures are *encapsulated* into structures termed *objects*, which provide defined input/output services through defined interfaces. An object's internal mechanism for providing these services is permitted to change freely, and as long as it supports the defined function through defined interfaces, its interaction with other objects in higher-level architectures is undisturbed. For an introduction to concepts and applications, see [36].

26 Whether buffering or amplifying the exposure of errors is an advantage can depend on population size. Krakauer and Plotkin [214] show in models that either behavior can itself be selected, and they argue, for a range of mechanisms observed in biology, that those actively provide either buffering or amplification.

27 The folding of a polypeptide chain into a three-dimensional functional protein is a complex process of packing in space subject to a network of interlocking constraints of molecular affinity both within the chain and with molecules (water or lipids) in the embedding environment. The search for a most-stable fold is a combinatorially hard optimization problem, and the fast and reliable folding of polypeptides is not a generic property. One method of fast and reliable folding starts with collapse of local regions into three-dimensional structures that will remain in the final folded state, and subsequent accretion of other parts of the sequence onto these kernels. Such folding avoids traps of locally stable but globally unstable (termed *metastable*) folds, so that the free energy landscape on which the polypeptide passes from the unfolded state to its final state resembles a funnel with mostly smooth walls, rather than a jagged surface with many local minima in which the folding process can lodge in a nonfunctional state. Some proteins that do not fold in such kinetic funnels may be aided by so-called "chaperones." These are helper proteins that sense signatures of misfolding (such as amino acids at the surface of a fold that are incompatible with the solvent), and either unfold the misfolded chain or in some other manner help guide it to the stable functional final state.

28 The paradigmatic examples of this phenomenon are active, negative-feedback control loops in amplifier design. Characteristics such as the response time or amplitude range in the setpoint of a controller create frequency bands of shocks that it can actively compensate. Outside this band, the active response of the controller can amplify rather than suppress shocks, leading to control loop failure. The "swing angle" (phase) in AC electric power distribution systems is such a variable controlled by phase adjustments among power plants driving a transmission line system. Failure of the swing angle control system can lead some power plants to drain the transmission line while others drive it, a situation that requires system shutdown to avoid catastrophic overload and destruction of the system components.

29 We mention carbon fixation because its innovations involve the most complex network changes and continued to arise for the longest time. For some other equally fundamental processes in primary production, the same assertion is true in even simpler form. The two primary mechanisms to produce energetic phosphates were likely in place by the formation of the first cells [74, 248, 289]. Nitrogen fixation appears to have evolved a single time, deep in the preoxygenic period [41, 303], and to have retained its core mechanisms for the remainder of history.

30 This comparison refers to the estimate of 1.06 percent of fixed differences in single-nucleotide polymorphisms (SNPs), for which such a numerical comparison may readily be made. Other changes include insertions, deletions, and chromosomal rearrangements, but these do not qualitatively alter the degree of similarity claimed from SNPs.

31 An existing estimate from Woodruff et al. is that the protein-coding footprint continues to scale as the 1/4-power of cell size found for whole-genome scaling in bacteria [368]. However, these data still are not published, and we do not know how much current work by Brown et al. may alter the claims.

32 The tiny numbers and overall universality of core genes that are metabolically essential to create a self-sufficient living ecosystem contrast with the enormous number and variability of gene variants and regulatory strategies used in ecosystems. Shotgun sequencing of genes from the Sargasso sea by Venter et al. [405] was interpreted as identifying more than 1.2 million previously unidentified genes.

33 The role played by selection in development as well as in population evolution is carefully discussed in developmental biology [45, 183]. Selection does not cease to function within development, but the emergence of organism-level organization changes the mechanisms that generate variation [158] and the selective context, thereby subsuming the "learning" aspect of selective dynamics within cell differentiation in the frame of single generations. Aligning the consequences of selection on cell populations within an organism's lifetime with the population-level selective forces that make the organism fit in its ecological context is one of the major problems that development solves, in ways that researchers still actively seek to understand.

Three widely recognized contexts in which selection grants significant autonomy to cell populations within a single organism include the function of the adaptive immune system, the perfusion and pruning of neuronal synapses in brain development, and the pathological proliferation of cells in cancers. Here the behavior of cell populations retains more of the manifest character of autonomy usually associated with organisms in ecological contexts.

34 We find Friedman's characterization here, like much of "social Darwinism," to leave much to be desired. R. A. Fisher famously opened *The Genetical Theory of Natural Selection* [131] with the statement "Natural selection is not evolution." Serious evolutionary studies [158, 169] are sensitive throughout to the structure in the mechanisms that generate variation, the units and levels of development and selection, the requirements for stability that limit viable developmental programs, and the coevolutionary dynamics in ecosystems that determine which ways of life can survive together. Darwin was, in the best of his tradition of natural history, a student of relations and system dynamics [70]. It can be cogent to argue that agents need not be rational in strategizing and planning if *ex post* selection can filter populations for strategies so that the survivors function "as if" they had chosen rationally. However, characterizing established power structures as "fit" simply by virtue of their prevalence is at best a statistical tautology if the assumptions underlying Fisherian fitness as a summary statistic are met [140], and at worst an analogy with no formal status if Fisherian fitness is not defined for the class of actors or strategies being described. Some analyses of recent banking failures [167, 168, 393] seem to us good examples of the kind of economic "ecological" depth that could support a serious application of evolutionary ideas.

35 It is worth noting that quantitative differences often are linked with qualitative differences in understanding the nature of the dynamics. A few frivolous orders of magnitude are observed here.

The number of people on earth is under 10^{10} and the number of ants is possibly 10^{15}. The number of stars in the Milky Way may be as high as 4×10^{11}, with the universe holding around 10^{13} or 10^{14} galaxies. The number of atoms in the galaxy may be around 10^{68} or 10^{69}. In contrast the number of firms in the US in 1992 was 23×10^6 of which 5.7×10^6 had a payroll. An oligopolistic industry has around 2–20 firms.

11 Mathematical Institutional Economics and the Theory of Money and Financial Institutions

11.1 Mathematical Institutional Economics

There is no royal road or philosopher's stone that will provide for an all-encompassing economic dynamics at the same level that general equilibrium answered the highly restricted but extremely pertinent questions it posed about the conditions required for the existence of a set of one or more efficient market-clearing prices.

The dynamics of a mass economy with government and laws poses a host of problems far more complex than the existence proof of an efficient price system in equilibrium in a preinstitutional economy with no public goods and either a utopian state of trust or an implicit referee or government that consumes no resources.

In chapter 6 we quoted F. Y. Edgeworth concerning the particular character of each real economic problem in its context. One might regard Edgeworth's comments as an observation of extreme pessimism, yet they contain a basic nub of truth when directed at application to economics. When dealing with application there is no substitute for knowing your business. The basic reason why applied economics is split into so many fields is that each of these specializations requires that relevant special details be added. The structure, mappings, functional forms, and parameters are ad hoc and require knowledge and expertise pertaining to the questions at hand.

11.2 What Is a Theory?

What is a theory? Different disciplines utilize the word differently. Furthermore "model" and "theory" appear on occasion to be used interchangeably. Several suggestions are noted below.

One might approach this question by querying currently institutionalized scientific authorities. The National Academy of Sciences of the United States [428] defines theory as:

> A plausible or scientifically acceptable, well-substantiated explanation of some aspect of the natural world; an organized system of accepted knowledge that applies in a variety of circumstances to explain a specific set of phenomena and predict the characteristics of as yet unobserved phenomena.

It also defines fact:

> In science, a "fact" typically refers to an observation, measurement, or other form of evidence that can be expected to occur the same way under similar circumstances. However, scientists also use the term "fact" to refer to a scientific explanation that has been tested and confirmed so many times that there is no longer a compelling reason to keep testing it or looking for additional examples [*pace* Black Swans].

Aristotle contrasted theory to "practice." *Praxis*, the Greek term for "doing," is concerned with application, while pure theory is not concerned with immediate application. An often used example comes from medicine. Medical research may be concerned with attempting to understand the causes of a disease without being immediately concerned with practice. In contrast good practitioners are more concerned with curing patients of a disease, and if they find a cure but not a deep explanation they are reasonably content (as are the patients). Central bankers may have the same view of the current financial system. Unfortunately, as yet their level of success appears to be far from that in medicine.

A mathematical view of a theory is deductive. A theory's (possibly full sensory or empirical) content is given by basic axioms, and a formal logic develops the theory. The logical consequences of the axioms are presented as theorems.

A semantic view of theories is as models providing a logical framework connected with some aspect of observation. They are abstractions or simplifications of some aspects of the real world.

In economics there are many subdivisions that tend to intermix theory and practice. Possibly the major rift is between micro- and macroeconomics.

There are many subdivisions of microeconomics (including the often not recognized applied field of operations research) where practitioners and theorists are highly intermixed.

A distinction often made to sort out the pure theorists from those highly involved with immediate empirical matters is between those devoted primarily to normative concerns ("what should be") and those more inclined to positive economics (stressing "what is"). Recently in finance and macroeconomics the term "engineer" has been used to indicate those involved with problems at hand. This may even include retreaded PhD physicists or top probability theorists devising complex derivatives or algorithms to take advantage of local correlations in time series in stock trading.

Small purist areas are the bastion of some game theorists and general equilibrium theorists devoted to exploring classical logical positivistic axiomatic and mathematical methods. Thus models abound varying the axioms on formal concepts of fair division, bargaining, and the mathematics of preference theory. The use of these models in experimental economics and social psychology is increasing.

11.2.1   Let a thousand specializations blossom!

Beyond the major divisions of micro- and macroeconomics, not only are there many economic theories with modifiers attached such as international economics, welfare economics, labor economics, health economics, and so forth; there are also divisions such as behavioral economics where the assumptions on behavior, including individual optimization and the standard models of utilitarian economic agents, are challenged. For example, some results in experimental gaming have indicated that the double-auction market is reasonably efficient even when operated by agents with limited intelligence.

The main thrust of macroeconomics is clearly operational. It deals with the dynamics of the whole economy, encompassing features such as inflation, economic cycles and growth, unemployment, and monetary and fiscal policy. An honorable employment for the macroeconomist is to give operational quantitative and qualitative advice to governments.

The political economists, economic historians, and historians of economic thought still provide broad insights utilizing the essay form as their way to deal with the imponderables.

Especially in application, the closely related disciplines of finance, accounting, and law intertwine with many economic investigations. The disciplines of sociology, social psychology, and psychology serve to challenge the behavioral axioms underlying many economic models. And recently the disciplines of physics, ecology, and biology have been considered as potential contributors to economic understanding of growth, innovation, and evolution.

As admirers of formal theories with clean axioms, interesting theorems and proofs, and concerned with invariant properties, we suggest that the strategic market game approach has offered a general modeling device which, when combined with expertise in understanding context and institutions, takes needed steps toward a mathematical institutional economics, one that may provide better understanding of the financial control of the overall economy that is called for by the complexity and evolution of the sociopolitical environment in which all economies must function.

11.3   Abstract Theory beyond General Equilibrium

This book's underlying goal has been to provide a basic theory of money and financial institutions and to link it with mathematical institutional economics in application. Several closely related but different subgoals must be dealt with in order to understand the way the control and evaluation system of a society is manifested in the private and public financial institutions of the sociopolitical economy.

Subgoal 1: One of our main goals has been to show that the natural preliminary step before dynamics is to transform and bring the observations derived from general equilibrium theory into a process model. This is provided in the structure of a game in strategic form. Such a game can be solved in many ways and the connection with and differences from the CEs established. In doing so a basic theory of money emerges, with money playing an important role in the emergence of an exchange mechanism. Utilizing the material in chapters 2–4, we are at the jumping-off point for dynamics.

Subgoal 2: A second subgoal has been to provide a formal analytical model of a process linking innovation and the breaking of the circular flow of money described by Schumpeter. This, as noted in chapters 9 and 10, is aided by an understanding of both various forms of increasing returns and the nonsymmetric distribution of agent size, power, ownership, and wealth in the economy.

Subgoal 3: A third subgoal has been to devise a general model-building methodology with stress on a fully defined state space and the utilization of the methods of physics in examining features such as dimensionality, conservation, symmetry, and scaling. This is noted in chapter 7. In particular the emergence of money appears to be related to the concept of symmetry breaking.

Tied in with this as a constant theme has been the call for the construction of models as *playable games* that can meet the test of operational specificity required for experimental gaming. Unfortunately there is a difficulty posed here. The pull between synthesis and analysis is ever present in political economy. A tradeoff must be made between concretion and abstraction. The more the political economy needs to reflect context, the less formal will be the mathematical model and the more the description and analysis will depend on the essay and the free-form type of game rather than one with rigid rules.[1] This is where the mixed scientific-art form of mathematical institutional economics enters. The ad hoc mixture of model building guided by context must be reflected in the modeling that precedes the analysis.

Subgoal 4: A fourth subgoal has been to frame problems of economic optimization in a way that naturally incorporates structure from the material world, whether physical, biological, cognitive, social, or institutional. The abstraction of costless and complete contracts covering all contingent circumstances [13] renders moot the relations within classes of goods, or even of the same good at different times, and optimization against simple linear budget sets can be used. An economy operating within material reality faces constraints ranging from the topology of space and time to distinctions between discrete and continuous classes of objects, to problems of concurrency and unavoidable by-products (such as waste streams), the finiteness of planetary resources, and limitations in human-social communication and computation. Each of these has rich structure, the study of which is most of the content of some dedicated science. The integration of what is known about these structures into any theory of decision making is essential for the theory to attain more than superficial validity.

11.4   Strategic Market Games and the Theory of Money

The simplest basic model of exchange is the one-period exchange economy, for which chapters 2–4 were devoted to constructing minimal process models. Here we recap several of our comments from there and set them in a more general and basic context involving markets, prices, and money.

There are only a few ways to construct minimal process models associated with the basic general equilibrium (GE) model. They are the highly decentralized *trading post* model that has formed the basis for several strategic market games [336, 339, 352] and the *windows* or *clearinghouse evaluation* model that leads to a game representation or a closed economy with a centralized clearing and price formation agency for the whole economy [311].

In 2003 Dubey and Sahi [98] were able to establish that both the trading post and windows models could be regarded as extreme members of a large class of mechanisms providing the basic structure of mass trade. They showed that these conclusions arise from four simple basic axioms underlying the structure of trade. These are noted below in section 11.5.3. Prior to discussing them and the strategic market games, basic modeling problems concerning the general equilibrium model are reiterated.[2]

11.4.1   Modeling a basic closed dynamic system

In going from the static, preinstitutional [211] highly abstracted formulations of general equilibrium by Arrow, Arrow and Debreu [12], and Debreu and McKenzie to a fully defined process model, care must be taken of both the modeling and its interpretation. In this discussion, for expository convenience references are made primarily to Debreu's 1959 book [79].

The formulation of modern general equilibrium price theory was achieved with an admirable and ruthless abstraction devoted to providing as lean and abstract a structure as possible, sufficient to catch the basic features of a price system and provide a mathematically tractable problem to prove the existence of an equilibrium.

The primitive concepts utilized were sets of price-taking consumer/traders; profit-maximizing firms; nonvoting shares in ownership of the firms; consumption/production goods; and their prices as well as the preferences of the consumer/traders. The existence of costless markets, clearing arrangements (clearinghouses, the commercial code, and accounting), and the rule of law were all implicitly assumed. Two ingenious assumptions concerning time and uncertainty were made that were sufficient to extend the mathematical analysis to include any finite number of time periods and any finite number of states of the system generated by stochastic events. Complications in common knowledge and information conditions were also implicitly abstracted away from the analysis.

Debreu stressed his use of the axiomatic method and mathematical rigor in his approach to the price system [79, p. viii]. The axioms require, as he noted, a selection from the observable world.

The concern here is with the economy as a fully defined game of strategy in strategic form. This involves a reexamination of the primitive concepts used in non-process-equilibrium-oriented models and appropriate additions to the assumptions. In particular attention is paid to the information processing conditions and the concept of the emergence of a market structure and to price formation mechanisms that precede the full formulation of a strategic market game.

11.4.1.1   The strategic and extensive forms   The economic structure presented in Debreu's book is closer to that of a game in strategic form rather than to one in extensive form. A game in extensive form displays the details of all moves and information conditions from the initial node of the game to all terminal positions. The simplest game in the potentially enormous set that will arise when information conditions are included is the game where all players have a single information set.[3]

11.4.2   Price taking and an NE solution

The GE formulation assumes price taking. All individuals regard themselves as without influence on price. A way to make this precise is to consider the consumer/trader agents as being composed of a continuum of small agents and demonstrate that the lack of influence on price is true. We may then show that with some additional modeling the GE and SMG solutions can be linked (see [97]).

11.4.2.1   Minimal mechanisms and multiple functions   The basic axioms or assumptions made in economic modeling may be regarded as minimal in one context but not in another; for example, Debreu's consumer is a consumer, trader, saver, investor, and worker all wrapped into one (as well as, implicitly, a sociopolitical animal). She has multiple functions.

A profit-maximizing firm may be, and is treated as, a primitive concept in the Debreu analysis; but in other analyses the firm is far from a primitive concept but is a complex, multiperson, multipurpose organism (see for example Williamson [417] or Padgett and Powell [281]).

If we use a mechanism approach to institutions and agents, we may try to create a serviceable, useful definition of "minimal" by defining the list of functions that the institution or agent is meant to provide and considering that any mathematical representation of an institution or agent is minimal if the removal of any part of the mechanism results in its inability to perform at least one of its functions.

It is in the spirit of considering the need for the addition of extra modeling assumptions or axioms to the basic GE model of exchange that we consider how to convert the GE model into a playable game.

11.5   Market Structures and SMGs

In the various publications on strategic market games there are two basically different types of exchange structures that have been considered leading to the formation of price. They are:

- The trading post structure,
- The window structure.

Dubey and Sahi [98] have shown that these two items can be studied as pure mechanisms for handling information even without having to formulate a full strategic game that explicitly involves players and preferences. By means of the four axioms noted below, they show that the trading post and windows mechanisms for price formation can be regarded as extreme cases of a general message model. The first has local clearing at each trading post. The second has an economy-wide clearing system and has no separate markets; instead it has a central message-gathering system that processes all messages and calculates prices as part of a centralized system that announces universal clearing prices.

11.5.1   Two stages to dynamics: structure and behavior

Setting economic dynamics on a sound basis requires the understanding that there is an interweave between the modeling and the mathematics. It calls for opening a methodology for model building of a mathematical institutional economics that permits the natural construction of the mechanisms of trade, followed by the specification of individual agents with ownership claims and goals that enable the modeler to define fully the strategy and payoff sets of each individual.

A fully defined SMG does not provide for actual dynamics. In order to obtain the equations of motion in any economy portrayed by an SMG, the concept of solution must be supplied. It is well known that no universal solution concept exists. Much work both in micro- and macroeconomics utilizes variants of the noncooperative equilibrium; but there are a host of other solution concepts involving learning, teaching, and various levels of communication. What these observations suggest is that from the viewpoint of application there is no substitute for knowing your business, and in the nonpejorative meaning of the term ad hoc modeling is called for. Relevant microeconomic, technical, behavioral, and contextual details must be supplied to account for the differences between the steel industry and growing cabbages prior to supplying the equations of motion.

11.5.2   The minimal trading model

We limit ourselves to considering a one-period mass trading economy E with m goods and n consumer/traders. We consider how many ways it may be remodeled as a set of strategic market games.

The exchange economy can be described as follows. Let $I_n = \{1, 2, \ldots, n\}$ be the set of traders, $I_m = \{1, 2, \ldots, m\}$ be the set of goods, and $\{p_1, p_2, \ldots, p_m\} \in R_m^+$ be the set of market prices for the goods.

Each trader α is assumed to have an endowment and utility function $u^\alpha : R_m^+ \to R$ that is continuous, concave, and nondecreasing and is assumed to maximize her or his utility. Consider $u^\alpha \left(x_1^\alpha, x_2^\alpha, \ldots, x_m^\alpha \right)$ to be the utility function of α. An individual α has an initial endowment of $a \in R_m^+$ or $\left(a_1^\alpha, a_2^\alpha, \ldots, a_m^\alpha \right)$; then each acts to

$$\max u^\alpha \left(x_1^\alpha, x_2^\alpha, \ldots, x_m^\alpha \right)$$

subject to

$$\sum_{j=1}^{m} p_j \left(x_j^\alpha - a_j^\alpha \right) = 0, \tag{11.1}$$

and the set of prices that clears all markets efficiently is shown to exist.

Even at this level of abstraction, either there have to be rules preventing the sellers of contracts from being unable to deliver or there must be failure to deliver settlement laws. In Debreu these are implicit in the strict budget constraints.

In contrast with the above, every strategic market game requires that the trading system be made explicit. For precision and in order to link our observations to an easily understood graph we restate several of the comments in chapter 4 somewhat differently. We represent a commodity[4] by a point. The existence of a direct exchange mechanism between two commodities is an arc directly connecting any two points representing commodities i and j.

An *exchange structure* of an economy is the configuration of a set of markets. In considering market structures there are two cases to be noted:

- Structures where the graph on the m points consists of two or more separate connected components. It is not feasible to trade some goods for some others.

- Structures where there is at least one path connecting any i to another j. If the graph is fully connected, an exchange of one commodity for another is always feasible, but not necessarily in one round of trade.[5] When there is at least one configuration in the form of a star, a distinguished commodity j

may be defined as a *money*. It has arcs connected directly to all the other $m - 1$ commodities. Dubey, Sahi, and Shubik [104] show that this has special minimal properties as noted below.

In the early development of SMGs the concentration of modeling and analysis was on games with $m - 1$ markets and a single money.[6] The usage was to call this the "trading post model" because a direct physical analogue could be made between a market and a physical entity where the messages and the goods were directly delivered and trade between a single good and money balanced locally. A market could be regarded as a trading post that accepts messages directly and provides local aggregation, computation, and disaggregation services that produce reallocations and prices.

At the other extreme the "windows trading model" informally suggested by Shapley and developed by Sahi and Yao [311] made use of a central computation and clearinghouse that reviews all messages and provides an algorithm to announce a set of consistent prices that clear all offers and bids.[7]

In the literature on SMG Sahi and Yao require a global solution given by a set of linear equations to guarantee global consistency of prices; in contrast Amir et al. [8] (ASSY) treated all markets as trading posts, leading to the possibility of type-symmetric noncooperative equilibria (TSNEs) that were not CEs.

The work of Dubey and Sahi [98] provides axioms that can be applied to any mechanism based on the network of trading posts. The axioms are directed toward the definition and characterization of the properties of a class of mechanisms and not directly toward the games that can be constructed using these mechanisms.

Clower [58] incorrectly described the structure in which m^2 trading posts exist as "barter." This misses the important functions of aggregation of many anonymous bids and offers to form prices, calculation, and then the disaggregation to produce the reassignment of ownership of the objects traded. When all trading posts exist with an aggregating and disaggregating price-forming device at each, then all commodities could be selected to act as a money. The complete graph can be descried as the union of m trees with $m - 1$ arcs or branches each.

Both in practice and theory the volume or broadness of a market as an aggregating device is critical in determining its viability and stability.

Although much of the analysis of strategic market games has utilized a finite number of agents, when considering large numbers of traders it is more convenient to regard an economy with n types of agent with a continuum of each, so that each agent views her influence on the aggregate aspects of exchange as negligible.

11.5.3   Trading post or other models?

Dubey and Sahi [98] utilized four axioms to establish the nature of trade in a broad class of mechanisms, entitled *G-mechanisms*, that provide structure not present in GE.[8]

A G-mechanism is defined as follows: "each trader α sends a signal which consists of nonnegative numbers a_{ij}^{α} for each arc (i,j) in G, where a_{ij}^{α} indicates the amount of commodity i that he is offering in exchange for commodity j. The prices and returns are given by the formulas for the windows mechanism, where we understand a_{ij}^{α} to be zero for nonexisting arcs."

The axioms are:

1. Aggregation,

2. Invariance,

3. Price mediation, and

4. Accessibility.

The set of all G-mechanisms may be regarded as consisting of the set of all connected graphs that can be constructed on m points. Figure 11.1a shows the complete graph for five goods where any good may be regarded as having the transactions property of a money. Figure 11.1b shows an irreducible graph with one money only.

Axiom 1 indicates that if a player pretends to be more than one player by splitting his signals, this has no influence on prices or returns.[9]

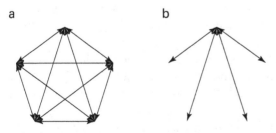

a   b

Figure 11.1

Graphs among goods: (a) a complete graph, (b) an irreducible graph with only one money.

Axiom 2 indicates invariance with respect to the scaling of units of measurement for the goods.

Axiom 3 indicates that returns to a player depend only on his signal and prices. Price consistency is assumed.

Axiom 4 describes the closed feasible set attainable by an individual given any configuration of the action of others.

The trading post and windows models are at the information processing extremes in the set of all G-mechanisms. A natural question to raise is whether there are any further considerations that would suggest that an economy would select the trading post model over the windows model or vice versa.

In a further investigation Dubey, Sahi, and Shubik [104] with somewhat different axioms (noted here) also defined two measures of complexity; the first is the number of exchanges required to complete a trade and the second the complexity in the messages required to guide the trade.

The axioms are:

1. Invariance,

2. Aggregation,

3. Anonymity,

4. Nondissipation, and

5. Flexibility.

The first two axioms are essentially as before. Axiom 3 says that the mechanism depends only on the message of the individual. Axiom 4 rules out that goods that have been bid or offered vanish from the system, and Axiom 5 indicates that if i is connected to j by any path, then any amount of i can be converted eventually completely into j.

Let $M(m)$ stand for the set of mechanisms that satisfy the axioms. For any mechanism we ask what is the minimum number of trades required to convert a commodity i into j. We denote by $\tau_{ij}(M)$ the *time complexity* for this conversion.

A further complexity defined as informational or more intuitively as price complexity is also considered. Having shown that prices will emerge, Dubey et al. [104] considered *price complexity* $\pi(M)$ to be the minimal number of components of the aggregate offer that are needed to compute exchange rates.

The axioms above are sufficient to show not only that markets and prices emerge as a consequence but that given the two complexity measures, time and price complexity, the trading post model mechanism emerges as the optimal

Table 11.1
Time and space complexities associated with markets in m goods

	Star	Cycle	Full
$\pi(M)$	4	2	$m(m-1)$
$\tau(M)$	2	$m-1$	1

mechanism when there are *many* commodities for trade. Table 11.1 shows the complexity levels for the two extreme cases, the star and the complete graph mechanisms, and between them the cycle mechanism where every commodity i has two neighbors (a circular arrangement).

We observe that as m becomes large the star mechanism or single money is dominated slightly by one component of the other two, but it dominates them in the other component by an arbitrarily large amount. The mechanism simplicity indicates little, if anything, about the complexity of individual strategies in an optimization as it deals only with mechanisms and messages, not individuals and optimization.

In physics the concept of "symmetry breaking" is well known. The emergence of a money in a situation where intrinsically there appears to be complete symmetry among all commodities is an exemplar of this phenomenon.

The proof of the formal theorem establishing the emergence of markets, prices, and the star mechanism of the single money as the structure with minimal complexity calls for some somewhat complex combinatorics, and the formal proof is presented in the study noted [104].

11.6   From Mechanisms to Games

Given any mechanism, in order to flesh out a fully playable game, players, endowments, and preferences (or some other behavioral condition) must be introduced explicitly.

The institutions of an economy provide a sufficient set of rules to support the processes the society requires. There are many institutional details that may exist only to accommodate the particular habits and customs of a specific society. Even though the general class of G-games may appear to be generally applicable to the abstractions of GE, they cover only a small part of the general socioeconomic processes of price formation. Many of these are embedded in time in such a way that our limitation to one-period exchange cannot do them full justice.

There is a literature on price formation in marketing (see for example [85, 425]) that apparently only weakly intersects the work of economic theorists. In economics recently the (unpublished) work of Bewley has been concerned with the intricacies of price formation.

A few of the natural divisions in price formation methods are noted.

11.6.1   A comment on general price formation

A rough categorization of different price formation mechanisms in a complex economy requires differentiating the various mechanisms and institutions found there.

In *finance*, private financial instruments involve primarily two or a few parties and may be hand-tailored by investment bankers, lawyers, and accountants over many months. In contrast there are mass markets for standardized instruments such as stocks, puts, calls, and standard derivatives where round-the-clock over-the-counter trading or double-auction markets exist. In these markets the expertise of principals and brokers, consultants, and experts may be high, but when the professionals play each other the game is close to constant sum. As evaluation of the issues of well-known companies improves, there are diminishing returns to expertise (see for example [239]). The individual direct stockholder is becoming a less common species.

Even better than in a poker game where the professionals live off the amateurs, in many of the markets many of the professionals not only have the opportunity to live off the errors and "animal spirits" of the amateurs, they also obtain "something off the top" in fees from running retirement funds, mutual funds, or hedge funds.

Then there are price formation mechanisms for *consumer goods*. Small fungible consumer items such as food, clothing, and household consumables are for the most part sold in stores and supermarkets with prices posted and moved by the seller. The sellers may use simple cost-plus-markup pricing, or algorithms based on sales. Then there are large consumer items such as automobiles and housing where there may be a posted price but there is leeway in bargaining and active middlemen and the Web play a role. Furthermore there is considerable legal work involving binary contracts. Overlaid on all consumer markets is an array of marketing messages in which an admixture of product information is combined with an array of messages designed to have sociopsychological influence on the preferences and behavior of the purchasers. This is hardly a setting for the customer as a simple rational optimizer of a fixed set of preferences.

Luxury items not only are subject to considerable taste-molding marketing, they include nonfungible items such as art that call for specialized dealers with high expertise and sales ability as well as auctions preceded by valuations.

Wages and salaries fall into a special category. They may be paid hourly, daily, weekly, monthly, or annually and represent a complex process involving technical, sociological, and economic factors with many shadings involving perquisites, bonuses, and many variants on the simple price (such as working at home, seniority, health and retirement conditions).

Producer goods reflect their institutional specifics, including in some instances cost-plus pricing and in many instances oligopolistic pricing that depends on technological specifics such as indivisibilities and capacity constraints. They also involve long-term supply contracts.

Government procurement provides yet another category. Here, especially when size is large, political and bureaucratic considerations are difficult to avoid. Thus even the use of sealed simultaneous bids poses considerable policing difficulties. Given the complexity in technological evaluation, the bidding may even involve a multistage process with the first round devoted to establishing the technological and institutional capabilities needed in order to qualify as a bidder in a final bidding process.

This brief overview of pricing is given to indicate that even the most abstract of theorists needs to acknowledge the unavoidably ad hoc aspects of economic dynamics. This is why we observe that even to establish consistency between general equilibrium theorizing and the process models of economic dynamics requires at least a study of minimal process models.

11.6.1.1   On the complexity and simplicity of strategies   In the market mechanisms of Dubey and Sahi, in order to construct fully playable games of strategy, player preferences and endowments must be introduced.

Looking for the simplest set of SMG that cover the GE trading model, we may ask, given a market structure, what is the minimal size of the strategy set of a player that can be utilized. It is one without contingencies permitted. In a one-period game without contingencies a message and the physical act it calls for can be regarded as the same; thus we may consider a strategy as shipping commodities and a commodity money or fiat to a trading post.[10] The message and the medium may coincide!

11.6.1.2   Quantity strategies   The message sent by a minimal strategy to a single simple market or trading post has to be one of two forms (b), (b, q). Continuing our observations from chapter 2, we define the first as *sell-all*, where all goods are up for sale and the individual bids money to buy each, and the second as *buy-sell*. They have been studied for m trading posts, as has been shown for bid-all and buy-sell in [339] and [102].[11]

When there are m^2 trading posts, any good can serve as a money. In the DSS [104] analysis all goods are intrinsically symmetric; hence there is no reason to select among them. Extra conditions, such as physical and legal properties as noted below, may serve to select a single money.

The debate on the use of the price system in a centralized economy versus the emergence of price in a decentralized economy was argued with vigor from the 1930s through the 1950s and was unresolved with the advent of general equilibrium theory. The Debreu book gives the existence proof for price that could equally well fit a centralized or decentralized economy.

The ideal centralized Soviet economy could be regarded as one utilizing even more than the windows mechanism, with the government claiming full knowledge of the rules of the game including all preferences and ownership claims and attempting an optimization to set prices and order allocations based on these prices. In actuality the information conditions were asymmetric, and the truth revelation games played primarily within a large bureaucracy may well have damaged the Soviet economy.

11.6.1.3   One basic and two modified price formation mechanisms   The *sell-all* and *buy-sell* mechanisms may be associated with Cournot and with noncontingent pure strategies involving quantities.

In the *buy-sell* models individual traders are assumed to be endowed with goods and some form of money (it could be a special good, fiat money, or personal IOU notes). In essence the basic *buy-sell* message covers the generality of one-move price formation without contingencies. It is the Cournot-style price formation mechanism.

11.6.2   On different monies

A *money* has been defined as a commodity that in an economy with m commodities is directly connected with trading posts to all the $m - 1$ other commodities, like the center of a star or the root of a tree. In describing the mechanism we made no distinction among commodities or any tradable financial instrument.

In constructing an actual SMG, the nature of the instrument that serves as a money may make a difference. There are two basic instruments that serve as a money in the construction of SMG models of trade (see chapter 5): *commodity money*[12] and *fiat money*. They serve somewhat different roles in the game construction, as is indicated below.

A commodity money is a tradable instrument whose node is connected directly to all other nodes. The amount of money in an economy sums to a positive number. Furthermore it has, or its services have, a consumption value.

A fiat money is a tradable instrument whose node is connected directly to all other nodes. It is placed into circulation by a government which may be modeled directly as an atomic player usually assumed to be large in comparison with other players. The amount of fiat in an economy sums to a positive amount. It has no consumption value.[13]

There are two near monies or credit instruments that serve as a means of payment or account for payments and are either explicit or implicit contracts. They are:

- Individual IOU notes issued by a natural person,
- Debt issued by a nonnatural legal person.

Each of them nets to zero.[14,15]

There is also an abstract or "ghost" money. It is an *abstract accounting money*. It is an implicit contract in the settlement of trade that nets to zero. It does not appear directly as part of a strategy. It is calculated (modulo selecting a free scaling parameter)[16] by an algorithm for the purchases and sales of each individual. Windows uses an accounting money.

An *individual-agent IOU money* is an instrument whose issue is under control of the issuing agent and is part of the agent's strategy. It is a promise to pay and in settlement can be calculated to net to zero by introducing and calculating exchange rates [391].[17]

A *nonnatural legal agent* other than government may issue its IOU notes as money, either by law or custom, but in general it requires the opportunity for the holder to redeem the note in fiat.

In common usage in macroeconomics, private bank debt is regarded as a major part of a country's money supply; but like all other financial instruments except for fiat it is issued with a counterparty instrument such that it balances to zero.

11.6.3   New institutions, instruments, and desired properties

In filling in the black (or gray) boxes in the GE formulation that enable us to formulate process models and eventually formulate equations of motion, we

may wish to impose extra specific properties suggested by modeling considerations such that markets are costly and one may wish to minimize the number
needed to obtain efficient trade. A commodity money in an economy with only
m simple markets may not be in sufficient supply for efficiency. Switching to
fiat money and loans that are policed may provide the simplest cure for such
inefficiency.

11.6.3.1   Some properties in the design of a minimal SMG   Some properties guiding the construction of basic SMGs are noted:

- Size limits for strategies,
- Information sets for each agent,
- Contingencies permitted in any strategy,
- Assurance that an efficient outcome for the associated exchange economy
  lies within the feasible set of the game,
- A minimal market structure for efficiency.[18]

In trying to categorize all financial instruments and institutions, one needs
a full linguistic or onomastic study that, as yet, has not been fully developed
(see [362]).

Many more complex instruments exist to handle problems that exist only
beyond the general equilibrium abstraction. They may provide fine shadings in
risk distribution (for example marine insurance); others provide for the financing of more or less indivisible items, such as expensive complex machines or
large buildings or large industrial firms. Still others exist to enable the purchasing of expertise and the pooling of investment risk, such as mutual funds. All
of these are ghosts without substance in a complete markets GE formulation.

The approach here is to strip away as many complications as possible in
the construction of SMG models to provide minimal process representations
of the GE and GEI (GE with incomplete markets) models. At even a highly
abstracted level the agents, institutions, and instruments required are:

- Traders: possibly buyers and sellers or both;
- Goods and services: possibly limited to fungibility and marketability;
- Money and/or credit: in forms noted above;
- Markets;
- Market prices and individual prices;

- Bankruptcy: reorganization or, more neutrally, inconsistency resolution rules;
- Clearinghouses: They exist primarily for settlement after trade. At the simplest level they provide the service of the clearing of agreed-upon contracts for trade. In fact they also need to deal with "fail conditions" and with information concerning delivery conditions;
- Goods delivery institutions: One may abstract this away by assuming that when a strategy involves quantities, the quantities are presumed to be physically delivered. In historical and technological fact the lags between financial and physical clearance have been different, calling forth a whole body of law, primarily the commercial code;
- Government: Even at the level of high abstraction, the government is the issuer of fiat and the enforcer of laws such as the commercial code. It is the largest player in the game and has always been such since the existence of an organized society with an economy;
- The law courts: The presence of the law courts is implicit in the resolution of repayment inconsistencies and in enforcement of contract.

11.7   The Basic Set of One-Period Strategic Market Games

The basic building blocks utilized in reviewing and constructing the SMG representations of the GE trading model are given below (with a number in parentheses indicating case distinctions):

- The trading post or windows models (2),
- Natural and other legal persons (2),
- A one-period model with quantity (Cournot) noncontingent or double-auction contingent (Edgeworth-Bertrand) strategies (2),
- Two types of asset or outside money[19] (2),
- Three types of inside money or credit (3).

An upper bound on the different models covering these four features could run to $2^4 \times 3 = 48$.[20] Fortunately there are good reasons to cut them down considerably. In particular there are strong reasons to favor the trading post SMGs over the windows model, as is shown below and proved in [104]. We nevertheless note that if we wish to have to model as few extra-institutional factors as possible, the windows SMGs based on central clearing and allocation are the most congenial. The reason is that when all allocations are made centrally involving the central knowledge of all supplies directly, there are (in an economy with a perfect, frictionless, honest bureaucracy) no liquidity problems.

Accounting money used in windows appears only as an accounting ghost because while omnipresent it does not serve any strategic purpose. It occurs in settlement where it balances the books and hence always nets to zero. In contrast, in the $(m-1)$-market trading post models where all trades in each commodity are aggregated against one money, liquidity problems often arise and one is forced to invent credit institutions.

11.7.1 SMGs with the windows mechanism

The SMGs that require the least addition of extra instruments or institutions utilize the windows mechanism. It is an ideal mechanism with perfect costless, instant clearing and centralized price calculation. The basic SMG is given by the work of Sahi and Yao [311].

11.7.1.1 The Sahi-Yao SMG Sahi and Yao [311] considered the game where a trader α submits a matrix B^α of bids subject to the constraints that all bids are nonnegative and do not violate their resource constraints. Prices are not formed in individual markets as all the messages concerning bids and offers are sent to a single location for price formation. Final settlement and price consistency require both a centralized final price calculation and a settlement or clearinghouse institution.

The price calculation requires solving m linear equations

$$\sum_{i=1}^{m}\left(\sum_{\alpha=1}^{n}a_{ij}^{\alpha}p_j\right)=p_j\sum_{i=1}^{m}\left(\sum_{\alpha=1}^{n}a_{ji}^{\alpha}\right)$$

to obtain m prices that balance sales and purchases, where a_{ij}^{α} are sales of i for j and a_{ji}^{α} are purchases.

Any attempt to construct a playable game with this market structure and pricing mechanism requires giving institutional meaning to an agency that centralizes messages and calculates prices. In essence the role of price formation is delegated to a centralized agency that aims at consistency of supply and demand, not optimality. The price formation in individual markets is no longer relevant.

11.7.1.2 The Sorin individual currency model Sorin [391] permits his agents to send individual IOU notes of any size to the central clearinghouse. It does a computation somewhat different from that of Sahi and Yao. It assumes the existence of m markets where, instead of the balance conditions of

$$p_i \left(\sum_\alpha q_i^\alpha \right) = b_i^\alpha,$$

because each individual is utilizing his own IOUs this condition is modified to

$$p_i \left(\sum_\alpha q_i^\alpha \right) = \sum_\alpha t^\alpha b_i^\alpha,$$

where the t^α are a vector of exchange rates, and the budget constraints become

$$t^\alpha \left(\sum_\alpha b_i^\alpha \right) = \sum_\alpha q_i^\alpha p_i.$$

No bankruptcy is needed in this model as it is avoided with the use of the clearinghouse and implicit enforcement of contract. It could also be called the "FX model" in the sense that all individuals are permitted to write their own IOUs to use as a money. There are n monies if there are n types of traders; more appropriately one could imagine n countries trading in m commodities but utilizing their own IOUs (currencies) and requiring a central mechanism to determine exchange rates. The concept of a tradable *personal IOU note* is added as an extra primitive concept.

Angerer, Huber, Shubik, and Sunder [10] utilized this model as an experimental game. The key result was to show experimentally that the economy can be run utilizing only individual credit, but that the control conditions on clearing and delivery are highly stringent and unrealistic. A second set of experiments illustrated that relaxing delivery conditions causes considerable losses in efficiency or requires a strong default punishment mechanism.

11.7.1.3   The socialized pricing economy: nonsymmetric information

Because the GE analysis provides only an existence theorem for an efficient price system, an immediate game-theoretic interpretation of the Debreu book is that it describes the dissemination of a set of prices to be utilized by all agents in an economy where the markets or trading posts are not really markets but merely information-gathering aggregation devices.

If we accept as a primitive (Soviet-style) the existence of a central government with knowledge of all preferences and production possibilities, the government takes all of this information and utilizes a computational process such as that of Lemke and Howson [217] and Scarf [316] and the efforts of Kantorovich [198] to announce its calculated prices; then all individuals utilize these prices to optimize individually. Within the appropriate axioms this logic is impeccable. Unfortunately, as the late Soviet Union found out, the idealization of the knowledge and information conditions together with a smooth honest costless efficient bureaucracy was a poor match for economic reality with a central agency calculating what it claimed to be a socially optimal set of prices consistent with the Debreu book. The key to understanding the difference between a competitive and a central government price system lies in the dynamics, and in particular in the information conditions, as has been observed by Hayek [180], Makowski and Ostroy [238], and others. At a formal level we need to consider a game with $n + 1$ players. The first n, as before, are the traders. The extra player is orders of magnitude bigger and better known than the others and is the government. If all agents other than the government were negligibly small, one could establish that truth revelation is consistent with individual behavior in an equilibrium; but the bureaucratic reality is far from the small agent ideal.

11.7.2 SMGs with the trading post mechanism

The earliest basic SMG models are given in [352], [336], and [339]; a commodity money is utilized, and lending and borrowing among the n natural persons who are players is feasible. A default rule is required to make it undesirable to default.

11.7.2.1 Sell-all and buy-sell trading post models with m markets and commodity or fiat money
The Shapley-Shubik analysis utilizes the sell-all market to simplify strategies. It indicates that borrowing and lending are needed to enlarge the feasible set. But even this may not be enough to have the CEs lie in the feasible set of the outcomes to the SMG.

Dubey and Shubik [102] studied the buy-sell game with n individuals, $m + 1$ commodities, and m markets where the $m + 1$st commodity is used as a money.

They showed the existence of an NE and the convergence of the TSNE to a GE price-taking model if the appropriate interiority conditions were met. In essence this amounts to there being enough money that is well distributed in the system. This is easily illustrated if the monetary commodity enters the utility function as a linearly separable term. Then "enough money" requires that the amount be

$$M \geq \sum_{\alpha=1}^{n} \sum_{j=1}^{m} p_j \left(x_j^\alpha - a_j^\alpha \right)^+,$$

or it may be regarded as the value of economic activity or national product in the period (see [356]).

The state of "not enough money" can be cured by the introduction of fiat money where each individual is supplied with an endowment of government money to act as the means of exchange; but this requires the existence of government and an axiom that the government money is accepted in trade. At this point the Knapp [210] proponents clash with the "Hahn paradox." This is far more a problem in modeling, evidence, and belief than one in mathematics. We argue in chapter 12 that both sides are right in context. Formally in a Knapp formulation we may regard its required acceptance as money in trade with no other means of payment as an axiom.[21]

Unfortunately the introduction of fiat money is insufficient to produce a set of SMGs that cover all of the GE exchange models. The distribution of fiat matters, and the "well-distributed" condition is not automatically satisfied for all models. For this to happen requires the addition of an added complexity in the form of a money market [356].

11.7.2.2   Trade with fiat, lending, and bankruptcy Papers by Shubik and Wilson [345], Dubey and Shubik [101], Shubik [353], and Dubey and Geanakoplos [96] all have considered m markets with inside and outside or fiat money and borrowing from a passive (strategic dummy) outside or central bank with some variations. Rather than discuss the details of these various papers, a simple example involving the initial conditions, the quantities of fiat and inside money, the money interest rate, and the bankruptcy penalty illustrates the basic structure and the support of fiat. A transparently simple example is selected.

A simple SMG modeled from a general equilibrium model: There are two types of individual, traders of type 1 and type 2, differentiated only by their initial assets. All have the same utility function of form $z = \sqrt{xy}$. Their initial endowments are $(2a, 0)$ and $(0, 2a)$. The unique competitive equilibrium has $p_1 = p_2 = p$ where $0 < p < \infty$ indicates that the price system is homogeneous of order 0. The final distribution of goods is (a, a) and (a, a).

The SMG with inside money only: fixed money supply: We now consider an SMG with an outside bank that is a strategic dummy and has M units of bank money to lend. The unit selected by the bank serves as numéraire. Initial endowments can be described as $(2a, 0, 0)$, $(0, 2a, 0)$, and $(0, 0, M)$. A strategy by a trader α of type 1 is a triad $\left(q_1^\alpha, b_2^\alpha, d^\alpha\right)$; similarly for type 2. Prices are formed as:

$$p_1 = \frac{\int b_1^\beta}{\int q_1^\alpha}$$

and

$$p_2 = \frac{\int b_2^\alpha}{\int q_2^\beta},$$

and the money rate of interest is given by

$$1 + \rho = \frac{\int \left(d^\alpha + d^\beta\right)}{M}.$$

We must modify the utility function to account for a default penalty against any individual who has a bigger overdraft of his IOUs than he can redeem in government-denominated credit. The modified form for α of type 1 is:

$$U = \sqrt{\left(a - q_1^\alpha\right)\left(\frac{b_2^\alpha}{p_2}\right)} + \mu^* \min\left[\left(p_1 q_1^\alpha + \frac{d^\alpha}{1 + \rho} - b_2^\alpha - d^\alpha\right), 0\right]$$

where μ^* can be interpreted as the marginal disutility of default,[22] and similarly for type 2. If the penalty is high enough, individuals will avoid defaulting, so that after the markets close no agent has fewer (or more) credits than she can pay back.

It is straightforward to check that an NE of this game yields a money rate of interest of $\rho = 0$ and a distribution of goods and credit of $(a, a, 0)$, $(a, a, 0)$, $(0, 0, M)$. Price, however, is no longer given by $0 < p_1 = p_2 = p < \infty$ as in the CE, but the introduction of M and the penalty $\mu^* < M$ have placed bounds on the equilibrium prices so that

$$p \in \left[\mu^*, \frac{M}{2a}\right].$$

The SMG with inside and outside money: fixed money supply: The previous model is modified in two ways. First we consider that the initial endowments are $(2a, 0, m)$, $(0, 2a, m)$, and $(0, 0, M - 2m)$. The rate of interest becomes

$$1 + \rho = \frac{M}{M - 2m} \quad \text{for} \quad 0 \leq m < \frac{M}{2}.$$

In essence the economy has become "cash-consuming." The $2m$ is fiat money owned with no offsetting debt against it; but the act of borrowing is a backward operator on time such that one can "buy now and pay later." As cipher or paper money has no value at the end of the game, the players might as well borrow to the point that any fiat money left over at the end of the game is utilized to pay off debt outstanding (see [96, 353]). The final holdings are $(a, a, 0)$, $(a, a, 0)$, $(0, 0, M)$.

This first simple example had the amount of fiat issued in proportion to the valuations of the individuals' initial holdings at the CE prices. Suppose this were not so. We consider the SMG where the initial holdings are $(2a, 0, m^\alpha)$, $(0, 2a, m^\beta)$, and $(0, 0, M - m^\alpha - m^\beta)$. We now observe that the fiat can be used to extract real resources from the economy. If $m^\alpha + m^\beta = 2m$ and $m^\alpha > m^\beta$ there is the same interest as before

$$1 + \rho = \frac{M}{M - m^\alpha - m^\beta},$$

but now the final distribution of resources becomes

$$\left(\frac{(M + 2m^\alpha)}{(M + 2m^\beta)} a, \frac{(M + 2m^\alpha)}{(M + 2m^\beta)} a, 0 \right),$$

$$\left(\left[2 - \frac{(M + 2m^\alpha)}{(M + 2m^\beta)} \right] a, \left[2 - \frac{(M + 2m^\alpha)}{(M + 2m^\beta)} \right] a, 0 \right),$$

$$(0, 0, M)$$

and there is a skewing of real income.

The SMG with inside and outside money: fixed rate of interest: The examples above were considered with a fixed money supply. Instead we could have frozen the interest rate and let the market forces pull in as much government money as called for. Now initial conditions are $(2a, 0, m)$, $(0, 2a, m)$, and $(0, 0, \infty)$ with $\rho = \rho^*$. The traders will each borrow $m^\alpha / (1 + \rho^*)$ and $m^\beta / (1 + \rho^*)$ respectively, and the price of each good will be

$$p = \left(\frac{\int m^\alpha + \int m^\beta}{2a} \right) \frac{(2 + \rho^*)}{(1 + \rho^*)}.$$

Trade with $m\,(m - 1)\,/2$ markets: The paper of Amir, Sahi, Shubik, and Yao [8] considered complete markets where nevertheless the information processing is all done at the trading posts. As with the windows model of Sahi and Yao [311], the bid by an individual α is a matrix B^α, but as there are many more trading posts the price formation becomes

$$
p_{ij} = \begin{cases} \dfrac{\sum_\alpha b_{ij}^\alpha}{\sum_\alpha b_{ji}^\alpha} & \text{if } \sum_\alpha b_{ji}^\alpha \neq 0 \\ 0 & \text{if } \sum_\alpha b_{ji}^\alpha = 0 \end{cases}.
$$

At this level of decentralization, even with a continuum of agents there are TSNEs that do not coincide with the CE. Amir et al. give two examples, of which the first (and simpler) is noted here.

Consider trade involving three commodities and four trader types with the utility functions and initial endowments given by

$$
u^0(x, y, z) = (xyz)^{\frac{1}{3}} \text{ and } (1, 1, 1),
$$

$$
u^1(x, y, z) = \left(yz^2\right)^{\frac{1}{3}} \text{ and } (0, 3, 0),
$$

$$
u^2(x, y, z) = \left(xy^2\right)^{\frac{1}{3}} \text{ and } (3, 0, 0),
$$

$$
u^3(x, y, z) = \left(x^2z\right)^{\frac{1}{3}} \text{ and } (0, 0, 3).
$$

There is a unique CE at $p_1 = p_2 = p_3 = 1$ with final holdings of $(1, 1, 1)$, $(0, 1, 2)$, $(1, 2, 0)$, and $(2, 0, 1)$. The CE is an NE; but there also is an NE at $p_1 = p_2 = p_3 = 2$ with final holdings of $(2, 2, 2)$, $(0, 1, 1)$, $(1, 1, 0)$, and $(1, 0, 1)$.

11.7.3   A deconstruction of trading post or windows models

Before considering the windows models further, a comparison is noted between the trading posts and windows, disaggregating somewhat further than we do in our formal models. There are physical acts of exchange where some amount of chattel A is actually given directly in exchange for some amount of chattel B, say 6 apples for 3 oranges. In the trading post models the goods delivered at the posts are the messages. Bids and offers in two commodities, one of which can be regarded as the money, come in to the post. They are aggregated and an exchange rate at that post is calculated. This is used to determine shipments, and the good and money are shipped to n destinations. m^2 exchange rates are formed, and as the models do not assume consistent prices, it requires proof that in equilibrium they are reduced to m consistent equilibrium prices.

In contrast with the simple trading post model, when a window receives all messages the trading posts no longer form price. In essence the market posts are irrelevant to the windows model. Symbolically it may appear that exactly the same strategy $\left(b_{jk}^i, q_{kj}^i\right)$ is being used, but now instead of this being interpreted as a shipment of goods, all bids and offers are messages used to calculate m consistent prices at a central agency, and a message is sent to each of the messages received[23] concerning goods shipments. The prices are denominated in an *accounting money* that has no physical existence. A full specification of price requires that a numéraire be set. The central calculation determines that all budgets are balanced globally; hence there is no need for default rules.

In both models the markets calculate prices, with no reference to utility or optimality. Whether windows is better or worse than trading posts depends on transaction features such as message costs and complexity as well as shipping costs. In a full multistage dynamics, the speed of convergence to some specified outcome may be relevant.

11.7.4   A summary of trading post models

A summary of the properties of seven trading post models is given in table 11.2. Column 1 lists the basic aspects of the three early papers on SMG [336, 339, 352]. Column 2 covers the buy-sell model with fiat [102]; 3 deals explicitly with fiat lending and bankruptcy; 4 considers all trading posts as generating decentralized prices [8]; 5 considers the bid-offer or double-auction mechanism.

A few comments on table 11.2 are called for. The first three papers all are based directly on a commodity money and all comment that the monetary commodity could be reinterpreted as a fiat. To do so, a justification for the acceptability of the fiat needs to be given. There are many ways to do this (for a listing see [298, chapter 7]. Among them are law, taxation, and the presence of an outside banking system.

Table 11.2

Properties of some trading post models

	1	2	3	4	5
Markets	$m-1$	m	m	$\frac{m(m-1)}{2}$	m
Agents	n	n	$n+1$	n	n
Money	commodity/fiat	commodity/fiat	fiat/accounting	commodity	fiat
Strategy	(b)	(b,q)	(b,q,d)	B^α	$(p,q;\bar{p},\bar{q})$
Loans	yes	no	yes	no	no
Money market	implicit	no	implicit	no	no
Central bank	no	no	yes	no	no
Default	not defined	no	yes	no	no
r/i	0	no	0	no	no

Note: The numbered columns represent the models identified in the text.

11.8   The Treatment of Bertrand-Edgeworth Models

The discourse so far has been limited to mechanisms and games based only on the Cournot or quantity bidding mechanisms. Except for the last column in table 11.2, the Bertrand-Edgeworth or double-auction mechanisms have been left out. Dubey [95] provided a full formal proof of the relationship between NEs and CEs.[24] In his treatment the strategies were enlarged for each commodity from two to four dimensions. This is tantamount to adding a contingent statement (in the form of a buy or sell price). Thus the windows model, which was not dealt with by Dubey or Sahi, can be extended by considering the strategy for a trader α to involve two matrices, the first being the conventional quantity (Cournot) strategy and the extra matrix involving exchange rates in the m^2 markets. This is a bid offer equivalent of the Sahi-Yao model; however, an open question that has not yet been answered is whether there is a natural extension of the Cournot-style results for a Bertrand-Edgeworth type of mechanism with an arbitrary number of contingencies. Mertens [259] has discussed many of the difficulties faced.

Given the existence of markets and money, the Dubey paper shows that the bid-offer method of clearing can lead to a strategic market game with efficient noncooperative equilibria [95]. However, an open problem remains; can one extend these results to bid-offer games with strategies with contingences such as: I will buy A bushels of wheat at or below p_1 if a ton of cement closes at or above p_2 and a barrel of oil is below p_3? We suspect, but have not adequately formalized the proposition, that if agents are permitted to utilize contingent bids involving more than one commodity, the complexity costs involved will rule out the design of mechanisms that use all information from the messages received to produce an equilibrium set of prices and allocations that dominate those obtained from the Cournot or quantity-without-contingency model.[25] Empirically, beyond limit bids in the stock market and commodities markets, we have been unable to confirm the existence of any successful mass markets where this type of bid exists.

11.8.1   An important modeling distinction:
simultaneous-sealed-bid and double-auction

We have described the mechanism above where two histograms are created and trade takes place at their intersection, or midway between a marginal pair of bids and offers, as a double-auction market mechanism. More precisely we need to distinguish between a double-auction market mechanism and a simultaneous-sealed-bid market mechanism. The distinction depends delicately on information conditions and the treatment of time and dynamics. We return to this point immediately at the beginning of chapter 12.

11.9   Concluding Comments

The general equilibrium model has frequently been looked at as the ultimate abstraction of the Walrasian description of a closed enterprise economy. It is an admirable abstraction that is both predynamic and preinstitutional.

The basic question it asks and answers is what the necessary and sufficient conditions are on agents, preferences, and commodities for the existence of a set of prices that efficiently enable all individual agents to optimize with these prices as signals.

Not asked with any generality is how the prices form and more generally whether we can describe equations of motion.

11.9.1   Quantity-competition-based SMGs and one Soviet SMG

In order to approach dynamics with the same level of rigor as GE theory, we have utilized the SMG as a natural extension. We have noted four features in the construction of minimally complex SMGs.[26]

11.9.1.1   Basic, minimal strategic market games   Prior to offering our final classification of the games we have discussed, we reiterate what we mean by a basic, minimal strategic market game.

An SMG provides a basic representation of a general equilibrium exchange economy if it is a playable game with at least one NE that is associated[27] with a CE of the exchange economy.

The game is minimal if it is basic as noted above and any simplification of the game would destroy its ability to perform some subset of the functions for which it is designed.

There are many features of the actual institutions of the economy that, when considered from the viewpoint of dynamics, call for parsimony or economy in design. The exchange and valuation mechanisms of an economy have many design problems involving microeconomic, technical, and cultural differences. In practice the specific institutional details matter, such as the important physical properties of gold as a money, or the cost structure of a local open-air market, or a supermarket or a wholesale (professionals only) trade fair.

Even without going into the institutional detail, we can consider as axiomatic that in many contexts it is reasonable to minimize the number of trading posts, or to minimize the complexity of messages sent or the number of turns of trade needed to complete a transaction converting some of commodity i to j, or to minimize the bookkeeping or accounting or other aspects of the drudgery that goes with completing various transactions.

Confining ourselves to the simplest step toward dynamics, we add a solution concept to the one-period exchange economies we have constructed as minimal SMGs. The noncooperative equilibrium solution is considered.

Given the constraint of one-period trade,[28] there appear to be a relatively small number of models; but even they require the invention of basic financial instruments and institutions designed to provide the functions (such as price formation and borrowing) required in guiding process. These are utilized in the games described below.

We begin with three centralized computation models. The three windows-based quantity strategy models are:

1. The Sahi-Yao model treated by windows (accounting money),

2. The Sorin individual currency model,

3. A fully centralized or Soviet pricing modeled regarded as a 1-person game.[29]

We then consider competitive decentralized market models. The four trading post models are:

1. The (b, q) trading post model [94] with a commodity money modified for inside money credit arrangements (see also [100]),

2. The (b, q) trading post model modified for inside money only,

3. The (b, q) trading post model modified for inside and outside money,

4. The Amir, Sahi, Shubik, Yao model with decentralized price formation with a strategy by trader α a matrix B^{α}.

We observe the structural differences in the games:

The basic windows games: The direct opportunity for all binary exchanges obviates the need for a loan market. All games are run with accounting scores that net to zero at settlement. Beyond the existence of a clearinghouse with additional abilities to do basic calculations and, (implicitly as in Debreu) a government to enforce the commercial code), no further institutions are required. This is emphatically not the case with the trading post basic models, where new institutions are required to balance accounts.

The basic trading post games: The cure to the limits on the feasible set of outcomes attainable by trading post games requires the introduction of a loan market. The loan market for one period could take the form of either a money market or a central bank. If we were to consider more than one period, the money market would be insufficient. Functionally the outside bank is more general than a money market. The former can change the total of the supply of the money and influence its redistribution, while the latter can only influence the redistribution.

11.9.1.2   The simultaneous price-quantity model   The price-quantity model of Dubey is the simultaneous-sealed-bid, low-information version of the double-auction mechanism. This relates to the open models suggested by both Bertrand [29] and Edgeworth [108].[30]

In this section we have argued that the basis for the theory of money and financial institutions lies in the first step into dynamics. The preinstitutional economic world was a world without time, uncertainty, or space. With the reality of time, process is called for.

Taking as a minimal interval the economic day, we can construct a minimal dynamic economic model playable in a gaming laboratory with two inactive periods and one active period. Even at this level of simplification a multitude of games can be built; but within this set we can be more restrictive and limit ourselves to the one-period simultaneous-move exchange economy where history is fully encompassed in initial endowments and the future is fully described in the valuation of terminal endowments.

With these stringent limitations, basic financial institutions and instruments emerge. They burst into prolific numbers as soon as the realities of many time periods and uncertainty are added.

Fortunately the relationship between the simultaneous-sealed-bid price-quantity game and the dynamic double-auction game can be studied; and it provides us with both an empirically important market structure and a natural introduction to the dynamics of mass financial and commodity markets, as is noted in chapter 12.

Notes

1 As one example, a summary of much of the work on the politico-military exercise is provided by a RAND study [44].

2 Many details concerning the literature on strategic market games that are not covered here are given in the comprehensive survey of Giraud [161].

3 This gives many players imperfect recall, but the agents still face a well-defined (but generally implausible) game of strategy.

4 The item could be a service or a financial instrument.

5 We regard the arc between i and j if undirectional as defining two exchange mechanisms, the one where i is exchanged for j and the other j for i, giving m^2 exchange structures in total. If the arc is regarded as bidirectional, then the upper bound on m commodities is $m(m-1)/2$.

6 With the money being either a commodity or fiat.

7 Note the difference between bids and offers, which are strategic concepts, and supply and demand, which are nonstrategic specifications of constraints imposed by preferences imposed on resources at any give price.

8 An exchange involves both the message sending and the shipment of goods; but at this level of abstraction we assume no transportation costs and no other physical features of goods delivery but concentrate on message and computational features of the trading mechanism prior to considering specific SMGs.

9 In actual market maneuvers in situations such as takeover fights, this is a relatively standard action in accumulating a position.

10 Although a level of "cheap talk" might accompany the message.

11 There is a strange but definable third basic game that can be called *bid-all*. The bid-all model simply requires that each individual is required to spend any commodity money or fiat that he has; thus the bid-all is strategically close to the buy-sell where each has a strategy of length $2m$, but the bid-all has the constraint that all money must be spent whereas the buy-sell does not have this constraint.

12 An interesting hybrid that has recently been manifested is Bitcoin (see *New York Times*, April 12, 2013, p. 1) in which skilled programmers and mathematicians can "mine" bitcoins, turning the currency into something between a super-hacker computer game and a potential international currency whose locations and transactions are independently highly protected. It is reputed to have generated a worth of the order of a billion US dollars and could possibly serve as means of transfer of funds for illegal operations, but as a universally accepted currency it would require both acceptance by custom and legal enforcement by government. Thus the long-term success of this enterprise is unlikely unless it is adopted by a world government.

13 Both the cartelist and intrinsic-value arguments concerning money may contain part of the truth. If the government is strong enough to provide the laws of the use of fiat money, including its ability to tax and enforce acceptance of fiat in the discharge of debts, then because it needs a bureaucracy to provide the enforcement but it pays the bureaucracy in fiat, it has created a utilitarian value for the fiat.

14 The addition of a credit instrument could conceivably be recorded as a pair of points with + and − attached to them. In actual economies, one, both, or neither of the instruments need be marketable prior to liquidation.

15 There is a gray area where, for example, the IOUs of a merchant banker may circulate either as notes of a trusted individual real person or as those of a legal person with unlimited liability. These depend on the institutional arrangements of a society's laws.

16 We stress that unlike the CE model, the SMG model with a bankruptcy condition does not have a scaling factor on the set $(0, \infty)$ but on the set $[p^*, \infty)$ where p^* is a lower level of prices at which strategic bankruptcy becomes profitable.

17 When legal persons such as commercial banks are introduced and may issue credit leveraged against reserves, this adds an extra level of complexity.

18 Ideally we might try to seek a measure that minimizes information flows while still providing for economic efficiency.

19 We deem both a commodity and a fiat money to be outside monies in the sense that they are assets with no counterparty operationally relevant. This does not conform wth common usage.

20 We encounter a problem in taxonomy here. The number 48 was derived by picking one instance from each of the categories. We could have argued that there are minimal models involving none or all of the features in each category. In this instance we would arrive at $4^4 \times 8 = 2,048$ models, many of which are vacuous. The point to stress is that even though this number is large, the number of minimal forms is not overwhelming.

21 If we require terminal holdings to equal or exceed initial holdings of fiat, we are required to introduce a penalty akin to a default penalty if terminal holdings are less than initial. At this point a distinction between accounting money and fiat money may be made. The total sum of accounting money nets to zero; but the sum of all government money holdings held by traders is

$$M = \sum_{\alpha=1}^{n} m^\alpha > 0$$

which is positive.

22 The justification for this form has been discussed elsewhere indicating that there is no loss of generality. See [356, chapter 11] or [102].

23 A trader may send more than one message. The message can be of any length the syntax supports.

24 A preliminary heuristic treatment was given by Dubey and Shubik [103].

25 Mertens [259] in a paper of over 100 pages explored a closely relate problem without success.

26 Conditions on symmetric or asymmetric knowledge can be introduced formally in the one-period model; but they are more appropriate to multiperiod analysis. Furthermore we have also abstracted away common knowledge problems.

27 Association by an appropriate limit process or by the assumption of a continuum of agents.

28 The strategic form of the game is taken as the primitive concept, not derived from an extensive form.

29 If we wished to consider nonsymmetric information, a natural extra model would be a fully centralized or Soviet pricing model where the power of the individuals is manifested in control over disclosure of information in an $(n+1)$-person game.

30 In terms of formal game theory, these two pre-game theory models with a finite number of players may have mixed-strategy solutions, but a convergence to a pure strategy as the number of players becomes large may occur [347]. Alternatively the presence of uncertainty may remove the mixed strategies.

12 Process, Strategy, and Behavior

12.1 Process Models and Dynamic Behavior

Chapters 2–4 and 11 have been devoted to the development of the basic set of minimal games to provide the elemental structure of money, markets, credit, and other financial instruments and institutions that are required as carriers of process in a loosely coupled dynamic economy.

Chapters 5–10 have been devoted to the first steps in providing proof in principle of how to utilize the basic procedures of building process models beyond the minimal structure of the one-simultaneous-move process model. The hyperastronomical explosion of special cases is to be welcomed as indicating that the initial timeless tight system when converted to a loosely coupled process model calls for both the specification of ad hoc questions and the supply of ad hoc model building of the detail needed to make it feasible to provide useful answers in any application.

We chose five different examples to illustrate the natural requirement for detail and the emergence of complexity in economic control. They are:

1. The endogenous introduction of gold or fiat into an economy;
2. Production and exchange in a small multigenerational economy with the lives of capital, labor, and finance on different timescales;
3. Bubbles, banking, and socioeconomic dynamics;
4. Innovation and the breaking of the circular flow of capital;
5. The variation of the money supply utilizing a central bank with or without commercial banks, national debt, and taxation.

The first, developed in chapter 5, involves how to endogenize the use of a money and to contrast an economy with the private production of gold with an economy with a government monopoly on fiat and a bureaucratic distribution and enforcement system. This bureaucratic system provides the guidance, support, and needed enforcement of the dynamics of the utilization of a fiat money system. Once the system is running, the dynamics provides, in part, its own bootstrapping to provide the expectations of enough acceptance, helped by potential enforcement, to maintain the volume of trade.

The basic new phenomena are the stress on the difference in timescales between everyday trade and selecting one's profession. Furthermore in the division of labor, once in motion the recruitment of the bureaucracy that is paid in fiat also provides a means to help enforce the acceptance of the use and valuation of the fiat.[1]

The second, in chapter 6, may be regarded as an essay in the mathematization of a slice of economic history, the need to finance a joint capital good in a relatively isolated farming community and the call for alternative methods of financing. Here much of the important economic detail depends on differences in timescale, and the role of finance comes in alleviating the disadvantages of these timing differences.

The third example, in chapter 8, deals with the dynamics of financial bubbles and extends the basic models of Diamond and Dybvig and Morris and Shin. In particular it develops the dynamics involved in the creation of the bubble.

The fourth example, in chapter 9, provides a mathematization that demonstrates the financial problems called forth by innovation where generically even under favorable circumstances the disequilibrium adjustment to an equilibrium state is highly dependent on the model structure and parameters. Furthermore, as indicated in chapter 10, the financing of innovation raises basic questions about the need for enlarging and varying the money supply and opens up fundamental questions concerning the problems involving economic and financial power, ownership and control in the investment process, as well as perception and expertise in the provision of financial support of innovation.

The fifth example, discussed in chapters 9 and 10, involves considering the construction of feasible and socially acceptable devices for providing mechanisms for changing the money supply in an appropriate manner.

We stress that each of these models requires one or more clear questions followed by considerable hand-tailored modeling to provide a process model, to which must be added a behavioral assumption or solution concept in order to yield equations of motion, or other (such as essay) descriptions of the behavior of the individuals and institutions.

12.2 Double Auction and Dynamics

In chapter 11 we observed that the double-auction mechanism was not central to the even more basic aspects of trade that called forth the emergence of markets, prices, and a money. Even a casual glance into economic history and anthropology shows that trade has existed for many thousands of years. Payment by weight in one or two special commodities such as barley or silver has existed for over $4,000$ years; economic contracts, banking, and bankruptcy laws date back to before 1800 BC (see [356] for a brief summary); coinage sponsored by a king to at least 520 BC; and one-sided auctions in some form for around $4,000$ years, if Herodotus' [243] story of the Babylonian "wife auction" is to be believed, and at least more than $2,000$ if not. In spite of the early existence of all of these mechanisms for the promotion and protection of trade, when we search for the origins of the double-auction mechanism it appears that it was preceded by the existence and growth of trade in the stock markets and commodity markets, which did not emerge until the seventeenth century with the Amsterdam stock exchange moving into the specially constructed building for trading in 1611. The building of the Amsterdam Exchange can be reasonably accurately dated, but the growth of trade is more or less organic and explicit dating is lost in social growth. The formalization of a London Stock Exchange may be dated from 1698 when John Castaing began publishing a simple list of stock and commodity prices used by the traders gathered at Jonathan's Coffee-house.

The Bourse in Antwerp founded in 1531 may be regarded as an earlier precursor of stock markets. It did not deal in stocks but in debt.

In New York the first formal agreement was on May 17, 1792, when 24 brokers signed an agreement under a buttonwood tree that stood at the current location of 68 Wall Street. Prior to that time trading had no formal home. Some trade remained on the street, giving rise to the Curb Market that eventually became the American Exchange.

When the exchanges opened, they did not utilize the double auction as we know it; for instance in the New York Stock Exchange the sequential calling out of bids and offers sufficed when there was light trading, and the call market was used from 1817 until 1871 when it was judged that the volume was too large to be handled this way and a continuous market with specialists replaced it. A brief review of the buildup of trade is shown in table 12.1.

Since the shift to the double-auction market in 1871, many modifications have been made to the rules of trade and the mechanism for the execution of

Table 12.1
The buildup of trade at the New York Stock Exchange

Date	Volume	Comment
March 16 1830	31	lowest day
December 15 1886	1,200,000	first above 10e6
October 29 1929	16,410,000	Black Friday
August 18 1982	132,681,000	first above 10e8
October 28 1997	1,201,346,000	first above 10e9
October 10 2008	7,341,505,000	Record up to 2010

Note: Trade volumes larger than 100,000,000 have been rounded to the nearest thousand.

the double auction. The growth has been evolutionary, adjusting to the forces of growth in volume and technology and influenced by politics, custom, and law.

During the twentieth and into the early twenty-first century the importance of the double-auction mechanism has grown until now it has a major role in the financial markets of the world, but as with other instruments and financial institutions, the function may mutate while the name stays fixed. With the oligopolistic growth in size of major financial institutions and improvements in technology, it could be that the double auction as we know it is nearing or even may have passed its peak usefulness, as special market networks to dispose of large blocks of stock have appeared and interaction with the control market for shares has influenced the nature of its functioning.

Our basic concern is what makes the double auction market so special in its role in economic theory in providing a natural minimalist link between statics and dynamics. We suggest that it depends delicately on the specification of the units of time involved. The work described in chapter 11 had essentially only one period. In terms of a stock market we might call it a trading day. Given this, the distinction can be made between the bid-offer model[2] and the double auction in terms of information, the number of moves, and the details on price formation. We first give a loose, heuristic discussion and then present formal definitions. For ease and clarity in exposition, suppose that within a trading period each of n individuals is permitted to make one bid and offer. A single price is formed by drawing histogram summaries of all bids and offers, and the single market price is formed by the marginal pair.

If, as is certainly the case for stock market trading, the bids and offers or reservation prices and quantities arrive in the market at random times during the trading day, then if a single price and amount traded are to emerge the individual actions must be summed over the whole interval. A simple example illustrates the mechanisms and the distinctions among the markets. We consider a market with 6 players. There are 3 sellers owning 1 unit of a good with reservation prices of $1, $2, and $3 respectively, and 3 buyers all of whom wish to buy 1 unit of the good at most, and who have reservation prices of $1, $2, and $3 respectively. One simple formulation is given, treating only trader time as limiting. Suppose that the interval of length 1 for the trading day is divided into 6 subintervals of length $\Delta t = 1/6$ where the interval is the time required for the mechanism to record one bid or offer; hence there are no ties in a time interval.

Figure 12.1 shows the sequenced bid and offer valuations. These have been drawn with the reservation prices on bids going up and those on offers going down. They could have been drawn with both histograms going in the same direction, or more generally they could have been drawn in the order received as shown in figure 12.2. The dashed line shows bid reservation prices and the solid line shows offer reservation prices.

It is well known from any elementary economics text that competitive equilibrium will be given where the cumulative supply and demand curves intersect. If the individuals truthfully bid their reservation prices and the mechanism aggregates all bids and offers, then a competitive equilibrium would exist with price $p = \$2$, and 2 units would be traded with the surplus of $2 split between the bidder with a reservation price of $3 and the offerer with a selling reservation price of $1.

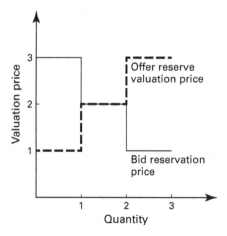

Figure 12.1
Sequenced bid and offer valuations.

The mechanism could be designed by the exchange to maximize trade rather than to maximize surplus, in which instance it should match the pair with the highest offer and bid reservation prices and continue until trade is exhausted. Here there will be a trade volume of 3 with the pairs $(3,3)$, $(2,2)$, and $(1,1)$ matched, and there is no surplus to be split. In both of these instances the full histograms of the arrivals of traders in the whole interval are considered. In figure 12.2 the dynamics of arrival is portrayed, but in the previous clearance no consideration is given to arrival time and the dynamics has no influence on price formation. Figure 12.2 shows the arrival priority but not the clock time. In actual trade, especially in financial instruments, the length of time for possible execution is down to microseconds. The double-auction mechanism in contrast with the sealed bid is highly dependent on the arrival times.

The double auction is designed to finalize trades as quickly as possible. In order to do this, instead of summing bids and offers over the whole interval it keeps creating two histograms until a trading pair is encountered and continues to do so after that trade has been satisfied. In the example in figure 12.2 the first pair is a pair that can trade, but the dynamics requires that a means for establishing a price between the bid and offer must be established. A reasonable convention is that they split the difference. In this instance it would be $p = \$2$. There will be no further trade until the bid to buy at $p = \$2$ or less comes in. As the sixth entry, it can be matched with the offer to sell at $p = \$2$ or more that came in as the third entry. Thus two prices are formed in the full interval; in this instance they both were $p = \$2$ but they could have been anywhere from $p = \$1$ to $p = \$3$, and there could be up to 3 different prices.

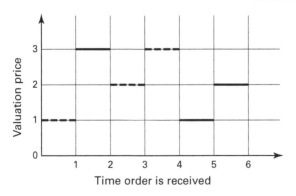

Figure 12.2
Time sequence of order arrivals.

This suggests that there are four criteria whereby two trading methods can be compared. They are:

- Amount of time required for trade,[3]
- Expected number of prices formed in the interval,
- Surplus generated in trade,
- Volume of trade generated.

Before we consider the different criteria for measuring the performance of a mechanism, we present formal definitions of the double-sided sealed bid and the double-auction mechanisms.

12.2.1   Comparative specification of three clearing mechanisms

The three mechanisms are:

1. Simultaneous sealed bids,
2. Random encounter,
3. Double auction.

In general, each of these models may introduce a unique parameter that limits capacity or efficiency in delivering surplus value to the traders. In order to make comparisons among models, we will set some of these parameters equal, in models where they are arbitrary, to the values in other models where they are fixed.

12.2.1.1   Timescales   There are three timescales that may be relevant to some or all of the exchange mechanisms.

1. The calendar day: This is the clearing interval for the simultaneous sealed bid, and for the random encounter if any trader is permitted to enter the market only once per day. The calendar day may also be an interval to clear the books on the double auction, depending on the minute details of the model specified.[4]

2. An individual response time Δt_I: This interval could be given many distinct meanings depending on the market context in which it is to be used. We will identify it with the time it takes individuals to perform one full cycle of the random encounter when they are permitted to enter the market repeatedly. A cycle consists of finding a partner, either executing a trade or determining that no trade is possible, and returning, to be ready to find the next partner.[5]

3. A mechanism response time Δt_M: This interval could also be given many distinct meanings in terms of computational complexity or execution time for clearing algorithms. Here we will operationalize it by supposing that the double auction receives orders serially at intervals which can only be integer multiples of Δt_M, and that with the receipt of each order, it updates the book by either queuing or clearing orders immediately. The important consequence of serial order receipt is that, per trading day, the number of traders that the double auction can serve is no more than $N_{\max} = 1/\Delta t_M$. For the sake of comparing markets, we will suppose that the capacity constraint $N_{\max}$ of the simultaneous sealed bid is set to the same value as that for the double auction.

Realistically in modern securities markets where the double auction is most widely used, $\Delta t_M \ll \Delta t_I$. Whether the two come into direct comparison will depend on whether traders can or cannot reenter the market for random encounters, and on the way the order books are updated in the double auction.

12.2.1.2   A simplifying assumption: one entry per trader   It is a structural limitation of the simultaneous sealed bid that, if any trader is limited to placing a single order, no trader can be served more than once in a trading day. For simplicity and for the sake of comparison, without burying ourselves in highly complex computations we impose the same restriction on the double auction.

12.2.1.3   Another simplifying assumption: unit quantities bought and sold   In general all three of the mechanisms above can accept price/quantity inputs, and the random encounter could naturally accept fully specified price/demand curves. To avoid the complexity of the resulting clearing rules, and to make the systems more directly comparable, we suppose that each trader comes to the market with a single unit to sell, or a demand to buy a single unit, of a single kind of good. The traders differ only in their sign (buy or sell) and in their reservation price, above or below which (respectively) they will not engage in a trade.

Simple models can be produced by declaring that there exist a minimum price $p_{\min}$ and a maximum price $p_{\max}$, and that both buyers and sellers are uniformly distributed on the interval $p \in [p_{\min}, p_{\max}]$. For the simultaneous sealed bid and random encounter, it is easier to take the price space to be continuous-valued, because with probability one all orders have a unique price, and priority rules do not need to be invoked for clearing. For the double auction, depending on how the book updating is handled, there may be advantages to using a discrete price space. If that is the case, however, tick size (size of the price increment) will become a quantitatively important parameter in the solutions.

12.2.2   Descriptions of clearing rules

12.2.2.1   Simultaneous sealed bid   A set of traders, randomly selected and fewer than or equal to N_{max} in number, submit limit-priced bids or offers. The market queues all orders, then clears them once per trading day using a supply/demand crossing rule. Orders that can be cleared are cleared at the crossing price, and all uncleared orders are canceled, so that the book starts empty on the following day. If there is always a surplus of traders beyond the market capacity, the number who enter will always be N_{max}. We suppose they are accepted first-come, first-served, and the remainder are turned away.

With a large number of traders, the expected number on both the buy side and the sell side will be $N_{max}/2$.

The expected number of either buyers or sellers with reservation prices in an interval $[p, p + \Delta p]$ will be $\Delta p N_{max}/2 (p_{max} - p_{min})$, for p in the allowed interval.

The cumulative distribution of eligible buyers at any clearing price p (those with bid prices at or above p) will therefore be

$$\Phi_{SSB,bid} = \frac{N_{max}}{2} \frac{(p_{max} - p)}{(p_{max} - p_{min})}. \tag{12.1}$$

The cumulative distribution of eligible sellers at any clearing price p (those with ask prices at or below p) will be

$$\Phi_{SSB,ask} = \frac{N_{max}}{2} \frac{(p - p_{min})}{(p_{max} - p_{min})}. \tag{12.2}$$

The bid and ask curves are expected to cross at $p_{clear} = (p_{max} + p_{min})/2$. The total number of units of goods to change hands will be $N_{max}/4$, and one half of the $N_{max}/2$ buyers and one half of the $N_{max}/2$ sellers will have trades executed.

A measure of the efficiency of the market to any trader who succeeds in executing a trade is the difference (in absolute value) of the trader's reservation price from the clearing price. The aggregate of these values over the full set of traders is an instance of consumer's surplus. The consumer's surplus for the set of buyers is

$$\int_{p_{clear}}^{p_{max}} dp \frac{N_{max}}{2 (p_{max} - p_{min})} (p - p_{clear}) = \frac{N_{max} (p_{max} - p_{min})}{16}, \tag{12.3}$$

and a similar surplus is captured in aggregate by sellers. The total over both buyers and sellers is therefore $N_{max} (p_{max} - p_{min}) /8$, and the average *per successful trader* is therefore $(p_{max} - p_{min}) /4$.

The simultaneous sealed bid has the property that the probability to have an order filled (in expectation) is *scale-independent*. It equals $1/2$ independent of the number N_{max}.

12.2.2.2   Random encounter   In random encounter, any agent can be either forbidden or permitted to attempt trade with more than one counterparty (in series) within the span of a day. In the former case, the individual-response interval Δt_I does not enter the solution, and the probability to have an order filled is scale-independent, as in the simultaneous sealed bid. In the latter case, the probability to have an order filled depends on the number of times a trader can enter the market in a trading day, which is limited by $1/\Delta t_I$. In either case the expected surplus captured by the trader is scale-independent.

Random encounter admits a simple clearing model. Two agents are randomly selected and paired. If the reservation price of the seller is at or below the reservation price of the buyer, they trade at the average of the two prices, and the surplus to each is half the difference in their prices.[6] If the bid and ask prices do not cross, they do not trade and are returned to the pool. If traders cannot reenter the market, the one-time probability to have a trade filled is the final probability. If traders can reenter, a trader with an unfilled order may seek another partner after an interval Δt_I. Traders whose orders are filled do not reenter. Since reentry is a conditional event, it leads to more complex probabilities to have orders filled, and (depending on other assumptions) more complex relations between the probability to have an order filled and the number of individuals served.

Properties of a single encounter: The state space from which traders are sampled is a square. The probability of a successful trade is given by the measure of pairs for which $p_{bid} \geq p_{ask}$:

$$\int_{p_{min}}^{p_{max}} dp_{ask} \frac{1}{(p_{max} - p_{min})} \int_{p_{ask}}^{p_{max}} dp_{bid} \frac{1}{(p_{max} - p_{min})} = \frac{1}{2}, \qquad (12.4)$$

the same as the probability per trader for the simultaneous sealed bid.

The total surplus extracted by any successful pair of traders is given by

$$\int_{p_{min}}^{p_{max}} dp_{ask} \frac{1}{(p_{max} - p_{min})} \int_{p_{ask}}^{p_{max}} dp_{bid} \frac{(p_{bid} - p_{ask})}{(p_{max} - p_{min})} = \frac{(p_{max} - p_{min})}{6}.$$

$$(12.5)$$

Since only half of the sampled trading pairs successfully execute a trade, the surplus per trade is then $(p_{max} - p_{min})/3$. Since it is split between the two traders, the surplus per trader per trade is $(p_{max} - p_{min})/6$, lower than that of the simultaneous sealed bid.[7]

Reentry of the market by unsuccessful traders: If reentry is permitted, several further assumptions must be made to define the probability space. In general, the assumptions that isolate the dependence of the market performance on individual parameters also preclude natural comparisons between random encounter and the other markets (as they should, because in most respects these clearing mechanisms are incommensurable without further ad hoc conditions).

The only case that is analytically simple is the assumption of a very large pool of traders on both the buy and the sell side, where "very large" is defined to mean that the exit of traders who carry out successful trades does not alter the price distribution of eligible trading partners over the course of the day. In this case, the probability to have an order filled for any trader becomes

$$\sum_{k=1}^{1/\Delta t_l} \frac{1}{2^k} = 1 - \frac{1}{2^{\Delta t_l}}. \tag{12.6}$$

Since the reservation price of the agent under consideration is sampled *ex ante* from a uniform distribution, independent of whether the agent enters the market once or repeatedly, and since the reservation price of the counterparty in each entry to the market is sampled independently from a large, uniformly distributed pool, the expected surplus per successful trade is independent of how many times the same trader may have entered the market previously, given the trader's *already specified* reservation price. Therefore the *ex ante* expected surplus per trader who successfully completes a trade is the same as in the single-entry case.

Both the expected surplus received by a trader and the number of times the trader enters the market are, however, dependent on the trader's reservation price, and therefore those two outcome properties are correlated with one another. Traders with reservation prices that are easy to meet receive a large surplus from most trades (they enter the market willing to buy higher or sell lower than the clearing prices they can arrive at with most counterparties), and they are also likely to execute successful trades within a few attempts. Traders with reservation prices that are difficult to meet will find fewer counterparties with whom a trade can be completed, and the counterparties are more likely to have reservation prices near their own, meaning that a smaller surplus will be split between the two.[8]

Note that, under the large-pool assumption, there is no natural way to assign a capacity constraint to random encounter without introducing a further independent capacity parameter. In the very large pool of traders, random encounter occurs in parallel, and the number of traders is not assumed to be limiting.

If the pool of traders is assumed to be finite, then a tradeoff can be introduced between the number of times a single trader enters the market as a partner and the number of possible partners who can be matched against a given counterparty. However, in this case the expected reservation prices of traders change through the course of the day, as those with prices that are harder to fill accumulate to become a larger fraction of traders reentering the market repeatedly. This property of accumulation of difficult-to-fill orders permits a more direct comparison with the double auction, where the same process inevitably occurs, but it is analytically more complicated; we do not pursue it here.

12.2.2.3 Double auction   There is a reason the double auction boasts a large literature, with long and often tedious papers each devoted to the development and analysis of some particular model and a variety of one-off cases. It requires several assumptions to specify, and almost no matter how these are made, the resulting models are analytically intractable. They provide grist for a mill devoted to experimenting with different applied behavioral ways of beating the market. The strategic treatment of interperiod information is the key.

The reason the analysis of the double auction is generically a hard problem is that it possesses properties of the random-encounter model with repeated entry and an always limited, but generally time-dependent, number of possible counterparties. The conditional probabilities of reservation prices are highly correlated with the history of both the order queues and the particular trader, and most clearing events and surpluses are conditioned on these. The mechanism has a property common to many computationally complex problems in number theory: that it is simple to implement (if one has the memory capacity for storage and accounting) but difficult to analyze because realizations of the process depend on the long memory made possible by a large state space [125, 160, 224–226].

Some of the important choices, and the consequences of each, are summarized here:

Daily reset or interday carry-forward: The double auction could be run starting each day with empty bid and offer books and accumulating orders through the day, or it could be run continuously, so that the uncleared parts of the queues at the end of each day pass to the next day. In the former case, the order books are nonstationary at all times, but the density is assured to remain bounded at all prices. In the latter case, the order queues may or may not settle to stationary distributions over long times, and the densities may or may not remain finite at all prices. Each of these depends on the way further choices about the model are made.

Discrete or continuous price grid: Many versions of the double auction with order books cleared at the end of each day will possess a regular continuum limit for the price grid, and in that sense whether prices are made discrete or continuous may be regarded as a nonessential feature of the group of models. In double auctions with order books that roll over across days, a discrete price grid permits a larger fraction of order clearing than a continuous space (because orders may not accumulate within arbitrarily small neighborhoods of the boundary prices p_{min} and p_{max}), but the properties of the density then depend on grid size. There may not be a bounded density if the price grid is taken toward its continuum limit. In that sense, discreteness becomes an essential property of the group of models. (In general, priority rules must also be introduced to specify an order of clearing, such as first-in, first-out, within a given price bin.)

Clearing only, or also spontaneous cancellation of orders: Both the simultaneous sealed bid and the random encounter can be analyzed with clearing or daily cancellation as the only mechanism by which demands, once introduced, are removed. It will not generally be the case that the double auction, with queues rolled over across days, possesses a stationary distribution if clearing is the only mechanism of order removal.[9] The problem of densities that are nonstationary (growing without bound) can be overcome by introducing a further process of spontaneous order expiration into the double auction with rollover, as was done in [69, 191, 377]. If a discrete price grid is also assumed (or if the price space is extended indefinitely), this can produce a stationary expected density for the order queues in the long term.[10] Spontaneous expiration requires specification of an additional parameter, which is the typical lifetime of unfilled orders before they expire.

Favoring order completion or favoring surplus: One of the most important choices that can be made, and also one of the most directly relevant to a performance tradeoff between capacity and efficiency, concerns the way crossing orders are chosen for clearing. The two limiting cases are a *minimum-surplus* clearing rule and a *best-price* clearing rule. The two are defined as follows:

The minimum-surplus clearing rule is one in which any new buy or sell order entering the book is cleared with the closest feasible counterparty in the book. (If there is no counterparty against which it can clear, it is queued.) This rule maximizes the number of executed trades and minimizes the accumulation of unfilled orders. We believe that it may be possible to show that this rule leads to stationary queues even with a continuous price space and without requiring spontaneous order cancellation. However, it also minimizes the surplus per trade.[11] It differs from mechanisms such as "fill-or-kill" order placement (which also produce bounded queues) in that a double auction with only fill-or-kill orders effectively recapitulates the random encounter, whereas a double auction with minimum-surplus clearing generates a qualitatively different tradeoff between capacity and per-trade surplus.

The alternative, best-price clearing rule matches any new buy or sell order with the best available counterparty's order. Under best-price clearing, orders placed near p_{min} and p_{max} are only cleared in rare cases where the book empties far enough to expose them. Since the events of such large excursions are exponentially rare in the number of orders in the queue, and since the rate of order addition per price increment Δp is constant in time, we expect that best-price clearing leads to the unbounded accumulation of orders and a nonstationary book, unless it is augmented by some other removal mechanism such as spontaneous cancellation.

12.2.2.4   Formal considerations   With either clearing rule, the price space in the double auction divides into three intervals with respect to any (instantaneous) state of the order book:

1. The interval between p_{min} and the highest bid, $p_{\text{best-bid}}$: The offer book is empty in this region. Arriving offers within this interval thin the bid queue, and arriving bids add to the queue. Where the thinning occurs, however, depends on the clearing rule.

2. The interval between the highest bid ($p_{\text{best-bid}}$) and the lowest offer or ask ($p_{\text{best-ask}}$), also called the *spread*: Both bid and offer books are empty in this interval. Either an arriving bid or an arriving offer adds to its respective queue, reducing the spread and changing either $p_{\text{best-bid}}$ or $p_{\text{best-ask}}$.

3. The interval between $p_{\text{best-ask}}$ and p_{max}: The bid book is empty in this region. Arriving bids within this interval thin the offer queue, and arriving offers add to the queue. Again, where the thinning occurs depends on the clearing rule.

We will refer to the average of the best-bid and best-ask prices as the *mid-price*. It is not a price at which any event happens, but it provides a general reference point for regions of the distribution near or far from the best-bid and best-ask prices.

The difference between the two clearing rules is that under the minimum-surplus rule, crossing orders thin the existing queue at interior locations, unless they fall between the best and next-best bid or ask, in which case they clear that best bid or ask and move the mid-price. In the case where N_{max} is large, the order density will be high, and both the spread and the interorder spacing within the queues will be small. Therefore most clearing under the minimum-surplus rule will thin the queues locally where the crossing order arrives. Movements of the midprice will be rare, but only in proportion to the smallness of the spread and the best/next-best price intervals, both of which should scale as $\sim 1/N_{\text{max}}$. Thus diffusion of the mid-price will slow only polynomially in the number of traders.[12]

Under the best-price rule, *all* crossing orders hit the best-bid or best-ask price and move the mid-price. Therefore almost all effects on the queue are nonlocal from the price of the crossing order.

An argument that the bid and offer queues under the two clearing rules have opposite asymptotic curvatures: With the assumption that both buy and sell orders arrive randomly and uniformly distributed in price, under the minimum-surplus rule the rates of queuing and clearing of both bids and offers at prices far from the mid-price balance in expectation. Therefore order cancellation creates no tendency for the density of the order book either to systematically increase or to systematically decrease. Such balance is consistent with a uniform density of the order book, and with density fluctuations that vary in the manner of a Poisson process. At every time, however, the bid and offer books are exactly empty, respectively above and below the spread. Connecting these two distinct behaviors for each book on either side of the mid-price leads to the prediction that typical configurations of both queues are concave away from the spread, and that in expectation they approach constant densities asymptotically (although they undergo large fluctuations about this expected profile). The values those constant asymptotes take likely require the solution of a highly nonlocal equation; since order arrival and cancellation are consistent with any constant value, it can only be the gradual propagation of interactions between the mid-price and the boundaries that sets its profile.

In contrast, we expect that under the best-price clearing rule the late-time profiles of the order books are strongly convex (curving away from zero) far from the mid-price. Queuing orders arrive with uniform density at all prices, but crossing orders all thin the books at the best-bid or best-ask price. The likelihood for thinning to occur decreases by a fixed *factor* with each price increment Δp, whereas order arrival is constant in each such interval. Therefore the rate of accumulation of orders, even at a fixed density, would increase exponentially with distance from the mid-price. As the density itself increases, the exponent for the decay of the probability of thinning becomes an increasing function of distance from the mid-price, and the rate of accumulation should increase faster than exponentially. Even an intuitive approximation of the behavior of queues in this model is difficult to estimate, however.

12.2.2.5   An analytic solution requires a master equation   In order to obtain any analytical results many approximations are usually required, to truncate the depth of memory that the variable inventory keeps. In previous joint work [377] one of us found that most of the difficulty was in obtaining approximations that would drastically reduce the dimensionality of the state space for the limit-order queues, and that could be checked against simulations to be sure they didn't deviate too far for the observables being calculated. Writing a simulator can in some cases yield scaling behaviors of interest more directly, but obtaining reliable sample points as a function of scale, and then fitting them to an approximate functional dependence, still requires care in the elimination of spurious model artifacts.

Gross scaling arguments or dimensional arguments can sometimes be used to estimate the fraction cleared and the surplus extracted. We suspect, but do not have a proof, that the following broad behaviors will be true.

Minimum-surplus clearing rule: The simplest case will be to take the continuum limit for prices and to roll the book over from one day to the next. We conjecture that this clearing rule produces an asymptotically finite density on the queues (or one that grows much more slowly than linear with time), which implies that asymptotically the same number of orders enter the book as leave the book within each day. Thus, the fraction of orders cleared approaches unity.

The density of the book must scale as some monotonically increasing (probably linear) function of the number of agents N_{max}, so the typical price interval between orders will scale (up to constant factors) as $\sim (p_{max} - p_{min})/N_{max}$. Since arriving orders are cleared with the nearest feasible entry in the queue, the surplus shared by the buyer and seller is no larger than the interorder interval on the queue, and thus also scales as $\sim (p_{max} - p_{min})/N_{max}$. Therefore the efficiency multiplied by the capacity approaches a constant at large N_{max}.

Fraction cleared and queue accumulation rate under the best-price clearing rule: Still considering the case where orders are rolled over across days, an upper bound can be placed on the fraction of orders cleared under the best-price clearing rule. Since all orders not cleared add to the queue, this is also a lower bound on the rate of accumulation of orders in the queue and thus on the slowing-down of fluctuations that expose orders near p_{max} or p_{min}.

The greatest clearing occurs when the spread is minimized. At an expected spread that goes to zero at large N_{max} or late times, the sum of the price interval above the best-ask, where bids come in and clear, plus the interval below the best-bid, where asks come in and clear, goes to the full interval $(p_{max} - p_{min})$. Since the density of the order rate for either bids or asks is $N_{max}/2 \, (p_{max} - p_{min})$ per trading day, the number of orders per day that clear approaches $N_{max}/2$ in this limit. Any nonzero spread that persists at large N_{max} or late times reduces the number per day that clear, as either bids or offers entering within the spread add to their respective queues—although this addition is transient, by the assumption that a nonzero spread remains open. Therefore a lower bound on the number of orders that must add to the queue is $N_{max}/2$ per day. The limiting fraction $(1/2)$ of orders filled is that of the simultaneous sealed bid.

12.2.3 The double auction market, econophysics, and game theory

The double auction mechanism and stock market rules provide just about as close a fully formulated formal game as one can find in economics. It is a natural hunting ground for econophysics methods and investigations of formal game theory solutions. Furthermore many of the difficulties encountered show how fast naturally deep modeling problems are introduced by what appear to be minor parameters in the system such as buying or selling large blocks, or placing limit orders. In spite of the stock market's being just about the richest source of detailed computerized numerical data in the whole of economics, the models quickly become intractable when the clearance system is intrinsically historical. Depending on the formation of two stochastic queues and the many combinations of individual knowledge of previous prices during the trading day, together with the state of the book, it invokes complex strategic behavior even for queues of length two.

12.2.4 Comments on trading mechanisms

In the future, how will the double auction market change or be displaced? An evolutionary change in the mechanisms certainly takes place when a trading capacity is reached and whenever a technological advance in computation and communication is made.

A reasonably full discussion of interesting and relevant variations of formal double auction models would require a separate volume. As this is not feasible we limit our remarks to a few salient features.

Even casual observation tells us that one individual does not know the reservation prices of all others. A complicated game-theoretic inference problem is posed in the double auction, where the strategy of an individual agent's bid or offer for sale of a quantity at a selected reservation price is made at a time depending on the previous history of prices. A further complication impinging on the market in process is the arrival of exogenous random events such as a strike against a particular company or a natural disaster such as an earthquake. There is a highly practical question concerning how quickly and by what paths this new information is absorbed by the market. This indicates that a basic purpose of the market is to serve as a perception device. The double auction is not only essentially to be considered in terms of dynamics, but an important part of its vital function is to incorporate new exogenous information. How efficient it is is still open to debate and calls for both new formal models and empirical work.

As game-theoretic models involving incomplete information and a high dependence on history fast become intractable, there is a great temptation to utilize simulation. We feel that this is essentially ad hoc and needs to be approached with caution unless there is a well-defined question with a theoretical basis to justify its merit as well as an empirical basis for justification. A more cautious approach, consistent with but different from a behavioral approach, is to concentrate on the mechanism per se, leaving out the description of the players and their goals and abilities but representing them as a set of messages to be processed. This concentrates more on mechanism design without emphasis on strategic detail.

The literature on auctions (primarily one-sided) is enormous. An excellent and voluminous coverage up until around 2000 is provided by Paul Klemperer [208, 209]. As much of this literature observes, many of the problems lie with nonsymmetric and incomplete information (as is evinced by the work of Robert Wilson [420]).

There are basic concerns about the dynamics of markets, as indicated in the work of Mandelbrot [240, 241] challenging the random walk dynamics going back to Bachelier [20] and underlying much of modern finance theory (see for example CAPM theory [228, 244, 269, 340, 402] and Black-Scholes options evaluation [34]).

In the last two decades there has been a considerable growth in an econophysics approach to the study of finance and the stock market in particular, stimulated by the double-auction mechanism of the stock market. An early article by Doyne Farmer [122] provides an excellent exemplar of how quickly special cases and detailed complexities crowd in. Originally his work led off with an attempt to derive equations of motion based on a concept of stock market pressure in terms of monetary profits and losses. However, Farmer stressed the viewpoint of behavior in terms of ecology and evolution, stressing the role of different timescales and adjustments in liquidity.

The work on the Santa Fe Institute Stock Market Model of Arthur et al. [17] provided an important demonstration of the ecological behavior of a large class of rules of stock market behavior. The work on value and herd investors by DeLong et al. [77] also provides an ecological example that casts light on why value investing can be destabilized.

A related and possibly more economist-friendly coverage was presented by Farmer and Geanakoplos [124], giving a broad presentation of the general equilibrium approach together with the concept of efficiency, including the linkage to finance via general equilibrium with incomplete markets. The distinction was made between the competitive equilibrium condition and the no-arbitrage condition, which derives from game theory and is far more general than the competitive equilibrium condition. The authors then turned to notes on disequilibrium and the inconvenient lack of match with economic theory of the power laws found by Mandelbrot and others. This paper was followed by an essay of Fabrizio Lillo [223] laying out the physicist approach to finance: for example, does the series of price changes pick up correlations of behavior?

These authors posed difficult problems in sorting out the difference between individual and market valuations. In actual market operations there has always been a tug between so called fundamental analysis and the attitude that the market tells all.

This and subsequent work is consistent with the basic theme of this book that the key problem in reaching economic dynamics from equilibrium theory is to recast the preinstitutional structure as a carrier of process. The subtle and often overlooked distinction between the simultaneous double sealed bid of Dubey [95] and the dynamics of the double auction in the stock market illustrates that carriers of process can be provided by the one-period market game, but even the double auction requires two or more periods to illustrate the complexity of information. Only here, along with complex information conditions, do the possibilities for behavior proliferate without bound, with the comforting sparseness of dynamic laws in physics replaced by an ecological and evolutionary richness. The game of Arthur et al. was only a precursor of simulations and agent-based models, as indicated by recent publications such as that of John Geanakoplos, Robert Axtell, et al. [151] on an agent-based model of the housing market.

12.3   Behavior, Innovation, and Process

12.3.1   The future of economic dynamics

The exhaustive treatment of the set of one-move[13] minimal strategic market games, as provided in this book, offers the first step toward dynamics by providing the construction of fully defined process models at a level of rigor at least as strong as that of general equilibrium theory while reinstating time and information explicitly. We purposely have only dealt in basic theory with what we term one-period minimal exchange models in order to stress that the problem of providing a process model is different from that of providing a process. Limiting ourselves to one-shot games places considerable limits on the complexity of behavior we can postulate. Our stress is on structure more than on behavior. There are not many behavioral assumptions one can make for how to play a one-shot game once. Furthermore if one wishes to consider the noncooperative equilibrium for the one-shot game, there are few embellishments that can be made beyond providing context. The considerable number of different behavioral assumptions appear as soon as a few periods and many information sets are considered.

When we proceed from the mechanism of the trading post models to the windows models, the paradox of the competition-based and the centralized socialist computed-price systems being the same is resolved. In a model without process (such as Arrow-Debreu) they cannot be distinguished. Social reality distinguishes them when one contrasts the requirements of a cumbrous centralized bureaucracy with great inducements to conceal information with a decentralized group of competitors. The system requirements lie with the calculus of administrative costs and not the existence of identical prices determined by fixed-point calculations ignoring context.

Because of the limitation to one-period models, most of the questions concerning what constitutes a solution concept adequate for playing a multistage game have been avoided. Our stress has been on structure, not behavior, except for the radically simple one-period competitive equilibrium and noncooperative equilibrium solutions.

By placing stringent restrictions on the class of SMGs, we obtain only a reasonably small number of fully defined process models of SMGs or playable games.[14] Limiting enquiry to applying the noncooperative equilibrium solutions to the class of SMGs in strategic form noted above, one may obtain all well-known general equilibrium results and more; but once information, time periods, and uncertainty are added, it is evident that the proliferation of feasible new structures indicates not merely a quantitative but a qualitative change. As more detail is added and the resource consumption aspects of financial instruments and institutions are considered, efficiency considerations call for the invention of new instruments and institutions. Transaction costs emerge as a logical requirement in attributing production costs to the information-processing, distribution, and control mechanisms of the institutions needed to run economic process.

The need for new instruments and institutions cannot be taken out of context of the customs and behavior of the political economy and society in which they are embedded. The type of instruments and laws designed for motivated sophisticated professional economic agents may need to be different from those whose main utilization will be by the average individual unschooled in economics or finance.

A process-oriented theory of money and financial institutions cannot avoid inventing instruments and institutions, as they are the carriers of process. This does not mean that there is no room for considering a mathematical structure. A mathematical institutional economics suggests that sound links between process models and the GE structure need to be and can be established via the methodology involved in the construction of SMGs. The economic principle still remains within the context of all the economic institutions, but its application requires an ad hoc recognition and description of the institution involved.

The building of the simpler SMGs already shows the critical roles of the various forms of money and credit.[15]

Unlike the laws of physics when applied to planetary motion, the laws of economic behavior when applied to a world of mutating institutions at best face the intractable prediction problems of the weather forecaster. The best predictions are both ad hoc and of short duration, combined with a highly parameterized description.[16]

This game-theoretic approach to money and financial institutions is devoted to building a loosely coupled system at a level of rigor equal to or higher than that of general equilibrium theory. The loose coupling opens the structure to the myriad of parameters and institutional details that empirically oriented ad hoc dynamics must acknowledge; but it does so in a manner that provides for the construction of complete, consistent control models. The approach to developing a theory of money and financial institutions via strategic market games stresses the control, information transmission, reception, computational and valuational aspects of financial control of a mass modern economy. The explosion of different models is due considerably to the information and perception conditions that are reflected in the activities of granting credit that involve search, negotiation, evaluation and control in the context of the many societies and polities that exist. Any attempt to provide a full formal game-theoretic model of the double auction illustrates the amazing complexity and flexibility that occurs when even the simplest of models is considered in multistage situations involving information.

12.3.2   Solutions, structure, and behavior

There is a groundswell of discontent with many economists brought up in the tradition of economic man. Economic man was further idealized in the last 60 or 70 years by the divorce of much mathematical economics and theory from political economy. Alongside this trend of mathematical idealization, however, there has also been a more recent proliferation of courses and seminars on behavioral economics and behavioral finance. While we applaud much of this effort, we believe that, to a great extent, a straw man has been set up (though this may have been needed).[17] The distinction between the economic and behavioral actors is a misleading and unfortunate one. One of the great services of game theory was to illustrate that the concept of the individual isolated rational actor could at best be extended only to two-person constant-sum games in strategic form. This is a minute segment of social reality.

Even for two-person non-constant-sum games in strategic form, there is no unique acceptable solution. The noncooperative equilibrium solution has little to recommend it beyond consistency of expectations. In general, properties such as uniqueness, symmetry, and efficiency are not necessarily consistent with the noncooperative equilibrium solution.

As soon as multistage games are considered, unless one imposes strong conditions such as the existence of the representative agent, symmetric agents, or a continuum of agents, it can be argued that many learning or teaching theories can be constructed that may find adherents among groups of theorists and other groups of experimentalists. But there is no universal theory. Which dynamic solution concepts appear to fit specific contexts is an open empirical question. There is a tug between normative and positive theories of strategic behavior.

Possibly one might wish to axiomatize best response. Having done so, the empirical question is in what domain behavior matches with the theory. The cooperative-game-theory solutions of core, value, and other solutions (such as the nucleolus [321]) and the noncooperative equilibrium can all be axiomatized. But the cooperative solutions are not mathematically congenial with dynamics unless considerably more modeling assumptions are added.

In a Forum on Bounded Rationality versus Behavioral Optimization presented in the *Journal of Economic Literature*, a paper by Harstad and Selten [178] notes that alternate models have offered limited challenge to the more or less standard paradigm, even though we are all aware from both psychology and marketing that a multidimensional utility function is not what Mrs. Jones computes with at the supermarket. Rabin's comment [300] on Harstad and Selten calls for the addition of both greater realism and inputs from psychology as embellishments to the economic optimization. Crawford [64] focuses more on strategic behavior and behavioral game theory. The three articles together provide a useful basic bibliography on experimental gaming in economics and signal the growing awareness and support for experimentation in the testing of economic theory, a sentiment with which we are in complete accord. Yet there are two items that we believe need far more attention than is currently given in either economic theory or experimentation. They are the role of fiduciary decision making and the controlling power of context. In chapter 10 we have already noted that the predominant form of decision making in society is fiduciary, whether by CEOs with other people's money or by politicians or generals with other people's lives.

In political economy the challenge is to modify conventionally titled models of rational economic behavior to reflect a contextualized rationality that includes the limits imposed by age, habit, perception, memory, and other factors of human behavior.

12.4   Dynamics and Complexity

The work in the previous chapters has presented a set of increasingly complex models as the size of the economy grows, specialization increases, and functions are differentiated.

Let n be the number of natural agents, m the number of real resources available, and τ the number of time periods involved.

1. The simplest model is the one-period Robinson Crusoe straight maximization $(n, m, \tau) = (1, m, 1)$; no distinction between natural and other legal persons is needed as Robinson is also his own government.

2. The many-period Robinson Crusoe model poses a straightforward one-person dynamic programming problem involving production and consumption where bookkeeping and accounting may be useful as external memory.

3. The one-period, two-person, one-commodity exchange economy $(n, m, \tau) = (2, 1, 1)$ extends the concept of individual rationality to a two-person game of pure opposition. All outcomes are by definition Pareto-optimal. This two-person situation is not a society, as interests are completely opposed. There is no potential gain from cooperation. The maxmin solution involves no trade.

4. The basic economic problem starts at $(n, m, \tau) = (2, 2, 1)$; this yields the Edgeworth-Bowley box diagram and the first nontrivial general equilibrium model. Already implicit in this is the assumption that government exists and that the commercial codes and contract laws are obeyed. The full mathematical apparatus of GE theory will produce efficient prices. A cooperative-game version produces the contract curve or the core. The model can also be recast as a strategic market game that yields inefficient noncooperative equilibria.

5. The fundamental GE and SMG models emerge when $(n, m, \tau) = (n, m, 1)$ where $n \geq 2$, $m \geq 2$. The quantitative and qualitative difference begins to show as n, m, or both become large. Whether these numbers are large or small makes no difference to the GE model as no process model is given. The axiom that covers behavior is that individuals are price takers. The same economy modeled as a strategic market game requires considerable elaboration of detail to provide the minimal mechanisms.

Without going into detail we summarize our approach to economic dynamics as involving a progressive differentiation of functions, instruments, and institutions. The numbers that count among the natural agents are 1, 2, few, many, and ∞. The numbers among the nonnatural legal persons are 0, 1, 2, few, many, and ∞.[18]

The one-person economy is still an economy, but with no basic need for institutions or financial instruments beyond an *aide-memoire* in bookkeeping and accounting.

Consumption and production are defined and a reasonable case can be made for welfare optimization by the single individual. Dynamics is reasonably well defined and is computationally tractable, if not analytically tractable.[19]

The two-person economy is where the economics of exchange starts.[20] The key feature of an economy is that there are joint gains available. But even with just two players in a non-constant-sum game, a host of new phenomena and problems appear. The laws and customs of needed institutions are called for. Rules for trade are called for to prevent kicking, gouging, cheating, fraud, and theft at the point of exchange. Thus when modeling even a two-person exchange, ownership conditions, a commercial code, and contract laws are all at least implicit if not explicit in the formulation. With just two persons the Edgeworth box presents a most attractive way of looking at the economics. But it can be misleading for the study of mass exchange. It portrays face-to-face exchange. No price formation mechanism is presented, no intermediary is present. Furthermore, Edgeworth, well before the formal invention of the theory of games [109], presented a contract curve solution that is far different from the GE price solution.

The full complexity of a mass economy first appears when looking at the Edgeworth model with two goods and two types of agent, but many agents of each type. A natural question for the economist to ask is how the models can reflect the mass data-processing and anonymity aspects of trade with thousands or millions of participants. Here the challenge involves modeling specific mechanisms to provide relevant detail. In section 11.7 we argued that the underlying one-period general equilibrium model of exchange is associated with a set of strategic market games of an order of magnitude of 50. This number was arrived at by considering distinctions among agents, market structures, price formation mechanisms, monies, and credit instruments. The argument is that although the number of SMGs associated with the basic GE model for one-period trade is moderately large, its size is not astronomical, suggesting that there are only a limited number of ways to convert the one-period general equilibrium model into a set of minimal process models. But these process models require the addition of a financial system to carry the processes. The constraint on the models to only one active period gives very little room for complex dynamics, yet is sufficient to enable one to see how to graft a complete financial control system on the general equilibrium structure. In doing so, not only do many financial instruments and institutions emerge as logical necessities, but the role of the government and financial structure as a control and evaluation mechanism emerges and suggests that the appropriate paradigm for studying the economy as a whole requires that government appear as a large agent in the game.

The cash flow constraints may be manifested in different ways depending on market structure; yet no matter how they appear, they serve as perception devices that signal the pressure points in the dynamics via their shadow prices.

Once one proceeds beyond the single simultaneous economy and permits eminently realistic items such as nonsymmetric information, one finds a hyper-astronomical proliferation of games that are associated with the general equilibrium system involving several time periods; but this proliferation is consistent with a flexible evolving dynamical system. This suggests that there are two stages in proceeding from GE to dynamics. The first is the conversion of the basic exchange model to a process model. This can be done exhaustively with the same if not a higher level of rigor than GE. The equilibrium results of GE can be obtained, but because the financial system is now reflected in the process model, parametric investigations can be performed to answer questions concerning the amount and distribution of money and credit in the system. The system has been opened up to be able to include parametrically a level of microeconomic detail not included in GE.

A further critical feature in the one-period process models is that the number of solution concepts that apply to the models has not greatly increased. The competitive equilibrium, the noncooperative equilibrium, best response, and entropic player are reasonably plausible and easy to define and apply, and a few others may be considered.

When we go beyond one period, leaving aside structural problems, behavioral considerations proliferate. Learning, teaching, and signaling all become important, and although one can limit oneself to the investigation of solutions such as the set of trembling-hand subgame perfect equilibria, the justification for the selection of a solution criterion becomes far more ad hoc. The phrase ad hoc utilized here is not necessarily pejorative. What it says, as noted in chapter 11, is that because of the overwhelming number of possible models and solution concepts in developing economic dynamics, there is no substitute for knowing your business. When constructing an economic model and selecting a solution concept, the selection must be made both in terms of logical consistency and empirical relevance.

Our conclusion is that there is no general abstract economic dynamics on a par with the physics of planetary motions. If there is an overall economic dynamic prediction model, it is more like a weather forecasting model than like the equations of motion of the planets.

In the last 80–90 years there has been a considerable proliferation of low-dimensional growth models ranging from Harrod to Solow, Phelps, Romer and Lucas and company. The theory behind each of them is relatively straight-forward; their success as very low-dimensional devices capturing a high-dimensional dynamics is up for debate on an individual basis. The 1950s and 1960s saw the growth of large Keynesian or neo-Keynesian models with dozens or up to hundreds of equations and parameters that required refitting every quarter. These models have almost disappeared. Yet from the viewpoint of economic theory the ad hoc justification of such a model is at least as good as, if not better than, a one-dimensional representative-agent dynamic-programming model of an economy if one is to proceed beyond parable.

Theory when applied to a dynamic economy for prediction requires a detailed ad hoc model. It may be checked for its logic, but it is validated by its predictive power. Theory when applied to problems in control has an easier task, because it does not have to deal with the details of specific time paths but with the possibility of influencing boundary conditions in such a manner that certain dynamic paths are prevented from occurring.

12.5   A False Dichotomy: The "Rational" or "Behavioral" Agents

In the analysis developed here, our prime concern has been the structure of political economies whose institutions support the dynamics generated by economic agents. Our concern has been to formalize the properties of the institutions and to link their relevance to a dynamic extension of the general equilibrium structure. As such we have utilized, as a "good enough approximation" to help define equations of motion, the neo-Benthamite gross simplification of individualistic human economic behavior referred to in the last one to two hundred years as *homo oeconomicus*, then "economic man" (to get rid of the Latin), then "economic individual" or agent (to get rid of gender bias).

This mythical individual complete with well-defined preferences (taken on faith) and combined with further approximations concerning individual motivation in mass markets, along with technical considerations concerning uniqueness of equilibrium, enables one to utilize the noncooperative equilibrium concept of solution to solve for equilibria in games in strategic form.

If one is investigating multiperiod economies, the simple definition of the noncooperative equilibrium solution is not enough to provide equations of motion, as is indicated by the studies of Fudenberg [147], Mailath and Samuelson [237], and others. The unqualified concept of the Nash NE solution to a game in strategic form is not able to provide fully defined laws of motion, both from the viewpoint of the logic of n-person game theory and from the many observations of human behavior in the social sciences.

All the solution theories including the noncooperative- and cooperative-game-theory solutions as well as simple response mechanisms are *behavioral theories*. We have to avoid being trapped in a false dichotomy: the noncooperative equilibrium solution concept and the rational-expectations solution concept are both behavioral. They call for action based on expectation. The implicit assumption is that coordination devices, learning, and teaching are needed to attain the equilibrium advocated.

12.5.1   The evidence from experimental gaming

The evidence from experimental gaming shows a mixed bag of results, as can be seen from the early work of Chamberlin [53] and Siegel and Fouraker [369], and also with Shubik [136], Smith [386], Plott [292], Shubik [349], Selten [329], Gode and Sunder [164], Roth [112], Huber, Shubik and Sunder [190], Bossaerts, Plott, and Zame [38], and many others. On the whole if the market mechanism is framed to call for mass market behavior, the individualistic view of competition in a simple, single market suggests that the rational-expectations (or NE) hypothesis is reasonably consistent with a substantial amount of the evidence.

Simple market models with a textbook economic story attached can be validated for simple noncooperative behavior, especially when there are many individuals and a unique equilibrium point.

Depending on context and complexity, the "economic principle" of individual isolated optimization does not provide an adequate account of behavior. The two-game and simulation examples of Brian Arthur on the El Farol [17] restaurant seating problem and the simulated stock market [15] provide examples of the basic difficulties with mass coordination and self-generated fluctuations.

12.5.2   The evidence from stock market studies

Possibly one of the best areas to test the power of rational expectations is the stock market. A modern stock market is a human construct more or less set up and constructed as a formal game with explicit rules of play. Because millions of individuals and thousands of their fiduciaries are participating with substantial sums of money at stake, the economic incentive to gather and analyze volumes of information is considerable. The work of Mandelbrot [240, 241], Taleb [397], Farmer [122], and others, as well as the imaginative simulation by Arthur et al. and the work of Shiller [341], provide an impressive answer that the rational-expectations model is inadequate for the description of financial dynamics.

12.6   Context Relevance and Economic Theory

We believe that across many contexts and in varying strength the economic principle of optimizing money earned is more or less consistent with observations. It remains an important explanatory variable in many situations. The fact that most of us go for "good enough" or "satisfice" is not at odds with the optimization. It merely reflects that the world is a highly complex place and that lack of common knowledge, information conditions, limitation on analytical ability, and social, economic, and political pressures in various strengths must be considered in application.

This is not meant as a pious avoidance of analysis, claiming that everything is involved, hence one can do nothing. On the contrary it says that context relevance determines the hand-tailoring needed; instances such as funding religion, defending abortion clinics, supporting casino gambling, checking on bank charges, and arguing for minimal wage legislation are all highly context-sensitive in the basic model building.

12.6.1   Our use of the NE or rational expectations

For most of our questions and models at a level of abstraction close to GE, the use of the NE allows us to demonstrate the basic way to convert the general equilibrium system's static structure into a set of process models and to argue that, where all agents are constrained to strategies that are single moves, there are relatively few such process models. Thus a fairly natural first step can be taken in bridging the gap between the basic timeless structure and its process relatives.

The insistence on games with the normal form and strategic form equivalence is utilized in order to be able to produce full process models while avoiding having to discuss immediately the many alternative solution possibilities that are called forth when confronting multistage games.

In our work we carefully select a few multistage games and still stick to the investigation of subgame-perfect NEs because, for the questions we address, this frequently unsatisfactory solution is sufficient to illustrate an item such as the breaking of the cash flow in Schumpeterian innovation and to point to the control problems raised.

12.6.2   Evolution and other solutions

The concept of a universal economic dynamics at the level of application is a pipe dream. Let a thousand question-specific models blossom utilizing essay, mathematized equilibrium models, full process models, or other ad hoc constructs. The low-dimensional dynamic programming models or the evolutionary game models provide, at best, some insights into context-specific questions; otherwise they provide metaphor and allegory on the nature of process. The revolution in models of the "satisficing" agent led by Herbert Simon [374] together with the spectacular growth of artificial intelligence and simulation methods promised a great breakthrough in the study of human and other behavior. The Carnegie School promised a sea change in the understanding of management and the growth of organization. Paradoxically the revolution took place, but not in the way its early advocates had expected. A hydra-headed explosion of new difficulties and new needed subdisciplines appeared in computer science, economics, sociology, psychology, biology, and elsewhere. Apparently trifling problems such as teaching a computer how to recognize and pick up a building block took many years. Early advocates of the relevance of biology to economics such as Marshall [245] and Kenneth Boulding [39] were voices in the wilderness, and the topic has called forth a dubious sociobiology with Edward Wilson [418] as well as the intersection of game theory and biology in the contributions of Dawkins [72], Lewontin [221], Maynard Smith [251], and collaborations between biologists and game theorists such as Hammerstein and Selten [175].

Programs in the characterization and the study of complexity have grown in the last 30 years, as evinced in the interdisciplinary work encouraged at the Santa Fe Institute and the journal *Complexity*; yet close connections between economics and biology have not yet been achieved. This is perhaps not surprising, and may be regarded not as a defect but rather as an acknowledgment that many relevant levels of structure exist. If one leaves aside the political struggles and sociology of the acceptance of evolutionary theory, one of the main points that has come to be understood within the syntheses of the twentieth century [296] is that the Darwinian dynamic of selection acting on heritable variations is an extremely general algorithm for producing order in dynamical systems, but by virtue of its very generality it contains almost no information about the solution to any particular problem. Evolution can act in parallel at many scales within each system [138, 169, 173, 174], and different levels of selection are all constructed ordered forms [132] maintained by evolution interacting within structures of constraints. Many levels already act within the sphere generally termed "biology," and a scope wide enough to include both biology and economics must span more levels in behavior, cognition, communication, sociology, and culture, each with inherent evolutionary contributions. Sometimes projections onto one or a few levels can effectively be modeled separately, and in these cases a subdiscipline grows to encode its own principles of order. However, the interaction across evolutionary levels tends to be denser and more complex than the relatively clean separations of scale to which scientists have grown accustomed in the physical sciences.

12.7   The Pure Theory of Money

In the chapters above a common theme at a high level of abstraction has emerged, and although it is of no immediate application to the many problems of the day, it has an import comment to make.

GE was essentially timeless. The clever trick of Arrow and Debreu killed time, uncertainty, and space. Our problem has been how to reintroduce them. In doing so the introduction of money is central. Many properties of money can be identified, but the most important appears to be its role as a means of payment.

We observe from [104] that considerations of efficiency in the trading mechanism call for a commodity money to emerge in an exchange economy. This involves breaking a symmetry in an otherwise essentially symmetric structure. Fiat money can be substituted for the commodity money, but a complex of institutional factors and the dynamics of trade are required to give worth to an intrinsically worthless commodity.

The economic process is ordered in time, and time is a distinguished dimension. The processes of production and exchange are carried out utilizing one or more monies and markets. The presence of fiat money in an economy provides for a mathematically sound construction of a limiting process that enables us to consider an economy of arbitrary length that approaches the infinite horizon smoothly and that does not unravel with a backward induction. The economy is "cash-consuming" in the sense that if it ends in any arbitrary finite time it will have consumed all of the initial fiat money if loans are permitted.[21] This is because borrowing provides a time shift in consumption and cash flow; thus all agents may plan to have precisely the amount left over at the end of the terminal active period T to be able to settle their debts at the day of settlement at time $T + 1$. The monetary system will always be in motion, and the rate of interest ρ must be greater than zero. If $\rho = 0$ then there is an essential discontinuity in the system and the model blows up. When $\rho > 0$ the society's price system is always in motion, and the initial injection plus any extra borrowing is extracted by the presence of a positive rate of interest.

The understanding of government as a combination of the major monetary player and the referee requires that we describe the uses of institutions such as a public debt, stock markets, commodity markets, risk markets, public goods, taxes, and subsidies. These are most easily understood abstractly, utilizing more or less context-free mathematical models concentrating primarily on their basic functions.

Unfortunately still lurking in the background are the powers of tradition and custom as contrasted with any immutable law. Added to these are the forces of technological change, especially in communication and computation. When these are considered, as the axioms for transactions money [104] suggest, there are possibilities for many monies having domains in subnetworks. The basic reliance on state money in the society is consistent with Knapp's views. It belongs to the biggest recognized and most highly policed network in the state. However, the other monies include the banks and any other subnet that can go into business for itself.

At the highest level of abstraction, a theory of the emergence of a transactions money is available. This together with institutional and technological reality indicate that the power of the central banks and the commercial banking system is in transition. The names of institutions called central bank and commercial banks will probably stay unchanged, but their functions and powers must change to adjust to a heavily mutating payments system. The theory deals with identifying and considering the basic functions of a money in an economy. The application to the current problems of the economy require a hand-tailoring and parameterization of the ad hoc problems at hand.

Notes

1 A slight modification to this model, adding a stochastic item to reflect the probability that the bureuacracy might be too corrupt, harsh, or greedy in its administration of the laws, could produce a class of models reflecting the expected length for a politico-bureaucratic structure to remain stable. We reiterate our observation from chapter 5 that the characterization of the bureaucratic output and connections with the political environment is a vital topic for empirical investigation.

2 This model is essentially identical to the double-sided sealed bid and offer. Although it is well defined, we do not know of any major actual use of the double-sided sealed bid.

3 In this heuriistic description this s not tightly defined as it does not distinguish between the time taken by a trader as contrasted with the tme taken by the mechanism. This is clariified in the more formal model.

4 A practcal example of how minute details emerge as operational problems is given by problems involved in announcing the closing price at the end of the New York trading day of a mutual fund based in New York that holds an international portfolio.

5 Other operational definitions of an individual timescale might come from the time it takes a trader to respond to information and place an order in a double auction, but to use such a timescale we would need to consider the role of the auction as a source of feedback signals, and the information-based responses of traders to those signals. That requires additional choices beyond those we will make in a minimal model. Note that, although plausible individual timescales for random encounter or the double auction are all slow compared to seconds or even microseconds, they might otherwise be much less than or much greater than a trading day, depending on the context modeled.

6 More complex models of the wealth exchanged by traders who may have different values, such as a wealth-dependent risk aversion, were considered in a fully stochastic model by Smith, Foley, and Good [379].

7 In terms of the performance measure of per-trade expected surplus, these minimal instantiations of the simultaneous sealed bid and the random encounter are qûite similar. Most trades are completed between counterparties that have prices far apart, and in that sense there is not a wide diversity between the mechanisms. In contrast, as is shown in section 12.2.2.3, the double auction admits instantaneous matching rules that range from distant-price clearing to adjacent-price clearing, and therefore permits a much wider diversity of mechanisms. Among rule sets of comparable complexity to one another, the double auction can thus produce values of per-trade expected surplus outside the (quite narrow) range spanned by the simultaneous sealed bid and the random encounter.

8 This correlation illustrates a property of surplus that can be counterintuitive. Traders who have difficult-to-meet reservation prices are *wealthier* as a result of trade if they can complete the trade successfully, because they buy lower or sell higher than those with easier-to-meet reservation prices. If the same good is repeatedly traded by agents who have no interest in actually *owning* the good, as is the case for the majority of trade in securities markets, greater wealth is achieved at the cost of more market entries and greater patience, which is an intuitive cost-benefit tradeoff. The notion of a reservation price as an *ex ante* property of a trader is a qualitatively different assumption that is a poor fit to the securities model of repeated exchange: it assumes that in absolute terms agents place more or less value on owning *the good itself*, and therefore declare more or less benefit from buying or selling it. The complex relation between wealth and surplus value can be captured to some extent in securities markets for multiple goods, in which the *relative* worth of owning one good versus another may depend on the trader's ability to acquire or dispose of the different goods in different markets in which he trades from a fixed budget.

9 A requirement of stationarity, which is only possible at all in cases where queues are rolled over, further limits the set of clearing rules that are admitted.

10 References [69, 191, 377] also introduced *market orders*, which cancel against the best price no matter where that price is found, so this constitutes a further model elaboration beyond those discussed here.

11 Whether the minimum-surplus rule is a pathological case, included only for game-theoretic completeness, or a potentially useful mechanism depends on the application domain and interpretation. We have treated the number of orders filled, and the consmer's surplus per order, as independent dimensions to acknowledge that there is no unique way to value a surplus computed from a reservation price against the value of completing versus not completing a trade. Minimum-surplus is a form of optimal sorting rule to maximize market accessibility under mechanism capacity constraints, and may be viewed as loosely analogous to the zero-profit horizon for efficient production in general equilibrium, or the Gale-Shapley optimal matching algorithms from cooperative-game theory [148].

12 This stands in contrast to the best-price rule, where slowing of movements in the mid-price will be exponential in N_{max}; see the discussion of this point immediately below.

13 Essentially one information set for each player.

14 We have not added the minimal exchange and production models as they are somewhat more complicated, but we conjecture that a case can be made for a minimal set of SMGs being only somewhat bigger than the exchange economies.

15 Much further structure is required to reflect the roles of public goods and to connect with not directly economic features of individual, social, and political behavior that provide the economy with its evolutionary impetus.

16 For better or for worse the parametric and functional form-updating of large macroeconomic models can serve as an exemplar of application and experimentation consistent with the development of a science, provided that the assumptions and structure are kept transparent and attempts are made to develop theory and a justification for the forms and assumptions employed.

17 It has been suggested that "Any stigma will do to beat a dogma." This is attributed to Philip Guedalla. Possibly one needs an overreaction to challenge the overuse of the super-rational economic agent.

18 Local institutions such as town governments and school districts add up to many thousands of institutions.

19 The expected length of life of a solitary individual in a multistage model must be specified.

20 In the set of all two-person games there is only a small subset of games of pure opposition; from the viewpoint of economics they have autarchic solutions as no gains from trade are available.

21 If there is uncertainty present and imperfect insurance at the last move, there will be some money left over.

13 The Guidance of an Enterprise Economy

13.1 The Prediction or Guidance of an Enterprise Economy

The Grail is in the seeking, not the cup.

The stock-flow distinction is at the core of understanding much of economic dynamics. The untrammeled flow determines the stock; but its guidance may produce stocks that minimize the damage caused by fluctuations.

Predicting the motion of an enterprise economy appears to be at least as difficult as, if not more difficult than, predicting the weather. This does not rule out the possibility that by adjusting constraints a government may be able to deflect the path of the economy from less desirable states.

13.2 Theory of Money and Dynamics

In chapters 1–7 our major thrust was to develop process models of exchange in a minimalist manner, avoiding as much as possible the specification and elaboration of special institutions, picking up only one or two of their essential functions. In chapters 8, 9, and 10 our concern was to take our first steps into dealing with disequilibrium and the breaking of the circular flow of capital. In all instances the models presented have been elementary, with the assumptions concerning parameters and behavior kept at a minimum.

Our intent throughout has been to avoid, when possible, vagueness in the verbal treatment of money and banking and fiscal behavior in order to concentrate on central physical and organizational aspects of the system. Given our ability to translate the static GE model into a process model, can we construct a guidance model for the economy that indicates the nature of the power and efficiency available to constrain the behavior of the private sector in accord with actions by the government sector?

We are not attempting to give immediately relevant direct operational advice to be applied to any specific ongoing economy. That is the job of the macroeconomist, whose central task is that of a practitioner dealing with the ad hoc institutions and other realities of an economy as it is.

Our more modest task is to consider basic abstractions such as "if there were an economy with all transactions paid in government money and/or bank credit where both the money and credit influence cash flow constraints, how well could these institutions control or guide growth and fluctuations?" Even this question is difficult to make precise and requires a host of explicit and often counterfactual constraints (such as the assumption that there are no other sources of credit beyond the central and commercial banks).

As is indicated in the analysis in chapters 9, 10, and 11, the differences in the control features of a commodity money such as gold as contrasted with fiat money are considerable. The introduction of commercial bank money (debt) introduces further complications in information processing and evaluation and control.[1]

13.3   Why Unify Macro- and Microeconomics?

In the discourse on modern economics one often hears calls for the unification of macro- and microeconomics into a satisfying whole. It is on par with a suggestion to unify physics with engineering. There are many subtheories in physics such as the theory of electricity, sound, quantum mechanics, relativity theory, and many others directed toward subfields of physics where special detail and structure must be considered. All of these theories are related to and manifested in the many engineering applications that are used in our societies. The understanding of the theories of electricity, sound, and light is manifested in the engineering that has produced items such as radios, television, and iPhones. The design of interplanetary rockets calls for an employment of many physical theories together with considerable engineering. The professors of physics and engineering recognize their symbiotic relationship and understand the gap between theory and practice. So it is with the many theories prevalent in economics.

There may be many subtheories, even in macroeconomics, but the economist as theorist should not be confused with the economist as engineer, consultant, and advocate. Unification per se is not a goal in economic theory.

13.4   Theories in Economics

A good theory is capable of bringing out the commonality that underlies the many models that can be grouped under it. The nature of the questions to be asked determines much of the detail of the model constructed to answer them. The questions at hand may be aimed at problems requiring direct immediately applied advice in running an economy or they may be devoted purely to theory, such as "Is it logically possible that under the basic axioms of this theory an equilibrium could exist with a constant flow of bankruptcies?"

Utilizing strategic market games and experimental gaming together with consideration of the methods of physics concerning scaling, conservation, and dimensional analysis, we have endeavored to construct a methodology aimed at building or joining models and theories in the broad subject of political economy with its many branches and ramifications. As matters stand today there is a broad collection of specialized theories many of which share at least the common assumptions of the presence of economic agents and institutions, and implicitly the existence of a modicum of law and order.

For most questions asked of the many subtheories and models that abound, the subdisciplines supply the special substructure, detail, and context needed to give answers, and no higher theoretical unification is needed. Some questions arise, however, that may fall between two or more of the subdivisions in political economy. For these one has to stitch together essentially diverse bodies of work and try to reconcile different gestalts.

Our concrete concern has been with a viable theory of money and financial institutions that involves at least three large subdisciplines of political economy (general equilibrium microeconomic theory, macroeconomics, and finance) as well as four allied disciplines (game theory, experimental gaming, econophysics, and accounting) and less directly economic history and oligopoly theory. There are many questions in trying to construct a viable theory of money and financial institutions that cannot be answered adequately without inputs from these diverse sources. A good example is the old chestnut going back to Adam Smith, the doctrine of "Bills only" that has been a source of controversy for nearly 250 years, with verbal comments and debates by many individuals such as Bagehot [21] and more recently Lucas [234] and Sargent [315]. This topic cannot be resolved without paying attention to the specific details required to construct a playable experimental game, with strict care taken in showing the different timescales assumed for the interactions of all parties and instruments, as well as the rules preserving or breaking conservation and the common knowledge and information conditions assumed.[2]

In chapter 11 we concerned ourselves with the meaning and usage of "theory" in economics. In essence the semantic view of theories appears to predominate, as a class of models providing a logical framework connected with some aspect of observation. Thus there are banking theory, the theory of international trade, oligopoly theory, welfare theory, and many others. In application of these theories it makes sense to hand-tailor ad hoc models to the problem at hand. The economist as doctor, consultant, or engineer [242] is called for. This is a role far different from that of the pure theorist. The economic theorist, the economic historian, the historian of economic thought, and the econometrician are a support team to the practitioner, advisor, and social engineer concerned with specific substance here and now rather than invariant properties, history, and technique.

13.4.1   Beyond general equilibrium

The theorist looks for invariant properties of systems. We believe that in economics there are invariants, but at a level far from immediate application. GE theory provided a basic starting point. The next level calls for process, and, even at its most abstract, process calls for mechanisms that provide the basic shaping of institutions. The new level of abstract questions calls for the search for invariant properties in the aggregation and disaggregation of information and of entities. A specific example is the emergence of markets and price noted in chapter 11.

General equilibrium theory should be looked at as providing the understanding of some broad basic idealized economic principles in a frictionless static preinstitutional world. It serves as a natural starting point for the development of dynamic models and theories to cover much but by no means all of everyday economic life. It provides only a narrow window on one aspect of human goals; it does little to cover sociopolitical life or provide insight into innovation, technology, individualities, and many public goods. The presence of bureaucracy and incentive systems is key to both the efficacy and cost of governance. As complexity increases, so do loci of governance.

13.4.2   On principles versus rules: regulation and its feasibility

With the enormous growth of population, advances in communication and computation, and the need for supervision of many institutions involving thousands, hundreds of thousands, or even millions of employees, bureaucratic structures have burgeoned, whether governmental or private. The problems of governance within these structures involves incentive systems and has not only been the study of sociologists [281], economists [417], and game theorists [179] but is showing up in accounting, where a shift in the treatment of Generally Accepted Accounting Principles (GAAP) from principles to rules and regulations can be seen. How much should professionals be held to a nondetailed and only partially written code of ethics, and how much should they be presumed to be required only to operate within the written rules? What is the optimal level of detail that needs to be present in the Commercial Code? These are ongoing questions that depend heavily on relevant ad hoc detail of a living mutating society. There are many case distinctions that emerge, and answers to the basic questions cannot be supplied without context. What is a bribe in one context is a present in another. One forgets at one's peril that custom trumps law. The economic theorist must simultaneously be aware of constraint and context and be honest enough to avoid presenting the economics as a theory of everything.

13.4.2.1 An aside on taxation One aspect of a mass anonymous society with a faceless bureaucratic system is that the payment of taxes is, for most members of the society, converted into a game of pure opposition. A delicate question in causality and culture is posed. Is the cooperative societal concept of the citizen recognizing and willing to shoulder her contribution to taxes pure mythology? Or is it "good economics" to destroy such a societal attitude, as it may be easier and cheaper to operate in a purely adversarial environment for a tax management system that may not have sufficient resources, incentives, organization, and accountability for prompt and cooperative redress of taxpayers mishandled by the system?

The proposition that the long-term economic forces do not produce dysfunctional organizations that may last for many decades, if not longer, remains unestablished and may be false. The long-term choice is probably not between smooth evolution and revolution; in context we may have both.

13.4.3 Optimality, efficiency, and context

Unfortunately, as is often the case, complex problems are complex. In a multi-agent society, only in the narrow bandwidth of easily decentralizable structures can individual and social measures of optimality coexist, unless one regards money as a sufficiently close approximation to a transferable utility.

The comfortable attractive umbrella of Pareto optimality holds only for a handful of the basic questions. Both the competitive equilibrium and the noncooperative equilibrium share the attractive property of no arbitrage; but although the competitive equilibrium has both the properties of no arbitrage and Pareto optimality, as is well known to careful theorists, the noncooperative equilibrium does not.

The concept of optimality in a mutating dynamic society can hardly be defined out of context. There is a danger in accepting a no-arbitrage condition as a surrogate for optimality. This may or may not be a reasonable approximation in an economy without innovation, as is noted in our discussion of the cost of government.

13.5   Data, Information, the Society and Economy, and Big Brother

In almost all of the work in this book we have used the convenient simplification of the more or less intelligent economic agent because it appears to provide reasonable answers to many pertinent questions on the existence of markets and prices; but this approximation to economic behavior is only justified in a context that it appears to fit moderately well. At best it may have only a partial explanatory power. Few economists doubt that other behavioral considerations are called for in many contexts. The buying of lottery tickets, the role of sloth, addiction, crowd behavior, the madness of crowds can all be skillfully beaten into the same bed of Procrustes[3] by some economists, but it may be that other behavioral interpretations offer a better explanation consistent with the context.

13.5.1   Intelligence, structure, and behavior

The Navy is a master plan designed by geniuses for execution by idiots. If you are not an idiot, but find yourself in the Navy, you can only operate well by pretending to be one. All the shortcuts and economies and common-sense changes that your native intelligence suggests to you are mistakes. Learn to quash them. Constantly ask yourself, "How would I do this if I were a fool?" Throttle down your mind to a crawl. Then you will never go wrong.
—Herman Wouk, *The Caine Mutiny*

Wouk may be taking some poetic license concerning the ship in which James Tobin is reputed to have served; but a reasonably intelligent design by skilled operations researchers and economists on how to amuse those standing in a Disney World queue, or American teenagers at a popular concert or Brazilian or British masses at a football game, can hardly be described as a candidate for guiding rational economic behavior.

Many economists do not give up utilizing their assumption of the rational economic agent because it appears to be almost miraculous that with such a simplistic view of the agent so much analysis can be done that appears to have some power of explanation. The model itself is behavioral, but of a personality-poor, simplistic agent in a mass market world. Constructing richer models of sociopolitical-economic agents is considerably harder than using the simplistic optimizer.

13.5.2   On the biological virtue of "bad guys"

When we view the economy as an ongoing ecology, up to a point the credit card thieves, the counterfeiters, the hackers, and other assorted scoundrels help to keep healthy the body economic and stimulate the production of social anti-bodies by improving codes and destroying weaknesses.

In essence the healthy economic system is not error-free. A stasis, if any, will be dynamic; a good example is provided by the legal battles arising in oligopolistic competition or in labor negotiations. A set of institutions such as firms and labor unions or firms and consumer representatives are in a reason-ably healthy relationship if there is always a backlog of legal cases against the firms along with a supply of countercases, where both sides win some and lose some and replenish the inventory with new cases. Different societies may be able to thrive with different numbers of lawyers, but the basic process is the same. Discovery, clarification, and change aid in the guidance of the dynamics.

A society requires an error correction capacity and an autoimmune system to react to invasion by foreign bodies.

13.5.3   The battle on information sources and sinks

The product of a modern society tends to be more and more information-intensive. The basic problems involving individual consumption and pro-duction of information are still growing. How large should be the rights of appropriation and protection of revenues from patents and copyrights? What is reasonable informational transparency in a corporation? Where do patents and industrial secrets fit? How are disclosure of personal records as well as surveillance to be limited? In a world with massive international trade and other forms of communication, the boundaries among economic, political, and societal activities are faint. Furthermore given the difference among political, bureaucratic, and judicial tenures the world over, the nature of the locus and deciphering of the data gathered raises questions about the distribution of polit-ical and bureaucratic power.

Raw data are not necessarily information. Overwhelming the opposition with low-level disclosure reminds us that much critical information may be hidden in plain sight when the recipients do not have the talent, time, or resources to mine the raw data.

13.6   Simecs, Ithaca Hours, Bitcoins, and Berkshares

The rage at the time of writing is an attempt to establish a broad base of acceptance for an individualistic virtual currency called Bitcoin. It comes with the attendant science fiction hype of a mystery Japanese superprogrammer, mystical and unbreakable codes, and the promise of a libertarian's dream. The ultimate denial of interference by any government in individual economic affairs appears to be part of its aim.

Bitcoin must be distinguished from other grassroots or individually generated private currencies, of which there have been thousands over the centuries. An object or symbol has a critical property of a money if it serves as a means of payment among a set of individuals. The set does not have to constitute everyone in a nation-state; it may be limited to a small subset. Three fairly recent examples are the Simec [396] from a town in Italy, Ithaca Hours in Ithaca, and the Berkshare [388] in the Berkshires around Stockbridge (http://www.berkshares.org/). Possibly the most interesting of the three is the Simec. It gave employment and enjoyment to Giacinto Auriti, a retired law professor who issued some of his Simecs in year 2000 as a currency in his home town of Guardiagrele. The Italian financial police impounded some of his Simecs, and he won the court case in Chieti on the argument that printing one's own money was not tantamount to counterfeiting the national currency. Auriti died in 2006, but his currency predeceased him.

Ithaca Hours were started by Paul Glover in 1991, evidently inspired by the notes issued by Robert Owen to his workers based on an hour of labor. The notes were accepted and circulated in some stores in Ithaca and were given in exchange for labor. By 2011 according to a local publication [206] only a few were still in circulation. The objective had been to stimulate trade in the local economy in a socially and ecologically responsible manner.

The Berkshare was first launched in September 2006 with the goal of stimulating the local economy and encouraging local trade. According to Berkshares, Inc:

> BerkShares are a local currency designed for use in the Berkshire region of Massachusetts and issued by BerkShares, Inc., a non-profit organization working in collaboration with participating local banks, businesses, and non-profit organizations.

The exchange rate of the Berkshare currently is fixed at 95 cents of a U.S. dollar; thus one might regard the scheme as a local 5 percent discount device. As of an interview in 2013 [388] there were around 130,000 Berkshares in circulation, which is a financial drop in the bucket, but with their organizational structure with Berkshares, Inc. they still thrive as a small hardy perennial.

Many monies have thrived on local information, trust, and power in company towns. Merchant bankers emerge from merchants with a reputation for trust. Walmart provides the latest example. But in spite of the dreams of glory of Professor Auriti, the local currency generators have been for local regions and/or special circumstances to satisfy modest needs, such as those generated in prisoner of war or concentration camps or in cities under siege. When we move closer to the world of 2010–2030, quaint minor paradoxes turn into new problems involving billions and potentially trillions in payments. All of the examples above involved physical representations of means of payment, but that is hardly what the ever-growing, more abstract payment system is about.

The fundamental difference between Bitcoin and the previous currencies is that, while the others have been heavily local, this is the first high-technology computerized attempt to aim for the globe. The basic problems with and opportunities for Bitcoin are based on subtle points in the theory of money, illustrated in part in chapter 11 and in [104], and unsubtle points in the economic reality of world trade, law, and sovereignty. The great danger is that Bitcoin provides a natural device for illegal trade in drugs and weapons, along with tax evasion and other aspects of an underworld economy. World gross product in terms of the United States dollar has been estimated for the year 2014 at $45.83 trillion and world trade at $24.2 trillion (http://clients.ibisworld.com). Figures such as these are fun to play with, helping us phrase and rephrase questions that are hard to nail down. These numbers suggest that, if we were to guesstimate the overall size of illegal world trade as anywhere between 0.5 and 5 percent of world legitimate trade, a virtually anonymous computerized transfer system could profit considerably on illegal trade alone. It could be regarded as an improvement of the hawala traditional Islamic payment system that was supported in part by the power of custom. As big as clandestine trade may be, however, the bigger prize that is coming into sight is the gains to be had through improvements in the legitimate payment systems of the world economy. Currently a reasonable estimate for the exchange and settlement processes is around 2–4 percent of world gross product. (The estimate depends heavily on how the service charges of many lawyers, accountants, auditors, insurers, bookkeepers, IT specialists, and other bureaucratic and supervisory personnel are included in the system, as well as FX costs and the services of

Paypal, Mastercard, Visa, American Express, and other expediters of the payments system.)

It is desirable to separate out, as much as possible, the exchange transaction costs from the pure transfer settlements as run through an institution such as the Clearing House Interbank Payments System (CHIPS). The changes in technology of both communication and computation make an assault on current payment systems highly likely.

13.6.1   On many monies and local information and trust

Any affiliation net if large enough and strong enough can invent its own submoney. We use the prefix "sub" to indicate that the submoney has its domain of operation over a subnetwork consisting of individuals or institutions known to each other and/or with a sufficiently large set of common interests for gains among themselves, together with joint expectations (and possibly some form of enforcement mechanism) that violation of implicit (or explicit) contract among the group will be low. The number in the special net may be as small as 2. For instance two international firms who regularly do considerable business with each other would have employed two banks in the 1950s. Today their treasury departments could be in direct contact, netting out payment in an agreed-upon fashion and setting up a more or less optimal settlement period by themselves. The subnet could also include millions. A recent development in transfer banking has taken place with Walmart. The chain has (in 2014) around 10,000 brick and mortar establishments around the world. It has a reasonably faithful lower- and middle-class clientele with many relatives elsewhere. Its entry into the money transfer banking business captures great hidden assets, provides a basic public service in a high-transaction-fee business, and can easily conform to all laws with respect to information disclosure and regulation. The computer net has offered a new way to cash in on both reputation and bricks and mortar.

The Walmarts, Starbucks, Disney dollars, Monte Carlo chips, Bitcoins, and Simecs will continue to grow in numbers and special purposes, each being a money in the context of its subnet. For the world community, whether Bitcoin per se survives is of little concern except to investors and supporters of Bitcoin. The key message is that large changes in the role of settlement technology may be in the offing (less so for the contracting and transaction technology).

Given the various improvements that must and will come from schemes such as Bitcoin, they must be made consistent with government concerns for tax evasion and illegal trade. The price for realizing these gains is to modify the libertarian dreams and to work out appropriate accommodations with all states involved that will enable new schemes for payment to improve the economy as a whole while conforming with the legitimate requirements of the state for taxation and the policing of illegal activities.

Good practice and good theory will and should remain apart, but they should never be far from each other. The new world of the electronic means of payment forces us to realize that the two theories of money, encompassing both custom and the evolution of trade with law and the legitimate power of organized society, are both consistent and necessary, as the future history of some LegitCoin will show; and an example such as Walmart shows that a net of trust can be built with people and bricks and mortar first used for other purposes.

The early growth of the computer strengthened the potential power of the central banks, but the growth of communication and the Internet has had the opposite effect; the subnets made feasible by the combination of political, social, and economic subgroups with the new technologies weakens some aspects of the control of the central banks.

13.7   More on Money Matters

Several other views of money are called for.

13.7.1   Money, finance, and language

Both money and language are phenomena associated with dynamics, communication, and evolution. Money along with financial instruments and markets is less complex than human languages, but provides a language for economic life.

The analogies between the two systems are not close in all respects, but language like money admits two levels of description: the first as an ensemble in which information is statistically contained in the instances of language production, the other as an *embedded* ensemble that is a component within a larger complex dynamic coordination process.

An adequate formalization of the information in individual locutions from among the possible constructions in a language was provided by Claude Shannon's theory of the information in symbol systems [332]. It is not possible to say that the information in a locution is inherent in its structure without further specification of context, but it is possible to assign information to fragments of language with a minimal representation of context by a probability distribution over all possible expressions. Shannon, in an effort to clarify the sense of information in his formalization, labeled it as *syntactic* information, which he contrasted with *semantic* information, referring to meanings of locutions outside the scope of simple ensemble representations of their likelihoods. Many commentators have misunderstood or misrepresented Shannon's disclaimer as an assertion that information theory cannot reflect meaning; an accurate statement[4] would be that the meaning in sentences resides in joint probabilities of their production along with events in the extralinguistic world. The representation of such joint distributions is a considerably more complex problem than mere estimation of the likelihood of a given utterance, averaged over contexts.

This view of language is not exactly static, but it does project onto a timeless ensemble the full scope of dynamics behind actual speech in context. The view of information as an attribute of a locution is distantly analogous to the view of a trade equilibrium as an inherent property, prior to institutional context, of the preferences and technologies of agents considered to compose an economy. Shannon's construction, like general equilibrium theory, provided an enormous advance in the precise characterization of structure, and is a fundamental tool of analysis throughout communication and computation theory [63, 406].

Not displacing the Shannon formulation, but considering independently those aspects of context that it does not address, are approaches to language as a system of tokens for coordinating loosely coupled systems. In these approaches, the emphasis is not on the structure of the tokens—it is taken for granted that many structures could be chosen and that many systems could be designed to use them for purposes of differentiation—but instead on the problem of coordination among partly autonomous processes. A formal theory of computation based on coordination is the "π-calculus" created as a language for concurrency theory [314].[5]

Even the production and recognition of linguistic acts decomposes into a coordination phenomenon among multiple loosely coupled systems. The most nearly formal statement of this position comes from Ray Jackendoff [192], who proposes that we understand phonological (including prosodic and phonetic), syntactic, and semantic dimensions of language as all being handled by partly autonomous processes, which are kept in loose synchrony during the process of producing or comprehending linguistic elements which have structure in all these dimensions.

Linguistic patterns straddle a boundary between inherited capabilities and culturally carried and evolved systems. For more than a century, the basic competence to understand and produce language has been attributed to specific (usually left-brain) areas[6] distinctive to humans.[7] At the same time, the seemingly open-ended variability of language systems argues for a component that is culturally constructed out of more primitive human social skills. It must be appreciated, however, that language as a construct within the social environment is an essential scaffold for the normal structure of the linguistic dimensions of human cognitive development. That is, it is a structure carried by the speech community, which the developmental program of humans has "offloaded" from strict genetic scripting to a much more complex but still highly stereotypical gene/environment interaction. The explicit role of developmental windows in language acquisition attests to a larger instinctive dimension within language than in most other social constructs, though the importance of developmental scaffolding for many social norms should not be underestimated.

Because each human language has an intrinsically culturally carried component, language evolution occurs across two or more widely separated timescales [48]. The structure (syntax, morphology, lexicon, phonology) of each particular language is carried by a pattern of cultural norms that evolve on multiple timescales intrinsic to the processes, which also vary widely but are all faster than the timescales of genetic change in the speaker populations.

As we noted in section 7.3, a language that is both sufficiently rich and precise to cover economic and financial activity is far from developed.

13.7.2 Big Brother and anonymity

Anonymity in one context is not anonymity in another. The computer age brings with it new possibilities not merely for freedom but for governmental control. The tracing of money flows is high on the list of means to trace individual activity. But the money flows are usually in credit of some form, not cash. Cash is far harder to trace.

13.7.3 On money and measurement: a reprise

Can and should we attempt to monetize everything? Money is associated with economic measurement.

13.7.3.1 Money and happiness? "What it happiness; can it buy money?" The answer, except for the misers and some poker-game-motivated moneymakers, appears to be no. "What is money; can it buy happiness?" Sometimes the answer is yes. The procurement of an income sufficiently high to be above a poverty level does influence happiness.

13.7.3.2   Money and power   The relationship between money and power is complex, and causality often goes in both directions. Money may buy power, and vice versa. But the mechanisms connecting money with power have many variants, as is shown in plutocracies, kleptocracies, and left- or right-wing dictatorships.

The struggle for corporate control raises problems in the relationship between votes and money. Operationally, the idea that corporate democracy is preserved by attaching votes to shares is part of mythology rather than economic reality. In essence the voting rights of a small passive stockholder are of zero worth to the stockholder.[8] Formally this can be seen by analyzing weighted-majority voting schemes. Although the direct sale of votes may be forbidden (depending on the country or state), there are many ways arrangements can be made to solicit blocks of votes from fiduciary holders. Considerable mechanism design is called for to change the power structure in corporate governance to go beyond self-controlled managements occasionally deposed by corporate raiders.

13.7.4   Utility or money as the measure?

For macroeconomics, finance, industrial organization theory, insurance, and many topics involving fiduciary decision making, the money measure serves as a better and empirically measurable alternative to the utility function.

The theory of consumer choice was elegantly developed using the utility function and was incorporated into general equilibrium theory, but marketing, experimental gaming, and psychology raise questions as to its use in application.

Even the axioms utilized by von Neumann hardly have a solid empirical basis, as is argued by Friedman et al. [141]; but in finance they are used predominantly.

13.7.5   An aside on NE and the cost of government

Prior to resuming our discussion on government guidance of an economy, a general question may be asked: How large an expenditure should independent decision makers be willing to make for government? This problem has been posed in a limited context in computer science as the "cost of anarchy." In essence the question asked is, if one has a money measure of the worth of playing a game in strategic form, what the monetary difference is between the worth of the cooperative solution and the worth of the noncooperative equilibrium solution.

We know that generically the NEs are inefficient; a reasonable question to ask is by how much. This requires the construction of a measure, and we propose a monetary measure as a crude, reasonable first approximation in many instances.

A study by Powers and Shubik [295] considered the set of all 144 ordinally, strategically different 2×2 matrix games. Although this number is large, it is associated with the only set of $k \times k$ games that can be studied exhaustively.[9] We produce a crude measure of inefficiency applied to any game with cardinal payoffs in one of the 144 ordinal categories. They naturally fall into three broad categories: games with natural coordination, mixed-motive games, and games of pure opposition.

A key question in the design of institutions is what the tradeoffs are between individual independence and supervision and coordination. The strategy of higher-echelon decision making is devoted to environment setting for and delegation to the lower echelons; but the overheads of this governance may be costly.

13.7.6   Refinancing sovereign and municipal debt

Virtually all of our mathematical models are parsimonious and low-dimensional relative to operational reality. Furthermore, the solutions considered have tended to portray the behavior of mass-market, individual low-communication agents. They would have been of little value to Alexander Hamilton in trying to consolidate the debts of the various states of the Union and trying to preserve some worth to the Continental dollars issued to the troops and others during the United States War of Independence. Neither would they have been of direct value in refinancing the debt of the city of Detroit. The study of debt renegotiation calls for a quasi-cooperative dynamic game.

A comment often made by the unwary is that when one reviews international and national economies, the incidence of sovereign or municipal debt defaults is surprisingly low, and hence bankruptcy is not very important. This misses the key point in refinancing with or without bankruptcy. From the viewpoint of the financiers, refinancing with or without formal bankruptcy is formally the same in the sense that they both entail a change in the previously agreed allocation of resources. However, in the larger sociopolitical game that is going on, the forms and euphemisms entailed in renegotiation without formal bankruptcy are directed toward preserving public confidence among those indirectly influenced but not active in the renegotiation. The illusion of stability offered by a renegotiation today may provide the reality of tomorrow when further borrowing is called for.

13.8   Toward a Theory of Organization

We regard our work here as a way station or small contribution to the far larger problem of eventually constructing a satisfactory theory of organization. The underlying economic principle appears to pertain to all organized systems, as do the features of tradeoff between local and global organization. In sections 10.8–10.9 we presented a brief biological viewpoint. In chapter 3 the stress was on economics in the light of basic physics. The separate core investigations of these three disciplines will continue, but by now the cross fertilization among them is going beyond analogy and rhetoric. An economic principle of minimization in the guidance of growth lies within all three. The common features of a developing economy proliferating new organizations, the organization of a galaxy, or the emergence of organs in complex biological organisms are part of the progression toward a general theory of organization.

13.8.1   Economic dynamics and new organizational questions

The economics of ad hoc problems brings a need for increasing numbers of parameters. Some of these arise from the more complex structure of optimization within the economic framework itself, and they may show convergence with problems of organization in other sciences. Other parameters result from the need for increasingly detailed integration of the economic decision process with dynamics in the physical or biological world, in which case relations to the other sciences become necessary to specify the structure of the state space.

The expansion of economics in the dynamical realm is not only one of parameter number and complexity. Economics also takes on new problems of understanding organization and comes to incorporate new principles. These can include problems of an increased role for sample variance, path dependence, or the extraction of robust phenomena from stochastic microdynamics. Some of these have counterparts in other sciences, and cross fertilizations may be possible.

The problem of formally modeling organization is one that exists in biology and physics as broad disciplines, and in more specific forms in a variety of narrower application domains. Here we note some of the specific contributions of other domains to an understanding of organization, and the relation to either concepts or applications of economic dynamics.

13.8.2   The economic principle in relation to the biology of population processes

The most immediate and apparent expansion of economic analysis leads to a coalescence with biological thought, as recognized already by Marshall [247]. To characterize the correspondence or convergence, it is helpful to identify levels of abstract description that are comparable in the two domains. The common character of economic models may be captured in an "economic principle," at a comparable level of abstraction to the abstraction of biological evolution, which is framed in terms of the dynamics of populations.

13.8.2.1   The economic principle   The *economic principle* is an abstraction that is more general than any specific case or model, one that unifies the problems and modes of description that are the domain of economics. It is not a theory but rather a common architecture shared by economic theories. It identifies economic problems as those which concern individual optimization in a context of optimization by other individuals. The application of the principle is heavily contextualized. Context specifies the nature of agents' identities, their roles, their available choices, the structure of the interaction, and the generators of behavior and choice.

13.8.2.2   Evolutionary population processes   The set of abstractions in biology that are comparable to the economic principle are those of *evolutionary dynamics*. The key abstractions in an evolutionary formulation of biological dynamics are *individuals* and *populations* [119, 220, 252].

Individuality is a complex concept [45], which entails a granular partitioning of the components of living systems into units (the individuals) that structure the growth and interaction of the components, a discrete generational organization in time that governs their replication, and shared hereditary trajectories for the components that jointly make up a viable individual.[10] Preconditions to formulating a biological phenomenon in terms of a population process are an identification of the levels of individuality that are possible and a typology of the forms that viable individuals can take. The evolutionary concept of the individual is similar in many respects to the economic concept of the agent or the game-theoretic concept of a player, and for many systems the same entity may fulfill each of these related, but conceptually distinct, roles.

The structural inputs needed to specify a theory for a particular biological population process are the mechanisms that generate individual variation and fitness [158]. The inputs that govern the types and mechanisms of variation of individuals are the domain of *development* (broadly construed), and the inputs that govern interaction and thereby reflect the structure at the population level are the domain of *ecology*.

Some questions that most evolutionary theories seek to answer are how selection acts in the contexts produced by variation and differential fitness, and what determines population dynamics when the space of possible configurations is much larger than can be sampled by actual populations. In such cases unpredictability and path dependence are routinely rather than only occasionally important, and evolutionary and ecological dynamics can be open-ended with respect to the generation of configurations not previously encountered and difficult to predict [169]. A major problem of understanding innovation in open-ended evolution is the *ex ante* description of the space of possible states. Configurations that are for practical purposes unpredictable nonetheless have important consequences for future trajectories.

Organizational problems about which some understanding has been gained include the roles of modularity and buffering [372–374], the nature of hierarchical organization and its role in control [60], and the mechanisms by which redundancy can enable error correction [333].

13.8.3   Biology as superset or as constraint on the economy

The dynamics of aggregate behavior by agents in the economy in some ways simply recapitulates problems of biological evolution and calls for the same conceptual organization. In other respects, it is necessary to understand the economy as a subsystem within the larger biological world which has organizational constraints of its own nature, not all of which are economic but which constrain economic activity. The following examples illustrate each kind of relation.

13.8.3.1   Economic dynamics as natural selection   The dynamics of the persistence, variation, and repeated interaction of economic optimizers often clearly calls for a formulation in terms of natural selection. This may take the form merely of financial Darwinism, as propounded by Friedman [142], or it may make much richer contact with evolutionary concepts by analyzing the role of state-space structure in determining evolutionary ascendency or extinction, or the complex persistent nonlinear dynamics of population states.

In biology selection acts on the variants that are produced by development acting on mutations, and it is selection that can concentrate actual populations within very small regions of the configuration space compared to the unfiltered output of random variations. When real markets are observed, they must be understood as the output of (often stringent) selective competition that has filtered a set of prior candidates for utility and reliability. From an evolutionary perspective, the interesting questions become what structure economic context gives to random inventions, how effectively filtering for utility and reliability works, and when it can be afforded given the monitoring and regulatory capabilities of the polity. It is essential in framing this question to recognize that the problem of concern is the aggregate outcome of selection acting on many agents of different types, to produce a restricted *structure of interactions* that results in stability rather than chaos.

An adequate theory that combines an understanding of the mechanisms of variation and of selection should account for the combination of regularity and complexity or chaos seen in actual economic dynamics.

13.8.3.2   Material biology and physics as boundary conditions for economic optimization   In the foregoing discourse the economy serves as an instantiation of principles of biological organization, and in that sense as an instance of a (hierarchically elaborate and highly institutional) biological phenomenon. A different interaction between economics and biology can arise when economic organization is distinct, but acts within a framework of constraint established by the biological or physical laws of the material world of which the economy is a part.

Fisheries, soils, and natural ecosystems are subject to a range of constraints ranging from input-output relations to stock-flow constraints. Economic optimization, which regards human consumption of inputs and production of wastes, energy flows, and impacts on both biological and physical natural capital, must occur within the set of realizable configurations [121], which may be far from a simple linear constraint.

Other constraints of behavioral origin similarly affect economic optimization as boundary conditions. Much economic decision making is not guided by contract negotiation and optimization of well-defined utilities, but by informal social norms or habits [182]. It is arguable that laws work well when they shape habit to such an extent that most of the time they do not need to be actively exercised—not as a result of the deliberative calculation of threat, but rather through the establishment of habits of behavior, often during key developmental windows in the human life course. More institutional dimensions of the reliance of the economy on noneconomic organizations might include the role of the organizations of civil society to establish reputation, to identify and prioritize tasks of shared interest, or as reservoirs of know-how or noncontractual insurance.

13.8.4   Other frameworks of organization

13.8.4.1   Convergence of core concepts from economics and physics   The attempt to extend the robust existence theorems of general equilibrium to dynamics in general, and stochastic dynamics in particular, leads to convergences of the needed core economic concepts with those that have arisen to fill similar needs in statistical physics. Here we note two examples.

One of the authors invented the strategic market game as a way to formalize the symmetry of strategic roles in economics at allocations away from the competitive equilibrium. This led to the basic role and nature of money as an additional quantity in the economy. The general origin of money as a result of spontaneous breaking of symmetries has now been axiomatized in the treatment of chapter 11. Symmetry breaking is a core concept in physics,[11] because it allows a similar axiomatization of the origin of order that is not imposed externally, in systems where many fine-scale parameters are inessential to the origin of order and may even change depending on the scale at which the system is observed [380].

A second example of the overlap of economics with core concepts in modern physics was provided in the analysis of multiple equilibria in section 8.4.1.1. Processes such as rare escapes from domains of attraction, although stochastic, may nonetheless have robust, generic properties that relate to the sizes of the basins and the intensity of attraction. The problem of extracting these general aspects of dynamics, from methods in the theory of large deviations [401] that directly extend the study of robust equilibrium states, has been an area at the forefront of development in modern statistical physics [376].

13.8.4.2   Learning to change the question   The early generation of work on nonlinear dynamics, chaos, and path dependence in the economy is summarized by Beinhocker [27]. It grew out of mathematical and physical study of complex systems which showed that trajectory prediction could be degraded in many systems to a point where it was lost rapidly, either on the approach to the infinite horizon or even over finite horizons. However, the lesson from nonlinear dynamics was not that the failure of prediction for trajectories was the end of science; rather it was that the useful questions changed, to concern features that could be predicted and were informative. These included the geometries of attractors or the action of iterated maps on distributions over these attractors.[12]

In a similar fashion in both economics and biology, the domain of complexity will combine operations research over the short term to produce time-local, adaptive management solutions, with possibly different questions about long-term or asymptotic constraints on the state space or the performance of control systems.

13.9   Nostradamus and the Economic Future

Much of the material in this book has dealt with economic theory and methodology intermixed, in an austere, abstract world with a minimum of the institutional richness that we confront in the everyday economy. Here we take the liberty of dusting off our crystal ball and devote the next sections to general commentary with few footnotes and references.

13.9.1   On prediction and reading the tea leaves

Looking forward to the next 200 years, there are many ways the world society and its apparent continuity could be wiped out. Meteors, deadly disease, inhospitable climate change, and massive nuclear, chemical, or biological war are among the candidates. The problem that besets economic forecasters and social commentators in general is that betting odds need to be supplied for many of these phenomena in order to help determine how to allocate funds.

A Cassandra by many measures is successful if she is able to trigger the social reactions that negate her prediction. The *Bulletin of the Atomic Scientists*, in this spirit, has set its Doomsday Clock since 1947, when it began with a reading of 7 minutes to midnight. It reached a low of 2 minutes to midnight in 1953 and a high of 17 in 1991. In 2013 it was at 5 minutes to midnight. Now it is no longer devoted solely to nuclear war but includes a consideration of global warming and other potential disasters.

13.9.1.1   War or a space race or another correlating device?   In chapter 10 we commented on war and innovation. We wish to reiterate that the societal coordination aspects of war may be of great economic importance and still need to be considered analytically. The influence on technology, innovation, and social structure of the American civil war and the subsequent two world wars was considerable.

Possibly a highly competitive space race aimed at establishing property rights and even weapon bases on the moon and Mars based on individual national occupation might yield more benefits in employment and innovation than would an international space cooperation program that would enable all parties to do little jointly.

The often-used phrase "A war on ..." indicates that an important use of war is as a high correlating device. Yet in a democracy the cohesion that can be generated for a patriotic war is difficult to achieve for a war on poverty or unemployment; Richard Nelson's discourse on the moon and the ghetto [271] provides an apposite example.

13.9.1.2   Population estimates and sociopolitical reality   Population estimates have been notoriously difficult to project for more than a few years into the future. A favorite topic for futurists is the upper bound for world population. Is it 10 or 20 billion, or more? Why just live on the surface? Why not have more cities underground? This is especially pertinent given the problems generated by climate change. How is the standard of living incorporated into these estimates? What is the new Malthus bound?

The more relevant aspect of population for the basic development and use of microeconomic analysis concerns at what level the various time periods must be taken into account. For today's markets, items such as "mark-to-market" yield reasonable approximations for some purposes, such as approximately what price I will get for 100 AT&T shares sold today. Yet the same measure may be fatally misleading for many other relevant questions, such as how changes in ephemeral current prices trigger a violation of reserve requirements for a bank.

For an economic theory in which population plays a role, a host of physical, biological, and societal process times are required to do justice to the dynamics if one is to provide equations of motion that are more than mere metaphor.

13.9.1.3   Length of life and retirement age   The socially accepted parameters of one era may be the policy variables of the next. For example, discourse on the bankruptcy of a social security system may depend on an implicitly accepted socioeconomic parameter such as a retirement age of 65 long after life expectancies and work patterns have clearly changed. Challenging yesterday's rules, parameters, and totemic facts is a necessity in order to avoid solving a current problem with inappropriate constraints (although the constraints may be widely accepted).

Many of the problems posed by life in a geriatric state are still unanswered, but the answers depend deeply on basic assumptions concerning what percentage of those over 65 can be added, at least in some aspects, to the work force. Henry Aaron has raised the basic question in "Longer Life Spans: Boon or Burden?" [1], but he did not deal with potential productivity in a world with a healthy enough population to move the retirement age from 65 (or to replace it with a more flexible procedure of gradual retirements up until any age, based on the viability of the individual).

A further set of problems exist for an extremely youth-dominated society. These involve the religious, social, and political aspects of birth control and education. Philanthropic improvements in child mortality in nations with limited administrative infrastructure may have the perverse effect of increasing the supply of child recruits for the army of the local dictator.

13.9.2 World government, law, and the economy

As communication, transportation, and computation have increased along with population, the world's economies are becoming an ever more unified system. The world's polities have no choice but to accept this set of circumstances. Yet each nation-state has its own set of laws, now increasingly intermixed with international economic and financial institutions and laws with varying levels of standardization and enforcement. The academic economist or lawyer leaving the halls of academe for the "real world" finds that a good living can be made in arbitraging the differences between legal codes, currencies, reputations, and customs.

As the boundaries of the nation-state become ever more porous, the fight between political and economic governance becomes more complex. Currency unions, and willingness to abide by the rulings of an international bank such as the Bank for International Settlement or the International Monetary Fund, both confound and meld economic and political purpose, and the euphemisms of diplomatic and political purpose are bolstered by the utilization of economists and lawyers to provide rationalizations for sociopolitical purpose under the rubric of sound economics.

The basic purpose of our discourse would be defeated by adopting a particular political viewpoint. As observers, however some general points can be made.

The power of the national central bank as an institution may have reached its peak fairly soon after the end of the second World War.

Institutions as multicelled organisms share their powers and functions with their subdivisions; thus for example the Federal Reserve system of the United States already involves at least three levels: the central bank in Washington, its regional Federal Reserve banks, and its client commercial banks. The system may eventually attain six if not more levels, with a world central bank, continental or other regional central banks, then the national banks and their subdivisions. The number of layers of institutions and their shape will be determined by allometric considerations involving the application of scaling laws.

Within the century the nature of the nation-state may be due for considerable evolution. The states become more and more porous to certain activities, such as international legal and illegal trade, new epidemics, toxic waste disposal, immigration, finance, and terrorism. Size increases the pressure for codification and aggregation of many rules that in turn lead to the anonymous treatment of the individuals, with an ongoing battle between the fine-graining needs for individual justice and the coarse-grained economy of mass treatment.

13.9.3   Entitlements and responsibilities

Welfare economics, philosophy, and religion all provide norms for what the citizens owe their state and vice versa. It is, however, the sociopolitical process that provides the current state of the ongoing process of assigning citizen entitlements and responsibilities. The fact that we have our own beliefs as citizens as well as varying professional abilities helps us more in phrasing appropriate questions concerning the system than it does in providing more than temporary answers.

Among the questions pertaining to entitlements we still need to make operationally meaningful such political slogans as the much-quoted phrase of Marx [249]: "From each according to his ability, to each according to his need."[13]

- How safe should a safety net be?
- What is an adequate definition of unemployment?
- Is there an optimal level of unemployment?
- What percentage of active bankruptcy is optimal for our society?
- How is innovation to be measured?
- What is the optimal rate of innovation?
- How is error generation and correction in a bureaucracy related to individual responsibility and incentives?

These are all questions that need first to be formalized adequately and then to be asked at least annually. They have no final answers. They all dwell in the penumbra of change. The dynamics of societal process calls for groups of lawyers, economists, and other expert witnesses to be in every shadowy spot trying to provide answers for the current time and jurisdiction.

It has been said, partially in jest, that economics is the only semiscience in which the questions remain the same from year to year but the answers change. This may be less jest than it is a description of process.

13.9.4   Technology, science and futurism

Most of our book has been devoted to relatively mundane examination of highly stripped down models derived from basic microeconomic theory and game theory. As soon as dynamics is considered, we are forced to acknowledge the interaction of processes on many different timescales. These timescales open the economic processes to the influence of the many social and political processes that interact with the economics, but on different and often longer timescales.

The next hundred years offers a myriad of paths to be taken. The futurist can at best offer vision and questions unconstrained by the realities of fundraising, resource finding, and organizing. In some ways the job of the futurist is like that of the visionary architect, involving the laying out of many plans that remain unbuilt but nevertheless provide the genetic code for a yet unrealized future. They are often offered with little or no concern for either cost or comfort.

We take massive highways loaded with cars and trucks for granted as a part of modern life, yet what we recognize as the automobile has been around for not much more than 140 years. The automobile highway started to grow in the 1920s, the superhighway in the 1930s in Nazi Germany in preparation for war and as a cure for unemployment. Is the argument for the prevalence of the current automobile and road system in 2015 much stronger than that for the horse and cart in 1850? When will the automobile die or transform to a new form of ground transportation? What is the future of the highway system?

We offer implicit if not explicit assumptions about what we believe to be the longevity of the physical instruments and institutions of today—the rules concerning pensions, insurance, savings, markets, and the current arbitrage between law and custom.

A question concerning the need for more or less government is probably the wrong question. It is not merely the size but the nature of governance that is in mutation. As the post-nation-state world approaches, many functions of government (law, order, defense, health, education, and economy) may be provided by consortia of globally dispersed institutions, with further overlapping of jurisdictions. The countercries of "small is beautiful" are consistent with "global is beautiful" when function, domain, and context are considered case by case. The future of the nation-state is not an either/or proposition. The name, language, and social identity of a particular country may persist for decades or centuries after many of its current functions have been absorbed into various levels of international structures.

The function of futurism is a blend of imagination, exhortation, advocacy, and the appreciation of practicality. It is most potent when spiced with a feeling for the concatenation of the possibilities for organizing resources, technology, and sociopolitical and economic will.

13.9.5 Goals before guidance?

We reiterate in discussing guidance that one also has to consider the goals behind the guidance. It is here that the whole array of considerations of fiscal and monetary policy enter and the conflicting and symbiotic roles of the central banks and the rest of the government must be considered.

This is not the place to argue priorities and how they should be split. The central bank is fairly clearly the locus for the control of the government monetary mechanism. However, the government as a whole has an array of potentially conflicting goals.

A book (or set of files) such as the *Statistical Abstract of the United States* provides a reasonably good listing of the laws, services, needs, and responsibilities that a set of citizens constituting themselves as a modern nation-state requires from the central or local governments or from private institutions. A brief listing includes:

- Health, education, and welfare,
- Defense or military power,
- Law administration and enforcement,
- Employment,
- Guidance of the financial sector, including banking and insurance,
- Transportation and communication,
- Business enterprises,
- Science and technology,
- International relations and trade,
- Arts, recreation, and travel.

Guidance concerning war, population control, health control, the atmosphere, and common problems involving the planet and outer space call for layers of international government that hardly exist.

13.9.6 Forecasting and guidance

Even if goals are well understood, an integral part of guidance involves knowing the level of forecasting that is supplied and called for. Here an understanding is needed as to when quantitative differences intermix with qualitative differences.

In an institution of any size, most forecasting for the next week to three months falls in the domain of routinized bureaucratic behavior, possibly flavored with a little operations research and other quantitative management where most imponderables can be set aside; routines are considered and the parameters bounding the system are taken as given.

Forecasting up to a year ahead already calls for the reevaluation of parameters and consideration of imponderables and sources of potential surprise.

Once corporate planning ventures out to three to five years, with a few exceptions [348, 355] due to the compounding of plausible contingencies the limits of operations research and economic long-range planning have been reached;[14] technique and statistics are preceded by moral imperatives and may be used only to bolster argument. Beyond five years there is little hard forecasting but there are statements of belief and intent.

13.9.7 The systems of a modern society

An economy operates within many smoothly operating systems. When they function well, we do not even notice their existence, but when they fail, we feel their absence acutely. In our society, 10 to 20 social, political, and economic systems cover much of our welfare. In this book we have limited our concern primarily to the monetary and financial aspects of the political economy; but the dynamics involved in overall guidance and protection of the systems of a society have certain basic similarities.

They all require: (1) the early detection of major instabilities in real time, whether a crash in a financial system or a terrorist attack on a power network; (2) effective public communications and relations at the onset and during the course of any disaster; and (3) an administratively feasible preplanned policy that facilitates swift flexible recovery from the disaster (a critical goal that is rarely met).

The world we live in is composed of a variety of interlocking systems. Among the social systems are religious, educational, recreational, and fraternal ones. The technical and administrative support systems for a complex society include communications such as the telephone system, television, the Web, roads, rail, air transport, and shipping. Energy delivery comes through the electrical grid, gas pipelines, and petroleum and coal distribution networks. Direct consumer support calls for water and food supply networks, health care, and disposal systems. The choreography of all of these systems requires sophisticated bookkeeping, accounting, and financial systems employing millions. All of these systems operate seamlessly under most circumstances. However, when disruptions occur, we become conscious of the coordination needed and the potential damage caused by coordination failure.

When a system fails, the damage that its failure causes to society depends considerably on both recovery time and the overall state of the society at the time of failure. Relatively pedestrian factors, such as the time of the year and direction of the wind, may make enormous differences in the damage inflicted by a system failure.

Systems damage must be considered from the viewpoints both of individual citizens and of the productive capacity of the society. For example, when considering the electrical grid's vulnerabilities, we need to determine how individuals, private firms, and the public institutions are influenced by electrical outages of two minutes, two hours, two days, two weeks, or more. In many situations, costs grow exponentially. A failure of two minutes, or even two hours for an individual at home on an early summer day, can have negligible costs. That same individual on a lung machine in a hospital with a faulty power backup system might view the outage differently. In summertime, after a few days, the damage to individual food inventories is considerable, and a day of electrical failure damages virtually all manufacturing establishments without backup systems. In some systems, the cost of backup sources is relatively cheap; in others it is highly expensive.[15]

Each system has its own detailed technical properties, but all have in common basic possibilities such as decentralization, production of excess capacity, and identification of substitutes. Current technology, science, and economics allow us to create reasonably good estimates of the social and economic consequences for different recuperation times in the event of many disasters.

A brief survey [367] considering defense problems with terrorist attacks on basic systems presented sketches of the requirements called for in recovery in several basic systems. The authors stressed (and we stress here) the need to bridge the gap between systems analysis and policy programs. The need calls for considerable dialogue between policymakers and systems experts. In the section below, we provide a suggestion for national policy concerning the levels of unemployment in the United States and suggest, as has been suggested in this section, that the operations research, economic theory, body of technical knowledge, and economic practitioners are all at hand; that the problem of unemployment policy lies far more in political will, the coordination of policy, and the administration of bureaucracy than it does in the economics. The prediction of future economic disasters still has many problems that are not understood by any theory of dynamics involving economic process; but we suggest that steps to alleviate much of the damage from the disaster of unemployment are available by building a speedy reaction system based on political and bureaucratic coordination assisted by economic knowledge. Such a system for the United States is sketched below. The principles for any country in the world are the same, but the institutional considerations may differ.

13.10   A Federal Employment Reserve Agency: A Practical Proposal

Efficient production and full employment must be central goals of any successful economy. A healthy economy is one that does not waste the real resources of goods and labor. These goals may not be sufficient for a great society, but they are necessary.

Enterprise is fostered by understood and accepted rules of the game, and the rules do not appear by magic or markets. They require the development and enforcement of items such as an accounting system, bankruptcy and default laws, a commercial code, and contract law. When the system is under stress, fail-safe measures must be available for swift adaptation to new circumstances.

The formulation, legislation, and enforcement of rules to set the environment for the functioning of a successful enterprise economy are critical. The process is a difficult ongoing evolutionary one produced by fallible and self-centered human beings.

The ideologues of both the right and left imagine utopian scenarios either with no government or with an ideal government. Neither of these states has ever existed nor ever will, except in political rhetoric aimed at entrapping the unwary. Reality and "good enough" economic efficiency reside not only in building the institutions and laws that provide the rules of the game but in answering the question: "Can they be implemented successfully at a reasonable cost?"

One of the more successful governmental economic institutions in the United States has been the Federal Reserve. It has manifested an interesting blend of public and private forces. It is clearly sensitive to both local and global concerns of the country. Unfortunately it and the Treasury are not enough. There are occasions when the financial control mechanisms of a society are not sufficient to stop serious damage to the underlying basic economy they are meant to protect. When this happens, the system requires a fail-safe mechanism that comes into play when the financial brakes do not work. Such a mechanism in the form of a Federal Employment Reserve Authority is discussed in this section.

Our financial institutions and instruments are part of a delicate overall guidance and control system for the political economy. The structure has to match the supply of public goods and taxation with the demands of the electorate, which calls for a blend of economic, political, bureaucratic, and social forces. The Federal Reserve System, created in 1913, has been evolving and adjusting for over a century and continues to do so. The overall organizational structure is laden with checks and balances and with diverse interests represented.

The Board of Governors is appointed by the President and requires confirmation by the Senate. Like the Supreme Court, the Board of Governors is the product of an interplay of political, economic, and legal forces. The number of governors reflects judgment calls on the balancing of powers and the ability of the institution to function.

It is suggested here that for the goal of keeping an appropriate socially acceptable index of unemployment below some specified level, a government agency similar in power and structure to the Federal Reserve System would be appropriate. Such an institution, the Federal Employment Reserve Authority, would require considerable hand-tailoring to provide the appropriate control details needed. But it could provide a permanent institution that would be an improvement over a last-minute disaster crash program such as the temporary WPA program utilized by the Roosevelt administration during the Great Depression.

In the design of an institution aimed at ameliorating the level of unemployment, it is highly probable that we need to hand-tailor a control structure with governance numbers different from either the Supreme Court or the Federal Reserve in order to fit the United States of the twenty-first century.

NAIRU or the non-accelerating inflation rate of unemployment is a product of the institutions, laws, customs, and technology of each society at a particular time. An institution such as a Federal Employment Reserve Authority would be devoted to monitoring the country's "natural rate of unemployment," natural in the sense that it is dependent on current institutions, laws, customs, and technology.

A few features of such an establishment may be sketched. The Federal Reserve System has of the order of 25,000 employees and 12 district banks. Instead of 12 district branches, this institution most naturally calls for a central or controlling authority in Washington and 50 branches, one in each state. A first cut at bounds on its size would be of the order of 6,000–11,000 employees, and a board of governors split among business and labor representatives from the states as well as academics and federal and state representatives.

Each authority would monitor unemployment in its state. It would also maintain a listing of potential public good or desirable infrastructure projects with priorities and potential revenue generation possibilities. The stress in priorities would be on self-liquidating projects from which some portion of the revenues would flow back to the state and/or the federal government.

A new Joint Assessment Financing Board would be required among the Federal Reserve System, the Treasury, and the Federal Employment Reserve Authority.

The duties of this board would be to monitor constantly the listing, evaluation, financing, and projected paybacks of projects-in-reserve proposed by each regional branch so that the structure of the financing can be set in place as soon as the employment level in any region passes the trigger value. A further duty of this board would be to determine how the unemployment in the state breaks down into recession unemployment or technological unemployment.

It is important to stress that constant monitoring and the ability to act quickly and deliberately are required. This will require that legislation be passed in advance to provide flexibility in emergency financing without having to go to Congress or state legislatures to trigger action.

Technological unemployment should not call for agency action except via an Educational Retraining Board acting in concert with the educational resources of the state and the federal Department of Education.

The governors of the regional (state) branches of the proposed authority would be selected from state government, the public, the universities, and top local employers and unions in the region who are subscribers. The regional authority and member firms would be responsible for the generation and maintenance of micro information on the state of unemployment, the valuation of local projects worthy of sponsorship in a high unemployment environment, and the distinction between recession and technological unemployment.

The Board of Governors of the central authority would be responsible for developing state and federal taxation and funding guidelines in concert with the Federal Reserve System via the Joint Assessment Financing Board.

There are several basic principles that should be adhered to by the authority.

It should never own assets that it does not have the in-house capability to evaluate. It should avoid supervision of projects where it does not have in-house expertise.

Its role would be to coordinate and stimulate activities promoting employment, not to employ individuals directly. Only under conditions of deep depression might a direct WPA employment approach be permitted as an act of last resort.

The authority must stress transparency in the availability of its information sources, evaluation of the regional economic and employment status as well as the projects to be implemented, and the bidding and procurement procedures employed.

Once unemployment goes above a fixed level, say 5 or 6 percent (to be adjusted by circumstances), the authority would put out bids for projects in coordination with federal and state funding authorities for the means for financing.

These comments are to be interpreted as a rough sketch pointing the way, not a detailed blueprint. There are many details to be worked out. The drafting of institutional rules is an evolutionary process. But this is offered as a start at building and institutionalizing a fail-safe system for the economy when the financial control structure fails the real economy. It stresses guidance and preplanned coordination, not prediction.

13.11   An Observation on Money and Voting in a Democratic State

It is not sufficient that the markets be provided with central guidance to protect against excesses; the political system also requires rules and guidance. There are many deep questions concerning the relationship between an enterprise economy and a democratic state. Although we incline to believe that a reasonable case can be made for the existence of a symbiotic relationship, in spite of much work in political science it remains a topic that still has neither been adequately defined nor answered. A democracy may be changed into a kleptocracy or a plutocracy without changing its name or formal arrangements. Just as it is difficult to maintain the functioning of a competitive price system in a market structure, it is difficult to maintain an unbiased voting system in the political system. Unrestricted campaign contributions can bias a voting system toward plutocracy.

We have argued that money is an important measure in economics. It would be technically feasible to design a system that utilizes it fruitfully as a measure in voting. At the time of writing, practically such a scheme has little legal or political chance of becoming law; nevertheless it merits noting, in spite of the difficulties that might be encountered in the United States with the First Amendment.

We subscribe to the belief that if individuals feel passionately about the political system, as information and communication are critical to the democratic process citizens should be encouraged to give; but there is a distinction between giving in order to control candidates and giving in order to help the democratic process as a whole. We may consider a system where giving in support of an election process is unrestricted, but concentrates on supporting the democratic process rather than buying candidates.

We can easily arrange that the disparity in funding between the top two parties never differs by more than some percentage we choose. Consider a system where giving in support of an election process is unrestricted, and to be encouraged, but giving to specific parties and candidates is limited only to a percentage of the contribution, for example 10 percent. The giving is directed to a trustee who takes all contributions and splits them into the party fund and the common fund. In this case it gives the 10 percent directly to the designated candidates and takes the remaining 90 percent and allocates them evenly to the top two parties determined by the previous election.

At the very (and highly implausible) worst, the largest spread in the funding of the two parties is 10 percent. If one party raises no money whatsoever, it would obtain 45 percent of the contributions and the other would get 55 percent. If we set the percentage to 100 percent to go to individual candidates, we are back to the system we have now. If we set it to 10 percent, the playing field is more or less leveled. The introduction of a single parameter is sufficient to provide the modification needed to fine-tune social choice.

If there are more parties, we sum the percentage of the vote obtained by the top two parties—say it equals $2k$, and there are n minor parties. The minor parties received $100 - 2k$ percent of the vote. Together they will be awarded that percent of the money collected, split in proportion to their previous vote. Suppose, for example, the major parties had 90 percent of the previous vote and the common fund holds a billion dollars to be split; the minor parties obtain 10 percent, split in proportion to their previous vote. A new party is given nothing. This prevents frivolous entry just to collect the allocation. However, this does not prevent an individual or set of incorporating individuals[16] from putting in their own money for the founding of a new party. After its seasoning by a vote it becomes eligible for sharing in the funds.

If previous third parties no longer exist, their allocation is split evenly among all participating parties.

The size of the overall contributions will be a measure of the public interest in funding the process directly rather than in buying candidates. The structure favors a two-party system, but is designed to prevent any party from being bought directly.

In keeping with promoting political participation, any individual would be able to contibute any amount of personal time to working directly for the party of his or her choice, but the purchase of the services of others to serve in the place of those who choose not to spend their own time would not be permitted.

As noted in section 6.2.2, Balinski and Laraki have suggested that a grading scheme be substituted for current party voting. The scheme suggested here is complementary with their suggestions to view voting in terms of measurement as best we can. They concentrate on changing the nature of the vote to a grading or evaluation scheme. We suggest changing the role of monetary contributions to remove the bias in influencing the vote, a different but relevant part of designing a democratic process.

In the light of current politics this proposition may be deemed utterly impractical, but as any review of a segment of history shows, context changes and the crackpot schemes of yesterday become the realities of today, as the nation as a whole starts to appreciate the dangers of having political power for sale to the highest bidder.

13.12   Static Theory and Dynamic Reality

The mixture of philosophy of Hume and Smith and insightful ad hoc nuanced observations of Smith provided the foundations for a formal economics. The approximations of Marshall provided for the insightful use of comparative statics along with "good enough" definitions of firm and industry, while some glimmerings of mathematization in the appendices provided economic insights that not only continued the British tradition of economic thought providing policy advice, but vastly expanded the popularity of economics as a topic for study. The works of Cournot, Jevons, Walras, Menger, Pareto, and Edgeworth provided much of the basis for the development of marginal analysis and mathematical economics. The formal development was oriented heavily toward equilibrium theory. Microeconomic advice and application were heavily based on marginalism and comparative statics.

The great influence of Keynes and of Schumpeter took off in other directions. The former led to the formal development of the applied field of macroeconomics, while the latter spurred the development of the view that innovation rather than price is the major driving force in an enterprise economy. Both in highly different ways were concerned with money, finance, process, dynamics and disequilibrium.

The position developed in this book is that the basic sociopolitical and economic realities are such that there is no general dynamic economic theory at the level of the well-developed static theory of general equilibrium. The closest approach to a parameter-free dynamic theory for a highly limited set of models was provided by von Neumann's fixed-proportions technology model and the work of David Gale.

The belief that there is a basic need to reconcile micro- and macroeconomics stresses the wrong question and provides answers that are at best metaphors for a complex world based on the behavior of grossly aggregated low-dimensional models. Their level of abstraction is sufficiently high that they may serve for experimental gaming or, at best, as a checking device to help to verify that more complex ad hoc models aimed at answering specific questions concerning the macroeconomy are logically consistent and complete.

As soon as one considers an economy with more than a few periods, the need for parametric models explodes. In the explosion many of the parameters required are time lags in the bureaucracy and in the speed and clarity of the politicoeconomic process. These considerations reduce the role of the economic advisor to predicting, at best, the trajectory of well-researched and supported ad hoc models. The lower-dimensional models may serve as a basis for qualitative advice and help to provide a link between a well-developed static theory and the underlying structure and behavior encountered in economic dynamics.

This book, utilizing political economy in touch with both physics and biology, has been devoted to providing a reasonably solid scientific basis for constructing the basic links between static economic models and the welter of behavioral dynamic models of the economy, stressing that, utilizing the device of minimal institutions and minimal information conditions, such a link can be constructed, with considerable abstraction. However, the application of a given process model to any part of the economy requires the addition of the appropriate parameters of structure, and the specification of the context-driven varieties of behavior cannot be avoided in application.

Mathematical institutional economics and econophysics are no oxymorons. Given the complexity of the political economy, an underlying appreciation of the logic and combinatorics of organization is required. In application this knowledge is manifested in the specific structure of the institutions that are the carriers of sociopolitico-economic purpose. Furthermore in the study of the key role of money and financial institutions the consideration of conservation, the rules of scaling, the derivation of measures, the selection of coarse or fine graining, and the roles for symmetry, coordination, and symmetry-breaking that appear in physics appear as the natural properties of a monetary system.

Notes

1 These do not take into account the many other near monies and submonies and other arrangements for transferring wealth [350, 360].

2 Even there, the sterility of the laboratory may miss the informal network of trust existing among local social and trade groups.

3 Many a reader born after 1950 may need to look this up.

4 Christoph Adami's writings [2, 3], though mostly dedicated to sequence information in biological structures, reflect such an understanding.

5 Although this section mostly deals with human language as both a cognitive and a social phenomenon, we are willing to draw from examples in formal language theory that were derived mostly for engineering applications, where these furnish the best exemplars of patterns common to the engineered and the biological notions of language.

6 These are the Broca and Wernicke areas in the frontal and temporal cerebral cortex of the dominant brain hemisphere. It should be appreciated, however, that refining very general associations in terms either of function or location has proved difficult and inconclusive. It is not contested within mainstream neuroscience that *H. sapiens* has brain area specialization for language comprehension and production. How much of language draws uniquely on these specialized areas, and how much expresses more general cognitive functions, remains uncertain, however.

7 This attribution also has an information-theoretic dimension, most strongly associated with arguments by Noam Chomsky [57]. The argument is that the set of linguistic events experienced by children is insufficient to define the rules of their language by exclusion. Therefore part of the knowledge of how languages should function must be an inherited character shared by each new generation of language learners.

8 They may be of negative worth if disposal costs are included. These include answering the calls of vote solicitors and reading or even just throwing away the proxy material.

9 Any game smaller than the 2×2 is too small to illustrate a two-person strategic situation with both sides having strategic freedom. Even the 3×3 game has too many case distinctions for an exhaustive search. The number of strategically different instances is given by $(9! \times 9!) / (3! \times 3!) = 3,657,830,400$.

10 This may be referred to as a dynamic of "shared fate" for the traits that are co-present in an individual. They may be lost together if the individual dies—even if the death is only due to one of the traits—or jointly passed on from a parent to its offspring if reproduction is successful.

11 Indeed, it underlies the entire modern theory of the hierarchy of matter [59, 415].

12 Similar ideas have been applied to the study of income and wealth distributions, with the assertion that the trajectories of portfolio wealth are poorly predictable and not the observables that enable the identification of correct theories; the relevant observables are instead distributions [91, 93, 133, 379].

13 As this Marxist slogan is so central, the original German should accompany its English translation: "Jeder nach seinen Fähigkeiten, jedem nach seinen Bedürfnissen!"

14 The number of formal alternative long range plans prepared rarely, if ever exceeds Miller's "Magic Number 7 ± 2" [261].

15 The costs of backup resources are often highly dependent on mass production. Thus if a society wishes to decentralize the temporary supply of electricity, mass-produced small generators will have a unit cost far smaller than the same generator with small production.

16 Limited say to 100 individuals, or some other number determined by experience and ad hoc circumstances after a few years of operation starting with 100.

Bibliography

[1] Henry J. Aaron. Longer life spans: boon or burden? *Daedalus*, 135:9–19, 2006.

[2] Christoph Adami. Sequence complexity in Darwinian evolution. *Complexity*, 8:49–56, 2002.

[3] Christoph Adami. Information theory in molecular biology. *Physics of Life Reviews*, 1:3–22, 2004.

[4] Sydney Afriat. The construction of a utility function from demand. *International Economic Review*, 8:67–77, 1967.

[5] Philippe Aghion and Peter Howitt. A model of growth through creative destruction. *Econometrica*, 60:323–351, 1992.

[6] Hirotugu Akaike. A new look at the statistical model identification. *IEEE Trans. Automatic Control*, 19:716–723, 1974.

[7] Maurice Allais. *Économie et intérêt*. Imprimerie Nationale, Paris, 1947.

[8] R. Amir, S. Sahi, M. Shubik, and S. Yao. A strategic market game with complete markets. *J. Econ. Theory*, 51:126–143, 1990.

[9] Andrew Ang. *Asset Management: A Systematic Approach to Factor Investing*. Oxford U. Press, New York, 2012.

[10] Martin Angerer, Juergen Huber, Martin Shubik, and Shyam Sunder. An economy with personal currency: theory and experimental evidence. *Annals of Finance*, 6:475–509, 2010.

[11] Kenneth J. Arrow. The economic implications of learning by doing. *Rev. Econ. Studies*, 29:155–173, 1962.

[12] Kenneth J. Arrow and Gerard Debreu. The existence of an equilibrium for a competitive economy. *Econometrica*, 22:265–290, 1954.

[13] Kenneth J. Arrow and Frank H. Hahn, editors. *General Competitive Analysis*. Elsevier, New York, 1971.

[14] W. Brian Arthur. *Increasing Returns and Path Dependence in the Economy*. University of Michigan Press, Ann Arbor, 1984.

[15] W. Brian Arthur. Inductive reasoning and bounded rationality. *Amer. Econ. Assoc.: Papers and Proceedings*, 84:406–411, 1994.

[16] W. Brian Arthur. *The Nature of Technology*. Free Press (Simon & Schuster), New York, 2009.

[17] W. Brian Arthur, John H. Holland, Blake LeBaron, Richard Palmer, and Paul Tayler. Asset pricing under endogenous expectations in an artificial stock market. In W. Brian Arthur, Steven Durlauf, and David Lane, editors, *The Economy as an Evolving Complex System II*. Addison-Wesley, New York, 1997.

[18] William Ross Ashby. *An Introduction to Cybernetics*. Chapman and Hall, London, 1956.

[19] Robert J. Aumann. Correlated equilibrium as an expression of Bayesian rationality. *Econometrica*, 55:1–18, 1983.

[20] L. Bachelier. Théorie mathématique du jeu. *Annales Scientifiques de l'École Normale Supérieure*, 3:143–210, 1901.

[21] Walter Bagehot. *Lombard Street*. Henry S. King, London, third edition, 1873.

[22] P. Bak, S. F. Nørrelykke, and M. Shubik. Money and goldstone modes. *Quant. Fin.*, 1:186–190, 2001.

[23] Per Bak, Maya Paczuski, and Martin Shubik. Price variations in a stock market with many agents. *Physica A*, 246:430, 1997.

[24] M. Balinski and R. Laraki. *Majority Judgment*. MIT Press, Cambridge, MA, 2011.

[25] W. J. Baumol. *The Free-Market Innovation Machine*. Princeton University Press, Princeton, 2002.

[26] S. D. Bechtel et al. Managing innovation. *Daedalus*, 125, 1996.

[27] Eric Beinhocker. *The Origin of Wealth: Evolution, Complexity, and the Radical Remaking of Economics*. Harvard Business School Press, Cambridge, MA, 2006.

[28] Roberto Benzi, Alfonso Sutera, and Angelo Vulpiani. The mechanism of stochastic resonance. *J. Phys. A*, 14:L453–L457, 1981.

[29] J. Bertrand. Théorie mathématique de la richesse sociale. *Journal des Savants (Paris)*, 68:499–508, 1883.

[30] Truman Bewley. *General Equilibrium Overlapping Generations Models and Optimal Growth Theory*. Harvard U. Press, Cambridge, MA, 2007.

[31] Truman F. Bewley. The optimum quantity of money. In J. H. Kareken and N. Wallace, editors, *Models of Monetary Economics*, 169–210. Federal Reserve Bank, Minneapolis, 1980.

[32] Truman F. Bewley. Stationary monetary equilibrium with a continuum of independently fluctuating consumers. In Werner Hildenbrand and Andreu Mas-Colell, editors, *Contributions to Mathematical Economics in Honor of Gerard Debreu*, 79–102. North-Holland, Amsterdam, 1986.

[33] Fischer Black. Banking and interest rates in a world without money: the effects of uncontrolled banking. *J. Bank Research*, 1:8–20, 1970.

[34] Fischer Black and Myron Scholes. The pricing of options and corporate liabilities. *J. Polit. Econ.*, 81:637–654, 1973.

[35] M. Boldrin and D. K. Levine. Perfectly competitive innovation. *J. Monetary Economics*, 55:435–453, 2008.

[36] Grady Booch, Robert A. Maksimchuk, Michael W. Engle, Bobbi J. Young, Jim Conallen, and Kelli A. Houston. *Object Oriented Analysis and Design with Applications*. Addison Wesley, New York, third edition, 2007.

[37] Grady Booch, James Rumbaugh, and Ivar Jacobson. *The Unified Modeling Language User Guide*. Addison-Wesley, Reading, MA, 1999.

[38] P. Bossaerts, C. Plott, and W. R. Zame. Price and portfolio choices in financial markets: theory, econometrics, experiments. *Econometrica*, 4:993–1038, 2007.

[39] Kenneth E. Boulding. General systems theory—the skeleton of science. *Management Science*, 2:197–208, 1956.

[40] William J. Boumol. The Neumann-Morgenstern utility index—an ordinalist view. *J. Polit. Econ.*, 59:61–66, 1951.

[41] Eric S. Boyd and John W. Peters. New insights into the eolutionary history of biological nitrogen fixation. *Frontiers Microbiol.*, 4:201:1–12, 2013.

[42] Rogier Braakman and Eric Smith. The emergence and early evolution of biological carbon fixation. *PLoS Comp. Biol.*, 8:e1002455, 2012.

[43] Rogier Braakman and Eric Smith. The compositional and evolutionary logic of metabolism. *Physical Biology*, 10:011001, 2013.

[44] Garry Brewer and Martin Shubik. *The War Game*. Harvard University Press, Cambridge, MA, 1979.

[45] Leo W. Buss. *The Evolution of Individuality*. Princeton U. Press, Princeton, NJ, 2007.

[46] Alessandro Caiani, Antoine Godin, and Stefano Lucarelli. A stock flow consistent analysis of a Schumpeterian innovation economy. *Metroeconomica*, online, January 28, 2014.

[47] Jean M. Carlson and John Doyle. Highly optimized tolerance: a mechanism for power laws in designed systems. *Phys. Rev. E*, 60:1412–1427, 1999.

[48] Luigi Luca Cavalli-Sforza. *Genes, Peoples, and Languages*. U. California Press, Berkeley, 2001.

[49] Bikas K. Chakrabarti, Anirban Chakraborti, Satya R. Chakravarty, and Arnab Chatterjee. *Econophysics of Income and Wealth Distributions*. Cambridge U. Press, New York, 2013.

[50] A. Chakraborti and B. K. Chakrabarti. Statistical mechanics of money: how saving propensity affects its distribution. *Euro. Phys. J. B*, 17:167–170, 2000.

[51] Anirban Chakraborti, Damien Challet, Arnab Chatterjee, Matteo Marsili, Yi-Cheng Zhang, and Bikas K. Chakrabarti. Statistical mechanics of competitive resource allocation using agent-based models. *Phys. Rep.*, 552:1–25, 2015.

[52] Damien Challet, Matteo Marsili, and Yi-Cheng Zhang. *Minority Games: Interacting Agents in Financial Markets*. Oxford U. Press, London, 2004.

[53] E. H. Chamberlin. An experimental imperfect market. *J. Polit. Econ.*, 56:95–108, 1948.

[54] Alfred D. Chandler. *Scale and Scope*. Belknap Press of Harvard U. Press, Cambridge, MA, 1990.

[55] Arnab Chatterjee, Sudhakar Yarlagadda, and Bikas K. Chakrabarti, editors. *Econophysics of Wealth Distributions*. Springer, New York, 2005.

[56] Arnab Chatterjee, Bikas K. Chakrabarti, and S. S. Manna. Pareto law in a kinetic model of market with random saving propensity. *Physica A*, 335:155–163, 2004.

[57] Noam Chomsky. *Language and Problems of Knowledge*. MIT Press, Cambridge, MA, 1988.

[58] Robert W. Clower. A reconsideration of the microfoundations of monetary theory. *Western Economic Journal*, 6:1–8, 1967.

[59] Sidney Coleman. *Aspects of Symmetry*. Cambridge U. Press, New York, 1985.

[60] R. C. Conant and W. R. Ashby. Every good regulator of a system must be a model of that system. *Int. J. Sys. Sci.*, 1:89–97, 1970.

[61] International Human Genome Sequencing Consortium. Finishing the euchromatic sequence of the human genome. *Nature*, 431:931–945, 2001.

[62] The Tomato Genome Consortium. The tomato genome sequence provides insights into fleshy fruit evolution. *Nature*, 485:635–641, 2012.

[63] Thomas M. Cover and Joy A. Thomas. *Elements of Information Theory*. Wiley, New York, 1991.

[64] Vincent P. Crawford. Boundedly rational versus optimization-based models of strategic thinking and learning in games. *J. Econ. Lit.*, 51:512–527, 2013.

[65] Ross Cressman. *Evolutionary Dynamics and Extensive Form Games*. MIT Press, Cambridge, MA, 2003.

[66] Vasco Cúrdia and Michael Woodford. The central-bank balance sheet as an instrument of monetary policy. 75th Carnegie-Rochester Conference on Public Policy: The Future of Central Banking, April 16–17, 2010.

[67] Herman E. Daly. Globalization and its discontents. *Philosophy and Public Policy Quarterly*, 21:17–21, 2001.

[68] Herman E. Daly and Kenneth N. Townsend, editors. *Valuing the Earth: Economics, Ecology, Ethics*. MIT Press, Cambridge, MA, 1993.

[69] Marcus G. Daniels, J. Doyne Farmer, Giulia Iori, and Eric Smith. Quantitative model of price diffusion and market friction based on trading as a mechanistic random process. *Phys. Rev. Lett.*, 90:108102, 2003.

[70] Charles Darwin. *On the Origin of Species*. John Murray, London, 1859.

[71] Eric H. Davidson and Douglas H. Erwin. Gene regulatory networks and the evolution of animal body plans. *Science*, 311:796–800, 2006.

[72] Richard C. Dawkins. *The Selfish Gene*. Oxford U. Press, New York, 1976.

[73] Richard H. Day, Gunnar Eliasson, and Clas Wihlborg. *The Markets for Innovation, Ownership and Control* (vol. 2 of *Studies in Economic Decision, Organization, and Behavior*). North-Holland, Amsterdam, 1993.

[74] Christian de Duve. *Blueprint for a Cell*. Neil Patterson, Burlington, NC, 1991.

[75] F. J. de Jong. *Dimensional Analysis for Economists*. North Holland, Amsterdam, 1967.

[76] J. Bradford De Long, Andrei Shleifer, Lawrence H. Summers, and Robert J. Waldmann. Noise trader risk in financial markets. *J. Polit. Econ.*, 98:703–738, 1990.

[77] J. Bradford De Long, Andrei Shleifer, Lawrence H. Summers, and Robert J. Waldmann. Positive feedback investment strategies and destabilizing rational speculation. *J. Finance*, 45:379–395, 1990.

[78] Gerard Debreu. The coefficient of resource utilization. *Econometrica*, 19:273–292, 1951.

[79] Gerard Debreu. *Theory of Value*. Yale U. Press, New Haven, 1987.

[80] Gerard Deckert, Patrick V. Warren, Terry Gaasterland, William G. Young, Anna L. Lenox, David E. Graham, Ross Overbeek, Marjory A. Snead, Martin Keller, Monette Aujay, Robert Huber, Robert A. Feldman, Jay M. Short, Gary J. Olsen, and Ronald V. Swanson. The complete genome of the hyperthermophilic bacterium *Aquifex aeolicus*. *Nature*, 392:353–358, 1998.

[81] Michael Denton. The protein folds as Platonic forms: new support for the pre-Darwinian conception of evolution by natural law. *J. Theor. Biol.*, 219:325–342, 2002.

[82] H. A. DeWeerd. Political military scenarios. Rand Corporation, Santa Monica, Rand P-3535, 1967.

[83] Douglas W. Diamond. Banks and liquidity creation: a simple exposition of the Diamond-Dybvig model. *Econ. Quarterly*, 93:189, 2007.

[84] Douglas W. Diamond and Philip H. Dybvig. Bank runs, deposit insurance, and liquidity. *J. Polit. Econ.*, 91:401–419, 1983.

[85] Peter R. Dickson and Alan G. Sawyer. The price knowledge and search of supermarket shoppers. *J. Marketing*, 54:42–53, 1990.

[86] E. D. Domar. *Essays in the Theory of Economic Growth*. Oxford U. Press, New York, 1957.

[87] Alexander Donath, Sven Findei, Jana Hertel, Manja Marz, Wolfgang Otto, Christine Schulz, Peter F. Stadler, and Stefan Wirth. Non-coding RNAs. In Gustavo Caetano-Anolles, editor, *Evolutionary Genomics and Systems Biology*, 251–293. Wiley-Blackwell, Hoboken, NJ, 2010.

[88] G. Dosi, G. Fagiolo, M. Napolitano, and A. Rovertini. Income distribution, credit and fiscal policies in an agent-based Keynesian model. *J. Econ. Dynamics and Control*, 37:1598–1625, 2013.

[89] G. Dosi, G. Fagiolo, and A. Rovertin. Schumpeter meets Keynes: a policy-friendly model of endogenous growth and business cycles. *J. Econ. Dynamics and Control*, 34:1748–1767, 2010.

[90] G. Dosi, C. Freeman, R. Nelson, G. Silverberg, and L. Soete. *Technical Change and Economic Theory*. Pinter, London, 1988.

[91] A. A. Dragulescu and V. M. Yakovenko. Statistical mechanics of money. *Euro. Phys. J. B*, 17:723–729, 2000.

[92] A. A. Dragulescu and V. M. Yakovenko. Evidence for the exponential distribution of income in the USA. *Euro. Phys. J. B*, 20:585–589, 2001.

[93] A. A. Dragulescu and V. M. Yakovenko. Exponential and power-law probability distributions of wealth and income in the United Kingdom and the United States. *Physica A*, 299:213–221, 2001.

[94] P. Dubey and M. Shubik. The noncooperative equilibria of a closed trading economy with market supply and bidding strategies. *J. Econ. Theory*, 17:1–20, 1978.

[95] Pradeep Dubey. Price-quantity strategic market games. *Econometrica*, 50:111–126, 1982.

[96] Pradeep Dubey and John Geanakoplos. Inside and outside fiat money, gains to trade, and IS-LM. *Econ. Theory*, 21:347–397, 2003.

[97] Pradeep Dubey, Andreu Mas-Colell, and Martin Shubik. Efficiency properties of strategic market games: an axiomatic approach. *J. Econ. Theory*, 22:339–362, 1980.

[98] Pradeep Dubey and Siddhartha Sahi. Price-mediated trade with quantity signals: an axiomatic approach. *J. Math. Econ.*, 39:377–389, 2003.

[99] Pradeep Dubey, Siddhartha Sahi, and Martin Shubik. Repeated trade and the velocity of money. *J. Math. Econ.*, 22:125–137, 1993.

[100] Pradeep Dubey and Lloyd S. Shapley. Noncooperative exchange with a continuum of traders. Rand p-5964 and Cowles Found. Discussion Paper 447, 1977.

[101] Pradeep Dubey and Martin Shubik. Trade using a borrowed means of payment with bankruptcy conditions. Cowles Found. Discussion Paper 488, 1977.

[102] Pradeep Dubey and Martin Shubik. Bankruptcy and optimality in a closed trading mass economy modelled as a non-cooperative game. *J. Math. Econ.*, 6:115–134, 1978.

[103] Pradeep Dubey and Martin Shubik. A strategic market game with price and quantity strategies. *Zeitschrift für Nationalökonomie*, 40:25–34, 1980.

[104] Pradeep K. Dubey, Siddhartha Sahi, and Martin Shubik. Minimally complex exchange mechanisms: emergence of prices, markets, and money. Cowles Found. Discussion Paper 1945, 2014.

[105] Darrell Duffie. The failure mechanics of dealer banks. *J. Econ. Perspectives*, 24:51–72, 2010.

[106] Jennifer A. Dunne, Richard J. Williams, Neo D. Martinez, Rachel A. Wood, and Douglas H. Erwin. Compilation and network analyses of Cambrian food webs. *PLoS Biology*, 6:e102, 2008.

[107] Francis Y. Edgeworth. An introductory lecture on political economy. *Economic Journal*, 1:625–634, 1891.

[108] Francis Y. Edgeworth. *Papers relating to political economy VII*. Macmillan, London, 1925.

[109] Francis Y. Edgeworth. *Mathematical Psychics: An Essay on the Application of Mathematics to the Moral Sciences*. C. Kegan Paul, London, 1932, original edition 1881.

[110] Evan N. Edinger and Michael J. Risk. Sponge borehole size as a relative measure of bio-erosion and paleoproductivity. *Lethaia*, 29:275–286, 2007.

[111] Edwin J. Elton, Martin J. Gruber, Steven J. Brown, and William N. Goetzmann. *Modern Portfolio Theory and Investment Analysis*. John Wiley and Sons, Somerset, NJ, ninth edition, 2014.

[112] Ido Erev and Alvin E. Roth. Predicting how people play games: reinforcement learning in experimental games with unique, mixed-strategy equilibria. *Amer. Econ. Rev.*, 88:848–881, 1998.

[113] Douglas H. Erwin. Macroevolution: dynamics of diversity. *Current Biology*, 21:R1000–R1001, 2012.

[114] Douglas H. Erwin and Eric H. Davidson. The evolution of hierarchical gene regulatory networks. *Nature Rev. Genetics*, 10:141–148, 2009.

[115] Douglas H. Erwin, Marc Laflamme, Sarah M. Tweedt, Erik A. Sperling, Davide Pisani, and Kevin J. Peterson. The Cambrian conundrum: early divergence and later ecological success in the early history of animals. *Science*, 334:1091–1097, 2011.

[116] Douglas H. Erwin and Sarah Tweedt. Ecological drivers of the Ediacaran-Cambrian diversification of metazoa. *Evol. Ecol.*, 26:417–433, 2012.

[117] Douglas H. Erwin and James W. Valentine. *The Cambrian Explosion: The Construction of Animal Biodiversity*. Roberts and Company, Englewood, CO, 2013.

[118] Stewart N. Ethier and Thomas G. Kurtz. *Markov Processes: Characterization and Convergence*. Wiley, New York, 1986.

[119] Warren J. Ewens. *Mathematical Population Genetics*. Springer, Heidelberg, second edition, 2004.

[120] Ray C. Fair. *Estimating How the Macroeconomy Works*. Harvard U. Press, Cambridge, MA, 2004.

[121] Joshua Farley and Herman E. Daly. *Ecological Economics: Principles and Applications*. Island Press, Washington, DC, second edition, 2003.

[122] J. Doyne Farmer. Market force, ecology, and evolution. *Ind. & Corp. Change*, 11:895–953, 2002.

[123] J. Doyne Farmer and John Geanakoplos. Hyperbolic discounting is rational: valuing the far future with uncertain discount rates. Cowles Found. Discussion Paper 1719, 2009.

[124] J. Doyne Farmer and John Geanakoplos. The virtues and vices of equilibrium and the future of financial economics. *Complexity*, 14:11–38, 2009.

[125] J. Doyne Farmer, Austin Gerig, Fabrizio Lillo, and Szabolcs Mike. Market efficiency and the long-memory of supply and demand: is price impact variable and permanent or fixed and temporary. *Quant. Fin.*, 6:107–112, 2006.

[126] J. Doyne Farmer and Szabolcs Mike. An empirical behavioral model of liquidity and volatility. *J. Econ. Dynamics and Control*, 32:200–234, 2008.

[127] J. Doyne Farmer, Paolo Patelli, and Ilija I. Zovko. The predictive power of zero intelligence in financial markets. *Proc. Nat. Acad. Sci. USA*, 102:2254–2259, 2005.

[128] J. Doyne Farmer, Martin Shubik, and Eric Smith. Is economics the next physical science? *Physics Today*, 58:37–42, 2005.

[129] Jin Feng and Thomas G. Kurtz. *Large Deviations for Stochastic Processes*. Mathematical Surveys and Monographs, vol. 131. Amer. Math. Soc., Providence, RI, 2006.

[130] I. Fisher. *The Purchasing Power of Money*. Macmillan, New York, second edition, 1931.

[131] R. A. Fisher. *The Genetical Theory of Natural Selection*. Oxford U. Press, London, 2000.

[132] Jessica C. Flack and David C. Krakauer. Evolution and construction of moral systems. In Simon Levin, editor, *Games, Groups, and the Global Good*, 1–41. Springer, New York, 2009.

[133] Duncan K. Foley. A statistical equilibrium theory of markets. *J. Econ. Theory*, 62:321–345, 1994.

[134] Jay Forester. *Industrial Dynamics*. Pegasus Communications, Waltham, MA, 1961.

[135] Lawrence E. Fouraker, Martin Shubik, and Sidney Siegel. The quantity adjuster models. Research Bulletin 20, Pennsylvania State Univ., Dept. of Psychology, 1961. Partially published in [137].

[136] Lawrence E. Fouraker, Martin Shubik, and Sidney Siegel. Oligopoly bargaining: the quantity adjuster models. Pennsylvania State Univ., 1961. Partially reported in [137].

[137] Lawrence E. Fouraker and Sidney Siegel. *Bargaining Behavior*. McGraw-Hill, New York, 1963.

[138] Steven A. Frank. The Price equation, Fisher's fundamental theorem, kin selection, and causal analysis. *Evolution*, 51:1712–1729, 1997.

[139] Steven A. Frank. *Foundations of Social Evolution*. Princeton U. Press, Princeton, NJ, 1998.

[140] Steven A. Frank and Montgomery Slatkin. Fisher's fundamental theorem of natural selection. *Trends Ecol. Evol.*, 7:92–95, 1992.

[141] Daniel Friedman, R. Mark Isaac, Duncan James, and Shyam Sunder. *Risky Curves: On Empirical Failure of the Expected Utility*. Routledge, London, 2014.

[142] Milton Friedman. *Essays in Positive Economics*. U. Chicago Press, Chicago, 1953.

[143] Milton Friedman, editor. *Studies in the quantity theory of money*. U. Chicago Press, Chicago, 1956.

[144] Milton Friedman. The permanent income hypothesis. In Milton Friedman, editor, *A Theory of the Consumption Function*, 20–37. Princeton U. Press, Princeton, NJ, 1957.

[145] Milton Friedman. *The Optimum Quantity of Money and Other Essays*. Aldine, Chicago, 1969.

[146] Drew Fudenberg and David K. Levine. *The Theory of Learning in Games*. MIT Press, Cambridge, MA, 1998.

[147] Drew Fudenberg and David K. Levine. *A Long-Run Collaboration on Long-Run Games*. World Scientific Publishing, Hackensack, NJ, 2008.

[148] D. Gale and L. S. Shapley. College admissions and the stability of marriage. *Amer. Math. Monthly*, 69:9–14, 1962.

[149] V. Gaur, M. Fisher, and A. Raman. An econometric analysis of inventory turnover performance in retail services. *Managment Science*, 51:181–194, 2005.

[150] J. G. Geanakoplos. Liquidity, default, and crashes: endogenous contracts in general equilibrium. In *Advances in Economics and Econometrics: Theory and Application, Eighth World Conference*, vol. 2, 170–205. Cambridge U. Press, Cambridge, 2003.

[151] John Geanakoplos, Robert Axtell, J. Doyne Farmer, Peter Howitt, Benjamin Conlee, Jonathan Goldstein, Matthew Hendrey, Nathan M. Palmer, and Chun-Yi Yang. Getting at systemic risk via an agent-based model of the housing market. *Amer. Econ. Rev.*, 102:53–58, 2012.

[152] John Geanakoplos, Ioannis Karatzas, Martin Shubik, and William Sudderth. The inflationary bias of real uncertainty and the harmonic Fisher equation. *Econ. Theory*, 28:481–512, 2006.

[153] John Geanakoplos, Ioannis Karatzas, Martin Shubik, and William D. Sudderth. Inflationary equilibrium in a stochastic economy with independent agents. *J. Math. Econ.*, 52:1–11, 2014.

[154] John Geanakoplos and Andreu Mas-Colell. Real indeterminacy with financial assets. *J. Econ. Theory*, 47:22–38, 1989.

[155] Murray Gell-Mann. *The Quark and the Jaguar: Adventures in the Simple and the Complex*. Freeman, New York, 1994.

[156] Andrew Gelman and Cosma Rohilla Shalizi. Philosophy and the practice of Bayesian statistics. *British J. Math. Stat. Psy.*, 66:8–38, 2013.

[157] Howard Georgi. *Lie Algebras in Particle Physics*. Perseus, New York, second edition, 1999.

[158] John Gerhart and Marc Kirschner. *Cells, Embryos, and Evolution*. Wiley, New York, 1997.

[159] John Gerhart and Marc Kirschner. The theory of facilitated variation. *Proc. Nat. Acad. Sci. USA*, 104:8582–8589, 2007.

[160] László Gillemot, J. Doyne Farmer, and Fabrizio Lillo. There's more to volatility than volume. *Quant. Fin.*, 6:371–384, 2007.

[161] Gaël Giraud. Strategic market games: an introduction. *J. Math. Econ.*, 39:355–375, 2003.

[162] John I. Glass, Nacyra Assad-Garcia, Nina Alperovich, Shibu Yooseph, Matthew R. Lewis, Mahir Maruf, Clyde A. Hutchison III, Hamilton O. Smith, and J. Craig Venter. Essential genes of a minimal bacterium. *Proc. Nat. Acad. Sci. USA*, 103:425–430, 2006.

[163] Dhananjay K. Gode and Shyam Sunder. Allocative efficiency of markets with zero-intelligence traders: market as a partial substitute for individual rationality. *J. Polit. Econ.*, 101:119–137, 1993.

[164] Dhananjay K. Gode and Shyam Sunder. Double auction dynamics: Structural effects of non-binding price controls. *J. Econ. Dynamics and Control*, 28:1707–1731, 2004.

[165] Nigel Goldenfeld. *Lectures on Phase Transitions and the Renormalization Group*. Westview Press, Boulder, CO, 1992.

[166] Terrence Gorman. Community preference fields. *Econometrica*, 21:63–80, 1953.

[167] Gary Gorton and Andrew Metrick. Getting up to speed on the financial crisis: a one-weekend-reader's guide. *J. Econ. Lit.*, 50:128–150, 2012.

[168] Gary B. Gorton. *Slapped by the Invisible Hand: The Panic of 2007*. Oxford U. Press, New York, 2010.

[169] Stephen Jay Gould. *The Structure of Evolutionary Theory*. Harvard U. Press, Cambridge, MA, 2002.

[170] Stephen Jay Gould and Elisabeth S. Vrba. Exaptation—a missing term in the science of form. *Paleobiology*, 8:4–15, 1982.

[171] R. Green. Real bills doctrine. In J. Eatwell, M. Milgate, and P. Newman, editors, *The New Palgrave*, vol. 4. Macmillan, London, 1987.

[172] Frank Hahn and Takashi Negishi. A theorem on nontatonnement stability. *Econometrica*, 30:463–469, 1962.

[173] William D. Hamilton. The genetical evolution of social behavior. I. *J. Theor. Biol.*, 7:1–16, 1964.

[174] William D. Hamilton. The genetical evolution of social behavior. II. *J. Theor. Biol.*, 7:17–52, 1964.

[175] Peter Hammerstein and Reinhard Selten. Game theory and evolutionary biology. In R. J. Aumann and S. Hart, editors, *Handbook of Game Theory with Economic Applications*, vol. 2, 929–993. Elsevier, Amsterdam, 1994.

[176] Roy F. Harrod. *Economic Dynamics*. Macmillan, London, 1973.

[177] John C. Harsanyi and Reinhard Selten. *A General Theory of Equilibrium Selection in Games*. MIT Press, Cambridge, MA, 1988.

[178] Ronald M. Harstad and Reinhard Selten. Bounded rationality models: tasks to become intellectually competitive. *J. Econ. Lit.*, 51:496–511, 2013.

[179] Oliver D. Hart and Berndt Holmström. The theory of contracts. In Truman Fassett Bewley, editor, *Advances in Economic Theory, Fifth World Congress.* Cambridge U. Press, Cambridge, 1987.

[180] F. A. Hayek. *Collectivist Economic Planning: Critical Studies on the Possibilitis of Socialism.* Routledge, New York, 1935.

[181] F. A. Hayek. *Road to Serfdom.* Routledge, New York, 2001, original edition 1944.

[182] J. Henrich, R. Boyd, S. Bowles, C. Camerer, E. Fehr, and H. Gintis, editors. *Foundations of Human Sociality.* Oxford U. Press, New York, 2004.

[183] Matthew D. Herron, Armin Rashidi, Deborah E. Shelton, and William W. Driscoll. Cellular differentiation and individuality in the "minor" multicellular taxa. *Biol. Rev.*, 88:844–861, 2013.

[184] J. R. Hicks. *Value and Capital: An Inquiry into Some Fundamental Principles of Economic Theory.* Clarendon, Oxford, 1946.

[185] John Hicks. Mr. Keynes and the classics: a suggested interpretation. *Econometrica*, 5:147–159, 1937.

[186] John R. Hicks. *A Contribution to the Theory of the Trade Cycle.* Clarendon, Oxford, 1950.

[187] Josef Hofbauer and Karl Sigmund. *Evolutionary Games and Population Dynamics.* Cambridge U. Press, New York, 1998.

[188] David Hounshell. *From the American System to Mass Production, 1800–1932: The Development of Manufacturing Technology in the United States.* Johns Hopkins U. Press, Baltimore, 1985.

[189] Juergen Huber, Martin Shubik, and Shyam Sunder. The value of fiat money with an outside bank: an experimental game. Cowles Found. Discussion Paper 1675, 2010.

[190] Juergen M. Huber, Martin Shubik, and Shyam Sunder. Three minimal market institutions: theory and experimental evidence. *J. Econ. Behavior*, 70:403–424, 2010.

[191] Giulia Iori, Marcus G. Daniels, J. Doyne Farmer, László Gillemot, Supriya Krishnamurthy, and Eric Smith. An analysis of price impact function in order-driven markets. *Physica A*, 324:146–151, 2003.

[192] Ray Jackendoff. *Language, Consciousness, Culture: Essays on Mental Structure.* MIT Press, Cambridge, MA, 2007.

[193] E. T. Jaynes. Information theory and statistical mechanics. *Phys. Rev.*, 106:620–630, 1957; reprinted in [308].

[194] E. T. Jaynes. *Probability Theory: The Logic of Science.* Cambridge U. Press, New York, 2003.

[195] William Stanley Jevons, editor. *Money and the Mechanism of Exchange.* Macmillan, London, 1875.

[196] Philippe Jorion. *Value at Risk: The New Benchmark for Managing Financial Risk.* McGraw-Hill, New York, third edition, 2006.

[197] Peter Jung and Peter Hänggi. Amplification of small signals via stochastic resonance. *Phys. Rev. A*, 44:8032–8042, 1991.

[198] Leonid V. Kantorovich. Mathematical methods of organizing and planning production. *Management Science*, 6:366–422, 1960.

[199] I. Karatzas, M. Shubik, and W. D. Sudderth. Construction of stationary Markov equilibria on a strategic market game. *Mathematics of Operations Research*, 19:975–1006, 1994.

[200] Ioannis Karatzas, Martin Shubik, and William Sudderth. Production, interest, and saving in deterministic economies with additive endowments. *Econ. Theory*, 29:525–548, 2006.

[201] Martin Karplus. Behind the folding funnel diagram. *Nature Chemical Biology*, 7:401–404, 2011.

[202] John Maynard Keynes. *A Pure Theory of Money*. Vol. 1 of *A Treatise on Money*. Macmillan, London, 1958, original edition 1930.

[203] John Maynard Keynes. *The Applied Theory of Money*. Vol. 2 of *A Treatise on Money*. Macmillan, London, 1958, original edition 1930.

[204] John Maynard Keynes. *A Tract on Monetary Reform*. Vol. 4 of *The Collected Writings of John Maynard Keynes*. Macmillan, London, 1971, original edition 1923.

[205] Ibn Khaldun. *Al Muqaddimah*. Franz Rozenthal, translator. Princeton U. Press, Princeton, NJ, second edition, 1967.

[206] Dana Khromov. Ithaca hour revival would require community support. Updated February 10 2012. www.ithaca.com/news/ithaca-hours-revival-would-require-community-support/article_175100c4-65d6-11e0-bd73-001cc4c002e0.html?mode=jqm.

[207] Charles P. Kindleberger. *A Financial History of Western Europe*. Allen & Unwin, Boston, 1984.

[208] Paul Klemperer. *The Economic Theory of Auctions*, vol. 1. Edward Elgar, Cheltenham, UK, 2000.

[209] Paul Klemperer. *The Economic Theory of Auctions*, vol. 2. Edward Elgar, Cheltenham, UK, 2000.

[210] G. F. Knapp. *Staatliche Theorie des Geldes*. Duncker and Humbolt, Leipzig, 1905.

[211] Tjalling C. Koopmans. Concepts of optimality and their uses. *Amer. Econ. Rev.*, 67:261–274, 1977.

[212] Tjalling Charles Koopmans. *Three Essays on the State of Economic Science*. McGraw-Hill, New York, 1957.

[213] David C. Krakauer and Joshua B. Plotkin. Redundancy, antiredundancy, and the robustness of genomes. *Proc. Nat. Acad. Sci. USA*, 99:1405–1409, 2002.

[214] David C. Krakauer and Joshua B. Plotkin. Principles and parameters of molecular robustness. In Erica Jen, editor, *Robust Design: A Repertoire for Biology, Ecology and Engineering*, 71–103. Oxford University Press, London, 2005.

[215] Thomas G. Kurtz. *Approximation of Population Processes*. Soc. Industrial and Applied Math., Philadelphia, 1981.

[216] Nick Lane and William Martin. The energetics of genome complexity. *Nature*, 467:929–934, 2010.

[217] C. E. Lemke and J. T. Howson. Equilibrium points of bi-matrix games. *SIAM J. Appl. Math.*, 12:413–423, 1964.

[218] Wassily W. Leontief. *Input-output economics*. Oxford U. Press, New York, second edition, 1986.

[219] David Levhari and T. N. Srinivasan. Optimal savings under uncertainty. *Rev. Econ. Studies*, 36:153–163, 1969.

[220] Richard C. Lewontin. *The Genetic Basis of Evolutionary Change*. Columbia U. Press, New York, 1974.

[221] Richard C. Lewontin. *The Triple Helix: Gene, Organism, and Environment*. Harvard U. Press, Cambridge, MA, 2000.

[222] Ming Li and Paul Vitányi. *An Introduction to Kolmogorov Complexity and Its Applications*. Springer, Heidelberg, third edition, 2008.

[223] Fabrizio Lillo. Econophysics and the challenge of efficiency. *Complexity*, 14:39–54, 2009.

[224] Fabrizio Lillo and J. Doyne Farmer. The long memory of the efficient market. *Studies in Nonlinear Dynamics & Econometrics*, 8:3:1–35, 2004.

[225] Fabrizio Lillo and J. Doyne Farmer. The key role of liquidity fluctuations in determining large price fluctuations. *Fluct. Noise Lett.*, 5:L209–L216, 2005.

[226] Fabrizio Lillo, Szabolcs Mike, and J. Doyne Farmer. Theory for long memory in supply and demand. *Phys. Rev. E*, 71:066122:287–297, 2005.

[227] Timothy A. Linksvayer, Jennifer H. Fewell, Jürgen Gadau, and Manfred D. Laubichler. Developmental evolution in social insects: regulatory networks from genes to societies. *J. Exp. Zoo. B: Mol. Dev. Evol.*, 318:159–169, 2012.

[228] John Lintner. The valuation of risk assets and the selection of risky investments in stock portfolios and capital budgets. *Rev. Econ. Stat.*, 47:13–37, 1965.

[229] Andrew Lo. Reading about the financial crisis: a twenty-one-book review. *J. Econ. Lit.*, 50:151–178, 2012.

[230] James Lovelock. *Gaia: A New Look at Life on Earth*. Oxford U. Press, London, 2000.

[231] R. E. Lucas. Equilibrium in a pure currency economy. *Economic Enquiry*, 18:203–220, 1980.

[232] Robert Lucas. Expectations and the neutrality of money. *J. Econ. Theory*, 4:103–124, 1972.

[233] Robert E. Lucas. Asset prices in an exchange economy. *Econometrica*, 46:1429–1445, 1978.

[234] Robert E. Lucas. Monetary neutrality. In Torsten Persson, editor, *Nobel Lectures*, 246–265. World Scientific, Singapore, 1997.

[235] Keynes J. M. *The General Theory of Employment, Interest and Money*. Macmillan, London, 1957, original edition 1936.

[236] Thomas Babington Macaulay. *The History of England*. Longman, Brown, Green, and Longmans, London, tenth edition, 1854.

[237] George J. Mailath and Lawrence Samuelson. *Repeated Games and Reputations: Long-Run Relationships*. Oxford U. Press, Oxford, 2006.

[238] Louis Makowski and Joseph M. Ostroy. General equilibrium and market socialism: Clarifying the logic of competitive markets. In P. Bardhan and J. Roemer, editors, *Market Socialism: The Current Debate*. Oxford U. Press, London, 1993.

[239] Burton G. Malkiel. Asset management fees and the growth of finance. *J. Econ. Perspectives*, 27:97–108, 2013.

[240] Benoit Mandelbrot. The variation of certain speculative prices. *J. Business*, 36:394–419, 1963.

[241] Benoit Mandelbrot and R. L. Hudson. *The (Mis)behavior of Markets*. Basic Books, New York, 2004.

[242] N. Gregory Mankiw. The macroeconomist as scientist and engineer. *J. Econ. Perspectives*, 20:29–46, 2006.

[243] John M. Marincola. *Herodotus: The Histories*. Penguin, New York, 1996.

[244] H. M. Markowitz. Portfolio selection. *J. Finance*, 7:77–91, 1952.

[245] Alfred Marshall. *Principles of Economics*, vol. 1. Macmillan, London, 1890.

[246] Alfred Marshall. *Money, Credit, and Commerce*. Macmillan, London, 1923.

[247] Alfred Marshall. *Principles of Economics*. Macmillan, London, eighth edition, 1926.

[248] William Martin and Michael J. Russell. On the origin of cells: an hypothesis for the evolutionary transitions from abiotic geochemistry to chemoautotrophic prokaryotes, and from prokaryotes to nucleated cells. *Philos. Trans. Roy. Soc. London*, 358B:27–85, 2003.

[249] Karl Marx. Critique of the Gotha programme. In *Marx/Engels Selected Works*, vol. 3, 13–30. Progress Publishers, Moscow, 1970.

[250] Andreu Mas-Colell and S. Hart. A simple adaptive procedure leading to correlated equilibria. *Econometrica*, 68:1127–1150, 2010.

[251] John Maynard Smith and George R. Price. The logic of animal conflict. *Nature*, 246:15–18, 1973.

[252] Ernst Mayr. *The Growth of Biological Thought: Diversity, Evolution, and Inheritance*. Harvard U. Press, Cambridge, MA, 1985.

[253] Mariana Mazzucato. *The Entrepreneurial State*. Anthem Press, London, 2013.

[254] T. M. McCollom and J. P. Amend. A thermodynamic assessment of energy requirements for biomass synthesis by chemolithoautotrophic micro-organisms in oxic and anoxic environments. *Geobiology*, 3:135–144, 2005.

[255] Forrest McDonald. *Alexander Hamilton: A Biography*. Norton, New York, 1979.

[256] Lionel W. McKenzie. Optimal economic growth, turnpike theorems and comparative dynamics. In K. J. Arrow and M. D. Intriligator, editors, *Handbook of Mathematical Economics*, vol. 3, 1281–1355. North-Holland, Amsterdam, 1986.

[257] Lionel W. McKenzie. *Classical General Equilibrium Theory*. MIT Press, Cambridge, MA, 2005.

[258] Karl Menger. The role of uncertainty in economics. In Martin Shubik, editor, *Essays in Mathematical Economics in Honor of Oskar Morgenstern*, ch. 16. Princeton U. Press, Princeton, NJ, 1967.

[259] Mertens, Jean-François. The limit-price mechanism. *J. Math. Econ.*, 39:433–528, 2003.

[260] M. Milakovic. *Towards a Statistical Equilibrium Theory of Wealth Distribution*. PhD thesis, New School for Social Research, 2003.

[261] George A. Miller. The magic number seven, plus or minus two: some limits on our capacity for processing information. *Psych. Rev.*, 63:81–97, 1956.

[262] John H. Miller and Martin Shubik. Some dynamics of a strategic market game with a large number of agents. *J. Econ.*, 60:1–28, 1994.

[263] Hyman Minsky. *Stabilizing an Unstable Economy*. McGraw-Hill, New York, 2008.

[264] Marvin Minsky. *The Society of Mind*. Simon and Schuster, New York, 1988.

[265] Philip Mirowski. *More Heat than Light*. Cambridge U. Press, Cambridge, 1991.

[266] Franco Modigliani and Richard Blumberg. Utility analysis and the consumption function: An interpretation of cross-section data. In Kenneth K. Kurihara, editor, *Post-Keynesian Economics*, 388–436. Rutgers U. Press, New Brunswick, NJ, 1954.

[267] Stephen Morris and Hyun Song Shin. Unique equilibrium in a model of self-fulfilling currency attacks. *Amer. Econ. Rev.*, 88:587–597, 1998.

[268] Melanie E. Moses and James H. Brown. Allometry of human fertility and energy use. *Ecology Letters*, 6:295–300, 2003.

[269] Jan Mossin. Equilibrium in a capital asset market. *Econometrica*, 34:768–783, 1966.

[270] Takashi Negishi. Welfare economics and the existence of an equilibrium for a competitive economy. *Metroeconomica*, 12:92–97, 1960.

[271] Richard R. Nelson. *The Moon and the Ghetto: An Essay on Public Policy Analysis*. Norton, New York, 1977.

[272] Richard R. Nelson. *The Sources of Economic Growth*. Harvard U. Press, Cambridge, MA, 1996.

[273] Richard R. Nelson and Sidney G. Winter. *An Evolutionary Theory of Economic Change*. Belknap Press, Cambridge, MA, 1985.

[274] Simon Newcomb. *Principles of Political Economy*. Harper and Brothers, New York, 1886.

[275] Makoto Nirei and Wataru Souma. Income distribution and stochastic multiplicative process with reset events. In M. Gallegati, A. P. Kirman, and M. Marsili, editors, *The Complex Dynamics of Economic Interaction: Essays in Economics and Econophysics*, 161ff. Springer, New York, 2004.

[276] William Nordhaus. Policy games: coordination and independence in monetary and fiscal policies. *Brookings Papers on Economic Activity*, 2:139–216, 1994.

[277] M. Arthur Okun. *The Political Economy of Prosperity*. W. W. Norton, New York, 1970.

[278] José Nelson Onuchik, Zaida Luthey-Schulten, and Peter G. Wolynes. Theory of protein folding: the energy landscape perspective. *Ann. Rev. Phys. Chem.*, 48:545–600, 1997.

[279] Guy Orcutt. *Microanalysis of Socioeconomic Systems: A Simulation Study*. Harper, New York, 1961.

[280] G. Owen and L. S. Shapley. Optimal location of candidates in ideological space. *Int. J. Game Theory*, 18:339–356, 1989.

[281] John F. Padgett and Walter W. Powell. *The Emergence of Organizations and Markets*. Princeton U. Press, Princeton, NJ, 2012.

[282] John M. Pandolfi. The paleoecology of coral reefs. In Zvy Dubinsky and Noga Stambler, editors, *Coral Reefs: An Ecoystem in Transition*, 13–24. Springer, Berlin, 2011.

[283] John C. Panzar and Robert D. Willig. Economies of scale in multi-output production. *Quarterly J. Econ.*, 91:481–493, 1977.

[284] John C. Panzar and Robert D. Willig. Economies of scope. *Amer. Econ. Rev.*, 71:268–272, 1981.

[285] Vilfredo Pareto. *Cours d'économie politique*. Droz, Geneva, 1896.

[286] Alan Pasternak. Global energy futures and human development: A framework for analysis. *Lawrence Livermore National Laboratory*, rep. no. UCRL-ID-140773:1–25, 2000.

[287] Don Patinkin. *Keynes' Monetary Thought*. Duke University Press, Durham, NC, 1976.

[288] Paul Krugman. Increasing returns and economic geography. *J. Polit. Econ.*, 99:483–499, 1991.

[289] Juli Peretó, Purificación López-García, and David Moreira. Ancestral lipid biosynthesis and early membrane evolution. *Trends Biochem. Sci.*, 29:469–477, 2004.

[290] Edmund S. Phelps. *Golden Rules of Economic Growth*. Norton, New York, 1996.

[291] Charles E. Plott. *Public Economics, Political Processes and Policy Applications*. Vol. 1 of *Collected Papers on the Experimental Foundations of Economics and Political Science*. Edward Elgar, Cheltenham, UK, 2001.

[292] Charles R. Plott and Vernon L. Smith. An experimental examination of two exchange institutions. *Rev. Econ. Studies*, 45:133–153, 1978.

[293] N. V. Plyasunova, A. V. Plyasunov, and E. L. Shock. *http://webdocs.asu.edu*.

[294] Joseph G. Polchinski. Renormalization group and effective Lagrangians. *Nuclear Physics B*, 231:269–295, 1984.

[295] Michael Powers and Martin Shubik. The value of government and the efficiency of noncooperative equilibrium. 2014. SFI Working Paper 14-11-040.

[296] William B. Provine. *The Origins of Theoretical Population Genetics*. U. Chicago Press, Chicago, 2001.

[297] Chen Zhong Qin and Martin Shubik. A note on uncertainty and perception concerning measurable utility. *Econ. Lett.*, 130:83–84, 2015.

[298] Tom Quint and Martin Shubik. *Barley, Gold, or Fiat: Toward a Pure Theory of Money*. Yale U. Press, New Haven, 2014.

[299] Naomi R. Lamoreaux and Kenneth L. Sokoloff, editors. *Financing Innovation in the United States: 1870 to the Present*. MIT Press, Cambridge, MA, 2007.

[300] Matthew Rabin. Incorporating limited rationality into economics. *J. Econ. Lit.*, 51:528–543, 2013.

[301] Frank P. Ramsay. A mathematical theory of saving. *Economic Journal*, 38:543–559, 1928.

[302] J. E. Rauch and P. B. Edwards. Bureaucratic structure and bureaucratic performance in less developed countries. *J. Public Econ.*, 75:49–71, 2000.

[303] Jason Raymond, Janet L. Seifert, Christopher R. Staples, and Robert E. Blankenship. The natural history of nitrogen fixation. *Mol. Biol. Evol.*, 21:541–554, 2004.

[304] Armon Rezai, Duncan K. Foley, and Lance Taylor. Global warming and economic externalities. *Econ. Theory*, 49:329–351, 2012.

[305] Jorma Rissanen. *Stochastic Complexity in Statistical Inquiry*. World Scientific, Teaneck, NJ, 1989.

[306] Joan Robinson. *The Economics of Imperfect Competition*. Macmillan, London, 1933.

[307] Paul M. Romer. Endogenous technical change. *J. Polit. Econ.*, 98:S71–S102, 1990.

[308] R. D. Rosenkrantz, editor. *E. T. Jaynes: Papers on Probability, Statistics and Statistical Physics*. D. Reidel, Dordrecht, Holland, 1983.

[309] Thomas Russell. Contact geometry, symplectic geometry, and the maximization hypothesis in economics: a new view of duality theory. Dept. of Economics, Santa Clara University, 2007.

[310] Thomas Russell. Symplectic geometry: the natural geometry of economics? *Econ. Lett.*, 112:236–238, 2011.

[311] S. Sahi and S. Yao. The noncooperative equilibria of a trading economy with complete markets and consistent prices. *J. Math. Econ.*, 18:325–346, 1989.

[312] Paul A. Samuelson. An exact consumption-loan model of interest with or without the social contrivance of money. *J. Polit. Econ.*, 66:467–480, 1958.

[313] Paul A. Samuelson. Structure of a minimum equilibrium system. In Joseph E. Stiglitz, editor, *The Collected Scientific Papers of Paul A. Samuelson*, 651–686. MIT Press, Cambridge, MA, 1966.

[314] Davide Sangiorgi and David Walker. *The π-calculus: A Theory of Mobile Processes*. Cambridge U. Press, Cambridge, 2001.

[315] T. J. Sargent. Where to draw lines: stability versus efficiency. *Economica*, 78:197–214, 2011.

[316] Herbert E. Scarf and Terje Hansen. *The Computation of Economic Equilibria*. Yale U. Press, New Haven, 1973.

[317] Herbert S. Scarf. Inventory theory. *Operations Res.*, 50:186–191, 2002.

[318] Marten Scheffer, Jordi Bascompte, William A. Brock, Victor Brevkin, Stephen R. Carpenter, Vasilis Dakos, Hermann Held, Egbert H. van Nes, Max Reitkerk, and George Sugihara. Early-warning signals for critical transitions. *Nature*, 461:53–59, 2009.

[319] Andrei Shleifer and Robert Vishny. A survey of corporate governance. *J. Finance*, 52:737–783, 1997.

[320] Andrei Shleifer and Robert Vishny. Fire sales in finance and macroeconomics. *J. Econ. Perspectives*, 25:29–48, 2011.

[321] David Schmeidler. The nucleolus of a characteristic function game. *SIAM J. Appl. Math.*, 17:1163–1170, 1969.

[322] P. S. Schnable et al. The b73 maize genome: complexity, diversity, and dynamics. *Science*, 326:1112–1115, 2009.

[323] Thomas D. Schneider. Theory of molecular machines I: channel capacity of molecular machines. *J. Theor. Biol.*, 148:83–123, 1991.

[324] Thomas D. Schneider. Theory of molecular machines II: energy dissipation from molecular machines. *J. Theor. Biol.*, 148:125–137, 1991.

[325] J. A. Schumpeter. *The Theory of Economic Development*. Harvard U. Press, Cambridge, MA, 1955.

[326] Joseph A. Schumpeter. *Business Cycles*. McGraw-Hill, New York, 1939. .

[327] Joseph A. Schumpeter. *History of Economic Analysis*. Edited from a manuscript by Elizabeth Boody Schumpeter. Allen & Unwin, London, 1954.

[328] Gideon E. Schwarz. Estimating the dimension of a model. *Ann. Stat.*, 6:461–464, 1978.

[329] Reinhard Selten. Ein Marktexperiment. In Heinz Sauermann, editor, *Contributions to Experimental Economics*, vol. 2, 33–98. Mohr, Tübingen, 1970.

[330] The Chimpanzee Sequencing and Analysis Consortium. Initial sequence of the chimpanzee genome and comparison with the human genome. *Nature*, 437:69–87, 2005.

[331] Cosma Rohilla Shalizi. Dynamics of Bayesian updating with dependent data and misspecified models. *Electronic J. Stat.*, 3:1039–1074, 2009.

[332] Claude E. Shannon. Communication in the presence of noise. *Proc. IEEE*, 86:447–457, 1949.

[333] Claude E. Shannon and Warren Weaver. *The Mathematical Theory of Communication*. U. Illinois Press, Urbana, 1949.

[334] Lloyd S. Shapley. On balanced sets and cores. *Naval Logistics Research Quarterly*, 4:453–469, 1967.

[335] Lloyd S. Shapley. Cardinal utility from intensity comparisons. 1975. Rand Publication R-1683-PR.

[336] Lloyd S. Shapley. Noncooperative general exchange. In S. A. Y. Lin, editor, *Theory and Measurement of Economic Externalities*, 155–175. Academic Press, Orlando, FL, 1976.

[337] Lloyd S. Shapley and Martin Shubik. On market games. *J. Econ. Theory*, 1:9–25, 1969.

[338] Lloyd S. Shapley and Martin Shubik. The assignment game I: the core. *Int. J. Game Theory*, 1:111–130, 1971.

[339] Lloyd S. Shapley and Martin Shubik. Trade using one commodity as a means of payment. *J. Polit. Econ.*, 85:937–968, 1977.

[340] William F. Sharpe. Capital asset prices: a theory of market equilibrium under conditions of risk. *J. Finance*, 19:425–442, 1964.

[341] Robert J. Shiller. *Finance and the Good Society*. Princeton U. Press, Princeton, NJ, 2012.

[342] M. Shubik and M. J. Sobel. On matching book: a problem in banking and corporate finance. *Management Science*, 38:827–839, 1992.

[343] M. Shubik and G. Thompson. Games of economic survival. *Naval Logistics Research Quarterly*, 6:111–123, 1959.

[344] M. Shubik and L. Van der Heyden. Logrolling and budget allocation games. *Int. J. Math. Econ.*, 7:151–162, 1978.

[345] M. Shubik and C. Wilson. The optimal bankruptcy rule in a trading economy with fiat money. *Zeitschrift für Nationalökonomie*, 37:3–4, 1977.

[346] Martin Shubik. A game theorist looks at the antitrust laws and the automobile industry. *Stanford Law Review*, 8:594–630, 1959.

[347] Martin Shubik. *Strategy and Market Structure*. Wiley, New York, 1959.

[348] Martin Shubik. Objective functions and models of corporate organization. *Quarterly J. Econ.*, 75:345–375, 1961.

[349] Martin Shubik. A note on a simulated stockmarket. *Decision Sciences*, 1:129–141, 1970.

[350] Martin Shubik. On different methods for allocating resources. *Kyklos*, 23:332–337, 1970.

[351] Martin Shubik. The dollar auction game: A paradox in noncooperative behavior and escalation. *J. Conflict Resolution*, 15:109–111, 1971.

[352] Martin Shubik. Commodity money, oligopoly, credit and bankruptcy in a general equilibrium model. *Western Economic Journal*, 11:24–38, 1973.

[353] Martin Shubik. The capital stock modified competitive equilibrium. In J. H. Karaken and N. Wallace, editors, *Models of Monetary Economies*, 97–130. Federal Reserve Bank of Minneapolis, Minneapolis, 1980.

[354] Martin Shubik. *Game Theory in the Social Sciences: Concepts and Solutions*. MIT Press, Cambridge, MA, 1984.

[355] Martin Shubik. What is an application and when is theory a waste of time? *Management Science*, 33:1511–1522, 1987.

[356] Martin Shubik. *The Theory of Money and Financial Institutions*, vol. 1. MIT Press, Cambridge, MA, 1999.

[357] Martin Shubik. *The Theory of Money and Financial Institutions*, vol. 2. MIT Press, Cambridge, MA, 1999.

[358] Martin Shubik. Innovation and equilibrium? In Dimitri B. Papadimitriou and L. Randall Wray, editors, *The Elgar Companion to Hyman Minsky*, 153–168. Edward Elgar, Northampton, MA, 2010.

[359] Martin Shubik. *The Theory of Money and Financial Institutions*, vol. 3. MIT Press, Cambridge, MA, 2010.

[360] Martin Shubik. Simecs, Ithaca hours, Berkshares, Bitcoins and Walmarts. Cowles Found. Discussion Paper 1947, 2014.

[361] Martin Shubik and Eric Smith. Structure, clearinghouses and symmetry. *Econ. Theory*, 30:587–597, 2006.

[362] Martin Shubik and Eric Smith. Building theories of economic process. *Complexity*, 14:77–92, 2009.

[363] Martin Shubik and Eric Smith. Varying the money supply of commercial banks. In Jean-Pierre Bourguignon, Rolf Jelstch, Alberto Adrego Pinto, and Marcelo Viana, editors, *Mathematics of Planet Earth: Dynamics, Games, and Science*, 609–667. Springer, Heidelberg, 2015.

[364] Martin Shubik and William Sudderth. Cost innovation: Schumpeter and equilibrium. Part 1: Robinson Crusoe. Cowles Found. Discussion Paper 1786, 2012.

[365] Martin Shubik and William Sudderth. Cost innovation: Schumpeter and equilibrium. Part 2: innovation and the money supply. Cowles Found. Discussion Paper 1881, 2012.

[366] Martin Shubik and Ward Whitt. Fiat money in an economy with one nondurable good and no credit (a noncooperative sequential game). In A. Blaquiere, editor, *Topics in Differential Games*, 401–448. North-Holland, Amsterdam, 1973.

[367] Martin Shubik and Aaron Zelinski. Network systems, protection, detection and recovery. *Contemporary Security Policy*, 2010.

[368] Brian J. Shuter, J. E. Thomas, William D. Taylor, and A. M. Zimmerman. Phenotypic correlates of genomic dna content in unicellular eukaryotes. *Am. Naturalist*, 122:26–44, 1983.

[369] S. Siegel and L. Fouraker. *Bargaining and Group Decision-making*. McGraw-Hill, New York, 1960.

[370] G. Simmel. *The Philosophy of Money*. T. Bottomore and D. Frisby, translators. Routledge, London, 1990, original edition 1911.

[371] Herbert A. Simon. A behavioral model of rational choice. *Quarterly J. Econ.*, 69:99–118, 1955.

[372] Herbert A. Simon. The architecture of complexity. *Proc. Am. Phil. Soc.*, 106:467–482, 1962.

[373] Herbert A. Simon. The organization of complex systems. In Howard H. Pattee, editor, *Hierarchy Theory: The Challenge of Complex Systems*, 3–27. George Braziller, New York, 1973.

[374] Herbert A. Simon. *The Sciences of the Artificial*. MIT Press, Cambridge, MA, third edition, 1996.

[375] Adam Smith. *An Inquiry Into the Nature and Causes of the Wealth of Nations*. Random House, New York, 1937.

[376] Eric Smith. Large-deviation principles, stochastic effective actions, path entropies, and the structure and meaning of thermodynamic descriptions. *Rep. Prog. Phys.*, 74:046601, 2011.

[377] Eric Smith, J. Doyne Farmer, László Gillemot, and Supriya Krishnamurthy. Statistical theory of the continuous double auction. *Quant. Finance*, 3:481–514, 2003.

[378] Eric Smith and Duncan K. Foley. Classical thermodynamics and economic general equilibrium theory. *J. Econ. Dynamics and Control*, 32:7–65, 2008.

[379] Eric Smith, Duncan K. Foley, and Benjamin H. Good. Unhedgeable shocks and statistical economic equilibrium. *Econ. Theory*, 52:187–235, 2013.

[380] Eric Smith and Supriya Krishnamurthy. *Symmetry and Collective Fluctuations in Evolutionary Games*. IOP Press, Bristol, 2015.

[381] Eric Smith and Harold J. Morowitz. Universality in intermediary metabolism. *Proc. Nat. Acad. Sci. USA*, 101:13168–13173, 2004.

[382] Eric Smith and Harold J. Morowitz. *The Origin and Nature of Life on Earth: The Emergence of the Fourth Geosphere*. Cambridge U. Press, Cambridge, 2016.

[383] Eric Smith and Martin Shubik. Strategic freedom, constraint, and symmetry in one-period markets with cash and credit payment. *Econ. Theory*, 25:513–551, 2005.

[384] Eric Smith and Martin Shubik. Endogenizing the provision of money: costs of commodity and fiat monies in relation to the valuation of trade. *J. Math. Econ.*, 47:508–530, 2011.

[385] Eric Smith and Martin Shubik. Runs, panics and bubbles: Diamond Dybvig and Morris Shin reconsidered. *Ann. Finance*, 10:603–622, 2014.

[386] Vernon Smith. An experimental study of competitive market behavior. *J. Polit. Econ.*, 70:111–137, 1962.

[387] Vernon Smith. *Research in Experimental Economics*, vol. 1. JAI Press, Greenwich, CT, 1979.

[388] Paul Solman. How to print dollars in your own backyard and keep them away from Wal-Mart. PBS Newshour, September 5 2013. http://www.pbs.org/newshour/making-sense/how-to-print-dollars-in-your-own-backyard-and-keep-them-away-from-wal-mart/.

[389] Robert M. Solow. *Growth Theory: An Exposition*. Oxford University Press, New York, 1988.

[390] Carsten Sørensen. Dynamic asset allocation and fixed income management. *J. Fin. Quant. Anal.*, 34:513–531, 1999.

[391] Sylvain Sorin. Strategic market games with exchange rates. *J. Econ. Theory*, 68:431–446, 1996.

[392] Wataru Souma and Makoto Nirei. An empirical study and model of personal income. In Chatterjee et al. [55], 34–42.

[393] Gary H. Stern, Ron J. Feldman, and Paul A. Volcker. *Too Big to Fail: The Hazards of Bank Bailouts*. Brookings Institution Press, Washington, DC, 2004.

[394] Nancy Stokey, Robert Lucas, and Edward Prescott. *Recursive Methods in Economic Dynamics*. Harvard U. Press, Cambridge, MA, 1989.

[395] Bruce J. Summers, editor. *The Payment System: Design, Management, and Supervision*. International Monetary Fund, Washington, DC, 1994.

[396] John Tagliabue. A legal tender of one's own. *New York Times*, January 30, 2001.

[397] Nassim Nicholas Taleb. *The Black Swan: The Impact of the Highly Improbable*. Random House, New York, 2007.

[398] Peter Temin. Real business cycle views of the great depression and recent events. *J. Econ. Lit.*, 46:669–684, 2008.

[399] R. Thompson. Economic perspectives on innovation. *Australian Economic Review*, 44:480–489, 2011.

[400] James Tobin. Money and finance in the macro-economic process. *J. Money Credit Banking*, 14:171–204, 1982.

[401] Hugo Touchette. The large deviation approach to statistical mechanics. *Phys. Rep.*, 478:1–69, 2009.

[402] Jack Treynor. Toward a theory of market value of risky assets. In Robert A. Korajczyk, editor, *Asset Pricing and Portfolio Performance: Models, Strategy and Performance Metrics*, 15–22. Risk Books, London, 1999, unpublished original 1961.

[403] Leigh van Valen. A new evolutionary law. *Evolutionary Theory*, 1:1–30, 1973.

[404] Hal Varian. *Microeconomic Analysis*. Norton, New York, third edition, 1992.

[405] J. Craig Venter, Karin Remington, John F. Heidelberg, Aaron L. Halpern, Doug Rusch, Jonathan A. Eisen, Dongying Wu, Ian Paulsen, Karen E. Nelson, William Nelson, Derrick E. Fouts, Samuel Levy, Anthony H. Knap, Michael W. Lomas, Ken Nealson, Owen White, Jeremy Peterson, Jeff Hoffman, Rachel Parsons, Holly Baden-Tillson, Cynthia Pfannkoch, Yu-Hui Rogers, and Hamilton O. Smith. Environmental genome shotgun sequencing of the Sargasso Sea. *Science*, 304:66–74, 2004.

[406] Sergio Verdú. Fifty years of Shannon theory. *IEEE Trans. Information Theory*, 44:2057–2078, 1998.

[407] G. von Dassow, E. Meir, E. M. Munro, and G. M. Odell. The segment polarity network is a robust developmental module. *Nature*, 406:188, 2000.

[408] L. von Mises. *The Theory of Money and Credit*. H. E. Batson, translator. Liberty Fund, Indianapolis, 1912.

[409] J. von Neumann. Über ein öconomisches Gleichungssystem und eine Verallgemeinerung des Brouwerschen Fixpunktsatzes. *Ergebnisse eines Mathematischen Kolloquiums*, 8:73–83, 1937.

[410] J. von Neumann. A model of general economic equilibrium. *Rev. Economic Studies*, 13:1–9, 1945. Translation of [409].

[411] John von Neumann and Oskar Morgenstern. *Theory of Games and Economic Behavior*. Princeton U. Press, Princeton, NJ, 1944.

[412] C. H. Waddington. Canalization of development and the inheritance of acquired characters. *Nature*, 150:563–565, 1942.

[413] Leon Walras. *Elements of Pure Economics*. W. Jaffe, translator. R. D. Irwin, Homewood, IL, 1954, original edition 1874, 1877.

[414] Robert G. Watts. *Engineering Response to Global Climate Change: Planning a Research and Development Agenda*. CRC Press, Boca Raton, FL, 1997.

[415] Steven Weinberg. *The Quantum Theory of Fields, vol. 1, Foundations*. Cambridge U. Press, New York, 1995.

[416] Knut Wicksell. *Lectures on Political Economy,* vol. 2, *Money.* Routledge & Kegan Paul, London, 1962.

[417] Oliver E. Williamson. The theory of the firm as governance structure: From choice to contract. *J. Econ. Perspectives*, 16:17, 2002.

[418] E. O. Wilson. *Sociobiology: The New Synthesis.* Harvard U. Press, Cambridge, MA, 1975.

[419] K. G. Wilson and J. Kogut. The renormalization group and the ε expansion. *Phys. Rep., Phys. Lett.*, 12C:75–200, 1974.

[420] Robert Wilson. Incentive efficiency of double auctions. *Econometrica*, 53:1101–1115, 2000.

[421] Edward Nathan Wolff. The asset price meltdown and the wealth of the middle class. 2012. NBER Working Paper No. 18559.

[422] David H. Wolpert and William G. Macready. No free lunch theorems for search. SFI Working Paper 1995-02-010, 1995.

[423] David H. Wolpert and William G. Macready. No free lunch theorems for optimization. *IEEE Trans. Evol. Comp.*, 1:67–82, 1997.

[424] Michael Woodford. *Interest and Prices.* Princeton U. Press, Princeton, NJ, 2003.

[425] Florian Zettelmeyer, Fiona Scott Morton, and Jorge Silva-Risso. How the internet lowers prices: evidence from matched survey and automobile transaction data. *J. Marketing Res.*, 43:168–181, 2006.

[426] *Statistical Abstract of the United States: 2001.* 121st ed. Government Printing Office, Washington, DC, 2002.

[427] *Statistical Abstract of the United States: 2003.* 123rd ed. Government Printing Office, Washington, DC, 2004.

[428] National Academies of Sciences, Engineering, and Medicine. Definitions of evolutionary terms. *Evolution Resources.* http://www.nas.edu/evolution/Definitions.html.

Name Index

Subject Index